# Global Politics
# in the
# Human Interest

FIFTH EDITION

# Global Politics
# in the
# Human Interest

## Mel Gurtov

LYNNE
RIENNER
PUBLISHERS

BOULDER
LONDON

Published in the United States of America in 2007 by
Lynne Rienner Publishers, Inc.
1800 30th Street, Boulder, Colorado 80301
www.rienner.com

and in the United Kingdom by
Lynne Rienner Publishers, Inc.
3 Henrietta Street, Covent Garden, London WC2E 8LU

**Library of Congress Cataloging-in-Publication Data**
Gurtov, Melvin.
Global politics in the human interest / Mel Gurtov.—5th ed.
Includes bibliographical references and index.
ISBN 978-1-58826-484-8 (pbk.: alk. paper)
1. International relations.   2. International economic relations.   3. World politics—
1989–   I. Title.
JZ1305.G87   2007
327.101—dc 22

                                                        2007003277

**British Cataloguing in Publication Data**
A Cataloguing in Publication record for this book
is available from the British Library.


Printed and bound in Canada

 The paper used in this publication meets the requirements
of the American National Standard for Permanence of
Paper for Printed Library Materials Z39.48-1992.

5   4   3   2   1

*For my daughters,*
*Alia, Marci, and Ellene*

*"In the bloom of life, like the sun*
*at eight or nine in the morning.*
*Our hope is placed on you."*

# Contents

# Tables

# Preface

Writing about what it means to view the world from the perspective of global citizenship is not easy when wars and large-scale degradations of human rights and the environment dominate the news. In the face of enormous violence, the tendency may be to dismiss the notion of global citizenship as either idealistic or irrelevant to what is happening in the "real world." Yet for me, nothing could be more vital than to try to communicate the practicality, not to mention the urgency, of thinking globally. We owe this to ourselves and to all who will come after us.

This is a book for those who believe in critical reflection and who are open to emerging ideas about human, environmental, and common security. It is for people who, like myself, reject the notion that "American" values should be universal and instead understand how important it is to look at the world through others' eyes—all the more so, those others with whom we most fervently disagree. In the end, the book is also for those who believe that the individual can (and *must*) make a difference.

Students should note that though the world becomes increasingly complex, tools for analyzing it are more available than ever. Virtually all major world newspapers are now online, as are the major journals of scholarship and opinion, the official positions of governments, and the reports of nongovernmental organizations (NGOs) and international bodies. Yes, the information available can be overwhelming; but there is no excuse for not going to the source. The notes and bibliography here reflect an effort to take into account these sources. But first and foremost, this book is a work of synthesis—drawing from the analyses of many specialists from many fields. My debt to them is enormous, and I again extend my thanks here.

I wish to thank Kristen Magis, Charles Pearson, and Tim Stoddard for research assistance on this edition, and Milton Leitenberg for his usual generosity in sharing ideas and materials. I also appreciate Alan Ely for his wonderful help with communications and other kinds of office support. Thanks to Rosemary Carstens for a wonderful copyediting job. Last, I am grateful to Lynne Rienner for her consistent support of this book and my other publications. I greatly value the partnership.

—*M.G.*

# Global Politics
## in the
## Human Interest

# 1

# Crisis and Interdependence in Contemporary World Politics

This dominant culture set the tone and standard for most of Shikasta. For regardless of the ideological label attaching to each national area, they all had in common that technology was the key to all good, and that good was always material increase, gain, comfort, pleasure. . . . And all this time the earth was being despoiled. The minerals were being ripped out, the fuels wasted, the soils depleted by an improvident and short-sighted agriculture, the animals and plants slaughtered and destroyed, the seas being filled with filth and poison, the atmosphere was corrupted. . . . These were maddened creatures, and the small voices that rose in protest were not enough to halt the processes that had been set in motion and were sustained by greed. By the lack of substance-of-we-feeling.
—Doris Lessing, *Re: Colonised Planet 5, Shikasta*, 1979

## Global Insecurity

Someone once defined fanaticism as "redoubling your efforts when you have lost sight of your original objective." The blind pursuit of national security fits this definition of fanaticism perfectly. As state leaders invest more and more political, human, and economic resources in weapons, aid programs, alliances, and the exploitation of resources, the security of persons, societies, and the planet as a whole actually seems to decline. In the industrialized, technologically advanced countries of the First and Second Worlds, insecurity is mainly reflected in acute anxiety about the efficacy of political systems and frustrations about any system's ability to deliver the "good life" except at very high social and ecological costs. In the underdeveloped countries of the Third and Fourth Worlds, where three-fourths of the world's population lives, insecurity takes a more basic form: the daily quest for survival. (The four "worlds" are depicted in Table 1.1.)

The causes and consequences of this pervasive insecurity, and the extent to which its different forms are interrelated and mutually reinforcing—the degree, for example, to which the quest for security in the industrialized world takes place largely at the expense of the underdeveloped

**Table 1.1    The Reshaping of World Politics**

|  | Cold War Era (1945–1990) | Post–Cold War Era (1990– ) |
|---|---|---|
| First World | US, USSR | US—"superpower"<br>EU, Japan—economic superpowers |
| Second World | Industrialized Europe,<br>Japan, Canada, Australia,<br>New Zealand | Canada, Australia, New Zealand, Russia<br>(first tier); industrialized<br>Eastern Europe (e.g., Hungary, Poland,<br>Ukraine), Israel (second tier) |
| Third World | Oil-exporting economies<br>High-income economies<br>Middle-income economies<br>Low-income economies<br>Fourth World economies | Oil-exporting economies<br>East Asian NICs, e.g., South Korea, Singapore<br>China, Mexico, Brazil, Turkey<br>Cambodia, India, Afghanistan, Angola<br>Other former USSR republics,<br>Africa/other Latin American,<br>South Asian, Middle Eastern states |
| Fourth World |  | Extremely impoverished countries,<br>e.g., Haiti, Somalia, Bangladesh,<br>North Korea, Chad |

world, yet also has profound economic and social impact at home—are the principal subjects of this study. The reasons are simple: The human costs of global insecurity are staggering; the narrow understanding of national security by most state leaders keeps these costs high and mounting; the penetration of every aspect of world politics (such as alliances, the ecosystem, global finance and trade, and people's movements and exchanges) by this global crisis has created great foreboding but equally great hesitancy to take bold remedial action; and, as a result, the prospects for planetary survival itself are not optimistic.

State leaders everywhere invariably seek to put the best possible face on their own situations, and many serious scholars persist in arguing that humankind will resolve today's problems just as it resolved yesterday's. After the Berlin Wall came down on November 9, 1989, there was cause for some optimism. German reunification was completed less than a year later. Massive demonstrations challenged the legitimacy of single-party states from China to Czechoslovakia and, in most cases, toppled them. The creation of a single market among the twelve countries of the European Community (EC), now the European Union (EU), was set to start in 1993. This radical alteration of the map of Europe took place against the background of revolutionary changes in Soviet-US relations. Soviet president Mikhail Gorbachev, whose "new thinking" essentially discarded the old rules of the Cold War game, was the single most important figure. His mid-1990 summit meeting in Washington, DC, with President George H. W. Bush continued US-Soviet arms talks that had already led to the first actual reductions, and destruction, of nuclear weapons in the postwar period. The peacekeeping role of the United Nations revived, with missions in diverse locations such as Afghanistan, Cambodia, and Namibia. Prominent human-rights activists were freed from captivity, including Nelson Mandela after twenty-seven years in South African prisons.

These events, when compared with the baleful character of international relations only a decade earlier, appeared to herald a new era of peace and security. Then, war and preparations for war dominated world politics, topped by the intense nuclear arms competition between the United States and the Soviet Union and a long list of civil and interstate conflicts in Africa, the Middle East, and Southeast Asia. Driven by this short-term comparison, some commentators were quick to proclaim the "end of history," in the sense that the demise of the Soviet empire and the seeming victory of Western liberalism in Eastern Europe had opened the way to a stable, if rather boring, epoch devoted mainly to technological development.[1]

The end of history? The breakup of the Soviet Union and the resurgence of ethnic and religious nationalism in central Europe and central Asia quickly revived history. A new world order? So President Bush declared at the conclusion of Gulf War I—Iraq's invasion and annexation of Kuwait in August 1990. Unfortunately, although the ideological battles of the Cold War were largely replaced by economic competition and led to a lessening of international tensions, there was no cause for celebration. When international and national security issues are evaluated from a planetary and long-term perspective, it remains that the quality of life in the underdeveloped world has barely improved and threats to global environmental security are more apparent than ever. As we will see in the remainder of this chapter, global insecurity is deepening and is beyond quick technological or diplomatic fixes, all the more so since the September 11, 2001, terrorist attacks in the United States and the onset of President George W. Bush's "war on terror."

The urgency of developing a global approach to security was first pressed by U Thant, then secretary-general of the United Nations, in 1969:

> I do not wish to seem overdramatic, but I can only conclude from the information that is available to me as Secretary-General, that the Members of the United Nations have perhaps ten years left in which to subordinate their ancient quarrels and launch a global partnership to curb the arms race, to improve the human environment, to defuse the population explosion, and to supply the required momentum to development efforts. If such a global partnership is not forged within the next decade, then I very much fear that the problems I have mentioned will have reached such staggering proportions that they will be beyond our capacity to control.[2]

In its essentials, the secretary-general's warning has come true. Although planetary extinction has thus far been averted, the depth and scale of the problems U Thant cited have indeed increased to nearly unmanageable proportions. In 1992 over 1,600 scientists from around the world, including 102 Nobel laureates, signed a "Warning to Humanity" that focused on the destructive environmental practices that threaten the planet's viability. They appealed for a new global ethic, including a commitment to eliminate poverty, war, and other causes of "social, economic, and environmental collapse."[3] Or, again in 2000, concerned that "our world is plagued by violence, war and destruction," religious and spiritual leaders of every faith published a "Commitment to Global Peace." It appealed not just for "agreement on fundamental ethical values" but also for "an attitude of reverence for life, freedom and justice, the eradication of poverty, and the protection of the environment for present and future generations."[4] Few government or major corporate leaders have shared these urgent calls; most have acknowledged one or another aspect of a global crisis but have not considered that the problems are symptomatic of a contagious and potentially fatal disease. Life and politics go on as before.

It is indeed strange that, at one and the same time, monumental leaps of scientific creativity occur for the benefit of humankind while political leaders stick to tired formulas and outdated rituals in pursuit of self-interest. The practice of politics has not kept pace either with scientific advances or with global ecological, economic, military, and social changes. U Thant appealed for a global partnership because he believed the future of the human species itself was imperiled. But the governments he addressed were not (and clearly still are not) ready to integrate global changes into narrowly national perspectives. And therein lies a crisis of our times that is equally as burdensome as any U Thant described: a crisis of political will in the nation-state system.

The emphasis throughout this book is on information, explanation, and argument. This chapter begins with some basic facts about the global crisis that are essential to understanding and interpreting the changed shape of world politics—its interdependence during, and globalization after, the Cold War. I introduce the two schools of thought that dominate writing and thinking about world politics—realism and globalism—along with a third school, global humanism, the values and analytical method of which I use throughout the present study. Chapter 2 is a critical examination of realism and globalism, especially the globalism practiced by transnational corporations. Three case studies of efforts to reshape the world order back up the discussion of how realism and globalism both compete and collaborate in the real world. Chapter 3 elaborates on global humanism as an alternative perspective—alternative with respect to meanings of development—*human* development—and meanings of security—*human* and *common* security. This discussion sets the stage for a more specific investigation of insecurity from a human-interest point of view, in the Third and Fourth Worlds (Chapter 4), in the United States and China (Chapter 5), and in Europe, Russia, and Japan (Chapter 6). The concluding chapter is policy oriented: It lays out an agenda for changes addressed to the main features of the global crisis.

## A Brief Report on the State of the Planet

The global crisis is apparent from the following facts and figures:

• Despite advances in world literacy, there remain thirty-four countries with over 80 percent illiteracy.[5]
• Approximately 1.1 billion people, overwhelmingly in sub-Saharan Africa, South Asia, and East Asia, were living in absolute poverty (usually defined as $1 a day) in 2001. The figure represents an improvement over the previous twenty years, when it was 1.5 billion people; but when added to the number of people living on between $1 and $2 a day, the total is a staggering 2.7 billion.[6] Put in terms of share of world income, in 2000 the poorest 20 percent of the global population accounted for a mere 1.57 percent, whereas people in the wealthiest countries, representing 15 percent of world population, accounted for 79 percent.[7]
• The world population, according to the World Bank, is expected to be over 8 billion by 2025, even though fertility rates are declining everywhere. In the mid-1980s it was commonplace to say that world population was growing by "another Mexico" (80 million) annually, whereas by 1990 the phrase had changed to "another Bangladesh," or about 100 million people every year.[8]
• At current rates of depletion, the Third World's forests, especially in tropical zones, will be reduced by one-half (thus intensifying an already serious shortage of firewood for fuel). Approximately one plant species of every eight—12.5 percent of approximately 270,000 species so far identified—is threatened with extinction.[9]
• Military spending worldwide roughly doubled in twenty years, reaching $940 billion in 1985—well over $2 billion a day. Over 80 percent of that amount was spent by the two superpowers. Global arms spending declined beginning in the late 1980s, but by 2005 it was soaring again. The United States accounts for nearly half the world total, over $1.1 trillion in current dollars.[10]
• Alternative uses of tiny fractions of the world's military spending could produce meaningful change in education, health care, and nutrition. For example, the cost of one new nuclear submarine (about $1.5 billion) could educate 160 million schoolchildren in twenty-three developing countries. World hunger affects over 850 million people; but only about $3 billion is estimated to be enough to enable the poorest countries to begin moving toward food self-sufficiency. Similar small amounts could probably prevent the deaths each year of about 15 million children from malnutrition, dehydration, and other easily curable conditions.[11]
• More and more people are moving into cities. The UN forecast that 47 percent of the world's population would be urbanized by 2000. Third World cities will grow 160 percent between 1990 and 2030 and will include seventeen of the twenty-one largest cities in the world.[12]

• The world's displaced population is rising at an astounding rate. About 2,700 people become "political refugees," refugees in their own country, or economic migrants every day.[13] Migration of workers has risen from 155 million in 1990 to around 191 million in 2005. Migrant workers are major contributors to their home as well as their host countries' economies, sending back $167 billion to developing countries in 2005.[14]

• Malaria, once thought to have been wiped out, is on the rise again. "Between 300 million and 500 million people now get malaria each year, and someone dies of it about every 15 seconds—mostly children and pregnant women. During the last decade, malaria has killed about ten times as many children as all wars combined have in that period." A $5 mosquito net, beyond the reach of most poor people who suffer from malaria, is considered to be the single best preventive measure.[15]

• AIDS infects an estimated 60 million people and has caused about 25 million deaths, making it "the greatest challenge of our generation," according to UN Secretary-General Kofi Annan. About $8 billion was spent to combat AIDS in 2005, a significant increase; but a UN General Assembly declaration said $23 billion would have to be spent annually by 2010.[16]

• About 1.1 billion people worldwide do not have access to clean water, 2.6 billion lack toilets or latrines, and diseases caused by impure water account for over 3 million deaths a year, mostly of children. Yet efforts continue to privatize water supplies, raising its costs and denying even more people access to quality water. The good news is that such efforts are failing as citizens and governments have rallied to vest water management in communities.[17]

• One large-scale study of global warming, by the US National Academy of Sciences, concludes that "recent warmth is unprecedented for at least the last 400 years and potentially the last several millennia."[18] As had been widely concluded in numerous earlier scientific reports, the new study attributed the dramatic temperature rise to carbon dioxide and methane, the principal greenhouse gases.

• Slave trafficking that forces women and children into brothels and sweatshops victimizes anywhere from 700,000 to 4 million people a year, and as many as nineteen countries reportedly are doing nothing to stop it.[19]

Statistics and facts of these magnitudes may be difficult to absorb at one sitting. But they give an immediate sense of what a global perspective on world politics does: It highlights the multidimensional and transnational character of a common crisis. And that is why we turn next to the phenomena of interdependence and globalization.

## From Interdependence to Globalization

Citizens in one country demonstrate for human rights in another. Genocidal wars in Cambodia, the former Yugoslavia, and Rwanda prompt proposals for a permanent UN court to prosecute crimes against humanity. The Indian government briefly arrests the chair of the board of Union Carbide, then sues the company in a US court, after a catastrophic gas leak from the company's branch plant in Bhopal kills over 3,700 people and injures 20,000. A worldwide emergency food relief effort begins in Ethiopia and Sudan after a BBC broadcast dramatizes the fact that several million people are starving to death. An Islamic terrorist group proclaims: "Let them know that sooner or later we shall reach the heart of the White House, the Kremlin, the Elysée, 10 Downing Street." A Japanese study of the effects of a major earthquake in downtown Tokyo predicts catastrophic consequences for the world's finances, inasmuch as Japan becomes the top creditor nation in the world.

These events of the 1980s and 1990s have one thing in common: They reflect the increasingly complex and transnational character of world politics. The line that once so neatly divided domestic from foreign affairs and foreign from global affairs is now much harder to find. Issues that once were the exclusive prerogative of governments, such as air and water pollution, now are matters of international diplomacy and sometimes social activism. Large numbers of ordinary people are being affected by world affairs as never before. Not only are advances in global information technology helping to create awareness of that fact, but, as the cost of acquiring information dwindles, far greater numbers of people have opportunities to affect world affairs.

Even the older patterns of inter- and intranational relations, in which conflict is the dominant feature, have new meaning today. Whether we are talking about wars between states, military and political interventions by one country in the affairs of another, nationalist and separatist struggles, or territorial disputes, the consequences of such conflicts carry well beyond their place of origin. As the two recent wars involving Iraq show, the impact transcends national boundaries to involve other economies, ways of life (consumer prices, cultures, food supplies, civil liberties, jobs), and international law and institutions.

The global agenda has become larger, more diverse, and more ominous. We need additional tools to analyze it. International affairs is still politics and economics, of course; but of special importance today is international political economy, the study of the ways certain systems (such as global capitalism) and structures (such as transnational corporations and military-industrial complexes) often decisively influence the distribution of wealth and power within and between nations, and therefore the character of national and international security.[20] In addition, biology (studying, for example, acid rain), anthropology (the demise of native cultures in the face of modernization), sociology (the international division of labor), feminist studies (women on the global assembly lines of transnational corporations), religion (the universal values of diverse spiritual paths), even sports (from

US-China ping-pong diplomacy to terrorism and fraternalism at the Munich and Los Angeles Olympic Games)—all have a place in the study of world politics. The transnational phenomenon requires an interdisciplinary approach to do justice to world politics.

And that is the approach of this book. I use the tools and insights of many disciplines in order to explore world politics in its fullest, global sense: across national boundaries, inside as well as outside societies, at many different levels of social activity (governing elites, races, ecological systems, economic classes, and bureaucracies, for example). Since the United States, despite all its vulnerabilities occasioned by global political-economic changes, is still the world's most influential actor, I emphasize its policies and behavior more so than any other state's. But most important are the humane values and norms that guide my analysis of national policies, social forces, and international institutions.[21] The point of departure here is that of the global citizen who looks at the world from the standpoint of the needs and interests of the planet, considered as a human community and as an ecological system, and makes assessments based on political and ethical standards that can be applied to all social systems.

This Global Humanist framework identifies inequality as the most prominent feature of world politics in our time. How the world works to the detriment of the disadvantaged, who benefits from that process, and what the disequilibrium means for the human condition are central to this study.

"We are stranded . . . between the inadequacy of the nation-state and the emerging imperative of global community," former US Secretary of State Henry Kissinger once said.[22] World politics today might be characterized as proceeding simultaneously along two tracks, with the distance between them getting wider all the time. The first track consists of the traditional statecraft of power politics, of which Kissinger has long been a highly visible exponent. The "engine" that propels movement along this track is commonly known as realism, a philosophy or paradigm of national interest and power politics that we will critically examine shortly. Running along the second track is globalism, which interprets world politics in terms of transnational forces. Globalism takes two politically quite distinct forms, one idealist and increasingly focused on corporate interests, and one humanist, reflecting the human interest within a global community. Both forms of globalism contend that politics-as-usual within the framework of competing national interests cannot cope with planet-wide problems. But whereas corporate globalism sees the world coming together on the basis of markets and the harmonizing of product and labor standards, global humanism sees the way forward in international cooperation that advances human rights, disarmament, and environmental protection.

All perspectives agree that world politics is highly interdependent and becoming more so all the time. No event in recent memory brought home this evolving perception more than the nuclear power plant disaster at

Chernobyl, near Kiev, in the former Soviet Union (now Ukraine), in April 1986. The Soviet leadership had to answer to the world, as well as to its own citizens, for the accident, the worst in the history of nuclear power. Leaders of individual states of course looked to their own interests in commenting on Chernobyl—either out of concern about radioactive fallout or out of a desire to exploit Soviet troubles for their own political benefit. But no one, including Soviet and US leaders, could avoid Chernobyl's global meaning. General Secretary (later president) Mikhail Gorbachev said it created the need for international monitoring and reporting of nuclear accidents. President Ronald Reagan said Chernobyl showed that some issues have implications that transcend the national interest. They and other state leaders seemed to accept that when it comes to species survival realist politics is severely handicapped.

"Interdependence" is shorthand for the transnationalization of world politics—not just events but also ideas, institutions, and decisions. It is a phenomenon that draws societies, and particular groups within societies, closer together, with both positive and negative consequences. There are at least six ways global interdependence may occur. One is through mutual dependence. The US economy, for example, is no longer as autonomous and uniquely powerful as it was at the end of World War II, when the dollar, backed by gold, was the only international currency. In 1985 the United States became a debtor nation for the first time since 1914: Its financial obligations to foreigners—from such things as investments and securities holdings—exceeded foreign obligations to the United States. Second, interdependence describes the integration of the world economy into a single unit. No longer are we talking about capitalist versus socialist (or market versus nonmarket) systems. Today, virtually all the major socialist economies, starting with China, are deeply enmeshed in the global capitalist system of trade, investments, and lending. Even an economy as closed as North Korea's depends heavily on imported food and other international aid.[23]

A third way of defining interdependence is in terms of global threats that seem beyond the capacity of states to control through traditional diplomacy. Terrorism, famine, ecological disasters, nuclear proliferation, and the eradication of whole species of plants and animals are examples. Fourth, interdependence may also be thought of as the spillover, typically unintended, of one country's (or region's) problems into another. Domestic issues become transnational ones. The Chernobyl disaster raised Soviet requirements for imported food, reduced Soviet food exports, pushed up world oil prices, put a damper on nuclear arms talks, and caused the biggest one-day drop in stock prices Wall Street had ever experienced. The accident also continues killing and poisoning people in Ukraine and other countries.[24]

Fifth, interdependence is the interrelationship of seemingly disconnected political-economic phenomena. The so-called greenhouse effect is commonly cited to illustrate this type of interdependence. The rapid buildup of carbon dioxide in the earth's atmosphere as the result of unprecedented large-scale use of fossil fuels (coal, petroleum, and natural gas), combined with the destruction of forests, is now widely accepted as being responsible for a warming of the earth's temperature. A leading scientific panel in 2007 reported "unequivocal" evidence that climate changes are profoundly altering sea levels and will have serious consequences for food production, world trade, human health, population movement, and even the stability of the polar ice cap.[25]

Finally, interdependence is manifest in the growing number and political importance of transnational movements and institutions. State-to-state diplomacy remains a fixture in international politics. But it is now supplemented, and in some cases even displaced or upstaged, by the activities of nongovernmental organizations (NGOs), for example, to promote human rights and people-to-people assistance; by popular movements for social change (such as the antinuclear, ecological, and women's movements that coordinate efforts around the world); by transnational religious, worker, and political movements (such as Catholic liberation theology, labor unions, and Green parties in Europe and North America); by powerful transnational corporations (TNCs), banks, and financial institutions (such as the World Bank and the International Monetary Fund [IMF]); and occasionally by individuals who act as transnational agents—world citizens, in effect—such as former US President Jimmy Carter when he traveled to North Korea in 1994 in hopes of short-circuiting a nuclear crisis.

Interdependence of whatever variety has one common consequence: It limits the nation-state's ability to conduct business without reference to any but its own interests. When that limitation cuts deeply enough to have lasting effects on, for example, a country's culture, language (speak English, please!),[26] social values, tastes, political processes, public policies, treatment of minorities, and market behavior, we have globalization.[27] Though the word itself (and equally, internationalization) is now so widely used that it may indeed amount to "globaloney,"[28] its intention is to describe a serious matter: the integrating and homogenizing effects that occur when national boundaries are penetrated by powerful forces acting above the state level. These forces are usually economic, driven by the TNCs and multilateral lending institutions such as the IMF that seek to regularize and stabilize world finance and trade in their own interests. But globalization is also technological, political and social, biological, and of course environmental, as we all know from the Internet revolution, the rise of civil society, and the rapid spread of viruses.[29]

In the abstract, globalization is neutral. It can promote social justice and cooperation within and between countries, such as public-private and international alliances on education, job retraining, unionization, energy conservation, and technology sharing. Through globalization, or in response to it, social forces such as protest movements, ethnic minorities, and NGOs can gain in their ability to combat or moderate economic, environmental, majoritarian, and other threats from above.[30] Or, globalization can primarily be the "global shopping mall," offering ever-greater opportunities for the richest countries and corporations to marketize the world at the expense of the poorest economies and social groups, the state, and whole cultures.[31] At the extreme, the consequences can be dire. Benjamin R. Barber captured these in "Jihad vs. McWorld": jihad being fundamentalist, violent, and opposed to any intrusion of the modern world (such as the Taliban in Afghanistan) and McWorld being universalist, commercial, and devoted to market conformism.[32]

The question becomes one of values as much as economics. From a dominant-culture perspective, globalization may appear to be an irresistible and righteous force capable of propelling societies into modernity—the contemporary equivalent of making "backward" societies "advanced," which was fashionable in the 1950s and 1960s. In fact, the new global way of life sounds suspiciously like a homogenization of US culture and values, fit only for people with money to burn. Maurice Strong said in 1992 as he opened the United Nations Conference on Environment and Development (UNCED, the so-called Earth Summit) in Rio de Janeiro, Brazil:

> The globalisation of capitalism is producing a new and universalising culture symbolised by CNN, brand-name consumer products like Coca-Cola, McDonald's and Levis, pop music, shopping malls, international airports, hotel chains and conferences. For the privileged minority who participate fully in this culture, it provides an exciting and expanding range of new opportunities and experiences. But for the majority, particularly in the non-Western world who live on its margins, and feed on its crumbs, it is often seen as alien and intimidating. Caught up in the dynamics of modernisation of which they are more victims than beneficiaries, it is no wonder that many react with anxiety and rejection, seeking refuge and identity in their own traditional values and cultures.[33]

Such a lopsided division of the fruits of globalization promises a future no more democratic, pluralist, equitable, or environmentally sustainable than that offered by globalization's fundamentalist opponents. If, instead, commonplace global values such as equal justice for all, the sanctity of life, respect for cultural diversity, and nonviolence were universalized, interdependence and globalization would probably look quite different from "Jihad vs. McWorld." And that was indeed the promise of the end of the Cold War and a "new world order."

## Trend Line 1: The New Structure of World Affairs

It seems an eternity ago that the first President Bush characterized Gulf War I as an "opportunity to forge for ourselves and for future generations a new world order, a world where the rule of law, not the law of the jungle, governs the conduct of nations."[34] Soon afterward, however, civil strife and humanitarian crises around the world revealed just how disorderly the post–Cold War world was going to be. Nevertheless, the end of the Cold War did result in important rearrangements of the world political economy.

What are these rearrangements? How new and substantial are they?[35]

Structurally, world politics is increasingly multipolar but with the United States first among equals, as Table 1.1 indicates. Political and economic power is more widely dispersed than at any time since the end of World War II, but not military power. Russia remains a major military power, but its political system, economy, and society suffer from a multitude of problems (see Chapter 6). The EU and China are now the primary other shapers of the global map, and "emerging market" economies (such as Hungary, Brazil, and Turkey) have political clout for the first time. Beyond the Second World and the top layers of the Third World, however, lie over sixty countries representing a majority of the world's population. For them there is no new order, and some in the Fourth World—states such as Somalia, Haiti, and Afghanistan—are considered "failed" or "quasi" states (see Chapter 4). Fourth World countries have virtually no influence over regional or global decisions unless, like North Korea, they develop a nuclear weapon.

A critical political reality of the post–Cold War world is the struggle for global authority between (US) unipolarity and multipolarity. As the only superpower, the views and actions of the United States are often decisive in determining the capacity and willingness of the international community to respond to crises such as Iraq's attack on Kuwait, genocide in Bosnia and Rwanda, and financial chaos in Mexico and Asia between 1994 and 1998. At the same time, only the United States is so consistently prepared to act unilaterally on major international issues regardless of other countries' views—such as the waging of preventive war against Iraq in 2003 and the rejection of an international treaty (the 1998 Rome Treaty that created the International Criminal Court) that a previous president had signed. No other country lectures other governments on how they should run their economies (as the United States did to Japan and Indonesia in 1998); how they should define and implement human rights (from China to Nigeria); or where their (Europe's) companies should not invest (Iran and Cuba). Yet when it comes to intractable disputes, such as between Israel and the Palestinian Authority (PA) and in Northern Ireland, it is the United States that is the essential broker. In short, one superpower dominates the international stage, and does so without worrying about double standards, such as not paying a good part of its UN dues while making full use of the UN's peacekeeping operations,[36] and preaching arms control while being the world's leading arms seller. But the United States cannot do as it pleases without consequences: The rest of the world went ahead with international agreements on global warming (the

Kyoto Protocol) and the International Criminal Court, and refused to provide funds or soldiers for the Iraq war.

A second essential new political reality is the tension between globalization and nationalism. The demise of nationalism has been regularly predicted by experts ever since the industrial age. Instead, we see that the more integrated the world economy becomes, the more frequently do nationalism and its offshoots, localism, ethnic nationalism, and transnationalism, assert themselves—for example, in weakened border security, restrictions on immigration and the entry of genetically modified organisms (GMOs) into the food chain, government takeovers of foreign companies, and formation of regional economic groups such as the North American Free Trade Agreement (NAFTA) and the Central American Free Trade Agreement (CAFTA). "They" prefer not to become more like "us" or to play by globalization's rules. Globalization can overwhelm cultures and economies, producing (in Kofi Annan's words) "greater vulnerability to unfamiliar and unpredictable forces that can bring on economic instability and social dislocation."[37] Angered by threats to sovereignty, indigenous rights, and cultural traditions, impotent to deal with the power of the global marketplace, or facing loss of one-time glory, nationalists of all stripes seek alternatives to globalization.[38]

Powerful economic and social forces are eroding the sovereignty and power of the nation-state, yet the state remains the essential actor in world affairs. On one hand, the nation-state is again under assault from "nations" demanding ethnic or cultural autonomy, and, less frequently, statehood. Literally hundreds of ethnic groups confront states that are determined to impose their authority at any cost. The opportunity for these groups came with two developments as the 1980s ended: the collapse of socialism, which (as a unifying vision that inspired the Russian Revolution) had sought to provide a new basis of national loyalty and international legitimacy; and sharp economic decline in much of the world. These forces unleashed long-suppressed ethnic and cultural antagonisms and aspirations capable of being seized upon by unscrupulous politicians, such as the former Yugoslavia's Slobodan Milosevic.

Transnational loyalties have also undermined the state, very much in response to globalization. Civil-society NGOs, one kind of transnational organization, act as watchdogs of human rights, the environment, gender equity, and many other social areas impacted by globalization. NGOs are said not only to be influencing debate on these issues; they often also provide settings for diversifying and universalizing the values and ideas that underlie such debate.[39] Terror networks such as Al-Qaida, on the other hand, rely on often arbitrary violence to destroy what is believed to have been imposed. Thus, while President Bush asked, "Why do they [Al-Qaida] hate us?" it seems clear that US policies and not US freedoms were the issue: policies that supported Israel and corrupt, faithless monarchies in the

Middle East. The multinational corporation is a third type of transnational organization. Leading corporate globalists see the nation-state as an anachronism in an interdependent world economy. Only the global corporation, they say, can deliver the goods and security people want. But the economic prominence of the Chinese, Jews, Indians, and other geographically dispersed groups demonstrates a fourth transnational loyalty—to "tribes" and networks that have staked their futures on values such as educational excellence, thrift, and family.[40]

The appeal and forcefulness of sovereign statehood remains substantial, however. After the Cold War ended, fifteen new states were carved out of the former Soviet Union (FSU) alone, such as Georgia, Ukraine, and Belarus. There were 167 states in 1988 (compared with 51 in 1945); today, there are 192. Even though nationalism turned against the multicultural state, bringing down the USSR and Yugoslavia in 1991, new political leaderships created new states or reestablished old ones, often on the basis of shared ethnicity. In the Baltic states of Estonia, Latvia, and Lithuania, the Soviet collapse permitted the recovery of lost sovereignty and led to attempts to kick out Russian minorities. Elsewhere, the quest for statehood, or at least greater autonomy from the state, found Chechens at war with Russia, Uighurs in conflict with China, and East Timorese successfully gaining independence from Indonesia.

Unprecedented opportunities are available for national economic renewal because of increased global interdependence in science, technology, trade, and investment. The world economy is a single capitalist system. At least in theory, with economic competition replacing Cold War competition, interdependence and globalization of markets ought to be able to propel national economies to higher levels of performance.

But several countertrends are apparent. Trade protectionism has intensified, making global trade arrangements more difficult to negotiate and enforce. Regional trading areas mentioned earlier, such as NAFTA, have become preferred routes to national prosperity. Moreover, real economic power in world affairs has not dispersed. It remains vested in the North— North America, Japan, and Europe—measured not just in terms of output and income levels but equally in terms of worldwide cultural influence, authorship of scientific papers and methods, technological solutions, telecommunications ownership, and political practices. Hence, the prospects for economic renewal continue to leave most of the underdeveloped South, especially Africa, out of the picture.

The intensifying competition for markets and profits has redefined the national interest. In the name of globalization, national economic policy has become synonymous with the downsizing of work forces and corporate megamergers. German businesses, in defiance of traditional practice, are increasingly exporting jobs to sustain "growth"; US and European businesses are casting off workers to satisfy stockholders and stay competitive; and corporate mergers between and among Japanese, European, and US firms are at record levels, greatly reducing competition in virtually every industrial and service sector. Meanwhile, "economic diplomacy" has supplanted ordinary diplomacy: Energy, technology, and investment interests, and opportunities to earn hard currency now dominate over strategic calculations in high-level decisionmaking, even when the transactions have military applications. (These matters are detailed in Chapters 2 and 5.)

Notwithstanding ongoing wars, military power, particularly in nuclear and other nonconventional weapons, is growing less salient to national and international security as other, global factors come into play. These include protection of land, water, and other natural resources; energy needs; economic management and productivity; scientific and technological innovation; and access to information. The ability to invest in these other sources of power was greatly enhanced by the end of the Cold War. Important reductions in national military-industrial complexes were made beginning in 1990, such as in the active-duty forces of the United States, its European allies, Russia, and China; in US and Russian nuclear-weapon stockpiles; in the real defense spending of those forces (China excepted); in employment at the world's largest arms-manufacturing firms; and in the value of conventional arms exports worldwide.

But these developments are a far cry from demilitarization and the abolition of war. Wars on every scale continue to be fought at enormous cost, for even though the number of wars and armed conflicts has gone down (from 62 in 1993 to 42 in 2003),[41] access to small arms and the resources (such as gems and timber) with which to purchase them has expanded. UN peacekeeping missions have sometimes been able to assist in bringing about cease-fires and temporary political settlements (in, for example, Cambodia, Mozambique, Haiti, and Angola), and accords have been reached in a few long-lasting conflicts, such as in Guatemala (1961–1996), Northern Ireland (1969–1998), and East Timor (1975–1999).[42] But many intractable conflicts remain so; the peacekeeping map is littered with examples of agreements that failed to become settlements. The most prominent is Israel and Palestine, despite agreements reached since the Oslo accords in 1993 that briefly held out hope of a land-for-peace agreement. (The 2003 "road map" pieced together by the United States, the UN, the EU, and Russia, we might recall, was supposed to lead to a "final and comprehensive settlement" by 2005.[43]) Other failed peace accords include North and South Korea, Sri Lanka's civil war, India-Pakistan, and Greek-Turkish Cyprus, all of which have seen minimal progress in genuine conflict resolution.

Since the 1990s, civil wars have resumed or escalated in Somalia, Afghanistan, Liberia, the Democratic Republic of Congo (formerly Zaire), and Sudan. Losses of life in these conflicts are enormous, and most of them continue whether or not there is UN mediation or monitoring.[44] But the most typical, and even more deadly, internal conflicts of recent times are along ethnic lines: the Turkish and Iraqi wars on the Kurds (over 100,000 deaths since 1961); Russia's intervention in Chechnya to prevent secession (around 50,000 deaths from 1994 to 1996); the Hutu slaughter of over a half-million Tutsis and moderate Hutus in Rwanda (1994–1995); the Tutsi slaughter of about 170,000 Hutus in Burundi (1988–1995); and "ethnic cleansing" in the former Yugoslavia, for the most part by Serbian forces against Muslims in Bosnia.[45]

As in the old order, too, international violence has been fueled by the spread of nuclear-weapons and missile technology and by a hyperactive international arms market. Led by the United States, the five permanent members of the Security Council—the very governments whose leadership is essential to a new military order—remain the major arms sellers. One circumstance that has changed, as Asia demonstrates, is the extent to which economic opportunities now drive arms spending and sales. Military budgets have risen along with gross national product (GNP) in several Asian states, starting with China but now including Japan. The Middle East, meanwhile, remains the largest market for arms by far.[46]

International approaches to global problems are increasing, but the insistence on state sovereignty continues to be a formidable obstacle to the realization of human and common security. Peacekeeping operations (PKOs) are an example. In 2005 the UN was carrying out seventeen PKOs, at a cost of roughly $4.5 billion. Altogether, of sixty peacekeeping operations since 1948, twenty-nine began in the 1990s and twelve are still in place (see Table 1.2). Their functions range from observation of cease-fires (such as between India and Pakistan) and monitoring of internal wars (Sudan) to support of political processes (East Timor) and "stabilization" of chaotic conditions (Haiti). The figures reflect a huge post–Cold War upsurge in resort to the UN.[47]

But the peacekeeping function has rarely evolved into the kind of collective security envisioned by the UN's founders, with the exception of the international coalition formed against Iraq in 1991. One reason is the end of the Cold War: Even though great-power interests no longer collide over territory or ideology, the stakes—particularly in civil wars—are usually insufficient to attract collective action. In this twilight zone, there is room for outrageous international behavior by petty zealots and terrorist organizations to pursue their objectives, which are often narrowly nationalistic and delusional. Among many examples, we may cite the Bosnian Serb leader, Radovan Karadzic, who sought to dismember Bosnia and went so far as to capture hundreds of UN peacekeepers in mid-1995 in response to the UN mission's efforts to stop the bombing of civilians; the campaign of the Armed Islamic Group in Algeria to kill allegedly pro-Western journalists (forty-six were killed in the course of civil warfare that claimed around 30,000 lives between 1992 and 1995);[48] Burma's junta, SLORC (the State Law and Order Restoration Council),[49] helped along with Chinese arms and

**Table 1.2  UN Peacekeeping Operations (2005)**

UNTSO                    Since May 1948
United Nations Truce Supervision
Organization
•Total strength (military and civilian): 384
•Appropriation 2005: $29.04 million

UNMOGIP                Since January 1949
United Nations Military Observer Group in
India and Pakistan
•Total strength (military and civilian): 114
•Appropriation 2005: $8.37 million

UNFICYP                 Since March 1964
United Nations Peacekeeping Force in
Cyprus
•Total strength (military and civilian): 1,198
•Approved budget 07/04–06/05: $50.69 million
(gross) including voluntary contributions of one-
third from Cyprus and $6.5 million from Greece

UNDOF                    Since June 1974
United Nations Disengagement Observer
Force
•Total strength (military and civilian): 1,174
•Approved budget 07/04–06/05: $40.90 million

UNIFIL                    Since March 1978
United Nations Interim Force in Lebanon
•Total strength (military and civilian): 2,387
•Approved budget 07/04–06/05: $92.96 million

MINURSO                Since April 1991
United Nations Mission for the
Referendum in Western Sahara
•Total strength (military and civilian): 465
•Approved budget 07/04–06/05: $44.00 million

UNOMIG                 Since August 1993
United Nations Observer Mission in
Georgia
•Total strength (military and civilian): 414
•Approved budget 07/04–06/05: $31.93 million

UNMIK                     Since June 1999
United Nations Interim Administration
Mission in Kosovo
•Total strength (military and civilian): 6,830
•Approved budget 07/04–06/05: $294.63 million

UNAMSIL               Since October 1999
United Nations Mission in Sierra Leone
•Total strength (military and civilian): 4,245
•Approved budget 07/04–06/05: $291.60 million

MONUC                Since November 1999
United Nations Organization Mission in the
Democratic Republic of the Congo
•Total strength (military and civilian): 18,903
•Approved budget 07/04–06/05: $957.83 million

UNMEE                     Since July 2000
United Nations Mission in Ethiopia and
Eritrea
•Total strength (military and civilian): 3,917
•Approved budget 07/04–06/05: $205.33 million

UNMISET                  Since May 2002
United Nations Mission of Support in East
Timor
•Total strength (military and civilian): 1,540
•Approved budget 07/04–06/05: $82.21 million

UNMIL               Since September 2003
United Nations Mission in Liberia
•Total strength (military and civilian): 17,558
•Approved budget 07/04–06/05: $822.11 million

UNOCI                     Since April 2004
United Nations Operation in Côte d'Ivoire
•Total strength (military and civilian): 6,864
•Approved budget 07/04–06/05: $378.47 million

MINUSTAH                 Since June 2004
United Nations Stabilization Mission in
Haiti
•Authorized strength (military and civilian): 8,322
•Total current strength (military and civilian):
8,939
•Approved budget 07/04–06/05: $379.05 million

ONUB                      Since June 2004
United Nations Operation in Burundi
•Total strength (military and civilian): 6,254
•Approved budget 07/04–06/05: $329.71 million

UNMIS                    Since March 2005
United Nations Mission in the Sudan
•Authorized strength (military and civilian):
14,579
•Total current strength (military and civilian): 645
•Commitment authority 07/04–06/05: $279.50
million

*Source:* United Nations Department of Public Information, DPI/1634/Rev.46, April 2005.

kept afloat with opium and heroin profits; Laurent Kabila, the Democratic Republic of Congo's leader, whose forces probably massacred Rwandan Hutu refugees and then prevented various UN missions from investigating the massacres; and the various terrorist groups that exploded a bomb under the World Trade Center in New York in February 1993, released sarin nerve gas (while also researching biological weapons) in the Tokyo subway in March 1995, in April 1995 planted a bomb that destroyed the federal office building in Oklahoma City, and flew airplanes into the World Trade Center and the Pentagon in 2001.

When it comes to the two most demanding kinds of peacekeeping—conflict prevention and response to genocide and mass murder—the UN (which is to say, the member states) has been found wanting. If Secretary-General Kofi Annan had had his way, that would have changed. During his tenure, Annan was on a personal crusade to redefine state sovereignty so as to open the door to preventive UN interventions in cases of crimes against humanity. Clearly motivated by the humanitarian disasters in Rwanda and the former Yugoslavia, he said: "Where such crimes occur and peaceful attempts to halt them have been exhausted, the Security Council has a moral duty to act on behalf of the international community. The fact that we cannot protect people everywhere is no reason for doing nothing when we can."[50] He also urged the acceptance of "an international norm against the violent repression of minorities that will and must take precedence over concerns of State sovereignty."[51] Annan was not calling for the authority immediately to order peacekeeping units into battle. But he *was* insisting that "in the face of mass murder [armed intervention] is an option that cannot be relinquished."[52]

The problems with responding positively to Annan's call rest more with the so-called international community. Cost aside, the idea of giving the Security Council authority to intervene in internal wars is unappealing to all three sets of actors: the countries where civil wars have already brought about a humanitarian crisis, the countries where internal fighting might lead to a humanitarian crisis, and the countries that would have to provide troops and logistical support. None is excited at the prospect of a foreign intervention that would probably last for several years. The international failure to respond to the genocide in Sudan's Darfur region—a case in which the Security Council voted for intervention but failed to dispatch forces when the president of Sudan protested—or to mass murder in the Democratic Republic of Congo is testimony to the lack of commitment to act.

Real peacekeeping, where blood as well as treasure might have to be expended on behalf of international security, either preventively or after the fact, is thus becoming more difficult to organize and requires more personnel at precisely the moment when there are so many communal and other types of internal wars—around twenty-five today. When it comes down to a choice between "respecting state sovereignty" and incurring moral and material responsibility to act, state leaders will choose sovereignty every time. National interests prevail today as they always have, so that even when states (notably the richest ones) agree to support PKOs, they are careful to limit their commitments. As a result, we find that whereas Third World countries have contributed the bulk of soldiers to UN-authorized PKOs—led by Bangladesh, India, and Pakistan—the United States and the EU have provided money and logistical help but usually deployed troops only in support of operations (wars in Bosnia, Kosovo, Iraq, and Afghanistan, and along the Israel-Egypt and Israel-Lebanon borders) *outside* UN control.[53]

"Civil societies" committed to democratic practices have become important in the politics of a number of formerly authoritarian governments, notably in the FSU and Eastern Europe, but also in some Third World countries.[54] In a few instances popular protests and civil-society groups have led directly to positive political change. In November 2005 Ukraine's "Orange Revolution" toppled an unpopular ruler who tried to steal an election.[55] In Nepal, after King Gyanendra seized power in 2005 and put an end to parliamentary government, arguing that tight control was needed in order to defeat a Maoist insurgency, young people took the lead in protests aimed at restoring democracy—and won to the extent that the king agreed to restore parliament and political parties. The Maoists will now compete for power by lawful methods. On the other side of Latin American corruption are heartening developments in the rule of law. In Mexico a team of researchers under the special prosecutor's office drafted a detailed account of a "genocide plan" carried out by the army from the late 1960s to the early 1970s against government critics.[56] The government of Luis Echeverría instigated the plan, and he was arrested in July 2006 despite the Fox administration's initial unwillingness to release their findings. The report on Mexico's "dirty war" follows on similar official admissions by the Argentine and Chilean governments, and on a greater willingness across Latin America to respond to the demands of human-rights groups for recognition of official crimes and the granting of compensation to victims.[57]

But the existence of civil society does not ensure that politics will be conducted in accordance with democratic norms. In fact, democratically elected governments in the post–Cold War era have often acted with total disregard for constitutional liberal traditions such as the rule of law, shared powers, and respect for civil liberties.[58] Thus, our second time line is on the limits of global democratization.

## Trend Line 2: Democratization's Rise and Fall

In a number of countries since the 1990s, dictators were replaced and the worst abuses of power were eliminated, but elements of democratic governance failed to materialize. From post-Soviet central Europe (such as

Latvia, Lithuania, Armenia, Azerbaijan, the former Yugoslavia, and Belarus) to Latin America (Mexico, Venezuela, Peru, Guatemala), Africa (including Côte d'Ivoire, Zambia, Kenya, Algeria, and Nigeria), and Asia (Cambodia), democratic experiments were overwhelmed by a multitude of pressures. One of them was the persistence of authoritarian political cultures and traditions. In Africa, for instance, the failure of democratization was attributed to "incumbents [who] have been rewriting the rules of the game, bullying opponents and restricting the press so as to be able to hold onto power regardless of their popularity or the success of their programs."[59] In the case of the FSU, former communists returned to power on the heels of separatism and civil war. Where political and economic reforms were promised, such as in Poland, Slovakia, and Hungary, the failure to deliver has led to populist reactions and the potential for a dangerous drift to the right.

One thing has become clear: Democracy understood narrowly in terms of elections is flawed. Rigged elections of presidents and parliaments are all too common; so are elections that merely confirm one-party rule, as in Singapore, or that are used by leaders to eliminate their opponents. Nearly all of Ukraine's and Russia's closest neighbors, such as Uzbekistan, Kazakhstan, Belarus, and Azerbaijan, have elected leaders who run their countries like dictators and expect to be presidents-for-life.[60] Or consider the Philippines, where the legacy of people power that drove Ferdinand Marcos from power in 1986 has not, despite all the elections since then, caused any real change in that country's pattern of elite domination.[61] After President Joseph Estrada was forced from office in January 2001 under questionable constitutional procedures, his vice president and successor, Gloria Macapagal-Arroyo, was able to mobilize street demonstrations and the military's support. As president, she ordered Estrada's arrest, which prompted his supporters to take to the streets in what she chose to call a "state of rebellion." That allowed for further arrests of her opponents. In 2005 and into 2006, however, she too faced pressure to resign after she apparently tried to fix an election result.

Free elections have experienced numerous setbacks in the new millennium: presidents in Indonesia (Abdurrahman Wahid), Argentina (Fernando de la Rùa), Peru (Alberto Fujimori in November 2000), Ecuador (Jamil Mahuad, 2000), Thailand (Thaksin Shinawatra, 2006), and Georgia (Eduard Shevardnadze, 2003) were beset by charges of corruption, cronyism, unconstitutional conduct, or incompetence; all were forced from office, though only one (Fujimori) was actually convicted of a crime. Haiti's elected president, Jean-Bertrand Aristide, was forced out in 2005 by mob violence and US pressure. Elections have occurred periodically in Cambodia, but under Hun Sen, the country's opposition parties and independent organizations have been intimidated and their leaders jailed or forced into exile.[62] In Mongolia, one of the few countries bordering Russia and China that seemed to have a successful democratic transition, leading democratic voices were strong-armed out of the parliament early in 2006 by former communists.

More than any factor, corruption sinks democratic hopes. Opinion polls show that widespread corruption has created a dramatic loss of confidence in democratic rule throughout Latin America.[63] Efforts to democratize (particularly if measured mainly in terms of free elections) cannot compete with official patronage, nepotism, and bribery. Both populist governments on the left, such as Luiz Inácio "Lula" da Silva in Brazil, and free-market regimes such as in Vicente Fox's Mexico and Alejandro Toledo's Peru, have been equally vulnerable to corruption on a grand scale. And these were reformists who came to power with the usual promises to clean up corruption.

To some extent corruption is in turn a consequence of economic globalization. Newfound wealth has turned political leaders into oligarchs, and vice-versa. Between 1995 and 1998, for instance, financial scandals in officialdom caused political upheavals in Italy, France, Japan, South Korea, Thailand, Colombia, Venezuela, and Peru. Russian politics, as pointed out in Chapter 6, has become overwhelmed by moneyed interests. Bribery and kickbacks are standard practices in international business, and experts say that large-scale foreign investment in emerging economies is a major reason that corruption in general costs an astounding $167 billion a year.[64] Even some of China's notorious "princelings," the sons and daughters of senior party and military leaders, could not be spared when payoffs to them were exposed. Old-time and new leaders alike, such as Mobutu of Zaire, the Salinas family in Mexico, President Suharto in Indonesia, Franjo Tudjman (president of Croatia), and the Bhutto family in Pakistan, exploited their power to amass great fortunes.[65] Trafficking and smuggling in drugs, nuclear materials, and weapons, and the virtual enslavement of women, children, and migrant workers were frequently in the news thanks to an expanding number of drug cartels, crime syndicates, and (in Burma, China, and Mexico) the military's involvement.[66] The Mafia now goes by many names, with Japanese, Russian, Chinese, Indian, and other national variations. Not surprisingly, the countries considered by international businesses to be the most corrupt are also prominent among those where democracy has failed.[67]

What such stories also tell us is that the barriers to exporting democracy, which is a fixture in US foreign policy, are very high. US-funded organizations that have sought to assist opposition politicians in the former Soviet Union—organizations that had a hand in successful pro-democracy movements in Ukraine, Georgia, and Kyrgyzstan—have been harassed, apparently with Russia's full support.[68] NGOs that seek to promote democracy are being restricted or forced to leave in Latin America and Africa as well.[69] On the other hand, exporting the US style of electoral politics, with its emphasis on telemarketing, political consultants, and image making, may have unfortunate consequences for democracy. As one study has found, the commercialization and engineering of elections means that a competition of ideas and genuine popular choice is seriously circumscribed.[70] Second, supporting democratization in a political system unused to it may be a waste of money that could be better spent on human-development projects. Third, governments that restrict foreign NGOs may sometimes be right in doing so. Just as the US government regards foreign involvement in its electoral process as intolerable, and makes it illegal, so other governments consider US-backed NGOs merely fronts for interfering in their political processes. As we will see in the Haiti and Venezuela cases (Chapter 4), supposedly pro-democracy organizations backed by the United States did interfere, and in destructive ways.

The growth of democracy and civil society is invariably impeded by political violence, whether carried out in the name of the state and "national security" or by terrorist and other anti-state groups. Studying the US war on terror is thus a suitable closing topic, for it reveals much about what the post–Cold War order has come to mean, for democracy building within countries, for the structure of international relations, and for the prospects of creating a humane world order.

## Case Study 1: 9/11 and the War on Terror

After the 9/11 attacks, US leaders launched the kind of crusade they had embarked on once before, against "international communism." But while "terrorism" was intended to concretize the main enemy, it actually distorted the nature and magnified the capabilities of terrorist organizations, which are not at all like those of regular armies encountered on battlefields.[71] The response to the attacks, the invasion of Afghanistan in pursuit of Al-Qaida's leaders, had near-universal support for the simple reason that it focused on destroying a particular terrorist organization that boasted of its responsibility for the attacks. But what should have been an international police action to kill or capture Al-Qaida criminals, in the manner of an Interpol operation against drug dealers or human traffickers, became merely prelude to—and justification for—the invasion and occupation of Iraq. With the invasion, the United States rapidly lost international support and the legitimacy of its response.

Since the 9/11 attacks terrorism has leaped to the top of the list of international security problems. But a clear understanding of terrorism is clouded by political biases. State leaders consider terrorists to be those groups, foreign or domestic, that use violence against them, as well as other states (typically labeled "rogues") that may support such violence. They thus omit not only terrorist acts that those same state leaders may sponsor, but also homegrown political violence by individuals. Such partial definitions are actually an old story that traces back to Europe immediately after World War II and throughout the Cold War, when debate focused on the violence of revolutionary parties and movements, as well as the states that opposed

them.[72] Were Algerian and Vietnamese revolutionaries terrorists or nationalists? Or were the Algerian and Vietnamese governments the real terrorists
for suppressing genuinely popular uprisings? Were the Nicaraguan *contras*
and the Afghani *mujahedeen* freedom fighters or terrorists? Was the Soviet
Union guilty of terrorism when it invaded Czechoslovakia and Afghanistan?
Was the United States guilty of terrorism when it bombed Libya and helped
overthrow governments from Guatemala to Iran? These questions had little
to do with clarifying the nature of terrorism; they were answered mainly in
accordance with one's political preferences in relation to acts of violence,
whether by groups or states.

The terrorism issue became further muddled by the character of Al-
Qaida, a transnational organization without a distinct headquarters or political program, but with a fundamentalist message and millenarian aims.
Washington contributed to the confusion not only by portraying Al-Qaida as
a monolithic entity, but also by exaggerating its links with other Islamic
groups and "rogue" governments in and beyond the Middle East. All mili-
tant groups were painted with the same brush, and the diverse causes of
political instability were conflated into one. Ignored were early warnings
from regional specialists that relying on military means risked having the
war on terrorism perceived as a war on Islam.[73] George W. Bush denied that
aim; but speeches by members of his administration consistently equated
terrorism with Islamic fundamentalism, thus dismissing the need to examine
dispassionately Al-Qaida's motives. As Chris Hedges has so eloquently
observed:

> By accepting the facile cliché that the battle under way against terrorism is
> a battle against evil, by easily branding those who fight us as the barbar-
> ians, we, like them, refuse to acknowledge our own culpability. We ignore
> real injustices that have led many of those arrayed against us to their rage
> and despair.[74]

The implications of these distortions of the terror issue are consequential for world politics. No sooner had Bush classified the search for Osama
bin Laden, Al-Qaida's leader, as part of an endless war on terror than other
state leaders began reframing their own wars. China's ethnic minority sepa-
ratists; Chechnya fighters in Russia; Kashmiris challenging India; antigovernment groups from Saudi Arabia to Colombia; and Hamas, Hezbollah,
and Palestinian groups fighting Israel—all were reclassified as terrorists by
those out to destroy them. (As Israel's minister of public security said, at a
time when Yasser Arafat headed the Palestinian Authority: "Arafat is of
course no different than bin Laden. The PLO [Palestine Liberation
Organization] and the Palestinian Authority are equal to the al Qaeda."[75])
This is not to say that terrorists are a figment of the imagination in these or
many other conflicts. But these conflicts predated the war on terror and are
highly likely to go on regardless of when or whether the war on terror ends.

They reflect national conditions, not some global master plan, just as did leftist revolutions during the Cold War.

The debate about what to do about terrorism proved equally as confounding and misleading as the debate about terrorism's identity. If counterterrorism meant war, what were the war's boundaries, which states were appropriate allies, and how long might the war last and cost? Bush promised that the war on terror "will not end until every terrorist group of global reach has been found, stopped, and defeated."[76] Some top US officials put forth a new interpretation of sovereignty that allowed the United States and others the right to intervene against states that "support terrorism."[77] That goal set an extraordinary agenda: launching military strikes against certain states (not just Iraq and Afghanistan but perhaps Iran and North Korea as well); financing unsavory groups that sought to overthrow "pro-terrorist" governments, as in Somalia;[78] or providing military assistance to governments that proclaimed their need of help against home-grown terrorists, as in Central and Southeast Asia. These approaches entailed large and oftentimes dysfunctional commitments, such as to undemocratic governments in Indonesia and Pakistan.[79]

The new US doctrine of "limited sovereignty" also spelled trouble for international security generally. If the United States gave itself permission to intervene against terrorists, so might other governments. A terrorist assault on the Indian parliament by gunmen who evidently belonged to an organization based in Pakistan brought the two countries to the brink of war as 2001 ended.[80] Further, "limited sovereignty" meant a limited role for the United Nations, since under the Bush Doctrine (see Chapter 2) the United States did not regard Security Council endorsement as essential to fighting terrorism or anything else. The United States did obtain the Security Council's passage of Resolution 1368 shortly after 9/11; it required all states to block the financing, recruitment, arming, and freedom of movement of terrorist groups. However, the document did not define "terrorist," and its lack of specific endorsement of action against countries believed to be harboring or abetting terrorists made it easier for Bush to justify unilateral intervention in both Afghanistan and Iraq.

The war on terrorism was containment redux. From Yemen to the Philippines to Colombia, the United States used the opportunity of the war to create the impression that internal conflicts of widely varying histories were somehow linked. The Revolutionary Armed Forces of Colombia (FARC)'s drug-financed war against the Colombian government, the thirty-year-old Muslim rebellion of Abu Sayyaf in the southern Philippines, and antigovernment violence in Yemen all were classified as terrorist conflicts. No credible effort was made to prove a relationship between any of these conflicts and Al-Qaida; it was simply stated by the Bush administration and generally reported as fact in the mainstream media. Yet, as a former chief of counterintelligence in the US Central Intelligence Agency (CIA) wrote, spreading the war increased the risks: "There is a difference between retaliating against Al-Qaida and its sponsors or affiliates, which can be understood as self-defense, and confronting a somewhat random series of armed groups. The difference may be that between finding enemies and making them."[81] By 2006 the assessment that the Iraq war had worsened the struggle against terrorism had gained acceptance throughout the US intelligence community.[82] Hezbollah's fight with Israel in mid-2006 may create another such situation.[83]

All the attention devoted to terrorism as a new threat to global security has come at a price: attention taken away from the more enduring sources of misery, conflict, and consequent despair that plague impoverished societies and peoples, certainly including Palestine.[84] This, despite the widespread view, to which top US government officials subscribe, that terrorism (in the words of Secretary of State Colin Powell) "really flourishes in areas of poverty, despair and hopelessness, where people see no future."[85] But the Bush administration evidently preferred the use of force to financing a war on poverty. Secretary-General Annan put the priority correctly when he said in 2003, with clear reference to US policy in Iraq:

> All of us know there are new threats that must be faced or, perhaps, old threats in new and dangerous combinations, new forms of terrorism and the proliferation of weapons of mass destruction. But while some consider these threats as self-evidently the main challenge to world peace and security, others feel more immediately menaced by small arms employed in civil conflict or by so-called soft threats such as the persistence of extreme poverty, the disparity of income between and within societies, and the spread of infectious diseases, or climate change and environmental degradation. . . . We now see, with chilling clarity, that a world where many millions of people endure brutal oppression and extreme misery will never be fully secure, even for its most privileged inhabitants.[86]

At one level Annan was sending the message that the immediate security concerns of the United States are not necessarily those of other countries. But at a deeper level, he was trying to gain perspective on the 9/11 attacks by reminding world leaders that come what may in the use of force to defeat terrorism, the root causes of international insecurity will still be with us and will require more sophisticated and long-term responses. And on that point he has been joined by a host of development experts who warn that if the United States and other major powers persist in "empower[ing] weak, autocratic, and corrupt states" rather than working to strengthen their legitimacy and effectiveness, such as by meeting people's basic needs, political violence is likely to spread.[87] That is a point worth remembering as we consider how differently realists, globalists, and global humanists evaluate world politics in general and the Third World in particular.

## Notes

1. Francis Fukuyama, "The End of History?" *The National Interest.*

2. U Thant, Address of May 9, 1969, "Ten Crucial Years," *United Nations Monthly Chronicle,* p. ii.

3. "World Scientists' Warning to Humanity," pamphlet produced by the Union of Concerned Scientists, 1992.

4. *New York Times* (hereafter, *NYT*), September 5, 2000, p. A13.

5. Willy Brandt et al., *North-South, A Program for Survival,* p. 58.

6. Jeffrey D. Sachs, *The End of Poverty: Economic Possibilities for Our Time* (New York: Penguin, 2005), pp. 20–21.

7. Yuri Dikhanov, *Trends in Global Income Distribution, 1970–2000, and Scenarios for 2015,* pp. 43, 47.

8. Ivan L. Head, "South-North Dangers," *Foreign Affairs,* p. 77.

9. According to a long-term worldwide assessment that concluded in 1998; see *NYT*, April 9, 1998, p. 1.

10. "Recent Trends in Military Expenditures," Stockholm International Peace Research Institute (SIPRI), at www.sipri.org/contents/milap/milex/mex_trends.html (2006).

11. The estimate on world hunger is from a United Nations report cited in *NYT*, December 8, 2004, p. A5. On the spending alternatives, see Ruth Leger-Sivard, ed., *World Military and Social Expenditures 1983: An Annual Report on World Priorities,* p. 5; Brandt et al., p. 14.

12. World Bank, *World Development Report 1992: Development and the Environment,* p. 27 (hereafter, *World Development Report 1992*); study by the World Health Organization and the UN Environment Program reported in *The Oregonian,* December 2, 1992, p. A7.

13. David Keen, *Refugees: Rationing the Right to Life,* p. 3.

14. Warren Hoge, "Nations Benefit From Migration, U.N. Study Says," *NYT*, June 7, 2006, p. A8.

15. Nicholas D. Kristof, "Malaria Makes a Comeback, and Is More Deadly Than Before," *NYT*, January 8, 1997, p. A7.

16. Lawrence K. Altman and Elisabeth Rosenthal, "U.N. Strengthens Call for a Global Battle Against AIDS," *NYT*, June 3, 2006, online ed. at www.nytimes.com.

17. Elisabeth Malkin, "At World Forum, Support Erodes for Private Management of Water," *NYT*, March 20, 2006, p. A11.

18. John Heilprin (Associated Press), "Earth's Temperature Is Highest in Centuries," AOL News, June 23, 2006, online at http://news.aol.com.

19. Todd S. Purdum, "Several U.S. Allies Criticized in Powell Report on Slave Trading," *NYT*, June 6, 2002, p. A13.

20. See Robert A. Isaak, *International Political Economy: Managing World Economic Change,* p. 2. There are several different emphases to "international political economy," reflecting narrower or broader understandings of what "politics" comprises. For a sense of the diversity, see R. Dan Walleri, "The Political Economy Literature on North-South Relations: Alternative Approaches and Empirical Evidence," *International Studies Quarterly;* James Petras, *Critical Perspectives on Imperialism and Social Class in the Third World,* ch. 1; and Robert J. Gilpin, *U.S. Power and the Multinational Corporations,* ch. 1.

21. Humane values and norms, as key elements in the global-humanist (or "world order") perspective, are discussed in the following major works: Richard A. Falk, *A Study of Future Worlds* (the introduction includes discussion of the World Order Models Project); Richard A. Falk, Samuel S. Kim, and Saul H. Mendlovitz, eds., *Toward a Just World Order,* vol. 1; Samuel S. Kim, *The Quest for a Just World*

*Order;* Saul H. Mendlovitz, ed., *On the Creation of a Just World Order;* and Johan Galtung, *The True Worlds: A Transnational Perspective.*

22. Kissinger, quoted in Charles W. Kegley Jr., and Eugene R. Wittkopf, *World Politics: Trend and Transformation* (1981 ed.), p. 29.

23. About 90 percent of North Korea's total imports in 2003 consisted of food and other foreign aid. See Stephan Haggard and Marcus Noland, *Hunger and Human Rights: The Politics of Famine in North Korea,* fig. 2, p. 15.

24. Total deaths from the accident may be in the range of several thousand. The impact of radiation on children, notably a high incidence of thyroid cancer, has been particularly severe. "Chernobyl will be with us forever," said Ukraine's health minister (*NYT,* April 23, 1998, p. A5), although the plant itself was shut down for good in 2006. Medical sources from around the world can only guess how many additional people will die, become ill, or suffer genetic disorders, in Ukraine, neighboring Belarus, and worldwide, from the radiation. See Harvey Wasserman, "In the Dead Zone: Aftermath of the Apocalypse," *The Nation.*

25. This is the report of the Intergovernmental Panel on Climate Change. See *NYT,* February 3, 2007, p. 1. The full report is expected to be released in late 2007, and will be available at www.ipcc.ch.

26. For a European view of English as the language of globalization, including on the World Wide Web, see Jeanne Peiffer, "The Plurilingual European Tradition as a Challenge to Globalization," in Inoue Nobutaka, ed., *Globalization and Indigenous Culture.*

27. Wolfgang H. Reinicke, "Global Public Policy," *Foreign Affairs,* pp. 127–38. With reference to economics, Reinicke proposes that interdependence is macroeconomic in its consequences, and globalization is microeconomic.

28. Richard J. Barnet and John Cavanagh, *Global Dreams: Imperial Corporations and the New World Order,* pp. 13–14.

29. Two other excellent sources on the meaning of globalization are P.J. Simmons and Chantal de Jonge Oudraat, eds., *Managing Global Issues: Lessons Learned,* and David Held et al., *Global Transformations: Politics, Economics, and Culture.*

30. One example is the cooperation between US and Mexican labor unions that has occurred as a direct result of NAFTA. Global environmental changes have also enhanced the influence of NGOs and other social activists vis-à-vis the state; see Ronnie D. Lipschutz and Ken Conca, eds., *The State and Social Power in Global Environmental Politics.* Grassroots responses to economic globalization are documented by Jeremy Brecher and Tim Costello, *Global Village or Global Pillage: Economic Reconstruction from the Bottom Up.*

31. As in Barnet and Cavanagh, *Global Dreams.*

32. Benjamin R. Barber, "Jihad vs. McWorld," *The Atlantic,* pp. 53–63.

33. Maurice Strong, "The 'New South,'" *The World Today,* pp. 215–19.

34. Speech of January 16, 1991, in Micah L. Sifry and Christopher Cerf, eds., *The Gulf War Reader: History, Documents, Opinions,* p. 313.

35. For an excellent summary and evaluation of the issues, see Richard Falk, "In Search of a New World Model," *Current History,* pp. 145–49.

36. In mid-1998, the United States was in arrears by between $1 billion and $1.5 billion in payments to the regular and special (peacekeeping) budgets of the UN. Consequently, under the UN Charter, it was in danger of losing its vote in the General Assembly. *NYT,* June 28, 1998, online. Once the George W. Bush administration took office, a deal with Senator Jesse Helms freed up funds for repayment.

37. Annan, "'We the Peoples': The Role of the United Nations in the 21st Century," chapter 3 of his Millennium Report to the UN, at www.un.org/millennium/sg/report/ch3.htm (hereafter cited as Annan, *Millennium Report*).

38. William Pfaff, "Ideology Still Looms Large in the World," *International Herald Tribune*, January 6, 2000, online ed. at www.iht.com; John Ralston Saul, "The Collapse of Globalism," *Harper's*, March 2004, pp. 33–43.

39. This is the argument of Elise Boulding, "The Old and New Transnationalism: An Evolutionary Perspective," *Human Relations*, pp. 789–805.

40. See Joel Kotkin, *Tribes: How Race, Religion and Identity Determine Success in the New Global Economy.*

41. Michael Renner, "Violent Conflicts Unchanged," in Lisa Mastny et al., *Vital Signs 2005: The Trends That Are Shaping Our Future*, pp. 74–75.

42. In Guatemala, the war was largely the work of a ruthless military apparatus. About 150,000 people, mostly of Indian ethnicity, lost their lives, and another 50,000 people disappeared (*NYT*, April 28, 1998, p. A8). Approximately 3,200 people were killed in Northern Ireland's violence, which may finally have ended with the signing of a power-sharing agreement in March 2007.

43. Text in *NYT*, May 1, 2003, p. A7.

44. The civil war in Somalia (1988–1995) caused around 355,000 deaths; in Afghanistan since 1991, over 1 million; in Liberia (1990–1995), about 100,000; in Congo (since 1998), about 3.8 million; and in Sudan (since 1984), upwards of 2 million, including about 200,000 in the Darfur region from 2003 to the present. Milton Leitenberg, "Deaths in Wars and Conflicts"; Sivard et al., *World Military and Social Expenditures 1996*, pp. 18–19; Philip Christenson, "Fall of Mobutu Is No Guarantee of Peace," *Los Angeles Times World Report,* May 24, 1997, p. 5; Marc Lacey, "Beyond the Bullets and Blades," *NYT*, March 20, 2005, sec. 4, p. 1; Renner, "Violent Conflicts Unchanged," p. 74.

45. Figures from Sivard et al., *World Military and Social Expenditures 1996*, pp. 18–19, and Center for Defense Information, "The World at War," *The Defense Monitor*, table 3, p. 4.

46. Stockholm International Peace Research Institute, ed., *SIPRI Yearbook 1992: World Armaments and Disarmament*, tables 8.1 and 8.2, pp. 272–73. Since 1987 China has been the fifth largest arms exporter, and Japan the fourth largest arms importer in the world.

47. By contrast, in 1988 the UN's annual peacekeeping budget was $230 million for five operations; and in 1992 the budget was about $1.7 billion for eleven peacekeeping operations. *NYT*, January 6, 1995, p. A3.

48. *NYT,* May 31, 1995, p. A6.

49. SLORC, which has governed since 1988, redesignated itself the State Peace and Development Council. I use the original name to avoid confusion, and out of deference to the Burmese peace forces (which also prefer "Burma" to SLORC's creation, Myanmar).

50. Annan, *Millennium Report.*

51. Speech at the University of Michigan, April 30, 1999, at www.un.org/News/Press/docs/1999/19990430.SGSM6977.html.

52. Annan, *Millennium Report*, ch. 3.

53. For example, in 2002 the United States had a total of 9,166 military and civilian personnel assigned to international peacekeeping. Of those, only about 700 were under UN command, including a single soldier. See the chart in *NYT*, July 3, 2002, p. A4.

54. As a shorthand definition, we may think of civil society as "a political space, or arena, where voluntary associations seek to shape the rules that govern one or the other aspect of social life. . . . Civil society associations bring together people who share concerns about a particular policy area or problem." It should be noted that by no means are all civil-society groups devoted to progressive causes. See Jan Aart Scholte et al., *Democratizing the Global Economy: The Role of Civil Society.*

55. See Adrian Karatnycky, "Ukraine's Orange Revolution," *Foreign Affairs*, pp. 35–52. The ousted president, Leonid Kuchma, had once been tape-recorded ordering the elimination of various political enemies. He also engineered the removal from office of his reform-minded prime minister, was implicated in the murder of a reform-minded journalist, came under fire for vote rigging and illegal arms exports, and manipulated the country's supreme court to secure a third term in office. Even so, Ukraine's new leadership fell on hard economic times and charges of corruption. President Viktor Yushchenko's reform government suffered heavy losses in parliamentary elections that were widely hailed, including by the president himself, as exceptionally free.

56. See Ginger Thompson, "Report on Mexican 'Dirty War' Details Abuse by Military," *NYT*, February 27, 2006, p. A3. For the draft report, see the National Security Archive for February 2006 at www.nsarchive.org.

57. Larry Rohter, "After Decades, Nations Focus on Rights Abuses," *NYT*, September 1, 2005, p. A4.

58. Fareed Zakaria, "The Rise of Illiberal Democracy," *Foreign Affairs,* pp. 22–43.

59. Howard W. French, "Africa's Ballot Box: Look Out for Sleight of Hand," *NYT*, October 24, 1995, p. A3. See also French's later report, "Sure, Africa's Troubled; But There Is Good News," *NYT,* June 15, 1997, online.

60. Douglas Frantz, "Fresh Dynasties Sprout in Post-Soviet Lands as Democratic Succession Withers," *NYT*, February 20, 2001, online ed.

61. Seth Mydans, "Political Turmoil Again Thwarts Progress in Philippines," *NYT*, February 26, 2006, p. 3.

62. Mydans, "Cambodian Leader Cracks Down in Bid to Solidify Power," *NYT*, January 9, 2006, online ed.

63. Two excellent surveys are by Juan Forero, "Latin America Graft and Poverty Trying Patience with Democracy," *NYT*, June 24, 2004, online ed., and Larry Rohter and Juan Forero, "Unending Graft Is Threatening Latin America," *NYT*, July 30, 2005, p. A1.

64. Paul Lewis, "International Community Takes Steps to Curb Corruption," *NYT*, November 28, 1996, online.

65. Mobutu became exceptionally wealthy during his thirty-odd years as the unchallenged ruler of Zaire. A civil war finally forced him into exile, and led to his death, at one of his French estates in 1997. Raúl Salinas, brother of Mexico's president (Carlos Salinas de Gotari) in the mid-1990s, evidently received payoffs by cocaine traffickers in return for political favors. He was later arrested on corruption charges and found to have stashed millions of dollars in overseas bank accounts (Sam Dillon, "Fugitive Lawman Speaks: How Mexico Mixes Narcotics and Politics," *NYT,* December 23, 1996, p. 1). Suharto, who was forced to step down in May 1998 after thirty-two years in office, was an exemplar of crony capitalism, which enabled him and his family to amass a fortune once estimated at $30 billion (Philip Shenon, "For Asian Nation's First Family, Financial Empire Is in Peril," *NYT,* January 16, 1998, p. 1). Karadzic and Tudjman, as various newspapers reported in 1997, were essentially war profiteers who enriched themselves and their supporters through control of the government-run alcohol and cigarette market, and through prostitution and drug trafficking. Their "governments" more closely resembled a Chicago mob. As for the Bhutto family (see John F. Burns, "Bhutto Clan Leaves Trail of Corruption," *NYT*, January 9, 1998, p. 1), Benazir Bhutto, whose father had served as Pakistan's prime minister until his execution, twice was prime minister herself—the first female to head a Muslim country. She and her husband seem to have profited from a number of multimillion-dollar bribes paid by foreign companies and then banked abroad to facilitate deals with the Pakistani government.

66. On the involvement of organized crime in illegal immigration, see *NYT,* June 14, 1995, p. A8.

67. Voted most corrupt in 1996 were Nigeria, Pakistan, Kenya, Bangladesh, China, Cameroon, Venezuela, Russia, India, and Indonesia. Barbara Crossette, "Yearly Survey of Businesses Rates Nigeria Most Corrupt," *NYT,* June 2, 1996, online, and *NYT,* June 3, 1996, p. A4. The other face of the corruption problem, however, is that businesses have continued to *pay* bribes as an ordinary cost of doing business.

68. Joel Brinkley, "Pro-Democracy Groups Are Harassed in Central Asia," *NYT,* December 4, 2005, p. 3.

69. Thomas Carothers, "The Backlash Against Democracy Promotion," *Foreign Affairs,* pp. 55–56.

70. See Gerald Sussman and Lawrence Galizio, "The Global Reproduction of American Politics," *Political Communication,* pp. 309–28.

71. For an excellent critique along these lines, see Jeffrey Record, *Bounding the Global War on Terrorism.*

72. See, for example, Maurice Merleau-Ponty, *Humanism and Terror: An Essay on the Communist Problem.*

73. See Ahmed Rashid, "New Wars to Fight" (on Central and South Asia) and Bruce Wain, "Unfriendly Fire" (on Southeast Asia), both in *Far Eastern Economic Review,* September 12, 2001, pp. 14–22.

74. Chris Hedges, *War Is a Force That Gives Us Meaning.*

75. *NYT,* June 19, 2002, p. 1.

76. Speech to Congress of September 20, 2001, in *NYT,* September 21, 2001, p. B4.

77. See Nicholas Lemann, "The Next World Order," *The New Yorker,* pp. 45–46.

78. The groups in question were warlords whose efforts, funded by the CIA, were defeated by an Islamic government that took power in Mogadishu in June 2006. See John Prendergast, "Our Failure in Somalia," *Washington Post,* June 7, 2006, online ed. at www.washingtonpost.com.

79. In Indonesia, US counterterrorism aid was accompanied by pressure to arrest local Muslim leaders, creating perceptions of undue interference in the country's internal affairs. See, for instance, Michael R. Gordon, "Indonesian Scolds U.S. on Terrorism Fight," *NYT,* June 7, 2006, online ed. US aid to Pakistan's army in order to contain the presumed danger of radical Islamists not only exaggerated that danger; it also overlooked the assistance the Pakistan military has itself provided to violent Islamic groups in Afghanistan and Kashmir. See Frédéric Grare, "Pakistan: The Myth of an Islamist Peril," *Policy Brief,* pp. 1–7.

80. See the account of Steve Coll, "The Stand-Off," *The New Yorker,* pp. 126–39. The attack put enormous pressure on President Pervez Musharraf of Pakistan to take direct action against extremist groups as well as against the religious schools (*madrasas*) that were believed to be training terrorists. Facing a huge Indian military buildup along the border, and under US pressure to take strong action against domestic sources of terrorism, Musharraf announced in January a ban on all such organizations and schools.

81. Vince M. Cannistraro, "The War on Terror Enters Phase 2," *NYT,* May 2, 2002, p. A27.

82. A classified National Intelligence Estimate of April 2006, leaked to the press, states: "The Iraq conflict has become the cause célèbre for jihadists, breeding a deep resentment of U.S. involvement in the Muslim world and cultivating supporters for the global jihadist movement." *NYT,* September 27, 2006, p. A6.

83. By supporting Israel's bombing of Lebanon in retaliation for Hezbollah raids, the United States is likely to face a new round of suicide bombings and other violent acts of retribution by new recruits.

84. A report in 2001 by Terje Roed-Larsen, the United Nations Special Coordinator for the Middle East Peace Process, indicated the numerous signs of decline and inequity in Palestine: an economy that was losing $8.6 million a day; about 250,000 Palestinians, representing 38 percent of the workforce, unemployed; 32 percent of the population living in poverty; and a fiscal crisis for the Palestinian Authority (PA), due in large part to Israel's withholding of revenues that it collects for the PA. Roed-Larsen made the prescient argument that it was "in the interest of Israel that the Palestinian Authority doesn't collapse, because that will produce a situation of anarchy that will make a difficult security situation." He went on to say: "People have lost faith not only in the peace process but in any dialogue with Israel, which is fueling now a support for and participation in violence." *NYT*, February 13, 2001, online ed.

85. *NYT*, February 2, 2002, p. A8.

86. *NYT*, September 24, 2003, p. A11.

87. This is the major conclusion of a study commissioned by the Center for Global Development in Washington, DC. See Commission on Weak States and US National Security, *On the Brink: Weak States and US National Security* (June 8, 2004), at www.cgdev.org.

# 2

# Realism and Corporate Globalism in Theory and Practice

*power & security.*

## The Realist Perspective

The process of globalization under way in the world needs to be oriented in the direction of equity and solidarity to avoid the marginalization of people and groups. . . . Will everyone be able to take advantage of a global market? Will everyone at last have a chance to enjoy peace? Will relations between states become more equitable or will economic competition and rivalries lead humanity toward even greater instability?
— Pope John Paul II's 1998 New Year's message

Throughout the postwar years, realism has reigned as the dominant way of looking at the world among state leaders and their advisers.[1] But corporate globalism, centered in the United States, Japan, and the other major industrialized countries that are home to the world's largest corporations, became a powerful force in its own right in the second half of the twentieth century. Realism speaks to the interests of state power, corporate globalism to the market needs of transnational institutions, mainly business and finance.[2] In the next two sections, I want to assess these two perspectives with specific reference to the global crisis and the issues of interdependence they raise. With the help of case studies of postwar US economic planning, the global financial crises of the 1990s, and the US war on Iraq, I hope to show that— despite important differences of emphasis—realism and corporate globalism embrace common values and aims, many of which run counter to human interests.

For realists, power is the essential ingredient of politics. It is the instinctive goal of persons (who are considered to be naturally evil-minded and aggressive); and it is the unavoidable objective of nations (since international relations is a jungle). The best leaders seek to maximize their country's power, believing that the national interest is thereby served. The standard operating precepts of realist diplomats are to construct and defend a

stable balance of power among rival states; to evaluate the costs and benefits of state actions in strictly national terms; to operate on the basis of what
is, not what has been or might be; to disregard expressions of good intentions by other leaders; to trust no one (not even allies) and nothing, other
than the justness of one's own national cause; and to rely on coercion rather
than moral suasion, diplomatic agreements, international law, or an open,
democratic decisionmaking process to protect and enforce one's interests.

Table 2.1 displays what seem to be the principal values that guide the
social behavior of realists, corporate globalists, and global humanists.
While there undoubtedly would be some differences between realists in different socioeconomic systems—for example, realists in the West would say
they value individualism and liberty, whereas socialist realists would give
priority to collectivism and social conformism—I maintain that in general
realists everywhere share most of the values listed. Clearly, the emphasis is
on authoritativeness: decisiveness, competitiveness, and elitism.
Transferred to the level of official work (institutional), these values are typically expressed in a determination to defeat the opponent (other bureaucracies and other states) in the game of nations, and thus to preserve the
national interest. But on closer examination, we find that there is nothing
"national" about this interest. In any political system, the national interest
usually defines the political-economic priorities of an elite—that set of
interests that *it* decides national power ought to promote. Realist leaders (as
well as corporate-globalist leaders) do not usually count cooperation, participation, accountability, and social responsibility among the values they
apply to national or international politics. With the onset of globalization,
those kinds of social values, so central to global humanism, are even more
likely to be sacrificed to competitive, win-at-all-cost values.

Realism's guiding norm, and corporate globalism's too, is system maintenance. Both seek, while relying on different tools, to preserve a favorable
status quo. In the realists' case, the national interest must be preserved;
accommodations to political change are acceptable, but only so long as the
underlying structure of power is retained. "Them versus us" is another classic realist norm, used by US realists to justify the Vietnam War[3] and, most
recently, the Iraq war. But some realists have disputed those and other war-
making decisions, not on moral grounds but on the basis that *that* war did
not threaten the global balance of power, or that the benefits of *that* war no
longer justified the costs. In spite of these differences, realists, like their
corporate-globalist counterparts, concur on the need to preserve the "rules
of the game" by which the system itself (capitalism, socialism, pan-
Arabism) maintains hegemony.

Realism is a paradigm of the philosophy, strategy, and objectives that
define the national security state, that complex of institutions, special interests, and powerful bureaucracies that govern all societies. And for the

**Table 2.1    Alternative Values**

| Realist | Corporate Globalist | Global Humanist |
|---|---|---|
| **Personal values** | | |
| action | action | androgyny |
| adaptation | adaptation | appropriateness |
| aggressiveness | aggressiveness | authenticity |
| ambition | ambition | community |
| amorality | amorality | compassion |
| competition | competition | cooperation |
| disingenuousness | disingenuousness | diversity |
| elitism | elitism | enoughness |
| invulnerability | invulnerability | equality |
| leadership | leadership | harmony |
| loyalty | loyalty | honesty |
| materialism | materialism | idealism |
| perseverance | perseverance | integrity |
| power | power | morality |
| pragmatism | pragmatism | naturalness |
| progress | progress | nonviolence |
| success | success | personal power |
| toughness | toughness | responsibility |
| | | self-reliance |
| | | service |
| | | spirituality |
| | | spontaneity |
| | | tradition |
| | | trust |
| | | vulnerability |
| **Institutional values** | | |
| bargaining | access | accountability |
| competition | bigness | appropriate technology |
| control | consumption | autonomy |
| diffused accountability | control | collectivity |
| flexibility | diffused accountability | decentralization |
| gamesmanship | efficiency | democratic management |
| hierarchy | growth | equal opportunity/ rewards |
| influence | hierarchy | networking |
| mission | influence | openness |
| order | laissez-faire | participation |
| pluralism | loyalty | shared power (empowerment) |
| prestige | order | small scale |
| racism | profit | voluntary simplicity |
| secrecy | racism | |
| security | secrecy | |
| sexism | sexism | |
| stability | specialization | |
| standard operating procedures | (division of labor) | |
| team play | stability | |
| winning | team play | |
| worst-case planning | technological solutions | |

national security manager who runs the system, as Richard Barnet observes, "the basic premise . . . is that international politics is a game."[4] A game has stakes, rules, winners, and losers. Peace is threatening to realists, not because it is undesirable in the abstract, but because it is inherently suspect: Since conflict, not harmony, is believed to characterize the "real world," the national interest is better served by emphasizing positions of strength based on military power rather than diplomacy in resolving disputes. As Henry Kissinger once wrote, "No idea could be more dangerous" than that peace "can be aimed at directly as a goal of policy."[5]

International security in realist terms is the ability to deter or neutralize threats to national power, rendering them harmless. Hence the realists' constant emphasis on stability and order, preferably through a balance of power among the major states. But a balance of power, as early "idealists" like Norman Angell (writing in the first decade of the twentieth century) first observed, is inherently unstable. In the absence of common values and ideas, states will seek superiority, not balance, with their rivals.[6] That is precisely how the United States has behaved since 2001.[7] To speak of a new post–Cold War equilibrium, therefore, only makes sense to those few governments that make the rules and whose interests can be satisfied by orderly change.[8] For the rest, equilibrium is likely to be bitterly contested among the major powers themselves as well as between them and weak states or political movements. In such circumstances, realists may resort to other devices, such as military and economic alliances, containment, threats of economic sanctions, spheres of influence, dependent relationships with weak states, or anything else that ensures hegemony and promotes manageability and a measure of predictability in the system as a whole.

Should these methods fail, the maintenance of empire requires that realists be prepared to use force (to "up the ante" and play "hardball," as they like to say). Destabilization of opponents, sometimes including friendly governments, comes first, by exerting external and internal pressures such as embargoes, suspension of credits, disinformation campaigns, support of political and military opponents, and impositions of sanctions. Next up the ladder are unilateral interventions and intimidation using military power to weaken or eliminate those whose actions are believed to undermine a major power's sphere of influence. For example, Soviet forces backed the Communist Party coup in Czechoslovakia in 1948 and intervened directly in 1968. Moscow maintained about one million soldiers along the border with China for about twenty years. Soviet tanks crushed uprisings in Hungary and Poland in 1956; they lurked in the background when the Solidarity movement of Polish workers threatened to topple communist authority in 1981. Soviet forces also intervened in Afghanistan (1979–1989) and in the 1990s in Chechnya, Tajikistan, and Georgia. US forces were sent to Lebanon (1958), the Dominican Republic (1965), Vietnam (1965–1973), and Grenada (1984) to prevent the dominoes from falling in those regions. In Panama

(1989), US forces intervened to seize a dictator and bring him to the United States for trial. Indirect US pressure proved sufficient to cause changes of government in Iran (1953), Guatemala (1954), Brazil (1964), Chile (1973), and Australia (1975). The Chinese have proved they can practice realist politics, too. In 1979, their troops crossed into Vietnam in order, their leaders said, to "teach a lesson" to their once close allies. And in 1996 China's military conducted a series of missile tests near Taiwan to intimidate its leaders and dissuade them from seeking independence.

In every one of these cases, state leaders justified their actions by clothing them in doctrines of national interest. To realists, principles of sovereignty and self-determination have their limits when national security is believed threatened. But is there really any essential difference between, say, the Brezhnev Doctrine that was used to rationalize Soviet intervention in Czechoslovakia in 1968, on the basis that Czech political liberalization might infect the rest of Eastern Europe, and the US-backed overthrow of Chile's Salvador Allende in 1973, on the basis that (as Secretary of State Kissinger said then) "we [shouldn't] have to stand back and watch a country go Communist because of the irresponsibility of its own people"?[9] Just as the Czechs dared to talk about democracy, the Chilean people had the audacity to elect a socialist president, leading President Richard Nixon to decide that Chile should be "squeezed until it 'screamed.'"[10] Reasons of state tend to sound the same everywhere.

Indeed, self-righteous doctrines of the "just war" are among the hallmarks of realist politics. And herein lies the essential flaw of realism itself. For, clearly, if all states live by the iron law that might makes right and that success is the only arbiter of action, then international politics is indeed a jungle governed only by survival of the most heavily armed—a self-fulfilling prophecy. Even disastrous uses of force—the United States in Vietnam, the Soviet Union in Afghanistan, China in Vietnam—did not lead great powers to reassess interventionism. The United States in Iraq seems destined to repeat that script. Realism thus contributes to perpetuating the disorderly world that justifies itself, in the manner of a doctor who keeps a patient on medication in order to ensure future visits. Little room is left for developing alternatives to power politics and limiting the reach of aggrandizing states. Even in the post–Cold War period, where international hardball is played multilaterally more often than before, the conclusion is the same. The war with Iraq in 1991, the invasion of Haiti to oust a military dictatorship in 1994, the North Atlantic Treaty Organization's (NATO) use of air power against the Serbs in the late 1990s, and sanctions on North Korea in 2006 all had United Nations approval. Yet such uses of force and pressure are not necessarily justified by that approval. Each case has its own background that might have made the use of force and sanctions avoidable. And in each case, the actions taken mainly served national, not common-security objectives.

As realism is typically practiced, national security conflicts directly with global security: The search for absolute security that preoccupies realist leaders intensifies interstate violence and legitimizes open-ended military spending and buildups. Enough is never enough. James Woolsey, on being appointed director of (US) Central Intelligence in 1993, defended his $30 billion post–Cold War budget by saying, "Yes, we have slain a large dragon [the USSR]. But we live now in a jungle filled with a bewildering variety of poisonous snakes. And in many ways, the dragon was easier to keep track of."[11] Many other bureaucratic leaders shared this mixture of Cold War nostalgia for the predictable enemy and zeal to protect an agency that thrives on threats to national security. Inasmuch as costs and benefits are weighed in terms of state power, ordinary citizens often are left out of the equation. "In politics the nation and not humanity is the ultimate fact," as Hans Morgenthau, the most-cited realist, once conceded.[12] As we will see in Chapter 5, citizens pay dearly for extravagant national-security programs.

Perhaps it is already apparent how difficult it must be for realists to adapt to an interdependent world system. The more transnational politics becomes, the less relevant (and effective) are policies based on one-sidedly promoting the national interest. While realists persist in interpreting the world in terms of strategic choices and capabilities, the key issues are increasingly developmental and compel mutual cooperation. Thus, realism did not anticipate the Soviet attempt to fend off collapse by adopting perestroika, Russia's efforts to democratize, and China's decision to embrace an open-door, market-oriented development path. Political leaders there recognized their countries' backwardness and incapacity and chose to break with the past. In doing so, both countries moved closer to longstanding enemies in the West. Domestic needs chiefly motivated those historic decisions, not (as realism would have it) power politics.[13]

As secretary of state, Henry Kissinger once lectured a Chilean foreign minister, even before Allende's election, that "nothing important can come from the South. History has never been produced in the South. The axis of history starts in Moscow, goes to Bonn, crosses over to Washington, and then goes to Tokyo."[14] It is as if the strategic balance is the only game in town, and small states can only be bit players in it. Realists typically underestimate the enormous impact that developments in the Third World have on world politics, beginning with political and ethnic nationalism (as in Latin America and Africa), economic nationalism (as in Middle East oil), and trade (the emergence of Pacific Rim countries such as South Korea and Taiwan as technological competitors). They also overestimate, as in Kissinger's remark above, the ability of big powers to control and manipulate Third World politics. The United States, for example, could no more determine the outcome of Vietnam's, Cuba's, Iran's, or southern Africa's revolutions than the Soviet Union and Russia could dictate the course of events in China, Afghanistan, or the Horn of Africa.

Excessive attention to military and ideological issues, and the persistent belief that history belongs to the great powers, have diverted the resources of the major powers from other areas besides armaments that affect national security and international influence. "Imperial overstretch," as Paul Kennedy's monumental history shows, invariably undermines the real security of the states that engage in it.[15] In an interdependent world, real security must take statecraft beyond the diplomacy of war and peace. Famine, global warming, job flight, toxic waste dumping, and massive refugee flows may threaten societies from without and within simultaneously. Realism's response, however, often treats global problems episodically. Each is managed behind closed doors, finessed until the next eruption, or election. Thus, we had the energy and inflation crises in the 1970s, the recession and unemployment crises in the early 1980s, the food and debt crises in the mid-1980s, the financial crisis in the 1990s, and the crises of terrorism and global warming today. Crisis management, however, is woefully inadequate to the scope of the problems, like putting Band-Aids on gaping wounds.

One reason realists prefer to treat the symptoms of global disorder rather than search for basic cures is that they recognize and fear the revolutionary potential of deeper structural change. Aid programs, arms sales, food relief, and repression of unrest are more appealing as political tools than are programs that address fundamental inequities in landholding, political power, law, and income. Kissinger recognized the underlying issue when he said, with reference to human rights, "Making [human rights] a vocal objective of our foreign policy involves great dangers: You run the risk of either showing your impotence or producing revolutions in friendly countries—or both."[16] Better to contribute to state security at the top and placate repressive governments than take concrete steps to enhance the security of billions of people at the bottom. This approach to "solving" problems is a familiar one in any system wrenched by convulsive, sometimes violent, and always unpredictable change. But if we accept that states exist to serve human communities, such an approach is politically and morally irresponsible. Centralized, elite-managed, efficiency-minded, technical mechanisms seem quite inappropriate considering the size and depth of humanity's crisis.

Until the outbreak of World War I, realist state leaders could usually count on balance-of-power politics to keep the lid on unwanted violence. When the balance was shattered by two world wars, an uneasy East-West condominium dominated by the superpowers took its place. By the post–Vietnam War era in 1975, however, that structure was already characterized by imbalance, disunity, and fragility in relationships among allies. Ideological allegiances were proving insufficient, in the West, to resolve trade disputes (such as between the United States and Japan), preserve unity in NATO, or prevent Western and Eastern Europe from having commercial dealings. Old allies of the United States like Canada and Mexico became bolder in their criticisms of US interventions and energy and environmental policies. Alliances pieced together by the United States during the Cold War, such as the Southeast Asia Treaty Organization (SEATO), the Central Treaty Organization (CENTO), and ANZUS (Australia, New Zealand, and the United States), were all reduced to insignificance. On the Soviet side, the Warsaw Pact, even before the crumbling of communist authority in Eastern Europe, was weakened by the Solidarity resistance in Poland, Eastern Europe's substantial financial and technical dependence on Western banks and trading firms (leading Hungary and Poland to sign up with the IMF), and the Soviets' own poor administrative and economic performance.

Three lessons might have been learned from these discordances. One, superpowers could not give orders and expect to have them followed as they once were. World politics was already becoming multipolar. Second, military superiority was not proving as decisive as in the past in ensuring control of events. When Iraq invaded Kuwait in 1990, therefore, it was a test of realism's viability in the post–Cold War era. "We are striking a blow for the principle that might does not make right," said President Bush (on August 15, 1990) as US forces were deployed in Saudi Arabia. The third lesson, in Kissinger's words, was that "fragmentation" and "globalization" would be the chief contending forces in efforts to construct a new world order, and that no government was really well equipped to handle such complexities.[17] The case study of the Mexican and Asian financial crises illuminates his point.

## Corporate Globalism and the World Economy

"All freedom is dependent on freedom of enterprise," said President Harry S Truman. "The whole world should adopt the American system. . . . The American system can survive in America only if it becomes a world system."[18] The globalization of US capitalism has surely exceeded Truman's hopes: The stock value of foreign direct (private) investments (FDI) abroad by US–based corporations has climbed from about $12 billion in the late 1940s to over $400 billion in 1993 and $1.8 trillion in 2004.[19] By 2004, US FDI was running just under $250 billion a year and US-based TNCs were accounting for 24 percent of all private US business output.[20] What began as a very tentative postwar corporate expansion now is a global movement of capital, technology, labor, information, and culture in which US transnational corporations play a leading, but no longer unchallenged, part.

The importance of foreign trade and investment to US political and business leaders was well recognized as early as the 1920s, when the United States fully emerged as a major player in the international economy. Even before World War II ended, as the first case study in this chapter shows, systematic planning began for overseas expansion. Investments abroad then were considered highly risky, and foreign trade from domestic industries was the preferred route. Now, foreign investment is considered a business necessity. The corporation lives or dies by expansion in the global marketplace; banks depend on making overseas loans; individual investors count on emerging markets for current and retirement income. Besides, the profit margin on investments and interest on loans is considerably higher abroad than at home. The risks of loss have increased, and terms of investment are less favorable to TNCs than before; but the tax rates, the trend of privatization of formerly government-run services, and general conditions of operation (especially in times of recession at home or high labor costs) are superior. No wonder, then, that the top ten US banks had 169 percent of their equity (about $44 billion) tied up in loans to the Third World in the early 1980s.[21] Or that the services sector has become more attractive for the major investing countries than manufacturing and primary products.[22] Or, lastly, that the investment pattern of many of the world's largest corporations, such as General Motors, is changing—from the United States, where it had been spending around $5 billion a year to upgrade plants, to Mexico, China, and other Third World locales, where investments are about $4 billion a year but in *new* plants for auto assembly and parts. Unskilled, low-cost, non-unionized labor, cheaper-to-build structures, and a huge market of new car customers are what count at GM.[23]

The key to success for corporate globalists is the free flow of goods, skills, and services around the world, without hindrance from governments and civil-society groups. Management, not national security, is the governing ideology. Making the world "safe for interdependence" was the main reason that in 1972 David Rockefeller, chair of the board of Chase Manhattan Bank, initiated formation of one of the best-known and most influential corporate-globalist organizations, the Trilateral Commission.[24] Composed of representatives from business, media, politics, and labor in the United States, Western Europe, and Japan, the Trilateral Commission's objective is to promote cooperation through the removal of barriers to trade and investment worldwide. The commission first gained attention during the administration of President Jimmy Carter when he, himself a member, appointed several other commission members to his cabinet. Ronald Reagan did the same when he took office, showing that corporate globalism spans the political spectrum. No conspiracy here; rather, what we have is the normal tendency of US leaders to appoint people with corporate connections or values to key positions, just as George W. Bush did with numerous appointments of energy officials and lobbyists.

For corporate globalists, interdependence has a particular meaning: augmenting the power of the global corporations and, if necessary, decreasing that of governments. Their identity, as Coca-Cola's chief executive once admitted, is global: "We used to be an American company with a large international business. Now we are a large international company with a sizable American business."[25] Not accidentally, the Trilateral Commission was founded soon after President Nixon shocked the corporate community in 1971 when he announced a number of steps to halt and reverse the US trade deficit, including taking the dollar off the gold standard and imposing a surtax on imports. To corporate globalists, such protectionist steps are poison; they compromise the free flow of currency and trade. Later, beginning in 1974 and extending into the 1990s, new obstacles to world trade emerged: recessions, the formation of regional markets, increasing protectionism, and the inability of the major trading states in the GATT (General Agreement on Tariffs and Trade) regime to resolve disputes over lowering trade barriers. TNC leaders have usually been able to turn these adverse developments into opportunities, however.

First, in 1995 state and corporate leaders replaced GATT with the World Trade Organization (WTO), which is composed of 150 member countries (Russia is the biggest nonmember) and occupies GATT headquarters in Geneva. The WTO's chief advantage over GATT is a binding dispute resolution mechanism that promises to resolve accusations that a state engages in unfair trade practices. For global corporations, the WTO fits its agenda perfectly.[26] There are around 69,000 TNCs and nearly 700,000 branch plants in the world, representing about $8 trillion in assets and employing nearly 15 million people.[27] TNCs dominate global exports of goods and commercial services, which in 2005 were valued at $10.1 trillion in the former and $2.4 trillion in the latter.[28] In fact, about one-half of the exports of the major economies are actually intra-TNC (usually intra-firm) transactions.[29] Among other things, the WTO promises liberalization of national regulations governing trade, which makes it a boon to TNCs. So far it has also meant that one country's higher labor and environmental standards will usually not be allowed by the WTO to stand in the way of another country's exports.[30] Nor will TNCs have to pay much heed to workers' rights, for the WTO makes no assurances to the millions of workers, increasingly skilled,[31] whose jobs are being lost to corporate restructuring as global trade competition intensifies.

Restructuring relates to the second major option: TNCs and TNBs (transnational banks) have accelerated mergers of corporate giants, such as Exxon Mobil and ChevronTexaco. More striking is the prominence of cross-border joint venturing and mergers. These began in the 1980s when, for example, Chrysler and General Motors invested in Mitsubishi, Honda, and Isuzu in Japan and joint production enterprises were formed, such as between GM and Toyota and between US Steel and Korea's Pohang Steel. Joint ventures such as these became the norm, not only cross-nationally but also intranationally, by TNCs headquartered in the same country. Now, under the pressures of globalization for companies and banks to cut costs, raise profits, boost earnings for investors, and take advantage of a looser regulatory environment, strategic alliances and megamergers are the name of the game. In the first category, we find NEC Corporation of Japan and

Samsung Electronics of South Korea agreeing in 1995 to collaborate in making microcomputer chips so as to improve their competitive position with the industry leader, Intel, in the United States. Megamergers are especially noteworthy: Around $500 billion worth of corporate mergers and acquisitions are taking place worldwide *every quarter*—in other words, $2 trillion a year. Among these, cross-border mergers are still in the minority; they came to $297 billion in 2003.[32] If the US situation is any guide, however, they may account for more than half of all FDI in recent years.[33] The effect can be contagious: Once one TNC does it, others in the same industry are likely to follow. In the automotive industry, for example, no sooner did Daimler-Benz A.G. announce its acquisition of Chrysler Corporation in 1998, in a record-breaking $39 billion deal, than the British firm of Vickers P.L.C. agreed to a $710 million takeover of its Rolls-Royce division by Volkswagen A.G.

A third trend among TNCs is to create various types of production networks or commodity chains. Here, the truly global corporation carries the integration of operations among parent and affiliates to a higher level, by creating a division of labor, from manufacturing to advertising, within the firm itself.[34] The objective, as always, is increased efficiency, higher profits, management flexibility, and control from the top, typically accompanied by a sizable reduction in the work force. We can see the different ways such integration works, for example, in Nike Corporation's production and marketing of athletic shoes, in the Korean automobile industry's expansion from domestic to international markets, and in IBM's layoff of over ten thousand workers in 2005 so that accounting and other desk work could be parceled out to low-wage countries.[35] Japanese TNCs in Asia since the mid-1980s provide another example of networks. They have shifted from low-cost manufacturing to labor- and technology-intensive production networks, using Japanese and local affiliates, and the location has changed from South Korea and Taiwan alone to the emerging-market economies of Southeast Asia such as Thailand and Malaysia. Japanese TNCs seek flexibility in meeting market demand and want to avoid (as in 1998) a sudden collapse of local markets. In effect, they export their production processes to subcontractor companies.[36]

Fourth, TNCs have formed business ties with "region-states"—large consumer markets that straddle borders, such as the Pearl River Delta that is the geographic hub of Greater China. By targeting regional-transnational markets, TNCs and their local partners hope to appeal over the heads of government bureaucrats who seek to regulate them.[37] They are being helped by another aspect of globalization: the porosity of borders and creation of ever-larger border zones—a process one writer calls "de-bordering and re-bordering"[38]—that has made border control increasingly difficult. This circumstance lends itself to a fifth trend favorable to TNCs: the widening flows of skilled and migrant labor across frontiers, discussed further below.

All these efforts reveal the exceptional maneuverability of TNCs as they seek to expand markets and defend themselves against competing corporations and governments.

Rapid growth in transnational business has had the most striking results for the US economy. It has literally internationalized industry, cutting into the once unchallenged role of the United States in world trade. While the shares of world trade of Western Europe and Japan rose sharply (to about 39 percent and 7 percent, respectively, in the mid-1970s), that of the United States declined just as sharply (from nearly 17 percent of world exports in 1950 to just under 10 percent in 1982). By the end of the 1980s, the US share had recovered to 13.5 percent, the world's largest, with West Germany just behind at 13 percent and Japan third at 10 percent.[39] This ranking continued into the late 1990s; but by 2005, although the United States remained the largest trading nation (imports included), it dropped slightly behind Germany on the basis of exports alone. The new element is the rise of the East Asian economies, notably China and South Korea, to positions among the top dozen trading states, with China surpassing Japan and poised to surpass the United States as well.[40] Also significant, but hardly new, is the ever growing US balance-of-payment deficit. The deficit (the difference between imports and exports) was $156 billion in 1986. Currency revaluations in the late 1980s, which had the effect of cheapening US exports, brought the deficit down to $65 billion in 1991, but it was back up to $84 billion in 1992, $115 billion in 1993, $148 billion in 1995, and $829 billion in 2005. The negative US trade balance with China alone accounts for about a quarter of the US trade deficit.

As is evident from Table 2.2, multinational business is highly profitable. Earnings by US TNCs on investments abroad have been able to make up somewhat for the outflow of dollars brought about by the trade deficit. These earnings amounted to $74 billion in 1995 and $474 billion in 2004 (out of total global profits for the top one thousand TNCs of $1.049 trillion).[41] US branch plants overseas, which today handle over one-third of all US imports and exports (47 percent and 32 percent respectively),[42] allow TNCs to leapfrog over tariff walls and other national impediments. By the early 1970s, US government income from the returned profits of TNC branch plants began to exceed income from exports by domestic companies.[43] Just how significantly TNCs depend on overseas operations can be gauged from the fact that in 1980, sixteen of the top fifty US TNCs earned half or more of their revenue abroad.[44] By 1997, the number had climbed to twenty-two of the top fifty.[45] The importance of TNC activities to all economies is among the reasons that TNC advocates believe trade gets the attention that TNCs deserve.[46] China's leap to trading prominence would not be possible, for instance, were it not for TNCs: About 60 percent of "Chinese" exports are produced in foreign enterprises.

The prominence of global corporations in the world economy can be

Table 2.2    The Fifty Largest Transnational Businesses (2004)

| Rank | Company | Home Country | Market Value | Profits ($US billions) |
|---|---|---|---|---|
| 1 | General Electric | US | 328.1 | 15.0 |
| 2 | Microsoft | US | 284.4 | 9.9 |
| 3 | Exxon Mobil | US | 283.6 | 20.9 |
| 4 | Pfizer | US | 269.6 | 1.6 |
| 5 | Wal-Mart Stores | US | 241.1 | 8.8 |
| 6 | Citigroup | US | 239.4 | 17.8 |
| 7 | BP | UK | 193.0 | 9.5 |
| 8 | American International Group | US | 191.1 | 9.2 |
| 9 | Intel | US | 184.6 | 5.6 |
| 10 | Royal Dutch/Shell Group | Netherlands/UK | 174.8 | 11.4 |
| 11 | Bank of America | US | 169.8 | 10.8 |
| 12 | Johnson & Johnson | US | 165.3 | 7.1 |
| 13 | HSBC Holding | UK | 163.0 | 11.6 |
| 14 | Vodafone Group | UK | 159.1 | 11.3 |
| 15 | Cisco Systems | US | 152.2 | 3.5 |
| 16 | IBM | US | 150.5 | 7.5 |
| 17 | Procter & Gamble | US | 139.3 | 5.1 |
| 18 | Berkshire Hathaway | US | 136.8 | 8.1 |
| 19 | Toyota Motor | Japan | 130.6 | 10.5 |
| 20 | Coca-Cola | US | 125.5 | 4.3 |
| 21 | Novartis | Switzerland | 125.5 | 5.0 |
| 22 | GlaxoSmithKline | UK | 124.0 | 8.7 |
| 23 | Total | France | 122.9 | 8.9 |
| 24 | Merck | US | 105.2 | 6.8 |
| 25 | Nestlé | Switzerland | 104.8 | 4.9 |
| 26 | Wells Fargo | US | 99.8 | 6.1 |
| 27 | Altria Group | US | 98.2 | 9.2 |
| 28 | ChevronTexaco | US | 96.7 | 7.4 |
| 29 | Roche Holding | Switzerland | 95.9 | 2.4 |
| 30 | Verizon Communications | US | 95.7 | 3.5 |
| 31 | Royal Bank of Scotland | UK | 94.3 | 8.5 |
| 32 | NTT DoCoMo | Japan | 92.1 | 5.8 |
| 33 | PepsiCo | US | 91.2 | 3.5 |
| 34 | Dell | US | 90.0 | 2.6 |
| 35 | UBS | Switzerland | 84.7 | 5.0 |
| 36 | Eli Lilly | US | 83.2 | 2.5 |
| 37 | ENI | Italy | 82.0 | 6.8 |
| 38 | Home Depot | US | 81.7 | 4.3 |
| 39 | United Parcel Service | US | 80.6 | 2.8 |
| 40 | Nippon Telegraph & Telephone | Japan | 79.0 | 5.8 |
| 41 | SBC Communications | US | 78.4 | 5.9 |
| 42 | AstraZeneca | UK | 78.3 | 3.0 |
| 43 | Time Warner | US | 77.6 | 3.1 |
| 44 | J.P. Morgan Chase | US | 75.2 | 6.6 |
| 45 | Telefónica | Spain | 72.0 | 4.2 |
| 46 | Samsung Electronics | Korea | 71.0 | 5.0 |
| 47 | Gazprom | Russia | 70.7 | 0.9 |
| 48 | Deutsche Telekom | Germany | 70.5 | 0.2 |
| 49 | Amgen | US | 70.0 | 2.2 |
| 50 | Nokia | Finland | 66.9 | 4.5 |

*Source: BusinessWeek,* July 26, 2004.

further gauged by noting their size and market dominance. The global trend for some time has been bigness and concentration of control.

> The world's 500 largest industrial corporations . . . control 25 percent of the world's economic output. The top 300 transnationals, excluding financial institutions, own some 25 percent of the world's productive assets. The combined assets of the world's fifty largest commercial banks and diversified financial companies amount to nearly 60 percent of *The Economist*'s estimate of a $20 trillion global stock of productive capital.[47]

Commentators often point out that the largest TNCs have total sales greater than the GNP of most states. At the end of the 1990s, for example, TNCs represented one half of the one hundred leading national economies.[48] It is frequently remarked today that Wal-Mart Stores is China's eighth-largest trading partner. A mere fifteen TNCs, and in most cases only three to six, control world trade in all basic commodities, from food to minerals.[49]

Transnational investments and loans have always gone mainly (70 percent today) into manufacturing and financial services in the richest economies—the thirty countries of the Organization for Economic Cooperation and Development (OECD)—and not into the Third World.[50] With the rise of China and other emerging-market economies, however, that situation may change: In 2003 China, and not the United States, was the top choice of foreign investors, at $54 billion.[51] Still, one of the chief characteristics of global corporations is that their capital mostly originates in and ends up in the same few places. Their headquarters are overwhelmingly in the largest economies (in fact, 62 percent of the headquarters are in English-speaking countries: the United States, Britain, and Canada), and their corporate branches in the major economies invest mainly in other major economies.[52] US companies were still the leading source of FDI in 2001 (20 percent of the total), with British and German companies in second (15 percent) and third (8 percent) place.[53] China's rise notwithstanding, since 1984 the United States has usually been the preferred country in which to invest because of high interest rates and profit margins on capital. In the decade from 1994 to 2003, for instance, foreign direct investment in the United States came to $1.3 trillion; it was $113 billion in 2005 and $190 billion in 2006, compared with $79 billion and $86 billion for China in those years.[54] As a result, foreign holdings of US assets—approaching $4 trillion in 2000, mainly in prime real estate, securities, farmland, and businesses—increased far more rapidly than US ownership of foreign assets, and sales to US consumers by non-US TNCs exceeded sales by US businesses.[55] That is how the United States became a net debtor in 1985—to the tune of $663 billion by the end of 1989 and around $1 trillion in the late 1990s.[56] Britain, Japan, and Canada were the leading sources of investments in the United States during those years. Some in the United States reacted with the same alarm as Third World leaders to this supposed loss of control over the country's economy. Others, noting that US foreign investment now is twice the level of foreign investment in the United States, see the large influx of foreign money as just another sign of the times: global economic interdependence. And still others see it as a positive contribution to the US economy that not only helps lower the budget deficit but also finances much of the gross investment in US business modernization.[57]

Overall, the spread of global capitalism means that the locus of international finance and production is gradually, but inexorably, becoming less US-centered. At the start of the 1980s, the United States was home base for 42 percent of TNCs, followed by the United Kingdom (14.5 percent), Netherlands (7.8 percent), West Germany (7.4 percent), and Japan (7.3 percent).[58] But a decade later *Fortune* magazine's list of the top "Global 500" TNCs showed US and British firms down to 31 percent and 8 percent, respectively, of the total. Japanese firms had risen to 23 percent, with German and French firms at 6 percent each.[59] Of the 100 largest transnational industrial firms, 67 were US-based in 1963, 58 in 1971, 47 in 1979, 25 in 1990,[60] and only 22 in 1997. Japanese TNCs headed the top 100 list in 1997 with 30, including 5 of the top 10, and German TNCs held 15 spots. (Table 2.2 shows, however, that if all global businesses are taken into account, those based in the United States far outpace the others.) In banking, US-based transnationals, led by Citicorp, Bank of America, and Chase Manhattan, held 44 of the top 100 positions (and 53 percent of all bank deposits) in 1956. By 1978, however, the US position had slipped to 15 of the top 100 positions and 15 percent of deposits.[61] Since the 1990s, stiffer competition and mergers among European and Japanese banks have further reduced the US position. In 1995 Japanese banks occupied 15 of the top 20 TNB positions by assets, and in 2004 Mitsubishi Tokyo Financial Group, thanks to takeovers, was slated to become the world's biggest bank (though US-based Citigroup was the sixth-largest global corporation in that year).[62] State- and privately owned companies in Asia and Latin America have also emerged to compete with firms of the Trilateral Commission countries. Among the top 1,000 global businesses are 93 from Third World countries, led by 21 from China and Hong Kong, 18 from Taiwan, 11 from South Africa, and 10 from South Korea.[63]

Intimately related to the growth of TNCs has been the expanded influence of multilateral financial institutions, notably the IMF and the World Bank. Commanding multibillion-dollar budgets, they are the key institutional links between the Trilateral states on the one side and borrowing countries on the other.[64] The World Bank's functions include low-interest loans and assistance on economic development projects proposed by underdeveloped countries in two classes: middle-income and "creditworthy" poor countries able to pay near-market interest rates, and the poorest countries, which are eligible for interest-free loans.[65] In recent years the Bank has committed between $20 billion and $22 billion in loans; about $8–9 billion of that has gone to the poorest countries.[66] Governments and government agencies receive the loans, which are then used to contract with private firms on development projects. In the 1990s, responding to widespread criticism of its disastrous record of loans for dams that displaced (or would have displaced) millions of rural poor and led to popular protests, the Bank placed a moratorium on financing dam construction. It now seems to be back in that business, though it also gives substantial funds for sustainable development projects such as reforestation, pollution control, and family planning.[67] Decisions on Bank policy and programs rest with its shareholder contributors, 45 percent of which are the seven major industrialized countries—the Group of 7, often now the Group of 8 to include Russia—headed by the United States with a 17 percent share. Thus, in an organization of 184 member countries—only North Korea and Cuba are not members—the United States can and does wield considerable influence, including a veto power on some matters and the ability to steer business in the direction of US banks and other private entities.

The IMF, whose initial responsibilities were to help countries keep their international payments in balance and their exchange rates stable, has gained notoriety in the present era of global indebtedness by making "structural adjustment" loans—loans granted on condition of major changes in social and economic policies by the recipient government. Founded in 1946 with thirty-nine members, the Fund now has 184 member countries that by 2006 had paid in over $300 billion.[68] The US share is $37 billion, which again gives it predominant voting power: 17 percent, as compared with 6.13 percent for Japan, 5.99 percent for Germany, and 4.95 percent each for France and Britain. (The quota distribution is also reflected in the Fund's leadership; traditionally, the president is an American, and the managing director is a European.) IMF loans and credits, which take the form of special drawing rights (SDRs, which represent the average worth of the five major contributors' currencies), have grown astronomically. They were around $4 billion in 1970, $14 billion in 1980, and $39 billion (about $26.5 billion in SDRs) in 2006.

Since the mid-1960s, direct aid in grants and loans by the industrialized states to the underdeveloped countries has declined from 55 percent to less than 20 percent of worldwide economic assistance. There is no longer a free lunch and money is power. Private capital flows have largely taken the place of aid, especially since the 1990s when indebtedness has soared and the end of the Cold War has lifted the lid on many economies. Private sources accounted for 85 percent ($243 billion) of all financing to Second and Third World countries in 1996.[69] In 2005 the World Bank reported that net private capital flows, mainly FDI and portfolio equity, came to $491 billion. Other multilateral agencies, such as the various regional banks (the Asian Development Bank and the Inter-American Development Bank, for instance) and their commercial bank partners remain critical in the financing picture, dispensing additional tens of billions of dollars each year to developing countries. There too, the record shows that private enterprise, not grassroots development needs, has priority when it comes to loans.[70]

With the overwhelming amount of development assistance tied to decisions in corporate-style board rooms, politics is inescapable. The claim of the IMF and the World Bank that loans and advice are based on strictly economic criteria simply does not stand up to the evidence.[71] As one journalist quipped, referring to the new prominence of a country's credit ratings: "You could almost say that we live again in a two-superpower world. There is the US and there is Moody's" (referring to Moody's Investors Service, Inc., which grades countries' investment climate).[72] The preponderant role of the United States—specifically the treasury and commerce departments—in these institutions ensures that its preferences will be fully aired and probably followed. In essence, those are consistent with the preferences of the transnational corporations and banks, as well as the European and Japanese representatives to the World Bank and the IMF—what has been labeled the "Washington consensus." The key objectives of the "consensus" are to promote stable, orderly growth and open markets in recipient countries, and maintain investor confidence. It has three unwritten rules: loan recipients must deregulate their markets, privatize state-owned enterprises, and remove barriers to trade ("liberalization").[73] Exemplifying the politics of the consensus, in 2000 the World Bank approved a $3.5 billion loan to construct an oil pipeline in West Africa linking Chad, a notoriously corrupt government and human-rights violator, and Cameroon. The pipeline's supporters? The United States and Exxon Mobil.[74] Similarly, in 2003 Indonesia received a new package of loans from the World Bank despite rampant corruption, apparently for two reasons: the government's support of US anti-terrorism policies, and Indonesia's agreement to improve the climate for private investment and privatization of state enterprises.[75]

As we would expect, "financial and private sector development" and related categories receive the largest proportion of multilateral bank loans. Necessarily, the IMF, the World Bank, and all others also insist on safe climates for investment, which typically means a "disciplined" labor force (i.e., no strikes), governments committed to law and order, tax advantages for foreign investors, and soft labor and environmental standards. Since the governments these TNCs and multilateral institutions deal with usually are running balance-of-payments deficits and are deeply in debt, the recommended policy (if they want a loan) is to sharply cut back on social welfare spending, step up exports to earn foreign exchange, and open the manufacturing and services sectors to foreign interests. As we will see in the case study of two recent financial crises, such a recommendation from the IMF or the World Bank directly serves the interests of TNCs, which dominate the exporting industries, and commercial banks, which can buy up government debt at a discount and will make foreign loans only because the discipline the IMF imposes on lenders affords a hedge against their default.[76]

The IMF's history of moving from facilitator to lender demonstrates its increasingly political role. When the fixed-rate system of international exchange, under which all currencies were pegged to the US dollar, collapsed in 1971, the IMF abandoned its original mission of helping countries bring their international payments into balance. Major changes in the world economy—the Latin American debt crisis of the 1980s, the shift of the former Soviet Union and Eastern Europe to market economies, the large loans in 1995 to bail out Mexico ($17 billion) and Russia ($6.2 billion), and the East Asia currency collapse of the late 1990s—all empowered the IMF to become a socioeconomic engineer. In each stage, it used the heavy hand of the lender to prod the borrower, not always successfully, to accept structural adjustments. (The World Bank's new name for this demand is "development policy operations"!) In Egypt in 1997, a new land law took effect, "largely at the behest of the World Bank and the International Monetary Fund," that overturned the practice, dating from the 1950s, of freezing rents on land owned by (often absentee) landlords. The main reason reported for the legal change, whose effect was to drive poor farmers from their land, was the Egyptian government's insistence that farmers produce more for export and profit.[77] In Côte d'Ivoire, the IMF forced the government to cut subsidies and get out of the commodities business—including the number-one export crop, cocoa—and privatize state-run companies in basic services, such as water and telephone, in order to obtain loans. Yet the IMF's and World Bank's own records in sub-Saharan Africa show that such austerity programs do not result in higher incomes or GNP.[78] When, in April 2001, the United States (presuming to speak for the IMF) announced a third round of multibillion dollar loans to Turkey, it coupled it with a warning that Turkey could not expect any more. Turkey would have to comply with a long list of desiderata, including privatizing certain industries, cutting back state-financed programs, allowing the lira to float freely, and reorganizing its banks.[79] But compliance does not always happen, as Argentina's recovery from collapse at the end of 2001 shows. Instead of following the IMF's economic orthodoxy, the government taxed exports and promoted domestic consumption—and the economy grew by 8 percent annually in 2003 and 2004, enabling Argentina to begin paying off its debts.[80]

In the upper reaches of big capital, what others might regard as self-serving is justified as promoting global well-being. Corporate globalists see interdependence as an opportunity not only for profit making but also for economic development in the Third World. They have traditionally labeled TNCs "engines of development" that transfer technology, management skills, and capital to industrialize agrarian societies, fuel growth, universalize information, promote productivity, and extract raw materials for export. In promoting free trade and investment, TNCs contribute importantly to world peace, it is said.[81] A scholarly argument can certainly be made that trade *sometimes* helps countries expand their economies and *sometimes* stabilizes relations between states. But these are weak arguments.[82] As the case studies in later chapters will show, neither trade nor aid nor FDI has been crucial to growth or poverty alleviation in the Third World, much less a panacea for conflict.

TNCs are also regarded as transmission belts of corporate-global values and culture: competition, growth, materialism, freedom of enterprise, efficiency. In their pathbreaking book on TNCs and their global managers, Richard Barnet and Ronald Müller quote an IBM executive:

> For business purposes, the boundaries that separate one nation from another are no more real than the equator. They are merely convenient demarcations of ethnic, linguistic, and cultural entities. They do not define business requirements or consumer trends. Once management understands and accepts this world economy, its view of the marketplace—and its planning—necessarily expand. The world outside the home country is no longer viewed as a series of disconnected customers and prospects for its products, but as an extension of a single market.[83]

We see here the kind of thinking that created the industrial revolution in the eighteenth century and motivated creation of the single European market and NAFTA trade blocs: centralization of large-scale operations, rationalization of market strategy and labor, and the subordination of the objectives of state managers to those of business managers. As Barnet and Müller wrote, the corporate globalists' power comes not from a gun but "from control of the means of creating wealth on a worldwide scale."[84]

To be sure, this borderless-world conceptualization may be a US myth, and it probably obscures important differences in perspective and corporate strategies among TNC leaders of different nationalities.[85] That is probably one reason why mergers of corporations representing different cultures and management styles are not automatic successes and are not preferred over mergers or buyouts between national firms. (Another reason is economic nationalism, as governments will sometimes block takeover efforts of a strategic industry by a foreign TNC.) Japanese and German heads of TNCs no doubt want to advance their own countries' as well as their firms' interests when trade policy in the WTO or EU is discussed, or when investment decisions about, say, Southeast Asia or China are made. As just one example, in 1996 Chinese firms were found to be producing pirated versions of music and video recordings that were causing an estimated loss of $2 billion in royalties for US affiliates of Bertelsmann A.G. and Sony Corporation. Washington pressured the Chinese government to close down the factories. But at the headquarters of the two companies in Germany and Japan, the view was totally different. They wanted to continue doing business with China and therefore were not at all interested in going along with US pressure tactics. Their response to the situation was dictated not by their US subsidiaries' interests but by the promise of Chinese authorities to throw more business Europe's and Japan's way.[86]

So corporate nationality does matter. But the global view, the big picture, seems even more important. When Third World economic nationalism surged beginning in the mid-1970s, behind calls for a "new international economic order" (NIEO), some corporate global leaders reacted sympathetically.[87] Their concern was that unless some of the NIEO's agenda was adopted, such as improved terms of trade and debt reduction, global underdevelopment would lead to more revolutionaries rather than more customers. Those days now seem long past. Dramatic changes in the world economy since the 1970s have enhanced the TNCs' opportunities for controlling economies. One change is the way the work force can be mobilized. At one end of the scale, that of skilled technical people, TNCs have been able to forge networks of researchers, engineers, advertisers, and other specialists who work in offices located throughout the industrialized countries and, increasingly, in emerging-market countries such as India. With advanced laboratories and computers and high pay scales, TNCs have no trouble recruiting talented Third World people. As these specialists contribute to the production and marketing of high-technology products, it has been argued, they become IBM or Volkswagen people rather than Americans or Germans.[88] At the other end, that of unskilled labor, TNCs have profited from the enormous increase in migrant workers brought about by poverty, recessions, population growth, and political upheavals. A 1992 report estimated that there are "at least 35 million people from developing countries [who] have taken up residence in the North in the past three decades" and that their numbers are increasing by 1.5 million a year.[89] At one time these "economic migrants" were concentrated in three regions—Mexicans in the United States, north Africans and southern Europeans in Western Europe, and Asians in the Middle East oil-producing states. Now one also finds Vietnamese in South Korea, Indonesians in Taiwan, Filipinos and Iranians in Japan, and Russians, Turks, and Romanians in the EU countries. TNCs are not just using this cheap, unorganized labor as it comes their way; they are also, and especially, investing (often in electronics assembly) where it is—for example, Japanese plants in Indonesia and Thailand, Taiwanese and Hong Kong plants in southeast coastal China, and US plants in the border area with Mexico.

Further tying together the world market is control of information. Ever since the days of colonial empires, information—financial, legal, marketing, advertising, labor, natural resources—has been central to the acquisition of wealth worldwide.[90] Today, the advent of microprocessors has greatly accelerated the pace of information gathering and centralization of its control in the major global corporations. IBM, Texas Instruments, AT&T, and McGraw-Hill dominate in computers, data processing, and telecommunications, the technology for which is overwhelmingly in the developed world.[91] Western news agencies (Associated Press in the United States, Reuters in Britain, and Agence France-Presse in France) supply 90 percent of all the foreign news in the media of the nonsocialist world.[92] Western book publishers, film companies, advertising agencies, and radio and television corporations dominate their respective markets abroad as they do at home.[93] Control of these markets has become highly concentrated: A mere five conglomerates—two US, one French, one German, and one Australian—exercise extraordinary influence over publishing and electronic media.[94] Satellites for broadcasting, data transmission, and remote sensing of geophysical changes within countries are mainly under the control of the richest economies, which also use 90 percent of their geostationary orbit.[95]

Globalization has impacted media and telecommunications as it has every other industry, by contributing further to the power of multinational business. By early 1997, the WTO had opened telecommunications to competition, sparking a flood of alliances and joint ventures between the corporate media giants.[96] Many crossed borders, such as Rupert Murdoch's News Corporation, based in Sydney—its many holdings include Star TV (Hong Kong), the *London Times* and *The Sun* (Britain), and Fox Broadcasting and 20th Century Fox studios (US)—and Bertelsmann A.G. of Germany, which in 1998 took over Random House, sometimes called the crown jewel of US publishing. But there were also media megamergers within countries, such as between Time Warner and Turner Broadcasting (followed by the even bigger Time Warner–AOL alliance), and Disney with Capital Cities–ABC (and later with NBC and CNBC), thus forming the two largest media conglomerates in the United States. For the US government, the WTO was an unmatched opportunity to use national deregulation of telecommunications to export democratization and other US values "to try to open up societies," as a top official said.[97] State telephone monopolies from Germany to Japan were forced into competition in a market estimated at $600 billion and 43 million customers as the new agreement permitted foreign firms to own local companies. Sprint Corporation allied with France Télécom and Deutsche Telekom, and AT&T with the Europeans' Unisource.[98] Commercialization of NASA spy satellites opened the heavens to giant corporations in the same way they had to military power.[99]

Such concentrated control of communication channels and information means power: the retention, for sale or manipulation, of market data; the definition of news, ideas, and images; the molding of political and social choices; and the export of homogenized Western cultural values. It is the kind of power that serves realist and corporate-globalist interests equally well, enhancing a large state's leverage against the consumer state and building profits and market control for a giant corporation. To Third World and many Second World countries, however, it smacks of cultural imperialism, another form of dependence, in this case on (mainly US) entertain-

ment, news equipment and reports, sales techniques, and editorial training—all of which are infused with the perspectives and biases of their country of origin. But the Third World's insistence on a "new international information order" (NIIO) fell flat. With economic globalization has come the
presumed right of TNCs and their governments to search for and transmit
data across national frontiers (the "free flow of information") as against the
proclaimed right of Third and Second World states to protect their sovereignty and identity, to make data gathering accountable to some authority,
and to share in the fruits of the information explosion.[100] The outcome of
this debate was never in doubt.

There is a third player in the struggle over information rights: people.
The telecommunications revolution has clearly expanded the scope of political expression and has broad implications for human rights. In China at the
time of the Tiananmen crackdown on dissenters in 1989, faxes and e-mail
messages sent by students enabled the world to know what China's leaders
desperately hoped to hide. The Chinese government's inability to cover up
the AIDS and SARS epidemics in the 1990s also owes much to the new
communications, as well as to individual heroics. In 1996, the Serb
(Yugoslav) government refused to accept the results of local elections and
then silenced an opposition radio station when it became the principal
source of uncensored news. Thanks to publicity on the Internet, the station
was able to get back in business. And in Burma, the military government's
repression led the democratic opposition to establish an Internet site, called
the Free Burma Coalition, as the essential means of getting information into
and out of the country. An official with one human-rights organization said:
"Cyberspace spawned the movement to restore human rights to Burma. The
proliferation of information has put Burma higher on the US policy agenda
than it ever would have been otherwise."[101]

Of course governments have their web sites too, and the Chinese gov-
ernment has proven rather adept at blocking undesirable information. Still,
repressive governments that seek to limit access to computers, modems, and
satellite dishes must contend with technology that they themselves rely on.
In a word, the Internet has become indispensable for acquiring information.
In popular hands, it may also constrain the excesses of global corporations.
In a number of instances involving labor abuses by subcontractors of major
TNCs—such as Nike's suppliers in Vietnam, Walt Disney's in Haiti, and
various carpet makers in Pakistan and Bangladesh who use child labor—the
Internet has been a powerful tool of human-rights organizations for exposing the companies and changing some of their practices. To one observer,
this "spotlight phenomenon" has changed the calculus of international business. Cheap labor and other low costs of overseas production must now be
measured against the sometimes higher costs of adverse publicity back
home. Thus, according to this view, TNCs may actually be in the process of
*promoting* human rights they had once been repressing in partnership with

other governments.[102] But such a conclusion seems much too optimistic. For every discovered and corrected human-rights abuse to which a TNC is a party, there are doubtless thousands more that go undetected; and for every company that pulls out of a country, such as the garment firms and oil companies that heeded criticism of their investments in Burma, many more stay put.

Though the assets and global organization of TNCs give them formidable power, not all governments that allow in foreign capital are dependent on them.[103] Interdependence has widened but also diffused corporate power, above all in East Asia.[104] There, governments have improved their bargaining terms with TNCs by steering foreign investors into industries that promote exports and by placing limits on their ownership shares. Even then, export-led industrialization in East Asia has been significantly financed by local capitalists (especially Chinese family networks) and banks, which have formed their own powerful conglomerates.[105] Three of the four East Asian newly industrializing countries (NICs) (Singapore is the exception) have relied much less than the Latin American NICs (Brazil and Mexico) or China on foreign direct investment for capital. These qualifications may only prove the rule, however—and were weakened because of the IMF's conditions for loans to South Korea and Indonesia in 1997 and 1998. Wherever they become established, TNCs acquire considerable political and economic power by virtue of the extensiveness of their operations. They hold a particular advantage over host governments because of their control of labor markets in manufacturing.[106] The fact that the presence of foreign-based TNCs is less direct and dominating than in previous decades is not equivalent to saying that they now exert significantly less influence.

## Rivals or Partners?

One thing the conflict over trade, investment, and information dependence shows is that globalists understand the politics of interdependence much better than realists. They know that people, as customers, can be brought into line far more efficiently by changing their tastes, habits, and ways of thinking than they can if treated as potential revolutionaries who have to be forcibly suppressed. Coca-Cola, powdered milk, Levi's, and CNN make more sense than a machine gun if one wants to get people willingly to adopt a particular way of life. Gunboat diplomacy represents old-style international politics; domination of information, advertising, entertainment, and philanthropy is the new style. Greater political openness in China, it can be safely predicted, will more likely occur because of the Internet, Wal-Mart, and Star TV than because of pressure tactics by Western governments.

This sizable difference in perspective was often on display during the Cold War. Corporate globalists in the West at the heads of TNCs and in government commercial bureaucracies tangled with government and military leaders over economic relations with the socialist countries. Interests in expanding markets, promoting trade, and helping the balance of payments clashed with the realists' fears of helping the enemy's economy and giving away state secrets. TNCs often were forced to abandon business opportunities, though they sometimes ignored government directives when the profit was irresistible. After all, corporate leaders have always taken the position that global business is more farsighted and adaptable than states. Money talks with people of any political stripe—as has been demonstrated from Angola to China.[107] Indeed, said an international banker during Poland's debt crisis in the 1980s, "Who knows which political system works? The only test we care about is: Can they pay their bills?"[108]

With the waning of the Cold War, corporate globalists see even less relevance either for realism's geopolitical perspective or, in the United States, its more recent concern about "rogue states." For them, the key items on the global agenda should be liberalizing trade and investment policies, and preventing trading blocs from becoming discriminatory. They have been behind efforts, therefore, to reform the IMF and strengthen the WTO. By implication, although governments direct these regimes, TNCs are the key instruments for securing and distributing their benefits.

The self-confidence of TNC leaders comes from their belief that in a world whose future depends on markets and technology, superior management on a world scale will be decisive. Harvard University's Robert Reich, secretary of labor under President Bill Clinton, has offered a forceful presentation of this view. National economic interests, the GNP, and the nationality of corporate headquarters do not matter much any more. Products, like firms, are increasingly the sum of many parts and many minds from many countries: "global enterprise webs," in Reich's phrase. The Japanese car and the US tank are things of the past. Nor is "foreign" ownership of "national" property, such as Sony's purchases of CBS Records and Columbia Pictures in the late 1980s, important. In a single world economy, what counts is the creativity and adaptability of individual firms whose staffs, spread out around the globe, add value to the market.

Governments become the corporate globalists' enemy when they interfere with transnational management, such as by imposing tariffs and surcharges on imports, subsidizing home industries, forcing their own TNCs to make investments on national security grounds that dollars and cents do not justify, placing sanctions and embargoes on trade with particular countries, enacting controls against capital and job flight, nationalizing foreign businesses, threatening to repudiate external debts, and forming cartel-like organizations (such as the eleven-member Organization of Petroleum Exporting Countries, or OPEC) to recapture control of precious resources. To some corporate globalists, these interferences by home and host countries undermine the national interest and international security just as surely as a popular uprising strikes fear in the hearts of realists.

Corporate leaders further argue that government interference with global business is useless, and sometimes contradictory. Take some recent cases of sanctions: During the second term of Bill Clinton, when containing repressive states had a high priority, sanctions were imposed on Burma, banning US investments and preventing the Unocal Corporation from carrying out contracts for gas field explorations. The US Congress also enacted sanctions that affected certain companies doing business with Cuba, Libya, and Iran. Sanctions against China were debated as well. In the Burma case, Unocal pointed out the contradiction in the Clinton administration's policy between engaging China through extensive economic ties and punishing Burma. The company also noted that, as with Iran, sanctions would only hurt US businesses; French and other energy companies would happily step in.[109] In addition, no US ally, least of all Japan (which buys about 17 percent of Iran's annual production), was willing to cooperate on Iran. (In the 2006–2007 confrontation over Iran's nuclear program, China and Russia were among the countries that opposed sanctions, reflecting their business ties with Tehran.) As for Cuba and Libya, European and Latin American businesses and governments alike protested, forcing Clinton (who, largely for domestic political reasons, supported the sanctions) to abandon implementing them.

Confronted with these assessments, realists retort that TNCs are often the culprits when the smooth functioning of the global system is upset. TNCs, they say, export jobs and capital abroad instead of investing at home. They use tax havens and other tricks of the transnational trade to avoid making their full contribution to national treasuries.[110] They increase a nation's dependence on strategic minerals by going abroad to find them rather than searching for them at home. They fail to appreciate that the domestic political setting in which realist state managers operate sometimes requires a positive response to demands for protection of home industry and jobs. They get in the way of traditional diplomacy, and they even compromise national security by contributing to the economies of, and turning over high technology to, enemy states and potential rivals. When McDonnell Douglas Aircraft's president for China operations said, "We're in the business of making money for our shareholders. If we have to put jobs and technology in other countries, then we go ahead and do it," we can be sure that state leaders in Washington no less than US unions winced.[111]

All of this carping may give the false impression that corporate globalists and realists are deadly adversaries. Indeed, there is a school of thought that suggests that TNCs are essentially "on their own" in world politics— powerful, autonomous forces that realist governments ought to leash before they get any more out of control. To the contrary, I argue that the two parties, though having different senses of mission, jealously safeguarding their respective turf, and occasionally clashing over particular issues, *cannot do without each other*. Their overall relationship is symbiotic. No clearer statement to that effect is likely to be found than that of Jeffrey E. Garten, who has worked in both camps. In the era of globalization, he writes,

> The hallmark of involvement with big emerging markets is that American business depends on Washington's help to liberalize trade, protect intellectual property, remove regulatory barriers, and encourage continued economic reform. It needs government's help to win major contracts [abroad]. . . . And Washington needs business more than ever to reinforce its goals. The executive branch depends almost entirely on business for technical information regarding trade negotiations. . . . In all emerging markets, America's political and economic goals depend largely on the direct investments in factories or other hard assets that only business can deliver. . . . Moreover, there are areas of great strategic significance where U.S. diplomacy and business could not succeed without each other. Take, for example, the Caspian Sea region.[112]

The statement is a simple acknowledgment that corporate globalization is a matter of dollars, cents, *and politics.* Exchange rates, intensified competition, protection of property, barriers to trade and investment, TNC and TNB mergers and acquisitions, promotion of sales abroad—in none of these areas can international business proceed without government support.[113] Garten's example, the international competition for the affections of the oil-rich Caspian Sea states, is one of many. As Paul Doremus and colleagues convincingly argue, the work of creating trade regimes, the WTO being the latest example, shows that TNCs "depended not on some automatic market mechanism promoting deep structural convergence, but on painstaking and often painful political negotiation."[114]

At the level of values (Table 2.1), as has been pointed out previously, there is little to distinguish realists and corporate globalists. Both groups set high store on order and stability and, rhetoric aside, share a disdain for democracy.[115] Nor is either group moved by moral impulses. A revealing insight to the consensual worldview of realists and corporate globalists has been provided by two writers for *Der Spiegel,* Hans-Peter Martin and Harald Schumann.[116] Behind closed doors in San Francisco, some of the world's most powerful men gathered in 1996. Their vision for the next millennium is "20/80": Twenty percent of the population will be able to produce all the goods and services for the other 80 percent. No more middle class; people will either "have lunch or be lunch," one US executive suggested. So the major challenge as these men see it is how to keep all those redundant workers occupied. Some combination of welfare—but *not* from corporations—and mind-deadening entertainment—"tittytainment," suggested Zbigniew Brzezinski, former national security adviser to President Jimmy Carter—is one answer. Nor was this meeting an isolated incident. At the World Economic Forum held annually in Davos, Switzerland, some leaders of the drive for globalization worried about those who are losing out. But others took comfort in the bright job outlook for plumbers, electricians, and personal trainers![117] In short, the people who are shaping the next century have a place for the 80 *and* the 20 percent, one that ensures a comfortable life for them.

But it is at the policy level that mutually supportive ties between realists and corporate globalists take concrete form. "Live and let live" seems to be their common credo. And why not? As numerous studies have pointed out, governments benefit from TNC operations in many ways, including:

- TNC remittances of their overseas profits, which help to balance a government's international payments;
- the ability to reward, punish, and thus influence small states, which major governments acquire by virtue of TNC, IMF, and World Bank loans and investments (the kind of leverage the United States has long exercised in Latin America);
- the access and control TNCs provide governments over the extraction and marketing of strategic resources, such as oil, natural gas, and precious metals;
- the support from corporate lobbies and media when dealing with critics of government policies, such as human-rights violations in countries where both TNCs and governments want to continue doing business;[118]
- the bonds forged by corporate-globalist officials with political and military elites abroad (sometimes by bribery), which create opportunities for their governments to acquire intelligence, strengthen friendships, neutralize enemies, and repress labor;[119] and
- the transmission through these corporate bodies of political and cultural norms, for example, the "American (Japanese, French) way of life."

The deal cuts both ways. Realist practices also make vital contributions to the corporate way of life, promoting and protecting TNC investments. The "safe climate for investment" that corporate globalists often require includes the military backing they sometimes call upon or like to have near at hand—such as US protection of oil tankers in the Persian Gulf during international tensions in 1987 and 1990, and US military training of the Colombian army in 2002 to protect a vital oil pipeline from rebel attacks. It may also involve economic retaliation governments can use or threaten against countries that do not fairly treat "their" TNCs or that seek to weaken a TNC's investment position relative to that of local firms. Increasingly, this component of government's safety net for corporations includes legal support when, as in Burma and Indonesia, US companies (Unocal and Exxon Mobil respectively) are defendants in labor exploitation cases.[120] Lastly, a safe climate most definitely means the personal involvement of senior government officials to strike huge business deals on behalf of their nationals.

Once it became clear that the former Soviet republics of Central Asia situated around the Caspian Sea, such as Azerbaijan and Kazakhstan, were sitting atop hundreds of billions of dollars' worth of oil and natural gas, a veritable gold rush ensued. Oil company executives and former and present government officials from several countries (the United States, China, Iran, Russia) descended on the area, attracted not just by the potential profits but just as much by the geopolitical bonanza—an alternative to reliance on OPEC's oil and a chance to influence the political complexion of the entire region.[121]

Governments are not only facilitators for TNCs; they often *create* market opportunities for them. For instance, their "aid" to food-poor countries may be tied to the purchase of TNC machinery, processing equipment, and seeds, or to growing cash crops that can be consumed locally (such as tobacco) or exported (from avocados to strawberries). The US food aid program, for instance, is a bonanza for the handful of giant corporations that ship and sell the commodities.[122] Promoting its own nationals' trade, private investment, weapons, and loans is part of a foreign embassy's business, not to mention a president's.[123] That task extends to standing up for corporations when international agreements seek to regulate their behavior, as when the US government at first refused to sign the Framework Convention on Tobacco Control in 2003 because it imposed too many restrictions on US cigarette manufacturers and advertisers.[124] Governments also encourage overseas investment through favorable tax policies;[125] export credit agencies (ECAs) that underwrite and insure large construction projects and other foreign investments;[126] legislation to deny bilateral and multilateral aid to a government that nationalizes private investments (the US Congress's Hickenlooper and Gonzalez amendments); antitrust relief (which enabled the major US oil companies to become dominant in the Middle East); direct subsidies (such as of the nuclear and oil industries in the United States and agricultural exports in Europe); deregulation and nonregulation of production and commerce (oil in the first case, the dumping of unsafe and unproven products abroad in the second case); removal of bureaucratic obstacles to corporate sales (such as the Clinton administration's approval of militarily sensitive technologies and information to China for its aerospace program); pressure on governments to implement elements of the Washington consensus, such as privatization of state-owned enterprises; and noninterference in those corporate practices (such as transfer pricing and Eurodollar market borrowing) that cost national treasuries and taxpayers huge sums of money.

One does not find corporations complaining about these benefits—nor about domestic law that is typically enforced loosely to permit multibillion-dollar mergers and acquisitions among the largest corporations; interlocking directorates among the biggest banks, insurance companies, energy corporations, and related institutions; tax-deductible lobbying and research; and personnel movements between the private and public sectors that (as in the case of US military officers who move from the Pentagon to military industries) smack of conflicts of interest.

Nor do TNCs quarrel with direct government interventions in their behalf, as when the then–West German government came to the rescue of its industrial giant, AEG Telefunken; or when Washington decided to bail out Lockheed Aircraft, Chrysler Corporation, and Continental-Illinois National Bank when they declared bankruptcy; or when President Carter froze and then permitted Chase Manhattan Bank to seize $6 billion in Iranian assets during the 1979 hostage crisis; or when President Reagan, despite his opposition to the Polish government's crushing of Solidarity, floated an agricultural loan to Warsaw rather than see it default on its $27 billion debt to US and other banks; or when the US government in 1984 aided the transnational banks with an $8.4 billion increase in its commitment to the IMF, enabling several Latin American governments to make payments to the banks and thus (in the strange world of international finance) qualify for additional loans and a rescheduling of old ones; or when the German government, in 1995, awarded Dow Chemical a subsidy of nearly $7 billion to enable Dow to take over a giant petrochemical complex in the former East Germany, the second largest bailout in Europe, behind France's $9.3 billion to keep Crédit Lyonnais, Europe's largest bank, afloat; or when the OECD joined with the World Bank and the IMF in pushing through rules to combat bribery in business dealings, a common practice that TNCs finally decided it was in their interest to regulate because it limits economic growth.[127]

TNCs and government officials traditionally cultivate close ties with political and economic elites who, out of self-interest, welcome foreign aid and investment and the arms to protect them (and themselves). Thanks to these elites, special foreign-trade zones offering labor, tax, and tariff concessions are available to TNCs in major ports (such as Masan, South Korea; Kaohsiung, Taiwan; and Shenzhen, China) for product assembly and export. The same intimacy may exist in a government's direct support of home-grown businesses, a partnership model made famous by Japan and widely considered to be a principal factor in the dynamic economic growth of South Korea and other Asian states. The state's careful nurturing of these conglomerates has today yielded world-class TNCs bearing names such as Hitachi, Toyota, Samsung, and Daewoo. But excessive state-corporate closeness was also a factor in Asia's currency crisis.

Sensitivity in some societies to large-scale foreign investment does on occasion create resentment and resistance. But most corporate globalists treat such reactions as a cost of doing business. They have confidently asserted—and the evidence supports them—that, on balance, elites in underdeveloped countries can be "co-opted into senior decisionmaking roles in the management structure of the international economy." "For the most part," this writer, a US State Department official at the time, candidly admits, "Third World elites are even less committed to human equality as a general condition of humanity than we are. They are talking about greater equality between states."[128] So long as corporate globalists and realists can keep the dialogue over global problems at the level of governments and the elites who run them, and away from people's needs, they believe they have a stranglehold on the future.

That conclusion points to another: the often unholy alliance between TNCs and governments to undermine, or simply ignore, human rights in host countries. The oppressive conditions under which women and children work throughout Asia for Nike, Esprit, Reebok, and numerous other clothing manufacturers are by now well publicized.[129] In Burma, Unocal and its French partner, Total, were charged with using essentially slave labor dragooned by the SLORC. The TNCs not only denied the charge; they pleaded ignorance—they didn't want to know where their money came from or to what purpose its profits were put—and noninvolvement—they didn't regard human rights as any of their business. Chevron's oil production in Angola practices avoidance: Oil workers live and work in a secluded enclave, guarded by Angolan soldiers and totally divorced from Angola's desperate poverty and political corruption—corruption that evidently is fed by the skimming of oil profits by government officials.[130] Or take US-China relations: The opportunity to sell China nuclear power plants, commercial aircraft, and supercomputers evidently has priority over China's appalling treatment of prisoners, which includes arbitrary detention of dissidents, sales abroad of goods produced by prison labor, and sales to foreigners of organs transplanted from executed prisoners.[131] Shell International, the major foreign oil company in Nigeria, also kept quiet when the government defied international criticism and hanged nine dissidents, including Ken Saro-Wiwa, in November 1995. Saro-Wiwa was a prominent writer who had led his Ogoni people in environmental protests against Shell's operations. Shell holds a 25 percent stake in a $3.8 billion natural gas project in Nigeria. It was widely rumored to have close relations with the military government at that time, which was voted as the world's most corrupt in a survey of international businesses.[132] In response to the hangings, the United States adopted rather mild sanctions against Nigeria. Not only did Shell join with various organizations representing TNCs in protesting the sanctions; it announced that it would be developing new offshore oil fields for Nigeria.[133] Summing up the corporate attitude on such matters, the president of Levi Strauss & Company said (in explaining a reversal of a previous decision not to invest in China because of human-rights violations): "Levi Strauss is not in the human rights business. But to the degree that human rights affect our business, we care about it."[134]

The head of Levi Strauss is apparently correct: TNCs do protest when business is hurt by a rights issue. When the Chinese government announced in 1996 that its official news agency would have to approve (i.e., censor) information from Dow Jones, Reuters, and other news services, the companies, joined by the US government, strenuously objected. But protests even in those circumstances are not certain. Some corporations prefer not to bite the hand that feeds them out of larger market considerations. Thus, Rupert Murdoch politely accepted Beijing's insistence that British Broadcasting Corporation news be removed from his Star TV broadcasts; and when the former (and last) British governor of Hong Kong, Christopher Patten, wrote a manuscript under contract to one of Murdoch's publishing houses that was highly critical of China, Murdoch refused to allow its publication. In the China pirating case mentioned earlier, non-US corporations, concerned to protect their market position, decided not to join in Washington's protest. Despite professed misgivings, Google, Yahoo, and Microsoft wanted access to the Chinese market enough to agree with the government on limiting use of their search engines. They agreed to remove e-mailing and blog capabilities, and to filter undesirable words and ideas (such as "democracy" and "Falungong") on the Internet, even going to the extent of reporting the names of users critical of the government.[135]

In summary, then, the principal criticisms of transnational commercial institutions (businesses, banks, and multilateral aid agencies) are that they, usually in cooperation with their governments, have been instrumental in promoting global *under*development and human insecurity. These dominating institutions have specifically contributed to sustaining Third World indebtedness, social injustice, economic inequality, environmental destruction, and the undermining of indigenous cultures, all of which promote conflict within and between countries. At bottom, finally, transnational institutions refuse to confront the implication of these failings for global political-economy as a whole: that system reforms of the kind corporate globalists (and realists, too) typically propose cannot touch the deep structural roots of the crisis, which begin with gross inequities of power and consumption in the industrially advanced countries and extend to privileged elites in the underdeveloped countries. This last is the point of departure for the discussion of global humanism in Chapter 3.

## Case Study 1: Postwar Planning for the "American Century"

By all accounts, the postwar United States represented the most extraordinary concentration of national power in history. World War II had claimed the lives of some 15 million soldiers and 65 million civilians, over 3 percent of the world's population. Europe and Asia were in ruins. But the United States, Pearl Harbor and many casualties aside, had not been touched by the war. In fact, its economy had benefited in several ways, including the start of systematic government-business cooperation on military production, the large-scale entry of women into the work force, and an unrivaled degree of productivity and production. Two years after the war, in 1947, the United States accounted for half of total world output; it also held nearly 65 percent of the world's gold currency, making the dollar central to all economic transactions. Finally, the United States had a nuclear monopoly: the "secret" (or so its leaders thought) of the atomic bomb and, obviously, the willingness to use it. Henry Luce, magnate of *Time* magazine, had every reason to argue that the rest of the twentieth century should belong to the United States.

The dollar and the bomb were considered the foundation of the "American century" by the policy planners who, well before the end of the war, met to outline the future.[136] Each element represented an essential tool for remaking the postwar world. For corporate globalists, the dollar meant free trade and export-led growth, the integration of world markets, the primacy of Europe (including a revived Germany) as a market for US goods, hostility to national socialist experiments in Western Europe, and, within the United States, big business and small government. For US realists, the bomb represented the ability to contain Moscow, rebuild Europe's defenses (NATO, in 1948), and centralize military-scientific-industrial cooperation at home. Heavily influenced by Roosevelt's New Deal, however, the realist camp leaned toward big government, antitrust actions to undermine big business, and priority to US capitalist goals (such as full employment) over foreign economic expansion.

The working out of a compromise agenda that could incorporate both realist and corporate-globalist priorities took place roughly between 1944 and 1947. Both the Marshall Plan for European recovery and President Truman's aid program to Greece and Turkey to contain international communism symbolized a historic synthesis. Multilateralism and anticommunism, as Alan Wolfe has observed, made for a new and enduring political consensus:

> Once anticommunism was grafted onto the multilateralism program, the political logjam in the United States was broken. Free trade, an inherently elitist notion, transformed itself into an ideology with mass appeal when it adopted anticommunism as its rationale. Every one of the limitations of the free-trade position could be overcome by an emphasis on the threat that the Soviet Union posed to the United States.[137]

In emphasizing that the shaping of the postwar world was equally the handiwork of realists and corporate globalists, I should further note the different but compatible lessons each side brought to its task. For realists, the main lessons of two world wars were that there is no appeasement of aggression and that military preparedness prevents war. Their key untouchable item was (and remains) the military budget, and their central accomplishment in the years prior to the Korean War was National Security Council document NSC-68, which called for a major US rearmament program to deter the presumed and exaggerated Soviet threat. For the corporate globalists, on the other hand, the world wars had taught that closed national markets led directly to the Great Depression. Only open economies in an open world market could prevent a repeat of that experience and the rise of fascism in Europe that followed it. Their greatest achievement was the 1944 Bretton Woods (New Hampshire) Conference, at which the major capitalist allies agreed to create a new international financial system to ensure currency and trade stability. The plan was US-made by government and business leaders who had earlier carved out a "Grand Area" strategy of global trade. The strategy called for creating two new institutions, the World Bank and the IMF, in each of which the United States would have more than a third of the votes.

How was it possible for corporate globalists to accept anticommunism and rearmament—"military Keynesianism" (government pump-priming through heavy spending on arms), as Fred Block has called it? Or for the realists to swallow world economic integration? After all, each agenda would be expensive and would orient the US government toward a different set of priorities, one international and one national.

The brief answer is that liberal (or Cold War) internationalism, as Wolfe's above-quoted remark indicates, satisfied the main constituencies of both groups. Within the US Congress, for instance, European recovery promised new markets and jobs based on expanded US exports. The Marshall Plan would not be a giveaway program. For the emerging breed of Cold Warriors, in Congress and in the administration, the plan meant a tough but also cost-effective stance against the Russians. In the country's higher circles, the combination of the Marshall Plan and containment had additional significance: European dependence on US military equipment for their defense; the undermining of powerful communist-backed labor movements and of national socialism; the sealing off of Western Europe from Soviet penetration; and the first step toward European economic (Common Market) and military (NATO) integration. It was the kind of "growth coalition" that liberals and conservatives could get behind. And once the country was hit by the "Red scare" tactics of the far right—the attacks on the US Foreign Service for "losing" China; charges of atomic spying for the Russians; and Senator Joseph McCarthy's allegations of a pro-Soviet conspiracy in high places—the era of isolationism was over.

A quick look at the key individual actors and what they said in these pivotal years is instructive. The guiding principle of the open door was succinctly stated by Secretary of State James F. Byrnes in August 1945: "In the field of international relations we have joined in a cooperative endeavor to construct an expanding world economy based on the liberal principles of private enterprise, nondiscrimination, and reduced barriers to trade."[138] After George C. Marshall became secretary, he argued (in his address of June 5, 1947, to inaugurate the Marshall Plan) that it was "logical that the

United States would do whatever it is able to do to assist in the return of normal economic health in the world, without which there can be no political stability and no assured peace." This made perfect sense to the international corporate community, which, in the words of one leading bank executive, was "extremely troubled about the future of free enterprise" in noncommunist Europe. To him the Marshall Plan to provide $17 billion in economic aid was "a smart gamble" because it would enable those who might otherwise take the socialist path "to play the game under the rules we adhere to."[139]

But sending money abroad did not make nearly as good sense to realists as did tough talk about the Russians. It was one thing for Truman to wax euphoric about the mission of US capitalism and quite another, politically, to say: "Unless Russia is faced with an iron fist and strong language another war is in the making. Only one language do they understand—'how many divisions have you?'"[140] One of his key advisers, Clark Clifford (a later secretary of defense), had given him the consensus of opinion in Truman's inner circle that "the language of military power is the only language which disciples of power politics understand." Clifford advised that the United States, with its military superiority, "should entertain no proposal for disarmament or limitation of armament as long as the possibility of Soviet aggression exists."[141] Here was a prescription for rearmament—not merely the $13 billion military budget of 1950 but, as one of the chief architects of NSC-68, Paul Nitze, was even then urging, a $50 billion budget (which was adopted three years later).

By early 1947 a general agreement had been reached within the US elite that both elements of liberal internationalism—multilateralism and anticommunism—would be needed to ensure a "peaceful" future. On the eve of Truman's containment address to Congress, his secretary of defense, James Forrestal, told him that since "the Russians would not respond to anything except power"—a bow to realism—the only option was to bring government and big business—the corporate globalists—together "in a single team," deterring the Russians and uplifting the Europeans in one coordinated effort.[142]

This neat division of labor was not cemented, however, until the onset of war in Korea. The US economy went into a recession late in 1948, and there was resistance to increasing imports of European goods. Congress was in no mood to refinance the Marshall Plan. The administration unveiled a new rationale for sending more money to Europe: to provide a defensive umbrella, in NATO, for the reconstruction of Europe. This approach also did not have lasting effectiveness; economic problems at home and abroad continued. The Korean War, and NSC-68, finally bailed out the Marshall Plan and gave liberal internationalism clear sailing. The war demonstrated the document's wisdom in urging a rapid US military buildup as part of an overall political and economic offensive to counter the Soviet peril. NSC-68 argued that "the integrity and vitality of our system is in greater jeopardy than ever before in our history." A "total struggle" would be necessary—both for economic reasons, to develop "a successfully functioning [trade and aid] system among the free nations," and for military reasons, to restore world order, lest the United States be "overcome" by the forces of totalitarianism.[143]

The postwar partnership of realism and corporate globalism in the United States has had profound consequences, some already hinted at and others to be explored in later chapters. Most fundamentally, the partnership gave birth to the national-security state—a joining of military-industrial interests with a nationalistic, expansionist great-power ideology. Protecting and promoting national security became the rallying cry. This structural phenomenon, which can be found in many other political-economic systems, spurred ever higher US military spending on behalf of allies and led to a number of direct and indirect US interventions against "communism." But the economic costs of these activities—in reduced productivity, inflation, the flight of gold-backed dollars abroad, and the military's absorption of scientific know-how—quickly began to erode the US competitive advantage in foreign trade. The EU and Japan caught up with and then surpassed the United States as societies on the leading edge of technology and skills. Before the first Eisenhower administration was over, it was clear that national security would have to mean not merely arms buildups and interventionism but also the expansion of private enterprise abroad. A business-government alliance representing both parties was crafted under Eisenhower to develop a "world economy" strategy specifically oriented to fighting communism with transnational capitalism.[144]

Eisenhower premised pursuit of national security on his awareness of how interdependent the US economy had become with the world economy. Twenty years later, in the Carter administration, Andrew Young, ambassador to the United Nations, marked the profound impact that corporate globalism was having on realism when he said that the "rightful role [of the United States is] as the senior partner in a worldwide corporation."[145] But the war in Vietnam lay in the background. With its enormous costs in blood and treasure, the Vietnam War challenged the realist–corporate-globalist assumption that the United States could indefinitely finance both "guns" (anticommunist crusades abroad) and "butter" (domestic well-being within an ever-growing global market). Since Vietnam, the "senior partner's" position in the world economy has gone through many convolutions. As other industrialized countries became competitive with the United States in high-technology exports, "a noticeable shift in emphasis [took place] in US trade policy, from a concern with more ambitious (and ambiguous) global objectives to a focus on more identifiable and short-term national economic interests."[146] The shift was propelled by other developments too: the oil crisis of the early 1970s; recessions in the mid-1970s and early 1980s; and the

Reagan administration's monetary and fiscal policies, which resulted in a strengthening of the dollar that made US exports uncompetitive and contributed to the first of many huge trade deficits with Japan.[147] The end result was to politicize trade policy as never before: Protectionist pressures from the Congress and business rose, which were countered by demands from abroad (especially Japan and Europe) for the United States to restructure its economy if it expected them to be more hospitable to US exports. The "American century" was replaced by a tripolar world economic order, and the struggle for market position on a global basis was on.

## Case Study 2:
## Capitalist Dominoes—The Mexican and Asian Financial Crises

Economically, the top story in the post–Cold War era is emerging markets. Mexico and Indonesia were slated to be among them, moving up the ladder from low-income developing countries to NICs and ultimately, like South Korea, perhaps even to OECD membership. Glowing growth forecasts for these markets were commonplace, right up to the time things came apart.[148] But the currency collapse was only a part of the story; the rest of it had to do with strategic interests. By briefly focusing on the experiences of Indonesia, Mexico, and South Korea, we can highlight a number of troubling features of realist and corporate-globalist practices when it comes to planning for the post–Cold War era. (A fuller examination of South Korea's political and economic development is in Chapter 4.)

Mexico's rise came to a crashing halt on December 20, 1994, when its new president, Ernesto Zedillo, announced that the value of the peso had plunged, setting off an economic crisis that threatened to put Mexico in default on its massive bond and other international obligations. By March 1995 the peso's value was down to about 18 cents (it was worth 29 cents on December 19), and the Mexican stock market went into a tailspin. The US government took the lead in organizing a financial rescue plan. It committed $12 billion of a total international credit line to Mexico, under the IMF's management, of around $50 billion. US and international banking officials talked about saving the peso the way they used to talk about saving friendly governments from communism: the need to prevent falling dominoes ("avoiding contagion effects to other emerging markets"), to uphold US credibility ("the feeling in the rest of the world would be that we are a nation in disarray, a country incapable of addressing a crisis"), and to preserve international system order ("the potential for global financial apocalypse").[149] The crisis was also an opportunity to publicize the point that all globalization is local, for any American with investments had to be concerned about Mexico's fate.[150]

The story of the Mexican peso is not, however, about an unexpected economic emergency. Nor is it fundamentally about the esoteric world of bonds and interest rates. Far deeper issues of global and national import were (and still are) involved. The inequitable pattern of Mexico's development; the unresolved contradictions of its internal political crisis; the continuation of the 1980s debt crisis in new forms; the weak foundations of NAFTA; and the perils of privatization, export-led growth, and overreliance on foreign investment to finance it—these were the issues that made an international crisis of the peso's decline and the US effort to rescue it.

In the 1980s, Mexico became a leading Third World debtor country as it sought to overcome a multitude of economic problems by borrowing. From 1982 on, Mexican authorities were engaged in constant negotiations with the IMF, the World Bank, and the US Treasury Department over how (and whether) to discharge the country's debt obligations. Specifically, the burning issue was what social costs—increasing poverty, inflation, lower domestic output, and unemployment—the Mexican government was willing to pay in order to satisfy the lenders' demands. Those came down to three: liberalize tariffs and investment laws, cut the budget, and privatize state-owned enterprises (SOEs).[151] It was the usual structural adjustment package that, by the late 1990s, would make Mexico the single largest borrower in the IMF's history. The pain of the IMF's medicine was felt mainly by the poorer segments of the population: cuts in food subsidies and support of agriculture, with consequent price rises and reduced consumption;[152] a further widening of the gap between rich and poor;[153] a significant increase in the number of poor people; negative growth in real wages; and no noticeable progress in land reform and other government programs in the 1990s that were supposed to help alleviate poverty.[154] However, opportunities opened up for wealthy Mexicans and foreign businesses to make fortunes, sometimes in questionable ways, particularly from the sell-off of state enterprises.[155]

NAFTA, which got under way in 1993, offered a way out of Mexico's development dilemma: how to attract foreign capital, promote exports, create jobs, and avoid feeding social unrest from the IMF's victims. Both Mexican exports to and imports from the United States went on a steep upward climb. By the end of 1994 Mexico had matched Japan as the number-two market for US products. Transnational corporations from the United States, Japan, and the EU flocked to Mexico in anticipation of the end of most tariffs and other trade-limiting barriers.[156] Comparing 1980 with 1995, Mexico's trade (as a percentage of gross domestic product [GDP]) and private capital inflow approximately doubled.[157] The Clinton administration was predicting the creation of 100,000 new jobs in the United States (and only several thousand jobs lost) due to NAFTA, though its figures were challenged by the US labor movement and other sources.[158] Mexico's economic restructuring was cited by some US bank executives as an example of how the debt crisis had been defused through an adroit combination of financial instruments to reduce debt and encourage privatization. But while a glorious future for Mexico's economy was being trumpeted, and the Mexican president (from 1988 to 1994), Carlos Salinas de Gortari, was being feted as a hero of free-marketization, a different picture was unfolding: a widening trade deficit (from an $8 billion surplus in 1985 to a $15 billion deficit in 1993);[159] increasing debt (roughly $120 billion, about half owed to US stock and bond holders and around $18 billion to US banks);[160] and excessive reliance for capital to offset these deficits on sales to foreigners of very large amounts of risky short-term government bonds, pegged to the peso-dollar exchange rate, rather than on FDI as in other countries.

There were warnings from US officials (but evidently not the IMF) to the Salinas government of impending financial trouble.[161] But those only became known later. At the time, both the Bush and Clinton administrations evidently sought to hide Mexico's troubles. Had it been widely known that the Mexican peso was greatly overvalued, Mexico's suitability as a partner in NAFTA would have been in doubt, and Congress might never have approved the agreement. An overvalued currency means weakened ability to generate exports, offer profitable returns and opportunities to foreign investors, and keep poor workers from migrating (north, in Mexico's case). It also lowers expectations of larger markets and more jobs for the major economies (here, the United States). According to one source, "the central demand of US fund managers [was] that Mexico keep the peso artificially inflated" so as to give both Mexican businesses and foreign investors advantages in the conversion of pesos to dollars.[162] The actual peso crisis ought to have occurred long before 1994–1995; that it did not is tribute to the combined behind-the-scenes efforts of the US government and international lenders, which always recognized that the peso's collapse would have devastating consequences for the Mexican system.

Clearly, from the standpoint of international business interests alone, a quick and generous response to the peso crisis was preordained. Mexico's economy was too important, the size of its debt was too large, and the possibility of Zedillo's declaring a debt moratorium was probably real enough.[163] It was a financial domino. But the stakes went beyond economics, as the above-quoted comments about contagion effects implied. Mexico's political stability was the fundamental concern. At the start of 1994, Indians of Mayan descent, long impoverished and neglected by the central government, began an insurrection in Chiapas state under the leadership of the Zapatista movement. In addition, two top-ranking members of the ruling party (PRI: Partido Revolucionario Institucional) were assassinated later in the year; one of them was the PRI's presidential candidate. When Zedillo was chosen to replace him and was elected in December, he ordered the army to move against the Zapatistas.[164] These events turned out to be only the tip of the iceberg. By 1998, eleven states showed evidence of popular unrest over repression orchestrated by local officials and their police or gangster hirelings. In short, a corrupt, violent, and traditionally authoritarian political system was tottering and, unless it was shored up, not only would foreign investors abandon Mexico but the United States would have a civil war on its southern border.

In one year, Mexico thus went from being an emerging market to becoming a virtual ward of the United States and the IMF. Foreign monitoring of its bank-lending policies to prevent runaway inflation, and placing oil and petrochemical export earnings in escrow (in a New York bank) in case of default, were only the most public (and demeaning) of Mexico's sacrifices to stay afloat.[165] To survive and satisfy its foreign creditors, the Mexican government, which is to say the PRI and the richest Mexicans it represents, had to clamp down on the Zapatistas and other opposition forces; the situation in Chiapas has been volatile ever since. As many political observers foresaw, the bailout drew Mexico more closely within the US orbit, not only in its economic policies, but also in sensitive political areas such as drug trafficking and prosecution along the border. In short, the penalty for Mexico's skewed "emergence" was a further erosion of sovereignty and surrender of the only recently imagined possibility of sustained economic growth. The government had to impose another round of austerity and structural adjustment, just as in the early 1980s, involving (in the IMF's words) "wage, price, and credit restraint," "acceleration in export growth," and further privatization.[166] That meant more bad news for Mexico's rural poor and for workers, who were devastated by the erosion of the peso's value and had no social safety net to rely on. Mexico was able to repay the $12.5 billion it had borrowed from the United States ahead of schedule, in January 1997; but that spelled no relief for most Mexicans.[167]

Just as the IMF failed Mexico, so has NAFTA. On one hand, overall trade figures for the United States, Mexico, and Canada since NAFTA have shown consistent growth, and some Canadian and US companies certainly have profited from increased competition by becoming export-oriented, which often meant moving to Mexico and exporting from there. But the market has not worked for the poor. Corporate gains mask NAFTA's failure to do what was advertised: create many more jobs than would be lost, improve the quality of life for all, keep poor Mexicans productive on their land, and provide legal recourse for maltreated workers. To the contrary, Mexico's poverty and social inequality have deepened, political violence has increased, and the cleavage that "separates those Mexicans plugged into the US economy from those who are not" has widened.[168] A report of the Carnegie Endowment reaffirms that assessment: Rural Mexicans are the biggest losers, but *all* sectors of the Mexican economy are worse off in employment than before NAFTA. The day after the report came out, it was announced that Mexico's ambassador to the United States had been dismissed for saying that Washington regarded his country as its "backyard."[169]

In fact, Mexicans are flocking to the United States in ever greater numbers, and even in the *maquiladoras,* where employment rose during the 1990s, low-wage jobs in China are helping take away the gains.[170] Meantime, the lure of NAFTA contributes to a weakening of unions, lowering of wages, depressing of community economies, loss of health and other benefits, and undermining of environmental standards. NAFTA is making Mexican agricultural products uncompetitive, allowing cheaper US corn, grains, poultry, and other food products to flood the market and TNCs to increase their exports from Mexico of processed food.[171] Mexican workers, particularly poor subsistence farmers, have the choice of being stuck in poverty or risking a border crossing to the United States.

Whereas NAFTA has never penalized any foreign-invested company for violations of labor standards,[172] it has done wonders for corporations investing in the three countries. One reason is an overlooked provision, Chapter 11, that was heavily lobbied by US-based TNCs. Chapter 11 compensates a company whose foreign investment loses money because of another country's environmental or other rules. Private property trumps social concerns, in short. This has come to mean that if a US state seeks to protect its air quality to the detriment of a foreign company's profits, as California has done by banning a Canadian-produced chemical additive to gasoline, or if a US firm in Mexico is forced to leave for dumping dangerous wastes in violation of local law, companies can expect compensation. Moreover, the tribunal created under NAFTA to decide such issues bars public participation, just like the WTO arbitration panel.[173]

The long-term importance of the peso crisis is that it sharpened the focus on the Mexican political system's serious defects, which had been overlooked (especially in the United States) in the rush to liberalize and privatize the country's economy. Corruption is at the heart of Mexico's failure either to democratize or to develop in equitable ways. It infects the national police, the military, state government, and the banking system; corruption money from drug trafficking and bank bailouts has implicated senior figures in all these institutions.[174] It has crippled the legal system: "Prosecutors rig evidence and judges sell verdicts according to the highest bidder." With graft and lack of accountability endemic in the system from top to bottom, it is no wonder Mexicans have the least confidence of any Latin American population in their legal system.[175] And corruption has stifled political competition, for despite the ending of the PRI's domination of government in 2000, recent presidential elections—notably the exceptionally close one in 2006—have raised serious charges of fraud and ballot-box tampering.

By the late 1990s, Mexico's realist and corporate-globalist saviors were touting its rehabilitation as an emerging market; but deep down, senior officials in the United States and probably elsewhere reportedly believed they were watching a powder keg. Mexico is politically and economically far out of balance, and its best hope would seem to lie in a grassroots movement for democracy and social justice.[176] Meantime, the Mexico bailout forced international financial leaders to ponder the prospect of additional defaults by Third World countries. As Alan Greenspan, then chairman of the Federal Reserve, said in 1995, "In today's world, Mexico became the first casualty . . . of the new international financial system."[177] How many more casualties waited in the wings? The answer came soon enough in East Asia.

This was supposed to be the era in which market forces would determine economic and social outcomes. The Asian financial crisis showed otherwise. Why, beginning roughly in mid-1996 and extending into early 1998, did the very same economies that had been extolled for their consistently high growth rates and technological leaps forward—economies that had seemingly shown the virtuousness of "Asian values" such as discipline, order, and hierarchy—suddenly become so vulnerable? A reasonable short answer might be "a potent mix of globalization, poor governance, and greed."[178] These factors betrayed structural problems common to fast-growing economies.

First, the Asian countries were done in by easy money—domestically, by loosely regulated banks too quick to lend, thus driving up the price of real estate beyond all reason, and internationally, as in Mexico, by overreliance on foreign portfolio and direct investments. Very large sums of money poured into the so-called Asian tigers in the 1990s: $318 billion from European banks, $260 billion from Japan, $46 billion from the United States, plus another $38 billion in mutual-fund investments and around $50 billion in foreign investment.[179] Few investor institutions could see beyond the prospects of huge profits to the possibility of overextension. For the recipients—including Thailand, the first "domino" to fall in 1997, and Indonesia—these funds provided a temporary escape from serious economic problems. But they also created dependence on foreign funds to cover mounting trade deficits; and hence they represented debts and vulnerability. When Japanese investors in particular shifted to other Asian locations in the early 1990s, Thailand had to fall back on short-term financial devices, and corrupt practices, to raise money. It faced the same debt crunch that Mexico faced. Investors fled and currency took a dive.[180] The story was different in the details but not the fundamentals in South Korea.[181] There, an economy that had grown spectacularly on the strength of exports and close state–big business ties, but *not* foreign investment, confronted new obstacles in the 1990s. Trade competition intensified, especially with Chinese exports and Japanese multinationals in Southeast Asia, causing very large deficits. The United States pressed Korea to reduce trade and investment barriers. Korea's dominant business conglomerates, *chaebol*, began to lose their competitive edge and, in some cases, their viability as labor and other costs jumped. The state and its ruling party, always politically beholden to the *chaebol* and dependent on its economic predominance, ignored market discipline in favor of huge bailout loans, engineered via friendly banks. The banks wound up with $100 billion or so in nonpayable debts. Corruption and cronyism, as well as the wavelike effects of the currency crisis that started in Thailand, brought the house down by the end of 1997.

A second basic factor in the currency collapse was poor governance. Though the state in Asia is often assumed to be the guiding force in disciplining the economy, following the Japanese model, it was rather the weakness of government regulations that helped catapult these states into eclipse.[182] That weakness opened the doors wide to commercial transactions based mainly on personal relationships and payoffs among government leaders, bureaucrats, and business tycoons. It also made possible the ownership of key businesses and state monopolies on the basis of blood and friendship ties—as in the case of Indonesian President Suharto's six children and various cronies. Such coziness also led to bad business decisions, such as redundant production, showpiece construction projects, and huge debt run-ups. Some Asian leaders, notably Mohamed bin Mahathir of Malaysia, fumed about the nefarious influence of Western currency speculators and other moneyed interests who, he insisted, manipulated the financial crisis so as to cut the Asian tigers down to manageable size. But while such talk had a receptive audience in some parts of Asia, especially as it made the IMF and the United States convenient targets, it really seemed to amount to an effort to deflect attention from the greed, lack of accountability, and dependence on foreign capital of many Asian economies.

How governments and international agencies handled the Asian financial crisis is instructive. They not only intervened when markets failed; the IMF converted a problem into an opportunity for the TNCs and TNBs. In Korea, instead of "providing a temporary bridge loan and then organizing the banks into a negotiating group,"[183] the IMF chose a direct approach: a $57 billion bailout (including an initial commitment of $17.2 billion to which the World Bank, the Asian Development Bank, and several governments contributed) of Korea's failing banks and *chaebol*. One can only assume the IMF took the interventionist course at the behest of Washington, which initially had decided against making a direct loan to Korea. It reportedly saw the major US banks (which were far less exposed in Korea than were Japan's) and TNCs as the ideal replacements for bankrupt Korean institutions. Moreover, an active US role was considered strategically necessary given the importance of South Korea's political stability to US security interests in Northeast Asia.[184] Foreign corporations and banks such as Chase Manhattan, J. P. Morgan, and Citicorp finally got access rights to the Korean economy that Korean leaders had long denied them, such as the right of majority ownership of corporations and partnership in bank mergers and takeovers.[185] The *chaebol* had lost so much value, and so many Korean banks had turned belly up, that there was little resistance to these new sources of dollars and yen. Korean unions were told to prepare their workers for massive layoffs such as Korea had not seen in decades. President-elect Kim Dae Jung, supported by organized labor for the presidency, had promised that no jobs would be lost in exchange for IMF help, but had to backtrack even before taking office. No layoffs, no loans, said the IMF. Budget-cutting and limitations on economic growth were other IMF-dictated steps that would primarily impact working families.[186]

The rapid downfall of Indonesia's economy, like that of Mexico and South Korea, was treated by the IMF and the United States as a *strategic* decision.[187] Indonesia was too big to be allowed to fail economically, and it was too important politically to be allowed to descend into chaos. As Indonesia unraveled in 1998, US officials engaged in a war-room–style debate (with the Pentagon's participation) about Indonesia's potential social instability if prices continued to rise. There was grave Vietnam-era talk about the global stakes—the IMF's credibility, a test of US leadership, and dominoes falling if Indonesia were to go under. Suharto, under pressure from student and other demonstrators to step down, responded by reinventing himself as a radical nationalist who was resisting the foreign devils seeking to run Indonesia's economy.[188] Largely lost in the contest of wills was the repressive Indonesian political system built around Suharto and the armed forces that was designed to stifle the broad-based opposition aroused by the country's crumbling economy. Remarkably, Suharto did step down in May 1998 under pressure from his military and the United States, leaving an economy that the World Bank predicted would require $50 billion in emergency loans and have 40 percent of the population living below the poverty line.

A few corporate globalists took the IMF to task for forcing "fundamental structural and institutional reforms on countries."[189] But the more common view was of a triumph on a par with the crumbling of the Berlin Wall. It was not just that the creditor banks avoided having to pay for their mistakes, which would have required (for example) bearing the costs of bad loan decisions and making lending and other policies more open.[190] Perhaps the largest victory of all was articulated by Alan Greenspan: the presumed discrediting of the Asian model of late or state capitalism. When Asian economies were growing at 10 percent a year, he said, their "faulty" economic structures could not be demonstrated. Now, one can see "a consensus towards the . . . Western form of free-market capitalism as the model which should govern how each individual country should run its economy."[191] With socialism also buried, only the US model was left standing. Asian governments probably disagreed; but in any case, some reversed themselves and opted to join the WTO. They needed the money. "The difference from just two years ago," Lawrence H. Summers, the US deputy treasury secretary, said, "is that in many countries the problem has shifted from managing capital to attracting capital." Another senior US official noted that "these are countries that for two decades have followed the Japanese model—keep a tight control on your financial institutions and you control your economy."

Now, he said, "they have discovered the dark side of that strategy," the risks of ignoring sound lending practices.[192]

As the fallout from the crisis spread to South Africa, Russia, and Brazil between mid-1998 and early 1999, a number of proponents of globalization began to wonder if the IMF's medicine had worsened the disease. Yet few changes of policy or practice occurred. The IMF did not significantly change the way it operates. Asian leaders opened their economies somewhat more to US and other foreign investors,[193] but without making structural changes. By 2006, in fact, Asia was again receiving huge capital inflows from foreign investment in its stock markets and large borrowing at cheap rates. And few people talked of risk or of 1997.[194]

Lost amid the tumult of stock market tailspins and strategic calculations was the fact that the financial crisis became a human-rights crisis.[195] Hardest hit were the poor; no social safety net for them. In Indonesia, for instance, prices of household commodities skyrocketed; people in outlying islands reportedly were reduced to eating just about anything that grew. In urban areas, sometimes violent protests were often directed at the minority Chinese population that dominates the entrepreneurial class. In South Korea, the traditional family structure was undermined by salarymen suddenly turned out of work and ashamed to admit it to their families. Korean women professionals were the first to be laid off by their companies. In Thailand, Indonesia, and other countries, rural people bore the brunt of unemployment. Migrant workers were the first to be laid off; families sold daughters to brothels to earn money; and workers who had graduated from sweatshops returned to them or faced having no work at all.[196] As US strategic planners were well aware, the real possibility existed that an unresolved financial crisis, unprecedented unemployment, and widespread despair could turn into an ugly series of social upheavals.

## Case Study 3:
## Another American Century? The Invasion of Iraq[197]

> The war began on my watch, but it's going to end on your watch.
> —President Bush, speaking to the West Point class of 2006[198]

Gulf War I in January 1991 was a classic tale of realism and corporate globalism: the US effort to impose a new world order; the importance of territory, sovereignty, and access to a vital resource; the trade of US money and intelligence for influence with Saddam Hussein; the roles of historic and personal animosities, duplicity and megalomania, and contending nationalisms. Gulf War II was in some ways a continuation of the first war: the US decision to finish the job left undone, namely, the removal of Saddam Hussein from power in Iraq; the continuing concern over Iraq's possible possession of weapons of mass destruction (WMD); the role of oil and

Israel's security in US decisionmaking. But in several other respects, Gulf War II was an entirely different conflict. It was a preventive war, decided upon opportunistically and carried out unilaterally and deceitfully, leaving realists and globalists open to heavy criticism.

George W. Bush entered office in the company of people determined to fulfill a new doctrine of US supremacy. The Bush Doctrine was the product of a group of neoconservative officials (neocons), former officials, national-security specialists, and journalists. Many of them had been associated with the Project for the New American Century (PNAC),[199] an organization dedicated to ensuring that in the post–Cold War era, the United States would have no peer. The neocons' strategic conception, vigorously pushed by Vice President Richard (Dick) Cheney and Secretary of Defense Donald Rumsfeld, found expression in *The National Security Strategy of the United States of America* (NSS), issued in September 2002.[200] Like NSC-68, NSS sought to redefine US global strategy in terms of a singular threat, terrorism. Unlike NSC-68, NSS posited that the United States must act unilaterally whenever necessary to meet the threat; that preemptive attack on enemies might well be required, since the old strategies of containment and deterrence were no longer adequate; and that "regime change" was a necessary objective for dealing with rogue state leaders.

In truth, these three policy goals—unilateral action, preemptive attack, and regime change—are not novel features of US foreign policy. All post–World War II US administrations resorted to them at times. The novelty lay rather in the ideological zeal with which Bush's administration carried out these policies, the faith-based certainty with which the president acted, and the willingness to act before hard evidence was in hand on the slightest suspicion (the "one-percent doctrine") of a threat to US national security.[201] The Bush administration made what for traditional realists is a cardinal error: turning a response to the 9/11 attacks into a global crusade. In numerous public statements, administration figures defined the invasions of Iraq and Afghanistan in apocalyptic terms: a fight for "civilization itself," a battle of good versus evil, "the decisive ideological struggle of the 21st century," the equivalent of the wars against Nazism and communism. Alliance relationships and coalition politics were downgraded; policy would no longer be made "by committee," Rumsfeld said. The quest to legitimize US actions by squaring them with international law and seeking UN endorsement was largely abandoned. The Department of Defense usurped the State Department's policymaking functions. All the risks of a crusade were assumed, and came to pass—overextension, overconfidence, underestimation of the consequences of victory, and conflation of a diverse enemy into a monolithic one, "Islamic terrorists."

The war on Iraq clarified the practical meaning of the Bush Doctrine. Insisting that Iraq's possession of nuclear weapons was imminent, that it had stockpiles of chemical and bacteriological weapons, that it was in league with Al-Qaida, and that the United States had a sufficient mandate from both the UN and Congress to act, the Bush administration invaded Iraq in March 2003. In fact, Bush had no mandate from the UN. The Security Council agreed with him that Iraq was in "material breach" of its commitment to international inspections, but refused to endorse an invasion until diplomacy had run its course. Nor did the administration act under the terms of the 1973 War Powers Act passed by the Congress during the Vietnam War to restrain presidential war making. The administration presented the US attack as pre-emptive when in fact it was *preventive*, undertaken without evidence of an Iraqi capability or intention to use weapons of mass destruction. As would later become clear, Iraq actually had abandoned efforts to develop nuclear weapons and had no other ongoing WMD programs. Nor did it have plans to attack its neighbors, much less the United States. Nor, finally, did Iraq have any connection to Al-Qaida and its terrorist acts. In short, the United States acted on evidence that turned out to be worse than flimsy.

In reality, the Bush administration had the objective of regime change in Iraq almost from the day it took office. Perhaps the administration's worst sin is that it distorted the evidence on Iraq's WMD capabilities in order to win over doubters, prosecute a war, and avoid protracted negotiations. Bush officials fit the facts to suit a decision already made. They were determined to start the bombing of Baghdad regardless of how the Security Council voted, and the president was perfectly prepared to provoke a confrontation with Iraq.[202] Bush and Cheney knew full well that most people in the US intelligence community believed UN inspections of Iraq's weapons sites had worked and Saddam Hussein's ambitions had been stifled. Among several administration insiders who saw the situation for what it was and had the courage to say so is Paul R. Pillar, who served as the CIA's national intelligence officer on the Middle East at the time. He wrote:

> The Bush administration deviated from the professional standard not only in using policy to drive intelligence, but also in aggressively using intelligence to win public support for its decision to go to war. This meant selectively adducing data—"cherry-picking"—rather than using the intelligence community's own analytic judgments. . . . The intelligence community never offered any analysis that supported the notion of an alliance between Saddam and al Qaeda. Yet it was drawn into a public effort to support that notion.[203]

Invading Afghanistan, talking up Iraq's WMD capabilities, and alleging Iraq's support of Al-Qaida were justifications for a war based on a whole other logic. The United States went to war to complete the job that Gulf War I had not accomplished: regime change.[204] Ending Saddam Hussein's rule was essential to other US objectives, both realist and globalist. These were to strengthen US access to Iraqi and Middle East oil, acquire new military bases to replace those in Saudi Arabia, ensure that the next Iraqi government would be "democratic" (that is, friendly to US interests), and, above all, demonstrate US power and primacy in world affairs. These were all elements of the neocon agenda in the 1990s, when the PNAC believed the United States lost momentum in global leadership and devalued the role of military power to achieve political ends. Iraq, with its dictator, its oil, and its ambitions to be a regional leader, was the place to renew the American century, and the 9/11 attacks provided (as one neocon statement had put it years earlier) the next "Pearl Harbor" that would galvanize US nationalism in support of the neocon agenda.

President Bush declared victory on March 1, 2003. A dictatorship was overthrown, revealing horrid new details of Saddam's police state. But it was a hollow victory in many respects, and not just because the invasion occurred under false pretenses:

- The invasion was illegal under international law: It constituted preventive war, and it did not have Security Council endorsement.
- US military and intelligence services violated domestic and international law by abusing and torturing enemy soldiers, by practicing the "rendition" of some of those soldiers to third countries known to torture prisoners, and by unconstitutionally establishing military tribunals without congressional authorization.
- Planning for the postwar reconstruction of Iraq failed to anticipate an insurgency, a long-term occupation, and a host of serious social, economic, and political challenges in Iraq. This failure had much to do with the shift in power during the Bush administration to the Pentagon, which tended to ignore the State Department's extensive studies for the postwar period.[205]
- The invasion and occupation significantly hurt the US reputation abroad and the State Department's ability to effectively represent US interests abroad.
- The decision for war was part of a determined effort by US officials, led by Vice President Cheney, to expand the powers of the presidency and remove prior constraints imposed by Congress in the aftermath of the Vietnam War. Decisions, said Secretary of State Powell's chief of staff, were made by a "cabal [of Cheney and Rumsfeld] . . . that the bureaucracy did not know were being made."[206]
- The war did not spread democracy in the Middle East, and in some cases actually resulted in political developments adverse to democracy.
- The war's enormous financial cost undercut important social programs at home and deepened US indebtedness. Its privatization—the extensive role of private security forces and major US corporations operating under no-bid contracts—fed widespread corruption in Iraq.

In Iraq, the US victory was challenged by the limited capacity of Iraqi governments to govern. Though the US occupation officially ended in June 2004, the US presence in Iraq remained huge: 130,000 troops, the largest US embassy staff in the world, and nearly as many private contractors as soldiers. Such an overwhelming presence assured that the legitimacy of Iraqi authority would always be in question, not only because Iraq's new leadership seemed to be Washington's choice, but also because the future disposition of Iraq's oil and the open door to foreign investors were also products of the occupation. Commendably, parliamentary elections for a national government took place in December 2005 despite the insurgency. But increasingly the voting, like the fighting, followed sectarian divisions, showing that the population was a long way from identifying as Iraqis. They were also voting with their feet: Nearly 1 million had left the country since 2003, and another half-million had sought refuge within Iraq.[207]

By 2006 the struggle for Iraq had become two wars: an insurgency and a civil war.[208] The insurgents, mostly Sunni, commonly are estimated to number 15,000 to 20,000; only about 1,000 are from outside Iraq.[209] But their growth, audacity, cohesion, and terror have usually outmatched the security forces of the Iraqi government. The civil war is the sectarian struggle between private armies: militia belonging to Sunni and Shiite religious leaders and political parties; security forces embedded in Iraq's interior ministry; and Kurdish forces bent on defending their part of the country, which already has de facto independence.[210] Summarizing the increasingly adverse security situation, the commander of US forces in the Middle East told a Senate committee: "I believe that the sectarian violence is probably as bad as I've seen it, in Baghdad in particular, and if not stopped, it is possible that Iraq could move towards civil war."[211] For most independent observers, including some Iraqi leaders, civil war was already a fact of life.

By the fall of 2006 fighting in Iraq had claimed around 600,000 Iraqi lives.[212] Added to the daily violence of the insurgency was the reduced quality of life for the survivors. The future of the country had come to depend on factors the Americans who planned the war had ignored or downplayed: the formation of a broadly based coalition government, amalgamation of the armies and militias into a single force, the restoration of basic services, and Iran's cooperation in not supporting Shiite armies. In fact, by 2007 the Iran factor had assumed center stage in US planning. Concerned that Iran was capitalizing on its ties with the Shiite leadership in Iraq, the Bush administration reversed course and threw in its lot with "moderate" Sunnis, thus promoting further division in the Middle East between the Sunni- and Shiite-dominated states and movements: Iran, Syria, and Hezbollah on one side, Saudi Arabia, Jordan, and Kuwait on the other. The policy shift adds another ingredient to the mix of factors that might presage US-supported action against Iran.[213]

The emerging civil war in Iraq takes us back to our previous discussion of democratization. Building representative, accountable institutions is a long-term process; doing so in a country once ruled by a dictator, in the midst of communal conflict, and occupied by a foreign power is asking for the impossible. As one of the leading students of communal conflict wrote, years before Gulf War II:

> In democratizing autocracies . . . the opportunities for communal groups to mobilize are substantial, but states usually lack the resources or institutional means to reach the kinds of accommodations that typify the established democracies. In these states, democratization is likely to facilitate both protest and communal rebellion. The serious risk is that the rejection of accommodation by one or all contenders will lead to civil war and the reimposition of coercive rule.[214]

George W. Bush was right to reject nation building as an element of US foreign policy before he assumed the presidency. But he forgot the "pottery barn rule" that Colin Powell recited: "You are going to be the proud owner of 25 million people [in Iraq]. . . . You break it, you own it."[215] The temptation to try anyway evidently proved too great.

The US occupation of Iraq also failed where it was proclaimed by the Bush administration to have succeeded: creating and nurturing pro-Western democracies that would send a message to authoritarian leaders throughout the Middle East. In fact, the occupation gravely wounded prospects for that kind of democratization. King Abdullah of Jordan abandoned plans for political reform. Hezbollah did well in 2005 elections in Lebanon. Hamas candidates won legislative elections in 2006 that gave it a decisive voice in the PA.[216] Presidential elections in Iran amounted to a leap backward with the victory of a hard-line anti-Western leader virulently opposed to Israel. In Egypt the longtime president, Hosni Mubarak, agreed to allow opposition parties to contest for the presidency. But Bush's lauding of the decision proved premature: Government-sponsored violence kept many people from voting in parliamentary elections in 2005, despite which the radical Muslim Brotherhood scored major gains. Following presidential elections later that year, the runner-up to Mubarak, who had received a mere 7 percent of the vote, was jailed for five years on trumped-up charges. The parliament then (in May 2006) renewed a detention law that has been in existence for two decades to provide a legal basis for imprisoning opponents of the government. Nor did promised constitutional changes materialize that would have opened up political competition.

Meanwhile, Afghanistan bears all the earmarks of a failing state despite having held national elections. It suffers from three intersecting crises: massive human-development requirements, the resumption of the opium trade, and a continuing threat from the resurgent Taliban. The resettlement of over 3 million people who fled the country during Taliban rule, and over 1 million who were internally displaced, is one element of the human-development crisis. The international community's commitment to Afghanistan's economic needs has proven shaky. Only a fraction of the promised development assistance has materialized. Many farmers have gone back to cultivating opium poppy, which the Taliban had once banned but now reportedly is encouraging. Poppy sets new production records each year, leading some UN officials to refer to Afghanistan as a "narco state."[217]

NATO, with about 32,000 troops, leads the peacekeeping effort in the country's interior, supplemented by 8,000 troops under US command. Some 22,000 additional US troops roam the borderlands looking for Al-Qaida remnants. But security remains a distant goal for Afghanis. Outside Kabul, warlords fight one another for territorial control. The Taliban are back in control of large swaths of territory, thanks in no small part to support from Pakistan's border villages and probably its intelligence service.[218] The country is awash in weapons, landmines, and unexploded ordnance. Afghanistan is perhaps the best example of why the 1997 landmine convention—officially, the Antipersonnel Mine Ban Convention—is needed, for it provides legal justification of a major UN-led effort to clear land that poses constant dangers to civilians.[219] It will take many years, at best, before the Afghan government has the capacity and the legitimacy to gain control of the country.

As happened in Vietnam, a protracted war in the Middle East has turned against those who prosecuted it and in the process divided the US populace. George W. Bush overextended himself, just as Lyndon Johnson and Richard Nixon did. As Bush entered the second half of his last term, his popularity plummeted and his administration had to deal with a Democrat-controlled Congress that was pressing him to set a timetable for US withdrawal from Iraq. Like his predecessors in Vietnam, Bush has relied on appeals to patriotism, national security, and the promise of ultimate triumph to sustain his policies. Yet despite US war casualties (over 3,200 in early 2007) that have surpassed those of 9/11, and perhaps $2 trillion in total costs for the two wars so far,[220] Congress and the public seem torn between keeping on in Iraq and withdrawing. While they ponder the matter, one thing seems clear: By the time the next president takes office in January 2009, the civil wars in Iraq and Afghanistan will be even more intense and the price tag, in blood and treasure, will be far higher than it is today.

### Notes

1. Among the most influential realist writings are Edward H. Carr, *The Twenty-Years' Crisis, 1919–1939: An Introduction to the Study of International Relations;* George F. Kennan, *Realities of American Foreign Policy;* and Hans J. Morgenthau, *Politics Among Nations: The Struggle for Power and Peace,* 5th rev. ed. For brief reviews of the literature, see Kegley and Wittkopf (1981 ed.), pp. 19–22; and Ray Maghroori, "Introduction: Major Debates in International Relations," in Ray Maghroori and Bennett Ramberg, eds., *Globalism Versus Realism: International Relations' Third Debate,* pp. 9–22.

2. Noncapitalist systems should also be considered to have their corporate globalists, however. They would be key figures in socialist and communist parties, state trading companies, and similar powerful bureaucracies that operate transnationally. Like their capitalist counterparts, these highly centralized organizations are also propelled by globalist ideas: the spread of market socialist economic models (such as China's), political institutions, and trading areas. Examples of the corporate-globalist world view are in Maghroori and Ramberg, eds., *Globalism Versus Realism;* Richard J. Barnet and Ronald E. Müller, *Global Reach: The Power of the Multinational Corporations,* part 1; Barnet and Cavanagh, *Global Dreams;* and Stephen Guisinger, ed., *Private Enterprise and the New Global Economic Challenge.*

3. As President Lyndon B. Johnson said in 1966: "There are 3 billion people in the world and we have only 200 million of them. We are outnumbered 15 to 1. If might did make right, they would sweep over the United States and take what we have. We have what they want." Quoted in Richard J. Barnet, *Intervention and Revolution: The United States in the Third World,* p. 25.

4. Richard J. Barnet, *Roots of War,* pp. 95–96.

5. Henry A. Kissinger, *Nuclear Weapons and Foreign Policy,* p. 244.

6. Lucian M. Ashworth, "The Great Illusion and the New World Order: Norman Angell's Approach to World Peace and Its Relevance to International Relations in a Post–Cold War World," paper presented at the annual conference of the International Studies Association, Acapulco, Mexico, March 27, 1993, pp. 21–23.

7. See David C. Hendrickson, "Toward Universal Empire: The Dangerous Quest for Absolute Security," *World Policy Journal,* pp. 1–10.

8. The emphasis on equilibrium may be found in Henry A. Kissinger, "The New World Order," in Crocker and Hampson, eds., *Managing Global Chaos,* pp. 173–181.

9. Kissinger, quoted in James Petras and Morris Morley, *The United States and Chile: Imperialism and the Overthrow of the Allende Government,* p. vii.

10. Henry A. Kissinger, *White House Years,* p. 673. This, despite the US ambassador's predictably paranoid admission that "Chile voted calmly to have a Marxist-Leninist state, the first nation in the world to make this choice freely and knowingly."

11. Quoted in *The Washington Spectator,* April 1, 1993, p. 2.

12. Morgenthau, p. 274.

13. For an excellent critique of realism on the issue of domestic forces that inspire leaders' preferences, see Andrew Moravcsik, "Taking Preferences Seriously: A Liberal Theory of International Politics," *International Organization.*

14. Seymour M. Hersh, *The Price of Power: Kissinger in the Nixon White House,* p. 263.

15. Paul Kennedy, *The Rise and Fall of the Great Powers: Economic Change and Military Conflict from 1500 to 2000.*

16. Kissinger, interviewed in "The Politics of Human Rights," *Trialogue,* no. 19 (Fall 1978), p. 3.

17. Kissinger, "The New World Order," in Chester A. Crocker and Fen Osler Hampson, eds., *Managing Global Chaos: Sources of and Responses to International Conflict.*

18. Truman, quoted in Noam Chomsky, *American Power and the New Mandarins,* p. 268.

19. John M. Stopford and John H. Dunning, eds., *The World Directory of Multinational Enterprises, 1982–83: Company Performance and Global Trends,* table 1.2, p. 5; David H. Blake and Robert S. Walters, *The Politics of Global*

*Economic Relations,* p. 79; *Statistical Abstract of the United States: 1992,* table 1324, p. 789; James K. Jackson, "U.S. Direct Investment Abroad: Trends and Current Issues," Congressional Research Service Report to Congress No. RS21118 (April 29, 2005), p. 2.

20. Jackson, "U.S. Direct Investment Abroad," pp. 2, 5.

21. *International Herald Tribune,* March 22, 1983.

22. Organization for Economic Cooperation and Development, *Trends and Recent Developments in Foreign Direct Investment,* pp. 9–10.

23. Keith Bradsher, "Subtext of the GM Strike Focuses on Global Strategy," *NYT,* June 23, 1998, online at www.nytimes.com.

24. On the Trilateral Commission's origins and development, see Holly K. Sklar, ed., *Trilateralism: The Trilateral Commission and Elite Planning for World Management,* chs. 2–4; and Laurence Shoup, *The Carter Presidency,* ch. 2.

25. John Huey, "The World's Best Brand," *Fortune,* May 31, 1993, pp. 44–54.

26. See Salil S. Pitroda, "From GATT to WTO: The Institutionalization of World Trade," pp. 231–34.

27. Erik Assadourian, "Transforming Corporations" (citing the UN Conference on Trade and Development, *World Investment Report 2005*), in Danielle Nierenberg et al., *State of the World 2006: Special Focus—China and India,* p. 172.

28. World Trade Organization, *World Trade Report 2006: Exploring the Links Between Subsidies, Trade and the WTO,* p. 3.

29. Robert B. Reich, *The Work of Nations: Preparing Ourselves for 21st-Century Capitalism,* p. 114; Murray Weidenbaum, "The Business Response to the Global Marketplace," *The Washington Quarterly.* Theodore H. Moran ("Trade and Investment Dimensions of International Conflict," in Crocker and Hampson, p. 157) reports that "multinational enterprises were responsible for more than 75 percent of United States merchandise trade, with approximately 40 percent of that trade consisting of intrafirm transactions."

30. Rulings in the WTO's binding dispute resolution process have thus far clearly favored trade over the environment, including protection of endangered species. Two examples can be cited. In the first, the US Clean Air Act was ordered changed because it set standards for gasoline that imported Venezuelan gas could not meet (David E. Sanger, "World Trade Group Orders U.S. to Alter Clean Air Act," *NYT,* January 18, 1996, p. C1). The act was considered discriminatory. A second case involved shrimp-exporting countries such as India. They won a ruling in April 1998 against the United States, which had prohibited shrimps caught by boats whose nets also caught endangered sea turtles. The US action was deemed to restrain trade rather than properly protect an endangered species (Elizabeth Olson, "Target Practice in Geneva on the Global Trade Body," *NYT,* May 16, 1998, p. C1). It might further be noted that although the WTO does have international environmental standards for exported products (called ISO 14,000), these are corporate driven and are not the result of consultation or collaboration with environmental organizations. For background, see French, *Costly Tradeoffs.*

31. See Keith Bradsher, "American Workers Watch as Best Jobs Go Overseas," *International Herald Tribune,* August 29, 1995.

32. Erik Assadourian, "Foreign Direct Investment Inflows Decline," in Lisa Mastny et al., *Vital Signs 2005: The Trends That Are Shaping Our Future,* p. 48.

33. *NYT,* May 8, 1998, p. C1.

34. Meier, *The International Environment of Business,* p. 11.

35. See Miguel Korzeniewicz, "Commodity Chains and Marketing Strategies: Nike and the Global Athletic Footwear Industry," and Hyung Kook Kim and Su-Hoon Lee, "Commodity Chains and the Korean Automobile Industry," both in Gary

Gereffi and Miguel Korzeniewicz, eds., *Commodity Chains and Global Capitalism,* pp. 247–65, 281–96.

36. Richard Stubbs, "Asia-Pacific Regionalization and the Global Economy," *Asian Survey,* pp. 791–93. By mid-1998, however, a number of Japanese companies had pulled in their horns as consumers at home turned away from buying and the weak yen made overseas operations less attractive.

37. The chief characteristic of region-states is "efficient economies of scale in their consumption, infrastructure and professional services," writes Kenichi Ohmae, "The Rise of the Region State," *Foreign Affairs,* pp. 78–87.

38. Xiangming Chen, *As Borders Bend: Transnational Spaces on the Pacific Rim.*

39. IMF statistics for 1989, reported in *The Oregonian,* September 13, 1990.

40. In 2005, Germany (exports of $971 billion), the United States ($904 billion), China ($762 billion), and Japan ($596 billion) held the top four positions in world merchandise exports. With imports included the United States topped the trade list with total trade of $2.6 trillion. WTO, *World Trade Report 2006,* p. 11.

41. *BusinessWeek,* July 26, 2004.

42. Chart, "Trade Within Firms," in *Foreign Policy* (January–February 2003), at www.foreignpolicy.com/issue_janfeb_2003/images/chart3.jpg.

43. These surpluses, as Robert J. Gilpin reminds us in *U.S. Power and the Multinational Corporations,* p. 157, are quite apart from income and from portfolio investments—stocks, bonds, and the like—which amount to several times the receipts from direct investments.

44. *Forbes,* July 7, 1980, pp. 102–6.

45. *Forbes,* April 1998, at www.forbes.com.

46. Joseph Quinlan and Marc Chandler, "The U.S. Trade Deficit: A Dangerous Obsession," *Foreign Affairs,* pp. 87–97.

47. David C. Korten, *When Corporations Rule the World,* p. 221.

48. Kegley and Wittkopf (2001 ed.), table 7.3, p. 231.

49. John Cavanagh and Frederick Clairmonte, "The Transnational Economy: Transnational Corporations and Global Markets," table 6, p. 25.

50. OECD, *Trends and Recent Developments in Foreign Direct Investment,* p. 1. The same figure also holds for US TNC investments; see, for instance, US Bureau of the Census, *Statistical Abstract of the United States: 1992,* table 1324, p. 789.

51. Ibid., p. 3; Assadourian, "Foreign Direct Investment," p. 48.

52. Jeff Harrod, "The Century of the Corporation," in Christopher May, ed., *Global Corporate Power,* pp. 26–28.

53. Ibid., table 2.1, p. 27.

54. Jackson, "U.S. Direct Investment Abroad," p. 2; *Financial Times,* September 6, 2006.

55. Quinlan and Chandler, "The U.S. Trade Deficit."

56. *The Oregonian,* July 3, 1990; Meier, *The International Environment of Business,* p. 174.

57. Weidenbaum, in *Christian Science Monitor,* August 23, 1988, p. 10.

58. Stopford and Dunning, table 1.3, p. 6.

59. *Fortune,* July 27, 1992, p. 176.

60. John M. Stopford, ed., *Directory of Multinationals,* vol. 2, pp. 1501–3.

61. *Los Angeles Times,* April 8, 1981, sec. 4, p. 1.

62. *International Herald Tribune,* May 29, 1995; *BusinessWeek,* July 26, 2004, pp. 68, 100.

63. *BusinessWeek,* July 26, 2004, pp. 76–93.

64. See Cheryl Payer, *The World Bank: A Critical Analysis,* and Charles F. Meissner, "Debt: Reform Without Governments," *Foreign Policy.*

65. The two institutions responsible for these classes of funding are the International Bank for Reconstruction and Development (IBRD) and the International Development Association (IDA). These and other basic facts on the World Bank are drawn from its web site: www.worldbank.org. A scholarly, detailed, and surprisingly critical history of the Bank and some of its activities, which the Bank itself commissioned, may be found in Devesh Kapur, John P. Lewis, and Richard Webb, eds., *The World Bank: Its First Half Century.*

66. Table, "World Bank Lending by Theme and Sector, Fiscal 2000–2005," *Annual Report 2005,* at www.worldbank.org.

67. Exemplifying the effort to change policy, the Bank decided not to help fund China's Three Gorges Dam project, the world's largest, and formed a World Dam Commission in 1998 to bring together NGOs, government, and industry representatives to advise on funding. (See G. Pascal Zachary, "World Bank Forces Battle of the Dams," *Wall Street Journal,* March 19, 1998.) The new Bank-supported dam projects are the Nam Theun 2 dam in Laos, also backed by the Asian Development Bank, which will provide electricity to Thailand (see Seth Mydans, "A Massive Dam, Under Way in Laos, Generates Worries," *NYT,* June 26, 2006, p. A4) and the Indus Basin Irrigation System that diverts waterways through a system of dams to provide power to Pakistan (see Peter Bosshard and Shannon Lawrence, "Pakistan's Rot Has World Bank Roots," *Far Eastern Economic Review,* May 2006, pp. 39–43). For a detailed, long-term critique of the environmental impact of Bank projects, see Robert Wade, "Greening the Bank: The Struggle over the Environment, 1970–1995," in Kapur, Lewis, and Webb, eds., *The World Bank,* ch. 13.

68. Basic data on the IMF may be found on its web site: www.imf.org.

69. All the following figures are from Meier, *The International Environment of Business,* table 4.6, p. 142.

70. See, for instance, Jeff Gerth, "In Post–Cold-War Washington, Development Is a Hot Business," *NYT,* May 25, 1996, p. 1.

71. Convincing cases are presented in Teresa Hayter, *Aid as Imperialism,* ch. 4; Payer, *World Bank,* pp. 19–21; and Cheryl Payer, *The Debt Trap: The IMF and the Third World,* ch. 10.

72. Thomas L. Friedman, "Don't Mess with Moody's," *NYT,* February 22, 1995, p. A15.

73. For a well-informed critique of the Washington consensus, see Joseph E. Stiglitz, *Globalization and Its Discontents.* Also see Dirk Olin, "New Washington Consensus," *NYT,* May 25, 2003, sec. 6, p. 21.

74. Christopher Marquis, "$3.5 Billion Africa Pipeline Expected to Pass," *NYT,* June 6, 2000, p. A3. The bank came to regret the decision; six years later it had to stop loaning Chad money when it became plain whose pockets the money was lining. Lydia Polgreen and Celia W. Dugger, "Chad's Oil Riches, Meant for Poor, Are Diverted," *NYT,* February 18, 2006, p. 1.

75. Jane Perlez, "World Bank Again Giving Large Loans to Indonesia," *NYT,* December 2, 2003, p. A14.

76. See Darrell Delamaide, *Debt Shock: The Full Story of the World Credit Crisis,* pp. 112, 227–28. As Meissner comments (p. 89), the efforts of Third World governments to restructure (postpone) their debts involve them in an elaborate game. It can only work if, in return for the governments' opening up their economies to foreign investments and increased trade, the transnational banks greatly liberalize lending policies, including a cap on interest rates. So far, only the debtors have been playing the game.

77. Douglas Jehl, "Egypt's Farmers Resist End of Freeze on Rents," *NYT*, December 27, 1997, p. A5.

78. Howard W. French, "Africa Resentful as Asia Rakes in Aid," *NYT*, March 8, 1998, online.

79. Joseph Kahn, "U.S. Backs Aid to Turkey Tied to Economic Overhaul," *NYT*, April 27, 2001, online ed. According to a *NYT* report (April 30, 2001, online ed.), "[US] Treasury officials have indicated that they see Turkey as a test case of their insistence on accountability, warning Turkish leaders that they should not return to the fund for more money if their financial overhaul, which includes bank reforms, privatization and budget cutting, fails to restore investors' confidence." Turkey became the IMF's biggest debtor in 2002; but it had the good fortune to be needed by the United States for prosecuting war in Iraq a year later.

80. Larry Rohter, "Economic Rally for Argentines Defies Forecasts," *NYT*, December 26, 2004, p. 1.

81. One TNC executive has said: "Retreating to fortress America isn't the answer. If we erect walls, we invite a battle. And there is enough tension in the world today without instigating trade wars. World peace, and its economic hand-maiden—international trade and development—are far better served by an open and free flow of investment." Quoted by Dexter F. Baker, "Foreign Investment—A Two-Way Street," *Vital Speeches of the Day*, vol. 48, no. 14 (May 1, 1982), p. 446.

82. See Moran, "Trade and Investment Dimensions," in Crocker and Hampson, eds., *Managing Global Chaos*, pp. 157–58, citing Edward D. Mansfield, *Power, Trade, and War* (Princeton, NJ: Princeton University Press, 1994); and Robert H. Wade, "Questions of Fairness," *Foreign Affairs*, pp. 136–43. Wade points out (p. 141) that the fastest growing economies since World War II, mainly in East Asia, defied the free-trade model and protected their economies from foreign competition. Though it is acknowledged that trade may also create international conflict, such as disputes resulting from trade imbalances and the adverse effects of FDI, the notion persists that countries intensively involved in trade learn to subordinate their rivalries. In the European context, such a view clearly has merit. Otherwise, the case remains open: Note, for example, the tensions between China and Taiwan, and the United States and China, despite substantial trade and investment relations. Moreover, the trade-peace connection ignores environmental, labor, and resource components of trade that can be sources of interstate conflict; and ignores the kinds of commodities traded, such as weapons and components.

83. Barnet and Müller, pp. 14–15.

84. Ibid., p. 15.

85. Such an argument is effectively presented in a study of American, German, and Japanese TNC leaders by Paul N. Doremus et al., *The Myth of the Global Corporation*.

86. David E. Sanger, "U.S. Blames Allies for Undercutting Its China Policy," *NYT*, June 12, 1996, p. 1.

87. Mahbub ul Haq, "Negotiating the Future," *Foreign Affairs,* p. 416. For a similar view from a Canadian, see Head, *Foreign Affairs*, pp. 71–86.

88. Reich, *The Work of Nations.*

89. United Nations Development Program, *Human Development Report 1992,* pp. 54–55. Hereafter, *Human Development Report 1992.*

90. See Anthony Smith, *The Geopolitics of Information: How Western Culture Dominates the World*, pp. 73–77.

91. Herbert I. Schiller, *Who Knows: Information in the Age of the Fortune 500,* pp. 30–33. US-based data banks hold about two-thirds of all organized data bases (ibid., p. 36). And see Howard H. Frederick, *Global Communications and International Relations*, pp. 72–77.

92. Anthony Smith, p. 73.

93. Ibid., ch. 2.

94. Ben Bagdikian, "Lords of the Global Village," *The Nation.*

95. Frederick, p. 72.

96. The transnational media giants are Disney, Viacom, News Corporation, Time Warner, and General Electric. Two other conglomerates have important media components: Vivendi/Seagram and Sony Corporation. What they all share is major stakes in a wide range of media, including book publishing, television, newspapers, magazines, and software. See the special insert of *The Nation,* July 3, 2006, and *NYT,* November 13, 2000, pp. C18–19.

97. David E. Sanger, "Playing the Trade Card," *NYT,* February 17, 1997, p. 1.

98. *NYT,* February 18, 1997, p. C1.

99. *NYT,* February 10, 1997, online.

100. See Herbert I. Schiller, "Transnational Media: Creating Consumers Worldwide," *Journal of International Affairs,* pp. 47–58.

101. Nigel Holloway, "Caught in the Net," *Far Eastern Economic Review,* November 28, 1996, pp. 28–29, quoting a member of Human Rights Watch/Asia.

102. Debora L. Spar, "The Spotlight and the Bottom Line: How Multinationals Export Human Rights," *Foreign Affairs.*

103. Stephan Haggard, *Pathways from the Periphery: The Politics of Growth in the Newly Industrializing Countries,* chs. 1 and 8; Steve Chan and Cal Clark, "Changing Perspectives on the Evolving Pacific Basin: International Structure and Domestic Processes," in Chan and Clark, eds., *The Evolving Pacific Basin in the Global Political Economy: Domestic and International Linkages,* pp. 1–26.

104. Thomas D. Lairson and David Skidmore, *International Political Economy: The Struggle for Power and Wealth,* pp. 269–70.

105. Danny Kin-Kong Lam and Ian Lee, "Guerrilla Capitalism and the Limits of Statist Theory: Comparing the Chinese NICs," in Chan and Clark, pp. 107–24; Haggard, pp. 193–206, 216–18. In the Korean case, if dependence was created, it was on foreign bank loans rather than foreign investments. Even then, these borrowings are nothing to compare with the heavy indebtedness to banks of Mexico and Brazil. See Haggard, p. 219, table 8.13.

106. Haggard, pp. 221–22.

107. For example, Gulf Oil (owned by Chevron) has for many years operated a refinery in Cabinda Bay, Angola, a socialist country. Despite pressure from US conservatives to pull out of Angola, where the United States was assisting rebel forces seeking to overthrow its government, Gulf stayed on. As the board chair and chief executive officer of Gulf Oil, James E. Lee, said: "The experience of Gulf Oil in Angola underscores the fact that ideological commitments—whether Marxist, Centrist, or Capitalist—can coexist with a quite responsible and pragmatic approach to business relationships" ("To Live in Interesting Times," in *Vital Speeches of the Day,* vol. 48, no. 24 [October 1, 1982], p. 743).

108. Quoted in Delamaide, *Debt Shock,* p. 81.

109. *NYT,* February 1, 1997, p. 4. US oil companies indeed complained about losing business because of the sanctions. But Stuart Eizenstat, under secretary of state for economic affairs, said, "This is a situation where the strategic interests of the United States are so great that they outweigh temporary advantages of American companies." Jane Perlez and Steven LeVine, "U.S. Oil Companies Chafe at Curbs on Investment in Iran," *NYT,* August 9, 1998, online.

110. Tax havens are low-tax countries such as Ireland and Bermuda that subsidiaries of TNCs use to reduce the taxes they pay on profits. The practice reduces the corporate tax base for home governments. Martin A. Sullivan, "Data Show

Dramatic Shift of Profits to Tax Havens," *Tax Notes*, September 13, 2004, pp. 1190–200, at www.taxanalysts.com/www/freefiles.nsf/files/sullivan2.pdf/$file/sullivan2.pdf.

111. Quoted in *Los Angeles Times World Report*, December 17, 1995, p. 6. For similar quotes from corporate leaders, see William Greider, "Pro Patria, Pro Mundus," *The Nation*.

112. Garten, "Business and Foreign Policy: Time for a Strategic Alliance?" in Eugene R. Wittkopf and Christopher M. Jones, *The Future of American Foreign Policy*, 3rd ed., pp. 107–8.

113. Jeffrey E. Garten, "Business and Foreign Policy," *Foreign Policy*.

114. Doremus et al., *The Myth of the Global Corporation*, p. 144.

115. See Michael J. Crozier, Samuel P. Huntington, and Joji Watanuki, *The Crisis of Democracy: Report on the Governability of Democracies to the Trilateral Commission*, pp. 113–15, on the need for greater "moderation" of democratic processes, including press freedom.

116. Hans-Peter Martin and Harald Schumann, *The Global Trap*, ch. 1.

117. Floyd Norris, "Win-Win? Tell It to the Losers," *NYT*, January 27, 2006, p. C1.

118. David Kowalewski, "Asian State Repression and Strikes Against Transnationals," in George A. Lopez and Michael Stohl, eds., *Dependence, Development, and State Repression*, pp. 77–81; Hilary F. French, *Costly Tradeoffs: Reconciling Trade and the Environment*, paper no. 113, Worldwatch Institute, pp. 31–32.

119. In the Philippines, Mexico, and other Third World countries, political leaders and TNC managers share a desire to control workers for purposes of maintaining both state and business security. When the matter of labor and human-rights repression in China has come up in the US Congress, for instance, both the Chinese and the US governments have gotten vocal support for "engagement" from Boeing, Motorola, Nike, Caterpillar, and numerous other TNCs that have large stakes in China's rise. Beijing also learned from the worldwide reaction to the Tiananmen crackdown that it was advisable to hire professional lobbyists, which it did. See Ken Silverstein, "The New China Hands," *The Nation*.

120. Juan Forero, "Foreigners Seek Rights Relief in U.S.," *International Herald Tribune*, June 27, 2003.

121. Stephen Kinzer, "A Perilous New Contest for the Next Oil Prize," *NYT*, September 21, 1997, online ed.; Stephen Kinzer, "Awash in Oil Wealth, but Just for the Few?" *NYT*, October 11, 1997, p. A4; Thomas Goltz, "The Caspian Oil Sweepstakes," *The Nation*, pp. 18–21.

122. In 2004, for instance, Archer Daniels Midland and Cargill were among just four US companies that sold half the food aid provided under the US Agency for International Development programs. See Celia W. Dugger, "African Food for Africa's Starving Is Roadblocked in Congress," *NYT*, October 12, 2005, p. A4.

123. President George W. Bush's high-profile embrace of India while maintaining strong ties with Pakistan is a perfect example. He decided to sell jet fighters to both countries in 2005, which was a boon to Lockheed Martin Corporation; and his decision to allow nuclear sales to India opened the door to a major increase in US investment in India. See, for instance, Saritha Rai, "Executives See U.S. Link as Crucial in India's Growth," *NYT*, March 3, 2006, p. C13.

124. Alison Langley, "U.S. Wants to Reopen Talks on Global Anti-Tobacco Pact," *NYT*, May 1, 2003, p. A6.

125. These may include a low corporate tax rate, a credit on foreign tax, and deferred or lower tax on repatriated profits—all granted to US multinationals in

recent years. See Edmund L. Andrews, "Why U.S. Companies Shouldn't Whine About Taxes," *NYT*, July, 9, 2006, sec. 4, p. 4. On the lower tax rates that subsidiaries of US multinationals pay, see US Department of the Treasury, Office of Tax Policy, *The Deferral of Income Earned Through U.S. Controlled Foreign Corporations: A Policy Study* (December 2000), at www.treas.gov/offices/tax-policy/library/subpartf.pdf.

126. ECAs provide loans and credits to developing countries for such projects. See Aaron Goldzimer, "Worse Than the World Bank? Export Credit Agencies—The Secret Engine of Globalization," *Food First Backgrounder* (Institute for Food and Development Policy), pp. 1–7. One such ECA in the US government, the Overseas Private Investment Corporation (OPIC), provided insurance and financing that was at the heart of the scandal involving Enron. See Richard A. Oppel Jr. and David E. Sanger, "New Inquiry Is Sought into Enron," *NYT*, April 2, 2002, p. C1.

127. Paul Lewis, "International Community Takes Steps to Curb Corruption," *NYT*, November 28, 1996, online. The OECD's ruling was designed to prevent TNCs from taking tax deductions on bribes, which they had previously been able to do in some countries. The World Bank is supposed to blacklist companies and governments that engage in large-scale bribery.

128. Tom Farer, "The United States and the Third World: A Basis for Accommodation," *Foreign Affairs*, pp. 79–97.

129. See, for example, Bob Herbert's columns in the *NYT* of March 31 and June 27, 1997.

130. Suzanne Daley, "In War-Torn Angola, U.S. Oil Workers Live in Bubble of Peace," *NYT*, June 25, 1998, online.

131. See, for example, Edmund L. Andrews, "German Company to Leave China over Sales of Organs," *NYT*, March 7, 1998, p. A5. The sale of prisoner-assembled goods and organs from executed prisoners was verified during a number of congressional hearings in 1998.

132. *NYT*, June 2, 1996, online. Since the ending of military rule in Nigeria, its government and Shell Oil continue to cooperate in the Niger Delta against popular protests. The protests arise from the government's failure to provide a fair share of development revenue to the local population and destruction of the air and water from flares and dumping.

133. For background, see *NYT*, November 16, 1995, p. A8; February 13, 1996, p. A1; March 12, 1996, p. A6.

134. *NYT*, April 9, 1998, p. C1. Coca-Cola and Eastman Kodak also "cared": They announced major new investments in China at the same time. For Levi Strauss, it was easy to evade responsibility, for it is a labor contractor, not a factory owner. Thus, responsibility for child and forced labor was placed on Chinese factory managers and the difficulties of policing *them*. Competitor multinationals such as Esprit, moreover, had already moved into China in the interim, evidently without any need to address moral arguments.

135. David Barboza, "Google Cuts 2 Features for China," *NYT*, January 25, 2006, p. C1; Philip P. Pan, "Chinese Media Assail Google," *Washington Post*, February 22, 2006.

136. This account of postwar planning is largely based on Fred Block, *The Origins of International Economic Disorder: A Study of United States International Monetary Policy from World War II to the Present;* Gabriel and Joyce Kolko, *The Limits of Power: The World and United States Foreign Policy, 1945–1954*, chs. 1–6 and 12–13; Alan Wolfe, *America's Impasse: The Rise and Fall of the Politics of Growth*, esp. pp. 9–31; Laurence H. Shoup and William Minter, "Shaping a New World Order: The Council on Foreign Relations' Blueprint for World Hegemony," in

Sklar, part 3, ch. 1; and John Lewis Gaddis, *Strategies of Containment: A Critical Appraisal of Postwar American National Security Policy,* pp. 60–65.

137. Wolfe, p. 114.

138. Byrnes, quoted in Kolko, p. 23. See similar quotes by Cordell Hull and Dean Acheson in Block, p. 40.

139. Quoted in Kolko, p. 24.

140. Truman to Byrnes, January 5, 1946, in Glenn Paige, *The Korean Decision: June 24–30, 1950,* p. 54.

141. Quoted in Barnet, *Roots of War,* p. 100.

142. Quoted in Walter Millis, ed., *The Forrestal Diaries,* pp. 251–52.

143. NSC-68 is reproduced in full in John P. Glennon et al., eds., *Foreign Relations of the United States 1950;* vol. 1: *National Security Affairs, Foreign Economic Policy.* The quoted portions are from pp. 262, 258–59, 262–63, in that order.

144. On Eisenhower's foreign economic policy, see Blanche Wiesen Cook, *The Declassified Eisenhower: A Divided Legacy of Peace and Political Warfare,* pp. 293–309.

145. Quoted in Holly K. Sklar, "Trilateralism and the Management of Contradictions: Concluding Perspectives," in Sklar, p. 564.

146. Michael Mastanduno, "Trade Policy," in Robert J. Art and Seyom Brown, eds., *U.S. Foreign Policy: The Search for a New Role,* p. 147.

147. Mastanduno, pp. 147–48.

148. Barnet and Cavanagh, *Global Dreams,* pp. 355–56, on Mexico; and a report of the World Bank's projections for China, India, Indonesia, Brazil, and Russia in *NYT,* September 10, 1997, p. C7.

149. Quotations from Ken Silverstein and Alexander Cockburn, "The Killers and the Killing," *The Nation,* March 6, 1995, p. 308.

150. Thomas L. Friedman, writing in the *NYT,* January 25, 1995; cited in Meier, pp. 223–24. Friedman was addressing members of the US Congress who considered the Mexican peso crisis too far away to justify a large loan.

151. Except where otherwise indicated, this paragraph relies on Carlos M. Urzúa, "Five Decades of Relations Between the World Bank and Mexico," in Kapur, Lewis, and Webb, eds., *The World Bank,* ch. 3; and Carlos Heredia and Mary Purcell, "Structural Adjustment and the Polarization of Mexican Society," in Jerry Mander and Edward Goldsmith, eds., *The Case Against the Global Economy—And for a Turn Toward the Local,* ch. 24.

152. Barnet and Cavanagh, p. 253.

153. In 1992, the lowest 40 percent of Mexico's households accounted for a mere 11.9 percent of all income, while the top 20 percent accounted for 55.3 percent (and the top 10 percent for 39.2 percent). World Bank, *World Development Report 1997: The State in a Changing World,* table 5, p. 223.

154. For figures on poverty and wages, and discussion of the antipoverty programs, see Urzúa, table 3-1, p. 56 and pp. 95–96.

155. Ibid., pp. 91–92. Urzúa adds (pp. 93–94) that by 1994, "Mexico had more billionaires than the United Kingdom and Italy." That was only possible at a time of economic stagnation, he concludes, because "those 'entrepreneurs' were earning rents from oligopolistic privatized industries and unregulated privatized monopolies." One such entrepreneur was President Salinas's brother, Raúl, who evidently used his relationship with the president to secure an enormous amount of money and send it abroad. See Julia Preston, "Mexico's Elite Caught in Scandal's Harsh Glare," *NYT,* July 13, 1996, online.

156. *NYT,* October 8, 1995, p. iv–14.

92      *Global Politics in the Human Interest*

157. *World Development Report 1997,* table 3, p. 219.

158. See Sarah Anderson and John Cavanagh, "NAFTA's Unhappy Anniversary," *NYT,* February 7, 1995, p. A13. These writers report that "according to the Joint Economic Committee of Congress, NAFTA has caused a net loss of 10,000 U.S. jobs." Since the agreement, many US communities had lost businesses to Mexico; and some of those same businesses, once established in Mexico, violated Mexican environmental laws and replaced cheap labor with even cheaper labor.

159. Meier, table 5.8, p. 216.

160. Walker F. Todd, "Bailing Out the Creditor Class," *The Nation,* February 13, 1995, p. 193.

161. *NYT,* March 14, 1995, p. A7. The World Bank also was concerned about Mexico's overreliance on foreign capital. Urzúa, p. 106.

162. Silverstein and Cockburn, "The Killers and the Killing," p. 307.

163. Urzúa, p. 104.

164. Sam Dillon, "Rebels Strike in 4 Mexico States, Leaving 13 Dead," *NYT,* August 30, 1996, p. 1. In fact, by 1996 the Zapatistas, surrounded by superior military power, were persuaded to stop their rebellion. But insurgency itself did not stop; small guerrilla bands apparently belonging to a group called the Popular Revolutionary Army attacked Mexican army units in several states during 1996. The situation in Chiapas remains tense to this day, as the military maintains a strong presence in the state.

165. *NYT,* February 22, 1995, p. C16; Urzúa, pp. 103–4.

166. *IMF Survey,* February 6, 1995, quoted in Meier, pp. 220–21. In plain English, as David E. Sanger reported in the *New York Times* (February 22, 1995, p. C16), "The heart of the deal lies in requiring Mexico to pursue an extremely tight monetary policy, shrinking the country's money supply and preventing it from spending Government funds to stimulate economic growth. For Mr. Zedillo, who only a few months ago was talking of creating a million new jobs and sustaining a growth rate of 4 percent or more, that means selling Mexicans on a strict diet of austerity."

167. Julia Preston, "In Mexico, an Uneven Recovery," *NYT,* January 2, 1997, p. C13.

168. Jorge G. Castañeda, "Mexico's Circle of Misery," *Foreign Affairs,* pp. 92–105.

169. The Carnegie report is discussed by Celia W. Dugger, "Report Finds Few Benefits for Mexico in Nafta," *NYT,* November 19, 2003, p. A9. The ambassador's dismissal is reported in *NYT,* November 19, 2003, p. A5.

170. "Of the 700,000 new maquiladora jobs generated in Nafta's first seven years, 300,000 have been eliminated since 2000." Elizabeth Becker, Clifford Krauss, and Tim Weiner, "Free Trade Accord at Age 10: The Growing Pains Are Clear," *NYT,* December 27, 2003, p. A1; Elisabeth Malkin, "Manufacturing Jobs Are Exiting Mexico," *NYT,* November 5, 2002, p. W1; Mary Jordan, "Mexico Now Feels Pinch of Cheap Labor," *Washington Post,* December 3, 2003.

171. Ginger Thompson, "Nafta to Open Floodgates, Engulfing Rural Mexico," *NYT,* December 19, 2002, p. A3.

172. Edward Alden, "Human Rights Debates on the Downside of Nafta," *Financial Times,* April 20, 2001.

173. Justin Gerdes, "NAFTA's Chapter 11 Threatens Environment and Democracy," *Knight Ridder/Tribune Business News,* February 22, 2002.

174. *NYT,* February 22, 1997, p. 1; Sam Dillon and Craig Pyes, "Drug Ties Taint 2 Mexican Governors," *NYT,* February 23, 1997, online; Tim Weiner, "Mexico's New Chief Wants the Truth," *NYT,* September 29, 2000, p. A8.

175. *NYT,* April 15, 1998, p. A12.
176. For a similar view by a former official under Salinas, see Juan Enriquez, "Mexico's Cycle of Failure," *NYT,* March 11, 1997, p. A15.
177. Quoted in *NYT,* February 23, 1995, p. C3.
178. Nayan Chanda, "Rebuilding Asia," *Far Eastern Economic Review,* February 12, 1998, pp. 46–47.
179. Ibid., p. 47.
180. Martin Hart-Landsberg, "The Asian Crisis: Causes and Consequences," *Against the Current*; Walden Bello, "The End of the Asian Miracle," *The Nation.* Japanese banks held 32 percent of Asia's total debt of $389 billion in June 1997. *NYT,* January 28, 1998, p. C1.
181. I rely here mainly on Hart-Landsberg, Bello, and Lee Su-Hoon, "Crisis in Korea and the IMF Control," in Kim Eun Mee, ed., *The Four Asian Tigers: Economic Development and the Global Political Economy.*
182. Chalmers Johnson, "Cold War Economics Melt Asia," *The Nation.*
183. Martin Feldstein, "Refocusing the IMF," *Foreign Affairs,* p. 25.
184. David E. Sanger, "U.S. Joins Other Nations in New Bailout Plan for South Korea," *NYT,* December 25, 1997, online. The IMF's version is, of course, quite different. Sensitive to charges that the Mexican bailout really bailed out US investors, it argued that its policies were not designed to "protect" any financial institution or individual creditors but rather to stabilize and restructure collapsing economies. "Factsheet—IMF Bail Outs: Truth and Fiction," January 1998, online at www.imf.org.
185. For an overview, see Andrew Sherry et al., "State of Inertia," *Far Eastern Economic Review,* December 11, 1997, pp. 16–20. The key stumbling block for the foreign banks was whether the Korean government itself would, as in Latin America's financial crisis of the 1980s, guarantee the new loans. Eventually, it did, in exchange for rollovers of short-term into longer-term loans. For governments that, led by the United States, joined the IMF bailout by providing $10 billion in emergency loans to Korea, the risk was mainly political: Taxpayers would not take kindly to another Mexico-style bailout, especially when (in the US case) they had been promised "not a nickel" of their money would go to rescuing private investors and creditors from the product of their own risk-taking. That promise had been made by the US secretary of the treasury, Robert Rubin. It proved impossible to keep when the Korean won kept falling, and it became clear that unless government loans were provided to supplement the IMF funds, the Korean banks would default and a major US ally in Asia might be destabilized. See David E. Sanger, "Asian Crisis May Take a Painful Step," *NYT,* December 29, 1997, online.
186. The one (partial) victory for labor was when Kim presided over a historic three-way summit of government, business, and unions. They reached an agreement to permit future layoffs in exchange for increases in the government's unemployment insurance fund (to 5 trillion won, or about $3.1 billion) and in corporate contributions to their own worker safety nets.
187. David E. Sanger, "Indonesian Faceoff: Drawing Blood Without Bombs," *NYT,* March 8, 1998, online.
188. See the interview of the noted anthropologist and Indonesia specialist, Clifford Geertz, in *NYT,* May 9, 1998, online. Geertz observed how the IMF's confrontational approach to Suharto clashed with customary Indonesian conflict avoidance and parental protection of children.
189. See, for example, Feldstein, "Refocusing the IMF," p. 32. Feldstein's criticisms were that, as in Russia, the IMF insisted on detailed reforms in Thailand and Indonesia such as setting the price of certain commodities and ending corruption. In

Korea's case, he wrote that the IMF exaggerated the debt problem and imposed unnecessary limits on credit and government spending.

190. As Britain's Chancellor of the Exchequer, Gordon Brown, acknowledged at a meeting of EU and IMF officials: "We should do more to promote transparency in all countries about the operations of the economic policy, and economic developments and the operations of financial institutions. The better the understanding that the market has, the less will be the risk of sudden market readjustments," *NYT*, February 15, 1998, online ed.

191. *NYT*, February 13, 1998, p. C2.

192. David E. Sanger, "Asian Nations Strike Deal on Trade Agreement," *NYT*, December 14, 1997, online.

193. Nicholas D. Kristof, "Asia's Doors Now Wide Open to American Business," *NYT*, February 1, 1998, online.

194. Wayne Arnold, "Turmoil in Asia Doesn't Dent Investors' Enthusiasm for Its Markets," *NYT*, May 2, 2006, p. C4.

195. Human Rights Watch/Asia, "Human Rights Crisis in Indonesia: Statement to the Senate Foreign Relations Committee, Subcommittee on East Asia and Pacific Affairs," Washington, DC, March 24, 1998, pp. 1–10.

196. See, for example, Seth Mydans, "Thailand Economic Crash Crushes the Working Poor," *NYT*, December 15, 1997, p. A9.

197. This section relies mainly on my *Superpower on Crusade: The Bush Doctrine in US Foreign Policy*, chaps. 2–4. Only sources not cited in that book are cited here. The brief portions of this section on Gulf War I are taken from the fourth edition of this book (1999), pp. 60–66.

198. Quoted by Michael Barone, "Bush Knows His History," *U.S. News & World Report*, June 12, 2006, p. 36.

199. See www.newamericancentury.org.

200. The White House, *The National Security Strategy of the United States of America*. A later version with the same title was published in March 2006 and can be accessed at www.whitehouse.gov/nsc/nss/2006/index.html.

201. On this "Cheney doctrine" see Ron Suskind, *The One Percent Doctrine: Deep Inside America's Pursuit of Its Enemies Since 9/11*, pp. 150, 214.

202. The evidence of the administration's duplicity is overwhelming, but two previously classified British sources, both based on top-secret discussions with US leaders, should be mentioned. One is the so-called Downing Street Memo of July 23, 2002 (www.downingstreetmemo.com). The other, a memorandum of conversation between British prime minister Tony Blair and President Bush in January 2003, is in Don Van Natta Jr., "Bush Was Set on Path to War, Memo by British Adviser Says," *NYT*, March 27, 2006, p. 1.

203. Paul Pillar, "Intelligence, Policy, and the War in Iraq," *Foreign Affairs*, pp. 19, 21.

204. See the views of another former CIA official, Tyler Drumheller, in Mark Mazzetti, "Former C.I.A. Official Says Intelligence Was Ignored," *NYT*, April 22, 2006, p. A10.

205. This was the "Future of Iraq Project," November 1, 2002, portions of which were later declassified and released to the National Security Archive (www.nsarchive.org).

206. Lawrence Wilkerson, quoted by Bob Herbert, "How Scary Is This?" *NYT*, October 24, 2005, p. A23.

207. Sabrina Tavernise, "For Iraqis, Exodus to Syria and Jordan Continues," *NYT*, June 14, 2006, p. A11.

208. For example, see Eric Schmitt, "Iraq Facing Hurdles, U.S. General Warns," *NYT*, January 6, 2006, p. A10.

209. See Michael E. O'Hanlon and Nina Kamp, *Iraq Index: Tracking Variables of Reconstruction & Security in Post-Saddam Iraq* (Washington, DC: Brookings Institution, June 22, 2006), at www.brookings.edu/fp/saban/iraq/index.pdf.

210. Edward Wong and Sabrina Tavernise, "Religious Strife Shows Strength of Iraq Militias," *NYT*, February 25, 2006, p. 1.

211. Testimony of General John P. Abizaid, *NYT*, August 4, 2006, p. 1.

212. Based on the work of US and Iraqi public health specialists, in *NYT*, October 11, 2006, p. A16.

213. See Seymour M. Hersh, "The Redirection," *The New Yorker*, March 5, 2007, pp. 55–65.

214. Ted Robert Gurr, *Minorities at Risk: A Global View of Ethnopolitical Conflicts*, p. 138.

215. Quoted by Bob Woodward, *Plan of Attack*, p. 150.

216. US leaders were shocked by the Hamas victory and, along with Israel, rejected talks with it. To many opinion makers in the Middle East, as well as some in the United States, the US reaction belied its talk of democratization and showed ignorance of the importance of supporting civil society. As the editor of a Jordanian newspaper said: "Iraq has allowed people to say, 'Forget the American style of reform.' The Americans are not able to present anything to the reformers to encourage them." Quoted in *NYT*, April 10, 2006, p. A10.

217. Carlotta Gall, "Opium Harvest at Record Level in Afghanistan," *NYT*, September 3, 2006, p. 1.

218. Seth G. Jones, "The Danger Next Door," *NYT*, September 23, 2005, p. A19. Afghanistan's President Hamid Karzai has openly, and angrily, accused Pakistan of supporting the Taliban in hopes of destabilizing his country. See *NYT*, December 13, 2006, p. A14.

219. The UN Mine Action Programme for Afghanistan (MAPA) was established in 1989 when the landmine convention went into effect upon ratification by the fortieth country. A number of Afghani NGOs were established to help with mine clearance and education of the population about landmines. See MAPA, *Landmines* (July 2002).

220. Two distinguished economists made the calculation in mid-2006. See Linda Bilmes and Joseph E. Stiglitz, "Encore," *Milken Institute Review*, no. 4 (2006), pp. 76–83.

# 3

# World Politics in
# Global-Humanist Perspective

Injustice anywhere is a threat to justice everywhere. We are caught in an
inescapable network of mutuality, tied in a single garment of destiny. . . .
Whatever affects one directly affects all indirectly.
                                                        —Martin Luther King Jr.

## The Search for a Third Way

The Chinese word for "crisis" consists of two characters, the first (*wei*)
meaning danger, the second (*ji*), opportunity. The contemporary global crisis, as we have seen, holds within it many seeds of danger, including the
undeniable potential for species destruction. But from another angle, every
danger can also be an opportunity to transcend and transform the crisis. If
global humanism can be remembered for just one thing, it is this dialectical
understanding of the global crisis in terms of its two opposing elements.
The global-humanist outlook accepts neither the unalterable "givens" of
realism nor the inequitable one-world future of corporate globalism. Rather,
it persists in the conviction that doomsday is a real possibility that humanity
can yet overcome.

A number of realists and corporate globalists have acknowledged the
need for new concepts and values to deal effectively with global problems.
"Something beyond nationalism is slowly taking root in the world," a former
senior US official and foundation president wrote in 1977, "the signs of a
developing sense of common human destiny are present."[1] A World Bank
director said that "what the world badly needs today is a new vision for this
ailing planet."[2] *North-South,* the report of the Brandt Commission, agreed.
Generations of people are needed, said the report, who will be "more concerned with human values than with bureaucratic regulations and technocrat-
ic constraints."[3] Clearly, thinking about international politics is evolving.

But whether such movement will be fast enough to head off one or
another kind of global catastrophe is very much in doubt. The margin of
survival is sometimes very thin, as was apparent at the height of the nuclear

arms race in the early 1980s; and the number of state and corporate leaders who determine the fate of the planet is very small. For global humanists, the central question is, Who speaks for the planet? "Could we," as the late Professor Roy Preiswerk inquired, "study international relations as if people mattered?"[4] To do so requires directing attention to the human and environmental consequences of global interdependence, fixing accountability for decisions, and increasing local-level involvement in policymaking. These objectives pervade global-humanist analysis, whose core element is the primacy of the human interest above any other—state, ideological, economic, or bureaucratic.

The human interest frames the main issues in world politics that global humanism studies. Professor Yoshikazu Sakamoto has defined them in terms of four interrelated world crises of our times: human rights, participation (democracy), conflict, and underdevelopment (including destruction of the environment).[5] These crises shape the priorities of the global agenda: investigating and seeking to change conditions of oppression and repression; defining the inequalities among states, classes, and persons; critically assessing policies justified by "national security"; and weighing the human and environmental consequences of economic growth.

To speak of priorities is to draw attention to their underlying values and norms. In contrast with realism and corporate globalism, which claim to be merely frameworks for understanding the international system, global humanism openly acknowledges the principal values and norms that determine its orientation. The task of defining core or preferred values has not been an easy one:[6] It has required coming to grips with cultural and class biases that reinforce one's awareness of how differently blacks and whites, intellectuals and workers, Third World and industrialized world, and socialists and capitalists interpret the world. Nevertheless, initial efforts have been made (see Table 2.1 for one such effort). We can now explore how these values and norms enable us to analyze crisis and change in global politics.

### Values, Methods, Measurements, Objectives

In this section I explore global humanism's distinguishing characteristics, which might be divided according to nine main beliefs and approaches.

First, certain values are primary: *peace*—meaning the minimization of violence and the institutionalization of nonviolent ways to resolve conflict; *social and economic justice*—movement toward equity in reward and opportunity for all without the imposition of arbitrary distinctions; *political justice*—civil liberties guaranteed in law and fact; *ecological balance*—including resource conservation and environmental protection; and *humane governance*—popular participation in, and the accountability of, government.[7]

Although these "preferred values" grew out of a multinational forum called the World Order Models Project in the late 1960s, they are more than the handiwork of intellectuals. A number of international documents, adhered to by most of the world's states, enshrine these values—such as the Nuremberg Principles derived from the Nazi war crimes trials (1945); the Universal Declaration of Human Rights (1948); the Convention on the Prevention and Punishment of the Crime of Genocide (1948); the International Convention on the Elimination of All Forms of Racial Discrimination (1965); the International Covenant on Economic, Social, and Cultural Rights (1966); and the International Covenant on Civil and Political Rights (1966).[8] Humane values also underpin the UN Development Program's (UNDP) periodic reports. These use a "human development index" (HDI) to rank countries on the basis of how well they fulfill basic human-security needs such as literacy, life expectancy, access to clean water, and an adequate diet. In addition, interviews with leading thinkers of all political persuasions and diverse cultures have found that there are shared values or ethics—such as love, fairness, truthfulness, and respect for life—that fit within the global-humanist paradigm.[9]

Second, these values carry with them a set of positive assumptions about the nature of humankind and optimism about the prospects for humane change. Although it is tempting to explain global-humanist optimism with reference to the idealism of the 1920s and after (see below), there is more substantial philosophical bulk to it. Among its diverse sources are humanist psychology (e.g., the works of Sigmund Freud, Erich Fromm, Abraham Maslow, Rollo May, and Carl Rogers); Eastern philosophy and spirituality, as well as Western syntheses of them (e.g., Zen Buddhism, Taoism, mysticism, Gandhian *satyagraha* or "truth force," and the writings of J. N. Krishnamurti, Carl Jung, and Alan Watts); early and more recent feminist writings (from Rosa Luxemburg to Kate Millett); the physical and social sciences (e.g., the works of Margaret Mead, Ashley Montagu, Rene Dubos, Fritjof Capra, E. F. Schumacher, Carl Sagan, Kenneth Boulding, and Amartya Sen); and political philosophers across the spectrum, from Karl Marx's "Economic and Philosophical Manuscripts" to Thomas Jefferson's community democracy and John Stuart Mill's essay "On Liberty."

From this eclectic (and sometimes contradictory) collection comes a positive conception of humanity, conviction in the human potential for cooperative living, and an understanding of politics that integrates spiritual and material development. Global humanism, in direct contrast to realism, assumes that human beings are by nature good hearted, peaceful, sharing, and infinitely creative; that lawful, equitable, cooperative societies that live in harmony are realizable, and, in fact, have already been created;[10] that narrow nationalism—belief in permanent enemies, intractable conflicts, and competition for power—is the product of social conditioning that can be redirected into trusting behavior patterns;[11] that the differentness of peoples and cultures should be celebrated as one of the most enriching features of human existence; that our personal insecurities in large measure account for our fear of differentness, our defensiveness, and our reluctance to trust others ("We have met the enemy and they is us," in the comic character Pogo's classic formulation); and, therefore, that the struggle for power and profit that goes on at the international level is very much a struggle within each person to determine just what it is that makes us feel secure.

Third, global humanism has an explicitly normative approach to politics: "It seeks to shape and inspire a world movement for systemic change, and is not content with understanding how the present system operates."[12] With Karl Marx, global humanists contend that "the philosophers have only *interpreted* the world in various ways; the point, however, is to *change* it." System transformation, not simply reform, is the global humanists' ambition. The nation-state is the key world political structure to be transformed, although whether its authority should devolve to smaller political units, be supplanted by international regimes or even a world government, or coexist with a new global structure is a matter of ongoing debate among global-humanist theorists.

Fourth, global humanism is prompted by both idealism and a hardheaded political-economic concern about structural violence. Idealism as a school of political philosophy exerted its greatest influence between the two world wars. It was an effort to direct moral outrage and political reforms at those national institutions that were believed responsible for war making. To combat state rivalries and aggression, idealism emphasized the development of a system of international collective security and the realization of national self-determination. The Kellogg-Briand Pact of 1928 outlawing war as an instrument of national policy, the League of Nations, and, after World War II, the United Nations and the Universal Declaration of Human Rights were all products of idealism's search for the conditions of peace.

Global humanism retains idealism's moral content, its optimism about human nature, and its suspicions of balance-of-power, state-centric politics. It also shares idealism's preeminent concern about peace. But global humanism takes these concerns several steps further. Peace is not merely the absence of war. Even if all the conflicts currently going on around the world were miraculously to cease tomorrow, violence would still be the order of the day for most of the world's people. Global problems such as poverty, hunger, environmental destruction, terrorism, and the arms race point to additional, equally prevalent and malevolent forms of violence— and to the need for analyzing their structural roots, without regard to the political or economic character of states.

Why a structural approach? Because the most common explanations of inequity, oppression (both visible and invisible),[13] and violence within and between societies—in terms of personal, bureaucratic, or social and cultural practices—while useful, are often superficial. They do not probe deeply enough into the mechanisms and institutions that tend to perpetuate conditions of inequality. Glaring and widening gaps exist worldwide between the wealthy and the impoverished, the well-fed and the malnourished, the heavily armed and the physically weak—all *despite* overall increases in production, income, and knowledge. Understanding how poverty, the arms race, or authoritarian rule become so institutionalized in societies as to be immune to mere reform can significantly advance analysis of problems and the search for their solution.

Fifth, precisely because oppression is so universal while the means of attaining personal and group security are so inequitably distributed, global humanism takes a critical look at the policies for national security of state leaderships. What it finds is that as their objective power increases, states, regardless of their social systems, will embrace increasingly expansive conceptions of their national-security "needs," their enemies, and their military and other interventionist capabilities. Ultimately, as with the United States and the former Soviet Union, the entire globe must be secured in order for national leaders to feel confident about domestic security. This was precisely the point of Pope John Paul II's encyclical letter in 1988. He said that the greatest obstacle to ending underdevelopment was "an unacceptably exaggerated concern for security" on the part of the US and Soviet blocs, "[each of which] harbors in its own way a tendency toward imperialism."[14]

Global humanism offers an alternative approach to national and international security. It rejects the inevitability of war, permanent enemies, and permanent crisis. It seeks to bring the needs of national security into line with the needs of the global community, particularly the Third World's powerless and marginalized. It seeks to bridge the chasm between cultures—established by the language as well as the materiality of dominance—that Edward Said so poignantly describes in his classic study of orientalism: the kind of mindset about the "other" that stereotypes, dehumanizes, and justifies superiority over "them."[15] To inject realism into its idealism, global humanism looks for points of identity and mutual interest between different communities—between nation-states and international regimes, between workers at home and workers abroad, and between cultures in and across borders. The objective is to make the world safe for diversity in the process of transforming it along equitable lines.[16]

More specifically, global humanism embraces three concepts that attempt to redefine security within and between states: human development, human security, and common security. Human development, in brief, "is the process of enlarging people's choices, by expanding human functionings and capabilities." Three "essential" capabilities are "for people to lead a long and healthy life, to be knowledgeable, and to have access to the resources needed for a decent standard of living." People living in poverty lack those capabilities and thus are severely limited in their capacity to (for example) live a long life and participate in their community's affairs.[17] Amartya Sen and, specifically with respect to women, Martha Nussbaum, are perhaps the best-known advocates of the capabilities-based approach to human development.[18] As Nussbaum writes, "What this approach is after is a society in which individuals are treated as each worthy of regard, and in which each has been put in a position to live really humanly."[19] That implies the need of human security: a government's responsibility to protect human life, promote human rights, and provide good governance so that human-development goals are attainable.[20]

Common security involves cooperative efforts by states to keep threats from arising rather than, as in collective security, assembling force to counter threats. The accent is on preventive steps such as transparency of military establishments and confidence and security building measures (CBMs and CSBMs).[21] Central to these ideas is that it is in the best interest of *all* sides to an international dispute to cooperate in preventive security measures. Nor are such measures necessarily limited to the military side of security. Common security may just as well include economic, cultural, and diplomatic forms of engagement, so long as they are undertaken as part of a conscious strategy of conflict prevention. These nonmilitary steps might include pledges of nonaggression, periodic meetings of senior leaders and civil-society groups, hot lines, mutually determined assistance programs, and joint development of disputed territories. The case studies that follow in this chapter of US relations with the USSR, North Korea, and Iran, and of US-China relations in Chapter 5, stress the importance of engagement strategies between adversaries in the search for common ground.

Sixth, peacemaking is therefore a crucial long-term project. Conflict may be unavoidable and can even serve positive ends; but when noble causes turn to violence, winning at all costs *becomes* the cause. Nor is violence automatically appropriate in response to the violence of others. Fortunately, the literature and mechanisms for peacefully resolving international disputes are growing rapidly, with creative ideas not only on negotiation and mediation strategies but also on formats (such as problem-solving workshops, confidence-building measures, and preventive deployments of troops) that may nip potentially violent conflicts in the bud and even transform adversarial relationships. Herbert Kelman, a pioneer in bringing communities of Arabs and Israelis together in workshops, has written:

> It is necessary to move beyond influence strategies based on threats and to expand and refine strategies based on promises and positive incentives. Conflict resolution efforts, by searching for solutions that satisfy the needs of both parties, create opportunities for mutual influence by way of responsiveness to each other's needs. . . . Parties can encourage each other to negotiate seriously by reducing both sides' fears—not just, as more traditional strategic analysts often suggest, by increasing their pain.[22]

Recent international responses to conflict have rarely displayed such sensitivity; the usual approach is based on carrots and sticks.

Seventh, global-humanist analysis seeks to go beyond left and right, state and society, us-versus-them dichotomies. Liberal capitalism and state socialism have become increasingly irrelevant tools for accurately explaining, much less resolving, global crises of human rights.[23] To be sure, each has made major contributions to human security: liberalism's emphasis on intellectual freedom, the rule of law, and the rights of the individual, for example; and socialism's emphasis on collective rights, the redistribution of the social product, and the creation (as Cuba and China once attempted) of a "new person" motivated by service to the community. But in the name of free enterprise and liberal political goals, regimes on the right commonly downgrade or dispense with social and economic justice, exploit the environment on behalf of powerful local and foreign interests, and promote crass commercialism that numbs people's awareness of their basic spiritual, cultural, and economic needs. In leftist and fundamentalist systems, collective welfare typically becomes a vehicle of state tyranny, extra-constitutional oppression of "the masses," and enforced conformity to rigid, unassailable bureaucracies. The state hierarchy represents correct thinking, and economics serves politics. The results are often great inefficiencies, unmotivated and poorly rewarded workers, a sharp gap in privileges between elites and everyone else, and the ruthless suppression of dissent.

Alongside these contradictions between theory and practice are several disturbing similarities between many market and statist systems. Both accept the widespread alienation of working persons and discriminate against women, ethnic minorities, and homosexuals. Nationalisms that take primary loyalties away from the state, religious, or ethnic center are considered threats. Both overcentralize control of technology and resources, resist the devolution of power to community levels, waste precious resources, and have increasingly remote forms of governance. Leaderships in these systems are materialist and rationalist: "The contemporary apostles of abundance through mastery of nature are as likely to be found at the chamber of commerce as at the Central Committee of the Soviet Communist party," wrote Richard Barnet.[24] The promise of satisfying people's basic needs, which are usually defined in strictly material terms, often becomes a smokescreen behind which elite politics goes on as usual. Meanwhile, both types of systems cling to concepts of national security that ensure perpetuation of the war system and global underdevelopment. As Johan Galtung has observed of capitalism and socialism, they are equally capable of pursuing imperialist policies, that is, maintaining the core country's dominance over its partners in the periphery through unequal and dependent ties.[25]

Beyond left and right may lie both a new political synthesis and a new realism. The synthesis would mean adapting socialist, liberal-capitalist, and other ideas: hence, the values of social and economic justice (from socialism) and political justice (from liberalism); the positive role of the state in promoting social well-being; the preference (under capitalism) for adjudicated, nonviolent change, but the acceptance (under socialism) of violent alternatives when oppression reaches unbearable proportions; the upholding of individual rights (as under capitalism), but the use of class analysis (as under socialism) to discern how self-interest can become a weapon of mass exploitation; the enormous potential of capital and technological movement worldwide to uplift societies, and their equal propensity for manipulation to create scarcity, destroy ecosystems, and "develop" some societies at the expense of others. Thus, at every step of humanist political analysis, we pause to ask, "Who benefits?" and "Who loses?" as the result of this or that social condition and change.

The new realism would lie in "thinking globally" (or interdependently) from an ethical foundation. Mass impoverishment, the terror of modern weapons, and the widespread deprivation of universally recognized human rights cannot be effectively dealt with as discrete social science "problems" that are best left to national decisionmakers to work out. These are interconnected global phenomena that demand a global response, both out of self-interest—in the sense suggested by Martin Luther King Jr. that "whatever affects one directly affects all indirectly"—and out of profound moral concern "to shape the relationships and rules of practice which will support our common needs for security, welfare and safety," as Catholic bishops declared during the nuclear arms race.[26] Václav Havel, the author and human-rights activist who became the first president of post–Cold War Czechoslovakia (now the Czech Republic), clearly articulated the new realism when he emphasized the global implications of postcommunism. As important as it is to measure progress in democracy and prosperity in the new Europe, he said, the real challenge lies in creating a "new politics" of global responsibility, "before it is too late":

> We must rehabilitate our sense of ourselves as active human subjects, and liberate ourselves from the captivity of a purely national perception of the world. Through this "subjecthood" and the individual conscience that goes with it, we must discover a new relationship to our neighbors, and to the universe and its metaphysical order, which is the source of the moral order.[27]

Eighth, global-humanist realism is activist: "not to conform with what is happening, but to be able to see what our present options mean, what could result from them, and what changes we have to envisage, drastic as they may be."[28] Popular national and transnational movements for social change, such as grassroots development NGOs, human-rights movements, and alternative energy groups, are part of an important trend in world politics. At their best, these organizations are generally characterized by political diversity, commitment to humane change, and decentralized organizational structure. They are prompted by a vision of greater self-reliance and local control of resources and decisions. They hold out the promise of a global future that remains interdependent but is less tightly linked economi-cally, much less militarized, and more attuned to the necessary balance of human and natural forces.

The imagined future world of the humanist-activist is a radical one, in the sense of the radical as "one who is permanently alerted to a gap between what is and what should be, between the suffering, waste, untruth and peril of the present, and the joy, plenitude, significance and security of a possible future."[29] A persistent theme in the writings of two great social critics of the twentieth century, Hannah Arendt and Herbert Marcuse, was that the con-duct of politics was frequently based on the lie. Truth for them was indeed (to quote Sri Ramakrishna) "the austerity of our times." Arendt saw in the big lie an essential feature of totalitarianism, in which the public realm was explicitly cut off from the mass by the manipulation of thought and symbols by leaders. Such domination of the mind is at once more possible and more subtle in an age of advanced telecommunications; and while there are opportunities for extending democracy via the "information highway," the ever-enlarging corporate control of media, the ceaseless drumbeat of con-sumerism in every medium, and the substitution of entertainment for infor-mation lead in the opposite direction.

Fulfilling a humane vision presents other challenges. Those who pro-mote social change must overcome the tendency to replicate precisely those rigidities of leadership, such as fear of opposition, dogmatic thinking, sex-ism, and elitism, that they fought to overthrow. Any "new" system is not new if it replaces the old guard with political values and institutions that are just as oppressive. The Brazilian educator of the poor Paolo Friere was elo-quent on this point, warning us about manipulative leaders who use revolu-tions to postpone genuine social transformation.[30] Friere was really talking about democracy: a system's openness to change, respect for diversity of cultures and opinions, and receptivity of leaders to people's involvement in their own destiny (self-determination). He invited us to reject authoritarian-ism of all stripes, to support a high level of political participation by citi-zens, and to resist the notion of limited democracy—the idea, put forward with equal vehemence by industrialized and Third World state and corpora-tion leaders, that too much popular participation is a dangerous thing.

Finally, ninth among global humanism's distinguishing characteristics, is that human progress is measured in terms of human rights. The indicators consulted by global-humanist analysts differ markedly from those used by realists and corporate globalists. The former look for signs of qualitative advances in well-being for popular majorities and in the environment, as Michael J. Sullivan has done in a compendium that ranks states and regions in terms of their progress toward fulfilling global-humanist values.[31] The latter prefer gross measurements of state or corporate achievement, with emphasis on the bottom line: power and profit. No wonder that the two groups cannot have a constructive dialogue about political and social trends; they are like two ships passing in the night. Making use again of our four global crises (human rights, democracy, conflict, and underdevelopment), we can illustrate the wide disparity in measurements that inform these opposing views of global issues.

The gulf in interpreting progress in human rights was most clearly revealed in the late 1970s, when President Carter announced that human-rights achievement would be a cardinal element of his foreign policy. Carter's policy had the great merit of putting human rights on the global agenda. But it ran into two formidable problems. One was that the traditional US emphasis on individual civil liberties clashed with the Third World's and the socialist countries' insistence that collective economic rights should take precedence. Second was a glaring contradiction in US policy itself. When it came to choosing between human rights and national security, such as on the question of whether or not to sell arms to a repressive but economically and strategically important government, national security invariably won out. And the US record on human rights, several governments charged, was hardly exemplary.

What emerged out of that period was the not surprising discovery that governments interpret human rights in self-serving ways—to promote their own domestic and international interests while undermining the interests of adversaries, whether ideological foes abroad or ethnic minorities at home. The debate in the 1990s over "Asian values" in response to Western definitions of human rights was typical: The real issue was only superficially philosophy and principally politics, an attempt to use "culture" to deflect attention away from government abuses of power.[32] No government spoke for human beings or the sacredness of other living things. Every government that invoked "human rights" upheld itself as the sole arbiter of "rights." Each government's list of acceptable rights was not only very partial—liberty, social justice, a multi-party system, a new international economic order, disarmament—but seemed designed to respond to any other government's list.[33] The whole process was a classic example of realist self-righteousness garbed in humanitarian verbiage.

The debate over human rights, especially between the developed and underdeveloped countries, obscured more than it revealed. There is no necessary contradiction between political liberties and economic development; social justice can be promoted by both. What ought to matter is not the origin of particular values and norms but their suitability for addressing specific needs, such as protection of speech for minorities or of property rights for those victimized by corruption.[34] In the end, creation of a definitive, universally acceptable list of human rights is probably impossible. Yet a number of covenants broadly defining the scope of human rights have been widely endorsed by governments. Needless to say, endorsement and implementation are two entirely different matters. By relying on governments rather than independent bodies to initiate action and ensure compliance, the covenants limit legal options for citizens, especially the poor and women. National experiences are too diverse, moreover, to expect agreement among state leaders on which rights have priority. (Is it more important to end hunger or arbitrary arrests?) Nevertheless, a few guidelines concerning human-rights priorities can be suggested.

First, they should be rights fundamental to all political systems, that is, divorced from a particular ideological preference. Ending racism, violence against women and children, starvation, and ethnic cleansing are especially important objectives in this category. Second, they should have universal applicability and not be specific to a culture. Third, they should take account of the different levels at which human rights are threatened—global, state, and individual. Fourth, they should include nonmaterial as well as material human needs. Finally, they should be specific enough to point to political action that will realize them—not just, for example, the right to a healthy life, but the right to live in conditions that are "sustainable" for future generations.

Fouad Ajami[35] and Richard Falk[36] have proposed somewhat different lists of "core" human rights. Ajami's are:

- The right to survive; hence the concern with the war system and with nuclear weaponry
- The right not to be subjected to torture
- The condemnation of apartheid
- The right to food

Falk's list comprises five categories of rights:

- Basic human needs ("food, housing, health, and education")
- Basic decencies (including freedom from "genocide, torture, arbitrary arrest, detention, and execution, or their threat")
- Participatory rights ("including choice of political leadership, of job, of place of residence, of cultural activity and orientation")
- Security (the right to "minimal physical well-being and survival," including "ecological security")
- Humane governance ("the rights of individuals and groups to live in societies and a world that realizes the rights depicted in [Falk's four previously listed rights]")

Except for the absence of nonmaterial (spiritual, emotional) needs from Ajami's list, and the unimplementable nature of Falk's fifth item, it would seem that both listings satisfy the five criteria laid out above. They flow clearly out of the writers' common commitment to global-humanist values. Perhaps most important, the rights they propose neither draw from nor depend for their implementation upon government or party sanction. They rest instead upon an interpretation of the human interest, the most profound of which, given the nature of the global crisis, is security.

The crisis of democracy, or participation, should likewise be measured with due regard for ideological and cultural biases. Should we talk only about parliamentary democratic norms and exclude social and economic democracy? Global humanists think not, for reasons discussed in Chapter 1. It is important, using the Western tradition, to measure democratic progress in terms of political competition, press freedom, constitutional rights and duties, and the manner and extent of representation. It is equally important to identify signs of participation and accountability elsewhere than in the formal institutions of government. Grassroots democracy in the workplace and the community is vital, too, and in some societies is more meaningful to people's livelihoods than elections and constitutions. Access to public services, such as health care; people's involvement in local decisionmaking groups, such as educational boards; restrictions on ownership, management, and political activity in corporations, such as mass media; and unofficial but influential channels of communication between people and their leaders—these, too, should count as democratic practices. And, of course, we should take account of when appearances of democracy are a cover for an undemocratic reality, as underscored in the first chapter's timeline on democracy's backsliding.

The global-humanist approach measures conflict, the third global crisis, in the manner of a doctor holistically examining a patient. Armed disputes and structural violence are symptoms of a planet-wide disease whose consequences extend well beyond the usual toll of human casualties, territory gained or lost, incidences of war and terrorist acts, effects on the balance of power, and weapons in national arsenals. The notion of common security points to the need of an epidemiology of global violence—the full psychological, social, ecological, and economic costs of conflict and preparation for conflict.[37] War is not merely stupid—invariably destructive to winners and losers alike, and (as Eisenhower said) a "theft" from social programs. It is also psychologically self-defeating and delusional; it dirties rather than cleanses us, gives us a false sense of national pride and superiority, and subordinates the rule of law to the law of the jungle.[38] As Jonathan Schell has written, what made the fall of the Berlin Wall so "historically consequential" is that it led to a nonviolent revolution—the demise of an empire without war.[39] Common security evokes that idea: the peaceable transformation of violence-prone states.

If we analyzed conflict with these ideas, we would (for example) take account of the trade-offs of global militarization: What the money spent on weapons might buy in jobs, nonmilitary research and production, health care, and other kinds of real social security. We would consider the number of persons trapped in the war machine—as combatants; as employees involved in military research, production, and administration; as citizens living under military-controlled governments; as refugees fleeing war, dictatorship, and other forms of oppression; and as potential victims caught in the middle of conflict. And we would calculate the psychological and ecological damage that has been, and might be, done as the result of mass violence and preparation for it—for example, the cratering of countries by bombing (as in the Vietnam War, when the United States dropped "the equivalent of one Nagasaki bomb per week for seven and a half years");[40] the destruction of communities and environments by chemical warfare, such as Iraq carried out against the Kurds in the 1980s; the trauma to civilians (especially children) and soldiers exposed to war, terrorism, and torture; and the public-health effects of highly toxic military wastes produced in military reactors and on military bases.[41]

The last of our four global crises, underdevelopment, may provide the clearest case of how differently realists and corporate globalists, on the one hand, and global humanists, on the other, evaluate a central issue in world politics. For the former, development and underdevelopment can everywhere be measured in terms of gross production and average distribution, using indicators such as gross national product, gross profit, per capita income, total exports and imports, and, in centrally planned economies, production targets.[42] Such indicators can be useful general guides to economic performance, but they have been roundly criticized for many years. Among other things, they distort the real-world picture of losers and beneficiaries from economic growth. "Growth for whom?" is a question that goes unexplored. Gross and average measurements typically draw attention from the mass of impoverished people to whom economic benefits rarely trickle down. They usually discount the ecological and environmental (including public-health) consequences of economic growth, with respect both to the costs of production and the consequences of consumption. Furthermore, an increase in a gross measure such as GNP may not be the most desirable kind of growth in a society filled with malnourished, unhealthy, uneducated people. Focusing on economic globalization's imposing figures can easily miss the way it may overwhelm traditional village life, transforming bearable poverty into unbearable "destitution."[43]

Overall, global humanists seek to inject equity, social justice, and environmental considerations into their calculations of development. A truly developed society, as distinct from an economy that is growing, would have low infant mortality; a small percentage of population below the poverty level; low (and declining) pollution levels; high (and increasing) access to public services for all citizen, gender, ethnic, and age groups; and high levels of educational access and achievement for each age group.[44] (The UNDP's HDI and Sullivan's global values framework enable countries to be ranked using these criteria.) Prosperity would be distributed from the bottom up rather than from the top down, focusing (as discussed above) on human capabilities and basic human needs and not on further enriching the privileged few. How well governments perform in providing the elements of human capabilities and meeting basic needs would then be the true measure of development and the recommended target of development assistance. Where those conditions are minimal, either because of government policy or international constraints, a failure of state responsibility has occurred: People are kept from pursuing an authentic, humane existence to which they are entitled as a matter of fundamental freedom.[45]

These present-time criteria would be governed by a larger "sustainable vision" based on principles such as stewardship of resources, global community, appropriate scale, and sufficiency.[46] Hence, global humanists want to know what percentage of a national budget serves public services, military programs, and interest on external debts. How are people taxed, how has the value of money changed, and who might be subsidizing whom? They will take a close look at exports and imports: Are food and other commodities capable of being produced at home being imported, or exported despite a local need? Do local or foreign entrepreneurs control foreign trade, and which sectors of it? To what extent is export promotion serving human development needs such as employment? Are transnational corporations sharing technology with the host country, reinvesting profits, and producing goods or services that are meeting the needs of an underdeveloped economy?

Ecopolitics—assessing the environmental costs of growth and the simultaneous underdevelopment of both economies and environment—especially needs study in the case of global corporations.[47] They contribute to the ecological devastation of Third and Fourth World countries by encouraging farming for export and by setting up factories there that pollute the environment or become dumping grounds for pesticides, electronic trash, and other toxic wastes.[48] Industries whose output of wastes goes beyond permissible levels in their home countries find safe havens abroad, encouraged by local authorities eager for foreign investment and perhaps open to a bribe. The pesticide leak at the Union Carbide plant in Bhopal, India, in December 1984 is one such instance of a pollution-dumping tragedy. Its lessons about fair compensation to the victims, adequate information to the host country and community, and sharp limits on the export of extremely dangerous processes and technologies have not been learned to this day.[49] Canada sells Third World customers a type of nuclear reactor that has been shut down at home because of safety and environmental problems.[50] Nor can the state be exonerated when the poor are victimized by environmental disasters. Just weeks before Bhopal, an explosion in Mexico City of liquefied gas tanks owned by the government oil corporation, Pemex, killed about 450 slum-dwellers. The shipment of hazardous waste and rubbish from industrialized to cash-poor countries is becoming increasingly routine.[51] In the industrialized countries, meanwhile, we likewise find ecological nightmares and near-disasters. The names of Three

Mile Island, Love Canal, Stringfellow, and the *Exxon Valdez* in the United States; of Chelyabinsk and Chernobyl in the Soviet Union, sites of nuclear disasters in 1957 and 1986; of Seveso, Italy, scene of a major dioxin spill in 1976; of Germany's treasured forests, where one in three trees has now been damaged by acid rain—these evidently represent only the tip of an ecocidal iceberg.

Finally, global-humanist analysis of underdevelopment considers the costs and benefits, from a human-interest standpoint, of alternative production, consumption, and investment patterns. In what ways can more self-reliant, autonomous development take place? (Since *any* concept of development may be viewed as management by and dependence on outsiders, should it be abandoned as an unwarranted interference in people's basic right to autonomy and in their self-determined efforts at cultural regeneration?[52]) Is a better balance between economic growth and environmental protection achievable, or even desirable, given the realities of a rapidly deteriorating global environment on one hand and the incessant demands of rich and poor countries for higher levels of production and consumption on the other? What needs to happen politically, as well as economically, in order for people's basic needs to be met? How can foreign trade and aid be altered so that they serve, rather than are merely served by, the working population? These kinds of questions will probably only be asked by analysts who accept the necessity of political transformation. Until now, the dominant models of modernization employed in the West and adopted in much of the Third World reflected Western capitalism's own development, stressing the virtues of the private sector, bigness, and stable, steady-state politics. There is undoubtedly merit to the argument that such models have been directly encouraged in the United States and elsewhere by government and foundation research support.[53]

This review of the global-humanist methodology has emphasized the special importance of human-centered values, norms, and assumptions to the definition, not to mention the analysis and potential solution of global political problems. The methodology has emerged alongside and has been shaped significantly by the global crisis. The consequences of that evolution are both positive and negative. It has shown the need—indeed, the urgency—to break down intellectual barriers to cross-disciplinary research and to science with ethical content. It has helped to redirect political inquiry to human beings while raising critical questions about prevailing categories of political-economic analysis, including models of development, definitions of national security and human rights, and left-right ideological distinctions. It has infused the notion of "interdependence" with new meaning—not simply "interconnectedness" or "multilateralism," but shared insecurities about life on a planet facing simultaneous threats from rampant expansionism. Finally, global humanism reflects optimism about the human prospect that may point to entirely different ways of providing for human security, concrete and potential examples of which are mentioned in the last chapter.

On the negative side, global humanism must take account of several important criticisms. Realists take aim at its excessive idealism and deemphasis of interstate power politics. They remind us that as much as world politics has become infused with greater complexity, its dominant actors remain states locked in competition with one another. From corporate globalists comes the charge that global humanism is anticapitalist and disregards the many positive contributions transnational corporations make to both national and international well-being. The global corporation can be a positive force for material progress and global exchange. The radical left, on the other hand, often considers global humanism too "soft" on capitalism, reformist rather than revolutionary, and (in agreement with the realists) unjustifiably idealistic about the prospects for humane change. All three groups of critics take global humanism to task—rightly, in my view—for failing thus far to propose a coherent world or national policy agenda to effect the transition "from here to there," that is, from global crisis to global community.

Criticism of global humanism has also come from the Third World. Some groups committed to a new international economic order see the basic-needs approach as yet another foreign (Western) intervention in Third World affairs, or at least as a diversion from the central task (as they see it) of rectifying inequitable trade and investment relations between underdeveloped and industrialized states. Others in the Third World express misgivings about global humanism's equal emphasis on social-economic and political justice (and its concern about human rights generally), seeing that, too, as an ill-informed intervention. And there is hostility to any implication that the Third World, having already sacrificed its development to the industrialized world's, should now cut its economic growth in order to contribute to reversing global ecological problems such as pollution, toxic waste, and resource scarcity.

Finally, global humanism must contend with controversy within its own diverse ranks. One prominent issue is sustainable development, a norm that is intimately associated with a planetary perspective but eludes clear definition. Having got sustainable development onto the global agenda and into mainstream dialogue on development, global humanists must grapple with some difficult questions. Do humans and nature, including wildlife, have equal priority? Should the object of environmental protection be the return to a pristine era? Is it appropriate to use violence to protect natural resources? Is management of the environment antithetical to protecting nature and the cultures living in harmony with it? Exactly how much, if any, growth is sustainable? And taking account of the vast differences in quality of life between indigenous peoples, rich and poor in the Third World, and citizens of the industrialized world, sustainability for whom?

## Case Study 1: The US-Soviet Arms Race During the Cold War

Security in the nuclear age means common security. Even ideological opponents and political rivals have a shared interest in survival. There must be partnership in the struggle against war itself. . . . International peace must rest on a commitment to joint survival rather than a threat of mutual destruction.
—Independent Commission on Disarmament and Security Issues, 1982

The rise and fall of empires is a favorite theme of historians. The twentieth century witnessed the passing of the British Empire, the destruction of Nazi Germany and Imperial Japan, and most recently the breakup of the Soviet Union, now the Russian Federation. As the new century begins, the United States stands alone as a superpower and, arguably, an empire, though in military and economic terms rather than in territory. The common theme of this case study is the insecurity bred by the US-Soviet arms race during the Cold War: the costs it imposed on their societies, the dangers to which they and the world's peoples were exposed, and the enduring legacy of their competition—in the squandered opportunities to move toward the elimination of nuclear weapons; in the ongoing problem of proliferation of all weapons of mass destruction (nuclear, chemical, and biological); in the largely unrestrained and profit-oriented conventional weapons trade; and in the tensions still evident in US-Russian relations (elaborated in Chapter 6).

The Cold War absorbed human, capital, and technological resources in the United States and the Soviet Union to a degree probably unmatched in history. By one count, world military spending from 1960 to 1990 was $21 trillion, of which perhaps $7 trillion was expended by the superpowers and another $1 trillion by US and Soviet allies in NATO and the Warsaw Pact.[54] During the forty-five years of Cold War, their leaders consciously chose to make "national security"—preparedness for war—the highest priority, sacrificing human needs at home and economic order abroad. As a United Nations report stated in 1982, "the world can either continue to pursue the arms race—or move consciously and with deliberate speed toward a more sustainable international economic and political order. *It cannot do both.* The arms race and development are thus in a competitive relationship." The report cited President Eisenhower, who drew the same conclusion in 1953: "Every gun that is made, every warship launched, every rocket fired, signifies, in a final sense, a theft from those who hunger and are not fed, from those who are cold and are not clothed."[55] Yet Eisenhower was no more able to stem the arms race than any other president.

As the 1990s began, however, Soviet "new thinking" in foreign policy, combined with US budget deficits and the breakdown of Cold War alignments in Europe, laid the basis for a dramatic transformation of superpower relations. The June 1990 summit meeting in Washington, DC, found the two governments in unprecedented agreement. "We are proceeding from the assumption that anything that is not good for the United States . . . will not be good for us either," said President Gorbachev. To which Secretary of State James Baker replied: "While the Cold War might be characterized by the balance of terror, today I think US-Soviet relations stand on the steadier ground of a balance of interests." This auspicious beginning to the post–Cold War period, which was followed in 1991 by even more dramatic events—the end of Gorbachev's rule, the collapse of the USSR and of the Warsaw Pact, and the first of several steps to reduce nuclear arms (the Strategic Arms Reduction Talks, or START)—seemed to set the stage for halting and even reversing the arms race.

But although nuclear arms racing stopped, and a number of arms-reduction treaties were concluded with the end of the Cold War, the dangers posed by nuclear weapons have by no means gone away. Nor have US or Soviet/Russian society benefited from a peace divided. We may be able to learn why by looking back over the history of the US-Soviet arms race and identifying the driving forces behind it. My analysis will give primary attention to nuclear weapons. The numbers are deceiving: In the late 1980s the number of nuclear warheads and bombs in US and Soviet arsenals peaked at around 55,000, out of a worldwide total of over 65,000.[56] Roughly 20,000 US and Soviet weapons were long-range (strategic). In line with commitments under START I, US and Russian strategic arsenals were to be reduced to several thousand operational warheads each by 1997. Under START II (signed in January 1993) the number on each side was to be further reduced, to a maximum of 3,500 each, including a ban on land-based missiles armed with multiple warheads (MIRVs). Under START III (1997), each country was to have no more than 2,500 strategic nuclear warheads by the end of 2007. In 2002 there followed the Moscow Treaty (officially, the Strategic Offensive Reductions Treaty, or SORT), under which the United States and Russia pledged to reduce strategic warheads to between 1,700 and 2,200 by 2012. In spite of these agreements, the actual nuclear-weapon stockpiles remain very large (Table 3.1)—a total of over 27,000 nuclear weapons, including about 10,200 strategic warheads, in the possession of the Security Council Permanent Members (Perm 5) in 2002.[57] The weapons, operational and in storage, represent unimaginable destructive power[58]—power that, as always, is subject to human and technological errors and irreversible political miscalculation. When account is further taken of the spreading knowledge and materials for producing a nuclear weapon, the possible acquisition of such a weapon by a terrorist group, and the persistence of ideas for using nuclear weapons—matters covered in Chapter 5—we can look back to the US-Soviet competition to understand why. Albert Einstein's oft-quoted warning remains valid: "The splitting of the atom has changed everything save our mode of thinking, and thus we drift toward unparalleled catastrophe."

The nuclear question is the subject of an enormous literature that is

**Table 3.1   Worldwide Nuclear Arsenals (2006)**

| | United States | Russia | China | France | United Kingdom | Israel | India | Pakistan | Global Total |
|---|---|---|---|---|---|---|---|---|---|
| Strategic delivery systems | 1,039 | 855 | 32 | 132 | 64 | N/A | N/A | N/A | ~2,190 |
| Strategic nuclear warheads | 5,886 | 3,814 | 32 | 288 | 200 | N/A | N/A | N/A | ~10,828 |
| Total nuclear weapons | ~10,300 | ~16,000 | 410 | ~350 | 200 | ~100 | 70–110 | 50–110 | ~27,600 |

*Source:* Carnegie Endowment for International Peace, www.carnegieendowment.org/npp/numbers/default.cfm. North Korea's arsenal, generally believed to number 6–10 weapons, is excluded since it does not have strategic range.

often complex and even surreal in its discussion of strategy, weapons physics and characteristics, and the outcome of a nuclear exchange. In global perspective, however, answering one question may help us to rise above the clutter of numbers and arcane language: Do nuclear weapons, by virtue of their actual numbers, strategic doctrine, and the political economy of national security, promote or undermine the real security of states?

Dealing with any aspect of the arms race inevitably begins with assumptions about the causes of war that should be explicitly stated. The realists, for example, assume that the war system is a natural outgrowth of human beings' innate inhumanity and the corruption of the state system by, among other things, the enemy's expansionist ideologies. To them, nuclear weapons are a necessary evil, the logical outcome of technological sophistication that evolved to deter future (nuclear) war between the two great nuclear powers. Nuclear weapons paradoxically have both heightened and diminished the war crisis: Through mutual deterrence, they lend stability to the global balance of terror.

I find this view neither logical nor factual. It tells us we should learn to live with a weapon that all agree must never be used and, if used, might well mean the end of life as we know it. It assigns technology, rather than political economy, the central role in driving the arms race. It perpetuates the myth that nuclear weapons are merely defensive. And it helps sustain the belief that nuclear weapons can be controlled, when the evidence shows that even now, arms control is far behind the pace set by weapons development and strategies for using them.

My view is that the nuclear arms race had its roots in the domestic insecurity of the superpowers. Possessed of a particular way of looking at the world (a global ideology), and harboring the kinds of values previously identified, state leaders in the United States and the FSU were driven by self-preservation and expansionism. The social systems over which they presided contain vested bureaucratic interests in national security—the military-industrial complex—that exist independently of any actual threats to national survival. The combination of ideological self-righteousness, conflict-oriented values, and bureaucratic momentum made preparedness for war a dominating feature of political life. It led to deliberate exaggeration of the other side's capabilities ("We overstate the Soviets' force and we understate ours, and we therefore greatly overstate the imbalance," said former US secretary of defense Robert McNamara in 1982).[59] It created fears about the other side's intentions and lofty presumptions about one's own. It prompted planning for the worst case, which maximized opportunities for miscalculation and misperception of the other side's actions.

Ultimately, Cold War politics generated an expansionist interpretation of the national interest, leading to ever larger military budgets; incentives to develop more deadly weapons; disincentives to negotiate arms reductions; increasingly tight identification of the work force, education, and popular culture with the military; restrictions on information and civil liberties in the name of national security; and constant efforts to attract allies to one's side in the worldwide struggle against "them." As we witnessed in the US-Soviet arms deadlock of the early 1980s, each side saw itself embarked on a noble crusade that of necessity was justified in stereotypic images. "We" were always the epitome of virtue, while "they" were evil incarnate: angels versus devils. Thus, in 1977, President Leonid Brezhnev declared that the USSR "will never embark on the path of aggression and will never lift its sword against other peoples"[60]—this, one year before the invasion of Afghanistan—while in 1983 President Reagan characterized the Soviet Union as the "focus of evil in the modern world," at the very time his administration was seeking to topple the government of Nicaragua. Such mirror imagery has long been noted by psychologists; it was one element of mutual reinforcement of the superpowers' domestic insecurity, the specifics of which I come to shortly.

This way of looking at the phenomenon of war has specific relevance to understanding the purpose of nuclear weapons. It suggests that politics, rather than either technology developing independently of political will or careful calculation of the number and character of weapons actually needed for national defense, is the driving force behind strategic weapons programs.[61] But still more fundamentally, this perspective leads us to question—and reject—the concept and morality of nuclear war itself. It is not thinkable.

The central issue of nuclear weapons is not numbers and dollars; it is human life and the survival of the species. And what makes nuclear war unthinkable, as Jonathan Schell pointed out in *The Fate of the Earth*,[62] is that it is not *war* at all. For war is governed and ended by political decisions, whereas the use of nuclear weapons presages the end of politics and the onset of a global medical, ecological, and social catastrophe without foreseeable end.

At the height of the Cold War, enough nuclear weapons were at the disposal of the superpowers to incinerate every populated area in the two countries down to the level of a town of 1,500 people, and still have an ample reserve. The US and Soviet arsenals included thousands of warheads in each part of their so-called strategic triad: long-range intercontinental ballistic missiles (ICBMs), intercontinental bombers, and submarines. Any one of these parts—in fact, even the warheads delivered by a few submarines—could effectively obliterate another society. Figures inevitably vary on how many people might be killed instantly, die later of radiation poisoning, or be disfigured, genetically mutated, blinded, and so on. Comparisons with the experiences of Hiroshima and Nagasaki are absurd, since today's one-megaton bomb (1 million tons of TNT) is equivalent in destructive power to eighty Hiroshimas. In addition, weather conditions and the number and location of the weapons dropped determine the extent of casualties. Suffice to say that had a US-Soviet nuclear exchange occurred involving at minimum several thousand megatons of weapons, it would have caused appalling numbers of deaths—perhaps 200 million in the two countries alone—injuries in the range of 60 million persons, and disease and destruction of unparalleled, hence unimaginable, scope. From a medical as well as a military standpoint, it would have been the "final epidemic."[63]

Even if a nuclear weapon is never again fired in anger, it already poses health and safety dangers.[64] People who lived near the plants that produced its components—during the Cold War, seventeen facilities in thirteen US states and twelve nuclear reactors and other plants in the FSU—faced a multitude of hazards. The technical difficulties of storing or burying radioactive plutonium, U-235, and tritium remain unsolved, guaranteeing periodic leakages of extremely toxic materials into the air and water. At the Hanford Nuclear Reservation in southeastern Washington State, for instance, some of these leakages over a forty-year period, and without public knowledge, have emptied into the Columbia River. Hanford, along with two other major plants, has been shut down; but the cleanup bill for all of them may be $150 billion, and the chosen method of waste disposal has proven to be dangerous.[65] Nuclear waste disposal in Russia was far worse. Half of all that was ever produced for weapons was—and, some Russian scientists say, still is—simply buried underground near rivers, without containment shells. Leakages are occurring, prompting one renowned US physicist to call it "the largest and most careless nuclear practice that the human race has ever suffered."[66] The plants themselves are a serious danger: Most of them are old and unsafe. A Chernobyl-like meltdown is certainly repeatable. And in the United States, numerous accidents finally led the US Department of Energy in 1988 to shut down all reactors that produce weapons-grade materials. According to a former assistant secretary of that agency, "a military culture" prevailed, "a bunker mentality" that always forced environmental and safety concerns to take a backseat to the maximum production of warhead material.[67] The changeover to processing nuclear waste has not led to a different mentality.[68] With its more recent decision to recycle 34 tons of plutonium from nuclear weapons, including Russia's, for use as fuel in civilian nuclear power plants, however, the department is risking theft, though the decision is a boon to the nuclear industry.[69]

Yet official and, to a great extent, public debate on the nuclear issue was dominated until the 1990s by arguments about numbers: Which side has more weapons, the biggest weapons, the highest military spending? Such arguments had merit when the United States had a nuclear monopoly (1945–1949) and then clear superiority over the USSR (1949–1962). Once the USSR started to catch up, however, the numbers game distorted far more than it revealed. For by then, according to Robert McNamara, in spite of maintaining a strategic superiority over the USSR of "at least three or four to one"—enough to destroy a third of the Soviet population and half its industry with only a fraction (about four hundred bombs) of the US stockpile—the United States could still be "effectively destroy[ed]" by a Soviet retaliatory blow.[70] And that continued to be the case for the remainder of the Cold War. "What in the name of God is strategic superiority?" asked Henry Kissinger in 1974. "What is the significance of it, politically, militarily, operationally, at these levels of numbers? What do you do with it?"[71]

Indeed, what do you do with so many weapons? McNamara and his boss, President Kennedy, were among those who recoiled at the unusable capability for overkill, particularly targeted against cities. Yet the change that came about was not to stop the production of nuclear weapons but to move toward a different mixture of targets. A "countercities" nuclear force became "countervalue" (directed mainly at economic targets) and still later "counterforce" (directed at military, communications, and political targets as well as economic assets). And as the number of all these targets grew—to about 40,000 in the 1980s from 2,600 in 1960 and 25,000 in 1974—the number of warheads and weapons needed to "cover" the targets also mushroomed.[72] The rationality of such planning had lost touch with reality: Many millions of civilians would still be killed even in the most selective nuclear attacks (since nonmilitary targets, after all, often are located near population centers); the number of warheads (in the *hundreds*) actually needed for deterring attack (convincing an enemy, that is, that it would be destroyed if it attacked the United States) was *thousands* fewer than the number available; and the targeting of several or more warheads on a single industrial plant, city, or other facility defied imagination.[73]

Not only did target lists and weapons arsenals grow, they also, perhaps inevitably, became more refined. Military planners and scientists, foremost in the United States, began emphasizing the technical characteristics of nuclear weapons and the means of delivering them. "More" would have to be coupled with "better." And so for nearly two decades, the decisive military factor in the US-Soviet strategic competition was the relative technical quality of the weapons: their accuracy, reliability for delivery, and vulnerability to attack. It was the advances in weapons technology, in which the United States always had an edge, that accounted for the dangerous new threshold of the arms race in the early 1980s.[74] For despite the widely held view at the time, which this analysis shares, that the United States and the Soviet Union had roughly equivalent strategic striking power—each side had several thousands of deliverable nuclear warheads, enough to destroy the other several times over, and neither side had a usable margin of superiority over the other—they both deployed weapons that moved beyond deterrence of attack to potentially offensive capabilities. The US strategic force had the advantage, however, because roughly half of it was deployed on virtually invulnerable submarines and all elements of the force were far more accurate than Soviet weapons. US military leaders acknowledged but rarely mentioned these advantages in public discussions.

The nuclear competition was also more than the sum of its parts. The net strategic result of nuclear-weapons development was to alter the logic that underpinned it: deterrence. Nuclear deterrence refers to the ability of one side to make a nuclear attack on it too costly for an opponent to contemplate rationally. In theory deterrence is achievable because the defending side can sustain a nuclear attack and still have the second-strike capacity to retaliate devastatingly against valued targets of its opponent—population centers, industry, strategic and other military assets, and the leadership itself. But even in theory, deterrence is a weak reed on which to rest the planet's survival. It is largely a state of mind; there is no certainty about the military forces needed to deter an adversary until (possibly) *after* being attacked, at which point deterrence has failed. Precisely what deterred the Soviets from attacking the United States or its allies, and vice versa, was a matter of conjecture, of educated guesswork; and from conjecture sprung the belief that increasing numbers and types of nuclear weapons were essential to deterrence. It was an irresistible logic for rationalizing continued research and development of additional nuclear warheads and weapons. For no one, the argument went, could be certain how much was enough to ensure deterrence.

So much for theory. In the real world, deterrence was fast eroding because of the nuclear technology itself, with respect to the US-Soviet competition and the proliferation of that technology worldwide. Deterrence rests on a certain stability akin to mind over matter, rational planning over technology run amok. In a deterrence relationship, what must work is confidence on all sides in the reality of deterrence. And this confidence is precisely what advances in nuclear weapons undermined, since the more accurate, destructive, and widespread nuclear weapons became, the more unpredictability of control and use they created. The overriding lesson of the Cuban missile crisis of 1962 for those decisionmakers who lived through it was that deterrence was irrelevant: "What you had was two small groups of men in two small rooms, groping frantically in the intellectual fog, in the dark, to deal with a crisis that had spun out of control."[75] Each side, Soviet and US, could only hope that the other was sane enough not to make a cataclysmic mistake and launch a nuclear weapon.

Technological advances in strategic weapons during the 1980s evidently created in the minds of some high-level leaders (particularly, but surely not exclusively, on the US side)[76] a conviction in the ability to fight, contain, win, and survive a "limited" nuclear war. Such careless thinking, even though discounted by other top US officials (such as the commander of NATO forces), alarmed many in Western Europe, one potential locale of a nuclear exchange. Both Soviet and US leaders periodically deplored the concept of a nuclear victory—former Soviet president Brezhnev, for instance, called it a "dangerous madness" that could only stem from a suicidal impulse[77]—but both sides nevertheless invested considerable resources in planning for a postnuclear future: improved communications among remaining national leaders, civil defense, and postattack economic and social recovery.[78]

Beyond limited nuclear war, weapons accuracy may also have made more conceivable a nuclear first strike, meaning the ability to decimate an opponent and not suffer a crippling retaliatory blow. One might think that the days were over when, as McNamara reported of the period just before the October 1962 Cuban missile crisis, the US Air Force could believe in its ability to carry out a disarming first strike on the Soviet Union.[79] But technology reopened that possibility. Sea- and air-launched cruise missiles, which were not covered by any arms-control agreement before START, are highly accurate and very difficult for radar to detect because of their smallness. If strategic targets can be pinpointed with weapons such as these, they could create in the minds of national leaders the belief that using them first is preferable to waiting to be attacked. Use of such compact, remote-controlled, and deadly nuclear devices is no longer conceivable in a US-Russia conflict; but they may be tailor-made for leaders of other states or political movements. In fact, several states already have cruise missiles in service, and several others are within technological reach of them. Deterrence theory has only textbook relevance in such circumstances.

Deterrence was also subverted by accident. Cases of drug and alcohol abuse among US missile personnel responsible for nuclear weapons were reported over the years. Computer failures became all too commonplace. For example, over eight hundred false alarms in the US strategic warning system occurred between 1979 and 1983.[80] US strategic forces went to high alert three times during a seven-month period in 1979 to 1980 because of computer failures in the North American radar system. President Reagan was not notified of the alerts, one of which left only four minutes for a decision on how to respond to a Soviet attack.[81] Over the years, accidents occurred involving nuclear weapons, though none in which a nuclear weapon was detonated. In 1981 the Pentagon reported on twenty-seven such accidents since 1950, most involving aircraft crashes.[82] Six of the previous US accidents occurred in foreign waters or over foreign territory. Deterrence theory takes no account of how one state's leaders may react to a reported nuclear accident in a highly tense period.

The dangers of technical and human breakdowns were all the more ominous because of the decreasing time between a missile launch and its arrival on target. Submarines lying off a coastline can accurately deliver nuclear weapons in a few minutes. Thousands of missiles—2,500 at this time—are on hair-trigger ("launch on warning") alert.[83] So little time to distinguish between a real and an imagined threat may mean that the grave decision to execute a nuclear strike will be delegated to military officers on the spot or even "loaded" into computers that automatically trigger retaliation. Nor have later bilateral agreements involving the United States, Russia, and China to de-target nuclear missiles aimed at each other solved the problem, because missiles can be retargeted very quickly.

The proliferation of nuclear weapons added yet another uncertainty to the nuclear-war issue, perhaps a larger one than the US-Soviet rivalry itself. Several states that either already possessed nuclear weapons or were trying to produce them—Brazil, South Africa, Pakistan, India, Libya, Iraq, and Israel—were closely tied to one of the superpowers and were involved in hostile relations with neighboring countries. A conflict involving one or more of these undeclared but nuclear-capable states could have embroiled a superpower partner. Several instances have recently come to light. In the late 1960s Israel's secret buildup of a nuclear-weapons stockpile became known to the United States. But Washington never pressured Israel, its key ally in the Middle East, to dismantle its facility or open it to international inspection.[84] When, in June 1981, Israeli jets bombed Iraq's French-built nuclear reactor, Washington expressed grave concern but privately applauded. A second case is South Africa, whose government had assured the United States in 1977 that it had no intention of developing nuclear weapons. In fact, South Africa was successfully doing so, thanks to a nuclear-exchange agreement with Israel—South African uranium ore and a nuclear-test facility for Israeli scientific help in building a bomb—that had started during the 1967 Six Day War between Israel and Egypt.[85] Pakistan is a third case. Throughout the Cold War years, Pakistan was a key partner of US intelligence agencies in surveillance operations against the USSR and (in the 1980s) in funneling arms to Afghani resistance fighters. The payoff for Pakistan was that its secret program to build a nuclear bomb was well known to and supported by the United States, which in the 1980s allowed Pakistani agents to buy high-technology materials while certifying to

Congress that Pakistan was a non-nuclear state. Not only did Pakistan develop a nuclear arsenal of six to ten weapons (a fact it finally disclosed in 1992), but in May 1990 it apparently came perilously close to a nuclear exchange with India over the long-simmering Kashmir dispute.[86]

International cooperation in the United Nations by Moscow and Washington officially was supposed to prevent the emergence of new nuclear states. Since the 1968 nuclear Non-Proliferation Treaty (NPT) and its regulatory body, the International Atomic Energy Agency (IAEA), came into force in 1970, no non-nuclear member state had gone nuclear. (The treaty is essentially a promise by signatories, now numbering 188, to "pursue negotiations" to end the arms race and achieve "nuclear disarmament." In exchange for agreeing not to acquire, manufacture, or seek technical assistance concerning nuclear weapons, non-nuclear states are promised access to nuclear-energy technology. The agency's purpose is to inspect atomic facilities and ensure that adequate safeguards have been installed to prevent the diversion of nuclear fuel to weapons manufacture.) But three of the six nuclear powers—China, France, and India—did not sign the treaty; and neither did five states that were developing or already secretly possessed nuclear weapons—Argentina, Brazil, Israel, Pakistan, and South Africa.

The line between peaceful and military uses of atomic power, which once seemed clear to many, had actually been erased: "*Every* known civilian route to bombs involves *either* nuclear power *or* materials and technologies whose possession, indeed whose existence in commerce, is a direct and essential consequence of nuclear fission power."[87] The IAEA was poorly equipped to deal with that problem. It lacked the enforcement powers, the personnel, and the right of unimpeded access that would make it an effective oversight agency. When, for example, Israel bombed the Iraqi reactor, which the IAEA had inspected, the agency could neither punish Israel nor absolutely refute Israel's charge that Iraq was diverting nuclear fuel for bomb-making purposes. In fact, Iraq was, though it never succeeded at making a bomb. In the case of South Africa, over one hundred IAEA inspections of its facilities failed to reveal what the government itself revealed in 1993: that it had produced six nuclear bombs between 1967 and 1990, when the program was scrapped. When we take up the Indian and Pakistani nuclear tests in 1998 in Chapter 5, it will be noted that both those secret weapons programs used plutonium from civilian reactors. So did North Korea in 2006. Iran may be planning to do the same.

The related problems of theft and covert acquisition of plutonium were even further beyond the IAEA's ability to control. Several cases of theft were reported from US nuclear plants, for instance. More ominously, the international availability of plutonium was nearly out of control. One creditable estimate by the Nuclear Control Institute based in Washington, DC, was that in the noncommunist countries alone there was enough plutonium in 1983 from conventional nuclear power plants to produce "at least 6,000 bombs, if separated out of spent fuel in reprocessing plants."[88] As we shall see, a great deal of plutonium remains potentially available despite nuclear-arms reductions.

But the most grievous weaknesses of the nonproliferation regime lay in the contradictory and hypocritical behavior of the superpowers, the United States in particular. Of all the NPT signatories, they were among the least responsible, for they failed to meet their commitment under the treaty to take "effective" steps toward an "early" end to the arms race and nuclear disarmament. Yet they wanted to universalize membership, supposedly to deny nuclear-weapons technology to the non-nuclear states. As Samuel Kim observed, "It is difficult to explain logically why nuclear weapons are good or safe in the hands of the great powers but bad or unsafe in the hands of the small powers."[89] *good point*

An even greater hypocrisy is that the United States, in order to promote the faltering fortunes of its nuclear-power industry and maintain good relations with Third World allies, provided several near-nuclear states with nuclear materials. It also looked the other way when, by hook or by crook, agents of these states surreptitiously exported such materials from the United States or elsewhere.[90] Here we have another example of how realism and corporate globalism come together to undermine a vital global interest.  The US government did not want US corporations such as Westinghouse, General Electric, and Bechtel to lose out in the competition with French and German nuclear-energy companies; nor did it want to slap the hands of its "strategic" friends, the Israelis, the Argentines, the Pakistanis, and the South Africans. So Washington, as we observed, did virtually nothing to prevent their moving closer to, actually acquiring, or expanding a nuclear capability—and, in fact, the US government sometimes facilitated matters.[91] Just how shortsighted such generosity can be was vividly illustrated in Gulf War I when the United States confronted an Iraqi army it and its European allies had helped, either with diverted aid money or with equipment, to work on developing a nuclear capability. Thus, Washington and Moscow led the retreat from nonproliferation by their actual practices, weakening deterrence horizontally (among countries) as well as vertically (by types of weapons).[92]

In such dismal circumstances, along came strategic nuclear defense to pose as an alternative to the mutual balance of terror. Both superpowers began investing heavily in space-based weapons that would be able to shoot down enemy satellites (ASATs) and direct powerful lasers or sensor rockets to knock out offensive missiles as they left the launching pad or were en route to targets. Missile defense was hardly a novel idea; the antiballistic missile (ABM) to defend land-based missiles was a major political issue in the United States when it was first proposed in the mid-1960s. The US-USSR ABM Treaty in 1972 prohibited the development, testing, and deployment of antimissile systems and their components. But under President Reagan's Strategic Defense Initiative (SDI, or "Star Wars"), shooting down Soviet missiles emerged as the solution to problems associated with deterrence.[93] It was not, for even at 99 percent effectiveness, the system would have failed to prevent a catastrophic attack. A sound missile defense on one side, moreover, looked like part of an offensive strategy to the other side. For these and many other reasons, SDI was scaled back.[94] But ballistic missile defense (BMD) is still alive in the United States, promoted by those who believe it can deter "crazy states" from launching a nuclear strike. (That is why the United States is working on a "theater" antimissile defense system in East Asia, presumably for deployment against North Korea but more likely with China also in mind.) BMD shows again how faith in a new military technology can divert political leaders from dealing with the sources of international conflict. If there are Third World leaders or terrorists who might use a nuclear weapon, it would seem more effective to take steps to prevent the proliferation of nuclear materials and technology in the first place rather than continue the costly and impossible search for a perfect defense. As it is, the US military has yet to succeed in a full-system test of BMD.

The belief that more is better and certainty is achievable was one of the driving forces behind the Cold War. So were advances in weapons accuracy and survivability, as we have seen. A third force needs to be considered as well: the deep institutional stakes the United States and the Soviet Union had in maintaining the arms race, and the political uses to which nuclear weapons were put.

On the institutional side, each social system created its own variation of the military-industrial complex. In the United States,[95] this grouping of public and private institutions is tightly interlocked: government agencies, the military services, and industries depend on one another for weapons research, planning advice, manufacturing, testing, and sales; many congressional districts are economically and politically dependent on military bases; and roughly nine million people (including soldiers, veterans, Department of Defense employees, and employees of military-industrial contractors) depend on the military budget for their livelihoods. The process transforms national security into more commonplace matters: careers, jobs, profits, and therefore political back-scratching and manipulation. The Soviet/Russian system unites industrial and military leaders (and the Communist Party before 1992) in a similar common interest. Although "complex" may not quite suit a society in which military affairs always has a central place, it does convey the inordinate role of military industries, research, and "needs" in the Soviet economy. For example, military (including space) research and development (R&D) accounted for roughly one-half of all Soviet R&D; military industries employed nearly 13 percent of all industrial workers and accounted for almost one-third of total Soviet industrial production; and "10–12 million people, or 15 to 18 percent of the labor force outside the armed forces," depended on the military budget. The full costs of Soviet-era defense remain incalculable to this day, as they were beyond questioning or a belief in any need for precise measurement.[96]

Defense planning determined industrial development rather than the other way around. Far from being an isolated sector of the economy, the Soviet military-industrial complex was the economy's linchpin—a circumstance created and backed by the party and armed forces leaderships.[97] This explains why the "complex" was behind the attempted overthrow of Gorbachev in August 1991; why as late as 1991 Soviet military spending was a staggering 52 percent of GNP; and why under the Russian Federation's first president, Boris Yeltsin, it was one of the powerful centers of conservative resistance to reforms.[98]

This situation of reinforcing interests, operating largely outside the rules of the civilian economy, amounted to a separate, state-run command system in both countries.[99] It enabled both sides to commit a large portion of their GNP to the military (from 1960 to the early 1980s, an average of 6.5 percent by the United States and at least 10.9 percent by the Soviet Union).[100] Each government devoted the bulk of its research funds to military work (close to 70 percent in the United States). Each maintained huge military forces and numerous bases abroad during most of the 1980s: for the United States, about 2 million service personnel, of whom about 284,000 were at sea and 460,000 were stationed overseas in 360 major bases; and for the Soviet Union, about 3.6 million soldiers, of whom over 700,000 were stationed (or fighting) abroad in twenty-four countries.[101] And the superpowers controlled well over half the world market in arms exports.[102]

Command of such resources creates bureaucratic and economic power that is the essence of the national-security state. Secrecy is one measure of such power. The separate military economies contained top-secret, so-called black weapons programs within them. On the US side, some of these programs were so tightly guarded that even their existence was rarely acknowledged.[103] Another measure is the political and economic functions performed by military spending. Comparative research suggests that despite the great differences in the way US and Soviet politics operated, military spending was used for similar purposes in both countries.[104] It responded to the needs of a powerful interest group, the military and civilian professionals who worked on national-security matters. It could be used to affect overall economic performance and thus either to influence elections (in the United States) or intra-leadership disputes (in the USSR). And in either society military spending became a quick fix to promote employment and increase or decrease consumer demand. Arms exports, for example, accounted for over 5 percent of total US exports and over 10 percent of Soviet exports in the 1980s.[105] For the Soviets, in fact, nearly half of their arms exports were either given away or artificially priced, suggesting the paramount importance of keeping factories going rather than making money.[106] Add to this list the inevitable military service rivalries, which led each service to covet a strategic role and the budget to sustain it, and we have the key elements of a deep-seated structural bias in favor of more weapons.

In the United States, the high cost and profitability of weapons and military technology supplied added political and economic incentives for more arms. The latest-model Trident submarines cost over $1.5 billion each. The B-2 "Stealth" bombers had a price tag of about $800 million each. Every ground-launched cruise missile cost over $6 million.[107] Contracts for such expensive weapons were dominated by the major military firms, companies such as General Dynamics and Lockheed (the main Trident contractors), Boeing (cruise missiles), and Northrup (the B-2), that do the bulk of their business with the Pentagon, including conventional arms, electronic components, and overseas sales. Cost overruns, government research and lobbying subsidies, and tax benefits add to the profit margins of the weapons. And with hundreds of thousands of jobs at stake and with the economic lifeline of specific communities (such as Seattle, Washington) and entire states (such as California) tied to those jobs, it is no wonder that the major military industries have always been politically active at election time. They have had every incentive to pressure legislators—and, through political action committees, the money to do it—for more and better weapons regardless of the actual military need. The selling of Star Wars is a case in point.[108] And the costs are huge.[109]

"National security" is the inevitable rallying cry of any military-industrial complex. They are the worldwide code words for ensuring a lion's share of a national budget—and for undermining those who might challenge high spending for defense. Because the business of national security is, moreover, esoteric and secretive; because it is heavily influenced by leadership ideology; and because it contains so many imponderable, unpredictable factors that lead to worst-case planning, enough is never enough for defense. Besides, national leaders sometimes believe, as Reagan said in an interview in 1982, that they can spend their opponents into submission.[110] Such wisdom is music to the ears of military-industrialists; it means a virtual blank check for weapons research and production. To judge from the leaps in US and Soviet military spending of the 1980s—an eight-year, $2.6 trillion buildup under Reagan; annual Soviet military budgets of roughly 12 to 15 percent of total central government spending—a blank check comes close to describing what the military-industrial complex received. In terms of nuclear weapons alone, from the 1940s to the mid-1990s, and thus embracing the entire Cold War period and a bit more, private experts calculate that the United States spent between $5.5 trillion and $5.8 trillion—a sum that dwarfs nearly all other government spending combined except welfare.[111]

These institutional forces go far toward explaining the consistent surge forward of nuclear and overall military spending and deployment. Still, the explanation is incomplete. It is not as though a technological monster was unleashed and then was subject only to the availability of dollars and rubles. Just as political priorities determined military spending, they also determined how nuclear weapons were used.

True, nuclear weapons were built in hopes they would never be used in war. But US presidents several times threatened to use them against other states, mainly the Soviet Union and China. Apparently the first instance was in 1948, when President Truman ordered atomic-capable bombers moved to bases in Britain during the first Berlin crisis. A second instance occurred in the final stages of the Korean War. According to President Eisenhower's memoirs, the United States conveyed to China its preparedness to employ nuclear bombs against it if the armistice talks dragged on. Had China violated the armistice with a "massive ground offensive," he was prepared in 1954 to use nuclear weapons against it.[112] Eisenhower also had tactical nuclear weapons sent to Taiwan in 1958 during a crisis with the People's Republic of China (PRC) over the Taiwan Strait. President Kennedy ordered nuclear-armed B-52s to prepare for a strike against China in 1961 during the crisis over Laos. It is also well known that Kennedy considered using nuclear weapons against Moscow during the 1961 Berlin crisis and the missile crisis over Cuba in 1962. President Nixon revealed in a 1985 interview that he had considered using nuclear weapons four times during his tenure, including in the 1971 India-Pakistan conflict over Bangladesh's independence, when he believed both the Soviets and the Chinese were threatening to become directly involved, and again in 1973, when he concluded the Soviets were prepared to intervene on Egypt's side in the war with Israel. On at least one of the four occasions where he considered the use of nuclear weapons—the 1973 conflict in the Middle East, in which the Strategic Air Command's B-52s were placed on full alert for twenty-nine days—he let Soviet leaders know he would use those weapons.[113]

US leaders privately pondered the nuclear option in several other conflicts.[114] So far as we know, Soviet leaders never directly threatened the United States with nuclear attack, although there is some evidence they tried to win US approval of an attack on China's nuclear facilities in the early 1960s.[115] Atomic diplomacy has apparently been the peculiar mainstay of the United States. A policy of first-use of nuclear weapons was in force not only in case of a Soviet conventional attack in Europe but also (and still today) in the event of a North Korean invasion of South Korea. The belief persisted in high US circles that nuclear weapons had an "extraordinarily salutary effect" for both superpowers in helping restrain conflicts between them. But such "restraint" merely channeled conflict into other countries at a high level of violence.[116]

The political utility of nuclear weapons, which the three military serv-

how NS when puts under hereover
at poss. of total death?
128     *Global Politics in the Human Interest*

ices compete to control,[117] not only helps to account for their ongoing production (far beyond conceivable need), it also enables us to understand US resistance to arms reductions. We can clearly date this resistance to the onset of Cold War internationalism in 1946 when (as discussed in Chapter 2) a high-level government consensus evolved against nuclear arms talks while the United States had a monopoly of mass-destruction weapons. The US government was far from reaching an agreement with Moscow that might put the nuclear genie back in the bottle, as some scientists were urging. The prevailing view, epitomized by then Army Chief of Staff Dwight Eisenhower in a top-secret memorandum of January 1946, was that "if there are to be atomic weapons in the world, we must have the best, the biggest, and the most."[118]

The political effect of such advice, which Truman and all his successors accepted, was twofold. One was to present the Soviets with proposals for limiting nuclear arms or tests that they were certain to reject. Examples are the Baruch Plan of 1946 for internationalizing control of nuclear weapons, Eisenhower's proposals in 1955 for "open skies" and on-site inspection of nuclear facilities, and Reagan's proposals in the early 1980s for mutual cutbacks of launchers. Each of these offers would have been to the US advantage and, in the Soviets' eyes, would have frozen the Soviets into an inferior position. When the Soviets finally accepted strategic inferiority in the START negotiations, the context of Moscow's decisionmaking had totally changed. Gorbachev badly needed an agreement to demonstrate his (and Russia's) authority over nuclear weapons at a time when the USSR's future was in the balance.

The second political effect of the consensus on arms control was to reach agreement only with assurances to the military-industrial complex of support for the next generation of weapons. All of the Cold War arms control agreements, such as the Nuclear Test Ban of 1963, the Strategic Arms Limitation Talks (SALT) I in 1972, the Vladivostok agreement of 1974, the never-ratified SALT II in 1979, and the Intermediate Nuclear Forces (INF) Treaty of 1987, left large loopholes for budgeting increases in weapons research, production, and deployment; for building up to specified limits; and for continued testing and replacement of nuclear weapons.[119] The test ban, for instance, permitted underground explosions, of which there were over seven hundred by the superpowers. SALT I largely limited antimissile systems, ICBMs, and submarine-launched ballistic missiles (SLBMs). At Vladivostok the Soviet and US leaders (Ford and Brezhnev) put a cap on certain categories of strategic launchers and the number of them that could be fitted with multiple warheads (MIRV'd). The INF Treaty provided for dismantling nearly 1,300 missiles deployed in Europe and set a precedent for their destruction using on-site means of verification. But the treaty did not restrict long-range missiles or destroy or reduce the number of US or Soviet nuclear weapons in Europe. These loopholes represented the failure, born of bureaucratic pressures in both political systems, to bring about real arms control through bilateral force reductions. Developing new strategic weapons consistently had the highest priority.[120]

The Soviets acted on the basis of similar rules of national and bureaucratic self-interest; having had to catch up in nuclear technology accounts in part for their rejection of various US offers. But once they did catch up in second-strike (if not counterforce) capability, the argument of self-preservation was not so compelling. Some general Soviet arms-control proposals— such as for a mutual nuclear freeze on weapons testing, production, and deployment; for a US-Soviet pledge of no first-use of nuclear weapons; and for a unilateral moratorium on nuclear tests that would continue if the United States also declared one—were interesting and ought to have been pursued by US leaders. But Moscow undermined its case with a rapid, strategically unjustifiable buildup to over four hundred intermediate-range missiles aimed at Europe. It seems safe to assume that a weapons lobby dominated nuclear policymaking there as here and, therefore, arms control, not to mention arms reductions, would always be outpaced by weapons development. This circumstance, along with historic Soviet mistrust of the West (dating from allied intervention in Siberia at the time of the Russian Revolution) and the ideology and values of Soviet leaders before Gorbachev, accounts for the paranoid style of Soviet, as of US, nuclear policy.

In summary, the superpowers' nuclear-weapons race brought the world to a dangerous threshold in the 1980s. During that period, weapons of mind-boggling destructive power were produced, refined, and deployed in unprecedented numbers by the superpowers. Yet, in answer to the question raised in the beginning of this section, nuclear weapons were found to *"serve no military purpose whatsoever. They are totally useless—except only to deter one's opponent from using them."*[121] The new decade began on a more hopeful note with an easing of Cold War tensions, not only in Europe but in many parts of the Third World. US and Soviet national-security planners could no longer presume to have a blank check for defense. Suddenly the myths of Soviet economic growth and military superiority were exposed for the bureaucratic invention they largely were. By 1990, conventional wisdom among official US Kremlinologists had completely reversed itself: Communism had failed, the Soviet Union was (as one newspaper put it) a "Third World economy with First World weapons," a Soviet attack on Western Europe was no longer conceivable, and the Soviets' very survival would depend on aid from the West. Indeed, the Cold War, at least in Europe, was over: "We have closed the book on World War II," said Soviet foreign minister Eduard Shevardnadze on signing the agreement in September 1990 that formally ended the four-power occupation of Germany. Two months later, on November 20, President Bush proclaimed: "The Cold War is over."

But is it? In the following case study, and in the continuation of the arms-race story in Chapter 5, we find that Cold War thinking and practices have by no means changed with the times.

### Case Study 2:
### North Korea, Iran, and Weapons of Mass Destruction

If human and common security, adherence to international law, and respect for human rights are vibrant elements of a new world order, how can these be applied when dealing with dictatorial governments that repress their citizens and develop (or seem to be developing) weapons of mass destruction? The US government provided one kind of answer when it invaded Iraq and toppled the Saddam Hussein regime. Iraq was one of three governments—Iran and North Korea were the others—that President Bush had identified as an "axis of evil" in his January 2002 State of the Union message. But in contrast to the politics of confrontation there is the politics of engagement, an approach that puts the use of force and pressure last among options and instead emphasizes a search for common ground. If violence can be avoided and a dialogue can be initiated, this line of thinking runs, opportunities may arise to advance the well-being of people and the security of regions—opportunities that will surely be foreclosed by violence.

Iran and North Korea share three characteristics that are relevant to their dispute with the United States in the early 2000s: a history of tension-filled relations, nationalism informed partly by that history and partly by identity, and insecurity. Both countries have had violent confrontations with the United States: Iran, as the result of a CIA-engineered coup in 1953 and Washington's attempt to prevent the 1978 revolution, which brought on the hostage crisis; North Korea, because of the 1950–1953 Korean War and numerous confrontations in and around the Korean peninsula since then. North Korean and Iranian nationalism flows from fierce pride, which comes not just from being able to withstand foreign pressure, but also from developing economically without reliance on the US-dominated world economy. Insecurity in both cases stems, obviously, from what is perceived to be the threat of US attack or encirclement—from Japan and South Korea in North Korea's case, from Israel in Iran's. The US invasion of Iraq intensified that sense of threat, and the incentive to acquire a nuclear deterrent. North Korea and Iran both benefited from the secret international nuclear technology network established by A. Q. Khan in Pakistan, a major US ally.[122]

North Korean and Iranian thinking converges in a shared presumption of the "right" to produce nuclear power—and, presumably, nuclear weapons. After its nuclear-weapon test of October 2006, North Korea is widely believed to possess anywhere from six to ten warheads, with the capability to develop many more. If Iran proceeds with its uranium enrichment program, which it successfully hid from view for many years, most estimates are that it probably could produce a nuclear bomb in several years. (Both countries also have missiles capable of delivering a nuclear weapon to a target at least several hundred miles away.) The right to nuclear energy is sacred to both leaderships: It connotes independence, security, and status. It also is legal to enrich uranium for energy purposes under the NPT. What it will take for either country to give up that right is at the heart of the dispute with the United States and other countries.[123]

The common-security path to a solution of the twin nuclear disputes supports direct dialogue between the principals. The opportunity is there: North Korean officials have repeatedly said that if the US threat ceases and normal relations are established, their country will give up its nuclear weapons.[124] Yet a senior US official twice turned down an invitation from the North Koreans in mid-2006 to visit Pyongyang for direct talks. Around that same time, the Iranian foreign minister said, "We won't negotiate about the Iranian nation's natural nuclear rights, but we are prepared, within a defined, just framework and without any discrimination, to hold dialogue about common concerns" with the United States.[125] But when Iran's president, Mahmoud Ahmadinejad, wrote directly to President Bush, in criticism of US policies but also in search of a spiritual dialogue, he did not get a response.[126] Nor did his predecessor, Mohammed Khatami, who was ignored when he visited Washington in 2006. Iran and North Korea commonly see the United States as central to any deal, even as both countries must also negotiate in multilateral settings—with the EU, Russia, China, and the IAEA in Iran's case, and within the Six Party Talks (the United States, China, Japan, Russia, and the two Koreas) in North Korea's case. The sticking point has long been the insistence of the Bush administration on avoiding direct, one-on-one talks such as the Clinton administration conducted with the North Koreans in the late 1990s. Even though US representatives have met with North Korean officials on a few occasions, the Bush administration has generally eschewed direct dialogue to resolve the nuclear impasse. The US view is that any agreement with either Pyongyang or Tehran must be within a multilateral framework—probably *not* because of US faith in multilateralism, but because of a strategic sense that if agreement cannot be reached with all the concerned parties, they will be prepared to vote with the United States to impose sanctions (as they did following the North Korean nuclear test and when Iran continued its uranium enrichment) or, at the extreme, stand aside as the United States uses force.

The other stumbling block to breaking the impasse, again the same for Iran and North Korea, is the sequence of steps that must be taken to implement an agreement. In the North Korean case, such an agreement has twice been negotiated: In September 2005 and again in February 2007 at the Six Party Talks, all sides promised a step-by-step process under which North Korea would return to the NPT and give up its nuclear-weapons program in exchange for security assurances, normalization of relations, and help with meeting its energy needs.[127] Immediately after the 2005 agreement, however, the United States insisted (as it did with Iran) that the nuclear-weapon program must cease first; any economic, political, or security incentives, including access to nuclear energy, may only come after the cessation is affirmed by international inspectors. That position is unacceptable to the North Koreans and the Iranians, since to them it means unilateral disarmament without certainty of compensation. Moreover, from North Korea's viewpoint, the United States failed to carry out its commitments under their previous "framework agreement" in 1994, which promised the North two new nuclear-power plants in exchange for a freeze on its nuclear facilities. Now, only IAEA inspections can give Iran and the Democratic People's Republic of Korea (DPRK) a clean bill of health; and previous IAEA experience with them gives little ground for confidence in the reliability of their promises.[128] It remains to be seen whether the 2007 agreement breaks the dangerous impasse that has come about.

The longer these disputes go on, the higher the risks. North Korea may expand its arsenal of weapons and share weapon technology with others. Iran will probably continue to seek the means of enriching uranium for weapons-making purposes. The secrecy of these programs will lend themselves to worst-case hypothesizing about their extensiveness and intentions. Governments in neighboring countries, notably Japan and South Korea on one end, Israel on the other, will be under pressure to respond, intensifying the dispute. (Israel has a substantial nuclear arsenal, and Japan and South Korea surely have the technical capability to quickly develop nuclear weapons.) The United States may try to keep the lid on new tensions among its allies; but it may also have to deal with internal pressure to take military action against North Korea or Iran, in the latter case in coordination with Israel.[129] As US leaders, including President Bush and Secretary of State Condoleezza Rice, said a number of times regarding Iran, although the United States prefers a diplomatic solution, all options are on the table.[130] The sanctions on North Korea voted at the UN in 2006 specifically exclude the use of force; in reluctantly voting for them, China and Russia urged continued negotiations and rejected interdiction of North Korean ships.[131] Should sanctions or multilateral diplomacy fail to yield a solution, the next step up is unilateral US pressure. Much depends on the fighting in Iraq and Afghanistan, which limits US options. But military action cannot be ruled out under a US leadership that is on a global crusade.[132]

There are important differences between the Iran and North Korea situations, aside from the obvious one that North Korea already possesses nuclear weapons and Iran does not. Iran has oil, a great deal of it, and thus has the ability to impact the global energy crunch if sanctions are imposed on it. North Korea is one of the world's poorest countries; since the famine of the mid-1990s, it has relied extensively on international agencies, NGOs, and bilateral assistance to meet its food needs—about $2 billion worth. Another difference has to do with the political space and opportunities for reform. In North Korea such space is extremely limited; yet in recent years the regime, following on visits to China by Kim Jong Il and his entourage, has been experimenting with markets, consumerism, and a South Korean investment zone. In search of hard currency during desperate economic times, Kim has evidently authorized all manner of illegal production, such as counterfeit US dollars and cigarettes, drugs, and money laundering. US policy has focused exclusively on sanctioning and interdicting these activities rather than looked for ways to promote economic reforms of the kind the Chinese have undertaken.[133] The large NGO presence in North Korea to deliver food and undertake other humanitarian projects could be much better utilized in support of North Korea's human security. Difficult though the delivery of aid to the DPRK is, it may still be the best basis (because it's non-threatening) on which to begin constructive international dialogue and put the North on a more productive development path.[134]

Reform opportunities are far greater in Iran, but here again, external pressure produces responses that undermine reform prospects. When the US president expresses hopes for regime change in Iran and (as he did in Iraq) authorizes financing of antigovernment groups,[135] he undercuts reformists and actually strengthens support of the regime. As one longtime European resident in Tehran wrote, Bush's "axis of evil" speech, and the invasion of Iraq,

> convinced Iran's clerical leaders that Bush was determined to try and topple the Islamic Republic. One of the ways they reacted was by intensifying their assault on liberalizing, reformist Iranians. The hard-line establishment depicted all democracy seekers as traitors; they were discredited, tortured, or jailed. Iran's pro-democracy movement could not survive in the atmosphere of protracted crisis that Bush helped create.[136]

Most striking are the similarities between Iran and Iraq before the US invasion.[137] US intelligence contains many informational loopholes. Thus, suspicion rather than hard evidence guides official US thinking. Like Iraq, Iran's intentions are worrisome, but they present no imminent danger to its neighbors. The diplomatic path to a resolution remains open, and some EU governments, as well as the IAEA, still see hope in it; but the United States, wedded to unilateralist power politics, seems to be holding out for tougher measures.[138] Except among military leaders, Washington's supreme confidence in its ability to orchestrate power is undiminished by the Iraq experience. Thus, as in the leadup to war with Iraq, Iran (and perhaps North Korea too) presents the possibility of a calamitous military adventure based on politically driven intelligence findings[139] and without clear appreciation of the consequences.

The common-security approach to dealing with North Korea and Iran was best articulated by a former US defense secretary, William Perry, who would subsequently write a book on the subject. Upon returning from a visit to North Korea on behalf of the Clinton administration in 1999, Perry said:

"We have to deal with the North Korean government not as we wish they would be, but as in fact they are." Perry urged that Americans take seriously the "very clear logic" of the North Koreans in having missiles for defense.[140] This was not an argument for learning to live with North Korean (or Iranian) missiles and nuclear weapons. Rather, it was an argument for creative diplomacy that provides incentives to move one's opponents onto a non-threatening path. As mentioned, international assistance to North Korea has saved its people from further calamity. The South Korean government believes (contrary to its US ally) that engaging the North is the only sensible policy, and has a $1 billion annual trade with the DPRK. Some kind of package deal that combines security assurances with economic aid and incentives is the only way out of the deadlocks with North Korea and Iran. But the US government may only be satisfied with strategies that result in regime change.

## Notes

1. William P. Bundy, "Elements of Power," *Foreign Affairs,* p. 26.
2. ul Haq, p. 417.
3. Brandt et al., pp. 8–11.
4. Roy Preiswerk, "Could We Study International Relations as If People Mattered?" in Falk, Kim, and Mendlovitz, pp. 175–97.
5. Sakamoto, "The Global Crisis and Peace Research," *International Peace Research Newsletter,* pp. 4–7.
6. On these values, see the introduction to Falk, Kim, and Mendlovitz, pp. 1–9. For the application of these values to Latin American political development, see Gustavo Lagos, "The Revolution of Being: A Preferred World Model," in Heraldo Muñoz, ed., *From Dependency to Development: Strategies to Overcome Underdevelopment and Inequality,* pp. 123–60.
7. Richard Falk, "World Order Values: Secular Means and Spiritual Ends."
8. These documents have been collected in US Department of State, Bureau of Public Affairs, Selected Documents no. 5, *Human Rights.* On the record of ratification by governments, see Kim, *The Quest for a Just World Order,* table 6.4, p. 232.
9. Rushworth M. Kidder, "Universal Human Values: Finding an Ethical Common Ground," *The Futurist,* pp. 8–13.
10. See Gerald Mische and Patricia Mische, *Toward a Human World Order: Beyond the National Security Straitjacket,* pp. 21–22 and 30–33, on the Tasadays in the Philippines and the Iks in Uganda. Also relevant are the Bushmen of southern Africa. See, for example, Laurens van der Post, *The Lost World of the Kalahari.*
11. Carl Rogers (*On Personal Power,* ch. 7) offers many insights from person-centered therapy that he has pioneered concerning communication among racially, economically, and politically different persons and groups. He refers, for instance, to the importance of perceiving others as humans, not symbols; of the unconditional acceptance of others' feelings; of listening closely as others express deep-seated rage. "It is being human which dissolves the barriers and brings closeness," he concludes.
12. Richard A. Falk, "Contending Approaches to World Order," in Falk, Kim, and Mendlovitz, p. 154.
13. Falk, "On Invisible Oppression and World Order," in Falk, Kim, and Mendlovitz, p. 44.

14. *The Oregonian,* February 20, 1988.

15. Edward W. Said, *Orientalism,* pp. 44–45.

16. As Elise Boulding has put it, there is a "new internationalism [that] not only incorporates the cultural, economic, and political diversity of that part of the Third World geographically located in the South, it also incorporates and gives a new visibility to the diversity of the Third World internal to countries of the North." She argues that this respect for diversity and openness to differing (non-European) values and solutions can especially be seen in the international women's movement, as well as in the peace and environmental movements. Boulding, "The Old and New Transnationalism," pp. 799–800.

17. UNDP, *Human Development Report 2000,* p. 17.

18. As examples of their work, see Sen, *Choice, Welfare, and Measurement,* and Nussbaum, *Women and Human Development: The Capabilities Approach.*

19. Martha Nussbaum, "Capabilities and Social Justice," *International Studies Review,* p. 130.

20. Commission on Human Security, *Human Security Now.*

21. See Ashton B. Carter, William J. Perry, and John D. Steinbruner, *A New Concept of Cooperative Security.*

22. Herbert C. Kelman, "The Interactive Problem-Solving Approach," in Crocker and Hampson, eds., *Managing Global Chaos,* p. 505.

23. Fouad Ajami, "Human Rights and World Order Politics," working paper no. 4. Also see Hazel Henderson's discussion of "flat-earth economics," which she contends is common to modern-day capitalist and socialist thought, in *The Politics of the Solar Age: Alternatives to Economics,* pp. 22–26.

24. Richard J. Barnet, *The Lean Years: Politics in the Age of Scarcity,* p. 299.

25. See Johan Galtung, "A Structural Theory of Imperialism," *Journal of Peace Research,* pp. 81–117.

26. The pastoral letter of the National Conference of Catholic Bishops appears in "The Challenge of Peace: God's Promise and Our Response," *Origins,* p. 322.

27. "The Post-Communist Nightmare," *New York Review of Books,* May 27, 1993, pp. 8–10.

28. Preiswerk, in Falk, Kim, and Mendlovitz, p. 179.

29. Liam O'Sullivan, "The Moderns: Herbert Marcuse and Hannah Arendt— 'Critics of the Present,'" in Brian Redhead, ed., *Plato to Nato: Studies in Political Thought,* p. 184.

30. Paolo Friere, *Pedagogy of the Oppressed,* trans. Myra Bergman Ramos, p. 74.

31. Michael J. Sullivan III, *Measuring Global Values: The Ranking of 162 Countries.*

32. Amartya Sen, "Human Rights and Asian Values," *The New Republic.*

33. Ajami, "Human Rights and World Order Politics," pp. 1–8.

34. Xiaorong Li, "'Asian Values' and the Universality of Human Rights," *Report from the Institute for Philosophy & Public Policy,* p. 20.

35. Ajami, "Human Rights and World Order Politics," pp. 28–29.

36. Richard A. Falk, "Comparative Protection of Human Rights in Capitalist and Socialist Third World Countries," in Falk, Kim, and Mendlovitz, pp. 424–25.

37. For example, see Kim, *The Quest for a Just World Order,* pp. 102–16.

38. Hedges, *War Is a Force That Gives Us Meaning.*

39. Schell, "Why War Is Futile," *Harper's,* March 2003, pp. 33–46.

40. Arthur H. Westing and E.W. Pfeiffer, "The Cratering of Indochina," *Scientific American,* pp. 21–29.

41. About 99 percent of all high-level radioactive waste in the United States comes from military reactors. At one time, the Department of Defense was produc-

ing roughly 400,000 tons a year of nuclear waste. See Joel S. Hirschhorn, "Toxic Waste," *Los Angeles Times,* October 10, 1983, sec. 2, p. 5; David E. Kaplan and Ida Landauer, "Radioactivity for the Oceans," *The Nation;* and "Military Nuclear Wastes: The Hidden Burden of the Nuclear Arms Race," *The Defense Monitor* 10, no. 1 (1981), pp. 1–8. It will take an estimated $3.4 billion to clean up fifty years of nuclear-weapons production in the United States. See Stephen Schwartz of the Brookings Institution, "The Hidden Costs of Our Nuclear Arsenal," June 30, 1998, online at www.brook.edu.

42. An example is Pam Woodall, "The New Titans," *The Economist,* pp. 3–34. This upbeat analysis of Third World economies is pitched at the level of national economies, using gross average measurements that slide by inequalities within and between countries. Even then, the emergence of China and India distorts the numbers for underdeveloped countries—all of which, by the way, are re-labeled "emerging countries." As for workers everywhere, they are "a big challenge to orthodox economies."

43. This is the argument of Ashis Nandy, "The Beautiful, Expanding Future of Poverty: Popular Economics as a Psychological Defense," *International Studies Review,* pp. 107–21.

44. Robert Theobald, *Turning the Century: Personal and Organizational Strategies for Your Changed World,* p. 224.

45. *UN Human Development Report 2000,* p. 21. This report's narrative section is entirely devoted to elaborating on the connections between human development and human rights.

46. See Stephen Viederman, "Sustainable Development: What Is It and How Do We Get There?" *Current History,* pp. 180–85.

47. For an early identification of this problem, see Osvaldo Sunkel, "Development Styles and the Environment: An Interpretation of the Latin American Case," in Muñoz, pp. 93–114.

48. On pesticide dumping see David Weir and Mark Schapiro, *Circle of Poison: Pesticides and People in a Hungry World.* The *Multinational Monitor* reports an estimate of Oxfam International that "375,000 pesticide poisonings, 6,700 of which are fatal, occur each year in the Third World" (in Robert Engler, "Technology Out of Control," *The Nation,* p. 489).

49. Toxic chemical accidents are on the rise worldwide. Several countries support the notion of prior informed consent when hazardous substances are being imported; but in India and elsewhere, business talks, such that regulations afford very little protection for communities even if governments are informed. Madhusree Mukerjee, "Toxins Abounding," *Scientific American.*

50. *NYT,* December 3, 1997, p. 1; Duane Bratt, "Candu or Candon't: Competing Values Behind Canada's Nuclear Sales," *The Nonproliferation Review* (Spring–Summer 1998), available at www.energyprobe.org/energyprobe/reports/bratt53.pdf.

51. North Korea and Vietnam, for example, have become repositories of German waste, the Philippines of Japan's, and China of Taiwan's. Taiwan's nuclear industry attempted to send low-level waste to North Korea in 1997, but the deal was discovered, protested by the South Korean government and Taiwan citizens, and canceled. Discarded computers and other electronic devices are increasingly being sent to China and other developing countries; see John Markoff, "Technology's Toxic Trash Is Sent to Poor Nations," *NYT,* February 25, 2002, p. C1.

52. This is the provocative question posed by a distinguished Mexican writer, Gustavo Esteva, in "Regenerating People's Space," *Alternatives,* pp. 125–52.

53. Irene L. Gendzier, *Managing Political Change: Social Scientists and the*

*Third World.* The role of the major US foundations in transmitting values and institutions to the Third World is well documented in Robert F. Arnove, *Philanthropy and Cultural Imperialism: The Foundations at Home and Abroad,* especially the essay by Edward H. Berman, "Educational Colonialism in Africa: The Role of American Foundations, 1910–1945," pp. 179–202.

54. Currency is in 1987 dollars. Sivard, *World Military and Social Expenditures 1991,* p. 11; Sivard, *World Military and Social Expenditures 1983,* p. 6. The Center for Defense Information in Washington, DC, estimates that total US military spending during the Cold War, in 1996 dollars, was $13.1 trillion. Online at www.cdi.org.

55. Quoted by Inga Thorsson, "Study on Disarmament and Development," *Bulletin of the Atomic Scientists,* p. 41.

56. Sivard, *World Military and Social Expenditures 1989,* p. 15; Natural Resources Defense Council (NRDC), Table of Global Nuclear Weapons Stockpiles, 1945–2002, at www.nrdc.org/nuclear/nudb/datab19.asp.

57. Carnegie Endowment for International Peace, Table of Worldwide Nuclear Weapons Stockpiles, at www.carnegieendowment.org/npp/numbers/default.cfm.

58. For example, the mid-1990s stockpile was "727 times the 11 megatons [millions of tons] of explosive power used in this century's three major wars which killed 44,000,000 people." Sivard et al., *World Military and Social Expenditures 1996,* p. 20. The combined destructive power of the nuclear weapons in Table 3.1 of this chapter is about 5,000 megatons.

59. Quoted in Milton Leitenberg, "The Numbers Game or 'Who's on First?'" *Bulletin of the Atomic Scientists,* p. 27.

60. Quoted in P. Edward Haley, David M. Keithly, and Jack Merritt, eds., *Nuclear Strategy, Arms Control, and the Future,* p. 166.

61. Two studies offer excellent case histories of how political priorities, values, and assumptions determined the development of nuclear technology: Greg Herken's *The Winning Weapon: The Atomic Bomb in the Cold War, 1945–1950;* and Jonathan B. Stein's *From H-Bomb to Star Wars: The Politics of Strategic Decision Making.*

62. Jonathan Schell, *The Fate of the Earth,* pp. 189–93.

63. Eric Chivian et al., eds., *Last Aid: The Medical Dimensions of Nuclear War,* p. 304.

64. "Nuclear Bomb Factories: The Danger Within," *The Defense Monitor* 18, no. 4 (1989), pp. 1–8; and "Defending the Environment," *The Defense Monitor* 18, no. 6 (1989), pp. 1–8.

65. *New York Times,* March 23, 1998, p. A10. Of 177 underground storage tanks at Hanford, 149 are single-shell steel. Sixty-eight of those have leaked, and the rest are expected eventually to leak. Most recently the US Department of Energy decided on vitrification, a process to immobilize the waste. But an independent government audit found that the process had a 50 percent chance of a major accident. Matthew L. Wald, "High Accident Risk Is Seen in Atomic Waste Project," *NYT,* July 27, 2004, p. A13.

66. William J. Broad, "Nuclear Roulette for Russia: Burying Uncontained Waste," *NYT,* November 21, 1994, p. 1. The words quoted were by Henry W. Kendall, a Nobel laureate at the Massachusetts Institute of Technology.

67. "Nuclear Bomb Factories: The Danger Within," *The Defense Monitor* 18, no. 4 (1989), p. 3; Dick Russell, "In the Shadow of the Bomb," pp. 20–21. The US government, in its search for a safe, final repository for high-level radioactive waste, finally settled on an area near Carlsbad, New Mexico, in 1998. The site will have to be capable of holding the waste safely for 10,000 years, which may be insufficient time in any case. (The half-life of plutonium is 24,000 years.)

68. Matthew L. Wald, "Report Faults Energy Dept. on Managing Nuclear Site," *NYT,* October 24, 1997, p. A10, concerning the findings of an independent group, hired by the US Department of Energy, at a nuclear plant in Ohio.

69. See *NYT,* June 19, 1995, p. A8 and January 15, 1997, p. A11, and Matthew L. Wald, "U.S. Settles on Plan to Recycle Plutonium," *NYT,* January 23, 2002, p. A15. The idea is to prevent reconversion of the plutonium for use in weapons, but concerns also include environmental and safety hazards, and the precedent of commercializing weapons-grade plutonium.

70. Quoted in Haley, Keithly, and Merritt, pp. 79–80.

71. Kissinger was right, but five years later he recanted this statement. See Richard K. Betts, *Nuclear Blackmail and Nuclear Balance,* p. 212.

72. *Los Angeles Times,* August 25, 1983, p. 4.

73. Dick Cheney, the secretary of defense under the first President Bush, reportedly recognized the absurd targeting formula and reduced the number of targets to 10,000 by 1989. General George Lee Butler, head of US strategic forces in the early 1990s, reduced them further to 2,500 (Steve Coll and David Ottaway, "Trying to Unplug the War Machine," *Washington Post,* April 12, 1995). But the notion of 2,500 nuclear targets defies the imagination just as much as does 25,000.

74. The Soviets were always playing catch-up, because most of the technological breakthroughs in weapons design (from the intercontinental bomber and the submarine-launched missiles to the multiple-warhead and the cruise missiles) were US-made. See "U.S.-Soviet Military Facts," *The Defense Monitor* 13, no. 6 (1984), p. 1; and R. Jeffrey Smith, "Soviets Drop Farther Back in Weapons Technology," *Science,* pp. 1300–1. This US research lead extends to areas critical to space-based systems. See "Star Wars: Vision and Reality," *The Defense Monitor* 15, no. 2 (1986), p. 7.

75. General George Lee Butler, in Jonathan Schell, "The Gift of Time," *The Nation,* p. 55. Butler also said: "I will tell you that in the Cuban missile crisis, the fact that we didn't go to war had nothing to do with deterrence. Talk to [Robert S.] McNamara and others." Schell did, and McNamara agreed with Butler; see Schell, "The Gift of Time," p. 26.

76. For evidence of past Soviet belief in nuclear victory, see the selections in Haley, Keithly, and Merritt, pp. 138–57. On the US side, see the quotations in Robert Scheer, *With Enough Shovels: Reagan, Bush and Nuclear War,* for example, pp. 253, 261–62; *Los Angeles Times,* August 15, 1982, p. 1 (on the Pentagon's secret nuclear-war plans); and "Preparing for Nuclear War: President Reagan's Program," *The Defense Monitor* 10, no. 8 (1982), p. 2.

77. Brezhnev's 1981 statement is in Haley, Keithly, and Merritt, p. 168.

78. Desmond Ball of the Australian National University offered perhaps the most decisive rebuttal of the logic of limited nuclear war. He emphasized the context in which *any* use of nuclear weapons might occur. Instead of a "relatively smooth and controlled progression from limited and selective strikes" to larger attacks and counterattacks, Ball observed the numerous difficulties a political leadership would have in maintaining control. Perfect rationality is hard to imagine when communication and command facilities have been disrupted or destroyed (and these are priority targets in a counterforce strategy, it will be recalled); when decision processes have become chaotic; and when popular feelings of confusion and hatred have run rampant. Indeed, as four former senior US policymakers contended, "there is no way for anyone to have any confidence that [a small-scale] nuclear action will not lead to further and more devastating exchanges." Desmond Ball, "Can Nuclear War Be Controlled?" in Haley, Keithly, and Merritt, pp. 107–13; Bundy et al., "Nuclear Weapons and the Atlantic Alliance," p. 757.

79. *Los Angeles Times,* April 8, 1982, p. 13.

80. Dean Babst, Robert Aldridge, and David Krieger, *Accidental Nuclear War Dangers of the "Star Wars" Proposal,* p. 3.

81. Robert C. Aldridge, "Fear Over U.S. 'War' Computers," *San Francisco Chronicle,* June 14, 1980, p. 34. President Carter was also nearly faced with the need for an instantaneous response to a false report. He, too, was not awakened by aides. See *The Washington Spectator,* September 1996, citing a new book by the then CIA director, Robert Gates, *From the Shadows.*

82. The Pentagon's list of "Broken Arrows" was first published by Stephen Talbot, "The H-Bombs Next Door," *The Nation,* p. 145.

83. Carnegie Endowment, "Nuclear Numbers," at www.carnegieendowment. org/npp/numbers/default.cfm.

84. Seymour M. Hersh, *The Samson Option: Israel's Nuclear Arsenal and American Foreign Policy.*

85. Ibid., pp. 263–68.

86. Hersh, "On the Nuclear Edge," *The New Yorker,* pp. 56–69; US State Department report cited in *The Oregonian,* March 18, 1992, p. A4.

87. Amory Lovins et al., "Nuclear Power and Nuclear Bombs," *Foreign Affairs,* Summer 1980 (their emphasis).

88. Walter C. Patterson, *The Plutonium Business and the Spread of the Bomb,* pp. 156–57.

89. Samuel S. Kim, *The Quest for a Just World Order,* p. 123.

90. These were krytrons, which are used in making nuclear triggers. See Charles William Maynes, "When Israel Jumped the Nuclear Firebreak," *Los Angeles Times,* June 9, 1985, sec. 4, p. 2, and Harold Freeman, "Pakistan: Joining the Nuke Club," *Los Angeles Times,* December 1, 1985, sec. 4, p. 2. Another case involving illegal nuclear technology exports to Pakistan broke in July 1987 and caused a rift in US-Pakistani relations.

91. Samuel S. Kim, *The Quest for a Just World Order,* pp. 126–27; and Gurtov and Maghroori, *Roots of Failure: United States Foreign Policy in the Third World,* pp. 42–44. The Reagan administration's support of nuclear sales was concisely summarized by a senior State Department official: "To achieve our nonproliferation goals, we must also maintain a position as a leading and reliable nuclear exporter" (US Department of State, Bureau of Public Affairs, *Current Policy,* no. 434, November 17, 1982, p. 2). Such support, for example to the Philippines under Marcos, included substantial loans to Third World countries to finance nuclear-plant construction—for instance, $5.8 billion from the US Export-Import Bank as of 1982 (*Los Angeles Times,* April 5, 1982, sec. 4, p. 1).

92. William Walker and Mans Lönnroth, "Proliferation and Nuclear Trade: A Look Ahead," *Bulletin of the Atomic Scientists,* pp. 29–33; Gerard C. Smith and Helena Cobban, "A Blind Eye to Nuclear Proliferation," *Foreign Affairs.*

93. Fred Charles Iklé, "Nuclear Strategy: Can There Be a Happy Ending?" *Foreign Affairs,* p. 824.

94. For evaluations of Star Wars, see William E. Burrows, "Ballistic Missile Defense: The Illusion of Security," *Foreign Affairs;* "Star Wars: Vision and Reality," *The Defense Monitor* 15, no. 2 (1986), pp. 1–8; Gary L. Guertner, "What Is Proof?" *Foreign Policy,* pp. 73–84; Babst, Aldridge, and Krieger, p. 3; *NYT,* March 7, 1985, p. 1; and *Los Angeles Times,* September 22, 1985, p. 1. Illustrative of the pro–Star Wars position is Keith B. Payne and Colin S. Gray, "Nuclear Policy and the Defensive Transition," *Foreign Affairs.*

95. The best source is Gordon Adams, *The Iron Triangle: The Politics of Defense Contracting.* See also Gurtov and Maghroori, pp. 35–36.

96. Clifford G. Gaddy, *The Price of the Past: Russia's Struggle with the Legacy of a Militarized Economy,* pp. 2–3, 24.

97. Michael Renner, "Swords into Plowshares: Converting to a Peace Economy," pp. 13, 30; and *International Herald Tribune,* June 3, 1992, p. 2.

98. See Carey Goldberg and John Broder, "Putting Ax to Soviet Military," *Los Angeles Times,* September 10, 1991, p. A1, on the complex's role in the coup; and, on Soviet military spending, see Alexander Konovalov, "Specific Aspects of the Conversion Problem in the Evolving Russia," in A. Brunn et al., eds., *Conversion: Opportunities for Development and Environment,* p. 176.

99. The point of Soviet and US similarities is made in a special supplement to the *Los Angeles Times,* "Servants or Masters? Revisiting the Military-Industrial Complex," July 10, 1983, p. 4.

100. Sivard, *World Military and Social Expenditures 1983,* p. 7. "At least" because by now experts agree that Soviet military spending averaged around 25 to 30 percent of GNP in the 1980s. Alexander Konovalov, in Brunn et al., pp. 176–77; Milton Leitenberg, "Soviet Resources in the Defense Sector and Their Availability for Economic Recovery," in Brunn et al., pp. 326–27.

101. Sivard, *World Military and Social Expenditures 1983,* p. 9.

102. The combined US-USSR share of arms exports was about 74 percent in 1963, 67.5 percent in 1979, and 54.6 percent on average between 1980 and 1984 (US Arms Control and Disarmament Agency, *World Military Expenditures and Arms Transfers 1985,* p. 20).

103. See *Los Angeles Times,* April 10, 1985, p. 1, which further reported that research and development in the United States for classified military programs accounted for about 20 percent of total Department of Defense spending.

104. Thomas R. Cusack and Michael Don Ward, "Military Spending in the United States, the Soviet Union, and the People's Republic of China," *Journal of Conflict Resolution,* pp. 435–38.

105. US Arms Control and Disarmament Agency (ACDA), *World Military Expenditures,* p. 15.

106. Gaddy, *The Price of the Past,* p. 91.

107. The costs of major strategic weapons are given in "More Bang, More Bucks: $450 Billion for Nuclear War," *The Defense Monitor* 12, no. 7 (1983), p. 9.

108. Like many other weapon systems, Star Wars involved the recruitment by military industry of former Department of Defense officials to advise, direct, and sell its programs; the lobbying of members of Congress and foreign governments to support SDI as a source of jobs and research funds; and the awarding of SDI contracts overwhelmingly to "states or districts whose Congressional representatives sit on committees with the most power over weapons acquisition and funding." See William Hartung and Rosy Nimroody, "Cutting Up the Star Wars Pie," *The Nation,* p. 201. See also *Washington Post,* October 20 and 21, 1985.

109. By 1992, SDI had cost $29 billion, of which $7.7 billion was wasted on projects begun and later dropped. Robert Burns, "Billions Gone Down Rathole of 'Star Wars,'" *The Oregonian,* May 25, 1992.

110. *Los Angeles Times,* January 21, 1982. Ballistic-missile defense still cost $4 billion in 1998.

111. The figure covers 1940–1996; see Stephen Schwartz, "The Hidden Costs of Our Nuclear Arsenal" (presentation at the Brookings Institution, Washington DC, June 30, 1998, online at www.brookings.edu), which is an introduction to his book, *Atomic Audit.* A lower figure of $3.9 trillion, covering 1945–1995, was produced in a study by the US Nuclear Weapons Cost Study Project (see *NYT,* July 13, 1995, p. C18). Both studies counted a much fuller range of costs than the Department of

Defense counts, including nuclear-weapons research, development, production, communications and control, environmental cleanup, and testing. In all, the United States built about 70,000 nuclear weapons from 1945 on.

112. *Washington Times,* December 13, 1994.

113. Sources on US "atomic diplomacy" include Herken, pp. 259–62; Daniel Ellsberg, "Introduction: Call to Mutiny," in E.P. Thompson and Dan Smith, eds., *Protest and Survive,* pp. v–vii; Gurtov and Maghroori, p. 39; *Time,* July 29, 1985, pp. 52–53; and Hersh, *The Price of Power,* p. 124.

114. President Truman, for example, twice privately considered using the bomb against the USSR and China in 1952, during the Korean conflict (*Riverside Press-Enterprise,* August 30, 1980). Kennedy and Johnson both weighed the idea of a joint US-Soviet strike against Chinese nuclear facilities (Gaddis, *Strategies of Containment,* p. 210; James Fetzer, "Clinging to Containment: China Policy," in Thomas G. Paterson, ed., *Kennedy's Quest for Victory: American Foreign Policy, 1961–1963,* p. 178). Nixon and Kissinger in 1969 ordered studies on using tactical nuclear weapons in Vietnam, according to Hersh, *The Price of Power,* pp. 120–29. For other instances, see Betts; Ellsberg, in Thompson and Smith, pp. v–vii; and Walter Pincus, "U.S. Repeatedly Considered Use of N-Bombs," *The Oregonian,* July 29, 1985, p. 2.

115. Betts, pp. 79–81.

116. Zbigniew Brzezinski, "How the Cold War Was Played," *Foreign Affairs,* p. 204. Brzezinski was President Carter's special assistant for national security affairs.

117. See Pincus, p. 2, on service competition.

118. The memorandum is quoted in Pincus, p. 2.

119. See Robert C. Johansen, *The National Interest and the Human Interest,* pp. 38–56; "SALT II: One Small Step for Mankind," *The Defense Monitor* 8, no. 5 (1979), pp. 7–8; "After the INF Treaty: U.S. Nuclear Buildup in Europe," *The Defense Monitor* 17, no. 2 (1988), pp. 1–8; Sivard, *World Military and Social Expenditures 1989,* p. 14.

120. See Milton Leitenberg, "United States–Soviet Strategic Arms Control: The Decade of Detente, 1970–1980, and a Look Ahead," *Arms Control,* pp. 213–64.

121. McNamara, "The Military Role of Nuclear Weapons: Perceptions and Misperceptions," *Foreign Affairs,* p. 79 (emphasis in original).

122. The president of Pakistan, Pervez Musharraf, revealed the link to North Korea in a memoir; see *NYT,* September 26, 2006, p. A10.

123. For excellent overviews see, on North Korea, Selig S. Harrison, *Korean Endgame: A Strategy for Reunification and U.S. Disengagement,* and on Iran, James A. Bill, *The Eagle and the Lion: The Tragedy of American-Iranian Relations.*

124. See, for instance, Burt Herman, "North Korea Says U.S. Threats Only Reason for Nuclear Weapons," *The Oregonian,* July 12, 2005.

125. In Michael Slackman, "Iranians Dismiss US Terms for Beginning Direct Talks," *NYT,* June 2, 2006, p. A12.

126. Text of the letter, with commentary, is provided by George Perkovich, "Ahmadinejad's Letter to Bush," at www.carnegieendowment.org/publications/index.cfm?fa=view&id=18317&prog=zgp&proj=znpp.

127. Text of the Joint Statement of September 13, 2005, at www.nautilus.org/napsnet/sr/2005/0577Agreement.html. The February 2007 joint declaration is available at www.nautilus.org/fora/security/07013Statement.html.

128. Both governments have at different times kicked out IAEA inspectors and limited or blocked certain nuclear sites. In each case there are important unknowns that international inspection could resolve—for Iran, that it does not have secret

weapon-making facilities and is not producing highly enriched (weapon-grade) uranium; and for North Korea, that it is not engaged in full-scale reprocessing of nuclear fuel, and that its nuclear-weapon equipment and material are not being exported.

129. By one account this coordination may already have occurred. In mid-2006, Seymour M. Hersh contends based on interviews, the Bush administration decided not to push for an immediate cease-fire between Israel and Hezbollah so as to allow Israel to eliminate Hezbollah "as a prelude to a potential American preemptive attack to destroy Iran's nuclear installations." As it was, Israeli bombing did not defeat Hezbollah, and Iran was thus not sent the warning Washington supposedly had in mind. See Hersh, "Watching Lebanon," *The New Yorker*, August 21, 2006, pp. 28–33.

130. See, for example, "Rice's Remarks on Iran," *NYT*, May 31, 2006, online ed. at www.nytimes.com, in which she said that if Iran rejected the package of incentives proposed by the EU and other countries, sanctions would be sought, Iran would be isolated, and "we have options that are very near-term options should they not make the right choice." After Iran failed to respond to a UN Security Council deadline (the end of August 2006) for terminating its nuclear enrichment efforts, President Bush said: "There must be consequences for Iran's defiance, and we must not allow Iran to develop a nuclear weapon." *NYT*, September 1, 2006, p. A10.

131. UN Resolution 1718, adopted October 14, 2006, condemned the nuclear test and decided that member states should prevent any transfer of heavy military goods to the DPRK, anything that might contribute to its WMD programs, and luxury goods. Text at http://daccessdds.un.org/doc/UNDOC/GEN/NO6/572/07/PDF/NO657207.pdf?OpenElement.

132. See Seymour M. Hersh, "Last Stand," *The New Yorker*, pp. 42–49.

133. Ruediger Frank, "The Political Economy of Sanctions Against North Korea," *Asian Perspective*, pp. 5–36.

134. This is the main argument of Hazel Smith, *Hungry for Peace: International Security, Humanitarian Assistance, and Social Change in North Korea*; and Stephan Haggard and Marcus Noland, *Hunger and Human Rights: The Politics of Famine in North Korea*.

135. Steven R. Weisman, "Rice Is Seeking Millions to Prod Changes in Iran," *NYT*, February 16, 2006, p. 1.

136. Christopher de Bellaigue, "Under the Olive Trees: Waiting for the War in Iran," *Harper's*, July 2006, p. 63.

137. Hersh, "Last Stand."

138. As President Bush said, "The Iranians should not have a nuclear weapon, the capacity to make a nuclear weapon, or the knowledge as to how to make a nuclear weapon." David E. Sanger and Elaine Sciolino, "Iran Strategy: Cold War Echo," *NYT*, April 30, 2006, p. 4. On US war planning, see Seymour M. Hersh, "The Iran Plans," *The New Yorker*, pp. 30–37.

139. Dafna Linzer, "U.S. Spy Agencies Criticized on Iran," *Washington Post*, August 24, 2006.

140. Perry, interview on the Public Broadcasting System, September 17, 1999; quoted in NAPSNet online at www.nautilus.org, September 20, 1999.

# 4

# The Third World and the Fourth: Human Rights, Environmental Decline, and Underdevelopment

> Market-based capitalism works well for the developed world, but our human values and compassion are needed to save these children. Markets alone won't do this.
>
> —Bill Gates, 2002

> The U.S. government view is that markets are always right. My view is that markets are almost always wrong, and they have to be made right.
>
> —George Soros, 2002

> Our nations must learn from the developed countries to avoid stumbling into the same pitfalls as they. It is absolutely essential that our creative endeavor should be directed toward the formulation of genuinely Latin American solutions. Hence there is no point in persisting in a race for development that takes no account of the values inherent in developed society.
>
> —Gustavo Lagos, 1981

## Defining the "Third World"

Anyone who has visited an underdeveloped country knows the scene: the sharp contrasts between rich and poor. At first sight, the modern capital city, with its international airport, skyscrapers, traffic jams, businesspeople, high-walled private homes, neon signs advertising luxury goods from every continent—and beggars, pollution, and shantytowns just beyond view of downtown. And then there is the rest of the country: unrelieved squalor, too many people for too little land, children with distended bellies and vacant eyes, the most primitive technology, thatched-roof dwellings, a closeness to death. Destiny or politics? Merely two societies, one modern and advancing, the other backward and decaying—or a structurally unequal system, the smaller part feeding off the larger?

The purpose of this chapter is to use the global-humanist approach in political economy to examine the crisis of human insecurity at closer range.

I present case studies of underdevelopment, environmental problems, and human rights in South Africa, Brazil, and South Korea, as well as briefer looks at three volatile Latin American countries: Haiti, Bolivia, and Venezuela. The first task, however, is to clarify what "Third World" means and does not mean.

Conventional definitions divide the 130 or so countries of the Third World according to a national average GNP per person, yielding high-, low-, and middle-income categories. The merit of this division is that it enables us to distinguish (as the World Bank and the UNDP do) the relatively more prosperous countries (such as Singapore and South Korea) from the middle-income countries (Brazil, Bolivia, Venezuela, South Africa) and the poorest (including Fourth World) countries (fifty, including Haiti). Nevertheless, an average-income classification such as this falls short of a human-interest point of view. Though it evidently is useful for international lending agencies and transnational corporations, since it assists them in making decisions about loans and investments, the classification says nothing about the quality of life and the distribution of social benefits within societies. Nor do average income figures provide more than an inkling of the true dimensions of poverty and the capacity of governments to tackle it. They do not convey money's true value—what it can actually buy in an economy in which the cost of living may be subject to wide disparities between rich and poor families, high inflation, subsidies, state controls, or great urban-rural and regional differences.[1]

A second way to define the Third World is quintessentially realist: It consists of the "developing" economies in relation to the "developed" ones, as measured by the value of their resources, markets, and strategic situation. Third World countries are objects of the major powers—defined either as threats to national interests or opportunities for advancing them. In the official US view of recent years, for example, the Third World has been threatening—a fertile ground for revolutions, mass emigration, ideological confrontations (Vietnam, Cuba, Iraq, North Korea), and terrorists. It may display nationalistic hostility to US investments, access to "vital" resources such as oil, and military bases. As opportunity, the Third World's importance to standard US interests goes far beyond the traditional geopolitical concern about allies and overseas bases. Third World countries purchase 40 percent of US exports; account for one of every twenty manufacturing jobs and one of every five acres of farm production; host about one-quarter of all US foreign investment and return one of every three dollars of overseas corporate profits; supply over 40 percent of all US imports, including many valuable minerals (such as bauxite, tin, and cobalt) and cash crops (coffee, rubber, cocoa); and offer TNCs cheap labor that allegedly reduces consumer costs for those in the United States.

Here again, the human interest, except insofar as the US lifestyle is concerned, is not taken into account. Who in the Third World benefits from all this trade and investment? What human price, at home as well as abroad, in the environment as well as the economy, is paid to preserve strategic and economic interests? This official version of the Third World is typically offered to justify economic and military programs before congressional and public audiences, and not in order to shape a consensus on behalf of the global poor.

Then there is the Third World's own version of the "Third World." Not much is left of it; globalization has created sharp distinctions between its richer and poorer members and different strategies for surviving in a one-world economy. There had been a time when Third World largely coincided with the countries—the so-called Group of 77 in 1964,[2] now numbering 132—that called for an NIEO in trade and development. Their meetings were opportunities to denounce the inequities of the global (capitalist) system. Meetings of the Nonaligned States occasionally still take place, though without their former significance. The inequities, meanwhile, go on: Although developing countries have doubled their share of world manufactured exports since 1980 (to about one-quarter of the total), for instance, the richest countries dominate such exports as usual, especially at the high-tech end.[3] The advances in production and exporting by a few Third World countries, such as China, India, and Mexico, are exceptions to the rule, which is that the Third World as a whole occupies the same subordinate position it has always occupied.[4] Developing countries continue to experience difficulties in marketing primary products, due to fluctuating prices and rising protectionism in the industrialized world; economic growth cannot keep pace either with population growth or help narrow the income gap with the industrialized world; and the costs of repaying or postponing repayment of debts remain very high.

More pertinently, increased trade—contrary to the corporate-globalist ideology—does not translate into improved income shares for developing countries or their citizens. The global pattern remains that of the inverted champagne glass, within and between countries and regions. The gap in shares of world income between the richest 20 percent and the remaining 80 percent of the world's people is huge and growing (Table 4.1). Likewise, the gap is great and growing in average personal income between people in the richest and poorest countries (the average US citizen today is 61 times richer, for instance, than a typical Third World citizen, compared with 38 times richer in 1990).[5] And rising inequality is also true within regions (Table 4.2) and countries (Table 4.3). While a number of Asian economies have soared, poverty in Latin America and even more so in sub-Saharan Africa has risen: In the latter region, "almost 100 million more people [were] living on less than $1 a day in 2001 than in 1990."[6] At the country level, the UNDP relates, "Of the 73 countries for which data are available, 53 (with more than 80% of the world's population) have seen inequality rise, while only 9 (with 4% of the population) have seen it narrow."[7]

**Table 4.1   Distribution of World Income Among People**

|  | Percentage Share of World Income | | | |
|---|---|---|---|---|
| Percentage of World Population | 2000 | 1980 | 1970 | 1960 |
| Richest 20 | 75.0 | 76.3 | 73.9 | 70.2 |
| Next 40 | 20.0 | | | |
| Next 20 | 3.5 | | | |
| Poorest 20 | 1.5 | 1.7 | 2.3 | 2.3 |

*Source:* UNDP, *Human Development Report 2002,* overleaf and table 3.1, p. 36; UNDP, *Human Development Report 2005,* pp. 36–37.

**Table 4.2   Trends in Income Poverty by Region, 1981–2001**

|  | Percentage of People Living on Less Than $1 (PPP) a Day | | | |
|---|---|---|---|---|
| Region | 1981 | 1987 | 1996 | 2001 |
| East Asia and Pacific | 56.7 | 28.0 | 15.9 | 14.3 |
| Central/East Europe and Central Asia | 0.8 | 0.4 | 4.4 | 3.5 |
| Latin America and Caribbean | 10.1 | 11.3 | 9.4 | 9.9 |
| Middle East and North Africa | 5.1 | 3.2 | 2.0 | 2.4 |
| South Asia | 51.5 | 45.0 | 36.7 | 31.9 |
| Sub-Saharan Africa | 41.6 | 46.9 | 46.1 | 46.4 |
| World | 40.4 | 28.5 | 22.3 | 20.7 |

*Source:* UNDP, *Human Development Report 2005,* table 1.2, p. 34.

**Table 4.3   Income Distribution in the Third World**

|  | Percentage Share of Household Income and Ratio of Richest to Poorest 10% | | | | |
|---|---|---|---|---|---|
|  | Poorest 10% | Poorest 20% | Richest 20% | Richest 10% | Richest:Poorest |
| Bangladesh | 3.9 | 9.0 | 41.3 | 26.7 | 6.8 |
| Brazil | 0.7 | 2.4 | 63.2 | 46.9 | 68.0 |
| El Salvador | 0.9 | 2.9 | 57.1 | 40.6 | 47.4 |
| Ghana | 2.1 | 5.6 | 46.6 | 30.0 | 14.1 |
| India | 3.9 | 8.9 | 43.3 | 28.5 | 7.3 |
| Morocco | 2.6 | 6.5 | 46.6 | 30.9 | 11.7 |
| Philippines | 2.2 | 5.4 | 52.3 | 36.3 | 16.5 |
| South Africa | 1.4 | 3.5 | 62.2 | 44.7 | 33.1 |
| South Korea | 2.9 | 7.9 | 37.5 | 22.5 | 7.8 |
| Vietnam | 3.2 | 7.5 | 45.4 | 29.9 | 9.4 |

*Source:* UNDP, *Human Development Report 2005,* table 15, pp. 270–72. Dates of survey figures vary from the late 1990s to 2002.

We are left with one firm conclusion about economic globalization: Its presumed benefits have yet to be demonstrated. Just as Bill Gates and George Soros said in the epigraphs at the beginning of this chapter, the global marketplace has enriched the wealthy and kept the poor poor—a view shared by many state leaders, not to mention Third World citizens.[8] Viewed from a human-security perspective, the global village of the imagination means inequality of two sorts in the real world: unequal distribution of resources and opportunities within countries, and unequal access to the means of well-being between countries. Reporting to the UN in 2000, Secretary-General Annan described a typical "global village" of 1,000 inhabitants: 780 people who live on less than $2 a day, with low life expectancy (52 to 64 years), high illiteracy (especially for women) and unemployment, and high incidences of malnutrition and infectious diseases; and 150 people who live in relative affluence that includes much longer life expectancy (78 years), access to health care and sanitary conditions, jobs, a computer or at least a telephone, and control of perhaps four-fifths of the village's wealth.[9] At the international level, this village is the Third World in microcosm—a world that attracts less than 1 percent of worldwide foreign investments, accounts for less than 1 percent of all exports, and—for its poorest populations (about 1.1 billion people)—lives in unrelieved misery. "The level of inequality worldwide is grotesque," the UNDP has concluded.[10]

The Third World's shared sense of weakness and vulnerability is compounded by the widespread conviction that advanced communications technology is further exploiting it. On one side come demands from the developed world's governments and TNCs for unimpeded access to Third World societies for advertising, television and radio programming, banking and financial services, data gathering (including news) and dissemination, and satellite-resource mapping. From another side, the major Western news agencies typically convey an image of the Third World that stresses disaster and violence. Their Third World consists of coups, mass starvation, the stereotypic restless natives whose cultures and dignities have long been buried. Progress in democracy and environmental protection never becomes the news stories it would if it happened in the industrialized world.[11]

But there is more here than meets the eye. However justified demands for NIEO and NIIO may be, they are meant only to bring about equity between states. Strengthening state power is the name of the game for most Third World leaders.[12] Many of those same leaders who make eloquent calls for a new international order are last in line when it comes to building new domestic orders that emphasize redistribution of income and human rights, such as self-determination for minorities and freedom of speech and press.[13] At that point they are likely to hide behind appeals to nationalism against foreign interference. They seem to fear that the First World view that capitalism promotes democratic values might be accurate, hence that economic growth should be kept separate from social equity. This may explain, for instance, why Third World elites frequently cite the widening income gap between rich and poor countries, but rarely the even wider income gap between rich and poor citizens in their own countries; or why some Third World governments that have poor records when it comes to protecting natural environments (such as Indonesia and Brazil) nevertheless demand payment from the industrialized world for environmental protection.[14]

Third World leaders in fact tend to use the same standards of social progress, such as average income and GNP, and the same arguments in favor of state power that are employed in the industrialized world. NIIO, which might legitimately be raised by Third World leaders as a defense against cultural imperialism, has also become a device for muzzling the press and minimizing political opposition. Likewise with NIEO: In some cases, André Gunder Frank asserts, NIEO has been merely a cover for mass repression. And since those who call for it represent a nation's dominant social and economic interests, any benefits from NIEO would go first to them, leaving the satisfaction of basic needs just where it now is—in the very distant future.[15] If anything, globalization has armed proponents of state power with a new justification. Regimes in weak states that are being squeezed by international pressures to liberalize economies and democratize politics, as well as by demands from citizens to meet basic needs, require increased coercive power if they are to make concessions.[16] That can be a recipe for disaster, since in most Third World countries regimes govern without the rule of law, accountability, or military subordination to civil authority. "The state that once loomed as salvation and for which men and women fought and continue to do so has too often become an instrument of terror and a means to self-enrichment," Fouad Ajami concluded.[17]

The NIEO version of the Third World is further weakened by important economic and political differences within the underdeveloped community. Some countries, notably the OPEC members, are not shackled with debts or plagued by a population explosion. They have accumulated multibillion-dollar surpluses, have substantial investments in the United States and Europe, and import labor from Asia and elsewhere. Others, like the "four little dragons" of the Pacific Rim (South Korea, Taiwan, Hong Kong, and Singapore), have become exporters of cars, steel, and advanced electronics. These countries have high growth rates, large export surpluses, and high average personal incomes—hardly the usual in the Third World. Politically, meanwhile, Third World unity remains largely a fiction. All may decry the arms race and at one time (during the Cold War) upheld nonintervention and nonalignment. But some Third World states have acquired or are believed to be developing nuclear weapons, take sides on international disputes, welcome the military aid or bases of the major powers, produce and export arms, and interfere in one another's internal conflicts.

To talk of these contradictions in Third World affairs is not meant to diminish the justifiability of its demands and aspirations. As already observed above (and further discussed below), even the most economically well-off Third World states are militarily vulnerable and dependent on major powers for security. Those with energy resources; cheap, labor-intensive consumer goods; and other commodities desired by the advanced economies must always remember that the larger economies determine currency values and can (and do) quickly erect tariff and other barriers to imports. Some Third World governments have gained controlling interest over production and extraction of their resources. But as we have seen, a handful of transnational corporations dominate the marketing and distribution of most goods, not to mention information and international credit. In this study the point remains, however, that such international inequities should not blind us to the internal inequities that turn state leaderships from victims into victimizers.

The plight of Third World peoples and the contradictory character of Third World states prompt the analysis here, which is founded on human interests and structural problems. Our Third World consists of that four-fifths of humanity—and especially the poorest 20 percent of it that lives in Fourth World countries—whose basic survival needs, cultural and spiritual identities, traditional social structures, and quite possibly personal self-esteem have been badly eroded by political and economic forces beyond their control. These forces, both internal and external to their communities and countries, have prospered at their expense. They form part of a comprehensive national, regional, and ultimately global system of production, distribution, and control whose purpose is to maintain and expand upon a fundamental inequality. Regardless of how one characterizes this system—imperialism, dependence, unequal exchange, a single (world capitalist) mode of production, corporate transnationalism—it amounts to basically the same end result: The world works to benefit the few at the expense of the many.

How that thesis gets played out in the real Third World requires further investigation. Notwithstanding the many important differences between underdeveloped countries, generalizations can and should be made about their political economies and the quality of people's lives. What follows is a synthesis of a typical Third World country's internal and external settings. Here and in the country studies that follow we can see how and why the global crisis continues.

## A Third World Country Profile

### A Typical Third World Country Has
### Substantial Poverty Embedded in a Clear Class Structure

We have already drawn attention to the huge income gap between households, but poverty is often rooted in the concentration of landownership, the main source of wealth. Table 4.3 shows income inequality in ten Third World countries, including most of those studied in detail later in this chapter.

What do statistics such as those in Table 4.3 tell us? First, large income gaps seem to come with increasing prosperity; this is the structural character of poverty. Whereas three poor countries—Vietnam, the Philippines, and Bangladesh—have fairly average income distributions, South Africa's and Brazil's are highly skewed in favor of the wealthy. Brazil is a notorious example of inequality in the midst of great material abundance. Nearly half the national income is earned by 10 percent of the households, while the bottom 20 percent of households earns only 2 percent. The gap between the richest and poorest households, 68 times, is the world's largest. Yet Brazil is often touted for its high rate of growth and per capita income, and for the size of its modern industrial sector, which exports steel, autos, and its own computers. Or take El Salvador, once considered a Fourth World country. There, average annual per capita income was $940 in the 1980s; it is over $1,600 today. But the unequal distribution of wealth—not much better than in Brazil—remains due to land control: Perhaps 2,000 families (0.002 percent of the population) own 40 percent of the land, and 10 percent of the landowners own 78 percent of the arable land.[18] The polarization of landed rich and landless poor was a major factor in the civil war in the 1980s.

Embedded in the figures is a second point: Democratization is no guarantee of equitable development.[19] While South Korea exemplifies improvements in income distribution with increased democracy—other examples would be Costa Rica, Ghana, and Mozambique—Brazil and India do not. Nor, to turn the matter around, does *lack* of democratic practices, for example in Cuba, China, and Vietnam, prevent improvements in income and other elements of human development. The reason for these seeming anomalies is simple: Governments, whether democratic or not, that invest in their people through (for example) education and health care are likely to have a fairer distribution of wealth—and therefore less poverty.

Third, as in the Americas, so elsewhere in the Third World: The rich are getting richer, the poor poorer, and the middle class is backing into poverty.[20] Development fails to trickle down as promised. Around 25 million additional people a year join the ranks of the absolute poor, and overall, poverty is increasing at approximately the same rate as population growth, or 1.8 percent a year.[21] Certainly, income poverty has been reduced in many countries, enough so that the UNDP stated in 1997 that "by the end of the 20th century some 3–4 billion of the world's people will have experienced substantial improvements in their standard of living."[22] India is a good example, having reduced the *percentage* of people in poverty from 50 to 33 during its fifty years of independence. The country's rise is now being talked about in the same breath with China. But it is with good reason that India's HDI is 127, well below Cuba and Mexico: The *number* of poor in India has more than doubled in that time, to about 380 million, and that is quite apart from appalling figures on other dimensions of human development, such as infant mortality, illiteracy, and malnutrition.[23] As former US president Bill Clinton said when he visited in 2000, India has 30 percent of the world's software engineers, but 25 percent of the world's malnourished (including 47 percent of children).[24] "Even under fairly hopeful assumptions about economic recovery in the rest of the [1990s]," reported the World Bank in 1992, "the absolute number of poor in the world at the turn of the century will probably be higher than in 1985"—that is, over 1.1 billion people.[25] It was, by about 200 million people.

Latin America hailed privatization and open markets for having pushed annual economic growth rates from below 1 percent between 1988 and 1990, to an average of 3 percent or better over the next four years. But the harsh reality is that the percentage of Latin American families living in poverty—that is, unable to afford even a minimum level of food, housing, and essential services—*rose* from 35 percent in 1980 to 39 percent in 1990. Despite the fact that in 2002 infant mortality rates in the region reportedly went down, and literacy improved, inequality continues to account for an extraordinary number of premature childhood deaths, spreading AIDS, and malnutrition among children.[26] "The resumption of economic growth has been bought at a very high social price," a specialist with the Inter-American Development Bank confessed.[27]

Chile, the darling of the development set—"the economic star of Latin America," according to the *New York Times,* an "emerging market" country, and possibly the next member of NAFTA—epitomizes the difference between economic growth and human development.[28] Despite improvement in the percentage of the population mired in poverty, Chile's richest 10 percent of its citizens has twenty-five times the income of the poorest 10 percent. A once-vibrant network of community services has given way to rampant consumerism by the wealthy and the evisceration of the middle class. The stock market, foreign investment, and exports are doing quite well; but education, social security, and health care are now privatized, hurting the working class (which has seen its salaries cut) and the poor generally. Thus the frequent references to "two Chiles."

### A Typical Third World Country Has High Unemployment and Underemployment in Both Rural and Urban Areas

Rural dwellers constitute the core of the Third World's most destitute. They sit in the middle of what the International Labour Organisation (ILO) calls the worst global employment crisis since the Great Depression.[29] These are people who lose their land to powerful landlords, the onset of rural technology and a money economy, the transformation from growing food to exporting it, and drought. Peasants in these circumstances may have a choice to

stay on in serfdom or as landless tenants, as in El Salvador and the impoverished northeast of Brazil. Or, as in China, massive migration to urban areas
in search of jobs may occur. Mexican peasants, equally desperate, have
crowded into the border area, where over two thousand mostly US-owned
assembly plants (*maquiladoras*) have been set up. These TNCs do provide
employment—for as many as 700,000 people—and have brought some
Mexicans into middle management. But they also pay workers (mostly
women) poorly and take full advantage of weak environmental and labor
protections.[30] Now, Mexico has lost half those jobs and hundreds of
maquiladora factories to China and other lower-wage countries. Local leaders must find ways to lure higher-technology businesses.[31] It's the old story
in globalization: move up or die.

   Poverty-reduction programs such as the World Bank administers have
failed to recognize the importance of employment to human development
and meaningful economic growth. A World Bank study in 2006 concluded
that its aid programs had largely failed to promote income growth in most
countries with very low to no income growth. In those countries, there was
less growth in 2000–2005 than from 1995 to 2000. Overall, the study found,
poverty stayed the same or increased in fourteen of twenty-five countries.
Macroeconomic growth, the Bank finally recognized, is not the same as job-
producing growth.[32]

   In urban centers, technology also dispossesses. Though many TNCs
have shifted operations to the Third World precisely in order to take advantage of cheap, unorganized, unskilled labor, the largest of them find automa-
tion to be even more cost effective. Yet a study of Kenya suggests to one
scholar that the main reason for the preference of capital-intensive over
labor-intensive production is political: A Third World government would
rather have a large, powerless underclass struggling for its daily bread than
have the rich, whose support is essential to regime survival, pay the true
costs of its education, health care, and low-priced staples.[33]

### Cities of the South Are
### Becoming the Centers of Underdevelopment

A historic shift in population is taking place worldwide from rural to urban
areas. In Third World countries, virtually all future population growth from
now on will probably take place in cities.[34] Seventeen of the world's twenty-one "megacities"—cities with populations over 10 million—are in the
Third World. Thirteen of them are in Asia. "By 2025, Asia's urban population is expected to rise to nearly 2.6 billion people, which will be just over
50 percent of the world's total."[35] These figures translate into extraordinary
social and environmental problems for urban authorities, such as in water,
sanitation, and health services, as well as compound the demands on rural
people and their environments. For as a UN study reminds us, urbanization
in the Third World mainly means slums:

Of every 100 new households established in urban areas in developing countries during the second half of the 1980s, 72 were located in shanties and slums (92 out of every 100 in Africa). Today, an estimated 1.2 billion people—almost 23 per cent of the world's population and 60 per cent of developing countries' city-dwellers—live in squatter settlements, often shantytowns made from cardboard, plastic, canvas or whatever other material is freely available. The number of urban households in developing countries without safe water increased from 138 million in 1970 to 215 million by 1988, and those without adequate sanitation rose from 98 million to 340 million.[36]

*The Status of Women Is Deplorably Low*
Women, as the Brandt Commission noted, suffer most in conditions of rural underdevelopment. They work in the home and in the fields, often putting in longer hours than the males but at a fraction of men's pay and without education, training, health and safety protection, child care, or access to credit. Women are far more likely than men to be displaced by technology, to work for subsistence rather than cash, to be illiterate (two-thirds of about 950 million adult illiterates in the world are women), and to suffer from malnutrition.[37] A UN agency reported in 2000 on what neglect of women's rights ultimately means: "80 million unwanted pregnancies each year, 20 million unsafe abortions, some 750,000 maternal deaths and many times that number of infections and injuries." Although the immediate cause of these calamities is poor obstetric care, including lack of access to family planning, in sub-Saharan Africa and other poverty-ridden regions the deeper cause is women's low status and consequent lack of power or education to make their own decisions.[38] As is discussed below, women also bear the brunt of dangerous methods of population control; and they are now just as likely as men in the poorest countries to contract HIV/AIDS. In some countries female children have literally been made to disappear. The status of women is therefore a sure indicator of how humane "development" really is.

Women are undervalued in the work force and in their own families. As workers, they are at the center of global shifts of production to cheap-labor sites. The Mexican maquiladoras were just mentioned. Another example is Indonesia's textile industry, where thousands of skilled young women sewers work for around $75 a month. This pittance has drawn Japanese, South Korean, and Taiwanese capital and technology away from higher-wage countries, contributing to Indonesia's industrialization and export growth.[39] The families of these women traditionally do not value them any more than their employers: They strongly prefer male children. In some Asian countries, including China and India, families have gone to inhuman lengths to ensure their preference, such as widespread use of fetal scanners during pregnancy, abortions of unwanted girls, sale of female children, and female infanticide. These practices explain why so many females are "missing" in these countries' male-to-female population ratios.

Law (as in the Arab states), culture (such as Latin American *machis-*

*mo*), and tradition (as in Africa) put the onus of harmful and discriminatory practices on women. Thus, the widespread practice in Islamic countries of enfibulation (removing a young woman's clitoris, sometimes called female circumcision) is traditionally justified by the need to inhibit her sexual desires;[40] Indian women are subject to criminal charges for prenatal tests to determine the sex of the fetus;[41] and in Afghanistan under the fundamentalist Taliban, repression of women, which was enforced by Muslim purity squads, applied in education, work, dress, contact, and many other aspects of social life.[42] The thinking behind such practices naturally extends to the political arena, where women are prevented from deepening their political involvement. Here we must talk about global trends and not only conditions in the Third World. With respect to the vote, only in New Zealand was women's suffrage achieved before early in the twentieth century. A survey by Susan J. Pharr found that at the next level of political activity—participation in voluntary political work—women have gained marginal acceptability in very few countries (the United States, Scandinavia, and Britain). When it comes to holding high office, aside from a few women elected to national leadership in 2005–2006 (including two presidents of Third World countries: Liberia and Chile), women have made exceedingly few inroads. If we consider one-third female representation in national parliaments to be a rock-bottom standard, only four Third World countries exceed or come close to that standard: Rwanda, Mozambique, Costa Rica, and Cuba.[43]

Perhaps most disturbing is that even when women do gain entry to political office, they tend to represent the same elite and class interests as their male counterparts. What has been written of Mexican women in politics may be generally true: "While women elites in Mexico deserve more political offices to represent their sex, they are no more representative of Mexican women than are male leaders of Mexican men."[44] This leads to the further conclusion that the values of such women are not representative of rural, low-income, working-class female populations but instead are the same traditional ones held by male politicians. Women in politics evidently must play by the same rules as the men.

### Children Are the First Victims

Malnutrition, early death from preventable diseases, and lack of education are three of the cruelest ways that poverty destroys children. Although marked progress has been made in reducing the gap between North and South in all these areas, children suffer at an alarming rate. For example, a child dies every eight seconds—11,000 a day—from malnutrition.[45] Another child dies every 2.5 seconds—over 12 million a year—from illnesses that are easily preventable, such as pneumonia and diarrhea.[46] Most such deaths, of course, occur in the poorest countries of Africa and South Asia. Serious infections, such as from vitamin A deficiency that affect about 200 million children worldwide, could readily be treated with vitamin supplements.[47] Children between five and fourteen years of age are employed in great numbers—around 250 million, according to an extensive ILO survey—even where laws exist against it.[48] Poor parents need their children's income; expenses even for public schooling can be prohibitive; and in a competitive world economy, cheap child labor is in high demand. By one estimate, "at least 15% of all 10- to 14-year-olds in Asia work, more than anywhere else in the world except Africa."[49] The numbers of children kept out of school run into the tens of millions. In India, which seems to have the most child workers, prostitution and AIDS are rampant; children of poor families often are forced to become sex slaves.[50]

Children are also the chief victims in wars. UNICEF (the UN Children's Fund) reports that about half the 3.6 million people killed in wars since 1990 have been children. When victims of AIDS and poverty are added to those of wars, children—over a billion of them, accounting for more than half of all the world's children—are the main sufferers.[51] In Congo's seemingly endless war, for example, one writer reports that for every combat death there are sixty-two other, war-related deaths (from disease and malnutrition), and that of these latter, thirty-four are children.[52] Sadly, this is considered progress, for in comparison with previous years children are not dying as quickly and are more frequently enrolled in school, as noted previously for Latin America.

*Because the Quest for "Growth" Typically Takes the Form of Top-Down Production and Distribution, the Political System Favors Those Already in Positions of Authority*

Preserving the political-economic status quo has priority over strategies for change, such as land reform and labor-intensive production that would feed and employ many more people. The Green Revolution that gained popularity with many Third World leaderships beginning in the 1960s illustrates this priority. The "revolution" worked insofar as the new seed varieties significantly increased wheat and rice yields. India is a prime illustration of this success. But to succeed required large amounts of water, chemical fertilizer, and, of course, seeds—hence also irrigation tubewells, capital, and mechanization. As a substitution of energy and money for land, the Green Revolution worked to the benefit of local power holders, their political patrons in the capital, and, in some countries, the TNCs that control international trade in fertilizer, seeds, and machinery.[53] The landholding system was preserved and, in fact, further consolidated, while peasants were forced onto marginal lands or forced to sell out to landlord-moneylenders.

Relatedly, TNCs have taken increasing control of Third World water supplies.[54] The French company, Vivendi Environnement, is the leader in this $200 billion a year business that already has a customer base the size of the US population. For urban dwellers around the world, privatization of water has significantly raised its price without necessarily improving water quality or delivery. Once again we find development banks providing the capital for private ventures, removing most of the companies' risk. But it has turned out that the real risk lies in popular protests, such as in Argentina and Bolivia, that have forced Vivendi to abandon its contracts.

### By Every Indicator, People's Basic Needs Are Very Far from Being Met, and the Consequent Waste of Human Resources Is Enormous

World Bank statistics show how misleading it is to talk about average improvements in (for example) Third World health and literacy, particularly since about 60 percent of the world's people live in the poorest countries (starting with China). In those countries, according to the UNDP, the average gap in literacy and health between Third World and First World countries had been reduced significantly by 1990.[55] For example, the gap in infant deaths per 1,000 births was cut in half between 1960 and 1990, from 123 to 61; in access to safe water, the gap went from 60 percent of the population down to 32 percent between 1975 and 1990; and in adult literacy, the gap dropped to 33 percent in 1990 from 49 percent in 1970. These gaps have continued to narrow since the 1990s.

But the bitter reality is twofold. First, the average First–Third World gap has widened over the years in other areas that pertain to literacy and health, such as years of schooling, basic education enrollment, and the percentage of the world's scientists, technicians, patents, and communications outlets. Second, when we look at particular countries, especially but not exclusively low-income ones, we still find disturbing figures.[56] Numbers matter more than gaps. The infant mortality rate, which averages 5 per 1,000 births in high-income countries, is many times higher in low-income countries—and much more than that in their rural areas. It is 109 in Mozambique, 112 in Malawi, and 98 in Nigeria. Even among so-called middle-income countries, the rate is 63 in India, 81 in Pakistan, 53 in Bolivia, and 33 in Brazil. The percentage of the population in low-income countries with access to safe water is 75 percent in Bangladesh, 73 percent in Tanzania, 60 percent in Nigeria, 73 percent in Vietnam, and only 22 percent in Ethiopia. Among richer Third World countries, the range includes 91 percent in Mexico and 94 percent in Argentina.[57] Public health spending by governments naturally reveals a huge gap between the thousands of dollars spent per person in the richest countries compared with between $25 and $250 per person spent in the poorest. Access to health care, measured by the number of physicians per 100,000 people, has similarly disturbing numbers in the low-income countries: 8 in Angola, 27 in Nigeria, 59 in Laos, 16 in Sudan.[58]

Finally, while most of the newly industrialized countries have school enrollments that are equal to those of the advanced industrialized countries, that is hardly the case for countries in lower-income groups. Moreover, when it comes to literacy rates and education at all levels, important gender differences are the norm. We must also consider that progress in educating young people in the Third World tends to be offset by the brain drain from the Third World. People with the rare opportunity to do advanced studies and research will look for more attractive conditions in the developed countries. Those who remain at home constitute a relatively small core of skilled people. For example, scientific talent in the Third World is about 95 out of 10,000 persons—in a range from 157 in Asia to about 10 in Africa—compared with 285 in the industrialized market countries and 308 in Eastern Europe. The difference is even more marked between developing and developed countries (a ratio of about 1 to 14) in terms of persons engaged in research and development.[59]

First World governments and TNCs like to focus on their efforts to rectify these imbalances through development aid. The amount of money needed to stabilize and reverse these trends is enormous, as Maurice Strong said at the Earth Summit: about $625 billion *a year,* of which the industrialized world would need to contribute about $125 billion, or under 1 percent of GNP.[60] Rather than doing so, the developed countries have used their commercial power to open up Third World markets at the expense of public health and well-being. The export of cigarettes, which are now universally understood to be an addictive drug, is a multibillion-dollar business for the major tobacco companies, and all the more so as the industry is finally being forced to pay at home for some of the health costs of smoking. In the name of free trade, and with the help of high-profile political figures, the US-based tobacco TNCs led by Philip Morris, R. J. Reynolds Tobacco Company, and Brown & Williamson have been able to pry open the door for their products around Asia, where smoking is already a leading cause of death. Experts foresee millions of new smokers and additional deaths from smoking as a result of the pressure tactics. The former US Surgeon General, C. Everett Koop, put it precisely when he said the US government and TNCs were knowingly "exporting death and disease to the Third World."[61]

Breaking the cycle of poverty and social decay is extremely difficult. The case studies of China and South Korea show different routes to largely positive outcomes. A third example, post-revolutionary Nicaragua, has been less successful but is noteworthy because of what was attempted and accomplished under highly adverse circumstances. The victory of the Sandinista movement in 1979 overthrew a forty-year-long dictatorship under the Somoza family. Nicaragua then fit perfectly the Third World profile of class domination of the economy, high indebtedness, widespread poverty, and desperate human needs.[62] But the Sandinistas' effort to transform these conditions met with armed resistance: a counterrevolution aided by the United States, which sought to overthrow the new government.

Another round of civil war, which lasted until presidential elections in 1990, devastated Nicaragua's economy and society. Nevertheless, the Sandinistas can be credited with some important human-development achievements. They launched a series of mass mobilization campaigns to implement social democracy.[63] The illiteracy rate was sharply reduced, rural school construction was emphasized, and public-health spending was increased to a striking 5 percent of GNP. Land reform was instituted to benefit small producers and end reliance on imported food. By the end of the 1980s, according to UN statistics, Nicaragua, despite a heavy military burden and very little outside aid, had also significantly reduced infant mortality and improved access to safe water and early schooling.[64] In the mid-1990s, however, Nicaraguans still faced formidable barriers to improvements in human development. Rates of infant mortality and malnutrition continued to improve and compared favorably with those of its Central American neighbors. But the population was growing at over 3 percent annually, faster than before, and the country was saddled with external debt—over $9 billion in 1995, nearly six times its GNP. Foreign aid accounted for almost half of GNP.[65] In 2002 debt was still high, accounting for 5 percent of GNP and for as much money to service as to pay for public health.[66] With its domestic politics still unstable, Nicaragua's social gains achieved through revolution remained vulnerable to powerful external forces.

### The Typical Third World Country Has Very High Population Growth Caused Mainly by Its Underdevelopment

While rates of population growth have slowed worldwide, in seventy-four of the poorest countries, populations are expected to double over the next thirty years. In thirty-three countries, twenty-five of which are in Africa, the fertility rate is still six children per woman.[67] Why? It has been well established that impoverished families, facing high infant mortality, little and marginal-quality land to work, limited (if any) educational opportunity, traditional restrictions on women, and no health care or old-age security, will seek to have many children, particularly males. That way, they perpetuate the family, have more hands to work the soil, and ensure care of the elderly.[68] Hence, poverty is the main factor in the Third World's population explosion, and not the reverse. The poorest Third World countries have the highest birth rates as well as the highest incidences of infant mortality and malnutrition. And while high population growth certainly exacerbates poverty, it can also be reduced in spite of poverty, as Bangladesh has shown.

Unless development gives prominence to meeting basic needs, above all female education, even the most affluent Third World country will still have high population growth, centered in its poorest regions. In Brazil, for instance, the population is growing rapidly alongside malnutrition that affects nearly two-thirds of the people. Food production is stagnant; yet Brazil exports soybeans, a major protein source. By the same token, a relatively poor country, such as Cuba, "which has benefited women with improvements in health care and education and has the most equal income distribution in Latin America, has halved its birth rate since the 1959 revolution, a record unmatched" in Latin America.[69] Recent research has even more sharply pinpointed female education as the critical variable in determining fertility rates and population growth. In Costa Rica, where adult literacy is 93 percent for both sexes, women are heavily involved in the work force, and the government has made significant investments in health care and other basic needs; family planning is widespread, and fertility rates have dropped sharply. Pakistani women have quite different prospects: very low social status, very high illiteracy (76 percent), and widespread poverty, especially in rural areas. The result is that the fertility rate is among the highest in Asia despite the availability of family planning services.[70] Demographic studies of regions of India and Kenya come to similar conclusions: "Women's status and education now appear to be far more significant than overall economic growth as a correlate of declining fertility."[71]

These facts provide insight into the relationship between population growth and hunger. If conditions of human development and agricultural policy were shaped with the family farmer in mind, the examples of China, Taiwan, and Cuba show that population growth would begin to slow down and agricultural production would increase dramatically.[72] Failure to invest in agriculture ensures that food dependency and large families will be the future. Checking population growth is certainly important in and of itself; but it sometimes gets caught up in politics, with disastrous results. Since the 1980s the US government, influenced by religious fundamentalists, has sharply cut aid for overseas family planning programs, notably those in China run by the UN Population Fund. Because US aid accounts for nearly half of all international support, the funding cuts may lead to many more births and abortions (800,000, according to UN officials) than Third World women would want.[73] Yet these same programs have also been pushed by the United States and other governments, international agencies, and TNCs whose interests were threatened by land reform. Population control—through, for instance, the US aid program in Bangladesh, which once promoted sterilization of women with the enticement of gifts of cloth, an exchange later urged upon poor Indian women by the government of Peru[74]—is often looked upon as an efficient way to prevent overpopulation from evolving into a revolution of the hungry.

## *The Development Strategy Established for the Typical Third World Country Is Industrialization Through Exports*

The frequent result of this development strategy is the neglect of agriculture and, notably in Latin America, a dominant role for transnational business in the country's economy. We typically see a country that, if it is especially poor, keeps to the traditional pattern of exporting primary products (usually only one or two) and importing the developed countries' processed and manufactured goods. The trade and investment practices of both capitalist and formerly socialist developed countries reinforce this pattern.[75] If the Third World country is already semi-industrialized, it probably has moved from the stage of import-substituting to export-promoting manufactures and begun importing financial services and advanced technology.

This "trade not aid" formula so popular among the leading economies is not succeeding for two fundamental reasons. One is that it does not deliver prosperity; the other is that the very countries that preach free trade have imposed substantial barriers to the exports of Third World countries—and more so to the poorest of them.[76] When President Bush met with heads of state of North and South America in January 2004 in order to set the stage for a Free Trade Area of the Americas, he got an earful when he proposed that "trade is the most certain path to lasting prosperity." Mindful of US policies that protect steel and farming interests from Latin competition, and of their huge poverty-ridden population, one Latin American leader after another rejected Bush's advice. They pointed to the growing gap between rich and poor, with the president of Argentina saying: "A [trade] pact that does nothing to resolve deep existing imbalances will do nothing but deepen injustice and the breakdown of our economies."[77] These leaders are not alone: A number of trade experts who have worked on the inside of the major global institutions share their gloomy assessment. "It is hypocrisy to encourage poor countries to open their markets while imposing protectionist measures that cater to powerful special interests," said the World Bank's former chief economist, referring to farm subsidies. The Bank's deputy managing director agreed, calling the subsidies "scandalous."[78] For a change, the Bank, the experts, and critics in the NGO community were on the same page.

The issue of trade subsidies goes far back, but it may best be remembered in the same breath as the Doha Development Round that began in 2001. Modest concessions by the EU and the United States could have freed up huge amounts of money that might redound to the benefit of the poorest countries and people. But the Doha talks promised low-income countries less than 2 percent of the gains from a package of proposals that included tariff cuts on their agricultural exports. While US and EU objections sought to protect textile and agricultural industries and their workers, the cost of protection is very high to consumers, and the costs are even higher to textile and farm workers in Third World countries. Significantly lowering tariffs on those commodities would, studies have shown, dramatically increase world income and especially the income of the poorest economies.[79] It was not to be; the talks, hailed five years earlier as having "removed the stain of Seattle,"[80] collapsed in July 2006 amid considerable rancor between US and EU negotiators.

The principal source of contention is the demand of developing countries for a lowering of rich-country barriers—meaning especially subsidies to their own farmers—to agricultural exports such as corn, rice, tomatoes, and cotton. The subsidies are huge—for the United States, around $9 billion a year on some eleven crops and for the EU, about $4 billion a year. But subsidies count for much more, politically as well as economically, in Third World countries. Take cotton, for instance, which accounts for roughly 40 percent of total African exports and is a major export of other developing countries, such as Brazil. As the president of Burkina Faso said, developed-country subsidies were 60 percent greater than his country's entire GDP, and "caused economic and social crises in African cotton-producing countries." Other African leaders called the subsidies threats to their national security. In the United States subsidies to cotton producers and cotton exporters run about $2.2 billion a year, and in the EU about $1 billion, keeping the price below what it costs an African cotton farmer to produce. Although programs exist to reduce tariffs on many African imports and to increase the productivity of African cotton farming, they can hardly keep pace with the political reality of farm subsidies in the richest countries.[81]

What the United States and other advanced economies have done is "kicked away the ladder" of protection that facilitated their own takeoffs in previous centuries.[82] As a consequence, the risk increases that Third World countries will become dependent on foreign funds and market decisions, and go deeply into debt. Brazil and Mexico are striking examples. Both relied heavily on TNC investments in their early industrialization that centered on consumer goods for the local market. Later, in the 1970s, they began borrowing heavily abroad as they moved into exporting manufactured goods. (The contrasting story of some Asian NICs was noted in Chapter 2; but while they avoided dependence, their post-1960 development came about under unusual conditions not found elsewhere.[83]) TNCs often moved in, buying out or outcompeting local manufacturing firms, a process called denationalization. The electrical, pharmaceutical, and automobile industries in Brazil are early examples of this external (mostly US) domination;[84] computers are a more recent one.[85] In Mexico the leading opposition politician claimed in 1991 that 75,000 local firms had been driven out of business by TNCs since 1983. He correctly predicted that passage of NAFTA would further enlarge the TNCs' power, leaving Mexican businesses with "nothing to gain because we have nothing to export."[86] The ensuing peso crisis intensified Mexico's reliance on foreign capital. In like manner, TNCs accounted for 90 percent of Singapore's exports in 1983, 25 percent of Taiwan's in 1982, and 18 percent of South Korea's in 1978.[87] Japanese TNCs are responsible for significant portions of the exports of Thailand, Indonesia, and other countries.

The net result for both the poorest and some of the richest Third World economies is that they become net importers of food and overall growth becomes unbalanced.[88] In the first instance, which characterizes much of Africa, agricultural diversification and productivity have been undermined by political and commercial opportunism, mainly on the part of local urban officials and traditional powerholders.[89] In the second, these same authorities have linked up with transnational business, banks, and their home government to give industrialization for export first priority. Foreign investors and banks get the red-carpet treatment: tax and other incentives to attract their money, supportive policies from the World Bank and IMF, and official "development" aid—a fair proportion of which winds up in the pockets of local officials or in secret foreign bank accounts—in order to stimulate manufacturing and convert food-producing land to cash crops such as tobacco and pineapples for export. Agriculture, once productive enough to meet local needs and generate a surplus for export, now must be supplemented by food imports (again, largely a US operation).[90]

### The Country Faces a Hunger and Health-Care Crisis

Hunger is a predictable result of agricultural neglect combined with rigid class structures. All other things being equal, there should be enough food for everyone, even under present conditions of increasing demand and lower production.[91] But production and distribution of food are not equal. Food may be prohibitively expensive (in the poorest countries, two-thirds of a family's income will be spent just on food); farmers are underpaid, making them reluctant to produce; increasingly large quantities of farmland and food will be used for nonhuman purposes, such as for animal feed, to pay for imported oil, or exported to fatten a richer country's cattle;[92] and food imports, including aid (notably, the US PL 480 program), have a history of winding up on the tables of the urban well-to-do and the military, or on the black market, rather than in the hands of the poor.[93]

We have already underscored the absence of health-care resources in numerous Third World countries, and the health consequences. Here we can observe what happens when epidemics such as HIV/AIDS and avian flu are encountered. The vast dimensions of the AIDS virus are by now well established, but it is worthwhile to point out how rates of infection will affect the future of certain countries and continents. AIDS will have major impacts on health-care costs, military preparedness, and education in Nigeria, Ethiopia, China, and South Africa, for example. The capacity of women to continue contributing to home life and local economy, especially but not exclusively in sub-Saharan Africa, will be severely limited now that women make up one-half the number of HIV-positive adults.[94] While as of early 2007 slightly more than three hundred humans have been infected with the particular virus known as A(H5N1) that is commonly called avian flu, the virus has made its way across three continents in three years and may well make the leap from migratory birds to chickens to humans in a major way. It is a difficult course but not impossible, experts say. Should that happen, though, it would probably have the same devastating consequences as AIDS in the poorest countries, where resources to identify, much less treat, the disease are limited or absent.[95]

The other side of the epidemic coin is control of drugs for treatment by TNCs. Here, the news is more positive thanks to the support of the World Health Organization (WHO) for production of safe generic AIDS drugs in India and Brazil, dramatically lowering treatment cost. It was the first time WHO had gone against global patent holders, which lobbied strenuously against production of generics.[96]

## Neglect of Agriculture in the Movement to Export-Led Development Has Profoundly Adverse Ecological and Environmental Effects on Natural Resources as well as on Human Development

Time and again it has been shown that the small family farmer, in any society, is more likely than an absentee landlord or large agribusiness to take good care of the land. Topsoil erosion, conversion of prime farmland to nonagricultural uses, overuse of fertilizers and pesticides, and escalating land and produce prices (brought on by concentrated private or state landownership and energy-intensive production methods) are among the consequences of pushing family farmers off the land.[97] In ecopolitical terms these practices deepen dependence on foreign grain suppliers and worsen hunger. Farmers are displaced onto marginal land and once-fertile land turns to desert, as seen throughout central and sub-Saharan Africa.

It is commonplace for these kinds of environmental tragedies in the Third World to be blamed on overpopulation. Such a view seems invalid, and not only because there are plenty of examples of environmental decline in areas of low population. The pressures of population on natural resources are real enough—in the contest for space between densely populated Cairo and the Nile Delta, with the delta steadily losing ground to urbanization (farmers selling rich soil for making bricks, industrial and agricultural runoff, and siphoning of water for drinking);[98] in the fight to cleanse the sewage-choked but sacred Ganges River, home to a half-billion Indians;[99] in the seemingly impossible struggle of Ethiopia's people, nearly all subsistence farmers without ownership rights, to meet basic food requirements at a time of rapid population growth, increased reliance on emergency food aid, and severe degradation of soil and deforestation.[100] But population growth, to repeat an earlier point, is most often consequential, not causal: It arises *out of* underdevelopment and the sharply reduced choices that powerful actors impose on ordinary people. Those actors may be public, private, or a combination of the two—as in the conversion of forestland to pasture for cattle, which occurs in many parts of Latin America and Africa;[101] the clear-cutting of tropical forests by transnational timber companies;[102] the competition for good land in Kenya that the government exploited for its own political purposes;[103] or the extensive mining conducted in Indonesia until recently by two of the world's biggest TNCs—Newmont Mining Corporation and Freeport McMoRan Copper and Gold—with the military's protection, causing great damage to people, nature, and local economies alike.[104]

How people who depend on farming will react to these pressures on their traditional way of life cannot be predicted. They may, for example, cut down trees for firewood, which is often the main source of fuel. They may organize against the corporation or government that seeks to move them off the land, as in West Papua. They may seek unity with their ethnic group against another ethnic group believed to be responsible for their plight. All such responses may be rational in the face of perceived necessity; and all have the potential to become violent.[105] On the other hand, and more probable, environmental pressures and ecological tragedies may simply victimize people who have no recourse. Pesticide poisonings are a case in point. WHO reports that there are about a half-million cases a year in the Third World. Dumping pesticides, many of which are banned for use in the country of origin, is a common corporate practice. The health consequences for the workers who use them, and for the consumers of the products sprayed with them, do not seem to enter the corporate equation.[106] Here is one example of what Sunkel called the "transnational style of development." Growth without public accountability and austerity programs that favor transnational (export) businesses give short shrift to ecological considerations.[107]

The story is similar in socialist Vietnam, illustrating the interconnectedness of development, environment, and population growth, and the difficult policy choices that the government of a very poor country faces. The market reforms (*doi moi*) since 1975 have benefited many people, especially in the entrepreneurial south; but around four-fifths of Vietnam, mostly the rural areas, lives below the poverty line. Poverty and high population growth have led to the destruction of forests, as large numbers of people who had been resettled in less populated areas have sought firewood.[108] More forest has been lost since the Vietnam War than during it. Total forestland declined from 40 percent in 1965 to 26 percent in 1994, and 40 percent of Vietnam is now classified as "bare land."[109] Soil erosion and forest fires are increasing. In the North, "growing food dependency" is becoming a reality.[110] With arable land dwindling, forests are also being threatened by the shift to cash crops (including coffee, sugar, and shrimp farming) and by new agricultural techniques (including extensive use of chemicals). These practices add to income but also promote soil erosion and contamination of fisheries and rice fields.[111] Vietnam is one of the world's major rice exporters; but with the country's membership in the WTO in early 2007 it must gear its industries for international competition.[112] The country thus faces a development dilemma: whether to promote cash crops and export-led industrialization, or conserve the ecosystem and increase investment in rural people.

*Development That Favors Narrow State and Elite*
*Interests in a Typical Third World Country Means a Huge Debt*
*Burden for All Except the Oil-Exporting Countries of OPEC*
Although all of these oil-importing countries together bring in less oil than
the United States, they suffered the most from the oil price hikes of the
1970s and after. As the 1980s began, these underdeveloped countries were
paying 5.3 percent of their GNP just for oil, almost twice what they had
paid only two years earlier.[113] The worldwide recession at that time cut still
more into these countries' ability to finance imports. As a result, they had to
borrow and borrow again in a desperate effort to pay for oil and other vital
imports and to make interest payments on existing debts. The big banks
were far from helpful: They had encouraged Third World countries to take
advantage of cheap money during the high inflation of the late 1970s, at a
time when they were awash in OPEC petrodollars. Since then, the banks
have been faced with numerous big-ticket customers who cannot even make
interest payments on their loans, let alone begin repaying the principal. By
2003 those payments came to $93 billion in interest on a total debt of over
$2 trillion.[114]

Many Third World countries, but particularly the poorest of them,
which have neither capital nor plentiful indigenous energy resources, have
essentially mortgaged their futures to the lending governments and the
major banks. In 1982, for example, Mexico owed $50.4 billion (31 percent
of GNP); Brazil, $47.6 billion (17 percent of GNP); South Korea, $20.4 billion (28.3 percent of GNP); Argentina, $15.8 billion (29.5 percent of GNP);
Turkey, $15.9 billion (29.7 percent of GNP); and Egypt, $15.5 billion (52.8
percent of GNP).[115] In the ensuing years, as interest rates remained high and
still more bailout loans were required, these debts piled up. The saving
grace for large economies such as Mexico, Brazil, and Nigeria was that the
banks were willing to roll over or discount their loans. By 2003 Mexico's
debt was down to 6.5 percent and Brazil's to 11.5 percent of GNP, still a
heavy burden. But Brazil got a new IMF bailout of $30 billion in 2002, and
Nigeria, a major oil producer, was able to repay its $30 billion debt in 2006
after receiving a 60 percent discount.[116] For most other debtors, there was
no such reprieve. Debt has eaten up almost all output since the 1980s.

The main reason is interest and service payments on external debt,
which take a large share of an underdeveloped country's export earnings
(e.g., about 24 percent of Mexico's exports, 177 percent of Turkey's, and
320 percent of Argentina's in 1995; 11.3 percent, 20.3 percent, and 34.7
percent, respectively, in 2003).[117] Only the strongest economy has any
prospect of repaying loans, even if (as has not been the rule) bank interest
charges hold steady or decline. What debt service means for the least-devel-
oped countries is this: Their governments and taxpayers pay more to service
the debt than to support health and education.[118] Even with debt relief,
which twenty-nine of the poorest countries were granted by the World Bank

and other creditors in June 2005, these countries still made debt service payments of $2.8 billion, equal to 15 percent of their government revenue on average.[119] Here is where developing countries feel the power of the IMF and the World Bank, for these institutions hold the keys to more credit and therefore, in most cases, the leverage to enforce cutbacks in social-welfare spending as the price of credit. Third World leaders have shown their displeasure with such pressure, but the great majority of them eventually accede—to the delight of the transnational banks and exporters.

Historically as well as in recent times, the big losers from this "debt trap" are the middle and lower classes, whose cost of living rises while wages and government social spending are cut back sharply.[120] Small businesses also suffer. Unable to compete with foreign-owned corporations, they are often absorbed by them or go bankrupt.[121] The poor lose the most. One large-scale study of the effects of IMF programs on Asian, African, and Latin American development in the first half of the 1980s is particularly revealing. Whereas a little more than half of the IMF-assisted countries were able to improve their balance-of-payments position, per capita growth stagnated or declined in 57 percent of the countries studied; "real" (inflation-corrected) investment by Third World governments stagnated or declined in 60 percent of the assisted countries; and, on average, IMF programs "tend[ed] to increase aggregate poverty, or in other words the number of people—and of children—living below the poverty line."[122] No wonder that there have been periodic riots in Third World countries against IMF austerity programs.[123]

Third World environments and ecosystems may also fall victim to debt. Forests, for example, may be virtually sold off to TNCs, as has happened in Brazil, Southeast Asia (Indonesia, Cambodia, and Malaysia), Central and West Africa, and the Russian Far East. Dams are constructed to provide hydroelectric power and irrigation, in the process destroying local ecosystems and uprooting hundreds of thousands of people. The World Bank's financing of such projects in Brazil, India, and Indonesia had calamitous results, as noted previously.[124] The world's fish stocks are being rapidly depleted by overfishing as demand for tuna, swordfish, and other large fish increases.[125]

A common misperception about this cycle of indebtedness is that Third World countries are soaking up huge amounts of capital in loans and other forms of aid and returning virtually nothing to lenders. The truth of the matter is quite different. For one thing, government and private capital flows to the Third World are significantly offset by debt payments. In 2003, developing countries received official development assistance (ODA) and private capital (mostly foreign investment) equal to 5.6 percent of their GDP, but together paid back 4.7 percent of GDP in debt servicing, leaving a mere 0.9 percent in external help. For Latin America, the bottom line is actually a negative 5.4 percent.[126] What this means is that the lenders are making a profit; loans are anything but giveaway programs. The trend of privatization since the 1990s has added to the reverse flow, as development banks have looked more to making money for investors than to allaying the costs of indebtedness.

Second, aid is meager and misdirected. ODA by developed-country governments to the Third World, while seemingly substantial at about $65 billion a year today, actually amounts to about 0.25 percent of their combined GNP. This is well below the UN's longstanding target (0.7 percent of GNP) for ODA. (The Scandinavian countries are the most generous, the United States and Italy the least. In 2005 the United States gave the most money, but the smallest share of GNP, 0.16 percent.[127]) Only in recent years has ODA gone mainly to countries most in need: About one-third of the total, compared with about one-fourth in 1990. Nor does it go mainly to basic human needs such as primary health care. ODA goes to governments, not necessarily to people, usually to repay debt or provide technical cooperation or emergency assistance. Only 10 percent or less of aid typically winds up in basic-needs programs.[128] Lastly, ODA is more than offset by rich countries' trade practices of subsidizing agricultural producers and tying aid to the purchase of their own companies' goods and services.

The Philippines is a tragic case of how internal elites, working with multilateral financial institutions, can bankrupt a political economy.[129] Internally, the dictatorship of Ferdinand Marcos, which lasted from 1966 to 1986, placed control of key sectors of agriculture, such as sugar and coconuts, with family members and cronies. The rural poor was (and is) over 60 percent of the population. Externally, the export-led development model made the Philippines a virtual stepchild of the World Bank and the IMF. By 1986, when Marcos was forced out by "people power" in a presidential election, the country was the sixth largest recipient of World Bank funds. These funds helped give agribusiness multinationals like Del Monte and Castle and Cook (Dole) pivotal positions in the Philippine economy; but they also contributed to soaring indebtedness and extraordinary corruption within the inner circle and in the military. Faced with rising political opposition and a guerrilla war, Marcos's regime operated under martial law for nine years, during which repression was widespread. The reform regime that followed under Corazon Aquino (1986–1992) never could recover from the awesome external debt—over $30 billion in 1990, or 65 percent of GNP—or break the historic pattern of landholding inequality and environmental destruction. The economy did make something of a turnaround later on.[130] But in a country still ruled by an oligarchy, still heavily indebted (12.8 percent of GNP goes to debt servicing),[131] still bearing many signs of a basic-needs crisis, and still dependent on female migrant workers' remittances for foreign exchange,[132] it is much too early to say that the Philippines will escape the debt trap.

Can a debt crisis such as plagues countries like the Philippines be ended? The UN membership pledged in 2005 to cut world poverty in half by 2015. The estimated cost to the industrialized countries would be fifty cents out of $100 of national income, one-half of one percent.[133] This is surely a pipedream; doubling aid to poor countries runs up against the priorities of most rich countries, which start with spending on arms and social security. Military spending by twenty-two OECD aid-giving countries was ten times their ODA in 2003.[134] Doubling aid also would not reflect their record of aid giving, which as noted has been one of increasing wealth not matched by increasing generosity. The alternative, and dominant, approach is that of US administrations since the 1980s. From the Baker Plan, named for then secretary of the treasury James Baker III, to the Millennium Challenge Account of George W. Bush, one plan after another has been introduced that tied new loans or reduced debt to changes in the economic and social policies of Third World debtor nations.[135] Such plans amount to an updated version of the Washington consensus: Third World nations that want some debt reduction must practice austerity economics in conformity with foreign needs. Except for AIDS assistance, the United States under George W. Bush has maintained that aid should only go to countries that have the ability to use it wisely, invest in education and public health, and encourage private investment. Even then, only a handful of countries that are eligible actually receive money.[136]

For those who, like Jeffrey Sachs, believe the key to Africa's problems lies in a major expansion of foreign aid programs, these are bad times. Although the EU has shouldered roughly half the global aid burden for Africa, and (along with Japan) agreed in 2005 to double aid to all poor countries for the next five years, the US share, though the largest, will remain at about one quarter of the total. This has resulted in a slowing of disbursements, leading Sachs to complain: "They're fighting wars for hundreds of billions of dollars and what they've done for Africa is start one program for AIDS."[137]

Priorities vary and people suffer. The Europeans have come round to the view that a substantial step-up in international aid to the poorest countries is essential, and they have put real money behind it. The United States is budget-conscious and also motivated by private-sector interests. Struggling Third World democracies like Niger and Mozambique rely on aid to sustain budgets. For Mexico and the Philippines, the remittances of their workers abroad are the most important source of income. States with failing economies such as North Korea need food and energy assistance to stave off disaster. Denying aid to weak and failing states can have dire consequences, as Iraq under Saddam Hussein showed when hundreds of thousands of children suffered from international sanctions. This happened in Afghanistan under the Taliban, when sanctions were also in place. When the UN and other bodies mobilized to attempt to spare ancient Buddhist statues in Afghanistan, the Taliban insisted they were destroying them out of outrage that foreigners would pay to save statues but not Afghani children.[138]

*Repression Becomes an Indispensable Tool of Social Order*
In circumstances of gross and obvious inequality, a Third World regime frequently falls back on police power to maintain itself. It has already alienated peasants, ethnic minorities, and the impoverished; now it starts to lose many traditional supporters of authoritarianism, such as local businesses, the church hierarchy, and sometimes nationalist elements of the military. "Social discipline"—that is, the national security state—becomes the order of the day: vigilantism in the form of death squads; censorship of the press and radio; disruption and elimination of political opposition and organized labor. In the post–Cold War years, besides the usual efforts to destroy political opponents, we see the repressive regime acting to stamp out religious fundamentalists, as in Algeria, or secular rivals to fundamentalism, as in Iran, or ethnic minorities, as in the former Yugoslavia, Iraq, and Turkey. Politics is encapsulated within a seemingly permanent state of siege. Foreign support (in arms, computers, economic aid, and numerous other means of repression and sustenance) becomes increasingly critical to the regime's survival.[139] The marriage of realism and corporate globalism is evident here, too, for the highest military spenders in the Third World receive, proportional to population, the biggest share of development aid.[140]

As has already been suggested, there are likely to be severe economic as well as civil liberties costs from the shift to outright authoritarianism. The military spending that supports repression and other defense functions siphons off scarce funds—on average, about 20 percent of Third World government budgets and 5 percent of GNP.[141] One careful study concludes that "the economic effects of military expenditure [in the Third World] have been negative. . . . To the extent that military expenditure does produce economic growth, the poorest members of Third World societies are the least likely to benefit from that growth."[142] It therefore makes no sense, an African scholar has argued, to funnel economic aid to authoritarian regimes, because "elites have simply carried out cosmetic reforms to please the donors and retained all the usual instruments of repression, manipulation, and intimidation for the domination of popular forces and their communities."[143] What is unfortunate here is that the corruption, repression, and other characteristics of a weak or failing state undercut the argument for more foreign aid to the poorest countries. Aid in the wrong hands is worthless; as a senior UN figure put it, when introducing a UNDP report on aid to impoverished countries, "governance is a critical building block for poverty reduction."[144]

*Repression Goes Hand in Hand with*
*the Further Concentration of Political Power*
The elite's base and its apex narrow. In some cases, it may assume the form of the absolutist state, as in Iran, Iraq, Cambodia, Nigeria, and numerous others. Should political order give way to social chaos, the military can be

expected to step in to "save the nation from the politicians" and other "enemies of the people." Military coups have become a trademark of Third
World politics: There were ninety of them (thirty-seven in Africa alone)
from 1960 to 1982, resulting in an average of sixteen years of military
rule.[145] Of the sixty-four military-dominated governments in 1989, fifty-
nine resorted to repression and fifty to torture or other brutalities to stay in
or close to power.[146] Not coincidentally, the most repressive Third World
governments, often military-run, have been the major arms importers of
recent years, mainly supplied by the FSU and the United States.[147] With the
United States now dominating the arms-export scene, it has been found supplying weapons to one or both sides in forty-five ethnic and territorial conflicts around the Third World, many (again) involving military-backed or
-run governments.[148]

The new element in post–Cold War authoritarianism is narcopolitics:
the incorporation of drug trafficking in state politics with the connivance—
and to the profit—of state, ruling party, and military leaders. The drug trade
takes corruption to another level; it not only subverts legal institutions, distorts the economy through investments of drug-related money, and promotes political violence, it can also undermine international security. The
impact of the drug trade in Mexico, in terms of violence and police and military corruption, has already been noted. In Turkey, drug traders apparently
operated as anti-Kurdish death squads for the government and its security
organs.[149] Under Burma's junta, the country has become "the world's leading producer of heroin and opium" from its part of the Golden Triangle. By
allowing some rebel forces to engage in opium growing, the government
neutralized a major source of armed opposition.[150] It also contributed to an
AIDS epidemic.[151] Drugs may be Burma's leading export, as well as a principal source of funds for domestic investment by members of the SLORC
and drug lords.[152]

### In Resource-Rich Countries, Resources May Be Used to Fuel Internal Conflicts

An abundance of oil, water, timber, diamonds, or minerals has become an
increasingly common factor in Third World wars.[153] Diamond wars have
occurred in Angola and Sierra Leone; opium poppy has been important in
Afghanistan; and in Colombia, a principal source of cocaine shipments to
the United States, the drug cartel has sought to enlist peasants and antigovernment guerrillas in coca production and to buy the neutralization of political leaders. In Nigeria, for instance, ethnic and religious strife, rooted in
poverty, authoritarian government, and social injustice, has often plagued
the country. Profits from foreign oil operations have found their way into
private pockets rather than into social services and jobs. None other than
Royal Dutch/Shell acknowledged that its oil operations were contributing to
popular protests over gasoline prices and other resentments: "We sometimes

feed conflict," said a Shell report, "by the way we award contracts, gain access to land and deal with community representatives."[154]

## Indigenous Peoples and Cultures Often Bear the Brunt of State Repression and Corporate Exploitation

Given that indigenous peoples rarely have political representation and, in fact, go to great lengths to avoid the reach of the state, it is hardly any wonder that intrusions into and takeovers of sacred lands, violations of human rights, despoiling of natural environments, and disruption of cultures occur around the Third World with little fanfare or outside protest. Governments normally protect states, not tribes, clans, or peoples. Previously, we have noted government repression of Indian groups in Mexico and Guatemala, and TNC investments that trampled on minority rights in West Papua, Ecuador, and Nigeria. Latin America alone has numerous other examples in Brazil, Peru, Colombia, and Ecuador, to name just a few.[155] In all of these instances, only the combination of indigenous peoples' organizing and support activities by NGOs prevented annihilation.

## Underdevelopment, War, and Environmental Degradation Lead to the Large-Scale Flight of People and Their Skills

The global refugee count includes the usual large numbers of people fleeing political persecution and war, such as those who escaped from Afghanistan (over 3 million people), Indochina (over 1.5 million), El Salvador (750,000), the Gulf War (2.8 million), and Rwanda (2 million). A UN source estimates there are about 14 million to 16 million political refugees. But there are also around 20 million to 25 million internally displaced people, refugees in their own country. Because they do not cross a border, they do not fall within the responsibility of any international agency.[156] The largest and fastest-growing group is the 35 million or more "economic migrants" from "developing countries [who] have taken up residence in the North in the past three decades." Their numbers are expanding at the rate of 1.5 million persons a year.[157] The new wave of refugees reflects the realities of the global political economy: 700 million unemployed or underemployed people in the early 1990s, and 1 billion by 2000;[158] rising population pressure on land and resources, as in Mexico and Sudan, and in Indonesia's resettlement of 6 million people to outlying islands;[159] rapid urbanization, especially in Asia; governments that are strapped for cash;[160] lack of full participation of women in development; environmental calamities brought on by use of unsafe substances and technologies as well as by outright destruction of people's surroundings;[161] and social upheaval such as produced around 2 million refugees in central Europe in 1990 alone, before the destruction in Bosnia. Migration is thus a function of structural violence; the countries that lose the largest percentage of educated people are among the poorest, such as Haiti (84 percent), Ghana (47 percent), and Mozambique (45 percent).[162] But for skilled professionals who find their way to North America and Western Europe, it is also a perceived opportunity for self-betterment. They are very unlikely to return to their native country—a gain for their adopted land but a costly loss in desperately needed skills for their home-land. This familiar brain drain adds to the already monumental human and social costs of underdevelopment and war.

## Case Studies of Crisis and Renewal

### South Africa: The Rise and Fall of the Apartheid Regime

Who could have predicted that South Africa would be one of the few bright spots in the post–Cold War world order? A barbaric social system based on racial domination—apartheid—was dismantled. In 1993 a new constitution with a bill of rights was written (parliament approved it in 1996),[163] the first all-races general election was held in April 1994, and South Africa's black majority now governs. Such an extraordinary turn of events will not wipe out the past, which is outlined below; but it does turn a new page in Africa's history: a peaceful transition to democracy.

In the Republic of South Africa, a white settler minority of under 5 mil-lion (mainly English and Dutch descendants) controlled all the instruments of power in a country of over 28 million Africans, 2.5 million persons of mixed race ("coloureds"), and over 800,000 Indians. In the face of mount-ing, increasingly violent resistance to its rule, the apartheid regime used every source of leverage at its disposal—from modest social reforms to indiscriminate terror—to maintain its power and recover international sup-port. By 1990, significant elements of apartheid had been removed under a reformist government. But the system itself was still intact.

South Africa was a pariah in the international community. Pledged to support the UN Charter and Declaration of Human Rights, it was consis-tently condemned by the organization for gross violations of their provi-sions. Blacks were not permitted to vote or hold political office. Until 1986 their movements were restricted by the infamous pass laws, or influx con-trol measures. These required that blacks carry small, passport-type identity books at all times, helping to restrict rural-to-urban migration. Persons without a pass book were arrested (on average, about 200,000 such arrests a year). The Group Areas Act, lack of housing, and government "emergency" legislation ensured, however, that, pass laws or no, nonwhites stayed in resi-dential and business areas the government designated for them. (Under its resettlement program, the government moved over 4 million nonwhites to new areas, many by force.) The still-larger official plan was to get Africans out of South Africa altogether. Ten Bantustans, or "homelands," were estab-lished within South African territory; four were proclaimed independent states but recognized as such only by South Africa. Africans were reduced in status to migrant workers, citizens without a country.[164]

Blacks who sought to express their human rights in South Africa ran a high risk of imprisonment, and worse. A variety of "internal security" acts legalized repression. Blacks who, for instance, protested or organized against apartheid or spoke out (in or outside the country) for economic sanctions against the government were guilty of subversion. At its discretion, the government could hold such persons without trial, charge, or communication with the outside.[165] Torture and isolation techniques were commonplace; several black leaders, such as Steve Biko, died in prison. Members of the South African military regularly carried out "dirty tricks" operations, including torture and assassinations, designed to intensify inter- and intra-racial animosity.[166] In some cases, persons and groups critical of the government were silenced by a form of internal exile known as banning. Rigid censorship laws made it extremely difficult for antiapartheid books to be sold or for those newspapers not intimidated by the government to report police detentions or quote black leaders without themselves being jailed. Arbitrary searches of people's homes by the police occurred frequently.

Denial of basic human rights to blacks and others extended to economic and social injustices. They were severely restricted as to where they could do business or own land. The homelands to which they were confined comprise about 13 percent of the land; they are the least arable and most environmentally devastated in the country.[167] Labor unions were exclusively for blacks and were subject to strict government regulation. Only a few of them had the funds or membership to be politically powerful. Racial segregation was extensive. It was complete in education and government and was only legally ended in public places and facilities in 1990. Segregation continued in small towns, however, either by making access too expensive for blacks or by converting facilities to private ownership, which the new law did not cover. Only in the early 1990s did the South African government repeal the Group Areas Act, the Land Act (which restricted black ownership of land and homes), and the Population Registration Act (which required racial classification at birth), each of which perpetuated segregation and inequality.

Racial injustice was most deeply reflected in the distribution of economic and social rewards and opportunities. South African whites typically earned ten times the pay of blacks and held the top positions in all industries. The average South African white could expect to live thirteen years longer than a black, eat twice as well, and be over fifty times more likely to have access to a doctor. A black child on average received about five times less money for education (an improvement over the 1970s, when it was twenty times less) and was about twenty times more likely than a white child to die in infancy.[168] Apartheid can also be measured in environmental terms. South Africa did much to protect wildlife but very little to protect blacks from toxic wastes, air pollution (from coal emissions), and lung diseases associated with mining.[169]

To understand why the white minority clung so tenaciously to

apartheid, we must briefly note its origins.[170] Apartheid evolved from colonial exploitation of native labor to the point where racism, like other forms
of inhumanity, became deeply structured into the country's way of life.
Contrary to both traditional and Marxist concepts of modernization, racial
distinctions in South Africa were neither eased nor erased by economic
growth. Instead, they intensified as South Africa developed. This occurred
primarily to accommodate changes in the economy and the emergence of
new social classes. But apartheid was also strengthened, as Biko explained
it, because racism took on a life of its own as whites came to "actually
believe that black is inferior and bad." In the modern era, apartheid,
although fundamentally a cover for exploitive racism, broadened into a
nationalist ideology designed to appeal to all of the country's whites.[171]

The first white settlers came to South Africa in 1652 in the employ of
the Dutch East India Company. Those who stayed took up farming, gradually penetrated the interior, and ousted the natives from the best lands. In
1806 the British occupied the cape and began to colonize it, pushing the
Dutch descendants (the Boers) into African tribal lands, which they seized
and proclaimed states. In the 1800s, when diamonds and gold were discovered in these regions, the British invaded. What had once been an agricultural (and largely subsistence) economy based on African labor was dramatically transformed into a mining economy based on foreign capital,
urbanization, and a cheap, reliable (therefore controlled) African work
force. After South Africa's independence from Britain in 1910, British
investors and Boer nationalists set aside their conflicts in a common effort
to maintain white authority, exclude Africans from the political process, and
ensure an adequate labor supply. All the restrictive race laws mentioned earlier flowed from these objectives.

South Africa's leadership until 1994, based in the National Party, owed
its political domination to successful appeals to white purity, nationalism,
and anticommunism. As its leader said in 1948, after the party had won the
general election and formed the first entirely Afrikaner (Dutch-descended
settler) government:

> [Will] the European race in the future be able to maintain its rule, its purity
> and its civilization, or will it float along until it vanishes for ever, without
> honour, in the Black sea of South Africa's non-European population? . . .
> Will the ever encroaching and all destroying communist cancer be
> checked, or will it be further allowed to undermine our freedom, our reli-
> gion, our own South African nationhood and our European existence, our
> honourable traditions and our racial and civil peace?[172]

Such an agenda demanded repressive methods for its fulfillment. By the
same token, it also invited resistance.

With a logic common to all repressive systems, exploitation in South
Africa met with increasing resistance, which set in motion more indiscrimi-

nate official violence, more restrictive laws, and better-organized resistance. Beginning with a strike of African mine workers in 1946, black resistance developed principally along two lines. The African National Congress, founded in 1912 on a policy of noncooperation, for years waged a guerrilla war directed from its headquarters in Lusaka, Zambia. It sought to make South Africa ungovernable through armed struggle in white areas and against black collaborators. Only after Nelson Mandela was freed in 1990 and the legal ban on the African National Congress (ANC) was lifted did it announce it would suspend armed struggle. Black trade unions were a second line of resistance. Representing upwards of 300,000 mine, food-processing, and metal workers, the unions focused on strikes and other job actions.[173]

Overarching these two forces was the powerful voice of nonviolent resistance of the black church, represented by the 1984 Nobel Peace Prize winner, Archbishop Desmond Tutu. Although Tutu distinguished his advocacy from Gandhian nonviolence, saying that one cannot turn the other cheek in the face of Hitlerian tactics, he urged "peaceful change" as the only alternative to "Armageddon." Tutu's message was until very late in the game spurned by the South African leadership, but it was picked up by other whites who agreed that a bloody civil war would engulf the country unless substantial concessions were made to black interests.

There were always South African whites, even in the parliament, who protested apartheid; from 1985 on some of them, major business and political leaders for the most part, defied the government by meeting with ANC leaders. The concerns of these whites evolved with the economy, that is, to an emphasis less on state enforcement of racism than on the assurance of labor stability and continued foreign investment.[174] But their concept of social reforms stopped short of challenging the racial order. Unlike Tutu, who insisted (like all black political leaders) on the complete dismantlement of apartheid and acceptance of the one-person, one-vote principle, white liberals emphasized economic gains that would eventually trickle down to blacks. Evidently fearing "another Rhodesia"—there, whites lost political privileges when black revolutionaries turned out the ex-colonial regime and proclaimed the new state of Zimbabwe in 1980—these whites argued that only continued "growth" and foreign investment could create a just society.[175]

In fact, economic expansion was crucial to the apartheid system, as becomes plain when we look at the role of foreign capital. The major transnational corporations and banks, principally British and US, did business in South Africa for all the usual reasons: a "safe" investment climate; high profitability (higher, in fact, than the worldwide average); cheap labor; and hard, convertible currency.[176] Retaining foreign business confidence was, certainly in the eyes of the white elites, the key to its continued predominance. "Another Rhodesia" to them meant not only a black revolution but, perhaps even more, the abandonment of foreign support, just as happened when Washington and London presided over the transfer of power in Zimbabwe. If most foreign, and especially US, investments and loans ceased or were withdrawn, the impact would be calamitous for the regime. A major source of investment capital would dry up (meaning over $4 billion in US loans and investments alone); the regime's ability to repay its substantial foreign debt (about $24 billion in 1986) and support very large military and police forces (which absorbed roughly 20 percent of the state budget and accounted for about the same percentage of all Africa's military spending) would be undermined; loans from multilateral sources, such as South Africa had received from the IMF, would be cut off; important markets for South African exports would probably shrink; and critical sources of both advanced technology (in, for example, mining, automobiles, and especially computers, which had internal security applications) and fuel (from the major oil companies) would be lost.[177]

Providing stability for foreign capital not only depended on the maintenance of apartheid in some form, it also required that governments support their corporations. In South Africa there was a happy marriage of corporate globalism and realism for about fifty years. Pro-Western governments consistently supported investments and loans in South Africa for two primary reasons, both rooted in "national security": the strategic minerals that South Africa exported, much of it to the United States, and the white minority regime's anticommunism, which always found a receptive audience among US policymakers concerned about black revolutionaries overrunning southern Africa. These factors gave Pretoria powerful political leverage that only increased after the overthrow of Portuguese colonialism in Angola and Mozambique and of British colonialism in Rhodesia. The apartheid regime exploited this leverage to suppress domestic political opponents (who were invariably labeled "communists" or "terrorists"); intervene in Angola, a socialist neighbor; and proclaim itself a "bulwark" of capitalist stability in Africa.[178]

US administrations from Truman to Reagan therefore subscribed to the call for evolutionary, peaceful change in South Africa made by liberal whites there and by transnational businesses. Clearly, the intersection of business and national-security interests explains that policy much better than concern about the fate of human rights for the majority population.[179] "Constructive engagement" and "quiet diplomacy," as US policymakers variously termed their approach, were oriented to preserving US stakes in South Africa—and even expanding them, as in the case of nuclear-energy cooperation in the 1980s—while nudging the Pretoria regime to implement reforms sufficient to keep the social pot from boiling over.

By the mid-1980s, full-scale civil war in South Africa had become a real possibility. It was avoided mainly because international pressure induced the ruling party to change course by softening apartheid. Initially, the pressure came from concerned citizens in the United States, Britain, and other countries whose TNCs were investing in South Africa. Responding to appeals from Tutu, these citizens caused a number of US city and state governments, universities, labor unions, and other institutions that owned the stocks and bonds of corporations doing business in South Africa to stop investing or divest altogether. The US Congress also responded. Over the opposition of the Reagan administration, it mandated US sanctions against South Africa, such as a ban on new US investments and on certain traded items. More than half of the US companies doing business in South Africa left the country, although many merely shifted ownership to local white-run affiliates. The sanctions, helped by an international oil boycott against South Africa, and the changes in Eastern Europe, worked.[180]

Seeing the handwriting on the wall, the National Party selected Frederik W. de Klerk as its new leader in September 1989. His strategy was to steer a midcourse between the complete dismantling of apartheid and the rigid opposition of white nationalists to any change at all. De Klerk sought to appeal to white and black moderates at home and abroad who would accept reforms as a substitute for a transition to a black-run government dominated by the ANC. Thus, for example, de Klerk's administration lifted the ban on the ANC in February 1990 and ordered Mandela and other key leaders released; but it did not release all the country's political prisoners, who may have numbered three thousand or more. It also ended emergency rule in most provinces in 1990, but kept it in one. As just mentioned, it repealed some laws governing racial segregation while leaving the main ones intact.

The process, thus begun, moved fitfully toward a new governing structure and basis for citizenship. Late in 1991 direct negotiations between de Klerk's government and the ANC established CODESA, the Convention for a Democratic South Africa, in which most other political forces also participated. The idea was to agree on a formula for a transition to a one-person, one-vote system, with guarantees of civil liberties and a new parliamentary structure. Then, early in 1992, de Klerk took a major gamble: He called for a whites-only referendum on (as the ballot measure stated) "continuation of the reform process . . . which is aimed at a new constitution through negotiation." The gamble paid off: De Klerk won approval with 69 percent of the vote; and he acceded to the notion of a transitional administration that inevitably would be headed by Mandela.

South Africa's new federal structure goes halfway toward meeting the concerns of whites and blacks—those of the former, for substantial autonomy for individual states, out of fear of the black majority, and those of the latter, for a strong central government, reflecting the 5-to-1 ratio of blacks to whites in the population. In such a scheme, the greatest threat to South African unity will no longer be white minority racism but tensions between center and state governments, both of which will be dominated by blacks. At the level of governance, the ANC surprised many observers with its resiliency, and in particular with the choice of white businesses and the military to work with it.[181] The greatest challenge was dealing with the violent past. Here, the government came up with a creative, and controversial, approach, one that has since been adapted in Argentina, Guatemala, and other postconflict societies. It established a Truth and Reconciliation Commission, headed by Archbishop Tutu, to hear testimony from former officials and others, in return for which the commission was empowered to grant immunity from prosecution. By spring 1998 several thousand people had applied for amnesty. Though the commission was unable to get South Africa's previous presidents, P. W. Botha (1978–1989) and de Klerk, to admit their personal responsibility for or full awareness of assassinations, torture, and other terrorist acts, it succeeded at exposing details of the work of the security forces that clearly pointed to their culpability.[182] The ANC also admitted to having used torture and bombings against opponents, as Tutu insisted; and when the government tried to issue a blanket amnesty for ANC members, the supreme court rejected it, compelling some members to testify in return for individual amnesties.[183] Granting amnesty to killers and torturers is never popular; but it has been fairly applied and seems essential for a society to heal and move on.

Likewise, eliminating an oppressive system is only the first step in a long rebuilding process. Apartheid's undoing marks the start of an extremely difficult and very expensive confrontation with underdevelopment. In a society historically based on deep-seated inequality, it will take extraordinary resourcefulness to bring nonwhite incomes, education, skills, health, housing, and environmental quality up to reasonable levels—even with white cooperation. Today, whites still control the economy, dominating business, banking, and farming, whereas blacks must still cope with high illiteracy (16 percent) and limited capital for investment.[184] AIDS, which the government initially denied was an epidemic, is a monumental problem that afflicts not only poor blacks but also public servants, raising questions about the future governance of the country.[185] Whether or not a black-majority government can transform South Africa without the kind of instability that Zimbabwe has undergone is the great challenge now before it.

*South Korea:*
*The Successes and Contradictions of an "Economic Miracle"*
South Korea, along with Brazil, is one of the most frequently cited examples of successful capitalist economic development in the Third World. Both have enjoyed periods of high growth rates, both have high average incomes, and both rank at the top among NICs in average levels of health and education. The overall performance of South Korea—officially, the Republic of Korea (ROK), as distinct from the socialist Democratic People's Republic of Korea (DPRK) in the North—is all the more impressive when we consider that its population is five times less than Brazil's and

that ever since the Korean War (1950–1953), national security has dominated political and economic affairs. But to call South Korea an "economic miracle" of laissez-faire capitalism and a model of Third World development, as it frequently is called, ignores several things: the preponderant role of the state in managing the economy, the special advantages that South Korea had as it moved into export-led development, and economic distortions, social inequities, and political weaknesses that have accompanied the country's dynamic growth and democratization.

From 1962, the year in which the government in Seoul introduced its first five-year plan, to 1983, the GNP of South Korea rose from $2.3 billion to $75 billion. In fact, GNP grew an average of 12 percent a year in the 1980s. Per capita GNP rose from $87 in 1962 to $1,800 in 1983. By 1989, GNP had reached $210 billion, or $4,968 per capita.[186] Prior to the currency crisis, these last figures had approximately doubled, so that the average Korean was earning just over $10,000 annually. Now the figure is over $16,000. A striking feature of this income increase is its relatively broad distribution; the income gap is closer to Canada's than to Brazil's. Add to these facts that average wages in Korea have risen dramatically over the past twenty years and that the level of educational attainment is unusually high (as is government spending on education), and it appears that the ROK leadership has found a way to achieve both rapid economic growth and social equity.

The driving force behind this economic growth was the rapid expansion of industrial production for export, which was the cornerstone of the development strategy adopted in 1962 by the iron-fisted president, Park Chung Hee. As a result, the weight of the manufacturing sector in the economy steadily increased, and exports moved to skill-intensive goods such as electronics and textiles. Total export volume grew by 31.7 percent annually between 1965 and 1973, with manufactured goods (which now make up over 90 percent of exports) leading the way.[187] High-technology exports constitute about one-third of manufactured exports. By 1992 Korea was the fifteenth largest economy in the world and in the top ranks of world trade—the main reasons for its elevation to membership in the OECD, the "rich countries' club," in 1996, a first for a Third World country. Today South Korea, with about $475 billion in merchandise exports, is the twelfth largest exporter.[188]

Some of the reasons behind Korea's success as an exporter make it a doubtful model for other developing countries, however. As Durning wrote, "the foundations of equitable growth [in Korea] came before the export boom" in the form of radical land reform in the late 1940s and heavy state investment in education in the early 1960s.[189] The Japanese colonial heritage of state-directed development is also generally acknowledged as an important source of rapid growth. As an ally of the United States throughout the Cold War, Korea received special treatment. US economic aid alone averaged $270 million a year, or 15 percent of South Korea's GNP, from 1953 through 1958.[190] Military aid (excluding sales) totaled $9.3 billion from 1950 to 1979.[191] Finally, Korea received US military and Japanese technology transfers, and preferential access to US markets. This combination of self-made and externally created advantages is simply not duplicable today.

There are also complicating factors in evaluating the South Korean economic advances. One is the growing neglect of agriculture. South Korean peasants, once the backbone of the economy, have been hard hit by export-led development. Prior to 1962, peasants had benefited from a large-scale land-to-the-tiller program and state intervention to ensure adequate prices, fertilizer, and credit. Since then, state investment in agriculture has sharply declined, and so have agricultural production, employment, and income. The social consequences are by now familiar to us.[192] Farmers who were not forced into tenancy migrated to the cities, taxing the resources of government and industry. They remain vulnerable to foreign competition under the WTO.

Second, relative income equality "may be a consequence not so much of equitable sharing in the fruits of economic growth as of very high levels of labor extraction among low-income workers and families."[193] The South Korean work force, women assembly-line workers in particular,[194] was unfairly treated and historically repressed prior to the start of civilian rule. The repression of labor in South Korea was in fact a central aspect of export-led development under state direction.[195] Korean industrialists (mostly meaning the *chaebol*) kept wages down and work hours high to make the price of Korean exports more attractive.[196] Korean governments even now, in an era of independent unions, assign a high priority to maintaining a "disciplined" work force, one willing to subordinate the improvement of wages and working conditions to company and national goals. Wages have indeed risen rapidly since the 1970s, but in recent years they have usually been offset by increases in the cost of living. Chaebol leaders nevertheless moved manufacturing plants to lower-wage countries, first to Southeast Asia and more recently to China.

Korea's economic rise has always been closely tied to the fortunes of the chaebol. The top ten dominate sales, exports, and bank loans. In the 1990s, sales of the thirty largest chaebol accounted for about three-quarters of Korea's GNP.[197] Such a concentration of market and financial power points up the crucial role of the state in economic planning. As several specialists have emphasized,[198] the state, far from being a neutral player in the economy, has guided and nurtured industrial development through control of credit, protection of domestic firms from competition with foreign investors and banks, decisionmaking on key investments, and various subsidies and awards to exporters. Korea may be a growth miracle, but it is certainly not a miracle of free-market competition. The chaebols' economic power translates into difficult times for Korean small businesses and, politically, into huge financial contributions to the ruling party and slush funds for politicians that simultaneously corrupt the growth process and progress in democratizing. The conviction of the head of Hyundai Motor Company in 2006 on bribery charges shows that the Korean "disease" of corruption continues.

Until the late 1980s, South Korea's enviable overall economic performance was managed in the confines of the national-security state. The country's spending on the military was substantial: over 6 percent of GNP (in North Korea it was about 22 percent) in the 1980s and over 35 percent of the government budget. Despite the Korean armistice of 1953, armed clashes on land and at sea occurred periodically. Each Korea drew extensively on the resources of its major-power partners—the United States for the South, the USSR and China for the North—to acquire the latest military hardware. A state of war existed throughout the peninsula, justifying not only arms buildups but also widespread domestic repression. The national-security state in South Korea comprised an extensive police and intelligence apparatus that employed the "communist threat" to intimidate, jail, and torture political opponents; to muzzle the press; and to keep intellectuals, students, and labor leaders in line. US officials looked the other way, excusing the repression as necessary to maintain stability in the face of the greater threat from the North. That attitude lent legitimacy to thirty-two years of military rule (from 1960 to 1992), during which direct military intervention in politics was always possible—as when General Chun Doo Hwan seized power and then, in May 1980, ordered special forces to suppress a popular uprising in the city of Kwangju. In short, South Korea was an authoritarian system, though much more open than North Korea, as evidenced by many years of student demonstrations and the parliamentary and presidential elections since 1984. Not until the remarkable events of 1987 did democracy begin to have meaning in Korea.

President Chun Doo Hwan had promised to step down at the end of his term in February 1988. The Olympic Games scheduled to take place in Seoul in the summer of 1988 would be a personal and national triumph. Chun's error was to assume that his successor as party leader would automatically also become the next president—that neither opposition leaders, such as Kim Dae Jung, nor Korean citizens and students could effectively challenge Chun's reliance on an electoral process that virtually ensured victory for the ruling elite. What actually happened is that student demonstrations throughout Korea for direct presidential elections were widely supported, notably by the middle class and the Buddhist, Anglican, and Catholic churches. When the demonstrators were assaulted and gassed by the police and army, public sympathy went entirely over to the opposition movement. Even US officials publicly questioned Chun's legitimacy. In an extraordinary development, Chun's heir-apparent, General Roh Tae Woo, pressured him not only to support a constitutional revision that would allow for direct elections but also to release some two thousand political prisoners, to commit to honoring civil liberties, and to free Kim Dae Jung from house arrest.

Roh Tae Woo won the 1987 presidential election with a little more than one-third of the popular vote in a three-way race.[199] He scored some major international successes, including hosting the Olympic Games, opening trade relations with the socialist countries and diplomatic relations with the USSR (1990) and China (1992), and making several overtures to North Korea that led in 1990 to the first exchanges of visits by prime ministers. North Korea became internationally isolated by virtue of its own rejection of Chinese- or Soviet-style reforms and by Roh's so-called Northern policy of flexible ties with the DPRK's allies. In September 1991 Pyongyang was forced to reverse its longstanding opposition to separate UN memberships for the two Koreas after China and the USSR agreed to support entry for both.

Even more dramatic steps followed. In November 1991, in line with US-Soviet nuclear arms reductions, all US tactical nuclear weapons were prepared for removal from South Korea. Roh then announced a Non-Nuclear Korean Peninsula Peace Initiative. Under it the ROK foreswore the manufacture, possession, storage, deployment, or use of nuclear weapons, and further stated it would not possess nuclear fuel and enrichment facilities. In the following two months, the two Koreas concluded two unprecedented agreements—one to reduce tensions (by pledging nonaggression, an end to attempts at subversion, and increased family and other contacts); the other, a declaration of mutual, verifiable non-nuclear policies.[200] For North Korea, these agreements were undertaken in the hopes of removing obstacles to US and Japanese diplomatic recognition and thus to their capital and technology. For the South the agreements would allay concerns about the North's possible development of nuclear weapons, silence opposition criticism of Roh for not pushing harder for reunification, and create the basis for an all-Korean solution to the peninsula's security problem. None of those hopes materialized, however, and may account for the North's decision to go ahead with its nuclear-weapons program.[201] A strategic crisis was avoided by virtue of a US–North Korean agreement in 1994 to freeze the DPRK's nuclear program in exchange for energy assistance. As the case study in Chapter 3 relates, the 1994 agreement was never fully implemented. But although North Korea has nuclear weapons, since Kim Dae Jung took office in 1998 (see below), South Korean governments have made engagement of the North a high priority, symbolized by the June 2000 summit between Kim and the North's supreme leader, Kim Jong Il, and South Korean investments in North Korea.

Efforts to reform the Korean political system and the iron triangle of the state, the banks, and the chaebol moved forward in December 1992 when Kim Young Sam became South Korea's first civilian president since 1960. Revelations of extraordinary corruption came out, including the chaebol chief executives' turnover of huge sums of money to previous Korean presidents, for their personal use and to support the ruling party's activities. Kim's administration found that Roh Tae Woo had accumulated a slush fund of about $650 million in numerous bank and investment accounts; that he had made payoffs to the opposition as well as his own party; and that all the chaebol leaders had contributed to this private war chest.[202] Eight chaebol chairmen were indicted on bribery charges.[203] Roh became the first Korean president to be jailed on corruption charges. Chun Doo Hwan was also indicted and jailed. (Both were later pardoned.) Chun's trial, and the arrest of fourteen generals, also provided an opportunity for Koreans to revisit the bitter legacy of Kwangju, where General Roh had led the troops, and the origins of Chun's 1979 coup.

In December 1997 Koreans went to the polls in the midst of an economic crisis and elected Kim Dae Jung, the first-ever member of the political opposition to win. Kim Dae Jung's presidency might have been a historic opportunity to create a new era in labor-management relations in Korea. Kim had long been an advocate of labor rights in the years of authoritarianism. But the financial crisis forced his hand. With the IMF insisting on restructuring the economy and therefore cutting back on work forces—some 37,000 companies went bankrupt during the crisis, including seven of the top thirty chaebol—Kim's representatives had to negotiate a twofold arrangement: organized labor's agreement to the elimination of 1 million to 2 million jobs, and agreement by the chaebol to fund job transition welfare payments. Essentially, Kim's incoming government had to do the IMF's dirty work for it and endure popular protests. The chaebol, whose common practice of borrowing heavily to finance expansion was a principal reason for the currency crisis, moved slowly to pare down their cross-holdings and affiliates. The big winners were foreign investors. Kim said Korea needed foreign competition, and TNCs were welcome to open up the economy.[204] Foreign investors responded to bargain-basement opportunities in banking and services, areas from which they had been excluded. But the role of FDI in the Korean economy remains small in comparison to some of Korea's neighbors, such as China.

Korea's economy recovered from the financial crisis: IMF loans were paid off, chaebol consolidated, and income levels resumed growing. Economic recovery, however, does not ensure political health: Korean democratization continues to be undermined by the Korean disease of buying favors, the "winner takes all" character of political rivalry, and the weakness of parties and parliament.[205] When the current president, Roh Moo Hyun—a human-rights lawyer, a disciple of Kim Dae Jung, and the first president to owe election mainly to young voters and the Internet—steps down in 2008, ten years of liberal rule are likely to end. But during that time, despite various scandals, Korean civil society has burgeoned and a multi-party system has become cemented—aspects of democracy that make South Korea more politically competitive than Japan.

### Brazil: Forests vs. Debts

Tropical forests are among the earth's most precious resources—and among the most endangered. They are home to a substantial proportion (at least half, perhaps as much as 90 percent) of all known plant, animal, and insect species—and probably to even more species that have yet to be catalogued. They are the source of spiritual and material sustenance and healing to the indigenous peoples who inhabit them; of rainfall that helps to regulate the earth's climate; and of much of the earth's oxygen supply. Large-scale depletion of tropical forests threatens all forms of life, and thus the planet's biodiversity. And the threat is very real: In contrast with previous epochs, when approximately one species became extinct every year, today tropical deforestation "condemns at least one species of bird, mammal, or plant to extinction *daily*."[206] It is thus one of many human actions that have accelerated species destruction almost beyond comprehension.[207]

Tropical forests have fallen victim to both human need and greed. Population density, the clearing of land for planting, grazing, and transportation, and the seeming imperatives of national and regional economic growth have put enormous pressures on wet and dry forests alike. One reliable assessment (in 1990) is that "the world is losing up to 20.4 million hectares of tropical forest annually," an amount equal to the area of Panama, and far greater than had been estimated a decade earlier by a UN agency.[208] Most of this loss is occurring in the tropical rain forests of Brazil, India, Indonesia, Costa Rica, Thailand, and Burma, at rates that vary from under 1 percent annually to an estimated 7.6 percent (in the case of Costa Rica).[209] Among the long-term consequences of this destruction is global warming: It is now believed that tropical deforestation accounts for about one-third of all human-caused emissions of carbon dioxide.[210] Saving tropical forests, on the other hand, is a major contribution to combating global warming: They act as a carbon sink, absorbing huge amounts of carbon dioxide produced by the burning of fossil fuels.[211]

The Brazilian case is worth special attention. Brazil's importance rests not only on its role in the world economy as an NIC. Brazil's rapidly growing population of over 180 million, larger than Russia's, is equal to about half of the total population of Latin America. The tropical forests within and outside the Amazon region are the world's largest and may contain as much as 22 percent of all flowering plant species alone.[212] Already, about 6 to 7 percent of the total rain forest is gone; and the smaller flooded portion, which is of unique scientific value, may be lost as soon as "the next decade."[213] Preserving such an enormous environmental and economic asset at a time of substantial external indebtedness and domestic inequalities has become the country's overriding dilemma. Politically, Brazil may be better prepared to cope with it, having emerged from a dark period of military rule (from 1964 to 1985), marked by extensive human-rights violations. But the political system remains unstable, corruptible, and sometimes violent. "Development" is more polarized than ever, as previously observed, and about 22 percent of the population lives on $2 a day.[214] Because of the sheer size of Brazil's economic, social, and environmental problems and possibilities, its future is a matter of global concern.

The pressures to extract the Amazon's riches have been both external and internal. Tropical hardwoods are in great demand worldwide, with Japan, the United States, and other industrialized countries being the leading importers. For the Brazilian government, as for other tropical countries, forest products are a major source of foreign exchange income. Until very recently, Brazilian leaders chafed at suggestions from abroad that the Amazon be treated as a global resource, arguing that the country's huge external debt and development needs ruled out "foreign interference" in how Brazilians should control their forests.

But the principal sources of Brazil's scheme to develop the Amazon region are internal. Most important among them are the social and demographic consequences of Brazil's underdevelopment. Poverty is especially pronounced in the densely populated northeast, where the rural poor have become significantly poorer in recent years. Seventy percent of rural households in Brazil are landless or near landless; 1 percent of landowners own 45 percent of all farmland.[215] Huge numbers of peasants flocked to Brazil's major cities beginning in the 1960s, driven by impossible dreams of employment and homes. (Between 1960 and 1990, Brazil's urban population grew from 45 percent of the total to over 75 percent.[216]) Instead, they added to already serious unemployment, homelessness, and slums.

The Amazonia project—the planned construction in the early 1970s of the Transamazon Highway, which would stretch some 3,300 kilometers on an east-west axis—thus provided the Brazilian government with a "safety valve" for channeling surplus labor, potential dissidents, and land-poor peasants out of Brazil's overcrowded cities.[217] For these people, clearing the seemingly boundless forests loomed as a way out of poverty, particularly after a severe drought hit the northeast. But many other interests were also involved. Amazonian development beckoned those who saw opportunities to profit from the unequaled natural resources in the region: cattle ranchers; tin, manganese, and gold miners; construction companies; and of course timber concerns. Some Brazilian civilian and military officials acted on fears of foreign intervention in the Amazon, great-power ambitions, and fulfillment of the dream of national integration.[218]

These factors converged disastrously with the willingness of international financial institutions, notably the World Bank, to subsidize Amazonian development. During the 1970s and 1980s the World Bank provided loans totaling over $2 billion for electric power and road construction that directly or indirectly contributed to the Amazonia project.[219] Only in the late 1980s did Bank authorities admit publicly the great environmental and human damage that had resulted from spraying with Agent Orange, flooding the forest, and uprooting communities.[220]

The overriding lesson of the project is that the search for short-term economic and social gain through an extractive and speculative form of development can lead to wanton destruction of the ecosystem and the human communities residing in it.[221] The costs of razing the Amazon region have far exceeded the gains. Mining, logging, and cattle ranching have depleted the land. Indian leaders have been killed with seeming impunity, and tribes have had their homelands come under legal challenge, as the government has responded to corporate interests in their lands.[222] The construction of roads and dams brought "civilization" into the interior but also resulted in ravaging fires, floods, and diseases previously unknown among tribal groups. In fact, these very activities brought the destruction of Amazonia to international attention. Forest fires in 1988 covered an area half the size of the United States. Vast clouds of smoke were visible in satellite photos. In the same year, Francisco Chico Mendes, leader of the rubber-tree tappers, was killed by ranchers who evidently feared his successful organizing. Mendes's efforts to end highway construction into his region had attracted support among environmentalists in the United States and elsewhere.

Worldwide criticism of Brazil's development policies in the Amazon eventually produced some positive outcomes. The fires were said to have caused President José Sarney great anguish. As a result, in October 1988 he suspended (and later ended) tax incentives to clear forestland. The rate of deforestation appeared to slow by 1989.[223] Brazil entered into arrangements with the United Nations and other groups to study the Amazon region and determine environmentally compatible land uses. International cooperation was recognized by the Brazilian government as being essential to managing the adverse consequences of deforestation, such as greenhouse emissions and species destruction.[224]

Yet any optimism then about the future of Brazil's forests must now be tempered by subsequent developments. Large-scale development projects continue to be approved in the Amazon. Indigenous tribes remain very much at risk. Cattle ranchers continue burning the forests, oblivious to legal restrictions and contrary to government promises of greater rain forest conservation efforts.[225] Earlier optimism about slowing deforestation is gone; fires and other causes nearly tripled the amount of deforested land between 1990 and the mid-1990s.[226] Under the popular-leftist government of Luiz Inácio "Lula" da Silva, Brazil has the ambition to be a leader of emerging democracies as well as a leader of Mercosur, a bloc that offers a regional alternative to the US-designed CAFTA. But Lula also wants to make Brazil an agribusiness superpower, the leading food exporter in the Americas. As a result, promised land reform has not occurred, swelling the ranks of a combative Landless Rural Workers Movement (MST) that squats on unoccupied private land to press its case for collectivizing agriculture.[227]

Nor has a fresh start been made to protect Amazonia's forests and its people. The rate of forest destruction has declined but remains very high—about 6,000 square miles a year, about the size of the state of Connecticut.[228] Instead, Lula's government has allowed more land to be cleared for soybean planting and, after much internal debate, authorized planting of genetically altered soybean seeds. It was a major victory for Monsanto over local and international environmental groups such as Greenpeace—and this from Lula, a hero of the labor movement.[229] Those decisions have intensified violence in Amazonia, as became clear early in 2005 when an American nun was shot to death by unknown gunmen who almost certainly represented ranching and logging interests. The sister had fought for peasants who are being cheated of their land rights by more powerful individuals who use fraudulent documents and, if they don't get their way, violence.[230] The forced recruitment of peasants into work gangs that fell timber and tend cows for export also occurs—as many as 25,000 men, often illiterate, who work under slave-like conditions.[231]

Clearly, not developing the Amazon region is inconceivable to Brazilian political leaders. That would make sustainable development the most globally responsible option. One approach is to create forest biodiversity reserves—Costa Rica has become a leader in these—with offsetting reduction of Brazil's debt (so-called debt-for-nature swaps). Other alternatives are forest reserves, "extractive reserves" such as Chico Mendes advocated to protect traditional forest industries,[232] identification of plants with medicinal (and therefore also export) value, carefully monitored tree cutting, implementation of reforestation laws, and international assistance to compensate Brazil for lost revenue. If these measures fail, however, Brazil and the international community should take note of the drastic, but necessary, course taken by Thailand: a complete ban on logging to save its greatly shrunken forestland.

Implementing reforms on a scale large enough to save Amazonia and its cultures may depend on global agreement, given the interlinked and transnational character of the issues involved. At the Rio Earth Summit, many government leaders from the South sought such an agreement: In return for the South's acceptance of strict regulations on pollution, greenhouse gases, and forest clearance—problems that, as the South sees it, have mainly occurred in the process of the North's enrichment—the industrialized countries would commit to paying (with development aid) for environmental protection and to making major revisions of the GATT/WTO system. Looking beyond Brazil at the situation for other exporters of tropical forest products, we can see the complexity of this idea and the reasons a forestry convention was rejected. Little has changed since Rio: Governments resist restrictions on their lumber industries, and environmental groups insist on the strongest possible safeguards.[233]

Extending concerns from a focus on Brazil, to include Southeast Asian countries such as Indonesia and Malaysia that also count heavily on exports of timber—raw logs and plywood—for foreign exchange earnings and debt relief, we find many of the same competing interests and problems. Indonesia alone has 10 percent of the world's rain forests. Even though the governments of both countries have claimed to be attempting to limit the felling of trees to sustainable numbers, this is not happening, and may be unachievable, for several reasons.[234] Some have to do with government practices, such as lack of enforcement of cutting regulations, insufficient taxation of timber companies, and permissions for poor farmers to clear forested land for agriculture. Other obstacles arise from conflict in villages for control of forest resources, which are a source of added income and therefore local power. International economics provides additional reasons: increasing timber demand in Japan, South Korea, the United States, and other countries; and high tariffs by Japan on processed wood, such as plywood, that compels exporting countries to cut down more forest to earn more money. As with Brazil, if Indonesia and Malaysia could add more value to the forest products they export, they presumably would not need to cut down as many trees as before.[235] At Rio, neither producing nor consuming states—and behind them the TNCs that extract, process, and market tropical woods—were prepared to make the concessions necessary to produce a sustainability-based agreement.

The consequence of failure to restrain commercial logging became apparent in 1997 and again in 1998, when dense smoke from forest fires on two Indonesian islands created serious health problems and caused some deaths as far away as neighboring Malaysia, Singapore, and Thailand. The fires were helped along by drought brought on by the El Niño weather pattern. The Indonesian government blamed small-scale cultivators who clear land, plant, and move on. In reality, the responsibility lies, as in Brazil, with government export and land-use policies, and corporate practices. These promote concentration of economic power in timber and agribusiness estates whose owners are politically well connected; unsustainable logging by the companies and their foreign partners looking to increase exports; and deliberate setting of fires to clear land, either for planting or to make way for oil palm, which is a highly profitable export crop.[236]

Even if an agreement on sustainable logging could be reached, questions arise about its desirability. It would be an agreement between governments, several of which have been known far more for their corruption in handling foreign aid money than for their commitment to protecting environments and indigenous cultures. NGOs and indigenous peoples would be left out in the cold as government bureaucrats and transnational corporations defined sustainable development and bargained over profits. This limited arrangement has happened before. The Global Environmental Facility of the UN, begun in 1991 and jointly administered by the World Bank and two UN agencies, has an Amazon Pilot Program for sustainable development. But NGOs and community groups have not been consulted on use of the program's funds, leading to suspicions the money will find its way into the usual pockets.[237] The situation is similar with respect to determining how the potentially great wealth from medical and drug patents based on wild plant species is to be shared. One estimate puts the commercial value worldwide at $40 billion a year.[238] As two writers present in Rio observed in connection with the proposed treaty on biodiversity, Indian groups would probably be cut out of patent rights and royalties on the fruits of their knowledge of the medicinal value of tropical plants. "Instead, the biodiversity treaty would compel the industrialized nations to compensate Brazil and other governments of developing nations where the raw materials are found." The large pharmaceutical firms headquartered in the industrialized countries would profit on the manufacturing end.[239]

Can tropical forests be saved? The experience of Brazil, Indonesia, and other Third World countries makes plain that, as the Brundtland Commission wrote, "species conservation is tied to development, and the problems of both are more political than technical."[240] The development process itself, including international aid programs, needs to be redefined so that significant new employment, land reform, and a slowing of population growth are the results. President Fernando Henrique Cardoso was right to say that "Brazil is no longer an undeveloped country, it is an unjust country."[241] There is broad agreement that equitable solutions are only achievable with the participation of local people in development planning.[242] In Amazonia, that means respecting the land rights, culture, and knowledge of the forests of various indigenous peoples and ensuring that they receive a fair proportion of income derived from their knowledge and labor. In the northeast and other impoverished rural areas, where the MST is most active, the resentments of the poor need to be addressed with meaningful land reform, not violence. Changes also are needed in the tariff policies and consumer demands of user countries. TNC extraction procedures need to be regulated to conform with rules of sustainability, strictly defined. Without wide-ranging changes such as these, Brazil and other states will continue to regard tropical forests as sources of debt relief and new wealth—until, that is, the forests are no more.

### Failing and Recovering States: Haiti, Venezuela, and Bolivia

"Failed states" is not a well-defined category; it refers generally to countries where governance is weak to the point where the country is barely holding together, as in Somalia and Iraq. Usually, economies in such states are fragile even if resource-rich (like Nigeria), human security is exceptionally low, and therefore prospects of widespread violence are high.[243] Authoritarian regimes in Fourth World countries, mainly in Africa and Central Asia, dominate the list of failed states.[244] These are "at-risk" states, meaning states in which a critical mass of indicators provides warning signs. The indicators include demographic pressures, such as major refugee movements and starvation; lack of democratic practices; and a sharp decline in the economy.[245]

Assessing which states are failing is difficult. By the indicators just mentioned, there are too many states at risk of failure, perhaps a third of the total. Few of them, though fragile in one way or another—for example, North Korea's widespread human insecurity; Liberia's destitution following the dictatorship under Charles Taylor; and Mexico's police and court corruption—seem unlikely to implode. "Recovering states," by contrast, may share some of the ingredients of those considered failing. But their governments have chosen to take economic development on a new course that just might enhance the quality of life and reestablish a national consensus. Of the three countries studied in this section, Haiti is a prime example of a high-risk state, whereas Venezuela and Bolivia show promise of being recovering states. What their experiences commonly reflect is the importance of preventive action against state collapse. Major increases in grass-roots-focused economic development and debt-relief assistance are one form of prevention.[246] Another, less often mentioned, is engagement that supports human and cooperative security. Failure by the major countries to act preventively, or prescribing the wrong medicine, often yields tragic outcomes, such as Rwanda, Somalia, Afghanistan, North Korea, and Haiti.

Haiti is the poorest state in the Western Hemisphere. It has a poverty rate of around 80 percent. Most of its college-educated citizens leave the country. Its politics is in constant turmoil, and violence linked to personal loyalty dominates over the rule of law. Nearly all the indicators of human underdevelopment cited in the first part of this chapter apply with special force to Haiti. Despite elections, Haiti is by any definition a failed state. It is also an example of how international aid does not work when it is lent with onerous conditions, not to mention lent to a government that cannot function amidst constant political violence. Haiti received $150 million from the IMF beginning in the 1980s and over $1 billion in World Bank loans since the 1950s. But the requirements of "structural adjustment" greatly restricted what any Haitian government could do for the poor.[247] Thus, following the US military intervention and occupation in 1994, Haiti was pressured by Washington and the foreign-aid community to sell off state enterprises as a condition of international assistance. The probable beneficiaries were the international bankers and TNCs.[248]

In Haiti President Aristide, ousted by the military in 1991 in a coup that was roundly condemned throughout Latin America, returned to power when the United States sent in troops three years later. He briefly retired from politics at the conclusion of his term in 1996, and was succeeded by René

Garcia Préval. Aristide was reelected in 2000. But the election was so one-sided that it led to suspension of international assistance programs. When efforts to negotiate failed, the opposition formed a shadow government, setting the stage for yet another crisis. By 2004 that crisis was in full bloom as pro- and anti-government groups, the latter led by elements of the previous terror regime,[249] took to the streets and demonstrations turned violent. Aristide's presidency had clearly failed, helped along by US interference in the guise of providing support for Haitian democracy.[250] Aristide was "advised" by the United States to leave the country, which he did—the latest in a long list of US interventions in Haiti.[251] A UN peacekeeping mission was sent in. But the violence did not end, and by 2006 new elections had to be postponed for a fourth time. Préval was eventually elected in a bizarre ruling by Haiti's electoral council; but whether or not he can persuade the international community to come through with pledged aid and debt cancellation is doubtful at a time of continuing economic decline, kidnappings and other violence, and an unsupportive, interventionist United States.[252]

In contrast with Haiti, a populist revolution seems to be sweeping over a large part of Latin America. As a Mexican scholar and statesman has assessed it, the revolution represents a "makeover of the radical left," with two variations: a more moderate version, such as in Chile and Brazil, and a more stridently nationalist version, represented in Venezuela and Bolivia. Both versions emerged from similar sources: inept, corrupt governance; the failure to reduce poverty; and US neglect of Latin America.[253] Under pressure from globalization and specifically the Washington consensus, another astute observer of the Latin scene has written, the region's social contract has been broken:

> A popular and political ground swell is building from the Andes to Argentina against the decade-old experiment with free-market capitalism. The reforms that have shrunk the state and opened markets to foreign competition, many believe, have enriched corrupt officials and faceless multinationals, and failed to better their lives. . . .Today the market reforms ushered in by American-trained economists after the global collapse of Communism are facing their greatest challenge in the upheavals sweeping the region.[254]

Under Hugo Chávez, who was elected president in 1999, Venezuela has become Latin American populism's most visible exponent. His government is seeking to reverse a long period of economic decline—twenty years of negative GDP growth by an oil-rich country.[255] Consistent with our Third World country profile, Venezuela had income inequality figures much like Brazil's before Chávez took power, such as an enormous gap between the richest and poorest 10 percent of households.[256] The Venezuelan "petrostate" that grew out of sudden oil wealth had squandered it. Various leaders used oil to create a myth of social progress while in fact consolidating the state, intensifying the power of oligarchs, and deepening external dependence.[257]

The political and economic power that comes from being a major oil producer also motivates Huge Chávez, but in a way quite different from his predecessors. Announcing the intention to build a "21st-century socialism," his government has spent around $20 billion in oil revenues to reduce what the UNDP calls human poverty—illiteracy, adult and child mortality rates, and child malnutrition, for instance—such that Venezuela ranks a very respectable fourteenth among 103 developing countries (just behind Mexico) on the UNDP's human poverty index, and had 10 percent economic growth in 2006.[258] Not all the human-development indicators show progress, to be sure; nor might his model, based as in past years on oil and state-run programs, be sustainable, especially if oil prices should fall.[259] Still, his social concerns seem genuine, a real break with Venezuela's, and Latin America's, past ignoring of the poor. But Chávez's appeal has also made him a pariah to the United States, for he, like Cuba's Fidel Castro, has directly confronted US hegemony. Castro did not have the oil weapon, however. Chávez does, and he has forced foreign oil companies in Venezuela either to sell it a majority stake or have its operations completely taken over. The royalties and taxes that the companies must pay have greatly increased.[260] Venezuela's oil riches have funded a sizable foreign aid program, not just in African nations but also, at cut-rate prices, in the Caribbean and Cuba. Chávez has helped Argentina pay off its debt to the IMF, established trade ties with Iran, and reached an oil deal with China.[261] Within OPEC, Venezuela has pushed for increasing oil production.

Oil is critical to Venezuela's budget and trade. It is also critical to the United States, which relies on Venezuela for 15 percent of total oil imports, behind only Canada and Saudi Arabia.[262] Those realities place Chávez in harm's way: US officials do not take kindly to governments that defy the Washington consensus, especially those possessing oil. In April 2002 US officials had a hand in a failed coup attempt against Chávez that has embittered relations ever since.[263] To the Bush administration, Chávez is "a demagogue awash in oil money [who] is undermining democracy and seeking to destabilize the region"—quite a charge by a government that sought to overthrow an elected and popular leader.[264]

Hugo Chávez is a controversial and enigmatic figure, a modern-day Simon Bolivar to some and part of an "axis of evil" to others.[265] Whether or not he can sustain a commitment to alleviating Venezuela's poverty and a foreign policy that cultivates opponents of the United States remains to be seen. But he is a nationalist and a populist leader who seeks new outlets for Venezuela's oil, and it is a mistake to dismiss him as another Cold War–era leftist dictator who should be ousted.

Similarly, in Bolivia, the anti-politics of globalization has produced

another populist, Evo Morales, a labor leader of indigenc
rose to the presidency in 2006 with an astounding (for Bol
of the vote. Morales had placed second in elections in 2002
kenness on behalf of coca growers, the poor Indian majorit
of economic liberalization put him on Washington's radar screen. w ɪɪ.,.,
upon election, Morales reiterated his intention to permit coca cultivation but
not cocaine production, the Bush administration placed him in the same category as Castro and Chávez.

Here again, Washington's view seems oblivious to Bolivian realities.
Bolivia is one of the poorest and politically unstable countries in Latin
America. Its economic situation has more in common with Haiti than with
Venezuela: a UNDP HDI ranking of 113 (Haiti's is 153; Venezuela's is 35),
based on severe problems such as income disparities, high illiteracy, poor
access to medical care, and low life expectancy. In the six years prior to
Morales's election, Bolivia had been ruled by seven presidents. Government
debt accounts for 20 percent of revenue and translates into debt servicing
that far exceeds what the government can spend on health care.[266] Yet, like
Venezuela, Bolivia has valuable resources, and any Bolivian government
interested in humane economic development must rely on its few assets,
mainly coca, natural gas, and oil. By the same token, it would have to reject
the traditional World Bank and IMF prescriptions for growth, prescriptions
that had been applied, with disastrous results, since the 1980s.[267] Morales's
rise to power came on the wings of defiant protests of the established order
and a promise to "end the colonial and neoliberal model" of development.[268]

In light of Bolivia's poverty and US insistence on coca eradication, it is
hardly surprising that Morales turned for support to Venezuela. Although
the United States remains the largest single aid donor (around $100 million
a year), the amount is paltry. Washington has rejected Morales's plan to
make legal, exportable products from coca, such as tea, shampoo, and flour.
Morales contends that his plan would benefit far more farmers, without the
coca being processed into cocaine, than would the US plan to pay farmers
for planting different crops.[269] The Bush administration also angered
Bolivia's military by cutting off nearly all military aid after Morales's victory, a step perhaps designed to encourage a coup. US agencies run development programs all over Bolivia, but Venezuela and Cuba have stepped in
with medical training, scholarships, rural education, and other more visible
grassroots programs.[270]

"We shouldn't be poor," Morales has said, and some prominent US
economists agree with Bolivian plans to demand a controlling interest in the
country's major oil and gas industries. Like Chávez, Morales is not opposed
to TNC investments, free-trade ideas, or even the IMF; but he wants a new
deal based on equity, not another "structural adjustment," and he is backed
by a citizenry that is tired of being maltreated.[271] If anything, Brazil and not

Cuba is Morales's model, as he demonstrated when he was able to win agreement from foreign energy companies in 2006 to expand the state's ownership stake, and thus its revenues. Yet the US treats Morales "as if he were the Osama bin Laden of Latin America," as one Latin America expert has put it.[272] US intransigence will make President Morales's task of delivering real development to his people all the more problematic. And he is likely to be followed by still other populist leaders.[273]

## Notes

1. Alan B. Durning, *Poverty and the Environment: Reversing the Downward Spiral*, Worldwatch Paper 92, pp. 12–13.
2. For background, see André Gunder Frank, *Crisis: In the World Economy,* ch. 5. On the full range of the NIEO agenda, see Frank, pp. 273–74.
3. Compare World Bank, *World Development Report 1984*, p. 6 (hereafter cited as World Bank 1984) with the *Human Development Report 2005*, p. 115.
4. *Human Development Report 2005*, p. 118.
5. Ibid., p. 37.
6. Ibid., p. 34.
7. Ibid., p. 55.
8. See Joseph Kahn, "Losing Faith: Globalization Proves Disappointing," *NYT*, March 21, 2002, p. A6.
9. Annan, *Millennium Report*, ch. 2, pp. 14–15.
10. *Human Development Report 2000*, p. 82; UNDP, *Human Development Report 2002*, pp. 18–19.
11. Anthony Smith, ch. 1; Lawrence Weschler, "The Other Democratic Revolution of 1989," *Utne Reader,* pp. 38–44.
12. Stephen D. Krasner, *Structural Conflict: The Third World Against Global Liberalism.*
13. See Rupert Emerson, "The Fate of Human Rights in the Third World," *World Politics,* pp. 201–26, on the denial by Third World spokespersons of ethnic and democratic rights in their own countries.
14. Patricia Adams, "Rio Agenda: Soak the West's Taxpayers," *Asian Wall Street Journal,* June 5–6, 1992, p. 8.
15. Frank, p. 271.
16. Mohammed Ayoob, "State Making, State Breaking, and State Failure," in Crocker and Hampson, eds., *Managing Global Chaos*, p. 47.
17. Ajami, "The Fate of Nonalignment," p. 370.
18. The income figures are from World Bank, *World Development Report 1990* (hereafter World Bank 1990), table 1, p. 178; and World Bank, *World Development Report 1997: The State in a Changing World* (hereafter World Bank 1997), table 1, p. 214. A similar situation exists elsewhere in Central America. See Billie R. DeWalt, "The Agrarian Bases of Conflict in Central America," in Kenneth M. Coleman and George C. Herring, eds., *The Central American Crisis: Sources of Conflict and the Failure of U.S. Policy,* p. 50.
19. See *Human Development Report 2002*, pp. 59–60; Sachs, *The End of Poverty,* pp. 312–15.
20. A. Kent MacDougall, "In Third World, All but the Rich Are Poorer," *Los Angeles Times,* November 4, 1984, sec. 6, pp. 1–3; Durning, *Poverty and the Environment,* pp. 15, 20.

21. From UNDP's "poverty clock," report 95–12 (1996), online at www.undp.org.

22. Overview of *Human Development Report 1997,* p. 2, online at http://hdr.undp.org/reports/global/1997/en/pdf/hdr_1997_overview.pdf.

23. *NYT,* August 14, 1997, p. A7; Amy Waldman, "Poor in India Starve as Surplus Wheat Rots," *NYT,* December 2, 2002, p. A3; Pankaj Mishra, "The Myth of the New India," *NYT,* July 6, 2006, p. A23.

24. For Clinton's remark, see *NYT,* March 25, 2000, p. A4; on childhood malnutrition, see *NYT,* May 3, 2006, p. A6, based on a UNICEF study.

25. World Bank 1992, p. 30.

26. *Human Development Report 2005,* p. 36; Ginger Thompson, "In Study on Children's Welfare, Latin America Is Most Improved," *NYT,* December 12, 2002, p. A12.

27. Nathaniel C. Nash, "Latin American Speedup Leaves Poor in the Dust," *NYT,* September 7, 1994, p. 1.

28. On Chile, see Marc Cooper, "Twenty-five Years After Allende: An Anti-Memoir," *The Nation,* pp. 11–23; Jack Epstein, "Chile's Economy Still Bustling," *Christian Science Monitor,* December 8, 1994, p. 8; and *Human Development Report 2005,* table 15, p. 270.

29. UPI report in *Korea Herald* (Seoul), March 8, 1994, p. 9.

30. Waste dumping and pollution are widely recognized as being responsible for illnesses on both sides of the border that are far above the average. But after five years, "not a single environmental project" has been started under NAFTA's financing arrangement. Sam Howe Verhovek, "Pollution Puts People in Peril on the Border with Mexico," *NYT,* July 4, 1998, p. A7.

31. Ginger Thompson, "Mexico Is Attracting a Better Class of Factory in Its South," *NYT,* June 29, 2002, online ed. at www.nytimes.com.

32. "Only two in five borrowing countries," said the World Bank report, "have recorded continuous per capita growth over the 5 years ending in 2005, and just one in five did so for a full 10 years." World Bank, Independent Evaluation Group, "Annual Review of Development Effectiveness 2006," at www.worldbank.org.

33. Barnet, *Lean Years,* p. 262.

34. By 2030, cities are expected to grow by 160 percent, rural areas by only 10 percent. *World Development Report 1992,* p. 27.

35. Hammond, *World Resources 1990–91,* p. 66.

36. UN, *World Social Situation in the 1990s,* p. 103.

37. Oxfam America, "Special Report: Women in Development," pp. 1–8; John-Thor Dahlburg, "Closing the Education Gap for Women," *Los Angeles Times World Report,* April 16, 1994, p. 1.

38. The quotation is from a UN Population Fund annual report, in Barbara Crossette, "Working for Women's Sexual Rights," *NYT,* October 2, 2000, p. A10. See also *NYT,* June 11, 1996, p. A1; *Washington Post,* June 15, 1996; and Save the Children, *State of the World's Mothers 2004.*

39. *Nikkei Weekly* (Tokyo), September 12, 1992, p. 13.

40. Barbara Crosette, "Court Backs Egypt's Ban on Genital Cutting of Girls," *NYT,* December 29, 1997, online. In banning the practice, an Egyptian court denounced the notion that it was authorized by the Quran.

41. John F. Burns, "India Fights Abortion of Female Fetuses," *NYT,* August 27, 1994, p. A5.

42. See, for example, articles in the *New York Times* during early April 1998, when the executive director of UNICEF, Carol Bellamy, visited Afghanistan expressly to determine the Taliban's treatment of women.

43. "The Complete Mothers' Index 2004," Save the Children, *State of the World's Mothers 2004*. See also Susan J. Pharr, *Political Women in Japan: The Search for a Place in Political Life*, pp. 174–77.

44. Roderic A. Camp, "Women and Political Leadership in Mexico: A Comparative Study of Female and Male Political Elites," *Journal of Politics*, p. 440.

45. According to the World Food Program; see *NYT*, November 13, 1996, p. A5.

46. World Health Organization (WHO) statistics; see John-Thor Dahlburg, "'Theirs Are the Silent Deaths,'" *Los Angeles Times World Report*, December 17, 1995, p. 1.

47. From a UNICEF study reported in *NYT*, June 12, 1995, p. A5.

48. *NYT*, November 12, 1996, p. 6.

49. Gordon Fairclough, "It Isn't Black and White," *Far Eastern Economic Review*, March 7, 1996, pp. 54–57.

50. Robert I. Friedman, "India's Shame," *The Nation*.

51. Celia W. Dugger, "Unicef Report Says Children in Deprivation Reach a Billion," *NYT*, September 10, 2004, p. A18.

52. Marc Lacey, "Beyond the Bullets and Blades," *NYT*, March 20, 2005, sec. 4, p. 1.

53. For analyses of the Green Revolution, see Susan George, *How the Other Half Dies: The Real Reasons for World Hunger*, especially ch. 5; Betsy Hartmann and James K. Boyce, *Needless Hunger: Voices from a Bangladesh Village*, pp. 48–54; and Vandana Shiva, *The Violence of the Green Revolution: Third World Agriculture, Ecology and Politics*. Kusum Nair's study, *In Defense of the Irrational Peasant: Indian Agriculture After the Green Revolution*, recounts the different results of the Green Revolution for inefficient rich landowners and efficient small farmers.

54. Sources for this paragraph include Maude Barlow and Tony Clarke, "Who Owns Water?" *The Nation*, pp. 11–15; and John Tagliabue, "As Multinationals Run the Taps, Anger Rises over Water for Profit," *NYT*, August 26, 2002, p. 1.

55. *Human Development Report 1992*, p. 39.

56. World Bank 1997, tables 6 and 7, pp. 224–27. Figures are for 1995.

57. *Human Development Report 2005*, table 10, pp. 250–52 and table 7, pp. 240–42. Health-care figures are for 2003; safe water figures are for 2002.

58. Ibid., table 6, pp. 236–38.

59. Head, p. 81.

60. Strong, "Consensus: If Not Now, When?" *International Herald Tribune*, June 1, 1992, p. 16. No such aid commitment was made by the industrialized countries at the Earth Summit.

61. The tobacco industry's efforts are recounted in a four-part series starting with Glenn Frankel, "Big Tobacco's Global Reach," *Washington Post*, November 17, 1996, online at www.washingtonpost.com. On smoking in Asia and its health consequences, see Anne Platt McGinn, "Preventing Chronic Disease in Developing Countries," in Lester R. Brown et al., eds., *State of the World 1997*, pp. 71–73.

62. Examples of these conditions were high malnutrition, over 50 percent illiteracy, high infant mortality, 30 percent of national income held by 5 percent of the population, extensive landlessness among peasants, and control of all major sectors of the economy by the Somoza family. See Richard Harris and Carlos M. Vilas, eds., *Nicaragua: A Revolution Under Siege*, pp. 299–302. The class system is documented in Peter Rosset and John Vandermeer, eds., *The Nicaragua Reader: Documents of a Revolution Under Fire*, pp. 122–27; DeWalt, in Coleman and Herring, pp. 50–51; and Carlos M. Vilas, *The Sandinista Revolution: National Liberation and Social Transformation in Central America*, pp. 56–81, 101–16, on rural and urban condi-

tions. Nicaragua's underdevelopment did *not,* however, include significant foreign investment (Vilas, pp. 81–83).

63. See Rosset and Vandermeer, pp. 341–46. On the social and economic character and nature of the Sandinistan program, see Harris and Vilas; Joseph Collins et al., *What Difference Could a Revolution Make? Food and Family in the New Nicaragua.*

64. *Human Development Report 1992,* table 4, p. 134, and table 17, p. 160.

65. World Bank 1997, tables 4, 6, and 17, pp. 220, 224, 246.

66. *Human Development Report 2005,* p. 89.

67. From a study of the Population Institute in Washington, DC, as reported in *NYT,* December 31, 1997, p. A7.

68. For a brief review of the evidence on overpopulation and underdevelopment, see Garvin and Rosenbaum, pp. 18–25. Cultural factors, of course, such as the status gained from having more children, also are among the reasons behind large families.

69. MacDougall, p. 3.

70. Krishna Ghimire, "Population, Environment and Development," *Tiempo,* no. 12 (1997), online at www.cru.uea.ac.uk/tiempo/newswatch. The female illiteracy rate comes from World Bank 1997, table 7, p. 226.

71. Timothy C. Weiskel, "Vicious Circles: African Demographic History as a Warning," *Harvard International Review,* p. 12.

72. See the comprehensive study by the International Fund for Agricultural Development, *Rural Poverty Report 2001,* at www.ifad.org/poverty/.

73. Barbara Crossette, "U.S. Aid Cutbacks Endangering Population Programs, U.N. Agencies Say," *NYT,* February 16, 1996, p. A6; Juliet Eilperin and Dana Milbank, "Bush May Cut U.N. Program's Funding," *Washington Post,* June 29, 2002.

74. Calvin Sims, "Using Gifts as Bait, Peru Sterilizes Women," *NYT,* February 15, 1998, online.

75. Frank, pp. 183–90.

76. *Human Development Report 2005,* p. 127.

77. Tim Weiner, "Bush Meets Skepticism on Free Trade at Americas Conference," *NYT,* January 14, 2004, p. A9.

78. *NYT,* September 30, 2002, p. A7. Another former chief economist for the Bank chided the Bush administration for its "one-sided" approach to trade issues in general, which he said merely serves special US interests and was sure to increase ill will toward the United States. See Joseph E. Stiglitz, "New Trade Pacts Betray the Poorest Partners," *NYT,* July 10, 2004, p. A29.

79. See Susan Sechler and Ann Tutwiler, "Trading Up," *NYT,* June 26, 2006, p. A23, citing a study by the International Food Policy Research Institute.

80. Robert B. Zoellick, the chief US trade representative, speaking at Doha (Qatar), *NYT,* November 15, 2001, p. A12. The reference is to the antiglobalization protests that took place at a WTO meeting in Seattle in December 1999.

81. Alexei Barrionuevo, "A Warning of Trade Suits over Farming," *NYT,* November 30, 2005, p. C1; Marc Lacey, "African's Burden: West's Farm Subsidies," *NYT,* September 10, 2003, p. A10; Elizabeth Becker, "African Nations Press for an End to Cotton Subsidies in the West," *NYT,* September 12, 2003, p. A5. Brazil wound up bringing cotton subsidies before a WTO arbitration panel, which found in its favor and ruled further that export credit guarantees on other products of about $3.5 billion a year were also illegal. But that didn't settle the matter. US protests continued (see Raymond Colitt and Edward Alden, "Brazil Joy at Ruling on US Cotton Subsidies," *NYT,* June 18, 2004, online ed.).

82. Ha-Joon Chang, *Kicking Away the Ladder: Development Strategies in Historical Perspective.*

83. These conditions included large amounts of US aid and military protection for Korea and Taiwan, the availability of Chinese and European money in Hong Kong and Singapore, a previous industrial base, and an early reliance on labor-intensive exports made cheap by repression of workers. See Haggard, ch. 8.

84. An excellent case study of denationalization caused by TNC takeovers of local firms is by Richard S. Newfarmer, "TNC Takeovers in Brazil: The Uneven Distribution of Benefits in the Market for Firms," *World Development,* pp. 25–43.

85. Brazil's multibillion-dollar computer market, long insulated from foreign competition by high tariffs, is now open for the taking. A new law passed in October 1992 will enable IBM and other microcomputer leaders to compete with local producers. Although some laws that favor local producers and sellers remain on the books, there is no way they can compete with the quality or marketing options of IBM, Apple, and Compaq. James Bruce, "Brazil's New Computer Market," *U.S./Latin Trade,* pp. 48–52.

86. "Trade, Debt and Plunder in Mexico: An Interview with Cuauhtémoc Cárdenas," *Multinational Monitor,* January/February 1991, pp. 25–27.

87. Haggard, table 8.11, p. 218.

88. Brown, *Building a Sustainable Society,* pp. 92–94. Some of the richer food-dependent countries today are in Asia: See Gary Gardner, "Preserving Global Cropland," in Brown et al., eds., *State of the World 1997,* p. 53.

89. See Robert H. Bates, *Markets and States in Tropical Africa: The Political Basis of Agricultural Policies.*

90. See Barnet, *Lean Years,* pp. 153, 156, 169. A US Department of State publication notes: "The US accounts for more than 65% of world coarse grain trade, 50% of world wheat trade, and about 60% of trade in soybeans and soybean products, and is an important factor in the world market in meat, poultry, and fruits and vegetables" ("Agriculture in US Foreign Economic Policy," *GIST,* November 1981, p. 1).

91. Lester R. Brown, "Facing the Prospect of Food Scarcity," in Brown et al., eds., *State of the World 1997,* pp. 23–26.

92. Barnet, *Lean Years,* pp. 152–53. In some of the richest countries, as much as three-quarters of all grain is fed to livestock. So is an increasing amount of soybeans. That makes meat an extremely expensive source of protein, and one that literally takes food out of the mouths of the poor. See Brown, *Building a Sustainable Society,* pp. 105–7.

93. On the corruption, inefficiency, and politics that bedevil food aid programs, see George, *How the Other Half Dies,* ch. 8; Frances Moore Lappé and Joseph Collins, *Food First: Beyond the Myth of Scarcity,* pp. 328–39; and Barnet, *Lean Years,* p. 155.

94. Lawrence K. Altman, "AIDS in 5 Nations Called Security Threat," *NYT,* October 1, 2002, p. A10; *NYT,* November 27, 2002, p. A10.

95. See the science section of *NYT,* March 28, 2006, for several informative articles on "Avian Flu: The Uncertain Threat."

96. Donald G. McNeil Jr., "New List of Safe AIDS Drugs, Despite Industry Lobby," *NYT,* March 21, 2002, p. A3.

97. Brown, *Building a Sustainable Society,* pp. 36–40.

98. Peter Theroux, "The Imperiled Nile Delta," *National Geographic,* pp. 8–9.

99. Alexander Stille, "The Ganges' Next Life," *The New Yorker,* pp. 58–67.

100. Donatella Lorch, "Even with Peace and Rain, Ethiopia Fears Famine,"

*NYT,* January 3, 1996, p. A3; Celia W. Dugger, "Overfarming African Land Is Worsening Hunger Crisis," *NYT,* March 31, 2006, p. A7.

101. On the Amazon, see Brown et al., *State of the World 1985,* pp. 12–13, and Barnet, *Lean Years,* p. 75. The loss of species is documented in Wolf, p. 14.

102. On TNC clear-cutting operations, see Norman Myers, "The Conversion of Tropical Forests," *Environment,* pp. 6–13.

103. Colin H. Kahl, "Population Growth, Environmental Degradation, and State-Sponsored Violence: The Case of Kenya, 1991–1993."

104. See the reports of Survival International at www.survival-inter-national.org, as well as John McBeth, "Company Under Siege," *Far Eastern Economic Review,* January 25, 1996, pp. 26–28, and Jane Perlez and Evelyn Rusli, "Spurred by Illness, Indonesians Lash Out at U.S. Mining Giant," *NYT,* September 8, 2004, p. 1.

105. The potential for conflict arising out of environmental changes, interacting with many other factors, is explored by Thomas F. Homer-Dixon in, "On the Threshold: Environmental Changes as Causes of Acute Conflict," *International Security.*

106. See David Weir, "The Boomerang Crime," *Mother Jones,* pp. 40–49. The serious health problems being posed by imported food in the United States are discussed by Jeff Gerth and Tim Weiner, "Imports Swamp U.S. Food-Safety Efforts," *NYT,* September 20, 1997, p. 1.

107. Sunkel, in Muñoz, pp. 99–109.

108. Average population growth is 2.4 percent annually nationwide, but much higher in rural areas, creating an expected population of 80 million by 2000. Judith Banister, *Vietnam Population and Dynamics,* pp. 31–38, 58–61; World Conservation Monitoring Centre (Britain) online at http://geo.unep-wcmc.org/infoserv/countryp/vietnam/chapter2.html, "The Socialist Republic of Vietnam," ch. 2. Thanks to Robert Leeper for research on Vietnam.

109. World Conservation Monitoring Centre (UK) online at http://geo.unep-wcmc.org/infoserv/countryp/vietnam/chapter2.html; World Bank Project Report, "Vietnam Forest Protection and Barren Lands Development," World Bank online at www.worldbank.org; Alexander S. Mather, *Global Forest Resources.*

110. Mark Selden, *Reinventing Vietnamese Socialism: Doi Moi in Comparative Perspective,* p. 241.

111. Alan Burnett, *The Western Pacific: Challenge of Sustainable Growth,* p. 80; M. Hiebert, "Food or Forests," *Far Eastern Economic Review,* April 7, 1994, p. 48.

112. Don Lee, "Eyeing WTO Membership, Vietnam Girds for Change," *Los Angeles Times,* August 19, 2006.

113. Althea L. Duersten and Arpad von Lazar, "The Global Poor," in Daniel Yergin and Martin Hillenbrand, eds., *Global Insecurity: A Strategy for Energy and Economic Renewal,* pp. 266–67.

114. IMF figures cited in Chris W. Scholl, "International Capital Flows and Institutions," in Michael T. Snarr and T. Neil Snarr, eds., *Introducing Global Issues,* 3rd. ed., p. 124.

115. World Bank 1984, table 16, pp. 248–49.

116. *Human Development Report 2005,* table 19, pp. 280–81; *NYT,* April 22, 2006, p. A6.

117. World Bank 1997, table 17, pp. 246–67; *Human Development Report 2005,* table 19, pp. 280–81.

118. *NYT,* March 7, 1995, p. A6.

119. *Human Development Report 2005,* p. 89. In 2006 the World Bank

announced that seventeen of those twenty-nine countries, mostly in Africa, would receive "irrevocable" debt relief amounting to $37 billion. *NYT*, April 22, 2006, p. A6; also see www.worldbank.org (May 10, 2006).

120. Summaries from country studies of the IMF in action may be found in Hayter, pp. 154–62; and Payer, *Debt Trap*, pp. 41–42.

121. For example, see the report on the World Bank's impact on small businesses in Chile, in Cynthia Brown, "The High Cost of Monetarism in Chile," *The Nation*.

122. Giovanni Andrea Cornia, "Adjustment Policies 1980–1985: Effects on Child Welfare," in Cornia et al., eds., *Adjustment with a Human Face: Protecting the Vulnerable and Promoting Growth*, pp. 60–68. The study was done for UNICEF.

123. IMF-mandated price increases on food and other necessities were frequent occurrences in the 1980s; they happened in Mexico, Brazil, Turkey, Egypt, Peru, and Venezuela, among other countries. Popular protests against IMF austerity programs occurred again in Brazil in 2000 and Bolivia in 2003.

124. See Peggy Hallward, "The Urgent Need for a Campaign Against Forced Resettlement," *The Ecologist*, pp. 43–44; Susan George, *A Fate Worse Than Debt*, ch. 10.

125. Ransom A. Myers and Boris Worm, "Rapid Worldwide Depletion of Predatory Fish Communities," *Nature*, pp. 280–83.

126. *Human Development Report 2005*, table 19, p. 283.

127. *NYT*, April 18, 2005, p. A10.

128. See *Human Development Report 1992*, pp. 41–45, and *Human Development Report 2005*, pp. 87–88.

129. Sources for this paragraph include Robert A. Manning, "The Philippines in Crisis," *Foreign Affairs*, p. 397; Amnesty International, *Human Rights in the Philippines: Hearing Before the Subcommittee on International Organizations of the Committee on International Relations, House of Representatives*, pp. 4, 17; Lawyers Committee for Human Rights, *"Salvaging" Democracy: Human Rights in the Philippines;* Walden Bello, "U.S. Sponsored Low-Intensity Conflict in the Philippines," p. 86; Walden Bello et al., *Development Debacle: The World Bank in the Philippines; Human Development Report 1992*, table 17, p. 160, and table 19, p. 164; and World Bank 1997.

130. See, for example, Edward A. Gargan, "Last Laugh for the Philippines," *NYT*, December 11, 1997, p. C1.

131. *Human Development Report 2005*, table 19, p. 281.

132. The roughly 3.5 million Filipino workers abroad, the world's largest such group of foreign migrant workers, send home anywhere from $3 billion to $6 billion annually, which is the government's main source of foreign exchange. See Jonathan Karp, "A New Kind of Hero," *Far Eastern Economic Review*, March 30, 1995, pp. 42–45.

133. Celia W. Dugger, "U.N. Proposes Doubling of Aid to Cut Poverty," *NYT*, January 18, 2005, p. 1.

134. *Human Development Report 2005*, figure 3.10, p. 94.

135. "Making the Brady Plan Work," *Foreign Affairs;* and James S. Henry, "Dance of Debt Isn't Over Yet," *U.S. News & World Report*, pp. 39–41.

136. *Human Development Report 2005*, p. 87.

137. Celia W. Dugger, "U.S. Challenged to Increase Aid to Africa," *NYT*, June 5, 2005, p. 8.

138. See *NYT*, March 19, 2001, online ed.

139. Michael T. Klare has written on both Soviet and US arms sales to the Third World. See "Soviet Arms Transfers to the Third World," *Bulletin of the Atomic*

*Scientists;* and Michael T. Klare and Cynthia Arnson, *Supplying Repression: U.S. Support for Authoritarian Regimes Abroad.*

140. *Human Development Report 1992,* p. 45.

141. World Bank 1990, p. 17.

142. Nicole Ball, "Military Expenditure and Socio-Economic Development," *International Social Science Journal.*

143. Julius O. Ihonvbere, "The State, Governance, and Democratization in Africa: Constraints and Possibilities," *Hunger TeachNet,* p. 5.

144. The official speaking was Secretary-General Annan's deputy, Mark Malloch Brown (*NYT,* April 5, 2000, p. A11), referring to "Overcoming Human Poverty: UNDP Poverty Report 2000,"available at www.undp.org/povertyreport/exec/english.html.

145. Sivard, *Military and Social Expenditures 1983,* p. 11.

146. Sivard, *Military and Social Expenditures 1991,* p. 19.

147. Ibid., p. 19.

148. William D. Hartung, "Nixon's Children: Bill Clinton and the Permanent Arms Bazaar," *World Policy Journal.*

149. Stephen Kinzer, "Scandal Links Turkish Aides to Deaths, Drugs, and Terror," *NYT,* December 10, 1996, p. 1. An investigation of a highway accident led to evidence of links between a heroin ring and high-ranking government officials and politicians of various parties. The key reason for this unholy alliance apparently was to assassinate Kurdish leaders, in exchange for the government's looking the other way on heroin trafficking.

150. Bertil Lintner, "Narcopolitics in Burma," *Current History.*

151. See Christopher S. Wren, "Heroin Puts Burma in Crisis over AIDS," *NYT,* May 3, 1998, p. 1.

152. Dennis Bernstein and Leslie Kean, "People of the Opiate: Burma's Dictatorship of Drugs," *The Nation.*

153. See Michael Renner, *The Anatomy of Resource Wars,* Paper 162.

154. *NYT,* June 11, 2004, p. W1.

155. See Donna Lee Van Cott, *Defiant Again: Indigenous Peoples and Latin American Security.*

156. Roberta Cohen and Francis M. Deng, "Exodus Within Borders," *Foreign Affairs.*

157. *Human Development Report 1992,* pp. 54–55.

158. Ibid., p. 54.

159. The resettlement program is designed to prevent migration to Java, the main island and the most overcrowded. See Seth Mydans, "Indonesia Resettles People to Relieve Crowding on Java," *NYT,* August 25, 1996, online.

160. Migration is often a safety valve for governments that cannot provide employment and see remittances from their citizens' overseas work as a way to compensate for low export earnings. *Human Development Report 1992,* p. 57.

161. See Jodi L. Jacobson, *Environmental Refugees: A Yardstick of Habitability.*

162. World Bank study cited by Celia W. Dugger, "Study Finds Small Developing Lands Hit Hardest by 'Brain Drain,'" *NYT,* October 25, 2005, p. A10.

163. Highlights of the constitution may be found in *NYT,* May 9, 1996, p. A7. It came fully into effect with national elections in 1999. The constitution provides for a government and a supreme court that are racially and gender sensitive, and have respect for human rights; a bicameral legislature; a five-year term for the president; various powers reserved for the provinces; and a wide range of individual rights that includes a host of basic needs.

164. On the discriminatory laws under apartheid, see Lawrence Litvak, Robert DeGrasse, and Kathleen McTigue, *South Africa: Foreign Investment and Apartheid,* pp. 19–24.

165. This is precisely what happened in 1986, after the pass laws were abolished to appease international opinion. A state of emergency gave the minister of law and order sweeping and uncontestable powers of arrest, search and seizure, and censorship in "unrest areas." South African sources conservatively estimated that 20,000 people, perhaps one-third of them children, were detained without charge during the year.

166. These operations probably included the assassination of anti-apartheid leaders, infiltration of civil rights organizations, and efforts to instigate black-against-black violence. When President de Klerk announced in December 1992 that a number of military officers were being suspended or dismissed, he as much as admitted to these activities. It marked a further breakdown of the white ruling elite, which had always been fortified by strong ties between the politicians, the military, and the security police.

167. Alan B. Durning, *Apartheid's Environmental Toll,* Worldwatch Paper 95, pp. 8–10.

168. Patti Waldmeir's article in the *Financial Times* (London), reprinted in *The Oregonian,* September 18, 1990.

169. Durning, *Apartheid's Environmental Toll*; Judy Christrup, "Of Apartheid and Pollution," *Greenpeace,* pp. 18–19.

170. The origins of apartheid are treated in Phyllis MacRae, "Race and Class in Southern Africa," *The African Review,* pp. 237–58; and Stanley B. Greenberg, *Race and State in Capitalist Development: Comparative Perspectives,* pp. 34–37.

171. Greenberg, pp. 6–12, 393–94.

172. Quoted in L.E. Neame, *The History of Apartheid: The Story of the Colour War,* p. 73.

173. Resistance efforts are briefly reviewed in Mike Calabrese and Mike Kendall, "The Black Agenda for South Africa," *The Nation,* pp. 393, 406–9.

174. On white reformism, see Greenberg, pp. 26–27 ff.; and Litvak, DeGrasse, and McTigue, pp. 34–36.

175. See, for example, Gavin W.H. Relly, "South Africa: A Time for Patriotism," *Washington Post Weekly Edition,* October 7, 1985, p. 29. Relly chairs the Anglo-American Corporation of South Africa.

176. See Ann Seidman and Neva Seidman, *South Africa and U.S. Multinational Corporations,* p. 6; and Desaix Myers, *Labor Practices of U.S. Corporations in South Africa.*

177. Litvak, DeGrasse, and McTigue, pp. 43–61.

178. US policy is reviewed by Kevin Danaher, *In Whose Interest? A Guide to U.S.–South Africa Relations,* pp. 80–83.

179. During the Nixon and Ford administrations, for example, human rights in South Africa—the "racial issue," as it was termed—were only considered important "because other countries have made it so" and because apartheid could lead to violence "and greater involvement of the communist powers." See Mohamed A. El-Khawas and Barry Cohen, eds., *The Kissinger Study of Southern Africa: National Security Study Memorandum 39,* p. 89. The quotations are from the once-secret memorandum.

180. See the report of a bipartisan US study of the sanctions in *The Oregonian,* February 9, 1990, p. A10.

181. Suzanne Daley, "A Divorce of Convenience," *NYT,* May 11, 1996, p. 5.

Not all the news from South Africa was good. There were persistent reports of corruption and favoritism within the ranks of the ANC, for instance (see, for example, *NYT*, October 9, 1996, p. 1), and of police incompetence (Suzanne Daley, "South Africa's Police Force Is Both Inept and Corrupt," *NYT*, March 25, 1997, online).

182. See, for instance, the testimony of a police torturer (*NYT*, November 9, 1997, online) and of a convicted police colonel (*NYT*, June 4, 1998, p. A11).

183. Suzanne Daley, "Party Led by Mandela Now Owns Up to Atrocities," *NYT*, May 13, 1997, p. A7; Suzanne Daley, "South African Court Voids Blanket Amnesties," *NYT*, May 9, 1998, online.

184. See Rachel L. Swarns, "Rarity of Black-Run Businesses Worries South Africa's Leaders," *NYT*, November 13, 2002, p. 1.

185. Four million of South Africa's 43 million people are infected with HIV/AIDS, and about 270,000 of 1.1 million public servants are also estimated to be HIV-positive. Nadine Gordimer, "Africa's Plague, and Everyone's," *NYT*, April 11, 2000, p. A31.

186. *Korea Annual 1990*, p. 199.

187. See Hyung Kook Kim and Guillermo Geisse, "The Political Economy of Outward Liberalization: Chile and South Korea in Comparative Perspective," *Asian Perspective*, p. 37.

188. World Trade Organization figures from http://stat.wto.org/CountryProfile.

189. Durning, *Poverty and the Environment*, p. 62.

190. Alice H. Amsden, *Asia's Next Giant: South Korea and Late Industrialization*, p. 39.

191. Klare and Arnson, p. 116.

192. Gavan McCormack, "The South Korean Economy: GNP Versus the People," in McCormack and Mark Selden, eds., *Korea North and South: The Deepening Crisis*, pp. 103–4. See also Parvez Hasan and D.C. Rao, *Korea: Policy Issues for Long-Term Development*.

193. Frederic C. Deyo, "State and Labor: Modes of Political Exclusion in East Asian Development," in Deyo, ed., *The Political Economy of the New Asian Industrialism*, p. 197.

194. See Chungmoo Choi, "Korean Women in a Culture of Inequality," in Clark, ed., *Korea Briefing, 1992*, pp. 97–116. Some positive legal changes have improved Korean women's conditions: The Equality Law of 1989 mandates equal pay for equal work at the same work site. The amended Family Law of 1991 gives women equality in marital property, child custody after a divorce, and inheritances. *Korea Annual 1990*, pp. 244, 247.

195. Jang Jip Choi, *Labor and the Authoritarian State: Labor Unions in South Korean Manufacturing Industries, 1961–1980*, pp. 308–9; Mark Clifford, *Troubled Tiger: Businessmen, Bureaucrats, and Generals in South Korea*.

196. Michael A. Launis, "The State and Industrial Labor in South Korea," *Bulletin of Concerned Asian Scholars*, p. 9; Amsden, pp. 200–5; Jang Jip Choi, pp. 299–305; and Martin Hart-Landsberg, *Rush to Development: Economic Change and Political Struggle in South Korea*.

197. *Los Angeles Times World Report*, December 17, 1995, p. 6.

198. Amsden, chs. 5–6; M. Shahid Alam, "The South Korean 'Miracle': Examining the Mix of Government and Markets," *The Journal of Developing Areas;* Chalmers Johnson, "Political Institutions and Economic Performance: The Government-Business Relationship in Japan, South Korea, and Taiwan," in Deyo, ed., pp. 136–64; Kim Dae Jung, *Mass-Participatory Economy*, pp. 38–39.

199. On Roh Tae Woo's administration, see Manwoo Lee, *The Odyssey of Korean Democracy: Korean Politics, 1987–1990*. Concerning his foreign policy, see

Melvin Gurtov, "Korea in the Asia-Pacific Community: Adapting Foreign Policy to a New Era," in Ray E. Weisenborn, ed., *Korea's Amazing Century: From Kings to Satellites,* ch. 1.

200. Texts in *Asian Perspective,* vol. 16, no. 1 (Spring–Summer 1992), pp. 157–62.

201. See Mel Gurtov, "South Korea's Foreign Policy and Future Security: Implications of the Nuclear Standoff," *Pacific Affairs.*

202. On the scandal, see *Far Eastern Economic Review,* November 30, 1995, pp. 66–72.

203. The total amount of payments made into the presidential slush fund by the eight men was $147.4 million. Several other chaebol were also accused of bribery but were not charged. *Los Angeles Times World Report,* December 17, 1995, p. 6.

204. Michael Schuman and Namju Cho, "Appealing to Foreign Investors Is Just the Beginning for Kim," *Wall Street Journal,* February 25, 1998.

205. Sook-Jong Lee, "Democratization and Polarization in Korean Society," *Asian Perspective,* vol. 29, no. 3 (2005), pp. 99–125.

206. John C. Ryan, "Conserving Biological Diversity," in Brown et al., eds., *State of the World 1992,* p. 9 (emphasis added). The figure for previous epochs is from Brundtland, p. 150.

207. Peter Raven, a leading US botanist, contends that "we are losing plant and animal species at between 1,000 and 10,000 times the natural rate," and "at a moderate estimate, we are now likely to lose around 50,000 species a year over the next few decades." Raven, "A Time of Catastrophic Extinction: What We Must Do," *The Futurist,* p. 39.

208. Allen L. Hammond, ed., *World Resources 1990–91: A Report by the World Resources Institute,* p. 102.

209. Ibid., table 7.1, p. 102.

210. Ibid., p. 109.

211. The scientific proof of the carbon-sink effect was published in *Science* and reported in the *NYT,* November 8, 1995, p. B7.

212. Ryan, in Brown et al., eds., table 2-1, p. 11.

213. Michael Goulding, "Flooded Forests of the Amazon," *Scientific American,* pp. 114–20. Flooded forests, which make up 3 percent of the Amazon rain forest, are home to an extraordinary diversity of wildlife, fish, and plants. Their uniqueness is due not only to differences with dryland forests but also to the enormous changes they probably have undergone to preserve species over time in flooded conditions.

214. *Human Development Report 2005,* table 3, p. 227. As a further example of the concentration of wealth, in 1994 the richest Brazilians, some 460 families, were for the first time subjected to income taxes. Their total wealth, the *New York Times* reported (November 10, 1994, p. 5), was equal to the GNP of Peru and Bolivia combined.

215. Durning, *Poverty and the Environment,* pp. 19, 28; Josué de Castro, *Death in the Northeast;* Tad Szulc, "Brazil's Amazonian Frontier," in Andrew Maguire and Janet Welsh Brown, eds., *Bordering on Trouble: Resources and Politics in Latin America,* p. 200.

216. Hammond, table 17.2, p. 270.

217. Nigel J.H. Smith, *Rainforest Corridors: The Transamazon Colonization Scheme,* p. 13.

218. Besides Nigel J.H. Smith, see Stephen G. Bunker, *Extraction, Unequal Exchange, and the Failure of the Modern State,* especially ch. 3; and Szulc, in Maguire and Brown, pp. 194–99.

219. Nigel J.H. Smith, pp. 14–15; George, *A Fate Worse Than Debt,* p. 157.

220. George, *A Fate Worse Than Debt,* p. 157; Szulc, in Maguire and Brown, p. 221. In the same period the World Bank was financing a similar but larger-scale "resettlement" plan in Indonesia to make way for a dam. As in Brazil, the strategy was to move land-poor tribal people from a densely populated region to an outlying area with the lure of jobs and land. The more than 3.5 million people thus moved cleared and logged the tropical forests to such an extent that a visiting specialist was reminded of post-atomic Hiroshima. George, *A Fate Worse Than Debt,* pp. 157–60.

221. This is the important thesis also of Bunker.

222. See, for instance, Diana Jean Schemo, "Brazil Furor over Ruling in the Death of an Indian," *NYT,* August 14, 1997, p. A5; *NYT,* January 10, 1996, p. 5, reporting the Brazilian government's rule changes allowing challenges to Indian reservation rights; and Diana Jean Schemo, "Brazil's Macuxi Indians Face Off Against Miners," *NYT,* July 21, 1996, online.

223. Hammond, p. 103.

224. Ibid., p. 105.

225. The government requires that Amazon region landowners set aside 80 percent of their land as tropical forest. In 1998, Brazil promised, with support from the World Bank and the World Wildlife Fund, to place 10 percent of the Amazon under government protection, which compares to around 3 percent up until then. *NYT,* April 30, 1998, p. A5.

226. *NYT,* September 12, 1996, p. A3, October 12, 1995, p. A3, January 27, 1998, p. 3. Following the last report, Brazil's congress voted to give the government's environmental protection agency the power to impose fines on those who damage the environment. But some legislators and environmentalists deplored the weaknesses in the bill. *NYT,* January 29, 1998, p. A8.

227. Larry Rohter, "Poor Press Brazil's Leader on His Promise of Land," *NYT,* July 27, 2003, online ed. On the landless workers movement, see Fábio L.S. Petrarolha, "Brazil: The Meek Want the Earth Now," *The Bulletin of the Atomic Scientists;* and Bill Hinchberger, "Land of No Return? Not Brazil," *The Nation.* The movement draws on liberation theology, professes nonviolence, and seeks (and has sometimes received) government sanction for the land seizures.

228. Larry Rohter, "Amazon Forest Still Burning Despite the Good Intentions," *NYT,* August 23, 2002, online ed.

229. Rohter, "Hard Realities: Brazil Drops Resistance to Genetically Altered Crops," *NYT,* September 28, 2003, online ed.

230. Rohter, "Brazil's Lofty Promises After Nun's Killing Prove Hollow," *NYT,* September 23, 2005, p. A3.

231. Rohter, "Brazil's Prized Exports Rely on Slaves and Scorched Land," *NYT,* March 25, 2002, p. 1.

232. Extractive reserves are sustainably harvested and locally managed. The World Bank endorsed the concept, and by 1992 the Brazilian government had created reserves embracing over 7 million acres. Brecher and Costello, *Global Village,* p. 92.

233. *NYT,* February 22, 1997, p. 4.

234. See Gareth Porter, "The Environmental Hazards of Asia Pacific Development," *Current History.*

235. Adam Schwarz, "Trade for Trees," *Far Eastern Economic Review,* June 4, 1992, pp. 60–62.

236. Kirk R. Smith and Michael R. Dove, "Indonesian Fires: Leaders in a Haze," *Asian Wall Street Journal,* December 8, 1997; *NYT,* September 25, 1997, p. A1, and February 23, 1998, p. A3; *Far Eastern Economic Review*, March 19, 1998, pp. 22–23.

237. Susanna Hecht and Alexander Cockburn, "Rhetoric and Reality in Rio," *The Nation,* pp. 852–53.
238. Brundtland, p. 155.
239. Jon Christensen and Jeremy Narby, "Treaty Favors Multinational Corporations," *The Oregonian,* June 11, 1992.
240. Brundtland, p. 153.
241. Cardoso made the statement in his 1994 election platform. See the *NYT* editorial, February 19, 1998, p. A20.
242. See, for instance, World Bank 1992, pp. 95–97, and Ryan, in Brown et al., eds., pp. 17–19.
243. See Commission on Weak States and US National Security, *On the Brink.*
244. For a systematic attempt to identify failed states, see "The Failed States Index," *Foreign Policy* (and the Fund for Peace) (May–June 2006, pp. 1–16, at www.foreignpolicy.com/story/files/story3420.php.
245. Carnegie Commission on Preventing Deadly Conflict, *Preventing Deadly Conflict: Final Report,* p. 44.
246. Commission on Weak States and US National Security, especially pp. 51–55.
247. Daniel Altman, "As Global Leaders Refocus, a Needy World Waits," *NYT,* March 17, 2002, online ed.
248. *NYT,* October 19, 1995, p. A7.
249. Tim Weiner and Lydia Polgreen, "Veterans of Past Murderous Campaigns Are Leading Haiti's New Rebellion," *NYT,* February 29, 2004, online ed.
250. The "support" was actually training of Aristide's opposition by the congressionally financed International Republic Institute, whose representative in Haiti acted apart from and against the wishes of the US ambassador. See the extensive account by Walt Bogdanich and Jenny Nordberg, "Mixed U.S. Signals Helped Tilt Haiti Toward Chaos," *NYT,* January 29, 2006, p. 1.
251. David Stout, "Administration Dismisses Rumors That U.S. Kidnapped Aristide," *NYT,* March 1, 2004, online ed.
252. See Kathie Klarreich, "The Fight for Haiti," *The Nation;* Debanyi Kar and Tom Ricker, "IDB Debt Cancellation for Haiti," *Foreign Policy in Focus* (December 7, 2006), at www.fpif.org.
253. Jorge G. Castañeda, "Latin America's Left Turn," *Foreign Affairs.* Castañeda makes plain his preference for the Chilean version.
254. Juan Forero, "Still Poor, Latin Americans Protest Push for Open Markets," *NYT,* July 19, 2002, online ed.
255. Sachs, *The End of Poverty,* table 2, p. 67.
256. 1998 figure in *Human Development Report 2005,* table 15, p. 271.
257. See Fernando Coronil, *The Magical State: Nature, Money, and Modernity in Venezuela.*
258. *Human Development Report 2005,* table 3, pp. 227 and 229, and table 10, p. 251; *NYT,* December 3, 2006, p. 18.
259. See Michael Shifter, "In Search of Hugo Chávez," *Foreign Affairs.*
260. Juan Forero, "Venezuela Seizes Control of Two Oil Fields," *NYT,* April 4, 2006, p. C15.
261. Forero, "Chávez, Seeking Foreign Allies, Spends Billions," *NYT,* April 4, 2006, p. 1.
262. Forero, "Venezuela's New Oil Law Is Seen as a Risk to Growth," *NYT,* December 4, 2001, p. A10.
263. Numerous press accounts of the US role in the coup, which ousted Chávez for two days, include: Larry Rohter, "Venezuela's 2 Fateful Days: Leader Is

Out, and In Again," *NYT*, April 20, 2002, p. A1; Christopher Marquis, "Bush Officials Met With Venezuelans Who Ousted Leader," *NYT*, April 16, 2002, p. A1; Christopher Marquis, "U.S. Bankrolling Is Under Scrutiny for Ties to Chávez Ouster," *NYT*, April 25, 2002, p. A8; Juan Forero, "Documents Show C.I.A. Knew of a Coup Plot in Venezuela," *NYT*, December 3, 2004, p. A12.

264. US White House, *The National Security Strategy of the United States of America*, March 2006, p. 15.

265. Franklin Foer, "The Talented Mr. Chávez," *Atlantic Monthly*.

266. *Human Development Report 2005*, p. 89.

267. William Finnegan, "The Economics of Empire: Notes on the Washington Consensus," *Harper's; NYT*, February 19, 2003, p. A5.

268. Juan Forero and Larry Rohter, "Bolivia's Leader Solidifies Region's Leftward Tilt," *NYT*, January 22, 2006, online ed.

269. Juan Forero, "Bolivia's Knot: No to Cocaine, but Yes to Coca," *NYT*, February 12, 2006, online ed.

270. Joel Brinkley, "Bush Budget Would Cut Military Aid to Bolivia by 96 Percent," *NYT*, February 9, 2006, p. A10; Juan Forero, "U.S. Aid Can't Win Bolivia's Love as New Suitors Emerge," NYT, May 14, 2006, p. 4.

271. Christian Parenti, "Morales Moves," *The Nation;* David Rieff, "Che's Second Coming?" *New York Times Magazine.*

272. Rieff, "Che's Second Coming?" p. 76.

273. Another is Rafael Correa, who was elected president of Ecuador in November 2006. He is the country's eighth president in ten years.

# 5

# The United States and China: Cooperation or Conflict?

The US-China relationship—one between a rising power and a superpower already risen—is becoming the most important to global security. This chapter explores the US transition from "free world" leader to lone superpower, China's transition from revolutionary state to rising economic power, and the unstable character of US-China relations today. We begin with US preeminence in military affairs, a discussion that picks up from the case study in Chapter 3 of the US-Soviet nuclear competition.

## Alone at the Top:
## US Domination of the Arms Race After the Cold War

With the two superpowers no longer enemies, nuclear-war scenarios based on deterrence were rendered meaningless. "The only rationale for maintaining nuclear weapons in the future," wrote one analyst, "is to deter others from using them. Minimum deterrence is no longer Utopian."[1] This assessment seemed entirely appropriate after START. In September 1991 President Bush announced unilateral cuts in nuclear forces that were matched by Gorbachev in October. These cuts removed (and destroyed) all US and Soviet short-range nuclear weapons in Europe and at sea, as well as removed US nuclear weapons from South Korea. Then, in January 1992, further reductions were announced: Bush canceled the Midgetman ICBM program and stopped production of the B-2 bomber and the MX ICBM, while President Yeltsin, in charge in Moscow, said production of two heavy bomber programs would be stopped and 130 ground and submarine missile launch systems would be destroyed. In all, the cuts in strategic weapons left the two sides with roughly equal numbers and the promise of further reductions. The US Congress voted to provide the FSU with funds to destroy the tactical nuclear weapons Yeltsin had promised to dismantle, reflecting concern that otherwise they might come under the control of Russian, Ukraine, or other nationalists in the former Soviet republics where the weapons were based.

A second significant development of the immediate post–Cold War period was conventional-force reductions, mainly in central Europe.[2] The context of these changes was an entirely new Europe-wide security structure that is discussed in Chapter 6. Third, during 1992, for the first time in thirty years, no nuclear testing took place anywhere in the world. It became possible for two reasons: The Russians unilaterally ceased testing, and the US Congress passed a nine-month testing moratorium that President Bush chose not to veto and subsequent presidents have maintained—though George W. Bush has authorized so-called virtual (laboratory) testing, as noted below.

Fourth, the US-Russia agreements promoted either new or extended international steps to control weapons of mass destruction (see Table 5.1). Two treaties are crucial to the future of nuclear weapons. In 1995, negotiations attended by nearly all the UN's membership led to an indefinite extension of the nuclear Non-Proliferation Treaty, which was up for renewal. Hopes were high, especially among the non-nuclear states, that the nuclear-weapon states would agree, in exchange for indefinite extension, to a firm declaration on disarmament linked to a stage-by-stage review process. In the end, the conference approved extension; but agreements were not reached on plugging loopholes in the nonproliferation regime, cutting the nuclear-weapons stockpiles of the major powers, or (as discussed below) preventing further proliferation of weapon materials.[3] The conferees did decide to conclude a Comprehensive Test Ban Treaty (CTBT) "no later than 1996." The UN General Assembly had called for negotiations on a ban as far back as December 1993. The treaty, which bans all nuclear explosions and thus poses a long-awaited barrier to weapons development, was concluded in September 1996. Once again, however, the US view prevailed: Third World states were unable to secure commitments to disarmament or sharing of nuclear-energy technology. India was particularly adamant that the nuclear-weapon states agree to destroy their weapons within a specific time. Its objections kept the treaty from entering into force, since it had to be ratified by all forty-four nuclear-capable states, including India and Pakistan.[4] Instead, in 1998 those two countries defied the "nuclear club" and tested nuclear weapons (see Table 5.2). Nevertheless, the CTBT's variety of verification methods for detecting violations of weapon-level magnitude, and provision for inspections of suspected nuclear test sites on short notice, provide some assurance against a nuclear breakout.[5]

As important as these steps were, the question remains: How much of a break with the past did they represent, with respect both to reliance on nuclear weapons for security and to beginning a reversal of the global arms race? Reagan and Gorbachev had agreed in 1985 that "a nuclear war cannot be won and must never be fought."[6] Why, then, are the principal nuclear-weapon states (the UN Security Council's Perm 5) still maintaining and refining very large arsenals at great cost, even as they and other states cooperate to ban other weapons of mass destruction?

Table 5.1   Major Post–Cold War and Related Earlier International Treaties
Governing Weapons of Mass Destruction

| Treaty (date) | Accessions (as of) | Related Treaty (date) | Accessions (as of) |
|---|---|---|---|
| *Chemical Weapons Convention* (1993; in force 1997) | 180 ratifications (October 2006); only 9 states have not signed | *Biological and Toxin Weapons Convention* (1972; in force 1975) | 155 ratifications (May 2006); 16 other states have signed |
| *Non-Proliferation Treaty* (1995 extension of 1968 treaty, in force 1970) | 188 signed (2006) | | |
| *Treaty of Bangkok* Southeast Asia Nuclear Weapon Free Zone (1995) | All 10 countries signed; protocol not signed by PRC or US | *Treaty of Tlatelolco* Latin American and Caribbean Nuclear Weapon Free Zone (1969) | All 33 countries signed |
| *Comprehensive Test Ban Treaty* (1996) | 176 signed, 135 ratified (2006) | | |
| *Treaty of Pelindaba* African Nuclear Weapon Free Zone (1996) | 50 of 53 countries signed (2003); has 18 of 28 ratifications needed to enter into force; protocols on testing signed by Security Council Perm 5 | *Treaty of Raratonga* South Pacific Nuclear Weapon Free Zone (1986) | 13 countries signed and ratified; protocols on testing signed by Security Council Perm 5 |
| Central Asian Nuclear Weapon Free Zone (2006) | 5 countries signed | | |

*Sources:* Stimson Center at www.stimson.org; Center for Nonproliferation Studies at http://cns.miis.edu/pubs/inven/index.htm; and United Nations Department for Disarmament Affairs at http://disarmament.un.org/TreatyStatus.nsf.

The short answer to these questions is that the military-industrial complex in the United States, as well as in Russia and other nuclear-weapon states,[7] has survived cuts in forces and budgets, and changed political circumstances brought about by the end of the Cold War. From the complex have emerged new justifications for holding onto nuclear weapons—and, in the United States, for maintaining the world's highest level of military spending by far and pushing military and nuclear sales abroad. In Washington since 1989, and especially since the 9/11 attacks, Pentagon heads, influential realists in Congress, and the largest military-industrial firms have suffered some defeats—such as a number of military base closures, reductions in military personnel, and reduced funds for some weapons programs—but the essence of the "iron triangle" is intact. We see this in several concrete ways:

212 Global Politics in the Human Interest

• *Military doctrine, influenced by the Gulf War but just as much by the Cold War, calls for a US capability to respond militarily to "rogue states" and "regional peer competitors" (namely, Russia and China) at every level,* including nuclear weapons that could (according to one study) be used pre-emptively;[8] preparedness to fight two major wars simultaneously; and readiness to face a multitude of new threats, such as biological terrorism, information warfare, and narcotics smuggling.[9] The weapons "requirements" such a strategy generates can easily be seen as self-justifying. The National Defense Panel, a group of retired senior officers and civilians, said just that of the two-war strategy, calling it "a means of justifying the current force structure—especially for those searching for the certainties of the cold war era."[10] After 9/11, the wars in Iraq and Afghanistan, the "war on terror," and the concerns about homeland security greatly enlarged the menu of threats—*and* the number of interest groups to lobby for additional weapons to meet those threats.

• *Military budgets are far beyond Cold War levels.* They averaged just under $300 billion a year for 1989–1992 under George H. W. Bush. Under Clinton, official US military spending in fiscal year 1996 was $264 billion, 33 percent of global official military spending.[11] By 2000 the $300 billion mark was passed. Following the 9/11 attacks, US military spending rose dramatically: The 2006 budget was 41 percent higher than the 2001 budget. Today, official US military spending is well over $500 billion.[12]

• *Military deployments, including nuclear weapons, still reflect the Cold War.* In Asia Pacific, for example, total US forces remain at around 100,000. Though US forces in Europe have been greatly reduced, nuclear weapons continue to be stored at air bases around the continent, thus making the United States the only country that deploys such weapons beyond its borders.[13]

• *Arms control still follows the interests of the weapons establishment and Cold Warriors.* For example, CTBT in the United States means more business, not less, for the weapons laboratories. At an estimated cost of $40 billion over ten years, government scientists in the marvelously titled "Stockpile Stewardship Program" will experiment with ways to ensure the potency of stockpiled weapons and use computers to simulate nuclear tests.[14] But while computer simulations avoid the need for explosions, they open up a whole new industry: "virtual" weapons. From these, new weapons can be, and are being, designed. For example, pure-fusion research has led to research on a miniaturized hydrogen bomb, the B-61 that is intended to burrow into the command bunkers of rogue-state leaders. In 2003 a ten-year-old ban on this class of weapons was lifted in the US Senate at the Bush administration's request.[15] Under Clinton, funding of "bunker busters" was regarded as a payoff for the complex's support of the CTBT.[16] The Bush administration, however, took CTBT, the ABM Treaty, and other arms-control staples off the table; the complex was fully back in charge.

Industry interests prevailed, as (see below) in the negative US attitude toward strengthening the Biological Weapons Convention. Bush preferred weaker approaches to WMD issues. In May 2002, the United States and Russia negotiated the Strategic Offensive Reductions Treaty (known simply as the Moscow Treaty), which provides for a major reduction of strategic nuclear warheads, but not until 2012, without international verification, and subject to reversal on three months' notice. Moreover, smaller (tactical) nuclear weapons are not included in the treaty.[17] And not a single nuclear weapon is to be destroyed under the treaty; the weapons will merely be warehoused.[18]

• *Military-industrial political influence continues to be felt in several ways.* Even though budgets for new weapons procurement declined 69 percent between 1985 and 1998, it is well over $60 billion a year.[19] And even as most of the major US prime contractors—the exception is Lockheed Martin—are shifting to civilian products for revenue, their leverage over the weapons-acquisition process actually seems to have increased.[20] Thanks to consolidation within the industry, weapons contracts have become less competitive than ever, and prices of weapons are therefore unlikely to decline. Between 1992 and 1997, mergers valued at around $55 billion reduced the number of military prime contractors to three: Boeing, which acquired McDonnell Douglas; Raytheon, which bought Hughes Electronics; and Lockheed, which bought out Martin Marietta. The industries' diversification of production had the effect of reversing the flow of dependence—from their dependence on the Pentagon to the Pentagon's dependence on them. ("We now think of the defense-industrial base as the US industrial base," said Jacques Gansler, under secretary of defense for acquisition and technology.) Decisions on which weapons to build may be determined more than ever before by the industries, as the case of the F-22 fighter jet shows.[21]

All the problems previously noted in the Pentagon–weapons industries connection remain. Cost overruns on major weapons systems, for example, came to $23 billion in 2006.[22] The latest weapons are very expensive: The US controller general noted in 2005 that the five biggest weapons programs alone cost over $520 billion![23] Yet the more the weapons cost, the fewer the number that can be purchased.[24] Meantime, older weapons systems survive budget appraisals, as military services and members of Congress lobby together to protect "their" weapons, no matter their relevance to the post–Cold War years. With the creation of the US Homeland Security Department, the costs of "national defense" become further embroidered with new spending on administration, intelligence, and port and border security. In short, no matter what the presumed threats to national security may actually be, and no matter how committed top officials may be to cost cutting, there seems to be no way to rein in US military spending.[25]

• *Arms exports and other military transfers have become increasingly commercialized.* As in the past, the overriding official justification for arms sales is to promote deterrence of national-security threats and regional stability. The reality, one suspects, is that the motives are increased market share and profits (dating from a presidential directive in 1995 that explicitly linked arms sales to foreign-policy goals), political influence abroad, a desire to please the defense contractors, and maintenance of force structures and budgets. US conventional arms sales have flourished in the post–Cold War years, buoyed by the Pentagon's robust threat assessments mentioned above, increased subsidization of arms sellers,[26] reduced competition from Moscow, NATO's expansion, and new buyers, such as in the rising economies of East Asia. As already noted, the United States is usually the dominant source of conventional weapons sales: In 2005, for instance, its arms agreements to all countries came to $12.8 billion, about a quarter of the worldwide total, compared with $7.9 billion for France and $7.4 billion for Russia.[27] As for developing countries, from 1990 to 1997, the value of actual deliveries of US conventional weapons came to over $53 billion, mostly (around 40 percent) to the Middle East.[28] From 2000 to 2004, the United States exported just under $30 billion in conventional weapons, slightly less than Russia.[29] But US arms transfer *agreements* soared to around $37 billion in 2004, of which nearly $22 billion were with Third World countries.[30] In eighteen of those countries (in 2003), there were military conflicts; thirteen of them were considered undemocratic by the US Department of State; and twenty of them were judged by the department to have serious human-rights problems.[31]

US small arms, which are not counted in the conventional-arms statistics, have become even more popular than artillery and tanks, which may help explain US resistance to an international treaty governing them. (The latest effort to reach agreement under UN auspices failed in 2006.) International small-arms sales are unregulated and difficult to track; an estimated one thousand companies in ninety-eight countries produce them, some secretively under government contract.[32] One estimate is that small-arms sales are running over $25 billion a year, often to police forces, crime syndicates, and rebel groups that have little regard for the lives of innocent civilians.[33]

These trends, so consistent with Cold War patterns, pose far more serious problems than merely advancing careers and distorting the economy. The possession of nuclear weapons greatly in excess of any conceivable national-security purpose, and reliance on them as an instrument of deterrence or retaliation; the abandonment of the major arms-control agreements by the United States, and its efforts to evade the requirements of others; and the promotion of arms transfers to authoritarian regimes in regions of conflict, are ethically wrong, contrary to professed interest in international peace and stability, and strategically dangerous. During the Cold War, it was possible to justify virtually any weapon in terms of the enemy; but now, there are no nuclear competitors of the major nuclear-weapon states, and nuclear weapons are simply irrelevant to combating terrorism and other transnational threats to security. For those and other reasons, a number of former high-level military and civilian leaders in the United States, the USSR/Russia, and other countries have voiced their support for major arms reductions (discussed in the next section).

The contemporary WMD danger is double edged: It embraces not only the weapons policies and programs of states, but also transfers to terror groups of the means to develop these weapons. A leading US defense official said in 1998 that twenty countries are actively developing nuclear, biological, and chemical (NBC) weapons. Now the figure is between forty and fifty.[34] The threat posed by terror groups is real, but would seem to be on a much lower level than the threat posed by states. The Japanese sect, Aum Shinrikyo, terrorized Tokyo in 1995 with its sarin gas attack in the subway. Yet despite huge financial resources at its disposal, the sect was unable to produce or procure biological agents. Transnational groups that are said to be seeking a nuclear weapon, such as Al-Qaida, have also been unsuccessful. One specialist therefore concludes that "the most serious threat [of biological weapons use] is from the proliferation of state-sponsored programs"; and the United States, by refusing to support a protocol to the 1972 Biological Weapons Convention that would have given it teeth to ensure compliance,[35] and by experimenting with "defensive" biological agents,[36] has greatly reduced the possibility of identifying and preventing threats. The same conclusion seems warranted with respect to nuclear weapons, as the India and Pakistan cases below indicate.

Against this background, the announcements by India and Pakistan in May 1998 that they had tested nuclear weapons—five tests by each—were a wake-up call for an international community that had become complacent about the nuclear peril. The two countries, which have fought three wars since 1947, became the sixth and seventh declared nuclear-weapon states (see Table 5.2). Their tests came fast on the heels of medium-range missile tests that indicated a mutual capability to hit any target in the other country and, for India, targets in China, too.[37]

There should have been no surprise about these countries' possession of nuclear weapons. India conducted a "peaceful" atomic test in 1974 and was widely known to be continuing work on nuclear weapons and missile delivery systems; and the United States, as noted earlier, knew at least since 1983 about Pakistan's plan to make an "Islamic bomb."[38] More to the point, neither country's bomb program could have succeeded without sustained international assistance, and both programs (as well as the bomb-making programs of other undeclared nuclear powers such as Israel) took advantage of strategic alliances with a superpower. Chinese and US nuclear assistance was indispensable to Pakistan's program. US training and provision of a

Table 5.2    **Known Nuclear Tests of the Declared Nuclear Powers, 1945–2006**

|             | US    | USSR/RF | Britain | France | China | India | Pakistan | N.Korea |
|-------------|-------|---------|---------|--------|-------|-------|----------|---------|
| Atmospheric | 215   | 219     | 50      | 21     | 23    | 0     | 0        | 0       |
| Underground | 815   | 496     | 159     | 24     | 22    | 5     | 5        | 1       |
| Total       | 1,030 | 715     | 209     | 45     | 45    | 5     | 5        | 1       |

*Sources:* United Nations; Physicians for Social Responsibility; *New York Times,* September 11, 1996, p. A3, and various issues in May 1998 and October 2006.

nuclear research reactor began in the 1950s, whereas PRC aid, such as weapon design and enriched uranium, went on for over twenty years.[39] A Canadian-made nuclear reactor, run with heavy water from the United States and by US-trained scientists, produced the plutonium for India's first bombs—including the device tested in 1974.[40] Several European countries' technology contributed to India's nuclear complex in later years.[41] What this amounts to is a pattern of duplicity about the Indian and Pakistani nuclear programs: Neither program ever had purely peaceful intentions, despite official promises to suppliers, and in all probability the supplier governments knew that fact somewhere along the way if not from the beginning. Now, India is commonly thought to have between thirty and thirty-five nuclear weapons, and Pakistan to have thirty to fifty, in both cases with enough weapons-grade plutonium or uranium to produce many more. It is therefore astounding that in 2006 the United States would reach a deal with India to sell it nuclear fuel and technology with exemptions from international inspection.

The Indian and Pakistani tests underscored the fragility of nonproliferation, the lack of a strong international will to punish proliferators, and the continuing and expensive allure of nuclear weapons, even for those states that (unlike those two countries) signed the NPT extension and the CTBT. Not one of the governments whose nuclear assistance was diverted by India and Pakistan to bomb making said a word about the repeated violations. When rather mild international criticism of the tests was made, India rejected it as hypocritical, rightly observing that the United States and other nuclear powers had failed to live up to their promise in the NPT of working toward disarmament.[42] Only a handful of governments imposed financial sanctions on India and Pakistan—mainly, blocking bilateral and multilateral development aid, most of which was released soon after. The absence of an outcry is not unusual: Among the Perm 5, France and China signed both the NPT and the CTBT, but not before conducting final nuclear tests in 1995. None of these tests drew particularly harsh reactions from other governments. France's sequence of tests in the South Pacific in 1995 aroused worldwide protests, and China's tests provoked US, Japanese, and some other negative Asian reactions. But no lasting sanctions were applied in either case, setting precedents for the rather mild UN-approved sanctions against North Korea in 2006 and Iran in 2007.

Stemming proliferation is harder today than ever before inasmuch as all the materials for making and delivering a nuclear weapon are available for a price. Theft, smuggling, and sales of nuclear plants, materials, technology, and equipment—such as supercomputers, missiles, and aerospace technology—by private and state corporations have greatly increased. The chaos of post-Soviet Russia is illustrative. As paychecks vanished, security eroded in the laboratories and storage facilities that handled nuclear materials, and some scientists decided to seek employment in China and Iran. This is why US-Russia cooperation since the mid-1990s to track and secure these materials, including weapons-grade waste sent back to Russia by its former republics (such as Uzbekistan), is so critical.[43] An even more daunting problem is the clandestine worldwide nuclear-materials network run by A. Q. Khan, who was finally exposed in 2005. Khan assisted the nuclear programs of Libya, North Korea, Iran, and possibly others by selling uranium-enrichment technology and weapon designs.[44] A hero in Pakistan, Khan may well have been protected by his government, a US ally; even when finally caught, he was merely placed under house arrest, and many details of his activities over the years remain hidden.

The increasing worldwide commerce in plutonium poses daunting problems. Despite post–Cold War reductions of nuclear arms, which reduced existing weapons-grade plutonium from around 270 metric tons to perhaps only 70, plutonium availability worldwide was around 930 metric tons in 1995 and was "expected to nearly double in the next decade."[45] Japan's import of reprocessed nuclear fuel for its plutonium-based reactors raises questions that are discussed in the next chapter. The United States, which in 1996 became the only country to provide a public accounting of its plutonium holdings, imports, and exports (nearly a ton) to other countries, has 99.5 metric tons and Russia is thought to have 100 or so tons.[46] (The core of a nuclear weapon requires a mere 2 to 4 kilograms of plutonium— 4.4 to 8.8 pounds.) Though the past US practice of exporting plutonium for use in nuclear-power reactors has ended, its use in US civilian power plants has only just begun.

A recent example of how, in the nuclear arena, globalization invariably trumps global responsibility is the 2006 US nuclear sales agreement with India referred to earlier. Evidently in order to promote US business interests as well as defense cooperation to contain China, Bush agreed that in return for India's willingness to put its civilian reactors under international inspection (but *outside* the NPT), the United States would sell it nuclear fuel, reactors, and equipment. Apart from the questionable value of nuclear power plants in meeting India's electricity needs, the deal could allow India to increase its nuclear weapons arsenal in two ways—first, by building fast-breeder reactors capable of producing weapons-grade fuel, but not under international inspection; second, by distinguishing between military and civilian reactors, and only placing the latter under inspection.[47] Not only did this deal send precisely the wrong message to Iran and North Korea about nuclear nonproliferation, but in trying to make India a special case because it is a democracy, the administration then had to deal with Egypt's request later in 2006 that it too should be helped to develop a nuclear-energy program.[48] Clearly, it is not only the ambitions of rogue states that are undermining proliferation; nuclear-weapon states and their corporations have selectively abandoned nonproliferation and the NPT regime when it suited their interests.

Nonproliferation since the Cold War ended can count some successes: the adherence of China and France to the treaty regimes; the transfer to Russia of over seven thousand nuclear warheads from Belarus, Kazakhstan, and Ukraine; the establishment in 2006 of the world's fifth nuclear-weapon-free zone (NWFZ) by Kazakhstan and four other Central Asian states;[49] the agreement with North Korea in 1994 that temporarily froze its nuclear program; and the decisions of Brazil, South Africa, Argentina, and Libya to terminate their nuclear-weapons programs and (for the first three) join their respective regional NWFZs. But the other side of the coin is the danger posed by additional nuclear-weapon states, thanks in part to nuclear-weapon states that do not practice what they preach about nonproliferation. The danger has less to do with the supposedly irrational behavior of Third World leaders who might possess nuclear weapons; as Richard Betts's study of nuclear coercion has concluded, US leaders had a "facile" understanding of them and never came to grips with what it would mean actually to employ them if deterrence or intimidation failed.[50] Rather, the danger lies in two other directions. One is that new nuclear powers will probably increase tensions, either tempting neighboring non-nuclear states to go nuclear (for example, Japan and South Korea in the case of North Korea) or increasing the likelihood that nuclear weapons will be used, perhaps preemptively. The second danger is that weak and isolated states, political movements, or terrorist groups may be more inclined than before to resort to a desperate act in the absence of mediation and incentives to act peacefully. When Pakistan and India came close to a nuclear conflict in 1990, only belated US diplomatic intervention corrected the misperceptions of their general staffs.[51] Iran and North Korea, on the other hand, have lost their major-power supporters. They have been treated as outlaw regimes and subjected to provocative military maneuvers and intrusive surveillance by their opponents. They have also drawn lessons from the invasion of Iraq in 2003, a country that did not have a nuclear weapon. Their options to behave "responsibly" have been limited; going nuclear (and *staying* nuclear) may strike them as being the logical road to security.

The great tragedy of the nuclear game for developing countries is that it is expensive. As India and Pakistan may already have discovered, becoming a nuclear-weapon state is only the beginning of a long road already traveled, at stupendous cost, by the big powers—a road that includes choices of delivery systems, command and control, scientific investment, service rivalries, safety, and environmental destruction.[52] The daily lives of literally hundreds of millions of destitute people will be affected by those choices. India, as noted before, is a classic case of immense poverty, a widening rich-poor gap, and an array of major public-health problems, all of which exist side by side with its new market-driven success, a reality pointed out by its own president.[53] Human development is declining in India, according to the UNDP's index. The US-India "strategic partnership" hailed in the aftermath of the nuclear deal cannot solve the dilemmas of that other India.[54]

## Reining in the Arms Race                    *seems so easy...*

From a human- and common-security point of view, the path to solving the WMD problem is for the nuclear powers to reduce and destroy nuclear weapons, thus setting an example while also, in fact, enhancing their own security.[55] Three of the key officials who originally conceptualized US nuclear strategy have made just such a case.[56] If, as they argue, nuclear weapons never had a true military purpose during the Cold War, other than to deter other nuclear powers, they have no larger purpose after the Cold War. "What this new [post–Cold War] era provides," they conclude, "is the opportunity to strive for truly collective security and an international rule of law, in which self-help by the use of military force for resolving conflicts among nations loses its legitimacy."[57] Retired US Air Force general George Lee Butler, former head of the Strategic Air Command, and retired Army general Andrew Goodpaster, former commander of NATO, issued a statement in December 1996 that called for "the complete elimination of nuclear weapons from all nations" as an "ultimate objective." Among their expressed concerns was the terribly slow progress of the United States and Russia in reducing nuclear weapons—recall from Chapter 3 that they still have over 18,000 nuclear weapons between them—when their strategic mission had vanished and the risk of nuclear terrorism has increased.[58] Sixty other retired generals and admirals from nuclear-weapon states, including Russia, joined Butler and Goodpaster in urging that the US and Russian nuclear arsenals be reduced to two thousand strategic warheads as a first step. No country would benefit more than the United States by doing so, Butler said: It would save billions of dollars and take more Russian warheads out of circulation.[59]

Though the specific recommendations of the antinuclear experts vary—*true* for example, on whether zero nuclear weapons, a minimum force of one hundred to two hundred weapons, or one thousand weapons should be the goal—there seems to be a consensus on several fundamental points. One is that possession of nuclear weapons for any purpose other than to deter their use by others is unacceptable. Second, the danger of an accidental launch of nuclear weapons is slim but real, notwithstanding nuclear detargeting agreements, and should be dealt with by taking nuclear forces off alert.[60] Third, instead of treating Russia and China as potential international rogues, policymakers should negotiate agreements with them that take many more nuclear warheads, launchers, and materials out of circulation, thus alleviating their, as well as US, concerns.[61] Fourth, the goal should be the elimination of nuclear weapons—by outlawing them and by implementing the Fissile Materials Treaty, which would ban production of nuclear-weapon material under international inspection and verification.[62]

Reducing the dangers from chemical and biological weapons and conventional arms transfers confronts obstacles similar to those encountered in the nuclear area. Two obstacles stand out: the continuing proliferation of chemical weapons, in spite of treaty obligations; and the lack of international will to enforce adherence to treaties or close loopholes in arrangements. Treaties banning the development, production, acquisition, transfer, and stockpiling of chemical and biological weapons have been overwhelmingly endorsed by states, as Table 5.1 shows. Nine states may have active programs of both kinds: Iran, Syria, Libya, Israel, China, North Korea, Taiwan, India, and Pakistan.[63] Yet five of them have thus far signed or ratified the Chemical Weapons Convention, whereas seven of them (Syria and Israel are the exceptions) have ratified the Biological and Toxin Weapons Convention (usually abbreviated BWC). With the exception of Syria, these are all states that possess or have shown interest in having nuclear weapons. Most dangerously, these are countries grouped in close proximity—in the Middle East, South Asia, or East Asia—and with active political disputes between them. Putting these elements together, there is every reason to believe that regardless of treaty adherence, these countries will continue working on producing chemical and/or biological weapons or maintaining a stockpile of them. The USSR, after all, had a clandestine biological-weapons program until 1992, President Boris Yeltsin revealed, in violation of the treaty it had signed.[64] Sanctions for violations, we have seen, are at best highly circumstantial, and commercial interests often prevail over national-security interests. Tightening the requirements of the relevant treaties is surely in order. The BWC, unlike the CWC, lacks obligatory inspection, verification, and enforcement procedures; the BWC requires a complaint to the UN Security Council, which must agree to initiate an investigation. Unless enforcement of the treaties can become automatic and thorough, a calamity such as Iraq's chemical-weapons attacks on Iran and the Kurds will happen again, and states (including the United States) will find ways to experiment with "defensive" biological weapons. Here again, the United States could lead by positive example.

With respect to conventional arms, outside of central Europe, efforts by the Perm 5 to curtail arms transfers, or at least make them more "transparent" (i.e., more open and subject to verification), have been feeble. The London guidelines of October 1991, for instance, promised to "avoid transfers" that "prolong or aggravate an existing armed conflict," "increase tension in a region," or "introduce destabilizing military capabilities in a region."[65] Yet the United States and others sharply escalated sales of combat aircraft, armored vehicles, and missile technologies to the Middle East long after Iraq's invasion of Kuwait was defeated. In the UN a Conventional Arms Register was established where governments voluntarily list weapons sold and purchased. Although the major arms exporters are submitting reports, important data such as the value of production, sales, and transfers of technologies with military applications are not recorded. The most recent, and most ambitious, effort to restrain arms exports is the Wassenaar Arrangement, which thirty-three states agreed upon in 1995. Its key provisions relate to reporting high-technology transfers with military applications. How much reporting actually takes place and how much restraint it puts on the arms trade remains to be seen. The glaring weakness of all arms-export control efforts is that they place no obligations on the weapons manufacturers and merchants, nor on their government subsidizers.

As one specialist has remarked, both Cold War militarization and post–Cold War commercialization have contributed to the hot pursuit by arms lobbies of clients in the Third World.[66] The increasing demand for high-technology components in tanks, jets, and bombs (so-called smart weapons) has made their export harder to control because these are commercial technologies, and more desirable to export because they add greatly to their cost and therefore their export value.[67] The tragedy is multiple: The arms sales are made on the pretense that they promote regional and international security; they can only add to the destructiveness of a conflict; allocations for them come at the expense of people's needs; and, considering that all the wars since 1945 have been conventional, "the single-minded focus of the nonproliferation community on weapons of mass destruction is misplaced."[68]

## The United States

> How America illustrates birth, muscular youth, the promise, the sure fulfillment, the absolute success, despite of people—illustrates evil as well as good, The vehement struggle so fierce for unity in one's-self.
> —Walt Whitman, "Thoughts," 1860

The United States is a nation deeply divided between wealth and poverty, new and old economic and political forces, the concentration of power in the center and its evisceration in the periphery. In a nation of such extraordinary diversity and shifting moods, it is always hazardous to identify trends. But the Reagan and George W. Bush years (1981–1988 and 2001–present)

were such a distinct departure from the moderate liberalism of previous
administrations, Republican as well as Democratic, that their imprint on US
political economy has been more lasting than any previous period since
Franklin Roosevelt's New Deal. Reagan's crusade against communism, and
Bush's against terrorism, were not really new, for foreign-policy crusading
has long been a staple of US foreign policy. What was new happened within
the country: the determined effort to dismantle the welfare state, including
its leading role on behalf of civil liberties, environmental protection, and
equal opportunity; the alignment of conservative politics with religious fundamentalism; the open identification of state power with big business and
the wealthy class; the seeming obliviousness to basic human-security matters such as the environment, universal health care, and education; and passage of the largest peacetime military budgets in US history, alongside
equally unprecedented budget deficits. All these contributed to a muscular
nationalism that sought to universalize US values and ideals.[69]

The eight-year interregnum of Bill Clinton (1993–2000) proved to be
something less than a reversal of the "Reagan Revolution." Clinton's policies on the environment, education, and women's rights reflected some
effort to shore up eroded federal support; and, in spirit at least, there was a
rededication to the liberal precept of government responsibility for social
needs. But just as the Clinton administration maintained Reagan-era levels
of military spending, it accepted some key social policies, if only because
they resonated with big business, a Republican-dominated Congress, and
the public. Believing that economic growth's benefits really do trickle down
to the lower classes, Clinton vigorously supported corporate downsizing
and megamergers, led the demolition of the welfare system, promoted
NAFTA with little regard for its labor and environmental consequences, and
slashed budget deficits rather than address social (especially racial) inequalities. Clinton could claim to have resurrected the US economy, which on
paper in 1998 was the world's strongest, with low inflation, low unemployment, and a fairly balanced budget. However, as one of his first cabinet officers, Secretary of Labor Robert B. Reich, whom we previously encountered
as a defender of globalization, said after leaving office, the Clinton administration seemed to have abandoned the traditional social compact under
which employee benefits and real incomes rise in proportion to corporate
profits.[70]

Neither Clinton nor Reagan nor Bush created the widening economic
inequalities and social problems in the United States. But on their watch,
the problems did intensify, in part because of US indebtedness. The federal
government debt reached about $2.6 trillion by the end of Reagan's tenure
in 1988. By the time George H. W. Bush left office, the federal debt topped
$4 trillion, or over $16,000 for every man, woman, and child. Interest on the
debt absorbed 15 percent (almost $200 billion) of each year's federal budg-
et, which meant that it "exceed[ed] the total of all federal spending for edu-

cation, science, law enforcement, transportation, housing, food stamps and welfare."[71] Under Clinton in 1996, the debt was over $5 trillion, and under George W. Bush it was over $8 trillion—including a $318 billion budget deficit by September 2006 and interest payments on the debt of $406 billion.[72] Meanwhile, the US international debt—the difference between payments to and receipts from foreigners—also skyrocketed. In 1986 it was roughly $250 billion; by 2003 it was $665 billion, equivalent to $5,500 a person and nearly one quarter of the entire GDP.[73] What the international debt created was dependence on Chinese, Japanese, and other lenders to continue financing it. Should the attraction of US interest rates change, the US economy could be in deep trouble.

Like many countries, the United States has increasing poverty alongside an increasing concentration of wealth. But the United States has the dubious distinction of being "the most unequal society in the advanced democratic world."[74] Although the existence of a "permanent underclass" in the United States was documented in the 1960s (at the time of President Lyndon Johnson's war on poverty), it grew by over one-third under Reagan, to 35.3 million persons in 1983, roughly 15 percent of the total population. A striking 40 percent of those persons were children. The poverty rate was highest for blacks (35.7 percent) and Hispanics (28.4 percent) and their children.[75] In the late 1990s, over 20 percent of children lived in poverty despite government assistance, by far the highest rate of any developed country.[76] Overall, the percentage of the population living below the poverty level (11.7 percent in 2001) keeps rising.[77] Unemployment figures tell the same story: Official unemployment was about 6 to 7 percent in the mid- to late 1980s, and around 4–5 percent thereafter; but for nonwhites the rate has been much higher, including nearly 50 percent of young blacks. Working people also experienced declines: The real hourly wages of the bottom 40 percent of the population went down during the 1980s; and a typical mid-1990s inflation-adjusted income showed no improvement compared with 1973.[78] By 2006, while corporate profits were at an all-time high and worker productivity increased, wages and salaries were the lowest ever as a share of the nation's GDP, moving the chairman of the Federal Reserve to warn that this unequal distribution of benefits could "threaten the livelihoods of some workers" and attitudes toward globalization.[79]

The structural nature of these growing class divisions is indicated by the fact that they took place at a time of increased wealth among the upper class and rising median income as a whole. In a word, the rich in the United States are richer by any measure than they have been since the Great Depression. One reason is that federal tax subsidies and tax cuts mainly benefit the affluent.[80] Poorer Americans do not earn enough to benefit from tax incentives, nor do they have access to pension plans and other tax-subsidized savings plans. A 1984 Federal Reserve Board study found that the richest 2 percent of families collected about 15 percent of all income, and that the income share of the top 10 percent had risen to 33 percent.[81] About a decade later, an OECD study found that the United States had the largest gap in after-tax income between rich and poor—5.9 times—of any industrialized country.[82] In 2000 matters worsened still more as the rich-poor gap was the largest since (and double that of) 1979. The gap is most meaningful when measured in terms of total wealth and after-tax (disposable) income rather than income alone. In 2003, the richest *one* percent of Americans (2.8 million people) had disposable income equal to 15.5 percent of the entire pie, and greater than that of the 110 million poorest Americans.[83]

At a time of soaring stock market values, unprecedented corporate profits and top-tier salaries, world economic leadership, and no Cold War, one might think US domestic achievements would match its number-one military ranking. But rising prosperity is not being distributed with human needs foremost in mind. For instance, the high US ranking in literacy and government expenditures on education does not pertain to functional (job-related) literacy, in which the United States ranks forty-ninth of 158 UN members.[84] The United States spends a good deal less than most EU countries on public health. It ranks low on infant mortality, and 60 million people lack health insurance at least part of the year.[85] Finally, in terms of environmental protection, the US ranking is quite low. One major international study ranks it forty-fifth among 146 countries, while the OECD ranks the United States seventeenth among the 29 richest countries.[86] The failure of the United States to support the Kyoto Protocol is a blight on its international reputation, all the more so because of official unwillingness to accept the strong consensus in its own scientific community that global warming is a real and dangerous phenomenon.[87]

Hunger, a basic cause of poor health, no longer affects only the poor in the United States. In a comprehensive report on hunger in 1985, a physicians' group called it a "public health epidemic."[88] By 1993, 26 million people were receiving food stamps, and the number of people (about 30 million) with below-minimum diets was 50 percent higher than in the mid-1980s.[89] Yet the United States ranks high in nutrition overall. Equally misleading is the education picture: The attractiveness of US schools to non-American families belied the findings of national surveys, such as one in April 1983 by the National Commission on Excellence in Education that said: "If an unfriendly foreign power had attempted to impose on America the mediocre educational performance that exists today, we might have viewed it as an act of war." In the 1990s, not much improvement occurred. The United States ranks ninth and tenth in the world, respectively, in public education spending per capita and per student; eighteenth in the percentage of school-age children in school; and thirty-ninth in the ratio of students to teachers.[90] Finally, regarding the status of women, the United States ranks only eighth among all countries on the UNDP's gender-sensitive human-development scale.[91] Although women now make up around one-half of total university enrollment, that figure does not describe the failure of (male-dominated) state legislatures to pass an equal rights amendment to the US Constitution; the unlikelihood that a woman (with or without a university degree) will earn a salary comparable to a man's (in 2005 the median earnings for women were still only 80 percent of men's earnings); and longstanding frustrations for women such as inadequate child-care facilities and unequal work and training opportunities, including professorships at the universities they attend.

There are other social "epidemics" in the United States, crime being principal among them. Lawlessness at every level—crime in the suites as well as crime in the streets; crime by and, especially, against children, and particularly violent crime related to drugs—dominates all media and affects an increasing proportion of citizens. "One in four young people ages 10 to 16 queried nationwide in 1993 reported being assaulted or abused within the previous year," the *New York Times* reported. Such assaults are believed responsible for increased alcohol and drug use among youth, thoughts of suicide, and pregnancy rates that are among the highest in industrialized countries.[92] The overall crime rate is one of the world's highest, the number of people in prisons of all kinds exceeds 2 million, and the rate of imprisonment (455 persons per 100,000) is more than ten times Japan's.[93] A murder takes place every twenty-three minutes—also among the world's highest rates.[94] Women are especially vulnerable: The greatest public-health problem for women is abuse and violence, usually from men they know. Yet white-collar crime is no less rampant—and several times more costly to society than street crime.

These factors contribute to staggering problems in the administration of justice. A telling comment on social priorities is that in 1995, California's spending on prisons (around $4 billion, or just under 10 percent of the state's budget) exceeded spending on its two public university systems.[95] By 2000, it cost US taxpayers $100 million a day to incarcerate prisoners, and prison construction has become a major funding source for small communities.[96] Almost inevitably, the rate of conviction and term of imprisonment vary greatly, often depending on the socioeconomic background and race of the defendant. As race relations have continued to deteriorate, the incarceration rate of black males has risen. Astoundingly, about 12 percent of black males ages 20 to 34 are in prison;[97] at nearly a half-million men, they exceed the number of blacks in college.[98] And the United States is one of a dwindling number of countries (78 in 2004) that retains the death penalty—and leads the world in the number of children it executes.[99]

Personal insecurity has a counterpart in the economic domain. There, too, an entire middle sector—small businesses, small banks, the family farm—is being squeezed and shrunk by economic forces that strengthen the upper stratum while weakening the lower level. Some elements of this concentration of benefits and power are inequities in the tax system—multibillion-dollar tax breaks for the largest corporations; large-scale corporate takeovers—$1 trillion worth in 1996, $1.5 trillion in 1997[100]—leading to further concentration of control in industry and finance; and huge work force reductions and shrinkage or elimination of workers' pension plans and other benefits as corporations focus on satisfying the bottom line.

These critical observations should be considered in the context of both the US dream and the US reality. To many millions of people abroad, the United States still represents a land of opportunity and personal freedom. The ongoing, huge flow of refugees and migrant workers into the country attests to that. So do the large numbers of students and specialists, from rich and poor countries alike, who seek (and find) their fortunes in the United States. They understand, even if many US citizens do not, that a US education is not only valuable but also a bargain investment in the economic development of whichever country they finally call home. And the United States continues to possess enormous talent, energy, and youthful dynamism, as Whitman's poem says. Even its most vociferous critics give credit to the country's history of social activism and openness to dissent and cultural diversity. US citizens are justly proud of their country—more proud, studies show, than citizens of any other country.[101] But the divisions within society and the economy are growing; the appearances of wealth and power are both real and deceiving. At the political center is an absorption with preserving privileges and power and a striking lack of political imagination to break clear of old shibboleths, left and right, in search of a new consensus appropriate to real security in a world in crisis. Even after the Cold War, the costs of empire hang like a dead weight over the country, obstructing opportunities to make such a break.

President Eisenhower once said: "The military establishment, not productive of itself, necessarily must feed on the energy, productivity, and brainpower of the country, and if it takes too much, our total strength declines."[102] We now examine the social costs of the arms race in terms of its direct impact—how military spending affects the US economy—and its indirect impact—how military spending siphons money away from other social sectors in which human need is great and growing.

Any discussion of the real costs of national security to a society must consider the full dimension of military spending. Some figures for the United States have already been given concerning the most obvious kinds of expenditures: weapons, armed forces, and bases at home and abroad. But other line items should be added, such as nuclear energy, veterans' benefits, the military component of space programs, the military reserve, homeland security, and interest payments on the national debt from past wars. The defense department budgets of all countries hide these costs—in the United States, in the budgets of other agencies. When these other costs are added to the bottom line of national defense, they account for very large proportions of government spending. At the height of Reagan's military buildup, defense spending was over 50 percent of all federal general spending out of tax revenues.[103] By fiscal year 1996, the real US military budget was $494 billion, still about one-third of total government budget outlays.[104] By 2005 the United States was spending about $530 billion, more than the rest of the world combined.[105]

The most glaring set of economic consequences of such profligate spending in the United States is in relation to indebtedness, interest rates, and taxes. Past and present military obligations have contributed far more than any other kind of public spending to the US national debt.[106] (Equally obvious to many observers is that only a sizable and sustained reduction in military spending can make a dent in the debt.) Economists generally agree that huge budget deficits drive up interest rates; and the military, having the largest claim on government borrowing, helps to keep interest rates high. Individual taxpayers are therefore hurt in three quite direct ways from high levels of military spending. First, as consumers, they pay high interest on credit purchases, from home mortgages to clothing. Second, families pay a substantial proportion of their income taxes for military spending. Third, because military spending accounts for about one-half of all discretionary spending by the US Congress—that is, money it can actually allocate beyond Social Security and other fixed costs—taxpayers are shortchanged on education, health care, and other government-supported programs.

A second set of direct costs of military spending pertains to economic productivity and competitiveness internationally. Here is the point of direct conflict between US political-military predominance and the erosion of US international economic hegemony. As Seymour Melman, among many others, has frequently pointed out, the Pentagon's inefficient way of doing business over many years—and, one should add, the congressional toleration, if not encouragement, of it—was a major factor in the loss of industrial advantage to the Japanese and the West Europeans. Large cost overruns, lack of competitive bidding on most prime contracts, production of unneeded weapons, scandalous waste and overcharges—and now concentration of military-industrial power in only three firms—all add up to very expensive military equipment very inefficiently produced by a very large sector of the economy—in short, reduced productivity and overpriced goods.[107]

As previously noted, US research money and talent have gone disproportionately into military work. In 1982 US research spending for nonmilitary purposes was only 1.9 percent of the GNP, considerably less than for West Germany (2.6 percent) or Japan (2.5 percent).[108] Several years after the Cold War's end, the US government was still devoting over one-half of its research and development spending to the military, whereas in Europe, two-thirds was going into civilian research on the environment, transportation, and other critical areas.[109] Simon Ramo, former president of TRW, a major military contractor, said then: "In the past thirty years, had the total dollars we spent on military R&D been expended instead in those areas of science and technology promising the most economic progress, we probably would be today where we are going to find ourselves arriving technologically in the year 2000."[110] Military work in the United States employs over 25 percent of all scientists and engineers, including 30 percent of all mathematicians, 25 percent of all physicists, 47 percent of all aerospace engineers, and 11 percent of all computer programmers.[111] "If the brightest engineers in Japan are designing video recorders and the brightest engineers in the United States are designing MX missiles," Lester Thurow observed, "then we shouldn't find it surprising that they conquer the video-recorder market"[112]—or, today, high-definition television.

Military spending is a two-edged sword in a third area: jobs. That it creates employment is self-evident. But the kind of employment created—skilled technical work for the most part—cannot tap into the much larger pool of semiskilled and professional workers that nonmilitary employment can. Thus, several studies comparing the number of jobs brought about by every $1 billion of government spending found that money used in (for example) education, public transportation, and health and police services produces thousands more jobs than spending on military development.[113]

While it is often argued on behalf of military spending that it contributes to the civilian sector through the technological spin-offs of research, notably aircraft and computers, there seem to be absolute limits to civilian applications.[114] In a word, the prospects for reducing unemployment in the United States, or anywhere else, are going to depend on the development of civilian goods and services. And when it comes to cutting into hard-core unemployment among the least-skilled, education and the expansion of human services, not military service or production, are the most effective remedies.

The military's absorption of resources represents yet another large social cost. Murray L. Weidenbaum, chairman of Reagan's Council of Economic Advisers, said in criticism of the 1980s military buildup: "What worries me is that these crash efforts rarely increase national security. They strain resources, create bottlenecks."[115] The US military's large-scale consumption of strategic materials such as oil and chromium adds up to two unpleasant possibilities: the use of force to gain or preserve access to valuable resources, or US government and corporate alignment with oppressive regimes that supply the resources. US energy policy has long been held hostage by a national-security strategy that relies heavily on Middle East oil. By emphasizing consumption rather than conservation, US administrations allowed the trade deficit to climb and dependence on Persian Gulf oil to increase to the point of going to war over it in 1991 and again in 2003.[116] Overall, then, a solution to the problem that would be in both the national and global interest would be to develop mineral and energy substitutes, to conserve and recycle, and to reduce the military's needs for weapons and resources.

As Eisenhower's remark quoted earlier suggests, excessive military spending indirectly draws human and material resources away from socially productive purposes. At precisely what point military spending becomes excessive is, of course, always a matter of debate. But when national security is redefined in global-humanist terms, it becomes possible to see the transfer of resources from military to civilian purposes as a contribution to defense. Widening income gaps, decreasing job security, childhood poverty, and an educational system in disrepair surely count as indicators of declining real security for generations to come. When these and other socioeconomic problems can be traced to particular causes, such as unprecedented levels of military spending, there is reason for judging the spending excessive and injurious to the national interest.

When Eisenhower, in his farewell address, issued his famous warning about the military-industrial complex, he specifically included two other areas: civil liberties and democracy. "We must never let the weight of this combination endanger our liberties or democratic processes," he said. "We should take nothing for granted." The warning is well taken. Fighting a war under false pretenses has led people around the world to regard the United States as the number-one threat to world peace.[117] Additionally, the shrouding of government activities with the mantle of national security has been detrimental to the US way of life in many instances, taking such form as secret warfare against other states; arming of governments that consistently violate the human rights and political liberties of their citizens; secretive contractual ties for military research between federal agencies and academic institutions; suppression of information that would embarrass and cause public criticism of government officials, rather than subvert national security; disinformation campaigns designed to mobilize public and congressional opinion against government enemies abroad; the prosecution of prominent former employees-turned-critics; expansion of presidential powers that violate civil liberties and international law (such as the secret prisons and use of torture since 9/11) while avoiding congressional oversight; the denial of entry from abroad of persons and films critical of US policy, or of "questionable" ethnicity; the insistence on a right of prior restraint on scientific and academic exchanges with persons from rival countries; and surveillance and infiltration of groups that peacefully protest US policy. The founding fathers foresaw this danger of the national-security state. "Perhaps it is a universal truth that the loss of liberty at home is to be charged to provisions against danger, real or pretended, from abroad," James Madison said in 1798.

## China's Rise: Revolution and Transformation

In a political fable familiar to every Chinese, Mao Zedong told in 1945 of "The Foolish Old Man Who Removed the Mountains." Defying the skeptics, the old man announced he and later generations would keep digging until the two great mountains that obstructed his way were leveled. Mao's point was that China's underdevelopment could likewise be conquered if the Chinese masses persisted in digging up the mountains, imperialism and feudalism.[118] The Chinese revolution won out four years later, and the equally difficult struggle began to implement the revolution's objectives: the transformation of the economy, of the political culture, and of the international order.

To appreciate the extraordinary changes that have occurred in post-revolutionary China, and particularly improvements in the quality of life of its 1.3 billion people, we must briefly take account of what China looked like on the eve of the communist victory. Its industry, transportation, and communications were in near-total disrepair. Inflation was rampant; paper money was worthless. "Government" had reverted to the traditional system dominated by clans and landlords and their private military forces. Landlord-class control in rural China meant that, taking the country as a whole, about 10 percent of the rural families owned just over half the land.[119] Poor and still poorer farmers were the mainstay of the population, constantly victimized by the weather, landlord usury, exorbitant rent and land taxes, and extortion—all of which conspired to force the sale of children, female powerlessness, hunger, illiteracy, indebtedness far into the future, and early death. Worst of all, poor peasants assumed these conditions were meant to be and were unalterable.[120]

The first business of the communist movement was to empower peasants to believe in the possibilities of change for the better. Central to that objective was the land question: landownership, organization, and increased production. For, as one witness wrote, "Without understanding the land question one cannot understand the Revolution in China, and without understanding the Revolution in China one cannot understand the world."[121] Before 1949, the Chinese Communist Party (CCP) carried out a modest land-reform and rent-reduction program in areas it controlled. The program mainly benefited poor and middle peasants at the expense of the landlord class. Afterward, between 1958 and 1962, the CCP instituted the Great Leap Forward, a radical and enormously costly collectivization of the countryside, where 80 percent of the people still live. (By most accounts, at least 30 million people starved to death in that period.) These people's communes were part of a self-reliant economic development plan in which agricultural growth would feed into, and be expanded by, heavy and light industry. Economic growth was based overwhelmingly on Chinese resources; foreign trade was kept small and in balance; and China's debts were paid off by the mid-1960s. State economic planning was highly centralized and inflexible, reflecting Soviet influence; but local initiative, by peasants and factory workers as well as party cadres, was strongly encouraged. Those who exemplified the revolution's ideals of self-reliance, initiative, thrift, and readiness to "serve the people" were held up as models of the "new socialist person."

Converting revolutionary ideals to reality was regarded as a fundamentally political problem and not merely a matter of economic management. The vehicle was class struggle through periodic mass movements or campaigns. Their purposes were to sustain people's devotion to the revolution, identify and weed out bureaucratic cadres and "bourgeois" intellectuals, and prevent China from becoming a "revisionist" socialist state like the USSR. But the constant campaigns badly disrupted the economy and education, caused social chaos, and depleted people's morale; they also caused enormous suffering. The Anti-Rightist Campaign (1957), by official admission, incorrectly labeled 550,000 intellectuals as bourgeois opponents of the Communist Party and ruined their careers. Many committed suicide. The following Great Leap Forward was undertaken at extraordinary human cost, as just mentioned. Perhaps a half-million people died during the chaotic decade surrounding the Great Proletarian Cultural Revolution (1966–1976), and untold tens of thousands more were erroneously accused of political crimes, persecuted, and sent into internal exile or to prison.[122] The Maoist faction was willing to accept these losses as the price of ensuring that future generations of Chinese would be reliable revolutionary successors. Some of Mao's comrades, notably Deng Xiaoping, came to disagree. Soon after Mao's death in 1976, they took charge.

Mao's successors strove for social unity and economic stability. Beginning in 1979, they relaxed social controls; sharply de-emphasized (and then abandoned) class struggle; substituted market and material incentives (profits, bonuses, managerial autonomy) for ideological ones; dismantled the communes; upheld individual achievement and specialization in education, the workplace, and management; and announced an open door for foreign capital and technology. These steps to promote production and expand the market extended into the military. A major program was undertaken to convert a significant share of military-industrial production (by the late 1990s, this share was officially claimed to have reached 70 percent by value) to civilian goods. As part of the program, official military spending was kept low for several years, the military-industrial complex was streamlined, and about 1 million troops were demobilized.[123]

The economic reforms have cut deeply into the meaning of socialism. Though China's economy remains subject to overall central direction, its driving forces are local and regional. Not only is there more scope than ever before for individual and corporate initiative, for competence and professionalism, and for personal enrichment, but also other forms of enterprise—private and collective—are growing more rapidly than the state sector and account for increasing proportions of China's commercial profit, employment, and tax revenues, not to mention consumer goods production and total industrial output (40 percent). The non-state sector accounts for about

80 percent of China's GDP. Anywhere from a third to a half of state-owned enterprises, by contrast, are deeply in debt, inefficient, and require huge subsidies to survive. Were it not for their large work forces (which, with their families, make up about 45 percent of China's urban population), most would be disbanded or sold off. Many already have been.[124]

Behind these shifts in economic strategy lay a broader vision.[125] Deng Xiaoping and his colleagues argued that China's security for the remainder of the century lay in rapidly increasing GNP, personal income, and technological levels. "To achieve genuine political independence," Deng said, "a country must first lift itself out of poverty. . . . It should not erect barriers to cut itself off from the world."[126] Economic strength had become the new basis of national power, the new leadership believed; the Cold War, especially after Gorbachev's accession to power, had largely abated, giving China a breathing space of perhaps ten to fifteen years to catch up economically. Its leaders marveled at the dynamic growth of the four Asian NICs, but they also worried about falling further behind them. If China could acquire significant foreign capital, technology, and training, the country's development would be greatly accelerated. A stable China would become a force for world peace, and the age-old goal of integrating Hong Kong and Taiwan into China proper would be completed in Deng's lifetime.

But just as this vision put an end to destructive mass campaigns, it also denied the alternative of political pluralism. Deng condemned both of these political options, saying they would sentence China to endless social chaos that would sabotage the economic reforms. Like so many other authoritarian leaders, Deng—again with an eye to the experience of the Asian NICs (such as South Korea's industrialization under authoritarian rule)—believed that tight social controls were essential to economic development. Within strict limits, he was willing to entertain ideas for political reform, including removal of the CCP from government work and multicandidate elections, for now restricted to villages. But Deng fully embraced Mao's principles of political centralization.

Until the spring of 1989, Chinese intellectuals were engaged in lively debate about how to democratize politics, including the CCP. They evidently enjoyed some high-level support, in particular from the party's general secretary, Zhao Ziyang. But it is now clear that ideas such as eliminating one-party rule, ending the system of lifetime tenure in office, and enabling China's parliament to check executive power were unacceptable to Deng Xiaoping. To the contrary, they were attacked as examples of "spiritual pollution" and "bourgeois liberalism," and official campaigns against them were carried out in the 1980s. Thus did Deng's reform program, with its almost singular emphasis on economics, differ from Mikhail Gorbachev's in Russia, setting the stage for the dramatic confrontation of June 1989 in Tiananmen Square.[127]

Defenders of the Chinese reform strategy emphasize the daunting demographic, social, and geographic problems facing any group of leaders—for instance, finding jobs for a very youthful population (65 percent of China's 1.3 billion people are under age thirty); raising the basic educational level (officially, China has 10 percent illiteracy); satisfying the demands for greater cultural and political autonomy of minority groups (of which fifty-five are officially recognized); and allowing for great (and growing) differences in land and water quality, mechanization, and income in rural areas. From this perspective, meeting people's basic needs is much more important to human rights in China than introducing Western-style democracy.

Considering China's history of exploitation from within and without, this view of human rights is understandable if decidedly incomplete. Socialism under Mao enabled huge numbers of people to have dignity, access to land, basic health care, and old-age insurance. It also earned China international respect. This foundation of impressive gains in social well-being has continued in the post-Mao period. As a recent World Bank report observed, China's high life expectancy (age sixty-five for men, sixty-nine for women), low infant mortality (34 per 1,000), universal primary education, and other social-welfare achievements are "enviable by much richer nations. . . . Consumption has more than doubled and the poverty rate has declined by 60 percent (200 million Chinese living in absolute poverty have been raised above the minimum poverty line)."[128] Surely reduced poverty is the most important accomplishment of the PRC leadership. While East Asia as a whole cut average income poverty in half between 1987 and 2001 (see Table 4.2), China did the same thing in the 1990s alone. As a UNDP report on human development states, "Between 1990 and 2001 the incidence of $1 a day poverty declined by 50%, with 130 million fewer people living below the international poverty line."[129] Including all other human-development indicators, China has much to be proud of: Overall, it ranks 85th of 177 countries (recall that India ranks 127th) on the UNDP's scale.

Remarkable as such figures are, the other reality is the huge numbers of Chinese who still live in poverty: About "600 million Chinese still live on less than $2 a day."[130] Moreover, the benefits of economic growth and human development have been unevenly distributed, in keeping with our Third World profile: between rich and poor, urban and rural, east and west, Han and non-Han Chinese. And these gaps are rapidly widening.[131] Still other major deficiencies are that about 140 million Chinese are malnourished; Chinese adults average only six years of schooling; and girls continue to be less well educated than boys.[132] Government investment in education in China puts it among the least-developed countries: just 2.1 percent of GNP. Meantime, the costs of education dominate both urban and rural household spending now that education is two-tiered.[133] Child mortality rates have fallen, but are still exceptionally high, with more annual child deaths than any country except India.[134] Chinese women are far from achieving equality with men; but the Chinese women's movement has made major gains in local-level leadership, economic opportunities and rewards, education, and family rights. The Marriage Law of 1950, revised in 1981, bestows a number of legal guarantees for women and children that are not found in many Western and most developing countries with respect, for instance, to marriage, divorce, and property disposition. Average rural incomes, thanks to the shift to a household-based economy, have risen dramatically, as have farm production and people's savings. Until recently, the imposition of numerous taxes and fees cut deeply into farmers' income, but these have now been (at least officially) abolished. Although generalizations about conditions in China and people's attitudes are always perilous, the observations of numerous visitors (myself included) and Chinese polls suggest that, on the whole, the great majority of Chinese welcome the social and economic reforms for the clear improvements they have made in the quality of their lives.

The crushing of Beijing student and worker demonstrations for democracy by PRC military forces on June 4, 1989, showed that the PRC leadership would not tolerate organized dissent from any quarter.[135] Restoring social order counted more than the probable consequences, such as damaging the PRC's international prestige, reviving anxieties in Hong Kong and Taiwan about rejoining the mainland (as Hong Kong would in 1997, under a 1984 British-Chinese treaty), and reducing overseas investment and tourism in China. All of these consequences came to pass, but they proved temporary; four years after Tiananmen, the love affair with China resumed. China's economy, measured in terms of purchasing power, is the world's third largest. In regional terms "Greater China" is already as large an economy as France. Precisely in line with Deng Xiaoping's strategy, China has grown at breakneck pace, led by coastal areas that rely on overseas Chinese capital from Hong Kong, Taiwan, and Singapore.

China is a major player in the world economy and, at the same time, is highly dependent on it for continued growth. It holds huge foreign reserves, which by 2007 may total around $1 trillion, much of which is invested in US securities. China typically runs a large trade surplus (over $100 billion in 2005), takes a sizable proportion of World Bank development loans to the Third World, and its growth rate continues to sizzle at around 9 percent annually despite government efforts to slow it. Foreign investment in China, now over $50 billion a year, made it the leading location of FDI in 2003, surpassing the United States.[136] TNCs account for about 60 percent of China's exports, as mentioned earlier. Such high levels of trade, investment, and economic growth put it in a special class within the Third World: China accounts for just under a third of all developing-country exports, and is the major factor in East Asia's income poverty reduction noted in Table 4.2 in the last chapter.[137] Yet its trade surpluses and some protectionist trade practices (despite membership in the WTO since 2001) have become a major headache for US and EU trade officials, while the Japanese worry about the hollowing out of industries that have moved lock, stock, and barrel to the PRC.

China's prosperity has importance in domestic politics. Because the leadership has thus far been able to deliver on promises of material gain for most people, political dissent in China is sporadic. Outside of Hong Kong, an organized constituency on behalf of human rights or political structural change does not exist. The very public and vitriolic campaign that began in the 1990s against the religious sect Falungong, and the breakup of Hong Kong–based noncommunist parties, show what may happen to any independent group that lacks official sanction. The legacy of Tiananmen lingers. As an editorial in the official party newspaper put it: "Protecting stability comes before all else. Any behavior that wrecks stability and challenges the law will directly damage the people's fundamental interests."[138] Political reform in China has been restricted to measures that promote efficiency, sustain public support of the CCP, and undermine party factionalism; but the authoritarian party-state system and official corruption remain very much intact. Public criticism of officialdom, dissenting votes in parliament, the role of nongovernmental organizations (which, however, must register with the government), and civil suits have all increased, but these are for the most part tolerated or encouraged by China's leaders only in the economic, environmental, and cultural arenas, where and when such acts promote their own agenda. Arbitrary arrests and detentions of political reformers and human-rights dissenters—political, religious, ethnic, labor—remain the rule.[139] Lawyers and journalists seem to be particular targets of the Public Security Bureau, evidently as a deterrent to defending dissidents and uncovering official crimes.[140] Torture, "though on the decline, particularly in urban areas, nevertheless remains widespread," according to a UN investigation.[141] Censorship of publications and the Internet is undertaken with official pride, and considerable success.[142] Capital punishment thrives in China, where nearly 2,500 executions were carried out in 2001, 3,400 in 2004, and at least 1,770 in 2005—in each year, about 80 percent of the worldwide total.[143] Official corruption remains a central problem of political and social life, leading to a high number of public executions. Kickbacks, excessive fees, and bribery all are commonplace. These developments no doubt explain why Presidents Jiang Zemin and, more recently, Hu Jintao launched image campaigns based on the idea of the Communist Party as the faithful representative of the people and standard bearer of a "harmonious socialist society."

Some observers see movement in China in the direction of civil society and eventual democratization. The fact that many Chinese city governments and the press now report pollution levels and their sources, for example; that the leadership finally acknowledged the extensiveness of China's AIDS problem, and allowed the WHO into the country upon the outbreak of the

SARS epidemic; and that quite a few members of China's parliament opposed the Three Gorges Dam project, scheduled for completion in 2009, suggest a gradual widening of permissible limits of public dialogue. Civil society has also made some progress, for example, in greater media freedom, to some extent assisted by marketization but also by intrepid reporting under official pressure; emerging new law on government-run labor unions that would given them bargaining power over working conditions in foreign enterprises; and the formation of environmental NGOs that work together with the State Environmental Protection Agency. Along with political changes initiated by Deng Xiaoping—such as the forced early retirement of senior party and government officials, a two-term limit on their positions, village government and party elections,[144] an increased number of court cases and lawyers, and an overall decline in political repression—it is argued that governance in China is reforming even though Western-style democratization is not yet in evidence.[145] Even that modest assessment may be prematurely optimistic, however. Still, in areas of personal life meaningful to ordinary Chinese, such as finding a job and saving for a home of one's own, freedoms have expanded beyond anything imaginable a decade or so ago.

With respect to international affairs, Chinese and foreign specialists agree that the PRC, thanks largely to its economic transformation and the end of the Cold War, has never been as militarily secure as it is today. But there is disagreement among the latter about what that sense of security portends.[146] One school of thought is that China's economic rise and increasing nationalism spell trouble for its neighbors, starting with Taiwan, which to most governments is still a Chinese province, and Japan. This school emphasizes China's improved weapons, its revised doctrine that focuses on rapid deployment to nearby areas, and its substantial annual increases in military spending. In 2006, official military spending was announced as about $35 billion, an increase of 14.7 percent,[147] putting China second in the world. Outside estimates are that actual spending is at least three times higher. A second school (to which my analysis belongs) does not dispute either the fact of China's assertive nationalism, represented across the leadership spectrum but more so in its military leaders, or its improved military capabilities and increased military spending. Nevertheless, China's economic successes have also created barriers to aggressive external behavior. The financial and social costs of rapid economic development command the leadership's attention and resources. Moreover, Chinese nationalism is constrained by internationalism—China's dependence on regional and international order to carry out its economic reforms, and its need of technology and capital from the advanced countries, TNCs, and multinational lenders— as well as by its own limited resources and weaknesses in its defense-industrial base. The PRC is years away from becoming a first-rank military power, though that is no doubt its objective.[148]

The PRC proclaims it is a "responsible great power," and there is considerable evidence in support of the claim. Since 1992 in Cambodia, it has contributed over 2,600 troops to eight other UN PKOs, including Lebanon in 2006.[149] China has many unresolved territorial issues with its neighbors, most importantly Taiwan, whose government seeks higher international status, and island groups in the South China Sea, over which several governments claim sovereignty. China has deployed military forces in both cases, but it has also exercised restraint and in recent years engaged in dialogue that has yielded agreement on codes of conduct and China's signing of a treaty of amity with its Southeast Asian neighbors. Beijing has also launched an impressively large aid program in that region, and has established a region-wide free-trade area.[150] Looking around China's rim, we find that Beijing since the 1990s has systematically established, restored, and strengthened relations with all its neighbors, including those such as Russia, India, and Indonesia that were once conflict ridden. Confidence-building measures have been put into place to enhance border security and promote economic interests, such as with the new Central Asian states that preside over oil and gas deposits to which China is buying access. Indeed, China's energy needs have become the core of its economic diplomacy in recent years, as discussed in detail in the next section. Thus, the notion of a China military threat has little basis; a rising China needs cooperative international relations, and the only situation that would probably compel China's use of force is a Taiwanese declaration of independence.

The principal challenges PRC leaders face for many years to come lie within. Many are a direct consequence of China's spectacular growth, and none are more daunting than environmental and ecological problems. One source is increased population pressure on cities, especially those in the special economic zones of the coastal provinces, where rapid growth has been fueled by foreign investment. (Five of the world's most polluted cities are in China, and pollution levels are well above WHO safety limits.[151]) Urban and rural areas are competing for land and water, reducing farm acreage and raising fears of food scarcity.[152] Other environment-damaging sources are large-scale development projects such as the Three Gorges Dam on the Yangtze River,[153] clearing of forestlands, chemical spills, and industrial and agricultural pollution of air, water, and soil. Because of rising coal use, China is the world's largest emitter of sulfur dioxide and second-largest of carbon.[154] By 2009 China is expected to surpass the United States as the number-one emitter of greenhouse gases.[155] Environmental and ecological costs are being passed back to people in the form of soil degradation and public-health problems such as significant rises in respiratory diseases and cancer.[156] Those costs are huge—roughly 10 percent of GDP, according to a top environmental official—and should require an adjustment of China's economic growth figures.[157] Like other developing countries, China is a latecomer to environmental protection and, in the minds of some Western specialists, too late to recover its forests, farmland, or water table. The Chinese government recognizes the costs and in some cases is committing large funds to remedy some of the problems.[158] But "development" usually takes first place, as in the government's ambitious plans for nuclear plant and dam construction, and for rerouting major southern rivers to meet the northern part of the country's water needs.

Agriculture is the Achilles heel of the communist government despite all the benefits farmers have received from the economic reforms. The income gap between rural and urban areas continues to grow. Tens of millions of people drift from countryside to city in search of work. Illegal seizures of land for resale to developers by local authorities in cahoots with police and the courts are a major scandal: According to one report, "the Ministry of Land and Resources admitted that in some cities more than 60 percent of the commercial land acquisitions since September 2004 had been illegal. In some places, that proportion had reached 90 percent."[159] The land seizures are a major cause of rural protests, quite a few of which have turned violent.[160] If neighboring India is any guide, democratization is one way out for China's farmers. The mobilization of Indian farmers and rural-related state bureaucracies have produced tangible gains for many rural people, though (as already discussed here) rural poverty is still widespread.[161] Yet India is the exception to the general rule that rural empowerment comes later in the development process. That may be too late for China's farmers, whose burdens (like those of Mexican farmers) come not just from decades of neglect by the state but now also from China's entry in the WTO, which will mean competition from cheaper agricultural imports.

China's rise has been favored by leaders totally focused on developing the economy, on an entrepreneurial culture that decades of Maoism could not erase, and on the lure of the China market that has made it the hot place for foreign investment. Delivering prosperity for hundreds of millions of people has ensured political stability, including a peaceful transfer of power to a "fourth generation" of engineers-turned-politicians. Nevertheless, China faces monumental problems in large part because of the rapidity of the changes and its size and diversity, as we have seen with respect to environmental degradation and income gaps. The PRC leadership needs to address popular anger, moreover, before it boils over and becomes more organized. By official count, over 80,000 "mass incidents" occurred in 2005, and while these are not all huge outbreaks, they reflect large year-to-year jumps.[162] As the numbers of Chinese connected to the Internet and carrying cell phones leap ahead, awareness of injustices will become harder to cover up.

The Chinese people, like people everywhere, want predictable, fair, lawful governance—more, perhaps, than they want multiparty systems and elections.[163] Can the Communist Party promote the rule of law and greater accountability in the economy while, in politics, preserving the one-party state? Or is the party on a collision course with the people? These developments speak to the real concerns of the average Chinese citizen—if it is possible to speak of such a thing—which are about economic opportunity and the obstacles to it, such as alienation from work—and for younger Chinese, about living life fully rather than for money[164]—much more than they are about civil liberties and the virtues of civil society. This is not to say, however, that the ordinary citizen is uninterested in politics. Studies of village elections, which are now universal in China, show that people want competent, honest government and officials who can represent their interests. Where such elections are truly competitive, as they are supposed to be, nonparty candidates stand a good chance of being chosen.[165] But not surprisingly, what is most on the minds of Chinese farmers and urban dwellers alike are quality-of-life issues: freedom of movement, jobs, health care, and opportunities for children.

These are only a few of the many worrisome features of China's rise. In a country that represents over one-fifth of world population, and is so large and diverse in population and resources, the impact of rapid growth could only be contradictory. Some of the forces it has unleashed, such as nationalism, widespread corruption, and the supplanting of party power by local interests, may prove uncontrollable. The best hope for bringing social justice to China probably lies not in the Communist Party's self-initiated transformation but in the growth of civil society. Already, informal protests, clubs, and religious organizations constitute a "slow-motion revolution."[166] Lawsuits, mass demonstrations, critical publications, and sometimes violent confrontations with authority all have the potential to coalesce in civil-society associations of one kind or another, not for the purpose of directly challenging the political system so much as its arbitrariness, stupidity, conflicts of interest, and violations of its own rules. Increasingly, the rule of law and transparent processes are important to the Chinese, and organizing against the system, though still dangerous these days, may not be far off. The PRC leaders will have to decide whether continuing to jail critics and closing down their activities, rather than tolerating them, is worth the prospective cost of even greater dissent.

One of Deng Xiaoping's greatest achievements was to avoid a succession crisis by putting in place a team of party leaders strongly committed to his vision before he died in 1997. They have inherited a China that has removed the two big mountains and is at peace. But new mountains are rising before their eyes.

## US-China Relations: Containment or Engagement?

US-China relations are the indisputable key to long-term regional stability in Asia. To hear senior US and Chinese officials tell it, relations between the two countries have never been better. The reality is quite different. Friendly relations are highly contingent on immediate events; each side sees the other as a challenger rather than as a partner. The United States wants a China that minds its own business and, through increasing globalization, starts to democratize. China, on the other hand, wants a United States that will continue to promote economic cooperation with it, will stop interfering in China's internal affairs (such as by pressuring it on human rights and arming Taiwan), and will treat China as an equal in addressing global issues.

China's "peaceful rise," as PRC leaders call it, poses an important question for US leaders: Will China's spectacular economic achievements, and its consequent rising nationalism, conflict with US interests in East Asia and elsewhere? Historically, according to some realists, a rising power that confronts an established superpower spells trouble. During the George W. Bush administration disputes with China have been muted by the terrorism issue; but US concern has been expressed about China's military spending, and aspects of China's global diplomacy—in particular its efforts to acquire new sources of energy and its refusal to side with the United States on genocide in Sudan and sanctions against North Korea and Iran. Chinese leaders, meanwhile, have acknowledged the fundamental structural difference between China and the United States but have insisted that China has neither the need nor the capacity to challenge the United States. Absorbed with the challenges of sustaining economic reforms while coping with their destabilizing consequences, the PRC leadership is significantly constrained from being a competitor. But some in the US leadership do not see things that way.

For all their obvious differences in wealth, political influence, and ability to project power, the United States and China have at least two things in common. One is a perception of the other as being an irresponsible (or at least unpredictable) great power. US officials have urged China to become a "responsible stakeholder" in the international system.[167] Chinese officials have criticized US "hegemonism" in the Middle East and elsewhere. Second, realists and globalists in both countries see the other as a very important economic partner but also as a major political and potentially military rival. The difference is that US leaders see trade and investment in China as a political tool for undermining socialism. As George W. Bush once proclaimed, very much in the same manner as Bill Clinton:

> When we negotiate for open markets, we're providing new hope for the world's poor. And when we promote open trade, we are promoting political freedom. . . . Look at our friends in Mexico and the political reforms there. Look at Taiwan. Look at South Korea. And someday soon I hope that an American president will end that list by adding, "Look at China."[168]

An asymmetry of power need not lead to conflict. If US leaders appreciate the immensity of China's development dilemmas and the limits of its ambitions, and if Chinese leaders continue to seek common ground with the United States on a range of issues, there is every reason to expect the relationship to evolve harmoniously. Certainly, differences will persist: The US-China relationship is to some extent prisoner to the past, historically and ideologically, and, even if that were not so, China's focus on rapid economic development creates needs and national objectives quite different from those of a highly developed global power such as the United States. As a Chinese official once explained: "China is most concerned with its own internal development and the United States is most concerned with trying to maintain international order."[169] Appreciating those differences can help to manage them; but accentuating them could easily bring on another Cold War. Thus, the US perception of China as a strategic competitor is potentially troubling. In the words of a 2005 US Defense Department report on China:

> China does not now face a direct threat from another nation. Yet, it continues to invest heavily in its military, particularly in programs designed to improve power projection. The pace and scope of China's military build-up are, already, such as to put regional military balances at risk. Current trends in China's military modernization could provide China with a force capable of prosecuting a range of military operations in Asia—well beyond Taiwan—potentially posing a credible threat to modern militaries' operation in the region.[170]

Quite aside from the needlessly alarmist tone of these comments—the report also states that "In the future, as China's power grows, China's leaders may be tempted to resort to force or coercion more quickly to press diplomatic advantage"—is the fact that US power and intentions more closely approximate the comments than does China's. The United States, not China, dominates global military spending, military modernization, arms transfers, and bases abroad. The US economy is approximately five times the size of China's. And it is the United States, not China, that has demonstrated both the will and the way to project power for coercive purposes. It is enough to lead at least one senior US military commander to lament that his bosses still seem to be fighting the Cold War, as though China is the Soviet Union of old.[171]

Thus, while US leaders urge China to be a "responsible stakeholder," the message Chinese leaders actually read is in a different language—the language of the senior partner addressing a junior partner. The message essentially amounts to telling the Chinese that if they play by the rules of the principal stakeholder, they will benefit; but if they misbehave, they will be confronted. (The 2006 NSS concludes on China: "Our strategy seeks to encourage China to make the right strategic choices for its people, while we hedge against other possibilities."[172]) According to the NSS, China should reduce its trade imbalance with the United States (at just over $200 billion, it represents about one-fifth of the total US trade deficit), moderate military modernization, promote freedom for its people, stop "locking up" global energy supplies, cease support of governments that have valuable resources but deny human rights to their citizens, and ensure that force or coercion are not used against Taiwan.

Prominent Chinese analysts who believe in the need for US-China cooperation nevertheless are quick to cite numerous troubling aspects of the relationship.[173] The "partnership" with China in the war on terror is paper thin; it simply gives each country more room to deal with *its* "terrorists" in its own way, without finger pointing.[174] Beyond that, from the Chinese perspective, US policy under Bush is at best inconsistent and at worst provocative. On Taiwan, a recent PRC defense white paper, *China's National Defense in 2004*, called the situation there "grim" because of President Chen Shui-bian's moves toward independence as well as US arms sales to Taiwan, which have been limited mainly by Taiwan's hesitancy to pay the roughly $15 billion bill. Even though Bush has opposed Taiwanese independence and stopped short of selling Taiwan some advanced weapons systems, he has consistently upheld a US obligation to defend Taiwan—and has enlisted Japan in that security interest. Japan's joint announcement with the United States in 2005 of a shared concern about Taiwan's security (which China seemingly answered with an antisecession law aimed at deterring any further Taiwanese moves toward formal independence) was apparently one of the issues that sparked an angry anti-Japanese Internet campaign in China.[175] President Bush and Prime Minister Koizumi Junichiro, in the Chinese view, became partners in a new containment strategy that includes research on theater missile defense, loosened restrictions on Japanese deployments and armaments, constitutional revision, and encouragement of Japan's rightists in their support of Taiwanese separatism.[176] Despite US pronouncements about nuclear nonproliferation, it has yet to protest occasional high-level talk in Japan about plutonium and developing nuclear weapons.

Nor is that all, from Beijing's perspective. The Bush administration's resort to sanctions against North Korea has been criticized a number of times by PRC officials. In line with South Korea, they believe in the need to provide energy assistance to the North, and argue for a continuing search for a diplomatic solution to the nuclear standoff.[177] US bases in Central Asia, on China's border;[178] US efforts to restart a military relationship with India and support India's nuclear energy program; differences over how to deal with Iran's nuclear program; and successful US pressure on the EU to delay lifting its arms embargo with China add to the list of issues that are undermining the relationship.

From Beijing's viewpoint, dealing with the United States may be summarized this way: In sharp contrast with the Maoist past, we in China have subscribed to global (capitalist) economic rules, signed on to numerous international arms-control arrangements, made numerous overtures to Taiwan's political leaders and opposition parties, and played the good citizen in relations with East Asian neighbors. Yet the United States, as the sole superpower, always demands more, for example by pressuring North Korea and continuing to arm Taiwan. Moreover, powerful forces in the United States now express the kind of alarm about China's "peaceful rise" that it did decades ago about China's support of communist insurgencies. Is the United States really interested in accommodation and peaceful competition, or is it interested in containing China? A well-known Singapore analyst has answered that "the United States is doing more to destabilize China than any other power."[179]

China is not about to confront the United States directly, however. Instead, as mentioned above, China is taking advantage of US preoccupation with the Middle East, specifically the military and diplomatic costs of that preoccupation, to build, mend, and strengthen fences with China's neighbors, particularly with a view to promoting China's rapid economic development. PRC leaders apparently are seeking to demonstrate that China is not just a good Asian citizen, but also a reliable partner in multilateral as well as bilateral undertakings. The contrast with the Bush Doctrine's emphasis on unilateral action and preventive war, and its growing security partnership with Japan, is left for other governments to draw.

### Energy

China's role in the global energy picture looms large, and reveals the potential for both conflict and cooperation. As China's economy has taken off, and an automobile market has emerged, energy security has jumped to the top of the leadership's priorities. The country has gone from energy self-reliance to becoming a major oil importer (imports account for about 40 percent of China's oil) and the world's second-largest oil consumer. Thus, even while China is still a leading oil producer, its oil dependence is rapidly rising—by some estimates, to 60 or 70 percent by 2020.[180]

China's energy diplomacy has major implications in several policy arenas. For one, it further elevates the value of access to oil and natural gas. Chinese officials have gone far and wide to find energy partners, either through acquisitions of oil companies, contracts for purchases, or pipeline construction. The search is global—to Canada, Brazil, and Venezuela, as well as Kazakhstan, Iran, and Russia—bringing China into direct competition with US, Japanese, and other large importers. Disputes are mounting— for example, with the United States when Washington blocked China's attempt to purchase Unocal, and with Japan over territorial boundaries in the East China Sea. Second, the price of oil is moving rapidly upward with rising demand, not only from China and the United States but also from India. Third, the environmental consequences of car ownership in China are staggering, for "If car ownership were eventually to rise to American levels, there would be 650m[illion] cars on Chinese roads—more than all the cars in the world today."[181] Last, there is the reality of geopolitics: Half of China's oil comes from the Middle East, putting China into the highly charged politics of the Persian Gulf—notably with Iran, which alone is responsible for over 10 percent of PRC imports.

China is not out to corner the market on oil, an impossibility anyway given the power of the energy conglomerates. But it wants its fair share, and preaches energy cooperation at the same time as it practices energy security. There is every reason for the major oil-importing countries to strive for cooperation, given how frequently oil politics has turned violent. But cooperation does not necessarily benefit the global environment, China's poor, or repressed populations. Global energy agreements promote further consumption, not conservation or energy alternatives. They benefit energy companies, whether private or state-run. Moreover, such agreements ignore the human-rights consequences of oil exploration and production, such as in Sudan, Ecuador, and Kazakhstan. Indeed, the Chinese government is no different from the energy giants such as Exxon Mobil in justifying its indifference to human rights by arguing that it should not meddle in the domestic affairs of the producer countries. All that matters is having access to their resources.

China's search for energy and its continued heavy reliance on coal point up the typical contradiction between a fossil fuel–based economic development plan and recognition of the immediate and long-term environmental and public-health costs. Much like the United States, China's decisionmaking on global environmental issues has sometimes adhered to scientific findings, such as on the Montreal Protocol, and sometimes (as on Kyoto) defied it in favor of economic growth. But then again, China's carbon emissions are about one-half those of the United States, and one-seventh as much on a per person basis.[182]

## The Future of US-China Relations

Dealing with China certainly is a challenge, just as dealing with the United States must be a monumental challenge for China. Human rights, trade, Japan, the environment, intellectual property rights, Iran, Sudan, and energy are important issues in dispute. How to engage China constructively on these issues is the difficulty, and it is here that the Bush administration has fallen down on the job. Part of the reason lies in the contradictory message it is sending Chinese leaders. The other part has less to do with China than with the fundamental ideas that the administration brings to world affairs generally—ideas that reflect limited faith in diplomacy and conflict resolution, arrogant assumptions about the preeminence of US values and institutions, and a conviction about the righteousness of using force and threat to advance the national interest. President John F. Kennedy's approach to the Soviet Union might well be applied to China. In a famous speech in 1963 at

American University, Kennedy said: "If we cannot end our differences now, at least we can help make the world safe for diversity." But that is not the current stance of the United States. "We are an empire now," a senior Bush official once told journalists, "and when we act, we create our own reality. . . . We're history's actors."[183] Until the idea of empire is discarded, it is hard to see how China can truly be engaged and encouraged to be a "responsible stakeholder."

## Notes

1. Adam Daniel Rotfeld, "Introduction: The Fundamental Changes and the New Security Agenda," *SIPRI Yearbook 1992*, p. 9.
2. During 1989 and 1990, large numbers of Soviet troops and weapons were withdrawn, including 73,500 soldiers from Czechoslovakia, 49,700 from Hungary, perhaps a quarter-million from the China border, and thousands of tanks from central Europe. Another 370,000 Soviet occupation forces in East Germany were also starting to head home.
3. For example, the conference did not tackle a number of weaknesses in the NPT regime that emerged from North Korea's conduct during its confrontation with South Korea and the United States in 1993 and 1994. These included the IAEA's difficulties in making inspections and demanding "special" inspections; dealing with a member that, like North Korea, decides to withdraw from the NPT or to suspend its withdrawal; and the lack of a ban on plutonium reprocessing. The conference also did not confront uncertainties in the Middle East over Israel's unsafeguarded nuclear facilities and Iran's nuclear prospects; agreement on a policy of no-first-use of nuclear weapons, which China sought; and enlargement of the number of nuclear weapon-free zones (NWFZs), such as in the Middle East. On these and other aspects of the conference, see *Disarmament*, vol. 28, no. 3 (1995), which gives a comprehensive review from a variety of national perspectives.
4. For background, see Rebecca Johnson, "The In-Comprehensive Test Ban," *The Bulletin of the Atomic Scientists*.
5. Sidney Drell, "Reasons to Ratify, Not to Stall," *NYT*, June 2, 1998, p. A21.
6. *NYT*, November 22, 1985.
7. On post-Soviet military spending cuts, see *SIPRI Yearbook 1992*, pp. 206–12. Gaddy (*The Price of the Past*, pp. 83–86) comments on the ability of the defense enterprises to "recover" from efforts to privatize them, and on the difficulties under Yeltsin of converting from military to civilian production, despite savings on weapons procurement and reduced military production. Of about 5,000 military industries in the FSU, only a little more than five hundred (including 460 in Russia) were actually tabbed for partial conversions of production. (See the Konovalov and Leitenberg essays in Brunn et al., pp. 175–82 and 325–33.) The arms industries are said to be engaged in the "mindless pursuit of private gain" and are basically out of control. Stephen J. Blank, *Why Russian Policy Is Failing in Asia*, p. 19.
8. This controversial article is by Keir A. Lieber and Daryl G. Press, "The Rise of U.S. Nuclear Primacy," *Foreign Affairs*, pp. 42–54. Their main argument: "It will probably soon be possible for the United States to destroy the long-range nuclear arsenals of Russia or China with a first strike" (p. 43).
9. The lack of a significant difference between the Bush and Clinton strategies is noted in the *NYT*, September 2, 1993, p. 1. US nuclear doctrine since the first Gulf War has been to deter or retaliate against others' use of weapons of mass destruction, or to use nuclear weapons in response to an invasion by certain non-

nuclear states. See Steven Lee Myers, "U.S. 'Updates' All-Out Atom War Guidelines," *NYT*, December 8, 1997, p. A3; William M. Arkin, "N.P.T.—Back to Ground Zero," *The Nation;* and *The Defense Monitor* 24, no. 8 (September–October, 1995), pp. 3–4.

10. *NYT*, December 2, 1997, p. A16.

11. "Official" spending refers to government-reported Department of Defense figures, which, in the US case, also include US Department of Energy spending on nuclear weapons. Center for Defense Information, online at www.cdi.org.

12. The official US total for 2004–2005 was $505.8 billion out of $1,025 billion worldwide; see Center for Defense Information, *The Defense Monitor* 35, no. 2 (March–April, 2006), p. 2.

13. Natural Resources Defense Council, *Taking Stock: Worldwide Nuclear Deployments 1998,* report (March), online at www.nrdc.org.

14. Walter Pincus, "New Methods Help Maintain Nuclear Arms," *Washington Post,* April 28, 1998.

15. Bill Mesler, "Virtual Nukes—When Is a Test Not a Test?" *The Nation;* William J. Broad, "Fusion-Research Effort Draws Fire," *NYT*, July 15, 1998, p. A5; Matthew L. Wald, "U.S. Refits Nuclear Bomb to Destroy Enemy Bunkers," *NYT*, May 31, 1997, online at www.nytimes.com; Carl Hulse, "Senate Votes to Lift Ban on Producing Nuclear Arms," *NYT*, May 21, 2003, p. A24.

16. William J. Broad, "Nuclear Arms Builders Shift Role from Developers to Care-Takers," *NYT*, January 6, 1997, p. 1.

17. The United States has an estimated 1,600 or so tactical warheads in the form of artillery shells, landmines, and bombs; Russia has anywhere from 3,800 to 18,000. Paul Richter, "Small Nuclear Arms Create the Most Fear," *San Jose Mercury News*, May 25, 2002.

18. See Gurtov, *Superpower on Crusade*, p. 198.

19. *NYT*, April 1, 2005, p. C3.

20. This paragraph relies on Leslie Wayne, "The Shrinking Military Complex," *NYT*, February 27, 1998, p. C1. See also *NYT*, March 10, 1998, p. C3.

21. Lockheed Martin's lobbyists reportedly drafted the language used in a US Senate bill to fund the F-22 and end a ban on its sale abroad. Leslie Wayne, "Washington Battles over Costly F-22 Jet," *International Herald Tribune*, September 12, 2006.

22. *NYT*, July 11, 2006, p. A4.

23. *NYT*, April 1, 2005, p. C3.

24. The case of the F-22 again is illustrative. At $361 million per aircraft, it is the most expensive ever, yet its cost-effectiveness is questionable.

25. Leslie Wayne, "White House Tries to Trim Military Cost," *NYT*, December 6, 2005, p. 1; David S. Cloud, "Pentagon Review Calls for No Big Changes," *NYT*, February 2, 2006, p. A15.

26. The extensive direct and indirect ways that the US government provides incentives for arms sales abroad are examined by William D. Hartung, *Welfare for Weapons Dealers: The Hidden Costs of the Arms Trade.*

27. In terms of arms sales agreements to developing countries, Russia led at $7 billion, with France at $6.3 billion and the United States at $6.2 billion. Thom Shanker, "Russia Was Leader in Arms Sales to Developing World in '05," *NYT*, October 29, 2006, p. 10.

28. Central Intelligence Agency, *Handbook of International Economic Statistics 1997*, table 127, online; Congressional Research Service report discussed in Tim Weiner, "Russia and France Gain on U.S. Lead in Arms Sales, Study Says," *NYT*, August 4, 1998, online. In the 1990s, Russian arms deliveries ranked second at $3.4 billion.

29. Stockholm International Peace Research Institute, ed., *SIPRI Yearbook 2005: World Armaments and Disarmament*, table 10A.2, online at www.sipri.org/contents/armstrad/at_data.html#chap.

30. "Annual CRS Report Shows Five Year High in Weapons Sales," *The Defense Monitor* 34, no. 5 (September–October 2005), p. 5.

31. See Frida Berrigan and William D. Hartung, *U.S. Weapons at War 2005: Promoting Freedom or Fueling Conflict?*

32. Elizabeth Olson, "Small Arms Proliferating, Study Finds," *NYT*, June 30, 2002, online ed.

33. Raymond Bonner, "For U.S., Gun Sales Are Good Business," *NYT*, June 6, 1998, p. A3. For background on the issue and international negotiations concerning it, see Michael Renner, *Small Arms, Big Impact: The Next Challenge of Disarmament*. Renner (p. 11) gives a rough estimate of $3 billion a year in international trade of small arms. With Canada and Norway leading the way, the first international meeting, involving twenty countries, took place in Oslo in mid-1998 to deal with legal and illegal traffic in small arms. These weapons, such as handguns, howitzers, and other conventional weapons handled by one or a team of soldiers, are the kind that fuel nationalist and ethnic conflict. The United States and some other major military powers that produce these weapons shied away from endorsing an international agreement to ban or limit their sales.

34. *Washington Post,* January 29, 1998; William J. Broad and David E. Sanger, "Restraints Fray and Risks Grow as Nuclear Club Gains Members," *NYT*, October 15, 2006, p. 1.

35. Milton Leitenberg, "Just How Bad Can It Get?" *Los Angeles Times*, October 28, 2001.

36. Judith Miller et al., "U.S. Germ Warfare Research Pushes Treaty Limits," *NYT*, September 4, 2001, p. 1.

37. For a good overview, see Jozef Goldblat and Peter Lomas, "Disarmament Watch: Nuclear Non-Proliferation, the Problem States," *Transnational Perspectives,* pp. 17–21. On the Pakistani and Indian missile capabilities, see *NYT*, April 11, 1998, p. A3. The best study on the motives behind India's tests is by George Perkovich, *India's Nuclear Bomb: The Impact on Global Proliferation*; it stresses domestic political pressures to test. But at least some Indian leaders were concerned about deterring China. A week before the tests, India's new defense minister had declared that China is India's "potential enemy No. 1" (*NYT*, May 12, 1998, p. A10). Later, an unnamed senior Indian official confirmed that fact, saying: "Our problem is not Pakistan," he said. "Our problem is China. We are not seeking parity with China. We don't have the resources, and we don't have the will. What we are seeking is a minimum deterrent" (*NYT*, July 7, 1998, online).

38. Norman Kempster, "U.S. Knew of Pakistani N-Program," *Los Angeles Times* (in *The Oregonian*, March 18, 1992).

39. Tim Weiner, "India-Pakistan Region Now Among Most Dangerous," *NYT*, May 17, 1998, online; Weiner, "U.S. and China Helped Pakistan Build Its Bomb," *NYT*, June 1, 1998, p. A6; R. Jeffrey Smith, "U.S. Aides See Troubling Trend in China-Pakistan Nuclear Ties," *Washington Post*, April 1, 1996.

40. Victor Gilinsky and Paul Leventhal, "India Cheated," *Washington Post*, June 15, 1998. The head of the India program in 1974 admitted to India's having lied about its intentions.

41. Tim Weiner, "India-Pakistan Region Now Among Most Dangerous."

42. A spokesman for the ruling Hindu nationalist party whose leaders authorized the nuclear tests shortly after assuming office said: "The American position is hypocritical. They are sitting on a mountain of nuclear arms, and they are pontificating to India and the world [about nonproliferation]" (*NYT*, May 14, 1998, p. A8).

Pakistan probably agreed; but in any event its position has always been that it would not sign the NPT without India's signature. Both governments promised following their May 1998 nuclear-weapon tests that they would not conduct additional tests, and they have not.

43. The US Department of Energy has been cooperating with the Russian Ministry of Atomic Energy (MINATOM) since 1994 to improve Russian security systems for weapons-usable material. US Information Agency press release, "U.S. and Russia Work Jointly to Secure Nuclear Materials," May 27, 1998. And see C.J. Chivers, "Uzbeks Ship Bomb-Grade Waste to Russia," *NYT*, April 20, 2006, p. A8.

44. Among numerous sources, see William J. Broad and David E. Sanger, "As Nuclear Secrets Emerge, More Are Suspected," *NYT*, December 26, 2004, p. 1; William Langewiesche, "The Wrath of Khan," *The Atlantic Monthly*, pp. 62–85; and David E. Sanger, "Pakistan Leader Confirms Nuclear Exports," *NYT*, September 13, 2005, p. A8.

45. William J. Broad, "Deadly Nuclear Waste Piles Up with No Clear Solution at Hand," *NYT*, March 14, 1995, p. B7. The article quotes one nuclear physicist, Dr. Arjun Makhijani, as saying, "Every four or five years we're making about as much plutonium in the civil sector as we did during the whole cold war."

46. William J. Broad, "U.S., in First Atomic Accounting, Says It Shipped a Ton of Plutonium to 39 Countries," *NYT*, February 5, 1996, p. 5.

47. Steven R. Weisman, "Dissenting on Atomic Deal," *NYT*, March 3, 2006, p. A10; Worldwatch Institute, "U.S.-India Nuclear Deal: Reckless on Every Score," March 3, 2006, at www.worldwatch.org.

48. In September 2006 Gamal Mubarak, the president's son and heir-apparent, made that suggestion, which, if accepted by the United States, would then have to contend with similar requests from South Korea, Taiwan, and others. But if the United States declines to assist Egypt, it is in the embarrassing position of putting an ally in the same category as Iran and North Korea—and thus denying an Islamic country access to nuclear energy. See Michael Slackman, "Son of Mubarak Eyes Succession," *International Herald Tribune*, September 20, 2006.

49. The treaty's other signatories are Kyrgyzstan, Uzbekistan, Turkmenistan, and Tajikistan. A provision of the treaty leaves open a 1992 agreement with Russia on transporting nuclear weapons through these countries' territories, leading to US and European opposition.

50. Betts, p. 213.

51. Hersh, "On the Nuclear Edge," pp. 66–67.

52. John F. Burns, "In Nuclear India, Small Stash Does Not an Arsenal Make," *NYT*, July 26, 1998, online.

53. Celia W. Dugger, "Rich-Poor Gap Endangers India, President Warns," *International Herald Tribune*, January 26, 2000.

54. Pankaj Mishra, "The Myth of the New India," *NYT*, July 6, 2006, p. A23.

55. See Daniel Ellsberg, "Manhattan Project II: The End of the Threat of Nuclear War," *Harvard Journal of World Affairs*, pp. 1–16.

56. Carl Kaysen, Robert S. McNamara, and George W. Rathjens, "Nuclear Weapons After the Cold War," *Foreign Affairs*, pp. 95–110.

57. Ibid., p. 101.

58. Other expert testimonies and documents that address the nuclear danger and propose major weapons reductions and related changes of nuclear doctrine and practice are *Report of the Canberra Commission on the Elimination of Nuclear Weapons*, January 1997 (an international commission established in November 1995 by the Australian government), online at www.dfat.gov.au; Federation of American Scientists, *Report of the Nuclear Policy Review Project*, 1997 (a group headed by

Morton H. Halperin that posed questions essential to a review of existing US nuclear-weapons policy), distributed by NAPSNet, February 5, 1997, and available online at www.fas.org/spp; Committee on International Security and Arms Control, National Academy of Sciences, *The Future of U.S. Nuclear Weapons Policy;* and the interviews in Schell, "The Gift of Time."

59. These and related statements by Butler, and official Washington's tepid response, were carried by NAPSNet, December 9, 1996, online at www.nautilus.org/napsnet.

60. A study by Physicians for Social Responsibility points to the breakdown of Russian command and control as the result of disarray in the armed forces as reason enough for concern about accidental or unauthorized launches of nuclear missiles, which are still automatically targeted at major US population centers and military facilities. *NYT,* April 30, 1998, p. A10.

61. One obstacle to this idea is precisely the disarray in the Russian military. For a number of Russian strategists and politicians, a large nuclear arsenal is desirable because *it's all they have left* to mark Russia as a superpower. David Hoffman, "Downsizing a Mighty Arsenal: Moscow Rethinks Role as Its Weapons Rust," *Washington Post,* March 16, 1998, online ed. at www.washingtonpost.com.

62. Hans Blix, the former UN weapons inspector, issued a report in June 2006 that urged the outlawing of nuclear weapons and, for states such as Iran and North Korea, international assurances against attack and support for their nuclear-energy programs. See Weapons of Mass Destruction Commission, "Weapons of Terror: Freeing the World of Nuclear, Biological and Chemical Arms," at www.wmdcommission.org/sida.asp?id=1.

63. Milton Leitenberg, "Biological Weapons, International Sanctions and Proliferation," *Asian Perspective,* pp. 11–12. Several of these states have openly admitted to possession of one or both classes of weapons. For the most recent status report on such matters, see the Stimson Center web site (www.stimson.org).

64. *NYT,* January 15, 1998, p. A9.

65. Text in *SIPRI Yearbook 1992,* pp. 304–05.

66. William W. Keller, "The Political Economy of Conventional Arms Proliferation," *Current History,* p. 182.

67. A good example is the US decision in 1997 to lift the ban that the Carter administration had placed on high-technology weapons sales to Latin America. Lockheed Martin and other US arms exporters were as happy as Latin American generals about the decision. See Calvin Sims, "Some in Latin America Fear End of U.S. Ban Will Stir Arms Race," *NYT,* August 3, 1997, online.

68. Keller, "The Political Economy of Conventional Arms Proliferation," pp. 179–80.

69. Minxin Pei, "The Paradoxes of American Nationalism," *Foreign Policy.*

70. See the interview in *NYT,* January 9, 1997, p. A9, and also Reich's "Broken Faith," *The Nation.*

71. Robert Pear, "Debt Puts Crimp in Clinton's Plans," *The Oregonian,* January 3, 1993 (from *NYT*).

72. See www.federalbudget.com and Rich Miller and Matthew Benjamin, "9/11 Left U.S. Economy on a Fragile Footing," *International Herald Tribune,* September 11, 2006.

73. L. Josh Bivens, "Debt and the Dollar," Economic Policy Institute, December 14, 2004, at www.epinet.org/content.cfm/Issuebrief 203.

74. Ray Boshara, "The $6,000 Solution," *Atlantic,* January–February 2003, pp. 91–95.

75. *Los Angeles Times,* August 3, 1984 and May 23, 1985.

76. Based on a comparative analysis done by the Luxembourg Income Study group and reported in *NYT,* June 1, 1996, p. 8.

77. Robert Pear, "Number of People Living in Poverty Increases in U.S.," *NYT*, September 25, 2002, online ed.

78. A particularly poignant and accessible source on economic decline (and corporate greed) during the 1980s is a special series by Donald L. Barlett and James B. Steele, "America: What Went Wrong?" *Philadelphia Enquirer,* October 20–28, 1991. It was later published as *America: What Went Wrong?* (Kansas City, MO: Andrews McMeel, 1992). See also David Moberg, "Decline and Inequality After the Great U-Turn," *In These Times,* pp. 7, 10. For the 1990s, see *The Washington Quarterly,* March 15, 1996, pp. 1–4.

79. Steven Greenhouse and David Leonhardt, "Real Wages Fail to Match a Rise in Productivity," *NYT*, August 28, 2006, p. 1.

80. See the charts in *NYT*, June 5, 2005, p. 17.

81. *Los Angeles Times,* October 4, 1984.

82. As reported in *NYT*, October 27, 1995, p. C2. By other income measurements, the gap between the richest and poorest 20 percent of the US population is about 13 to 1, only slightly better than in Mexico and twice as unequal as Great Britain's. Michael Renner, "Transforming Security," in Brown et al., eds., *State of the World 1997,* p. 121.

83. Lynnley Browning, "U.S. Income Gap Widening, Study Says," *NYT*, September 25, 2003, p. C2, based on a study of the Center for Budget and Policy Priorities. The gains in income made by the top 0.1 percent have been even greater; see *NYT*, June 5, 2005, p. 17.

84. See Jonathan Kozol, *Illiterate America.* Kozol proposed that 25 million Americans cannot read (a more commonly used figure is about 10 million) and that another 35 million can read only at a below ninth grade level.

85. Robert Pear, "New Study Finds 60 Million Uninsured During a Year," *NYT*, May 13, 2003, p. A20.

86. Yale Center for Environmental Law and Policy and Center for International Earth Science Information Network (Columbia University), *2005 Environmental Sustainability Index.*

87. See, for example, Andrew C. Revkin, "A Shift in Stance on Global Warming Theory," *NYT*, October 26, 2000, p. A18; James Glanz, "Scientists Say Administration Distorts Facts," *NYT*, February 19, 2004, online ed.; Andrew C. Revkin, "NASA Expert Criticizes Bush on Global Warming Policy," *NYT*, October 26, 2004, p. A12.

88. See *Los Angeles Times,* February 27, 1985, concerning a report by a twenty-seven-member Physician Task Force on Hunger.

89. Based on a Tufts University study; see *The Oregonian,* September 10, 1992.

90. Sivard et al., *World Military and Social Expenditures 1996,* p. 40.

91. *Human Development Report 2005,* table 25, p. 299.

92. *NYT,* June 7, 1995, p. A14.

93. On the imprisonment rate, see *NYT,* February 11, 1992, p. A12. The prison population figure is for 2002; see Fox Butterfield, "Study Finds 2.6% Increase in U.S. Prison Population," *NYT*, July 28, 2003, p. A8.

94. Nikki Meredith, "The Murder Epidemic," *Science '84,* excerpted in *Utne Reader,* no. 8 (February–March 1985), p. 80.

95. *NYT,* April 12, 1995, p. A11.

96. CNN, March 18, 1998, citing a report in *USA Today*; Fox Butterfield, "Study Tracks Boom in Prisons and Notes Impact on Counties," *NYT*, April 30,

2004, p. A15. There are now well over one thousand federal and state prisons in the United States, about double the number in 1974.

97. *NYT,* December 4, 1995, p. 8; Fox Butterfield, "Prison Rates Among Blacks Reach a Peak, Report Finds," *NYT,* April 7, 2003, p. A11.

98. *NYT,* February 11, 1992, p. A12. In 1998, the number of people in US prisons had climbed to 1.8 million. *NYT,* March 15, 1999, p. A12.

99. Amnesty International, "Facts and Figures on the Death Penalty."

100. In 1997, business mergers included 156, each worth $1 billion or more. Leslie Wayne, "Wave of Mergers Recasts the Face of Business," *NYT,* January 18, 1997, online.

101. Based on a study of twenty-three countries in 1995; see Tom W. Smith and Lars Jarkko, "National Pride: A Cross-National Analysis," National Opinion Research Center, University of Chicago, 1995.

102. Quoted in Kegley and Wittkopf (1981 ed.), p. 344.

103. Paul Murphy, "The Military Tax Bite 1986."

104. Center for Defense Information, online. Based on 1995 or 1996 official military spending figures.

105. *The Defense Monitor* (Center for Defense Information) 35, no. 2 (March–April 2006), p. 2. The figure includes supplemental funds for the wars in Iraq and Afghanistan.

106. Brown et al., *State of the World 1986,* p. 200.

107. Seymour Melman, "Profits Without Production: Deterioration in the Industrial System," in Suzanne Gordon and Dave McFadden, eds., *Economic Conversion: Revitalizing America's Economy,* pp. 19–32.

108. "Military Research and the Economy: Burden or Benefit," *The Defense Monitor* 14, no. 1 (1985), p. 2.

109. The US figures are from the fiscal year 1997 budget request; Center for Defense Information, online. On Europe, see Sivard et al., *World Military and Social Expenditures 1996,* p. 41.

110. Quoted in *The Defense Monitor* 14, no. 1 (1985), p. 6.

111. *Los Angeles Times,* supplement, July 10, 1983.

112. Quoted in ibid.

113. "Military Research and the Economy," *The Defense Monitor* 14, no. 1 (1985), pp. 2–3; Robert W. DeGrasse Jr., "The Military Economy," in Gordon and McFadden, eds., pp. 7–8; Marion Anderson et al., "Converting the American Economy"; *Los Angeles Times,* supplement, July 10, 1983 (citing a 1983 study by the Council on Economic Priorities).

114. "Military Research and the Economy," *The Defense Monitor* 14, no. 1 (1985), pp. 5–7; DeGrasse, in Gordon and McFadden, eds., p. 12.

115. *Los Angeles Times,* August 27, 1982.

116. Joseph J. Romm and Amory B. Lovins, "Fueling a Competitive Economy," *Foreign Affairs,* pp. 45–62. These writers point out that "oil imports alone have accounted for nearly three-fourths of the US trade deficit since 1970, or $1 trillion transferred to OPEC nations"; that from 1973 to 1986, however, energy conservation and increased use of renewable sources caused oil imports to drop even as real GNP grew; but that in the Reagan-Bush years, "imports of Persian Gulf oil surged more than sixfold. . . . Yet had the nation simply kept saving oil as fast as [before], the United States would not have needed any Persian Gulf oil after 1985."

117. Based on a fifteen-nation public opinion study by the Pew Research Center. See Brian Knowlton, "Global Image of the U.S. Is Worsening, Survey Finds," *NYT,* June 14, 2006, p. A9.

118. In Mao, *Selected Readings,* p. 321.

119. Lucien Bianco, *Origins of the Chinese Revolution, 1915–1949*, trans. Muriel Bell, p. 95.

120. For an eyewitness account, see A. Doak Barnett, *China on the Eve of Communist Takeover*, especially pp. 111–18.

121. William Hinton, *Fanshen: A Documentary of Revolution in a Chinese Village*, p. xii.

122. On the Anti-Rightist Campaign, see Frederick C. Teiwes, "The Establishment and Consolidation of the New Regime, 1949–57," in Roderick MacFarquhar, ed., *The Politics of China: The Eras of Mao and Deng*, p. 82. (The prominent journalist Liu Binyan in his autobiographical *A Higher Kind of Loyalty* [p. 90], says "the actual figure [of wrongly labeled 'rightists'] exceeded one million.") For the Great Leap Forward, see Jasper Becker, *Hungry Ghosts: China's Secret Famine*, where the figure of 30 million deaths from starvation is given; and Ma Jisen, "The Politics of China's Population Growth," *Asian Perspective*, where figures of anywhere from 17 million to 40 million excess deaths are given by Chinese and Western authorities. As for the Cultural Revolution, see the discussion in Harry Harding, "The Chinese State in Crisis, 1966–9," in MacFarquhar, ed., *The Politics of China*, pp. 241–44, where the estimate of a half-million dead is proposed.

123. Among the qualifications to this defense conversion program is that even as Chinese defense industries are producing more consumer goods, they are also earning hard currency and acquiring militarily useful high technology on the thriving international arms market. For an overall evaluation, see Mel Gurtov, "Swords into Market Shares: China's Conversion of Military Industry to Civilian Production," *The China Quarterly*, pp. 1–29.

124. Chen Xiaonong, "The Chinese Public Sector: Heading Towards Zero Profit?" *China Focus*, pp. 1, 4–5; Neil C. Hughes, "Smashing the Iron Rice Bowl," *Foreign Affairs*, pp. 70–71.

125. See, for example, Deng Xiaoping, *Fundamental Issues of Present-Day China;* Harry Harding, *China's Second Revolution: Reform After Mao;* and Lowell Dittmer, *China's Continuous Revolution: The Post-Liberation Epoch, 1949–1981*.

126. Talk of January 20, 1987 in Deng, p. 173.

127. Dittmer, ch. 8; Yan Jiaqi, "A Comparative Study of the Features of the Socialist Political System and Possible Reforms," in Mel Gurtov, ed., *The Transformation of Socialism: Perestroika and Reform in the Soviet Union and China*, ch. 5.

128. World Bank, "Country Brief: China" (September 1997), online at www.worldbank.org; World Bank 1997, various tables.

129. *Human Development Report 2005*, p. 34.

130. Christopher Flavin and Gary Gardner, "China, India, and the New World Order," in Nierenberg et al., *State of the World 2006*, p. 6.

131. See, for instance, the *Human Development Report 2005*, p. 59.

132. Ibid.

133. Benjamin Robertson, "China's New Education System," *Far Eastern Economic Review*.

134. *Human Development Report 2005*, pp. 29–30, 63.

135. Anywhere from several hundred to a few thousand people were killed in the military assault, and about ten thousand people nationwide were reportedly arrested. Some intellectuals high on the government's enemy list managed to flee the country. On the leadership's thinking regarding how to deal with the demonstrations, see Andrew J. Nathan, "The Tiananmen Papers," *Foreign Affairs*.

136. OECD, *Trends and Recent Developments in Foreign Direct Investment*, p. 3.

137. On exports, see the *Human Development Report 2005*, p. 117.

138. Quoted in Jim Yardley, "China Warns Citizens It Won't Tolerate Threats to Stability," *NYT*, August 1, 2005, p. A5.

139. Human-rights conditions in China are monitored by *China Rights Forum* and NGOs such as Amnesty International, Human Rights Watch Asia, and the Lawyers Committee for Human Rights. (See, for example, the Lawyers Committee for Human Rights' report, *Criminal Justice with Chinese Characteristics: China's Criminal Process and Violations of Human Rights,* as well as the official PRC position on human rights: Liu Huaqiu, "Proposals for Human Rights Protection and Promotion," *Beijing Review*, June 28–July 4, 1993, pp. 8–11.) China has ratified the UN convention on economic and cultural rights, which covers labor organizing. One prominent critic who was able to get a hearing is Bao Tong, who was Zhao Ziyang's chief of staff until the crackdown. See the interview with him in *Washington Post,* June 3, 1998, online. A handful of other critics, such as Wei Jingsheng, have been allowed to leave the country.

140. As just one example, see Ching-ching Ni, "Activist's Trial Proceedings Seen as Unfair," *Los Angeles Times*, August 19, 2006.

141. Joseph Kahn, "Torture Is 'Widespread' in China, U.N. Investigator Says," *NYT*, December 3, 2005, p. A3.

142. Clive Thompson, "Google's China Problem (and China's Google Problem)," *New York Times Magazine*.

143. According to Amnesty International reports cited in *NYT*, April 11, 2002, online ed., and November 1, 2006, p. A3.

144. Howard W. French, "China's New Frontiers: Tests of Democracy and Dissent," *NYT*, June 19, 2005, p. 6.

145. See Minxin Pei, "Is China Democratizing?" *Foreign Affairs.*

146. These following two paragraphs rely on Mel Gurtov and Byong-Moo Hwang, *China's Security: The New Roles of the Military.*

147. "Defence Spend in Tune with Economic Growth," *China Daily* (Beijing), March 16, 2006, online at www.chinadaily.com.

148. For excellent assessments of China's military, see David Shambaugh, "China's Military: Real or Paper Tiger?" *The Washington Quarterly*, and C. Fred Bergsten et al., *China: The Balance Sheet.*

149. David Lague, "An Increasingly Confident China Lends Clout to UN," *International Herald Tribune*, September 20, 2006.

150. The aid, clearly designed as much to support China's trade as to promote Southeast Asian economic development, is for road and bridge construction, power, and communications. See Jane Perlez, "China Becomes Major Player in Asian Aid," *International Herald Tribune*, September 18, 2006.

151. Elisabeth Rosenthal, "China Finally Confronts Its Air-Pollution Crisis," *NYT,* June 14, 1998, online.

152. Brown, "Facing the Prospect of Food Scarcity," in Brown et al., eds., p. 28.

153. The dam, which is nearing completion, also illustrates another aspect of the underside of rapid economic growth in China: the difficulties of resettling over a million people. Most of them face very hard times, and if China's prior history of resettlement to make way for dams is any guide, poverty is the probable consequence of moving. See Wu Ming, "Disaster in the Making?" *China Rights Forum*, and Erik Eckholm, "Relocations for China Dam Are Found to Lag," *NYT,* March 12, 1998, p. A8.

154. BBC News, August 3, 2003, in NAPSNet Daily Report, also US Department of Energy, "China: Environmental Issues" (July 2003), available at www.eia.doe.gov/emeu/cabs/chinaenv.html.

155. Keith Bradsher, "China to Pass U.S. in 2009 in Emissions," *NYT*, November 7, 2006, p. 1.

156. The combined cost of lost agricultural productivity and human health due to sulfur dioxide and other contaminants was estimated at $54 billion a year, or about 8 percent of China's GNP in 1995. Acid rain may affect 29 percent of the country, according to the Chinese government. See World Bank, "Country Brief: China," online at www.worldbank.org.

157. "Chinese Official Sees Private Role on Environment," *NYT*, June 6, 2006, p. A6. The official, deputy chief of the State Environmental Protection Agency, gave a rough figure of $200 billion a year in pollution costs.

158. For example, the government plans to spend about $125 billion in the next five years on wastewater treatment plants and water distribution equipment. It has appealed for foreign investment in these areas. *NYT*, August 23, 2006, p. C5.

159. Reuters, "Land Seizures Provoke Growing Anger in China," July 10, 2006, in NAPSNet Daily Report, same date.

160. A particularly brutal suppression of a peasant protest occurred in the town of Dongzhou, Guangdong Province, in 2006. See Howard W. French, "Visit to Chinese Anytown Shows a Dark Side of Progress," *NYT*, January 19, 2006, p. A4.

161. See Ashutosh Varshney, *Democracy, Development, and the Countryside: Urban-Rural Struggles in India.*

162. See, for example, Murray Scot Tanner, "China Rethinks Unrest," *The Washington Quarterly.*

163. The average income gap has risen to 3.3 to 1. As one leading economist said in an interview with a state-run business magazine: "If you establish a market economy in a place like China, where the rule of law is imperfect, if you do not emphasize the socialist spirit of fairness and social responsibility, then the market economy you establish is going to be an elitist market economy." Quoted in Joseph Kahn, "A Sharp Debate Erupts in China over Ideology," *NYT*, March 12, 2006, p. 8.

164. Gallup Poll of China, March and April 2005.

165. See David Zweig, *Democratic Values, Political Structures, and Alternative Politics in Greater China;* Anne F. Thurston, *Muddling Toward Democracy: Political Change in Grassroots China.*

166. Ian Johnson, *Wild Grass: Three Portraits of Change in Modern China*, p. 9.

167. See the speeches by Deputy Secretary of State Robert Zoellick at the US Embassy in Beijing on August 2, 2005 (at www.state.gov/s/d/rem/50498.htm) and to the National Committee on US-China Relations in New York City, September 21, 2005 (at www.state.gov/s/d/rem/53682.htm).

168. *NYT*, May 8, 2001, online ed.

169. Quoted by David M. Lampton, "A Growing China in a Shrinking World: Beijing and the Global Order," in Ezra F. Vogel, ed., *Living with China: U.S.-China Relations in the Twenty-first Century*, p. 121.

170. US Department of Defense, *The Military Power of the People's Republic of China*, p. 10.

171. Admiral William J. Fallon, commander of US Pacific forces, made the statement in proposing more military exchanges with China. See Michael R. Gordon, "To Build Trust, U.S. Navy Holds a Drill with China," *NYT*, September 23, 2006, p. A5.

172. US White House, *The National Security Strategy of the United States* (2006), p. 42.

173. See, for example, Wang Jisi, "China's Search for Stability with America," *Foreign Affairs*. Wang writes (p. 46): "The Chinese-U.S. relationship remains beset

by more profound differences than any other bilateral relationship between major powers in the world today."

174. One instance of their divergent views on terrorism came in the aftermath of the abortive revolt in May 2005 against the Karimov government in Uzbekistan. Whereas the US Department of State raised questions about the killing of hundreds of protesters by Uzbek security forces, China announced its unequivocal support of the regime for quelling what it termed a terrorist attack against the state.

175. Joseph Kahn, "If 22 Million Chinese Prevail at U.N., Japan Won't," *NYT*, April 1, 2005, p. A4.

176. Wang, "China's Search for Stability with America," p. 44; Wu Xinbo, "The End of the Silver Lining: A Chinese View of the U.S.-Japanese Alliance," *The Washington Quarterly.*

177. Even though China voted in favor of a UN Security Council resolution that condemned North Korea's missile test in July 2006, and supported a sanctions resolution following the North's nuclear test the following October, Beijing still urged dialogue with North Korea and made clear that China would not impose sanctions by interdicting North Korean shipping.

178. In the view of Chinese strategic analysts, Central Asia "has long been regarded by the United States as the pivot in realizing its global strategy," and the establishment of bases there is a "historic breakthrough" for US policymakers. See Xie Wenqing, "Post-'9.11' Asia-Pacific Security Situation," *International Strategic Studies.* The six-party Shanghai Cooperation Organization, to which China belongs, issued a statement in July 2005 that called upon the United States to withdraw from bases in Uzbekistan and Kyrgyzstan. Subsequently, US relations with the Uzbekistan government soured over that government's repression of demonstrations, and notice was served on Washington to leave its air base there in six months.

179. Kishore Mahbubani, "Understanding China," *Foreign Affairs*, p. 49.

180. See C. Bajpaee, "Setting the Stage for a New Cold War: China's Quest for Energy Security," *Power and Interest News Report*, February 25, 2005, online at www.pinr.com; E.S. Downs, *China's Quest for Energy Security;* P.K. Beng and V.Y.W. Li, "China's Energy Dependence on the Middle East: Boon or Bane for Asian Security?" *The China and Eurasia Forum Quarterly.*

181 "The Oiloholics," *The Economist,* August 25, 2005.

182 Seth Dunn and Christopher Flavin, "Moving the Climate Change Agenda Forward," in Flavin et al., *State of the World 2002: A Worldwatch Institute Report on Progress Toward a Sustainable Society,* p. 35.

183 Quoted in Gurtov, *Superpower on Crusade,* p. 210.

# 6

# Europe, Russia, and Japan in a Multipolar World

## The New Meaning of Power

When the history of the twentieth century is written, we can be certain that the rebirth of Europe and Japan after World War II, and of Russia marking the end of the Cold War, will be prominent chapters. One theme of the three stories is familiar: the transformation of war-ravaged economies, with Europe and Japan becoming dynamic centers of international business. Another theme is how these countries whose fates were intertwined with the Cold War competition have sought to play independent roles in dealing with the world's military, economic, and ecological crises. Each of them has had to adapt not only to the new era of globalization, but also to a new relationship with the United States.

European and Japanese politics have given new meaning to power. Unlike Russia, which lost an empire, the economic and social performance of the EU and Japan has demonstrated what can be accomplished when military considerations are not permitted to become dominant. This is not to say that these countries are minor participants in the global arms race. Britain ($47.4 billion), France ($45.2 billion), Japan ($42.4 billion), Germany ($33.9 billion), and Russia ($19.4 billion) rank second through sixth (in 2004–2005) in military spending, and Russia, France, Germany, and Britain rank second through fifth among the leading arms exporters.[1] In fact, business is booming for European arms sellers as much as for US companies.[2] France and Britain maintain strategic nuclear forces that continue to be modernized, and both countries have sizable, though diminishing, standing and overseas armies. Likewise Japan, which officially spends about 1 percent (in reality it is more like 1.5 percent) of its GNP on the military, and maintains around 240,000 armed forces. Now that the Warsaw Pact is a thing of the past, the East European states have also been able to lighten their military burdens, though the United States and its arms manufacturers have pressed them to acquire up-to-date weapons in their new home, NATO.

From 1960 to 1981, while the United States was spending an average of 6.5 percent of its GNP on the military and the Soviet Union was spending 10.9 percent, their European allies in NATO and the Warsaw Pact were spending, respectively, 3.7 percent and 3 percent of their GNPs.[3] The superpowers subsidized their partners' defense—the United States in that period accounted for two-thirds of NATO military outlays and the USSR for about 90 percent of Warsaw Pact outlays[4]—and, therefore, also their economic growth. This sacrifice of financial health for political allegiance continued to the end of the Cold War. From 1982 to 1991, the United States officially spent $2.79 trillion on the military, whereas the EC and Japan together spent $1.76 trillion. Europe and Japan thus accumulated over $1 trillion in additional spending power compared with the United States.[5] Today, the EU countries are spending perhaps a third as much as the United States on the military.

The international economic consequence was a decline in the US trade balance in manufactured goods that became permanent in 1968. US transnational firms moved to Europe, a powerful Eurodollar market emerged as more and more dollars found their way into European banking hands, and West European and Japanese industries began to outperform their US counterparts.[6] Their industries became more productive, innovative, profitable, and better managed than those of the United States.[7] The Soviets, meanwhile, watched as some East European economies became more efficient and flexible than their own, such as Hungary's, while others became massive headaches, such as Poland's. The Soviets' command-style system also bequeathed a legacy of environmental pollution and political repression that is only now being addressed.

Chapter 2 noted the increasing share of world exports being taken by Japan and what was then the European Economic Community (EEC; later simply EC) of West European states in the 1970s. Rapid growth in world trade in turn fueled overall economic growth. This relationship can be seen in figures for 1977, which indicate that international trade was 13 percent of Japan's GNP, 24 percent of West Germany's, and 25 percent of Britain's, compared with only 6 percent of the US GNP.[8] As the European economic union gained momentum in the mid-1980s (see below), the EC's share of world trade (18 percent) leaped ahead of the US and Japanese shares (which were 17 percent and 9 percent, respectively). Particularly dynamic growth occurred in the trade of the twelve EC countries with each other—it was nearly 60 percent of the members' total foreign trade in 1987—and in EC trade with other developed West European economies. By 1985, the EC had already become the world's largest trading bloc.[9]

Some elements of vulnerability accompany this economic strength. Dependence on foreign oil is one: The 1979 oil shortages, for example, drained Western Europe, Canada, and Japan of about $400 billion in that year alone to pay for higher-priced oil and reduced economic activity.[10]

These countries are also vulnerable to major recessions or inflations in the United States. The effects are always quickly felt, either in high unemployment and high interest rates, or in high unemployment and inflation ("stagflation").[11] And that is why, since the mid-1980s, European and Japanese leaders, as much as Third World leaders, have pushed the United States to reduce its enormous budget deficits. Their economies are hurt by weaknesses in the US economy, even though their exports are helped by the huge US appetite for European and Japanese products.

Despite these vulnerabilities, the EU countries and, even more so, Japan have proven quite adept at resisting US pressures to reduce tariff and other barriers to trade, eliminate government subsidies (such as on agricultural products) that may unfairly price exports, and substantially increase their shares of military spending—all measures that US administrations have argued would help reduce trade and budget deficits. Periodic, serious strains in the Western alliance have resulted from these perceived inequities. In the 1980s and into the 1990s, they inspired strong protectionist sentiment in the US Congress that led to pressure from the president on Japan and the EU to open up their economies to a long list of US products. Neither side in the dispute would admit to exaggerating its claims and scapegoating the other. For the reality would seem to be that Japanese and European markets are much more protected against other countries' products (including Japan's against the EU's) than they care to admit,[12] and that US trade problems are much less the result of such protectionism than of macroeconomic forces—low private savings, budget deficits, and high interest rates—that have fostered long-term US neglect of its industrial base.[13]

The erosion of US leadership and competitiveness in world trade has, as stressed above, coincided with its enormous investment in arms and global alliances. In Chapter 5 we observed the social and economic costs for the United States of this investment. In contrast, Europe and Japan have put a significant portion of their savings on the military into long-term economic investment and social well-being. Consider, for instance, how R&D money is allocated. The United States spends much more on scientific research, as a proportion of GNP, than any other industrialized country. Yet until 1993, US industrial productivity ranked very low in comparison, one reason clearly being the high proportion of federal R&D invested in the military.[14]

The EU countries and Japan have always been known for their high quality of life: efficient, well-ordered societies, progressive environmental policies, a cradle-to-the-grave health and welfare system (and high taxes to pay for it)—and for being leaders in most areas of human development. But the post–Cold War shift to globalization, the liberation of Eastern Europe, and (for Japan) the bursting of the real estate bubble forced governments, businesses, and publics to reexamine traditional practices and values. It has been a painful transition, full of unanticipated crises and setbacks.

In Western Europe the precipitating factor was a recession severe enough that in 1993 the EU suffered its first economic contraction since the peak of the oil crisis in 1975.[15] About 22 million workers—one in every nine—were unemployed. Budget pressures and concerns about trade deficits forced every European state to cut back on social welfare benefits. In France, for instance, unemployment went from 9.4 percent in 1991 to 12.7 percent in 1996; combined with an aging society, it made for very high social insurance costs that no one, least of all organized labor, wanted to give up. Knowing that high-technology industries were losing their competitive edge, and that budgets would have to be pared in anticipation of a common European currency by 1999, the French still quailed at the thought of embracing the US formula for productivity: downsizing and privatization. The rise of the anti-immigration, antiglobalization right-wing National Front, led by Jean-Marie Le Pen (he won 15 percent of the vote in the 1995 presidential election, and continues to be a force in French politics), was in direct proportion to France's high unemployment and low growth.[16]

And so it was across Europe: Bleak times provided fertile ground for racism and discrimination against "foreigners," mainly economic refugees and migrant workers from southern Europe, North Africa, and other poor regions. Their cheap labor had fueled the rapid postwar recovery of Germany, France, Britain, and other EU countries. Many became permanent residents. But in the early 1990s, at a time of economic downturn, these workers became convenient political targets of extremist groups and the object of restrictive legislation. Starting in Germany, which was already beset by the unexpectedly high costs of rebuilding the eastern zone, and spreading to France, laws were passed greatly restricting immigration and asylum.[17] Yet immigrant populations in both countries, and throughout Europe, are very large, posing challenging problems for implementing multiculturalism and resisting anti-foreign propaganda.

In Eastern Europe, economic and social problems have been just as serious as in eastern Germany, and without the infusion of western German funds and technology that the east obtained. High unemployment, one-third of the region (120 million people) living in poverty,[18] a public-health crisis,[19] and bewilderment at the enormity of the changes since communism's demise coexist with newfound freedoms, prosperity and consumerism in major cities, and business opportunities.[20] Today, in spite of (and to some extent because of) EU membership, the former communist states have income levels far below those of West Europeans.[21] The number of people in Eastern Europe living on $2 a day has risen dramatically, "from 23 million in 1990 to 93 million in 2001, or from 5% to 20%."[22] Economic growth has generally been stagnant and real incomes have fallen dramatically—for example, by 10 percent in Ukraine and 40 percent in Georgia.[23] Hence the figures in Table 4.2 that show declining income poverty in Eastern Europe at $1 a day really should be interpreted as merely reflecting improvement from absolute to "ordinary" poverty. Amidst such deepening divisions, democracy and civil societies have had difficulty taking root. The return to political prominence of remolded Communist Party officials, human-rights abuses, anti-Semitism, and anti-foreignism are serious problems in the east. To one degree or another, these developments originated in the post–Cold War economic dislocations.[24]

These destabilizing trends came at a time when Europe was dealing with longstanding, mostly transnational, environmental issues. "Forest death," as the Germans refer to acid rain, is extensive in both parts of their country, as well as in Scandinavia and Poland. When Germany united, sulfur dioxide emissions became the highest in Europe, further damaging its neighbors' air.[25] Acid rain has also harmed more than half the forests of the Czech Republic and Slovakia, Greece, and Great Britain and has caused severe damage to fish in the lakes of Finland, Norway, and Sweden.[26] Seventy percent of Czech and Slovene waters are officially considered heavily polluted, and 28 percent have no fish.[27] Last, several European countries (including Germany, Britain, and Italy), along with Japan, are major sources of carbon emissions that contribute to global warming.[28]

In comparison with Eastern Europe, however, the West European states have the resources and the political will to take action at home and exert leadership internationally on issues such as global warming.[29] Germany, for example, is the world's fifth-largest carbon emitter because of its reliance on coal; but it reduced carbon emissions by over 10 percent in the first half of the 1990s through a combination of efficiency incentives, taxes, industrial restructuring, and public concern about climate change.[30] By 2003 Germany, Britain, and France had either met or exceeded the Kyoto Protocol's targets for emissions cuts. (But several other EU countries had not.[31]) Eastern Europe is an environmental disaster area, as exemplified by Poland. Like the other onetime members of the Soviet bloc, Poland after World War II adopted the Soviet economic model that emphasized central planning, development of heavy and extractive industries, and collectivized agriculture. The country's health care and nutrition ranked high worldwide, but over time public services went into decline and created serious air and water pollution.[32] A 1985 report of the Polish Academy of Sciences offered the somber prediction that "the long limitation of investments may have in the near future social and ecological consequences on an unimaginable scale."[33] Indeed, Poland's precarious environmental situation seriously threatens the country's future.[34] Years of overexploitation of natural resources, emphasis on heavy industrialization to the exclusion of its environmental costs (especially air pollution), bureaucratic indifference to environmental issues, and plain lack of environmental technology and enforcement have exacted a heavy toll on public health.[35] Even though democratization has opened up Poland's political system to "green" voices, harsh economic realities impinge on its ability to create a healthier society.

## Toward a United Europe

> We want to belong to a Europe that is a friendly community of independent states, a stable Europe, a Europe that does not need protection from superpowers because it is capable of defending itself by constructing its own security system.
>
> —President Vàclav Havel

Jean Monnet, France's architect of European recovery after World War II, had a dream: to create a strong European economic union that would someday evolve into a political federation. That dream is close to being realized: By the end of 1992, all barriers to the movement of people, capital, goods, and services had been removed, paving the way for economic and political union. The EU in 2007 comprises twenty-seven countries with a combined population of about 450 million people.

European cooperation has progressed from a limited partnership to a union in several stages: the European Coal and Steel Community (ECSC) of six member states (France, West Germany, Italy, the Netherlands, Belgium, and Luxembourg) in 1952; the Rome Treaties of 1958, by which the same six nations established the European Atomic Energy Community and the EEC, or Common Market; expansion of the EEC in 1973 to include Britain, Denmark, and Ireland, in 1982 Greece, and in 1986 Spain and Portugal (bringing the membership to twelve); in 1986, the signing by "the Twelve," the European Community, of the Single European Act;[36] the admission of Finland, Sweden, and Austria in 1995; in 2003, the signing of the EU accession treaty and a jump in the organization's membership by ten; the admission of Bulgaria and Romania in 2007 and Turkey knocking on the door.

The single-market plan was born of economic motives: to eliminate all remaining internal barriers that were proving costly to further growth; to stop the fragmentation of research and production in twelve national markets and instead create economies of scale based on uniform standards, fewer regulations, and combined efforts; to increase Europe's global competitive power, and therefore global market share; and to increase savings, GNP, and employment.[37] These objectives clearly reflect the interdependence of Europe's various domestic economies with the global economy—and the determination, therefore, to combat the perceived US and Japanese challenges to Europe's future prosperity.[38]

With a combined world trade of over $2 trillion, the EU is a formidable challenger for world economic leadership. In accordance with the Maastricht Treaty of 1992, the EC set a timetable for establishing a common currency (the euro), central banking system, and common citizenship (commonly called "Europe 92"). One reason the direction of a single market was considered necessary was that the breakdown of national economic barriers would place new demands on transnational institutions such as the European Parliament and Court of Justice. These were created under the

ECSC and adapted by the Common Market countries. (Europe's Convention on Human Rights, created subsequently, requires the signature of states that seek to join the EU.) As a single Europe evolves, the parliament and court will be more frequently resorted to for legislation and the adjudication of disputes. Continentalism—a vision of Europe stretching "from the Atlantic to the Urals" (in Charles de Gaulle's words), a "common home" (in Gorbachev's)—is taking hold. Not every government accepts the full implication of this vision—should there be a "united states of Europe" or a "united Europe of states"?—but one Europe and a European identity are widely shared beliefs.

Europe 92's train was delayed, though not derailed, by nationalism and economic stresses that began appearing in 1991. Many Europeans became skittish about surrendering national sovereignty under Maastricht. As regional economic woes increased, so did anxieties about tight integration.[39] For the harsh reality of currency union was that bringing government spending down to 3 percent of GNP, which Germany had insisted on as one criterion of membership, would compel governments, Germany's included, to slash social welfare and put working people on the street.[40] But in the end corporate globalism scored another victory: French voters barely approved the treaty, and Danes voted for it only on the second try (in May 1993). The British House of Commons followed suit in midyear, but only after Britain, like Denmark, was exempted from provisions governing monetary and security cooperation. Reaching consensus on currency values proved especially vexing because of the Bundesbank's protection of the mark, leading some observers to write that the whole Maastricht process was in danger of being overwhelmed by narrow national interests.[41] The strains of warfare in central Europe also played a part, for they revealed political differences among key states over a course of action and the EU's consequent inability to stop the violence around it (discussed in the next section).

Britain's vote for Maastricht meant that all twelve members had ratified it, paving the way for implementation. But complete political integration is likely to be further off than once appeared. A draft European constitution, approved by the EU leaders in 2004, failed to gain ratification by all the parliaments or publics in 2005. Yet meantime, the area of European economic unity has actually widened. The euro came out on schedule January 1, 1999, although only eleven countries (not Britain, Sweden, Denmark, or Greece) initially used it.[42] With a value higher than the dollar at present, and some countries wanting to hedge against the dollar for political reasons, the euro might one day become its rival as the world's principal reserve currency.

## The Changed Strategic Picture

Until the Gorbachev phenomenon swept over Eastern Europe, the continent's longstanding concern had been its vulnerability to a conflict between the superpowers. In the early 1980s, high-ranking US officials were publicly mentioning Europe as the potential setting for a "limited" nuclear exchange that might result from an escalation of conventional fighting with Soviet forces. Approximately 10 million NATO and Warsaw Pact soldiers were on duty in Europe at that time, and each side controlled thousands of nuclear weapons all over the continent intended for battlefield use.[43] This circumstance became the source of constant tension within NATO—tension that reached a crescendo during the Reagan presidency. On one hand, Europeans were well aware from studies done within NATO dating back to 1955 that if nuclear weapons were used to defend against a conventional Soviet attack, all of Europe would eventually be destroyed.[44] European fears were running so high that then chancellor Helmut Schmidt of West Germany remarked in 1981 that "in some situations it seems that Europeans are even more afraid of the Americans than they are of the Russians."[45]

On the other hand, European leaders constantly questioned whether or not the United States really would put its own cities at risk of a Soviet nuclear attack to defend its NATO allies. The more the United States and the Soviet Union built up so-called theater (medium-range) nuclear forces, the more European confidence in the US commitment eroded. What Europeans wanted was ultimately impossible to provide: an ironclad promise from the United States to defend them to the death by providing "strategic assurances that we cannot possibly mean, or if we do mean, we should not want to execute because if we execute, we risk the destruction of civilization."[46]

The contradiction between fearing nuclear arms and believing in their deterrent value did not prove NATO's undoing. But it did play an important part in promoting European independence of action. In 1966 France left NATO's joint command structure, although it remained a member of the North Atlantic Council. (France rejoined NATO command in 1995.) Spanish voters, in a 1986 referendum, decided to pull out of NATO's joint command and prohibit the stockpiling of nuclear weapons on Spanish soil. US nuclear deployments to Europe in 1983 gave new life to the nuclear disarmament movement in Britain, Germany, the Netherlands, and part of Eastern Europe. Massive demonstrations did not stop the deployments, but they did spur parliamentary oppositions in Western Europe to adopt antinuclear platforms. They also showed that popular support for groups like the Greens and the British Campaign for Nuclear Disarmament extended to the middle class. (These protests had better results in New Zealand, whose government decided in 1985 to bar US nuclear-powered or nuclear-armed ships from visiting its ports. The ANZUS alliance was effectively reduced by one member as a result.) Even in Eastern Europe, antinuclear sentiment was not restricted, as Moscow had hoped it would be, to opposing only US missile deployments. Antiwar demonstrations, church meetings, and protests took aim at Soviet deployments as well, most strenuously in East Germany.[47]

Europe's rapid movement toward full integration, and the equally rapid disintegration of communist authority in much of Eastern Europe, changed the terms of debate about security—from "national" to "continental," and from military to economic. The fact that Communist Party dictatorships in Eastern Europe were overthrown without challenge from Soviet armed forces represented a dramatic departure with the past. Unified Germany pledged to remain a non-nuclear member of NATO. Hungary pulled out of the Warsaw Pact and began dismantling Soviet missiles. Inside the Soviet Union, parliaments in many of the republics that declared their independence adopted antinuclear platforms. For a time, it appeared that military conversion programs, which started in Britain's defense industry in the mid-1970s, might spread across the continent with the end of Cold War spending levels. But except for a few successful experiments in Sweden and Italy, conversion did not catch on; but stepping up arms exports did.[48] Nevertheless, with so many signs of the Cold War's disappearing, some European leaders, such as President Havel, talked—overoptimistically as it turned out—about creating an entirely different security system.

The new security structure contains three elements: the Conference on (now Organization for) Security and Cooperation in Europe (OSCE), actually a series of conferences and resulting formal agreements—it began in 1973 with thirty-four states and now has fifty-six member states (including Russia and most of the former Soviet republics); the Treaty on Conventional Armed Forces in Europe (CFE), which entered into force in 1991 with twenty-two signatories; and the 1992 Open Skies Treaty, signed by twenty-five states.[49] Taken together, these instruments provided for large-scale troop and weapons withdrawals from central Europe, mostly by the Soviet/Russian army; extensive reduction and destruction of conventional arms; major reductions and redeployments of national armies, and reduction of military budgets; limitations on arms transfers; exchanges of military data; and aerial and other kinds of monitoring of military activities, such as large exercises, to prevent surprise attacks or miscalculations. The OSCE is particularly relevant today in terms of early warning and conflict prevention, such as tensions between Russia and Georgia.

As impressive as these measures are, they do not amount to a full-fledged European security system. The EU, after all, has no army, and NATO does not have overarching structures like the EU's. What the member states accomplished were arms limitations and confidence-building measures within a defined zone of Europe to reduce the danger of war across state boundaries. The agreements, in company with earlier US-Russia strategic-weapons treaties, may justly be called "a triumph of arms control" and "a third method [common security] for achieving security."[50] CFE and the other treaties introduced "predictability and assurance in military relationships" and brought a halt to the conventional arms race. But they neither demilitarized Europe nor equipped it to deal with wars within states or outside the established zone, especially once these broke out.[51] Would common security apply in ethnic and other "new-order" conflicts? CSCE's first test, perhaps an unfair one given its timing—the onset of economic troubles in Western Europe, the negotiations at Maastricht, the disintegration of the USSR, and the Persian Gulf crisis—was the breakup of Yugoslavia.

The critical moment may have been in 1991 when Germany took the ill-fated step of granting diplomatic recognition to Croatia and Slovenia. The decision has been sharply criticized for having misused the self-determination principle, pushing the button of ethnic violence. Instead of speaking out forcefully on behalf of human rights in Yugoslavia, it opened the way to Serbian attacks on Croatia and the ensuing ethnic cleansing.[52] Such a harsh judgment is tempered in other accounts that paint a picture of collective failure: an absence of leadership, clear signals, and well-defined objectives on all sides, an unwillingness by any government to put the human crisis in Bosnia ahead of its own domestic political concerns, and missed opportunities for diplomacy and preventive military deployments by the UN or NATO before any of the parties, last of all Bosnia, was recognized as a separate state.[53] Not until August 1992 did the UN Security Council decide that the Bosnian situation was a "threat to international peace and security," fourteen months after the war began. And only in 1994 did Bosnia become a national-security interest of the United States and its NATO partners, when bombing was used to force the Serbs to the bargaining table.

The wars in Bosnia and Kosovo showed the severe limitations of the post–Cold War security system, not just in Europe but also internationally: the inability of regional states and great powers to prevent large-scale, even genocidal violence in their midst. It was a moral as much as a political failure. The inaction raised questions about the usefulness of CSCE and the UN as peacemakers (questions about peace*keeping* came later); about NATO's reason for being; about whether "common security" has meaning beyond defense of national interests; and, for some observers, about the reality of a European community.[54] President Havel called Europe's failure in the Balkans war every bit as great as its failure to respond to the Nazi and Soviet threats.[55]

In sum, European integration and common security are ideas whose time has come. But practice lags behind aspiration. NATO has twenty-six members, with five others seeking membership as of 2007 (Croatia, Macedonia, Albania, Georgia, and Ukraine); and the EU, as mentioned, has twenty-seven. But both organizations face major challenges. In the EU, the constitution remains to be ratified; Turkey's membership is opposed by France and others; treatment of migrant workers and Muslim immigrants differs greatly from one country to another, especially since 9/11; in many countries historical memory, notably of the Holocaust and the communist era, remains elusive;[56] tensions persist between globalization and nationalism, on issues such as job security, takeovers of national banks and firms, and European integration itself, making more people receptive to right-wing populist appeals;[57] and most countries have fallen short on meeting global warming targets. Capital punishment, genetically modified organisms (GMOs), immunity from war-crimes prosecution for US soldiers in peacekeeping operations, engagement with Iran and the Palestinians, secret CIA prisons in Europe for terrorism suspects, and US leadership in world affairs generally are persistent sources of Euro-US differences.[58]

Within NATO, the scope of its security responsibilities outside Europe lacks consensus, despite the peacekeeping mission in Afghanistan, as does the concept of universal membership in NATO for all democratic states, European or otherwise.[59] Military spending by the Europeans, notably the Germans, in NATO is far below US levels, leaving their armies underequipped and undermanned.[60] Moreover, deep divisions have emerged with the United States since 9/11, as Germany and France, as well as large majorities of European citizens, joined in rejecting participation in the Iraq war and the unilateralist predilections of the Bush Doctrine. Though the fear of some observers that such mistrust meant "the end of the Atlantic alliance as we have known it" has not panned out, since all parties agree that NATO should survive, the US reputation in Europe is at an all-time low.[61] The real issue, in the words of a former US ambassador to NATO, is that "Europeans believe that U.S. actions merely reflect the country's immediate preferences as opposed to their judgment about its underlying interests."[62] But that means the United States must practice genuine multilateralism and seriously consult with allies rather than, as in Iraq, lean on a "coalition of the willing" and denigrate (as Donald Rumsfeld did) "old Europe."

It is not easy for Europe to speak with one voice because national institutions and loyalties still vie with central European ones. Pressure from and policy differences with the United States exacerbate that difficulty. War in the Balkans provided only negative lessons about bringing economic integration and common security to bear on a collapsing situation. War in Iraq gravely weakened collective security with the United States; war in Afghanistan did little to strengthen it. We must wait to see whether the idea of a single Europe responsible for its "common home" can grow from these experiences. As a German government adviser said, "You have an overwhelming superpower on the one hand and an emerging Europe learning to articulate its interest on the other. That is the delicate post–Cold War equation we face."[63]

## Russia: The Rocky Road to Democracy and Development

The issue today is this: Either Soviet society will go forward along the path of profound changes that have been begun, ensuring a worthy future

for our great multinational state, or else forces opposed to perestroika will gain the upper hand. In that case—let us face the facts squarely—dismal times would be in store for the country and the people.
—Mikhail S. Gorbachev, at a Communist Party congress, July 1990

Assessing the current state of Russian affairs inevitably takes us back to March 1985, when leadership in the Soviet Union transferred to Mikhail Gorbachev. He soon unveiled a reform program based on two ideas: perestroika ("reformation," or "restructuring") and glasnost ("openness"). In his view, which proved to be accurate, the reforms would be as sweeping as the Bolshevik Revolution. In fact, the new Soviet leadership insisted (in direct contrast with China's reforms) that perestroika could only take root if greater social and political pluralism were permitted. Before noting what perestroika and glasnost promised, we need to take a hard look at Soviet political economy before and immediately after Gorbachev took office.

Against a background of underdevelopment, revolution, and two world wars, Soviet communism achieved some remarkable gains for its people— in education and health; in science, technology, and industrialization; in women's rights; and in improved educational and work opportunities for rural dwellers and ethnic minorities (who accounted for about 48 percent of the total population). The Soviet people went through some painful experiences, in war and politics, and yet attained a fairly high living standard in about seventy years.[64] But well before Gorbachev's appearance, the Soviet system had for many years shown the strains of aging leadership, economic wastefulness, and environmental neglect. The price of maintaining empire and achieving military parity with the United States was extremely high, reaching (according to a Soviet source) about $1 trillion between 1979 and 1984.[65] This figure presumably does not include the huge sums (perhaps $50 billion in the mid-1980s) paid beyond national defense to maintain Soviet military forces abroad and subsidize the economies of Vietnam, Cuba, Angola, Afghanistan, and Eastern Europe.[66] Rich in energy and mineral resources (such as oil, gas, coal, chromium, uranium), the Soviet economy was plagued by poor national economic management, inefficient allocation of labor, outdated industrial technology that wasted energy, transportation problems, and administrative inflexibility. Agricultural inefficiency was particularly important. Despite abundant cropland, Soviet agriculture was characterized by low productivity and rigid collectivization of production, making the USSR one of the world's largest grain importers.[67] Overall, the USSR produced half as much as the United States in terms of GNP and allocated less than half as much per capita of GNP.[68] It was a small factor in world trade, with combined imports and exports about one-third that of the United States and also far below West Germany and Japan.[69] "In fact," a Soviet economist wrote, "the Soviet Union lags behind the majority of developed countries in virtually every aspect of personal consumption. . . . Per capita goods and services consumption in the USSR is lower than anywhere else in Europe, save Albania, Turkey, and Romania." Military spending cut deeply into the amount of national income available for consumption.[70] Based on a wide range of social and economic perform- ance indicators put together by Ruth Leger Sivard, the Soviet Union on average ranked only nineteenth in the world, far below its number-two ranking as a military power.[71]

Like other older industrialized countries, the USSR emphasized rapid development of heavy industry with little regard for its environmental and ecological consequences.[72] Only after the start of glasnost did the full extent of the damage begin to be publicized. Some of it is irreparable, as in the case of nuclear reactors.[73] Serious air and water pollution, such as affects every industrial city, required standards and controls that no prior Soviet leader was willing to consider.[74] An ecological map compiled within the USSR Academy of Sciences identified 26 percent of the Soviet population in 123 cities as living within crisis areas.[75] Among the most severely affect- ed areas are those around the Aral and Caspian seas. The Aral, once the fourth largest inland body of water in the world, has been drained of nearly two-thirds of its water, mostly because of large-scale irrigation undertaken for cotton growing when the region was under Soviet authority. Now five Central Asian states rely on the Aral's precious water. Animal life in the sea basin has been extinguished, and a desert of salt and chemical residue was created that is blown into the air. The impact on humans includes increased illness, unemployment, and social problems for the towns that once thrived from the sea.[76] The Caspian Sea region has suffered from nearly the oppo- site effect: The sea level has increased since a dam was built in 1980 to block the flow to marshes. Within three years, the marsh regions, once rich in natural resources, had completely disappeared.[77]

Human rights stood out as the Soviet system's greatest shortcoming. The worst excesses of the Stalinist political terror receded under Gorbachev. But the leadership's Gulag syndrome, captured in Solzhenitsyn's writings, continued into the mid-1980s: the internal exile of political opponents and peace activists; the tight control of religious, media, and artistic expression; the pervasiveness of the secret police; the rejection of free emigration for Jews and other groups. All these actions violated provisions of the 1975 Helsinki Accords signed with the United States and the European countries. The approximately one hundred Soviet citizens in the Helsinki Watch Committee who attempted to monitor their government's compliance were often officially silenced. Such widespread repression was attributable to an extremely insecure and conservative party leadership, one that was rigidly hierarchical, hostile to reform, and fearful of the working class in whose name it ruled—a privileged class bent on self-perpetuation.[78]

As previously noted, Soviet (and, for that matter, East European) socialism on a transnational level was, in the words of one critic, "increas-

ingly an integral part of the capitalist world economy.[79] Promoting that
trend was, in fact, part of Kissinger's announced strategy for achieving
detente in the 1970s, a strategy welcomed by Brezhnev.[80] As traced by
André Gunder Frank,[81] East-West trade was the fastest-growing segment of
the socialist East European countries' total trade by the mid-1970s. The
Soviets and their East European partners in COMECON (the Council for
Mutual Economic Assistance) were importing technology and grain in
return for fuel and raw materials. But this exchange became increasingly
uneven and led to large annual trade deficits that put the COMECON countries, the USSR included, in significant debt to West European and US
banks: over $58 billion in 1981.[82] Thus, in terms of debt and trade patterns,
the Soviet Union and Eastern Europe occupied a position similar to that of
Third World NICs in the so-called international division of labor. What we
see here, in short, is an economic picture that was quite different from the
military competition that until the mid-1980s had dominated in East-West
relations. In keeping with the corporate-globalist vision of world order, the
Soviet Union and Eastern Europe became increasingly interlinked with the
global economy—at the very time when realist anti-Soviet hardliners such
as emerged in the Reagan administration were emphasizing the military
competition and the consequent need (which they attempted, largely unsuc-
cessfully, to implement) to weaken COMECON's access to Western credit
and technology.

Gorbachev's reforms sought to draw the USSR away from the precipice
of great-power obsolescence.[83] He appeared to be convinced that real Soviet
security had been emasculated by official corruption, loss of individual
effort and initiative, a stifling party-state hierarchy, excessive military
spending, and intolerance of intellectuals. Without dismantling the party or
state machinery, Gorbachev challenged it to make a radical change in the
way it did business. In Gorbachev's first two years, many old-line officials
were removed, a number of dissidents (some quite prominent, such as the
physicist Andrei Sakharov) were freed, literature and film began to reflect a
new realism (especially about the Stalin era), and the first steps were taken
to make state factories more autonomous and responsive to workers.

After only five years in office, however, the honeymoon was over for
Gorbachev. The powerful forces of nationalism, personal freedom, political
competition, and limited market socialism he had let loose came back to
haunt him. By 1990 Gorbachev was a politician struggling to retain control
over a system on the verge of collapse, his popularity stronger abroad (as
evidenced by his being awarded the Nobel Peace Prize) than at home, where
perestroika and glasnost upset long-established practices and patterns of
authority. The two most powerful bureaucracies, the Communist Party of 20
million and the armed forces, were forced to make sacrifices their leaders
resented—fewer privileges, reduced powers and budgets, more internal
democratization.[84] Radical reformists and conservative nationalists seized

the unprecedented openness to confront the political leadership and even to organize against it. Sharp challenges also came from the fifteen republics, including Russia itself (which comprised about three-quarters of Soviet territory and half its population). The army was called upon to quell large-scale demonstrations by Georgian and Armenian nationalists. By 1990 nearly all the republics had declared their independence in some form from Moscow. The Baltic states—Latvia, Lithuania, and Estonia—also broke with Moscow; independence for them meant the restoration of the sovereignty taken away by the USSR in 1940. Perhaps the broadest antagonism appeared daily in the streets, from a restive population demanding more goods in the stores yet fearful of what a free market would do to prices and job security.

Gorbachev's perestroika enjoyed greater successes in foreign affairs than in the economy. He showed sensitivity to global problems that transcend class and national interests, such as the environment and (after Chernobyl) nuclear energy. He followed through on his assertions that "security can only be mutual" and that "there can be no security for the USSR without security for the United States." The USSR made important initiatives on nuclear arms control, reduced troops and weapons in Europe and on the China border (the latter paving the way in 1989 for the normalization of relations), and cooperated with the United States during Gulf War I and in the resolution of several Third World conflicts. Gorbachev cut the military budget substantially and tried to persuade Soviet military industries to convert to producing more for the civilian market.[85] Finally, glasnost allowed particular foreign policies to be reevaluated in the press and parliament. Even the legitimacy of past actions, such as the secret Nazi-Soviet pact of 1939 that led to the annexation of the Baltic states, and the interventions in Czechoslovakia and Afghanistan, were challenged and overturned.

In the end, it was Gorbachev's inability to stave off revolt by the non-Russian republics and populations that did him in. Neither threats nor the use of force worked, and his formula for dealing with them as sovereign entities under a new union came too late. Not only had several of the key republics already opted for sovereignty on their own terms, but Boris Yeltsin, who was elected to head the Russian republic's supreme soviet in May 1990, was spearheading a drive that would culminate in an independent Russia.[86] The old guard responded with a coup attempt in August 1991; but when it was put down three days later, Yeltsin, not Gorbachev (who had been forced to leave Moscow), emerged as the hero. The USSR rapidly dissolved as the coup accelerated the drive for independence of the Balkans, Ukraine, Russia, and most other republics. By late 1991, amid acute economic problems in the Soviet Union—starting with a decline in GNP of 30 percent in 1991—even Gorbachev's greatest supporters in Europe and the United States held back on aid and prepared to recognize the independence of the republics. Yeltsin thereupon led the formation of an alternative political structure: the Commonwealth of Independent States (CIS), which eleven of the twelve republics joined. Gorbachev was forced to resign in December 1991; the Soviet flag ceased to fly over Moscow. All ministries were turned over to Russian authority, as was the USSR's seat in the United Nations.

Inevitably, Yeltsin, too, had to confront the harsh realities of a divided polity, a dysfunctional economy, and sixty years of central planning. Like Gorbachev, Yeltsin had to deal with powerful interest groups that had been hurt by the reforms and the foreign-policy changes—former Communist Party officials (who represented over 80 percent of the Russian parliament even as the party became illegal on the national level), military leaders of (now) a second-class power, captains of the armaments industries, and the heads of other state enterprises. Yeltsin was unmovable in his insistence on pushing ahead with privatization and centralizing authority in the name of democracy. But in doing so he made some major concessions. He allowed foreign, especially US, advisers and organizations to become deeply involved in economic and political planning, which "helped to create a system of tycoon capitalism run for the benefit of a corrupt political oligarchy."[87] When faced with resistance in parliament, he simply ignored it, revealing a certain shallowness of democratic values. He acceded to the military-industrial complex on slowing down the conversion of military plants and stepping up arms exports, as previously mentioned. And on the environment, Yeltsin showed no inclination to move dramatically against nuclear waste and fallout or to prevent the selling off to TNCs of large tracts of Siberia's timberlands.[88] Nor were the resources available to combat serious air pollution from industrial discharges.[89]

During his visit to the United States in 1992, Yeltsin reminded the US Congress that economic and political reforms in Russia were essential to prevent chaos and a restoration of authoritarian rule. But the thicket of economic and social problems seemed impenetrable.[90] A report on health care—"our No. 1 national security crisis," said Yeltsin—pointed out that reforms to address resource allocations and health-care priorities, thus eliminating inefficiencies and delivering needed services, were beyond reach. Entrenched interests and familiar ways of doing things made reforms the subject of much talk and even more resistance.[91] State and personal finances took a beating: The ruble lost half its value between mid-1997 and mid-1998; the government spent around one-third of its budget simply to make interest payments on its international debt; and funds allocated by various government organs never reached their destination, presumably having disappeared into private pockets.[92] Relevant to today's Russia is that "preventing insider deals in the auction of state businesses" was one of Yeltsin's most pressing challenges.[93] Although the Russian government received substantial assistance from the IMF and other multilateral lenders,[94] Yeltsin was constantly buffeted by the structural-adjustment demands of the IMF and his nationalistic supporters who resented the power of foreign capital. Having the money and being able to govern effectively and in keeping with democratic norms are different matters in Russia today. Corruption, extortion, and the power of money to move politics have reached obscene proportions. The *mafiya,* comprising numerous criminal gangs, defines much of what happens on a daily basis. In the upper reaches of politics, phrases such as "semi-criminal oligarchy" and "robber baron capitalism" are now commonly used by Russian as well as foreign critics to define the system.[95] Not only democratization and a market economy but also public morale are being subverted by a greedy elite that increasingly dominates the political economy. Such a "corporatist" Russia, in which parties and the rule of law have not taken root, may pose serious problems for the country's full integration into the international community. These problems have become even more acute under Yeltsin's successor, Vladimir Putin, as noted below.

A final matter of international concern with domestic roots is the Russian military and Russia's security. The sorry state of the Russian military since 1991—the demoralization of its leaders and its dramatic reduction in size, budget, and capabilities—poses potential dangers, including susceptibility to nationalist influences and reduced interest in arms control.[96] The disastrous Russian army intervention in Chechnya; the evisceration of the Far Eastern fleet; the sharp limits on Russian influence over events in Korea and the Middle East; Russia's limited ability to protect fellow Slavs in Yugoslavia—all these are taken as signs of national decline. Nuclear weapons have become one of the few symbols of grandeur worth preserving, it seems. The distress of some military leaders at Russia's reduction to second-class status has been a boon to the nationalists' cause.[97] They want to preserve Russia's sphere of influence (what it calls the "near abroad") over its former republics, and prevent secessions such as Chechnya's (a peace treaty was signed in May 1997, and by 2006 the rebellion seemed quelled at great cost). Under Yeltsin, Russia used military power to prevent secession in Abkhazia (Georgia), where the UN approved Russian enforcement of a cease-fire; kept troops stationed in Tajikistan; and concluded agreements with some CIS members such as Belarus that amount to a regional policing power.[98] But Russia has been just as active in promoting regional economic integration to assure continued access to vital resources.

Nothing undermined Russia's relations with the West so much as NATO's agreement in 1997, pushed by the United States, to expand its membership eastward. The Clinton administration contended that Russia had nothing to fear, that it was actually advantageous to Russia to have secure neighbors, just as NATO enlargement was a proper reward to the new market economies of central Europe and an encouragement for them to democratize. Russian concerns about having neighbors trained and armed as never before were dismissed as a "target of convenience for [post–Cold

War] Russian fears and resentments."[99] To Yeltsin, however, NATO enlargement made for a "cold peace," a resumption of "bloc divisions" in
Europe.[100] George Kennan, former ambassador to Russia and author of the
containment doctrine, agreed: It is "the beginning of a new cold war," "a
tragic mistake" in treating the new Russia as though it was still the
USSR.[101] But Kennan and other critics were drowned out by the voices of a
new realism that saw an opportunity to do what containment could not—
eliminate Moscow's influence and put emerging economies in its place. And
Yeltsin could do little but complain; he faced either accepting the new
Western hegemony or risking loss of Western aid. The fact that Russia was
included in a "Partnership for Peace" with the United States, in a new
NATO-Russia council and in the Group of 7, could hardly disguise the reality of its diminished status or its anguish over US domination.[102]

Russian leaders had probably hoped for a more symmetrical relationship with the United States and the EU in return for Moscow's cooperation
on major international issues. What they got instead, as they saw it, was
Russian cooperation being taken for granted, Russian interests being
ignored, and Russian dependence on loans being manipulated. In the words
of one prominent Russian commentator, NATO's eastward expansion was
"proof of the American desire to take advantage of Russia's present weakness and to complete what Americans see as their victory in the cold
war."[103] By 2001, US disenchantment with Russia's progress toward
democratization had spilled over into the security domain. The honeymoon
between the West and Russia was over, most experts agreed: The strong tendency of the Clinton and Bush administrations to ignore evidence of
Russian illiberalism and inequalities gave way to tough-worded criticism of
Russia's democratic backsliding and disagreements on everything from missile defense and global warming to NATO and Middle East policy. The CIA
director, George J. Tenet, warned in 2001 that Russia was seeking to restore
its great-power status and challenge US leadership. "There can be little
doubt," he said, "that President Putin wants to restore some aspects of the
Soviet past—status as a great power, strong central authority and a stable
and predictable society—sometimes at the expense of neighboring states or
the civil rights of individual Russians."[104] The 9/11 attacks pushed these
criticisms into the background, but only temporarily.

The driving force behind US-Russia differences today indeed seems to
be Putin's rejection of second-class status. "Russia's leaders have given up
on becoming part of the West and have started creating their own Moscow-
centered system," one knowledgeable observer concluded.[105] Denied full
membership in NATO, the EU, and (at least until 2007) the WTO while its
former satellite states became members, Russia's leaders evidently have
decided the Russian Federation (RF) can never be a special ally of the West.
It is all take and no give, Putin and others have been saying since the
Clinton years.[106] In Russian eyes the West is determined to transform

Russia within and, with an enlarged NATO, monitor and contain it with-out.[107] Like Chinese leaders, but unlike Yeltsin, Putin has responded force-fully. In 2004 he announced a new nuclear weapon in the Russian arsenal, one that he said had no equal in US arsenals. He put pressure on Ukraine, where his support of the pro-Moscow winner in a fraudulent presidential election had failed before the combined opposition of people power, the EU, and the United States, to accept a large price increase on Russian gas.[108] He joined with China in demanding that US forces withdraw from Central Asia, and rejected calls for sanctions on Iran as the nuclear issue heated up in 2006. Clearly, Russia's sudden oil and gas wealth—it has sur-passed Saudi Arabia to become the world's largest oil producer—gave it a new self-confidence to be confrontational.

The Russian counteroffensive was also on display when Putin, on the eve of a G-8 summit in July 2006, replied to mounting criticisms from Washington of Russian democracy by comparing them to the "arrogance" of the Western colonialists in Asia and Africa a century earlier.[109] Such a com-plaint, even if understandable in terms of Russian nationalist sensitivities, cannot account for Russia's democratic deficits. Domination of the political economy by oligarchs placed Russia's wealth outside the realm of social policy. As Stephen Cohen wrote, the oligarchs

> put Putin in the Kremlin to be a praetorian president safeguarding the sys-tem, its creators and its beneficiaries in business, politics, the media and even intellectual circles. . . . Even if some accounts of Russia's crisis are overstated, the only solution is a new economic course that uses the oli-garchs' enormous profits from the country's natural resources to rescue and develop the rest of the nation.[110]

Ignoring that advice, Putin has engineered state takeovers of the most prof-itable enterprises, notably in the energy sector. These represent not so much the decline of the oligarchs as an erasing of the boundary between state and private corporatism. Oligarchs who cooperate with the state are rewarded, economically and politically; those who do not are penalized, pushed out of business, and even imprisoned.[111]

Putin's presidency, though popular with the vast majority of Russians, displays many remnants of the old Soviet Union and even the czarist era. Putin runs a tight ship; there are no independent sources of authority.[112] Personal freedoms have expanded, but democracy has been undermined by sharp limitations on press freedom—thirteen journalists have been killed since he took office[113]—and his decision to appoint province governors and regional leaders rather than have them be directly elected. The rule of law leaves much to be desired; an independent judiciary is not apparent, and the arbitrary prosecuting power of the secret service—the Federal Security Service, a reincarnation of the notorious KGB that Putin once headed—has been restored.[114] Putin has little patience with his opponents in the media and politics, or with NGOs, whose role has been curtailed. On the very day that Putin received congratulatory messages on his overwhelming reelection in March 2004, a European team of observers came down hard on Putin's methods. "Esssential elements of [European Union] standards for democratic elections, such as a vibrant political discourse and meaningful pluralism, were lacking," said the report, which specifically cited biased news coverage, some voting irregularities (incredibly, Putin won 92 percent of the vote in Chechnya, for instance), and "a lack of a democratic culture, accountability and responsibility."[115]

In human-security perspective, however, Russia's greatest tragedy lies elsewhere—in the immensity of its economic and social problems, and (some maintain) equally in the inadequacy of the US response to it.[116] While Westerners may be dazzled by the new wealth on display in Moscow, the real Russian economy has the look of a richer Third World country: massive corruption, capital flight, concentration of wealth, deteriorating farms and factories, dependence on imports and oil exports.[117] Bribery is central to doing business; individuals are paying $3 billion annually in bribes, and businesses pay over $300 billion, far more than the government collects in revenue.[118] Ten percent of the population lives on less than $2 a day, and one-quarter lives below the national poverty line—this, *after* significant cuts in poverty between 1999 and 2002.[119] Malnourishment and high mortality rates for children, an emerging AIDS epidemic fed in part by rampant drug use,[120] and low life expectancy (only 59 years for males) are other serious matters. The public-health system is a nightmare for citizens.[121] Russia also has a declining population (the annual growth rate of population is negative); fewer marriages, increased divorces, and limited support for child rearing spell trouble ahead for the work force and even national security.[122] Russia ranks 62nd on the UNDP's human development index, just ahead of Brazil and Bosnia, but behind Panama and Libya. Perhaps the single most dramatic demonstration of Russia's decline is that whereas in the late 1970s Russia's economy was four times the size of China's, today China's economy is three times the size of Russia's.

## Japan's Quest for Normalcy

Japan presents the anomaly of being an economic superpower that depends for critical resources and military security on other countries. It has the world's second largest GNP and its overall human development ranking (11th) is just behind the United States. Japan is fourth among the world's top exporters, following the United States, Germany, and China, and it is one of the leading foreign-aid donors (about $8.8 billion in 2003, second to $16.2 billion in ODA for the United States).[123] In the 1990s Japan completed what has been called its third structural economic transformation—from textiles in the early 1900s, to heavy and chemical industries between the

1930s and the mid-1960s, and then to knowledge-intensive production.[124] It has demonstrated, perhaps better than any other society, an ability to make global economic interdependence work to its advantage. Yet Japan must still rely heavily on food and energy from abroad and on the United States for protection from attack under terms of a 1960 security treaty. As the only victim of atomic attack, Japan has a deeply ingrained "nuclear allergy" that has led it to forswear producing nuclear weapons even though it has the ability to do so. Article 9 of the Japanese constitution forbids war making as a national policy. This provision has been interpreted by successive governments to permit the maintenance and modernization of so-called Self-Defense Forces (SDF) (along with US bases), but to restrict their role to defense of the home islands to a distance of 1,000 miles, and (until the 2003 Iraq war) to noncombat service in UN-sanctioned peacekeeping operations. As a result, although Japan's total military spending has held steady at around $42 billion (fourth in the world) since 2001,[125] it is a tiny percentage of GNP, leaving it with considerable added spending power.

Observers have attributed the global surge of Japanese industry to many factors.[126] In the early postwar period, the imposition of a democratic system, partial elimination of the *zaibatsu* (finance-business combines) and their replacement by an interlocking ruling party–bureaucracy–big business complex, and the establishment of a US protectorate enabled Japan to concentrate on economic growth. Cold War politics ensured large US and Southeast Asian markets for Japanese exports. Japan also took advantage of its being a latecomer to use the newest technologies in rebuilding its industrial base. Leftist labor unions were contained or crushed, providing a period of enforced stability. Domination of national politics by a single party, the Liberal Democrats (LDP), lent continuity to the political system. By the early 1960s, Japan was prepared to take off economically, moving quickly from mere imitator and absorber of technology to producer of some of the highest-quality goods on the world market. Spurred by the vision of Yoshida Shigeru, who was prime minister from 1946 to 1954, Japan opted for a reactive foreign policy that included limited rearmament but, under the US security umbrella, emphasized the aggressive pursuit of economic growth and foreign exchange.

In this strategy to win the peace even though having lost the world war, investment in human resources, high-technology, and energy alternatives has been as critical a factor as any other. Incomes in Japan are extraordinarily equitable: The wide rich-poor gap in the United States has no counterpart in Japan; nor do the heads of Toyota and the other giant corporations command astronomical earnings.[127] The Japanese work force is the world's best educated, for example—although higher education as a whole does not encourage individual creativity. A paternalistic relationship between corporations and labor affords job security in the largest companies and promotes productivity. Japan's productivity increases in manufacturing can also be attributed to the accelerated introduction of new technologies by farsighted managers, advances in robotics, and the large number of engineers (far more than in the United States) who go to work for private industry.[128] Japan's nonmilitary research and development spending likewise contributes to its commercial success.[129] The Japanese have a high rate of domestic savings that contrasts sharply with the US penchant for buying on credit. A great deal of this money flows abroad in pursuit of higher returns than are available on investment at home. Energy-saving measures, such as extensive recycling of aluminum and use of compact refrigerators, go along with investment in a diversity of energy sources, including nuclear power that accounts for over one-third of Japan's electricity.

The quality of life in Japan is one of the highest in the world, reflecting a sense of national purpose that is seldom encountered elsewhere. Still, Japan has more than its share of social and political problems. The LDP that dominates this "elitist democracy"[130] is a political machine with deep roots in the society, a highly loyal constituency, and the ability to get out the votes in good economic times and bad. The opposition parties, by contrast, have consistently failed to take advantage of scandals, bureaucratic corruption, glaring incompetence, and unprecedented economic setbacks such as occurred beginning in the mid-1990s. While the media railed, the LDP ruled.[131] In a country where consensus counts more than policy preferences, the possibility of forming an effective opposition coalition, much less developing a two-party system, is still low. Democratic institutions exist; but they are constrained by the power of big business (which is helped by government regulation), by the bureaucrats who run the ministries, and by a self-perpetuating elite tied together by common schooling, intermarriage, and other social circumstances.

An aging population—Japan has the world's highest percentage of people (21 percent) over 65, and that figure may double by 2050—and a declining work force pose especially serious future choices, including a dramatic shrinkage of the country's economy. Unlike the EU, migrant workers, though needed in large numbers, are a very small portion of the Japanese work force. Women might help bolster the work force, but the status of women remains low: Japan only ranks eighteenth among twenty-two industrialized countries on a "gender-sensitive" basis.[132] Job opportunities and access to child care facilities are limited, reducing incentives to have more children. Thus, a very low birth rate coexists with the aging population. Women are also practically invisible in parliament and in central ministries. Even though Japan has largely recovered from the bursting of the real estate bubble in 1997, which triggered bank failures, a long recession, and unprecedented levels of unemployment, its long-term prospects are unclear. The era of guaranteed employment and social security is over, and for younger and older people that is a shocking circumstance.

Environmental issues are serious: Air pollution is hazardous in the major cities; the failure of manufacturers and consumers in the production and disposal of recyclable goods has created a throwaway society with a huge garbage problem;[133] Japan is the only industrial nation without an antismoking campaign or the requirement of environmental impact reports on major construction projects; land-use laws are strong when it comes to protecting rice lands, weak in protecting forests; and Japan's opposition to a worldwide moratorium on commercial whaling puts it almost in a class by itself. Politicians have learned to tread cautiously on the reform of many of these problems, so that when Prime Minister Miyazawa Kiichi staked his administration's future (in 1992) on making Japan *seikatsu-tai-koku,* "a great power in terms of quality of life," he and the LDP were unable to deliver. At bottom, Japan is a business society, not a consumer society.[134]

Japan's international perspective has been fundamentally shaped by geographic isolation, a strong (some might say exaggerated) sense of vulnerability, and economic nationalism. These influences account for Japan's single-minded pursuit of national objectives, as its international energy, trade, and foreign investment policies show.

Japan is highly resource-dependent: It relies on imports for about 50 percent of its food and over 85 percent of its total energy (including nearly 100 percent of its oil). Energy, therefore, is not just a commodity in trade but a strategic resource for Japan. Assurance of its continued supply must be planned as part of a comprehensive economic strategy. That explains why, in pursuit of its own energy needs, Japan has often run afoul of US policies, whether with respect to Middle East oil or Soviet gas or US supplies to Japan of nuclear fuel and technology.[135] As Japan further develops its knowledge industries, its energy priorities will be changing. Electronic and microprocessor goods will be research-intensive, therefore less resource- and energy-dependent (and less polluting) than previous kinds of production, which until the 1998 financial crisis were (and now again are) being transferred abroad. In the immediate future, Japan will continue to rely heavily on imported oil and nuclear waste reprocessed in Europe to meet growing electricity demand. That spells trouble in three ways. One is the ability to meet global standards for greenhouse gas emissions.[136] Japan is not doing so. The other two relate to nuclear power: Japan's fifty-two nuclear power plants have been accident prone and subject to mismanagement, making nuclear power plants increasingly unpopular;[137] and Japan's stockpiling of very large amounts of plutonium whose safeguarding has been questioned runs counter to international nuclear nonproliferation efforts.[138]

In the longer run, however, we may see even greater stress being placed on energy efficiency and conservation, with which Japan has had considerable success,[139] and on vigorously exploring renewable energy sources, such as solar and geothermal.[140] Government and industry will not be alone in making such decisions. Since the late 1960s, citizen-activists in local environmental and other protest groups in Japan have been instrumental in pushing an alternative energy agenda that reflects postindustrial values.[141]

Trade and investment policies reflect a major contradiction in Japan's approach: working for an open world economy, but putting Japanese economic interests first. The dominant view in Japan is that the contradiction is necessary. Resource dependence is one reason; it makes Japan vulnerable to the political stability and trading practices of others.[142] Another reason is that, while Japan enjoys a large surplus in trade with the United States, its senior partner, circumstance creates dependence on the openness of the US market to Japanese products. Over 22 percent of Japan's exports go to the United States—not as much as a decade ago, when it was 27 percent, but Japan's most important market after China.[143]

When it comes to foreign involvement in Japan's economy and to Japan's overseas investments, self-preservation again prevails. Japanese leaders lean toward monopoly control rather than unfettered competition. They tend to promote the most efficient and technologically advanced firms, national and transnational. Foreign ownership of domestic companies and foreign access to financial and equity markets are severely restricted, whereas Japanese investment abroad is heavily promoted.[144] The figures confirm the success of this strategy and the reasons for US and European chagrin over Japan's "neomercantilism." For in comparison with the US and EU economies, Japan's is indeed quite closed. Japan allows in only a fraction of what it invests abroad: Between 1994 and 2003, Japan's FDI came to $268 billion, as against FDI of $50.5 billion into Japan.[145] Japan hosts a minuscule proportion of worldwide FDI, and foreign firms in Japan account for much smaller percentages of total sales and employment than do TNCs in other countries. "One-way globalization," some specialists call it.[146]

In Third World investment, mainly in East and Southeast Asia, Japanese firms offer a textbook example of comparative advantage.[147] They shift along with changes in individual countries' skills, wage levels, and production capabilities. Increasingly, the products of Japanese TNC subsidiaries are exported out of China and Southeast Asia, either to Japan or elsewhere. In mid-2006 a milestone was reached when more automobile production was taking place abroad than at home—in China, Thailand, and numerous other locations in and beyond Asia.[148] Japanese trade works in conjunction with private investment and aid, moreover: Capital- and skill-intensive goods are exported from Japan; Japan imports processed goods from the more developed Asian countries and raw materials from the less developed countries. Aid programs and technology transfers are largely designed to promote Japanese-financed exports and "development" programs that will assist Japan's overall trade by building new markets for the next generation of Japanese products. At the corporate and government levels, these practices seem to benefit home and host country: For Third World hosts, they fit with the usual desire for more control over foreign investment, for greater employment opportunities, and for increased exports of processed goods; for Japan, they mean access to land and labor that are in short supply at home, and they compel the constant upgrading of Japanese production to meet competition that its own investments have helped to create.[149]

Thus, Japanese corporate globalism is as self-interested as any other. In banking, for example, Japan is a major contributor to the World Bank and various regional multilateral banks, such as the Asian Development Bank. But Japanese commercial banks, the world's largest, hold only half or less of Third World debt. This reflects their preference for investing where capital is most profitable, in the industrialized world, rather than where it is in desperately short supply. Only in 1987 did Japan indicate a major new commitment of funds to Third World development. Asia, where Japan's foreign investments are greatest, gets the lion's share (almost 60 percent in 1990).[150] When it comes to directing ODA to human priorities, Japan has one of the poorest records of any major aid-giver.[151] Given the opportunity to use or deny its foreign aid on behalf of human rights, Tokyo has often put commercial or other national interests ahead of ethical principles.[152] The story is similar on the environment: Japan has had a far from exemplary record in monitoring the environmental consequences of its ODA. Japan is the leading importer of tropical hardwoods, mostly for use in housing. TNCs such as Mitsubishi have become notorious for their clear-cutting of forests in ODA-recipient countries such as Indonesia and Malaysia.[153]

Japan's leadership is uncomfortably aware of the country's junior status, even though it seems to prefer things that way. Loyalty to the United States has frequently placed constraints on Japanese foreign-policy independence. Despite Japan's antinuclear weapon posture, until the early 1970s, US nuclear weapons transited through Japan, and their components were secretly stored in Okinawa. Until President Nixon's breakthrough trip to China in 1972 started the process of normalizing relations, Japan had been under consistent pressure from the United States to minimize economic and political ties with the PRC. And following the Asian financial crisis, US officials blocked Japan's initiative to create a new monetary fund for East Asia. All these forms of deference to US policy posed domestic political problems for Japanese leaders. Dependence on the United States has also put pressure on Japan to increase military spending and foreign aid, and either liberalize its trade and domestic investment policies or face rising barriers to Japanese exports to the United States. Occasionally, Japan's second-rank status has been reinforced by surprise moves by the United States, such as Kissinger's secret trip to China in 1971 and the "Nixon shock" the same year that imposed import surcharges and reduced US exports of soybeans, a staple of the Japanese diet. Surprises make for resentment when, as in Japan's case, a nation is frequently told how valuable an ally it is and then is neither consulted nor informed in advance about key decisions.

Until the late 1990s, when US and Japanese leaders signed off on new security guidelines, it had seemed that the end of the Cold War would bring lingering tensions, starting with the large Japanese trade surplus, to the surface. US claims of an unfair playing field were matched by Japanese claims of an overvalued US dollar and superior products and management techniques.[154] Trade tensions got so bad that when calls on Japan for voluntary restraints failed, Ronald Reagan "earned the dubious distinction of being the first postwar president to impose economic sanctions on Japan" in the form of retaliatory tariffs on some Japanese imports.[155] As late as 1990, opinion polls in the United States were showing more public concern about the "Japanese threat" than about the Soviet one. In essence, however, Japan's trade surplus is largely structural on both sides; neither US consumer tastes nor Japan's dense network of trading interests can be argued or legislated away.

What has "saved" Japan from further trade battles with Washington is China's much larger trade surplus. Instead, the US-Japan dialogue has moved to the security realm, over the question of whether or not Japan should assume a larger-than-economic role in world affairs. For with the Cold War over, it seemed that the principal reason for Japan's defense reliance on the United States had vanished and that Japan would finally be forced into a great debate over its lack of a foreign-policy vision.[156] The great debate never took place; the LDP never prepared Japan's public for one, and in any case the Japanese public overwhelmingly believes domestic affairs should remain the government's top priority and Japan's role in the world ought to be kept limited to economic contributions.[157] Nevertheless, elite opinion on the direction Japanese foreign policy should take was divided between passivists and activists, comparable to our realists and globalists.[158] One side argued that Japan should break from its self-centered foreign policy and behave in ways "commensurate with its enormous economic and technological strength."[159] Japan should remain in alliance with the United States, but should directly contribute to collective security.[160] Arrayed on the other side were those who believed that Japan should either remain lightly armed and dependent on the United States for its security, in accordance with the Yoshida Doctrine, or should explicitly take on the role of a "global civilian power" that makes its mark in the world through aid, trade, technology transfers, and other nonmilitary means.[161]

On balance, Japan's foreign policy during the 1990s was fundamentally in keeping with the Yoshida Doctrine—more internationalist, but still tightly aligned with the United States. For example, Japan, along with Australia, played a lead role in the formation of the Asia-Pacific Economic Cooperation forum (APEC), and decided to join ASEAN's regional political and security dialogue.[162] Tokyo sided with the EU in a number of disagreements with Washington over its unilateralism;[163] but it also became the only Asian participant to date in the planned US ballistic-missile defense system for East Asia, and, in the "New Guidelines for Japan-US Defense

Cooperation" of 1997, agreed to extend Japanese security responsibilities for the first time outside the scope of defense of the home islands.[164] Japan also became one of the major financial supporters of the UN's budget; sent minesweepers and contributed $13 billion to US war expenses in the Gulf War; and obtained parliamentary (Diet) approval in June 1992 of a peace-keeping operations bill, which then became the basis for the first-ever dis-patch of soldiers for service in Cambodia under UN command. A Japanese national then headed the UN Transitional Authority in Cambodia, itself an important new international undertaking.

Some of these foreign-policy actions turn out to prove the point of a largely passive, reactive Japan. Its strengthened security cooperation with the United States, its "checkbook diplomacy" following Gulf War I, and the PKO bill (which heavily qualified the terms of engagement for Japanese forces) were mainly in response to US prodding, and after wrenching inter-nal debate.[165] As the new century began, consequently, the bilateral security alliance remained the linchpin of Japan's security policy; Japan did not want to be a leader in East Asian or international affairs, contrary to the activists on the right, and it was thought that only a crisis of confidence in the US commitment to protect it could alter the relationship.

With 9/11 and a new government under Koizumi Junichiro, however, US-Japan relations became closer than ever, and the quest for "normal nation" status got under way. The Bush administration found an ally that, for its own purposes as much as out of partnership, would meet it more than halfway. The principal step taken by Koizumi was the unprecedented dis-patch of troops and other military support to Iraq and Afghanistan under emergency legislation, despite lack of a UN mandate and despite strong pub-lic disapproval. Other steps were planning for constitutional revision to give the armed forces official status and clear the way for military operations abroad;[166] the revival of public display of the Japanese flag and national anthem; willingness to confront Chinese and North Korean vessels in Japanese waters; and quest for a permanent seat on the UN Security Council. Under Koizumi, Japan also reduced its UN and ODA budgets to match its share of global GNP, which still meant paying 19.5 percent of the UN's regu-lar budget, but forfeiting its number-one standing among all aid givers.[167]

Koizumi's China policy may have the greatest long-term consequences for Japan and the region. Notwithstanding Japan's deep investments in China (about $5.6 billion in 2005, the highest amount so far),[168] its large trade deficit with China, its generosity in aid (around $20 billion in loans and grants since 1979),[169] and Koizumi's apology for Japan's wartime atrocities, high-level communications between the two countries have declined precipitously. The leaders did not hold a summit meeting between 2002 and the fall of 2006, when Koizumi stepped down. As Japan's con-cerns about China's rise have deepened, so has China's unpopularity with Japanese—a dislike that is mirrored in Chinese opinion polls.[170] Koizumi's

bow to the right wing by making annual visits to the Yasukuni Shrine in
Tokyo where fourteen Class-A war criminals are buried alongside all other
Japanese war dead has caused deep resentment in China (as well as in both
Koreas), including an Internet-based petition drive in 2005 started by young
Chinese that Beijing finally had to force to a halt. As symbolically significant as these visits to the shrine are, they would probably not arouse such
intense Chinese anger were there not so many competing issues of national
interest. Among these are territorial disputes in the East China Sea, China's
disapproval of a Security Council seat for Japan, Japan's identification of
China as a potential security threat in a defense paper of 2004, Japan's
agreement with the United States in 2005 to regard Taiwan as a common
security concern, constitutional revision in Japan,[171] and Japan's dispatch of
the SDF in support of US policy in the Middle East.

The trend to "normal nation" status is likely to continue under
Koizumi's successor, Shinzo Abe, who served under Koizumi as chief cabinet secretary and developed the reputation of being a foreign-policy hard-
liner.[172] Abe will need to be no less attentive to domestic matters than any
of his predecessors: Unemployment, immigration, the aging society, and
government debt are likely to preoccupy him. But he plans to carry out the
revision of Article 9 while strengthening the alliance with the United States
still more. Immediately on taking office in September 2006 he traveled to
China and South Korea to start mending fences, and left open the question
of visiting Yasukuni. Still, the prospects for China-Japan reconciliation any-
time soon appear remote.

To some leading PRC analysts, Japan is once again actively engaged
with the United States in the containment of China.[173] That would indeed be
a major blow to the stability of East Asia, for it would force other nations
once again to choose sides. It might also create new pressures for nuclear
arms in South Korea and Taiwan as well as in Japan, where influential voices have sometimes been heard calling for a nuclear-weapon capability. And
China-Japan rivalry would certainly have negative implications for reaching
a settlement of the North Korean nuclear issue and just about any other multilateral problem-solving effort.[174]

From a global-humanist perspective, Japan's preferred option is to be a
"global civilian power," even if it remains in alliance with the United
States. This path of "active pacifism," as some younger Japanese politicians
also call it, is one worthy of the permanent UN Security Council seat Japan
seeks. By virtue of having risen to First World status without pursuing hegemony, Japan might base its international role squarely on its capacity to do
good with its economic and technological assets.[175] Besides restoring
friendly relations with China and normalizing relations with North Korea,
Japan could help improve international security in numerous other ways—
sharing new technologies to improve the quality of life and environmental
protection; increasing the share of the government budget that is devoted to
relieving Third World debt, poverty, and other sources of human misery;[176]

and becoming more active in regional and international diplomacy on disarmament and human rights. Japanese energy and environmental technology can be especially useful. For example, Asia has become the world's principal source of carbon dioxide emissions, mainly because of rapid industrialization by China and other developing economies that use coal-fired power stations. These emissions account for a large proportion of global warming gases and pose a serious threat of transboundary acid rain.[177] Japanese technology can come into play in a number of ways, including energy conservation and pollution controls on power plants. METI, the powerful Ministry of Economics, Trade and Industry, is already working on new environmental technologies with Third World applications in areas such as air pollution and energy efficiency.[178] If, in addition, Japan were to be more generous with ODA (it ranks third from the bottom among industrialized countries in the percentage of national income it devotes to foreign aid);[179] if it were to increase the human-development component of ODA; and if the government were to take steps to stop destruction of the rain forests by Japanese TNCs, Japan would be doing much to heighten its stature as a reliable supporter of Third World development.

Generous policies such as those above would not only be departures from the past emphasis on economic self-interest. To be credible, they would also have to reflect, and require, a moral reevaluation, starting with a more systematic confrontation of the aggression and atrocities by the Imperial Army during World War II. Official apologies should not be undermined by denials or minimizations of the Rape of Nanking in China and the kidnapping of Korean and other Asian "comfort women" to serve in army brothels. (Shinzo Abe, for example, expressed sorrow to the women but said he saw no evidence of the military's role.) Japan's courts should stop blocking attempts by the surviving women to gain compensation.[180] Japanese nationalists should not be able to whitewash the history of World War II in school textbooks, which must be approved by the education ministry.[181] One of the most positive steps to reevaluate Japan's role in World War II and begin the healing process occurred in August 2006, when Japan's leading conservative newspaper, the *Daily Yomiuri*, published a series of editorials that pinpointed Japan's major errors and implicitly challenged Koizumi's visits to Yasukuni and right-wing historical revisionism.[182] Japan will need more such courageous self-reflection if it wants to achieve genuine normalcy at home and in relations with its neighbors.

## Notes

1. Arms spending figures are from the Stockholm International Peace Research Institute (SIPRI), and are cited in *The Defense Monitor* (Center for Defense Information) 35, no. 2 (March–April 2006), p. 2. On arms exports, see the *SIPRI Yearbook 2005*, table 10A.2, at www.sipri.org/contents/armstrad/at_data.html#chapt. From 2000 to 2004, Russia exported $26.9 billion in arms, France exported $6.3 billion, Germany $4.8 billion, and Britain $4.4 billion.

2. While US military and aerospace companies (Lockheed Martin, Boeing, Northrup Grumman, General Dynamics, and Raytheon) dominate the list, European companies such as EADS (European Aeronautic Defense and Space) and BAE Systems are growing rapidly in revenue and share value. See *International Herald Tribune,* September 16–17, 2006.

3. Sivard, *World Military and Social Expenditures 1983,* p. 7. See also Paul Kennedy, *The Rise and Fall of the Great Powers,* p. 384.

4. Sivard, *World Military and Social Expenditures 1983,* p. 7.

5. Based on figures in *SIPRI Yearbook 1992,* table 7A.2, p. 259.

6. Block, pp. 134–63.

7. World Bank 1984, tables 2.2 and 2.4, pp. 16, 17.

8. Kegley and Wittkopf (1981 ed.), p. 172.

9. Robert A. Isaak, *International Political Economy: Managing World Economic Change,* pp. 96–98; *Europe Without Frontiers: Completing the Internal Market,* p. 34.

10. The figure, from a statement by the Canadian secretary of state for external affairs, is cited in Barney et al., *Global 2000: Implications for Canada,* p. 58.

11. See Frank, pp. 34–35; and David P. Calleo, "Inflation and American Power," *Foreign Affairs.*

12. See World Bank 1984, table 2.5, p. 18, for comparisons of nontariff barriers to imports from developed and developing countries. See also the testimony of Clyde V. Prestowitz in the US Congress, House of Representatives, Committee on International Relations, subcommittees on International Economic Policy and Trade, Asia and the Pacific, and International Operations and Human Rights, "Hearings: The Future of U.S. Foreign Policy in Asia and the Pacific," pp. 204–11. The EC's exasperation over its trade deficits with Japan—about $16 billion in 1990, $25 billion in 1991, and $27 billion in 1992—is discussed in the *Los Angeles Times World Report,* April 9, 1994.

13. See the discussion in Meier, *The International Environment of Business,* pp. 227–28.

14. DeGrasse, in Gordon and McFadden, eds., p. 14.

15. For an excellent overview, see Craig R. Whitney, "Western Europe's Dreams Turning to Nightmares," *NYT,* August 8, 1993, p. 1.

16. See Roger Cohen, "For France, Sagging Self-Image and Esprit," *NYT,* February 11, 1997, p. A1; "A Survey of France," *The Economist,* November 25, 1995; and Daniel Bell, "The Future of Europe," *Dissent,* pp. 445–52.

17. The German Bundestag voted in 1993 to restrict entry to those victims of oppression and war who could claim political asylum. The French parliament opted for a "zero immigration" policy. These measures, politically popular at home, reversed a tradition of openness to all refugees, whether political or economic. As for the immigrant workers with longtime residencies, they were denied citizenship in almost all cases.

18. Defined as below $4 a day; see UNDP, "Overview of *Human Development Report 1997,*" p. 2.

19. A UNICEF report of August 1994 said: "The morality and health crisis burdening most Eastern European countries since 1989 is without precedent in the European peacetime history of this century." Poverty, stress, environmental decline, and budget cuts account for this circumstance. In some places, people said the health-care system was better in communist days, and some of its worst features, such as bribery of doctors and nurses to obtain care, have gotten even worse under the post-communist system (Jane Perlez, "East Europe's Health Care Is on the Danger List," *NYT,* November 23, 1994, p. A1). Drug use and drug trafficking have also become serious problems. *NYT,* June 5, 1995, p. 2.

20. See, for example, *NYT,* October 7, 1994, p. A1.

21. Tony Judt, *Postwar: A History of Europe Since 1945*, pp. 722–23. EU membership for these countries has meant rising labor and other costs, and thus loss of the cost advantage of their exports.

22. *Human Development Report 2005*, p. 34.

23. Ibid., p. 35.

24. For example, the disintegration of Yugoslavia was due less to ethnic hatreds than to the country's unsuccessful adjustment to globalization and austerity programs imposed to deal with mounting debts. By the end of the 1980s there was a sharp decline in living standards, high unemployment (especially among young people) and inflation, and widening regional economic differences. The middle class came apart. Ethnic differences came into play as people struggled to cope with the sacrifices they were forced to make. See Susan L. Woodward, *Balkan Tragedy: Chaos and Dissolution After the Cold War,* pp. 50–57.

25. Hammond, table 24.6, p. 24 (based on 1982–1984 statistics).

26. Hilary F. French, "Clearing the Air," in Brown et al., eds., *State of the World 1990,* tables 6-3 and 6-4, pp. 105, 108.

27. Tom Waters, "Ecoglasnost," *Discover,* p. 52.

28. Christopher Flavin, "Slowing Global Warming," in Brown et al., eds., *State of the World 1990,* table 2-1, p. 19.

29. Ibid., pp. 32–34. In November 1990 eighteen West European governments, representing about 19 percent of global carbon dioxide output, agreed to freeze carbon dioxide emissions at 1990 levels for the remainder of the decade. Some, including Germany, Denmark, and the Netherlands, also announced specific reduction targets and strategies. These actions finally found a positive response in the United States in 1993, when President Clinton reversed US opposition at the Earth Summit not only to European proposals on greenhouse gas emissions but also to the biodiversity treaty the Europeans favored. The United States signed the treaty in June 1993 and agreed to roll back greenhouse gas emissions to the 1990 level by 2000.

30. Christopher Flavin, "The Legacy of Rio," in Brown, ed., *State of the World 1997,* p. 11.

31. Emmy Daly, "Europeans Lagging in Greenhouse Gas Cuts," *NYT*, May 7, 2003, p. A10.

32. *Los Angeles Times,* February 12, 1986.

33. The report is quoted in Jerzy Milewski et al., "Poland: Four Years After," *Foreign Affairs,* p. 345.

34. John M. Kramer, "The Environmental Crisis in Poland," in Fred Singleton, ed., *Environmental Problems in the Soviet Union and Eastern Europe,* ch. 8.

35. World Bank, *Word Development Report,* 1997, table 6, p. 225.

36. Initially, Britain had been the prime mover in the creation of the seven-member European Free Trade Association (EFTA), whose members now are Austria, Finland, Iceland, Switzerland, Norway, Sweden, and Liechtenstein. Unlike the EC, EFTA aims only at eliminating trade restrictions among its members and not also at becoming a powerful export bloc (Isaak, p. 96). EFTA became linked with the EC as a single market in 1991.

37. *Europe Without Frontiers,* pp. 9–15; Paolo Cecchini, *The European Challenge 1992: The Benefits of a Single Market,* pp. 1–68, 97–98.

38. See, for example, the article by Carlo De Benedetti of Olivetti & Co. in *Wall Street Journal,* March 30, 1988.

39. An EU poll revealed a Europe-wide drop in support of European unity from 72 to 48 percent. William Drozdiak, "Unity Drive Is Faltering in Western Europe," *Washington Post,* July 4, 1997.

40. Edmund L. Andrews, "Stringent Rules on Euro Currency Cause Growing Turmoil," *NYT,* June 15, 1997, online at www.nytimes.com.

41. Whitney, "Western Europe's Dreams," *NYT,* August 8, 1993; Peter Gumbel, "Germany's Neighbors Are Bridling at Its Apparent Inward Turning," *Wall Street Journal,* August 3, 1993.

42. Nevertheless, other steps in the direction of a single monetary union are occurring, such as a joint London-Frankfurt stock exchange that was announced in mid-1998.

43. Wallace J. Thies, "The Atlantic Alliance, Nuclear Weapons and European Attitudes: Reexamining the Conventional Wisdom," p. 50; McNamara, pp. 68–69.

44. McNamara, pp. 70–71. One estimate is by Professor Henry Kendall of the physics department at the Massachusetts Institute of Technology. He calculated that a nuclear war in Europe in which one thousand one-megaton weapons were exploded would cause over 200 million fatalities directly and would contaminate several million square miles—not counting the Soviet Union. See "Nuclear War in Europe," *The Defense Monitor* 10, no. 7 (1981), p. 6.

45. *Los Angeles Times,* August 30, 1981.

46. Kissinger, quoted in McNamara, p. 59.

47. Robert English, "Eastern Europe's Doves," *Foreign Policy,* p. 44.

48. Renner, "Swords into Plowshares," pp. 40–58. The model conversion, or alternative-use, program was developed by workers at Lucas Aerospace, Britain's largest defense industry; Dave Elliott and Hilary Wainwright, "The Lucas Plan: The Roots of the Movement," in Gordon and McFadden, eds., pp. 89–107. Though rejected by Lucas management, the "Lucas Plan" was adapted elsewhere in varied ways, such as conversion of a military shipyard in Landskrona, Sweden. The idea was, and remains, to turn existing technology to civilian purposes and save jobs. Suzanne Gordon, "Economic Conversion Activity in Western Europe," in Gordon and McFadden, eds., pp. 108–29. As the experience of the former Czechoslovakia shows, potential earnings from arms sales abroad have tended to displace thoughts of reducing and converting military-industrial production. Milton Leitenberg, "Defense Industry Conversion: The Case of Czechoslovakia," in Brunn et al., pp. 312–14.

49. See *SIPRI Yearbook 1992,* pp. 477–95.

50. Michael Mandelbaum, "The Post–Cold War Settlement in Europe: A Triumph of Arms Control," *Arms Control Today.*

51. Jonathan Dean, *Ending Europe's Wars: The Continuing Search for Peace and Security,* pp. 306–19.

52. Carl Cavanagh Hodge, "Botching the Balkans: Germany's Recognition of Slovenia and Croatia," *Ethics & International Affairs.* Hodge notes that German support of human rights would probably not have prevented the ensuing bloodbath, "but such a policy would at least have engaged the debate" about liberal criteria applied to ethnic nationalism. Self-determination in Yugoslavia was the easy, and wrong, choice.

53. Dean, *Ending Europe's Wars,* pp. 368–74; Woodward, *Balkan Tragedy,* pp. 148–62.

54. Tony Judt ("Europe: The Grand Illusion," *New York Review of Books*) has written that the war in the Balkans shows that "the 'European' edifice is fundamentally hollow, selfishly obsessed with fiscal rectitude and commercial advantage. Just as there is no effective international community, so there is, for these purposes, no European one either."

55. Dean, *Ending Europe's Wars,* p. 369.

56. For a superb discussion, see Judt, *Postwar,* pp. 803–31.

57. See, for example, Alan Cowell, "Europe 'Is Rubbing Its Eyes' at the Ascent of the Right," *NYT*, May 18, 2002, p. A3; Elaine Sciolino, "French Youth at the Barricades, but a Revolution? It Can Wait," *NYT*, March 28, 2006, p. 1; Mark Landler, "Bank Deal Starts Debate on Polish Role in United Europe," *NYT*, March 27, 2006, p. A3.

58. For reporting on these issues, see as examples, Felicity Barringer, "U.S. Resolution on World Court Revives Hostility," *NYT*, June 11, 2003, p. A6; Elisabeth Rosenthal, "Biotech Food Tears Rift in Europe," *NYT*, June 6, 2006, p. C1; Dan Bilefsky, "Report Faults Europe in C.I.A. Detainee 'Web,'" *NYT*, June 8, 2006, online ed.; Lizette Alvarez, "Consumers in Europe Resist Gene-Altered Foods," *NYT*, February 11, 2003, p. A3. A poll by the German Marshall Fund found that 57 percent of Europeans consider US leadership "undesirable," not just because of Iraq but also because of distaste for the religious element in the Bush administration's approach to the world. "In the World of Good and Evil," *The Economist*, September 16, 2006, pp. 53–54.

59. The argument for universal membership has been made by Ivo Daalder and James Goldgeier, "Global NATO," *Foreign Affairs.*

60. Craig S. Smith, "Germany's Military Sinking to 'Basket Case' Status," *NYT*, March 18, 2003, p. A3.

61. Richard Bernstein, "Germany Hoping for Return of Strong American Bond," *NYT*, March 12, 2003, p. A13; Eric Alterman, "USA Oui! Bush Non!" *The Nation*; Stanley Hoffmann, "France, the United States & Iraq," *The Nation.*

62. Robert E. Hunter, "A Forward-Looking Partnership," *Foreign Affairs*, p. 15.

63. Quoted in *NYT*, June 1, 2000, p. 8.

64. See Sivard, *World Military and Social Expenditures 1991*, table 3, pp. 54–55.

65. From Soviet sources cited in Guo Simian, "'New Political Thinking' and the Soviet Union's Readjustment of Its Asian-Pacific Policy," *Comparative Strategy*, p. 139.

66. Frances Fukuyama, "Gorbachev and the Third World," *Foreign Affairs*, p. 718.

67. Brown, *Building a Sustainable Society*, pp. 94, 106–7; and Brown et al., *State of the World 1985*, p. 31.

68. This overview is based on John P. Hardt and Donna Gold, "Andropov's Economic Future," *Orbis.*

69. World Bank 1984, table 9, p. 235.

70. Sergei Gorbunov, "The Social Consequences of Economic Restructuring in the USSR," in Gurtov, ed., *Transformation of Socialism*, pp. 146–47.

71. Sivard, *World Military and Social Expenditures 1991*, table 3, pp. 54–55.

72. This section on the environment is based mainly on the research of Christina Burnside.

73. See Don Hinrichsen, "Russian Roulette," *Amicus Journal;* Jay M. Gould, "Chernobyl—The Hidden Tragedy," *The Nation.*

74. See Brown et al., *State of the World 1985*, pp. 51, 55 (on water), and p. 106 (on air pollution).

75. N. Zuyev, Novosti Press Agency, Moscow, in *Geographical*, vol. 62, no. 3 (March 1990), p. 14.

76. Michael Smith, "A Tale of Death and Destruction," *Geographical*, p. 13; Hammond, p. 171; Michael Wines, "Grand Soviet Scheme for Sharing Water in Central Asia Is Foundering," *NYT*, December 9, 2002, p. A14.

77. Ben Eklof, *Soviet Briefing: Gorbachev and the Reform Period*, pp. 133–34.

78. Daniel Singer, *The Road to Gdansk: Poland and the USSR,* pp. 78–80, 115–17.

79. Frank, p. 182.

80. Ibid., p. 318.

81. Ibid., pp. 6, 185–86, 188.

82. Timothy J. Colton, *The Dilemma of Reform in the Soviet Union,* p. 94.

83. The main features of Gorbachev's program are drawn from press reports and from Stephen F. Cohen's "Sovieticus" columns in *The Nation* (in particular the issue of May 31, 1986, p. 750); Robert C. Tucker, "Where Is the Soviet Union Headed?" *World Policy Journal;* Shireen T. Hunter, "Nationalist Movements in Soviet Asia," *Current History;* Karen M. Brooks, "Soviet Agriculture Under Perestroika," *Current History;* and *Transformation of Socialism,* chapters by Herbert Ellison, Rolf H.W. Theen, Guy Houk, Alexander Parkanskiy, Alexander Nagorniy, and Judith Thornton.

84. On Gorbachev's struggle with the CPSU, see Rolf H.W. Theen, "Party-State Relations Under Gorbachev: From Partocracy to 'Party' State?" in Gurtov, ed., *Transformation of Socialism,* ch. 4.

85. Renner, "Swords into Plowshares," pp. 30–36.

86. For a full account of these events, see Martha Brill Olcott, "The Soviet (Dis)union," *Foreign Policy,* pp. 118–36.

87. Janine R. Wedel, "The Harvard Boys Do Russia," *The Nation.* The article studies the Harvard Institute for International Development, which the Clinton administration chose as a principal administrator of over $300 million in economic aid to Russia. The main beneficiaries of the program appear to have been a few members of the Russian elite and their US colleagues.

88. An explosion of radioactive waste in April 1993 at the once-secret Tomsk-7, a military facility about 1,700 miles east of Moscow, underscored the ongoing problems of dangerous nuclear reactors. The cost of dismantling or modernizing such plants, perhaps $10 billion to $20 billion, is, however, prohibitive (*The Oregonian,* May 21, 1992). Huge quantities of radioactive waste have also been dumped into rivers, lakes, and oceans, such as the Sea of Japan. Nuclear submarine reactors, for example, were once dumped into the Kara Sea inside the Arctic Circle. See Nicholas Lenssen, "Confronting Nuclear Waste," in Brown, ed., *State of the World 1992,* p. 53; and William J. Broad, "Russia Acknowledges Ocean Dumping of Nuclear Waste," *The Oregonian,* April 27, 1992 (from the *New York Times*). On Siberian timberland, see Antony Scott and David Gordon, "The Russian Timber Rush," *Amicus Journal,* pp. 15–17, and John H. Cushman Jr., "Logging in Siberia Sets Off a Battle in the U.S.," *NYT,* January 30, 1996, p. A3.

89. *NYT,* November 9, 1994, p. A5. The Bank found that the discharges of sulfur dioxide exceed those in several EU countries *combined.*

90. On economic and social conditions, see Marshall I. Goldman, "Needed: A Russian Economic Revolution," *Current History,* pp. 314–20; and the collection of highly pessimistic essays by various Russian journalists in *Bulletin of the Atomic Scientists,* vol. 49, no. 1 (January–February 1993), pp. 12–46.

91. Michael Specter, "Citadel of Russia's Wasteful Health System," *NYT,* February 4, 1998, p. 1, reviewing a major hospital system for treatment of tuberculosis in Tomsk.

92. *NYT,* June 3, 1998, p. A10; Venyamin Sokolov, "The Virus in Russia," *NYT,* June 1, 1998, p. A19. Sokolov, a director of Russia's Chamber of Accounts, the oversight agency for public funds, wrote that 45 percent (not one-third) of the state budget was being used to service the debt.

93. Michael R. Gordon, "Yeltsin's New Outsider Team: Young, Reformist and Green," *NYT,* May 1, 1998, p. A12.

94. See Central Intelligence Agency, *Handbook of International Economic Statistics 1997,* table 125, online at www.eldar.org/~ben/scout/html/1083.html. For example, the IMF lent $10.2 billion for 1996 through 1998, and then around $17 billion more for 1998 through 1999.

95. See Grigory Yavlinsky, "Russia's Phony Capitalism," *Foreign Affairs.*

96. See Benjamin Lambeth, "Russia's Wounded Military," *Foreign Affairs.*

97. As the defense minister, General Pavel S. Grachev, said in 1994: "Not a single army in the world is in such a catastrophic state. I ask you [in parliament] to take this as a warning." *NYT,* November 19, 1994, p. 4.

98. Russia's policing effort is to some degree subject to international oversight and global norms. Its military forces are officially called peacekeeping forces, and it uses them officially at the behest of the UN.

99. See the article by the US deputy secretary of state, Strobe Talbott, "Russia Has Nothing to Fear," *NYT,* February 18, 1997, p. A15.

100. *NYT,* March 17, 1995, pp. A1, A5. The Russian view was that bordering countries might have more sophisticated forces and close-in bases (which would not be reduced), even with US assurances that an enlarged NATO would have fewer soldiers. See *NYT,* February 21 and 22, 1997, p. 1.

101. Quoted by Thomas L. Friedman, "Now a Word from X," *NYT,* May 2, 1998, p. A23.

102. At a summit meeting of the Conference on Security and Cooperation in Europe in December 1994, Yeltsin lashed out at the West, accusing the United States of wanting to dominate the world. *NYT,* December 6, 1994, p. A1.

103. "Eventually," this commentator wrote, "instead of having Russia as a long-term partner, the United States risks confronting not necessarily an enemy but a runaway train moving with growing speed in an unpredictable direction." Aleksei K. Pushkov, "The Risk of Losing Russia," *NYT,* January 21, 1997, p. A19.

104. *NYT,* March 8, 2001, online ed.

105. Dmitri Trenin, "Russia Leaves the West," *Foreign Affairs,* p. 87.

106. Peter Baker and Susan Glasser, *Kremlin Rising: Vladimir Putin's Russia and the End of Revolution,* pp. 219–21.

107. See, for example, Stephen F. Cohen, *Failed Crusade: America and the Tragedy of Post-Communist Russia,* pp. 6–9, 144–45; Steven Lee Myers, "As NATO Finally Arrives on Its Border, Russia Grumbles," *NYT,* April 3, 2004, p. A3; and Sergei Ivanov (Russia's defense minister), "As NATO Grows, So Do Russia's Worries," *NYT,* April 7, 2004, p. A21.

108. The rebuff of Putin signaled a "new cold war" to some observers: Ukraine seemed to be a test of Russia's ability to control events in its near-abroad. See Steven Erlanger, "Hungary's Premier Is Fearful of Turmoil in Ukraine," *NYT,* April 30, 2001, online ed.

109. Quoted by Steven Lee Myers and Andrew E. Kramer, "Group of 8 Talks, Like So Much These Days, Are All About Energy: Russia's Gas and Oil," *NYT,* July 13, 2006, p. A10.

110. Stephen F. Cohen, "The Struggle for Russia," *The Nation,* pp. 5–6.

111. See the essay by a former economic adviser to Putin, Andrei Illarionov, "Russia Inc.," *NYT,* February 4, 2006, online ed. An example is Yukos oil company, which was privatized in 1996; but then its assets were seized and sold off by court order, and its chairman was imprisoned, as the government took advantage of rising oil prices to bolster its budget. Now the number-one energy company is the state-run Gazprom, which has the world's largest oil reserves. (See Baker and Glasser, pp. 272–92.) On the political rewards, such as oligarchs running for office in the president's party, see Steven Lee Myers, "Big Business Plays Largest Role in Current Russian Vote," *NYT,* December 2, 2003, p. A3.

112. Dmitri Trenin, "Reading Russia Right," *Policy Brief* (Carnegie Endowment for International Peace); Anders Åslund, "Putin's Decline and America's Response," *Policy Brief.*

113. The best known of the journalists was the thirteenth—Anna Politkovskaya, who was a severe critic of Putin and of "state terror" in his prosecution of the war in Chechnya.

114. Baker and Glasser, pp. 237–60; Fred Weir, "Whistleblowers Face a Chill Wind in Putin's Russia," *Amnesty Now.*

115. Steven Lee Myers, "Observer Team in Russia Lists Election Flaws," *NYT,* March 16, 2004, p. A9.

116. One such observer is Stephen F. Cohen, "The New American Cold War," *The Nation.*

117. Cohen, *Failed Crusade,* pp. 149–51, 158; Andrew E. Kramer, "Russia Called Too Reliant on Petroleum," *NYT,* April 18, 2006, p. C10.

118. Steven Lee Myers, "Pervasive Corruption in Russia Is 'Just Called Business,'" *NYT,* August 13, 2005, p. A3.

119. *Human Development Report 2005,* p. 35.

120. Baker and Glasser, *Kremlin Rising,* pp. 180–84. Russia's military services have been hard hit by HIV/AIDS, leading the CIA to raise national-security concerns. See Lawrence K. Altman, "AIDS in 5 Nations Called Security Threat," *NYT,* October 1, 2002, p. A10.

121. Baker and Glasser, *Kremlin Rising,* pp. 187–96.

122. *NYT,* December 28, 2000, p. A1; C.J. Chivers, "Russians, Busy Making Shrouds, Are Asked to Make Babies," *NYT,* May 14, 2006, p. 4.

123. *Human Development Report 2005,* table 17, p. 278. On a per capita basis, Japanese ODA actually ranks higher than that of the United States.

124. See Kiyoshi Kojima, *Japan and a New World Economic Order,* pp. 120–24.

125. SIPRI statistics; see www.sipri.org/non_first/milex.php?/look_up_country =392.

126. Robert S. Ozaki, "Introduction: The Political Economy of Japan's Foreign Relations," in Robert S. Ozaki and Walter Arnold, eds., *Japan's Foreign Relations: A Global Search for Economic Security,* pp. 2–5; Kenneth B. Pyle, "In Pursuit of a Grand Design: Nakasone Betwixt the Past and the Future," in Pyle, ed., *The Trade Crisis: How Will Japan Respond?* pp. 7–9.

127. Kevin Sullivan, "Japan Questions Economic Equality," *Washington Post,* May 4, 1997.

128. Ezra F. Vogel, "Pax Nipponica?" *Foreign Affairs,* p. 753.

129. Ibid., p. 754. As one example, consider John Markoff, "Japanese Computer Is World's Fastest, as U.S. Falls Back," *NYT,* April 20, 2002, p. A1.

130. Donald C. Hellmann, "Japanese Politics and Foreign Policy: Elitist Democracy Within an American Greenhouse," in Takashi Inoguchi and Daniel I. Okimoto, eds., *The Political Economy of Japan: The Changing International Context,* pp. 345–78.

131. The examples are many, but consider the following editorial in the *Japan Times* (Tokyo) of November 22, 1996, concerning the revelation that the vice minister of health and welfare freely accepted gifts in return for political favors: "With corruption so rampant in the LDP and business circles, perhaps it was only a matter of time before the bureaucracy succumbed to the temptations of a money-mad society. . . . Civil servants were not likely to withstand forever the corrupting web spun so tirelessly by the politicians whom the public elected to the Diet. Even a reformed bureaucracy offers no permanent cure for a venal electorate and a corrupt Parliament."

132. *Human Development Report 1992,* p. 21.

133. "Japan: The Garbage Superpower—A Round-Table Discussion," *Japan Echo,* vol. 21, no. 1 (Spring 1994), pp. 86–92.

134. See Andrew Pollack, "Deregulation in Japan: Too Many Rules, but Not for All," *NYT,* November 16, 1996, online.

135. Charles K. Ebinger, "U.S.-Japanese Nuclear Energy Relations: Prospects for Cooperation/Conflict"; and Daniel K. Chapman, "USSR-Japan Energy Cooperation in Siberia: Implications for U.S.-Japanese Relations," both in Charles K. Ebinger and Ronald A. Morse, eds., *U.S.-Japanese Energy Relations: Cooperation and Competition,* pp. 147–62, 229–39.

136. Japan, on a per capita basis, produces 2.4 tons of carbon emissions, somewhat less than the average German's 2.9 tons and well below the average American's 5.3 tons. But Japan's carbon emissions grew nearly 11 percent in the 1990s, even though it had committed to reducing them by 6 percent under the Kyoto Protocol by 2008. Seth Dunn and Christopher Flavin, "Moving the Climate Change Agenda Forward," in Flavin et al., eds., *State of the World 2002,* p. 35.

137. The most serious accident occurred at a reactor in Mihama, north of Kyoto, when four workers were killed. Some Japanese communities have voted in referenda to bar nuclear power plants. See James Brooke, "Four Workers Killed in Nuclear Plant Accident in Japan," *NYT,* August 10, 2004, p. A3. See also Howard W. French, "Safety Problems at Japanese Reactors Begin to Erode Public's Faith in Nuclear Power," *NYT,* September 16, 2002, p. A10.

138. Frank Barnaby and Shaun Burnie, "Thinking the Unthinkable: Japanese Nuclear Power and Proliferation in East Asia," at www.nautilus.org/napsnet/sr/2005/0573Barnaby_Burnie.pdf.

139. Teruyasu Murakami, "The Remarkable Adaptation of Japan's Economy," in Yergin and Hillenbrand, pp. 142–43. Industry involvement in emissions reductions is noted in Christopher Flavin and Seth Dunn, "Responding to the Threat of Climate Change," in Brown et al., eds., *State of the World 1998,* p. 123.

140. Richard J. Samuels, "The Politics of Alternative Energy Research and Development in Japan," in Morse, pp. 134–62.

141. Joji Watanuki, "Japanese Society and the Limits of Growth," in Yergin and Hillenbrand, pp. 173, 178–82; Howard W. French, "Accident Makes Japan Reexamine A-Plants," *NYT,* January 13, 2000, online ed.

142. Ronald A. Morse, ed., *The Politics of Japan's Energy Strategy: Resources-Diplomacy-Security.*

143. The US market took in $134 billion in Japanese goods in 2005. Total trade with the United States was nearly $200 billion. Statistics from the Japan External Trade Organization (JETRO) at www.jetro.go.jp/jpn/stats/data/pdf/trade2005.pdf.

144. Robert S. Ozaki, *The Control of Imports and Foreign Capital in Japan,* chs. 4–5.

145. OECD, *Trends and Recent Developments in Foreign Direct Investment,* table 2, p. 4.

146. Doremus et al., *The Myth of the Global Corporation,* p. 77.

147. The following discussion is based mainly on Christopher Howe, "China, Japan and Economic Interdependence in the Asia Pacific Region," *The China Quarterly,* pp. 662–93.

148. Martin Fackler, "Japan Makes More Cars Elsewhere," *NYT,* August 1, 2006, p. C1.

149. Terutomo Ozawa, *Multinationalism, Japanese Style: The Political Economy of Outward Dependency,* ch. 7; David Arase, *Buying Power: The Political Economy of Japan's Foreign Aid,* ch. 6.

150. See *Nikkei Weekly* (Tokyo), May 16, 1992, p. 27. A fine overall analysis of Japan's foreign-aid program is by Robert M. Orr Jr., *The Emergence of Japan's Foreign Aid Power.*

151. In 1988–1989, only 2.7 percent of total Japanese ODA went for human priorities such as basic education and safe drinking water. By comparison, the US figure was 8.3 percent and Britain's was 8.8 percent. *Human Development Report 1992*, table 3.14, p. 43.

152. Examples are the Tiananmen crackdown in China, repression in Burma, a bloodless coup in Thailand, and the suspension of democracy in Peru under President Alberto Fujimori. See Robert M. Orr Jr., "Japan Winks at Peru's Coup," *Nikkei Weekly*, April 25, 1992, p. 7.

153. Richard A. Forrest, "Japanese Aid and the Environment," *The Ecologist*, pp. 24–32; Karl Schoenberger, "Wood-Revering Japan Accused of Pillaging Forests," *The Oregonian*, December 24, 1989.

154. Islam, p. 172; Vogel, "Pax Nipponica?" p. 759.

155. Islam, p. 174.

156. See Kishore Mahbubani, "Japan Adrift," *Foreign Policy*, pp. 126–44; Chalmers Johnson and E.B. Keehn, "The Pentagon's Ossified Strategy," *Foreign Affairs.*

157. Takashi Inoguchi, "Four Japanese Scenarios for the Future," *International Affairs*, pp. 16–18.

158. Kei Wakaizumi, "Japan's Dilemma: To Act or Not to Act," *Foreign Policy.*

159. Yoichi Funabashi, *Asia Pacific Fusion: Japan's Role in APEC.*

160. Kenneth B. Pyle, "Japan and the Future of Collective Security," in Danny Unger and Paul Blackburn, eds., *Japan's Emerging Global Role*, pp. 102–5. Pyle's contention is that Japanese leaders since Yoshida have been devious and manipulative in interpreting Article 9 of the constitution, using it to avoid contributing to Japan's defense and to international security even though they knew full well that, legally, Japan could at any time have cited UN membership as grounds for directly contributing to collective-security efforts.

161. Funabashi, "Japan and the New World Order," *Foreign Affairs.*

162. Yoichi Funabashi, *Asia Pacific Fusion: Japan's Role in APEC.*

163. Recent examples are sweetening negotiations with Russia on NATO expansion by inviting its attendance at the "Summit of the Eight" major economies in June 1997; refusing to accept any countries other than the Czech Republic, Poland, and Hungary into NATO; deciding to pay only $819 million of the United States' total debt to the UN of $1.2 billion, and attaching conditions to the repayment; refusing to commit to specific guidelines on greenhouse gases to reduce global warming; and rejecting an international ban, already joined by seventy-three countries, on the production, stockpiling, use, and export of land mines. See Steven Erlanger, "Yeltsin Basks at Summit; Some Europeans Are Cool to U.S.," *NYT*, June 21, 1997, p. 5.

164. Under the guidelines, the SDF would provide logistical backup for US forces in the event of regional "instability" in "areas surrounding Japan," which are generally presumed to mean the Korean peninsula or in the Taiwan Strait.

165. One criticism was over Japan's willingness to spend money but not lives in support of its overseas interests, unlike Germany, which has put soldiers and pilots in harm's way in peacekeeping operations. In fact, during 1995 the government decided to cut the SDF (to 145,000), the same day a newspaper reported that it had rejected as unconstitutional a US request during the previous year's tensions with North Korea for minesweepers and a squadron of antisubmarine aircraft in sup-

port of US naval operations. Nicholas D. Kristof, "Japan to Cut Own Military, Keeping G.I.'s," *NYT*, November 29, 1995, p. A5.

166. Anthony Faiola, "Japan's Draft Charter Redefines Military," *Washington Post*, December 3, 2005.

167. The main reason for the yearly reductions is swelling government debt. See James Brooke, "Japan to Cut Contribution to the Budget of the U.N.," *NYT*, January 22, 2003, p. A5.

168. *International Herald Tribune*, April 4, 2006.

169. David Arase, "Japan's ODA Policy Toward China," in Lam Peng Er, ed., *Japan's Relations with China: Facing a Rising Power,* p. 92. ODA to China will end, however, in 2008.

170. See Mindy L. Kotler, Naotaka Sugawara, and and Tetsuya Yamada, "Chinese and Japanese Public Opinion: Searching for Moral Security," *Asian Perspective.*

171. For background, see Hisane Masaki, "Where Is Japan Heading?" November 2005, at www://japanfocus.org/products/details/1586.

172. For example, see Norimitsu Onishi, "Japan's Likely Next Premier in Hawkish Stand," *NYT*, September 2, 2006, p. A5.

173. Wu Xinbo, "The End of the Silver Lining: A Chinese View of the U.S.-Japanese Alliance," *Washington Quarterly.*

174. For good ideas on how to reduce tensions in Sino-Japanese relations, including a more balanced role for the United States, see Minxin Pei and Michael Swaine, "Simmering Fire in Asia: Averting Sino-Japanese Strategic Conflict," *Policy Brief.*

175. See Ellen L. Frost, *For Richer, for Poorer: The New U.S.-Japan Relationship*, pp. 149–51; Masahide Shibusawa et al., *Pacific Asia in the 1990s,* especially ch. 7; Yoichi Funabashi, "Japan and the New World Order"; and Robert A. Scalapino, "The United States and Asia: Future Prospects," *Foreign Affairs,* p. 32.

176. In 2003, ODA accounted for 1.2 percent of the budget, compared with 5.7 percent for military spending. See *Human Development Report 2005*, table 3.1, p. 94.

177. *International Herald Tribune,* June 3, 1992, p. 2.

178. Jim Jubak and Marie D'Amico, "Mighty MITI," *Amicus Journal,* pp. 38–43.

179. Celia W. Dugger, "U.N. Report Cites U.S. and Japan as the 'Least Generous Donors,'" *NYT*, September 8, 2005, p. 8.

180. Other actions include the slave-labor conditions in many parts of Southeast Asia occupied by Japanese forces; and, most gruesome of all, the experimentation by doctors of army unit 731 on living persons in Northeast China. By now there are a number of scholarly sources for all these atrocities; but for a brief insight, see Nicholas D. Kristof, "Japan Confronting Gruesome War Atrocity," *NYT,* March 17, 1995, p. A1. Far from being apologetic, some senior Japanese officials have tried in recent years to justify past crimes by arguing that they took place during wartime; or, that the US atomic bombings and firebombing of Tokyo were just as horrendous as the Japanese atrocities (or even, as the mayor of Nagasaki put it, as awful as the Holocaust); or, as a former foreign minister said with reference to Japan's occupation of Korea, that it was invited by the Koreans! Even the offer to compensate victims has been tainted, as when the Hashimoto government proposed establishing a fund for the comfort women, but using private rather than official money.

181. To illustrate the difficulty of apologizing, during 1995, the year marking the fiftieth anniversary of the Pacific war, in a long-running drama in parliament, a resolution of "regret" (*hansei,* more precisely rendered, perhaps, as "introspection"

than "remorse") was finally forged in the lower house. Much stronger expressions of contrition and condemnation were proposed—an outright "apology" and recognition of Japan's "acts of aggression" and "colonialism"—but rightist politicians resisted. In the end the adopted resolution (which the upper house rejected) put Japan's official feelings in the wider context of (Western) imperialism: "Recalling many acts of aggression and colonial rule in modern world history, we recognize and express deep remorse for these kinds of actions carried out by our country in the past. They brought unbearable pain to people abroad, particularly in Asian countries." *NYT,* June 7, 1995, p. 1.

182. The editorials were backed by a year-long study, published in Japanese and English. The latter edition is by James E. Auer, ed., *From Marco Polo Bridge to Pearl Harbor: Who Was Responsible?*

# 7

# In the Human Interest: An Agenda for Transforming World Politics

Hate evil and love what is good; let justice well up as waters and right-eousness as a mighty stream.

—Torah

The only thing we have to fear is fear itself.

—Franklin D. Roosevelt

The ability to reach unity in diversity will be the beauty and the test of our civilization.

—Gandhi

Harold: You sure know how to get along with people.
Maude: They're my species.

—from the film *Harold and Maude*

## Lessons for the Future

In this chapter I search for a new realism that can address the multifaceted global crisis in positive ways—politically pluralistic, economically just, and ecologically sensitive. What, in a nutshell, have we learned thus far? We can begin by offering three general lessons. One stems from the enormity of the problems we have covered, their interconnectedness, and their transnational character. These problems can probably only be ameliorated by international cooperation, and only resolved by global system change. At the same time, as the many examples of individual ingenuity and selfless service cited below attest, personal commitment counts just as much. Unless the overarching crisis of unfulfilled human needs is transformed—and soon—we can expect more violent upheavals and environmental catastrophes, and therefore more fragile and failing states. If only as a matter of national self-interest, as many high-level reports have been saying for decades, state leaders must embrace the notion of global responsibility.[1]

Second, world politics in the new century seems to be characterized by powerful forces that have both decentralizing and centrifugal effects. Nationalism and identity politics seem to be the main reasons for decentralization, as seen for example in the demands for autonomy and statehood of nationalities and other minority groups within nation-states, in the declining importance of military alliances, and in the economic challenges of China, Japan, and Germany to historical US hegemony. At the same time, all national economies now must be responsive to a single set of rules and institutions governing global economic behavior. The trading state, as Richard Rosecrance has called it, is replacing the traditional territorial state.[2] So long as that trend continues, the prospects for peace improve. Take Germany, Japan, and China as examples: Their dependence for continued prosperity and social stability on global and regional trade, financial, and political networks and institutions greatly inhibits a return to militarism and expansionism. Much more likely is that they and other economically strong states will pursue new technological heights, seek new markets, and protect their resource base, all with an eye on ensuring domestic stability. As they do so, greater opportunities may emerge for the spread of knowledge and resources to Third and Fourth World countries.

Our third lesson is that the process for achieving "idealistic" objectives—peace, environmental protection, satisfaction of basic needs, democratization—should be both humane and grounded in political reality. Neither the theoretical argument for global humanism, nor appeals to conscience, nor programs to achieve a humane world order can ignore the interests that realist and corporate globalist leaders bring to the table. The global crisis has the best chance to end when consciousness of the human condition, the political will of national leaders, openness to increased trust, and new global structures cohere around concrete political-economic programs that benefit people, governments, and corporations. Put another way, the overriding challenge to global-humanist thinking is how to respond to the legitimate security and market concerns of states and TNCs while meeting human needs, eliminating weapons of mass destruction, and protecting planetary environmental resources. The challenge may seem insurmountable, but as threats to national security and corporate profits become primarily nonmilitary and transnational, or simply prove unmanageable, state and corporate leaders may feel compelled to invest more in cooperative, human-centered responses. And if they do not, they will face growing pressures from NGOs and popular movements.

There are many examples of global-friendly actions that have come about on the initiative of governments and corporations or by cooperation among them and concerned individuals. Some companies, such as BP, have found that the bottom line looks even better when they implement sound environmental practices.[3] Others practice fair trade (for example, Starbucks), develop fuel-cell–powered automobiles (Honda, Toyota, and others), invest in wind power (Shell), or donate drugs to fight river blindness (Merck) and trachoma (Pfizer) in poor countries. Government initiatives include the many US cities that have built light-rail systems (such as Salt Lake City, Utah, and Portland, Oregon), promoted solar and wind energy (Austin, Texas), and broadened recycling (Minneapolis, Minnesota); California's Global Warming Solutions Act that will cut emissions by 25 percent by 2020; British Columbia, Canada, which in collaboration with native peoples, timber companies, and environmental groups decided (after ten years of talks) to protect the black bears and 5 million acres of forestland; and East Timor, whose parliament established a petroleum fund to manage revenues so as to ensure that its health and education needs would be met.

These general lessons are backed by several more specific ones that ought to be incorporated into a human-interest agenda:

• *A new world politics begins at home.* The domestic enhancement of personal and collective well-being, improving human rights in the fullest sense, strengthens a leadership's ability and willingness to deal positively, and globally, with the great crises of our time. As Franklin D. Roosevelt once said, "America's own rightful place in the world depends in large part upon how fully [basic human] rights have been carried out in practice for our citizens. For unless there is security here at home there cannot be lasting peace in the world."[4] The more a national leadership is able to create real security at home, the less is it likely to seek security through expansion abroad.[5] That is why the success of political and economic reform in Russia and China is important to the world and not only to their own citizens.

• Mere increases in the means of global welfare (aid, food, refugee relief) not only are very unlikely to solve problems of inequity but are more likely to reinforce their structural foundations. Preventive approaches are preferable to constantly treating symptoms. Among them, increased self-reliance, in the First and Second Worlds as much as in the Third and Fourth Worlds, may be the single most important. Gandhi's maxim that "there is enough for every man's need, but not enough for every man's greed" provides a sensible guideline.

• *Specific human-interest policies will need to reflect a diversity of ideas and priorities.* No single formula or blueprint can adequately speak to the complexity of the human condition, no matter how humane its intent. Both public and private mechanisms and incentives will need to be considered in all societies. A strong role for government in social welfare, for example, may be essential to human development, as UNDP rankings of countries suggest.[6] But for human development to be humane, environmental protection (of nature itself) and resource conservation need to be valued as public goods in their own right. Economic growth and trade need to meet, and promote, environmental standards as much as they should create jobs and lead to a higher quality of life.

• Because state and corporate leaderships are likely to withhold support of human-interest policies for as long as possible, the most decisive force for humane change will probably continue to be popular, broadly based national and transnational movements. Although humane change is constantly being brought about by individuals, communities, and other elements of civil society, we seem to find NGOs providing the core of leadership when citizens press governments and corporations to do the right thing. Still, it will be the cumulative impact of all these efforts, not one of them alone, that will determine the course of world political change.

• Converting military-industrial complexes to research and production that meet human needs is essential to stopping the arms race. Among the many groups whose support is necessary for a conversion program to work are those persons whose jobs would be directly affected by the elimination of weapons contracts.

• Modest, workable programs that produce clearly beneficial results are preferable to grandiose schemes backed only by high ideals. Nor should the power of positive example be understated. Human-interest policies must widely be seen to serve everybody's interests rather than the interests of one segment of society, however numerous its members may be.

• The various elements of the global crisis are primarily the result of interlinked national and transnational political-economic forces; they are not mainly caused by haphazard occurrences in nature, "backward" cultural traditions, the wrath of God, or some singularly nefarious political doctrine. Awareness of the political roots of the crisis is grounds for both pessimism and optimism: pessimism about the historically powerful interests that must be confronted if the global crisis is to be resolved; optimism that what has been made to happen can also be made to transform.

### Thinking Globally

In this section I put the above lessons to use in outlining a human-interest policy agenda. I want to take note of the many positive achievements in creating human security that have occurred, and are being created now, worldwide.

### Toward Humane Economic and Social Development

Humane development embraces values such as equity, self-reliance, empowerment, dignity, love of nature, enoughness, and community; and norms such as decentralization, self-determination, and basic needs. To discuss development in these life-affirming terms is to cut to the heart of the question of inequitable distribution and wasteful use of resources, some of which (for example, oil)[7] are predicted to run out in less than fifty years at present rates of consumption. It is also to address directly issues of power, including globalization's overwhelming of indigenous cultures and the failure of male-dominated institutions to invest in women's futures. If development can be redefined to take account of both real and planned scarcities and of its human and environmental impacts around the planet, it may reward societies politically and economically. Humane development may be regarded as low-cost, preventive medicine for terrorism, ethnic conflict, and drug production—and as a preferable alternative to counterterrorism, repression, and limitless growth.

Implementing a humane definition of development raises a confounding question: Is "sustainability" enough to avert environmental catastrophe and ameliorate global poverty? Current and projected levels of production and consumption in the North are so high, some environmental systems (e.g., tropical forests and fisheries) are so seriously threatened, and the gaps between rich and poor are so wide that a sustainable, conservationist approach to development may already be inadequate, even disastrous.[8] The World Bank's prognosis in 1992 is cause for alarm. After noting impressive projections of output by all countries, the Bank stated:

> If environmental pollution and degradation were to rise in step with such a rise in output, the result would be appalling environmental pollution and damage. Tens of millions more people would become sick or die each year from environmental causes. Water shortages would be intolerable, and tropical forests and other natural habitats would decline to a fraction of their current size.[9]

What the Bank does not quite say is that greatly increased production will presumably be needed to match increased consumption, a notion that has distorted "sustainable development" ever since the term was first introduced in the 1987 Brundtland Commission report, *Our Common Future.* If, according to that report, sustainable development is nothing more than "meeting the needs" of present and future generations, the world's poor have no hope at all. The North's "needs" to consume will, as before, quite simply devour the South—not just its economies but also its cultures and value systems.[10] The Bank's optimism that the market and economic growth can produce a sustainable future is contradicted by its own projections of "appalling" consequences if the world continues to follow the development-as-growth paradigm. That kind of development is not sustainable; it poses immediate dangers to natural systems and basic human rights.

We are therefore compelled to search for policies that will provide sufficiency in development, "enough in order to be more, to be fully human."[11] A starting point might be to create a true global partnership for development. Policies might include, in the South, vastly increased aid for grassroots development and, in the North, measures to stop profligate consumption, if need be by taxing overuse of resources in order to fund global public goods such as peace projects and forest reserves.[12] The partnership would also seek ways to gain acceptance, even in the poorest countries, of the importance of avoiding malevolent patterns of energy use and growth, not only because of the real prospect of a global environmental collapse but also because protection of nature is in their own interest.

The highest priority of humane development is fulfillment of the right to food. Once that right is accepted as a global priority—and it has taken the African famines of the 1970s and 1980s to push world hunger to the top of the global agenda—it opens the door to debate about the political-economic forces behind hunger: unequal landownership, dependence-creating international aid programs, and oppressive national and transnational authorities. The previous discussion has addressed these questions in the context of global underdevelopment and environmental destruction. We can now turn to some policy implications of these findings.

Setting the conditions for food self-reliance may be the single most important human objective in world politics today. Giving people their own land offers hope of dramatic improvements in public health; of ending control of food for profit and political extortion; of new opportunities for small farmers, farming communities, and women; of the restoration of ecologically sound, energy-conserving farm practices (such as minimization of soil erosion and labor-intensive irrigation and plowing); of curtailment of the export of protein and overuse of cropland for export purposes, and, instead, use of local resources for local needs; and of the establishment of a better rural-urban balance in the resources provided by governments. Food self-reliance is therefore a multidimensional "human face" development strategy that has broad implications for a country's domestic and international politics.[13] To the extent the strategy is successful, it will help reverse the pattern of high population growth, unemployment, and migrations to cities and across borders that typically accompanies hunger; it will impede the power of authoritarian governments, landed oligarchies, and transnational corporations; and it will reduce reliance on the international trading system that, as we have seen, subsidizes growers in the richest countries at the expense of Third World farmers who seek markets abroad.

Embedded in the issue of hunger and land is opportunity. Many development experts, including those in the World Bank, now seem convinced that the single best investment that societies can make to promote food production and reduce population pressure on the land is in the education of women. Even if looked at in purely dollars-and-cents terms, it is a remarkably cheap investment.[14] Improving the status of women is a critical adjunct to education. In southern India, Bangladesh, and Kenya, projects to increase food production and bring down the fertility rate converged in the conclusion that the status of women—their leadership in family planning—was the key to realizing both objectives.[15] (Equally important is what these studies did *not* prove, namely, that development alone—increasing food production through the Green Revolution in India's case, raising incomes in Bangladesh's—will stabilize populations and reduce hunger, or that poverty and religion are insuperable barriers to women's social activism.) Lending seed money to poor people, women most of all, so that they may start up small businesses has also been a highly successful idea. They repay the loan as their projects (the purchase of a cow, for instance, or a small shop) make a profit. The idea originated in Bangladesh with the Grameen Bank, which began as a private NGO founded by Muhammad Yunus (winner of the 2006 Nobel Peace Prize) and has grown into a widely dispersed lender to several million villagers. The bank has achieved a near-perfect record of loan repayments and has demonstrated that rural people know how to use credit to create income and increase their self-respect and living standards in the process.[16] The Grameen experience has spawned a multibillion-dollar global industry, variously called microcredit or microfinance, that is being carried on by other NGOs with the support of governments, foundations, the UN, and corporations.[17]

Clearly, the key factor in moving to a food self-reliance strategy is the attitude of elites, their perception that, as a matter of self-interest and/or nationalism, ending hunger and malnutrition is vital to national security. Successful programs led by government agencies and by local and international NGOs can influence that perception. Home food production, such as Jamaica carried out in its "Grow Our Own Food" campaign, can sharply reduce malnutrition.[18] In Zimbabwe, as another example, farmers who have been given credit as well as a supply of high-yield seeds, fertilizer, and agricultural advisers have achieved dramatic production gains.[19] Shifting from large-scale governmental aid-giving to people-to-people programs that teach food self-reliance is yet another approach; among the NGOs that stress self-reliant development are Oxfam International, Grassroots International, the Plenty Project, Mercy Corps, and Church World Service.[20]

There has in fact been a veritable explosion of international development NGOs—Northern, Southern, and transnational. Altogether, their programs reach tens of millions of Third World peoples. Noteworthy about the NGO phenomenon is that "in terms of *net transfers* [of aid money] . . . NGOs collectively contribute more than the World Bank."[21] NGOs are not only seeking to protect people and the planet from the predations of states and corporations; they are also sources of new ideas and new ways of implementing them. A few examples may suffice. One concerns fair trade: The Fair Trade Federation and TransFair are groups active in the United States and Canada in promoting fair-trade practices through sales of Third World handicrafts and farm products direct from their producers. In 2004 these and other groups channeled nearly $400 million in sales to North American and Pacific Rim consumers.[22] Many NGOs have abandoned the confrontational approaches of the past in favor of working cooperatively, as in the cases cited earlier of the British Columbia set-aside of forestland and the California global warming initiative (both involved the Natural Resources Defense Council). The Rainforest Alliance, as another example, works with forest product companies in the United States and abroad to certify timber that is harvested using sustainable forestry practices. It also certifies sustainable cocoa in Latin America that is used by the giant Kraft multinational in its chocolate.[23] Some international NGOs focus on training, such as the Grupo de Agricultura Organica in Cuba (organic farming), the US-based Environmental Defense (water conservancy in China), and Mercy Corps (fisheries and farming in North Korea). The Nature Conservancy protects environmentally and ecologically valuable properties worldwide by purchasing them to convert into reserves. It also works with governments to design conservation plans.[24]

At the international level, administering world emergency food surpluses—and devising a method for compulsory food contributions by those nations and corporations that consume and transport most of the food—is another possible step. For example, a French doctor developed a ready-to-eat, candy-sized paste, called Plumpy'nut, that is high in nutrition and is being distributed by Doctors Without Borders in Niger to severely malnourished children. The results are unbelievably successful.[25] Why not *require* that the multinational food corporations provide Plumpy'nut to *all* hungry Third World children? Tax regulations governing TNCs could be changed to reward those corporations that invest in labor-intensive, energy-saving technology, promote women's and peasants' farm cooperatives, and offer opportunities for transferring patent and production rights to local ownership. Foreign economic aid could be conditioned on its use only for purposes that promote self-help in food production. Both international organizations and private nonprofit groups could disseminate the fruits of scientific research in plant pathology, energy conservation, and possibly (with safeguards) biotechnology.[26] The benefits would belong to countries and regions with the poorest resources for food production, while the discoveries would not be monopolized for profit by TNCs, as has been the case with Green Revolution seed varieties. Finally, technology sharing is important. A US computer researcher has developed a laptop computer specifically geared to Third World users that will cost a little more than $100.[27] The internationalization of satellite technology, which has thus far been resisted by the major powers that lead in its development, could enable the poorest countries to gain access to information on weather and crop prospects for their own use.

No less important than food (and other kinds of) self-reliance in the Third World is greater self-reliance in the richest countries. One reason was given by the British economist E. F. Schumacher: "We must live simply that others may simply live."[28] As one application of that idea, consider the popularity of calling upon Third World countries to reduce population growth while encouraging industrialized countries to increase population. The German state of Brandenburg, in fact, offered a reward of $650 for every new child. The Germans, suggested one writer, would do better to give that sum to Third World families, for "the average German uses roughly 35 times more resources and produces roughly 30 times as much waste as the average third-worlder."[29] If high-consumption countries would practice self-control, perhaps people in the South would be less suspicious of their motives when they talk about simpler living.

Specific changes in the richest countries might include stable commodity prices, increased loans, and land tax advantages that give preference to the careful family farmer rather than absentee landowners and the largest commercial farms; increased domestic production of food (such as many fruits and vegetables, fish, and beef) that is increasingly imported; reevaluation of the trend toward feeding animals food fit for human consumption; tax and other benefits to conserve soil and water and to prevent soil erosion, overuse of pesticides and fertilizer, and conversion of prime farmland to nonagricultural purposes; and increasing research support for and public interest in organic farming methods, grow-your-own-food programs, and new food-growing techniques (such as hydroponics, French intensive, and rooftop fisheries).[30] Finally, personal dietary changes in the food-rich countries away from excessive meat consumption for protein can also be important. Aside from the widely acknowledged health benefits, dietary changes on a large scale could reduce the use of land in the underdeveloped countries for the grazing of beef cattle. Cattle-raising is so resource-intensive that is has become unsustainable.[31]

Food self-reliance is also the principal element of health self-reliance. Mass preventive health-care programs, in which China and Cuba pioneered, mobilize an entire society to ensure effective outreach. Prevention and social mobilization are now being emphasized by WHO and UNICEF with dramatic results, especially among children and in war zones.[32] Even in the poorest African societies (Tanzania, Gambia, and Burkina Faso), early immunization and breast-feeding campaigns have been successfully implemented.[33] In Haiti an NGO affiliated with the Harvard Medical School provides a model program of care for people with HIV infections.[34] The Cambodian government has contracted with international NGOs to run entire public-health districts, thereby not only serving more people but also attracting its own doctors and nurses to return.[35] People-to-people medical care programs such as Rainforest Health Project, founded by a nurse in a small Minnesota community following a trip to the Amazon region, deliver basic care but also work with local shamans to promote and protect traditional healing practices.[36] As noted earlier, TNCs, although often a conduit of health hazards, such as tobacco and pesticides, sometimes play a positive role through donation of medicines. In the Andes mountain villages of southern Argentina and in Ceará state in Brazil's northeast, other successful preventive health programs are being carried out where medical attention had previously been unknown. These programs include low-cost treatment, a pyramidal structuring of facilities, local paramedical as well as professional providers, and an emphasis on basic health needs. WHO is already calling the Andes program a model for the Third World, and the Ceará program has cut the infant mortality rate by one-third in three years.[37]

Improving global wellness has prompted some billionaires to open their pocketbooks when government will not, perhaps inspired by Ted Turner's 1997 donation of $1 billion to the United Nations. The Bill & Melinda Gates Foundation has made huge donations to public-health causes.[38] Former US president Bill Clinton's Global Initiative and other fundraising endeavors have helped combat AIDS and promote public health in Third World countries, as well as alleviate poverty.[39]

Food and energy are intimately linked, as we have seen. The path of food self-reliance leads also to increased self-reliance in energy, along a "soft-energy path" popularized by Amory Lovins.[40] Soft-energy sources (solar, geothermal, hydro, biogas, and wind energy) have major advantages over the "hard" path of fossil fuels (petroleum, natural gas, and coal) and over nuclear energy. These soft sources are decentralized (many solar reflectors, for example, rather than a single giant utility), renewable and recyclable, job-producing, cost-effective, low- or nonpolluting, free of major health and safety problems, and far less of a drain on government treasuries and people's incomes because they do not require heavy subsidization. As with food self-reliance, the soft-energy path holds the promise—already fulfilled in many places[41]—of conserving precious global and local resources, strengthening community control, lowering user and government costs, and increasing productivity.

In the Third World, where the increased cost of oil and petroleum products (notably fertilizer) has been far more burdensome than elsewhere, a shift to soft-energy sources would clearly bring major benefits. Dung could again be used solely as a fertilizer, rather than also as a fuel. The enormous increase in tree-cutting for firewood, leading to deforestation and desertification in Africa and other places, could be reversed. In the search for alternatives, fuel-saving stoves have been introduced to farmers in Kenya.[42] Brazil has taken the lead in using sugar cane to produce ethanol as a replacement for imported oil. China and India, rich in coal but badly damaged by its emissions, could benefit from gasification, a process that produces electricity from coal, but by capturing the carbon dioxide and injecting it deep underground.[43] TNC investments in and transfers to the Third World of energy-saving technology and techniques, which their home governments' tax and trade policies could influence, would strengthen the attractiveness there of soft-energy strategies. Photovoltaic solar cells, for example, will eventually become economical enough to electrify every Third World village, while other forms of solar energy can provide for cooking and heating water.[44] These steps would likewise reduce resort to the nuclear option, with its high price tag in dollars and, potentially, in lives.[45]

In the end an investment in food and energy self-reliance is an investment in national solvency: Fewer loans and less money spent on imported food and fuel means more money available for reinvestment and repayment of debts. China set an example of this approach when it adopted a self-reliant development strategy in 1958. Seven years later, it had repaid its debts to the Soviet Union. To be sure, few Third World countries have China's resources to carry out such a strategy. But many are in a position to experiment with selective delinking from an international political economy dominated by Northern interests. This approach calls for increased South-South exchanges, to the extent possible, in trade, transnational investments, technology and skills transfers, and even aid.[46]

Delinking might also include alternatives to the repayment of debts, which have become a focal point of people's anger as human misery rises along with interest payments. During the 1980s, Bolivia and Ecuador put a moratorium on repayment. New governments in Peru and Argentina decided to limit repayment of external debts to a percentage of annual export earnings (in those cases, 10 and 30 percent, respectively). Brazil suspended payment of interest for a brief time. These actions forced several major international banks to increase their reserves to cover potential losses. In the end, however, only debt forgiveness seems realistic, whether by linking it to globally desirable actions by the debtor country (such as preserving its tropical forests[47]) or, as the British government succeeded in doing, by outright eliminating debts owed by the poorest eighteen (mainly African) countries.

Given the powerful pull of a globally interdependent economy, however, even a widely practiced selective delinking strategy is unlikely to improve conditions in the Third World as much as self-reliant trends in the richest countries. We may see this as we look at energy issues again. There is encouraging news of momentum in a self-reliant (and decentralized) direction in the North. By now roughly 20 percent of the world's energy comes from renewable sources. Investment in renewables has soared since the mid-1990s, starting with wind and solar power.[48] But we are reminded that many energy alternatives are themselves dependent on increasing energy production, not to mention high cost.[49] Corn production to produce ethanol, hydrogen, biomass, and gasification are among these problematic choices. Nuclear power, though important to some major economies (for example, France, where it accounts for about 65 percent of total electricity, and Japan, about 30 percent), is accident-prone, expensive, vulnerable to attack, theft, and diversion to weapons production—though with the high price of oil, nuclear power's popularity is rising in Europe and Asia.[50] In short, the search for the equivalent of a magic pill that will enable everyone to keep living the wasteful, materialistic, high-tech, resource-intensive lifestyles of the richest countries is illusory.

Conservation therefore must be uppermost in energy self-reliance. It has gained momentum in numerous countries: for example, the recycling of aluminum and steel in Japan and Norway; the building of more efficient automobiles, household appliances (the refrigerator in particular), and heat-conserving homes and offices in Japan and Western Europe; the reduction of energy use in making steel, as in Italy and Spain; and the new investments in many countries in solar and wind power, which do not require other energy sources to operate. As one authoritative study of the US energy picture has concluded, the objective of obtaining 25 percent of energy from renewable sources by 2025 has extensive support across the economic spectrum. And the savings from efficiency improvements are huge.[51]

Conservation, moreover, produces jobs while saving money for consumers and cutting down on bills for imported oil. These jobs will come from the new skills that will be in demand in resource management; from research, production, and construction of soft-energy facilities and equipment; and from increased consumer spending with money saved on energy bills. As one example, in the Ruhr region of Germany, employment patterns are changing as steel and coal, once the cornerstones of the economy, become uncompetitive. Today, businesses, local governments, unions, and universities are combining talents to produce industrial environmental equipment (such as for water recycling) that is energy saving.[52] Similar stories are being heard from neighborhoods and communities throughout the United States, Canada, and Europe—for example, in programs to weatherize homes, convert from oil to solar heating, co-generate heat and steam for industry, and reduce energy costs in hospitals and businesses through simple conservation techniques.[53] In the process, these programs are also demonstrating a global-humanist alternative to supply- and demand-side economics: end-use analysis, an approach to developmental issues that asks what the objective is before assuming that more is better.[54]

The third part of a program for humane development is environmental protection. Export of the North's development model has created an environmental crisis of massive proportions. Solving it is equally monumental and, as global warming illustrates, urgent. A report for the British government in 2006 cited the "risks of major disruption to economic and social activity, later in this century and in the next, on a scale similar to those associated with the great wars and the economic depression of the first half of the 20th century." The cost of inaction would be astronomical—an estimate of nearly $7 trillion over a decade—and many times greater than the probable cost of cutting greenhouse emissions by 2050 to between 60 and 80 percent below 1990 levels: around 1 percent of global GDP. Yet that cost compares favorably with global military spending, which is about 2.5 percent of global GDP.[55]

In the United States, Russia, Japan, and Germany, carbon emissions from industry, power plants, and automobiles account for about 39 percent of the global total. (On a per capita basis, Australia, the United States, and Canada lead the way in carbon emissions.) Fossil fuel use in the Third World now represents over one-quarter of the world total; and as tropical forest destruction continues, and the industrialized countries (including Eastern Europe and the FSU) move away from fossil fuels, that proportion of carbon emissions will rise significantly. China alone, with its heavy reliance on coal and its rapidly rising oil requirements, accounts for 13 percent of global carbon emissions.[56] How to wean this diversity of economies away from expensive, highly polluting, energy-intensive fuels and onto a truly sustainable path may be the greatest challenge currently facing the international community.

By now the evidence of the existence and dire consequences of global warming is no longer in serious question.[57] But few government or industrial leaders have yet been willing to adopt the ambitious energy-efficiency and carbon-reduction targets that are essential to solving the problem.[58] While action to reverse global warming and other environmental threats is taking place at local and regional levels, an international approach must be the centerpiece. The 1997 Kyoto Protocol is a starting point.[59] It took five years to get there from the Framework Convention on Climate Change at Rio, and it represents an important, though far from perfect, effort to cut greenhouse gas emissions. The protocol requires emission reductions below 1990 levels of 8 percent by the EU, 7 percent by the United States, and 6 percent by Japan. (The George W. Bush administration rejected US participation.) However, these and lesser deductions by twenty-one other industrialized countries—developing countries are excepted—will not have to occur before 2008; total reductions by the thirty-eight countries will amount to just over 5 percent under 1990 levels, rather than 15 percent as the Europeans and many NGOs had called for; countries that exceed targets will be able to trade quotas with those that do not; and penalties for protocol violations have yet to be established but will not be automatic.[60] Considering that 1990 global emission levels worldwide will be greatly exceeded by 2008—only some EU countries and Russia are meeting their targets, and overall, the industrialized countries are *increasing* their greenhouse gas output by 10 percent a year—the Kyoto Protocol may be considered a small step forward, limited by political bargaining in what needed to be accomplished.[61]

The shift to a pollution-free, soft-energy path has only just begun; it will take considerable time to take hold worldwide and to become practical for large industries. More immediate preventive and preservationist steps are called for, steps that would be sensible even if global environmental trends were to stabilize.[62] Such steps include a multinational planet climate watch to detect and attribute the sources of changes, reforestation (such as the greenbelts in north China and Kenya) and other soil-protecting programs, improved water management to cut waste and encourage conservation, development of crops more resistant to climate change, and restoration of damaged or destroyed natural areas.[63] Setting aside large tracts of forestland that are rich in species and in potential medical benefits, as Costa Rica has done, should also be considered, being mindful that indigenous peoples and cultures are not further victimized by a well-intentioned ecomanage-ment.[64] To avoid that result, one scholar has concluded after examining forest management in Asia, local community control of the land is essential. With that ingredient, a partnership with government can be effective; without it, sustainable development is impossible.[65]

But it is timely to consider even more drastic measures instead of adjustments of policies. These would include the outright prohibition of production of toxic chemicals and pesticides (unless demonstrated to be usable and disposable without danger to humans and wildlife);[66] a global moratorium on forest clear-cutting, even on private lands, in ecologically endangered areas; ending government subsidies of energy resources (coal, oil, and nuclear power) that have been proven to have destructive environmental consequences, such as overuse of water, pesticides, and chemical fertilizers;[67] and national and international legislation that prohibits or at least heavily penalizes the export by corporations of dangerous chemicals (as well as products that contain them), chemical plants, or pollutants whose production in the home country has been banned. There should be no more Bhopals, just as surely as there should be no more Three Mile Islands and Chernobyls. Finally, substantial taxation, with the revenues used to promote environmental protection, is long overdue. A UN agency has outlined several types of taxes, such as on trade (e.g., in tropical hardwood), on pollution (e.g., greenhouse gas emissions), and on consumption (e.g., on oil or coal).[68] The EU countries are already well advanced when it comes to environmental taxation.[69]

Global environmental problems have spurred the greatest advances to date in international cooperation.[70] The first such effort was the 1972 Declaration of the United Nations Conference on the Human Environment in Stockholm. The conference set the parameters of all subsequent discussion by introducing the concept of "sustainable development" and setting up a global environmental monitoring agency. Specific international agreements followed. The London Dumping Convention regulates the dumping of radioactive wastes at sea. In 1982 most of the sixty-four parties to it (but not the United States, Britain, France, South Africa, or Switzerland) agreed to an indefinite moratorium on oceanic nuclear-waste disposal. The London signatories also agreed in 1990 to ban the dumping of industrial waste at sea and recommended that a global mechanism be created to control marine pollution discharged on land. International disposal of toxic waste was also the subject of a treaty signed at Basel in 1989, which, as of 2006, has 169 parties (again, not the United States). It bans the export of hazardous wastes to Third World countries. The Law of the Sea Treaty, signed by 119 nations in 1982, established an important global-citizen principle—that the planet's undersea wealth is the "common heritage of mankind"—and a new implementing regime, the International Seabed Authority.[71] The treaty includes measures that hold states liable for pollution of both territorial and international waters, that tax members for pollution cleanup, and that create a court for settlement of disputes. Its weaknesses are that the major maritime states (the United States, Britain, Russia, Germany, France, and Japan) are not signatories—they all have reservations about the authority's jurisdiction over seabed minerals, and they have concerns about whether decisions will be made by consensus (as Third World states would prefer) or by weighted vote (as in the IMF and World Bank). Even without the major states, the Law of the Sea Treaty has been responsible for promoting cooperation on maritime boundaries and strengthening customary international law, such as on contiguous zones.[72]

In 1987, concerns about the buildup of chlorofluorocarbons (CFCs) in the atmosphere led to the signing of the Montreal Protocol. It commits governments, over 150 of which have ratified, to reduce CFC production from aerosols, foam products, refrigerants, and other sources; these are important contributors to global warming as well as to depletion of the earth's ozone layer and increased skin cancers. A fund was established in 1990 to enable Third World countries to obtain substitutes for CFCs. By the year 2000, global use of CFCs had declined 90 percent compared with the peak year of 1987.[73] The EU, Japan, the United States, and a number of Third World countries have entirely or nearly phased out CFC use. On the other hand, the FSU countries have reduced CFCs but not met targets, a black market in CFCs has arisen in Russia and a few other countries, and some of the largest Third World countries, such as China and India, have increased usage. If there is full compliance with the Montreal Protocol, the ozone shield should recover by the mid-twenty-first century.[74]

At least four important concepts for dealing effectively with global issues emerge from the Law of the Sea and Montreal treaties. One is international management of the planet's "common heritage," which ought to apply as well to food, energy, and other environmental and natural resources—not to mention peace. Second, taxation of offenders is a useful way to punish other crimes against the common heritage and, as a group of Japanese environmental specialists has suggested, set up an environmental trust fund to purchase nature preserves.[75] A third concept is the indispensable role of independent scientists and NGOs in the development of international public policy. As the lead-up to and amendments of the Montreal Protocol showed, hard scientific data is essential to tracking the course, causes, and remedies of environmental problems.[76] NGOs have played crucial roles in getting governments and industries to the negotiating table. Last, benchmarks are necessary to evaluate how well the parties and the agreement itself are performing toward achieving objectives.[77]

At the regional level there has also been progress on environmental protection. A reemergence of regional consciousness has occurred. In the United States it is referred to as bioregionalism, and in areas such as the Ozarks and the Great Lakes it takes activist political forms such as preserving watersheds and developing environmental policy platforms.[78] In a different vein, the United States and Canada subscribe to a long-established dictum prohibiting the carryover of air pollution from one country to the other. (It remains to be seen, however, what concrete action Washington and Ottawa take in accepting responsibility for acid rain and air pollution on both sides of the border.[79]) And in 1979, the thirty-four-member Economic Commission for Europe (under the UN) signed a Convention on Transboundary Air Pollution. But this effort to "limit and, as far as possible, gradually reduce and prevent air pollution" lacks the power needed to keep a major problem from getting out of hand. The convention does not establish pollution standards, lacks an enforcement mechanism, and does not stipulate accountability (such as in payment of damages) for polluting states or their corporations.[80]

The fourth component of humane development is employment. Equitability in this case should begin with revision of economic indicators such as GNP. Growth in jobs is more important than growth in the economy, as the World Bank's 2006 study cited in Chapter 4 has concluded. More specifically, the indicators should more accurately reflect who is producing in a society and at what social (including environmental) gain or cost. It seems particularly important to include the so-called informal sector: underground labor, unlicensed businesses, housework, child care, and volunteer labor—often work done by women and/or by the marginally employed. In many Third World countries, these forms of work are undervalued and officially discouraged even though they account for substantial actual employment and national income. If supported with access to credit, the informal sector could be an important source of business innovations and personal empowerment.[81]

We have already seen a few other ways that the unemployment crisis in the Third and Fourth Worlds can be addressed, starting with the redirection of government investment into agriculture and of transnational corporate investment into labor-intensive, energy-saving, ecologically responsible activities. TNCs have a particular responsibility to ensure that workers in their plants are not exploited, that child labor is eliminated, and that independent unions have a right to organize and bargain collectively. Alternatively, there are work cooperatives; one notable example is the Mondragon Cooperatives in the Basque region of Spain.[82] There, one finds local economic independence and control that has successfully incorporated democratic decisionmaking and worker ownership.

But employment is also a long-term structural problem in the advanced economies. Their one-dimensional focus on international competitiveness and privatization has led to high unemployment, especially among the young and unskilled, the exporting of jobs, and restrictions on migrant workers. The need is urgent for the United States, the EU, and Japan to reinvigorate their economies through an overhauling of public spending and tax priorities. A kind of legislative agenda based on human priorities would have to include, first, job retraining and corporate responsibility legislation to protect workers and communities in transition; second, appreciation of the positive role that migrant workers play in host economies, including the remittances they send home;[83] third, in the United States, sharp reductions in the military budget, particularly in new weapons procurement, nuclear weapons, and through cost efficiencies; fourth, tax incentives to corporations and banks that invest in job-creating, productivity-improving activities at home—and disincentives to those that do not or that continue to invest in countries where labor is repressed and human rights are discounted; and, fifth, greatly increased public funding of education, family farming, small business, resource conservation, and renewable energy sources.

An equitable approach to North-South differences over information is the fifth component of humane development. There appears to be room for bargaining. Governments in the South might accept that the electronic media cannot be kept out and that restrictions on press freedoms need to be loosened. But they have a right to expect that foreign reporters will be sensitive to their societies' cultures and histories (which might be assisted by enrolling reporters in local universities when they arrive). Both sides would benefit from improved reporting on the Third World, with more attention to long-term issues of underdevelopment and to positive efforts by governments and international agencies to deal with them. An international convention on media rights and responsibilities that lays out an agenda of mutual benefit might be in order.

## Toward Common Security

If movement toward a durable peace is to begin, the starting point must be the development of incentives for states and groups to avoid war in their political conflicts. The end point is disarmament within a system of global security. In between, what must be constructed is what Karl Deutsch, in his classic study of West European unity, called "a sense of community," meaning a shared belief that "common security problems must and can be resolved by processes of 'peaceful change.'"[84]

To create an agenda for moving to an alternative security system requires accepting certain fundamental premises. These flow from the previous chapters' arguments about the nature of the global crisis of international conflict. One is that our field of concern is the war system and not merely one country's military program. That means taking account of the political, bureaucratic, and economic forces in all societies that propel the arms race forward. A second premise is that system change will evolve out of a process of successful experiments that have popular support. Neither technical fixes (such as setting limits on types of missiles) nor ambitious rearrangements of the future (such as global disarmament and world federalism) stand much chance of being widely accepted in the foreseeable future.

A third premise is that alternatives to the arms race must address insecurity at several levels, including people's deep pessimism and fear that to reduce arms will invite attack; mistrust between national, ethnic, and religious leaders built partly on longstanding grievances; and the structural violence of underdevelopment. Fourth, every change in global security policy should strengthen the ability of the global community to move beyond state conflict toward new forms of identification, representation, communication, defense, and conflict resolution.[85] This premise further means that each change should have real substance and not be mere window dressing, as has often been the case with arms-control agreements. Last, our agenda should rest on optimism that war is not inevitable. Rather, war has become obsolete. With a new vision, the goal of general and complete disarmament under effective forms of inspection and control is achievable.[86]

Promising steps to an alternative security system are presented here in terms of four key areas: communications between adversaries, military issues, nonmilitary issues, and the public's role.

*Communications.*  A helpful beginning to creating a momentum for peace is for adversaries to agree to emphasize the positive aspects of their relationship. At the height of the Cold War, for example, the US and Soviet leaderships might have publicized the numerous agreements (major and minor, over one hundred in all) that they abided by. A noted international legal scholar reminds us of what Soviet and US leaders ignored: "how much international law and obligation applied and were effectively observed between the United States and the Soviet Union even when their relations were most strained."[87] Like it or not, these adversaries trusted each other all the time—to fulfill obligations under exchange programs and business deals, to keep military and political flare-ups around the world from escalating to a superpower confrontation, and especially to maintain nuclear weapons and communications in a fail-safe condition.

Some specific additional steps to facilitate communication between adversaries are:

• Substantially increasing people-to-people exchange programs, involving both professionals and ordinary citizens. These would be supported by networks of coordinating groups in and between the countries or territories concerned. Jordanian and Israeli scientists joined together in Bridging the Rift to create, along with two US universities, an environmental studies center along the desert border.[88] "Space bridges," which use satellites to link groups of children, musicians, doctors, and simply concerned citizens in hostile countries, exemplify the new possibilities that technology is opening up. Sister cities are another vehicle, one that already has wide international acceptance.

• Using a variety of negotiating and dialogue formats that have been developed to build trust and empathy, such as the Harvard Negotiating Project's approach that emphasizes interests over positions; Herbert Kelman's interactive problem-solving workshops in the Middle East; Raymond Cohen's work on cross-cultural sensitivity; and Harold Saunders's ideas for expanding the concept of negotiations to include an array of "pre-" and "circum-" negotiating processes that are crucial to effective official talking.[89] All these approaches may involve high-level officials or ordinary citizens. At Oslo in 1993, Arab and Israeli negotiators, forced to deal with one another over a long period of time away from the public spotlight, came to new levels of understanding about each other's cultures, security priorities, and humanness. "Everything that was security for us was dignity for them," said the chief Israeli negotiator. In the end, mutual respect accelerated the peace process; but, to state the obvious, it did not lead to a final settlement.[90] Years later, however, an unofficial group of Palestinian and Israeli negotiators took their cue from Oslo and developed a detailed "Geneva Accord" that constituted a rebuff to those who argue that an equitable agreement cannot be crafted.[91]

• Humanizing one's adversary. One of the unfortunate hallmarks of the Cold War competition was the invective, misrepresentation, and dehumanizing language that the United States and the USSR employed in their public discourse. Former ambassador George F. Kennan decried it as "the marks of an intellectual primitivism and naiveté unpardonable in a great government."[92] Name-calling cannot build bridges, as is apparent in US dealings with North Korea and Iran. Using civil language and in other ways treating one's adversaries as human beings just may have constructive results. The above-mentioned Arab-Israeli talks in Oslo paved the way for the famous handshake in Washington between Yasser Arafat and Yitzhak Rabin in 1993. When British prime minister Tony Blair shook hands with Gerry Adams, he said: "I treated Gerry Adams and the members of Sinn Fein [the political wing of the Irish Republican Army] in the same way I treat any other human being." The same principle, he added, should apply to the entire situation in Northern Ireland.[93] The gesture carried enormous symbolism and helped push the Northern Ireland peace process to a successful conclusion.

• Apologizing to those who have been wronged. In international affairs, as distinct from the personal realm, apologies are above all political acts, which make them rarities. Victors in wars and dictators never apologize; great powers and giant corporations, almost never. On a few occasions, governments have apologized to their own people: Germany's Chancellor Willy Brandt went down on his knees in the Warsaw ghetto to apologize for the Holocaust; the Canadian government apologized to indigenous peoples for its maltreatment of them; the US government apologized to Japanese Americans for interning them during World War II; and the government of Taiwan apologized to native-born Taiwanese for a massacre that occurred when the mainland Nationalists took over the island. But when President

Clinton apologized in 1998 for Washington's failure to respond to the unfolding genocide in Rwanda four years earlier, it was the exception to the rule. Does apologizing matter? Might not history have changed if Washington had apologized to the Ayatollah Khomeini for US training and support of the SAVAK and other costly interventions in Iran's political life? If Japan tomorrow offered China and all Koreans a credible, heartfelt apology for its aggressions and atrocities, might that not begin a process of healing, within as well as outside the country? Contrition is a uniquely human capacity. To apologize for having inflicted great pain and suffering on another people is the human thing to do. It does not end discussion; to the contrary, it is the pathway to historical explanation and the precondition of policy change. A truthful apology signifies a desire to understand and to behave differently in the future.

*Military issues.* The US-Soviet record indicates that carefully written arms agreements can build trust even in the tensest times. More than twenty related to nuclear arms, and as the Cold War ended, the two sides were in compliance with them.[94] Violations of arms agreements occur even with the best verification system. But satellites and other verification technologies are now advanced enough to ensure that major violations (those that would give one side a clear strategic advantage) cannot be concealed. Acceptance of on-site verification procedures is now almost universally regarded as critical to successful agreements. And they work, as witness the constraints that UN inspections placed on Iraq's WMD programs.

As we saw in Chapter 5, arms-limiting agreements only scratch the surface of the arms race. They tell us what negotiators considered was politically safe to do, not what the global interest indicated they ought to do. Consequently, there is a long way yet to go before we can feel secure in a world awash with nuclear and conventional weapons. Progress depends most of all on the United States, as the only superpower. Some specific areas for negotiation and diplomacy are:

• A multilateral declaration of no first-use of nuclear weapons. Parties making such a declaration would be agreeing to forgo the nuclear threat. (The Soviet government endorsed the no-first-use concept in 1981, as did the CIS members in 1991 and a number of former high-level US officials.[95]) A necessary component of abandoning the option to initiate nuclear attack is for the nuclear great powers to move to minimum deterrence—no more than a few hundred warheads. Such a small but highly accurate arsenal (for example, entirely based on submarines) would demonstrate that the only conceivable purpose of nuclear weapons is to deter their use by others.[96] It would also be a major step toward burying deterrence doctrine and reaching zero nuclear weapons.[97]

• An international convention on the elimination of nuclear weapons.

The UN General Assembly has twice (in 1996 and 1997) called for "an early conclusion of a nuclear weapons convention prohibiting the development, production, testing, deployment, stockpiling, transfer, threat or use of nuclear weapons and providing for their elimination."[98] The model for such a ban is the Chemical Weapons Convention (CWC): It applies to all countries without exception; it contains tough verification and monitoring provisions; and it is comprehensive in coverage. In short, such a convention would at one blow eliminate an entire category of WMD and thus would go well beyond the NPT and the CTBT requirements. It would also prevent nuclear transfers to nuclear and non-nuclear-weapon states alike; and it would presumably stop laboratory work that could improve or redesign nuclear weapons. Clearly, too, the convention's breadth would make it unacceptable in terms of current US nuclear policy. The convention would have to be accompanied by much stronger monitoring of nuclear plants than so far exists, and by an enforceable international agreement banning the production of all weapons-grade fissionable material, plutonium exports, the use of plutonium for any purpose, and the reprocessing of spent fuel from civilian reactors. International specialists should also be brought together to find an acceptable final resting place for existing spent nuclear fuel.[99] Pending conclusion of the convention, a number of sensible interim steps to reduce the danger of use of nuclear weapons have been proposed, such as separating warheads from launchers, removing the cores from warheads, and storing warheads far away from launchers.

• An International Satellite Monitoring Agency within the United Nations, as the French government first proposed in 1978. Aside from its economic development uses mentioned earlier, such a system could oversee military movements and help verify arms agreements. Internationalization of satellite technology for peaceful purposes is long overdue and represents a positive departure from proposals to "weaponize" the heavens.

• Additional nuclear-free zones, which are areas (from cities on up to countries and regions) within which nuclear testing, manufacturing, acquisitions, deployment, transit, and storage may be prohibited. Over forty countries and regions from Wales to Japan are nuclear-free, as well as outer space and the Antarctic, though not all in the same way. The challenge ahead is to make those regions nuclear-weapon-free where tensions run highest and where some governments already possess nuclear weapons: Northeast Asia, the Middle East, and South Asia.[100]

• Strategies for engaging rather than containing one's enemies. The use of force, sanctions, and other pressure tactics to compel another country's cooperation or bring about its capitulation rarely works in a globalized world. Our case study of the US confrontations with Iran and North Korea suggests that providing incentives for their cooperation is preferable to threats that might escalate to a general war. The art of diplomacy needs to be revived; force can always be used as a last resort in compelling circumstances. As the former US national security adviser, Zbigniew Brzezinski, said in advocating US talks with the Palestinian and Hamas leaderships: "I think we have to talk to everyone that's involved in this conflict, directly or indirectly. One doesn't gain anything by ostracism; it's a self-defeating posture."[101]

• Unilateral military initiatives, which may perform the same function as negotiated agreements more efficiently, provided the other side reciprocates within a reasonable time. The moratorium on nuclear testing came about in this manner. Similarly, a government's unilateral declaration that it will reduce its military budget by a certain percentage, or refrain from a particular military act (such as an arms transfer) if its opponent also refrains, can create a positive atmosphere for reducing tensions and arsenals.

• New or strengthened international institutions to monitor and enforce global standards of military (and nonmilitary) performance.[102] The United Nations Department for Disarmament Affairs might be empowered to supervise adherence to military agreements, including nonproliferation of nuclear technology, with information drawn from the kind of international satellite agency previously proposed. Conventional arms transfers are particularly important for an international regime to monitor and restrict. The Perm 5, as the major arms sellers, must take steps beyond reporting. Individually, they should greatly reduce their arms transfers and end subsidies to their arms-exporting companies. Within the UN and other international institutions, they should press for common restrictions on arms transfers to governments that (for example) fail to sign or violate specified arms-control treaties. World Bank development aid might be withheld from governments that have very high military budgets.[103] Conversely, incentives might be created for Third World arms sellers not to sell arms, such as swapping debt or providing human-development aid.

• An expanded and finalized Fissile Materials Treaty so that WMD materials can be monitored, secured, and kept out of the hands of terrorist groups. As former US senator Sam Nunn has said, "the threat is outpacing the response"; the number of unprotected research sites and arsenals that are vulnerable to theft far exceeds the money being spent to protect them.[104]

• Strengthened international capabilities for peacekeeping. As internal conflicts have moved to the top of the international security agenda, relying on collective security to combat them has lost its appeal among the major powers, for reasons discussed in Chapter 1. Despite the increased number of UN peacekeeping operations since the Cold War ended (refer again to Table 1.2), they remain the exception to the general rule of hands off. In most kinds of internal conflicts, that rule makes some sense, for they are far messier than an aggression of the Iraq-Kuwait type. Peacekeeping is, after all, intervention, and like all interventions, peacekeeping is risk-prone, from simple ineffectiveness to promoting greater violence.[105] It can hardly be accidental, then, that peacekeeping operations have mainly been facilitative rather than coercive, such as monitoring cease-fires and supervising elections.

Ideally, the best moment for peacekeeping is before violence breaks out. Chester Crocker speaks of "preemptive engagement in promoting negotiated alternatives to continued repression or expanding violence and upheaval."[106] Even more demanding is *preventive* diplomacy.[107] Michael Lund's study, which is a careful effort to specify the conditions for preventive action, actually shows why success is so unlikely. Prevention requires an unusual congruence of circumstances: harmony of interest among external parties and internal disputants, a convincing combination of carrots and sticks, and governing institutions in the warring territories strong enough to give legitimacy to moderating influences. In the end, facilitative operations would seem to stand the best chance of bringing about a negotiated peace, provided the warring parties want to negotiate. Simply put, political leaders have to want peace to get peace, as happened in Central America and (outside the UN) Northern Ireland.[108]

• A permanent UN force to intervene against humanitarian disasters. Winston Churchill once said, "The United Nations was set up not to get us to heaven, but only to save us from hell." The trouble is, the nation-state system that the UN reflects has sometimes ignored "hell," the unspeakable barbarities against whole populations that have resulted in huge numbers of deaths in a short amount of time. Ethnic cleansings, mass expulsions, deliberate starvation, systematic rapes, and other crimes against humanity and war crimes represent a special category of internal conflict that demands humanitarian intervention. Certainly, humanitarian interventions face the same kinds of obstacles that ordinary peacekeeping faces; good intentions are no substitute for clear objectives and adequate resources. Still, the UN system was established precisely to prevent new Holocausts; when political leaders see genocide directly ahead, is it not their duty to act? The tragedy of Rwanda is, in a sense, civilizational: By now the evidence is overwhelming that Rwanda—meaning both the slaughter there and in the refugee camps in Zaire to which so many people fled—was avoidable.[109]

In a truly new world order, the world community would not walk away from mass violence on the basis of narrow calculations of national interest. The central problem may be the need to make collective security genuinely collective and global, and thus different from previous UN peacekeeping missions.[110] The missing ingredient might be a permanent international peace force (IPF) acting under UN command in the event nonviolent measures fail to produce compliance with UN resolutions. The IPF concept dates back to the post–World War II years. Under Chapter VII of the UN Charter (Article 43), member states are supposed to conclude a "special agreement" to provide the Security Council, when called upon, with military forces and other assistance. Such agreements have never been made.[111] When UN

Secretary-General Boutros Boutros-Ghali proposed in July 1992 to establish a permanent peacekeeping force—one that would be composed of national contingents and have access to government intelligence on potential conflicts—only France's President François Mitterrand supported him.

A permanent IPF would bring national military contingents together for training in advance of actual need. The force would act on behalf of the international community, not an individual government or a regional organization. Its primary purpose would be rapid deployment to prevent or minimize large-scale threats to human life, such as by creating safe havens for civilians. A specific threshold of violence would automatically trigger the deployment. Secondarily, and not automatically, the IPF might be used in select instances of "peace enforcement," meaning the use of deadly force to assert the world community's will.[112] The UN Security Council's membership would probably have to be enlarged (such as by the addition of Germany and Japan) and its voting arrangements changed, both to add legitimacy to any use of collective force and to prevent an easy veto of a proposed peace action.[113]

A permanent UN force is not the only answer to mass murder. A multinational UN commission in 2001 focused on the conditions for forceful UN intervention, namely, when a state is unable or unwilling to protect people from large-scale loss of life, when the UN Security Council approves, and when the use of force is a last resort.[114] Inevitably, and appropriately, humanitarian intervention of any kind must answer to a large number of political and ethical questions, such as the precise circumstances that would trigger deployment, the scope of the mission, the likelihood of effectiveness, and possible abuses of authority.[115] Some governments, starting with the United States, will probably object to anything like an automatic response, even to genocide, as well as to financing a force and putting it under UN command. Unless effective answers are found to these issues, collective security will remain as dependent on national interests and geopolitical thinking as it was in the Cold War era.

*Nonmilitary issues.* Moving to a more secure world further requires strengthening law and diplomacy, and transforming the military economy. Some ideas here are:

• The strengthening of the international judicial system. Since 1970, there have been three universally acknowledged instances of genocide—the "killing fields" in Cambodia, Bosnia, and Rwanda—and possibly a fourth, Guatemala.[116] Very few political or military leaders with probable responsibility for mass slaughter have been apprehended and prosecuted. In Cambodia, for instance, the effort to preserve national reconciliation at all costs led to a pardon for one of the two top Khmer Rouge leaders, Ieng Sary, upon surrender to the central government of forces loyal to him. He was rewarded for his surrender with political power—the same man who oversaw the deaths of around 1 million people in the 1970s.[117] The senior Khmer Rouge leader, Pol Pot, was never apprehended; he died in the jungle after having been tried and convicted (of policy errors, not war crimes) by his peers. In Bosnia, NATO commanders, concerned about an outbreak of violence, refused to make seizure of the Bosnian Serb leaders part of their mission, contrary to the strong urgings of the chief justice of the International Court of Justice (ICJ), Richard Goldstone. Even though the UN tribunal created to handle war crimes in the former Yugoslavia has issued war-crimes charges against over 150 people, mostly Serbs, only about a third have been sentenced. A number of top Serb military and political leaders (other than Milosevic, who died while in confinement) remain at large.[118] The International Criminal Tribunal for Rwanda, which began work in 1997, has so far produced about twenty-eight convictions for genocide and other crimes, including some senior Hutu officials.[119] There and in Guatemala, punishment has been superseded by efforts at national reconciliation.

An international conference in Rome drafted a treaty for an international criminal court in July 1998. Two outstanding issues emerged: the Security Council's power to authorize charges of crimes against humanity, and the scope of the court's jurisdiction. On the first, only Britain among the Perm 5 argued for a fully independent body that ought not be dependent on the Security Council's will. Most countries agreed. As to the second, the United States was again in the minority in wanting the court's work confined to genocide and not, for example, extended to include mass rape and other war crimes that soldiers might commit, or crimes against humanity such as waging aggressive war.[120] The treaty passed, and the ICC came into being in 2002; the United States remains outside it, President Bush having "unsigned" the treaty that President Clinton had signed. A good indication of the ICC's value will be its handling of prosecutions for war crimes committed by Sudanese government leaders in Darfur—a process that began in 2007.

• The increased use of citizen diplomats—so-called Track II diplomacy. When hostages are taken and the lives of innocent persons having no official responsibility are at stake, unofficial mediators who can appeal on humane grounds may stand the best chance of succeeding. (Two examples: the Reverend Jesse Jackson's successful mission to Syria in 1984 to free a downed US pilot, and the efforts of Terry Waite, representing Britain's Anglican Church, to negotiate the release of hostages taken in Beirut by radical Islamic groups.) Jimmy Carter proved to be an extremely effective diplomat after his presidency, playing the roles of mediator, elections supervisor, and diplomat in several conflict situations, such as in Namibia, Nicaragua, and North Korea.

• The conversion of significant portions of military industries to nonmilitary production. Full-fledged conversion is as profound an economic and social undertaking as the shift from a command to a market economy. I define "conversion" as a comprehensive and conscientious (i.e., irreversible) shift of government resources from the military to the civilian sector—along with additional investment in the civilian sector—leading to the demilitarization of social and political life, and thus to socially useful, economically sensible, and environmentally sustainable uses of productive capacity. No society has attempted military conversion of such dimensions. Conversion in the United States and the EU countries has been highly localized—a shift to civilian production by a single company's management or by a community to save the defense facility and its workers.[121] Only in China has conversion been a matter of long-term national policy tied to economic development. Even then, conversion has not satisfied the other criteria, in particular demilitarization.

It matters what "swords" are converted into, how and where they are produced, who produces them, and why they are being produced at all.[122] Conversion is not the production of products with dual (military and civilian) use, products that are polluting, or products that are just as obsolete and costly as those converted from. Neither is conversion the production of arms for export rather than for one's own military, nor mere economizing, such as by reducing the military budget or armed forces, retraining some military-industrial workers, or eliminating costly or redundant weapons systems. Some of these changes may be steps to conversion, but they are not conversion per se. Conversion is a strategic decision, requiring, as some specialists have noted, not only planning for industrial and occupational transitions but two other major shifts: in government spending priorities and in the restructuring of national-security interests and military forces.[123]

Extensive post–Cold War military conversion thus further requires overcoming the same factors that lubricated the military-industrial complex during the Cold War: powerful alliances among politicians, industry, and the armed forces; opportunities for excessive profits under military contracts; the rallying cry of national security; and the dependence of individuals, industrial firms, communities, regions, and central governments on military contracts and arms exports. Even when some of these obstacles can be overcome, the costs of retooling assembly lines, developing product markets, and retraining workers may be prohibitive. Still, conversion programs represent an unusual opportunity for government-business-labor partnerships that shift employment—including demobilized soldiers—to nonmilitary work.[124]

*The public's role.*    The pervasiveness of war, its terrifying costs, and the slowness and weakness of the negotiating process have brought increasing numbers of people into the peacemaking arena. Popular rather than bureaucratic will is pushing the agenda of a non-nuclear, nonviolent world forward. Some national leaders recognize this human-interest potential. President Eisenhower once declared that people may one day "want peace so badly that governments better get out of their way and let them have it." Years later President Reagan agreed, saying in a letter to Brezhnev: "Sometimes it seems that the governments [of our countries] get in the way of the people." When General George Lee Butler implored listeners to seize the time and contain the "nuclear beast," he said: "I want to record my strong conclusion that the risks entailed by nuclear weapons are far too great to leave the prospects of their elimination solely within the province of governments."[125]

The influence of citizens depends on education and involvement, including the following:

• Education for a global citizenry. The incorporation of global-humanist values into world politics is conceivable only when large numbers of people, whether they are in policymaking positions or not, adopt a global perspective on national issues. That means educating people to think globally, on behalf of one planet.[126] Although this is a long-term project, it is already well under way. In the United States, for example, global education has taken shape in the introduction of peace studies to curricula at every level, in the founding of new conflict-resolution programs (such as Harvard's Negotiation Project), in congressional funding of a US Institute of Peace, and in a sizable increase in the number of teachers who use a global perspective in their courses.[127] In Africa, local and international NGOs are training people for peacebuilding roles such as post-conflict reconciliation in Rwanda and conflict mediation by women in Senegal.

• Demonstration of global humanism in everyday life. The role of global citizen is also evident on a day-to-day basis: in neighborhood and other decentralist programs of self-reliance and conservation (such as farmers' markets and household weatherization); in national and regional networks sharing information and ideas on environmental, economic, and other matters that are transnational in scope; in the many successful intentional communities that people have founded in urban as well as rural areas; in the increasing popularity of "socially responsible" investment programs (those that invest individuals' money only in companies that are engaged in ethical, environmentally sustainable practices); and in conscious efforts by untold thousands of people to lead simpler lives and (as is discussed further later on) cultivate their most human qualities.[128] As Paul Hawken reminds us, however, even the most progressive personal and business activities are likely to result in increased consumption. We who are privileged to live in postindustrial societies should therefore not delude ourselves that anything other than radical changes in the way businesses and public institutions operate will prevent large-scale environmental deterioration.[129]

• Exploration of preservative means of defense.[130] The peaceful transfers of power in Russia, South Korea, the Philippines, and Eastern Europe illuminate one of the great challenges to our imagination: finding ways of protecting societies while minimizing the likelihood of harming others—and destroying what one hopes to protect. Nonviolent resistance has a rich history that may be as relevant to weapons issues as it is to defense against tyrannies and foreign interventionists. Scientists who today refine instruments of war may tomorrow, working transnationally, develop nonprovocative instruments for repelling attack. In the meantime, it is left to citizens in threatened countries to act—and millions have, nonviolently, put their lives and positions on the line to say no to further violence.

Civilian nonviolent resistance will not always be sufficient or successful. The army in Burma brutally cracked down on unarmed demonstrators in August 1988 and continues to rule with an iron hand. The Soviet government economically strangled Lithuania's attempt to restore its sovereignty in 1990. In Romania the new socialist party that won the election after the overthrow of the previous dictator, Nicolai Ceaucescu, was dominated by members of his supporting cast. Even in those cases, however, the resisters displayed a moral superiority and popular support that attracted worldwide sympathy—and laid the basis for future political change in their countries. Regardless of the outcome, the potential of "people power" and nonviolent defense against tyrannical regimes calls for systematic research that may help determine under precisely what conditions oppressive rule can be peacefully eliminated.

### Toward Democracy and Human Rights

In most of the world, principles of widespread political participation and accountable government (democracy, in short), respect for individual freedom and civil liberties, and adherence by public authority to domestic and international law are ignored. All forms of government give priority to order over law and central authority over grassroots democracy. The usual justification is either national security—a foreign threat, a rebellion—or the need to postpone constitutionalism (such as free elections) and the resumption of civil liberties until economic and social justice has been implanted. Granted, in some cases threats to national security are real and economic and social development is a more immediate human need than, say, a free press. But the unpleasant reality is that governments that make a practice of ignoring, postponing, or trampling upon human political rights are highly unlikely to mend their ways. Which may explain Thomas Jefferson's famous remark that "a little rebellion now and then is a good thing."

Popular protests and movements for human rights have become the global counterpart since the 1970s to revolution in the 1950s and 1960s. Contrary to the expectations of many, persistent mass activism can produce results and yet remain nonviolent and nonideological. We saw this in the demonstrations in South Korea that forced a strong-armed regime to make major concessions to democratic procedures. In the Philippines in 1986, Roman Catholic bishops declared the Marcos regime lacked a "moral basis"; a citizens' boycott was organized against businesses owned by Marcos's cronies; people protected the ballot boxes and surrounded the tanks; soldiers and diplomats defected—and suddenly the dictator was gone. In Haiti, what had seemed to outsiders to be a passive acceptance of the Duvalier family's tyranny turned, seemingly overnight, into demonstrations and the dictator's removal—all brought about largely by small clandestine networks of students supported by the church and slum dwellers. ("There were no Communists, no capitalists behind [the movement]—just the people with a desire for change," said a teacher.[131]) During May 1992 in Thailand, students, civil servants, and workers of all descriptions took to the streets to protest an unelected general's assumption of the premiership. Perhaps a few hundred people were killed during the ensuing onslaught by the Thai army, and many more "disappeared," but eventually the people forced the general's resignation following the king's personal intervention. He used his moral force to insist that the two sides stop the destruction and amend the constitution in ways that limited the military's power.[132] Workers peacefully protesting against abominable conditions in locally owned and multinational factories have won acceptance of their basic rights.[133]

Even the most tightly controlled societies are vulnerable: In the USSR the voices of Solzhenitsyn, Medvedev, Sakharov, and other dissidents focused worldwide attention on human-rights abuses there. Demonstrating Chinese students, workers, and party members brought about a total reappraisal worldwide of their country's reforms when the tanks rolled into Tiananmen in 1989. In Eastern Europe, by the end of 1990 not one communist party leader who had been in power the year before had survived the popular revolutions. Except in Romania, no shots were fired. Once Gorbachev made clear that Soviet forces would not intervene to save communist party rulers, people took matters in their own hands, crossing borders, demanding that officials resign, and calling for elections. Police and border guards were wise to get out of their way. The winds of change carried to Africa. From Côte d'Ivoire to South Africa and from Zambia to Zaire, one-party states were going out of business in 1990; constitutional governments and market economies were being promised. As discussed in Chapter 1, however, in connection with Africa, Eastern Europe, and Central Asia, authoritarianism does not die easily and in fact made a comeback starting in the late 1990s.

As these stories of people power and attempts at democratic change unfold, they raise an important question: What accounts for rising popular demands for more democracy? A number of social scientists have long contended that capitalist economic growth is the chief prerequisite. With an eye primarily to East Asia, they see dynamic capitalism as the basis for an evolution from heavy-handed authoritarianism to competitive political systems. But the "economic miracles" in East Asia, as the case study of South Korea showed, were achieved under a repressive, dictatorial state that did not follow the rules of free-market capitalism, much less the road to democratization. In fact, economic growth was used to postpone democracy, just as is happening in China now. It took people power—not just the rising middle class, but also students, industrial workers, farmers, civil servants, priests, and NGOs—to initiate the dismantling of authoritarianism in South Korea.

Truth is, there is no firm connection between economic development and democracy: Countries that improve their economies are all over the political map, as China and India show. Nor does progress toward democracy ensure greater investment in human development, however positive other economic indicators may be.[134] This is not to deny the importance of a democratic dividend: Countries that are faithful to the rule of law, promote transparency in governance, and have independent political institutions (not just elections) are *more likely* than authoritarian regimes to have vibrant civil societies and responsive political systems, all of which are conducive to human well-being.[135] Such governments surely are deserving of development aid.[136] But focusing on a particular form of government may be putting the cart before the horse. If people are the real concern, it makes more sense when allocating aid or any other benefit to give highest priority to human development and not to "democracy," "capitalism," "socialism," or some other ideal type.

Building democracy is a far more complicated process than planting the seeds of economic growth. Market economics is the dominant trend in the post–Cold War order, but its inequities and dislocations are as important to note as its benefits. Both rising prosperity and unequal development may inspire social protest; neither may lead to greater political pluralism. The road to democracy, or some approximation of it, contains many detours that can lead astray politically mature and post-authoritarian societies alike. It seems, then, that no form of government or economic system is immune to corruption, social injustice, and environmental neglect. The simple lesson here may be that the fight for social justice, of which democratic institutions are a part, is a never-ending struggle. As Jefferson once said, "Eternal vigilance is the price of liberty."

And people are struggling for democracy and human rights everywhere. Some have received considerable media attention and international recognition, which are indispensable in pressuring governments to change. I think here, for example, of China's Tiananmen demonstrators; two leaders of East Timor's resistance to Indonesian rule, Bishop Carlos Ximenes Belo and Jose Ramos-Horta, who were awarded the Nobel Peace Prize in 1996; the Dalai Lama in Tibet (winner of the 1989 prize); Aung San Suu Kyi in Burma (the 1991 prize); and Rigoberta Menchú in Guatemala (the 1992 prize). By far, however, most citizens' groups go about their heroic work for social justice without any outside notice at all. Among them are the human-rights organizations in Burundi, the former Yugoslavia, Central America, and numerous other countries that record and report violations by military and police forces; the Grandmothers of the Plaza de Mayo, parents of the "disappeared" children during Argentina's "dirty war" from 1976 to 1983; the whites of South Africa who worked to end apartheid; members of military establishments and military-industrial facilities who attempt to bring humane understanding to the arms race; neighborhood and community groups in Brazil that protect street children from the attacks of police and right-wing gangs; the mothers in Nepal who spearheaded a national vaccination drive against measles; the Roman Catholic bishops of Canada and the United States, who have written astonishingly vigorous criticisms of economic injustice in their countries; and the Sarvodaya Shramadana movement in Sri Lanka, which since its founding in 1958 has been a village basic-needs development program based on voluntarism and nonviolence.

Consciously or not, these diverse national groups and entities are part of a growing transnational network.[137] Citizens in one part of the world are taking action on behalf of victims of repression and injustice thousands of miles away. The divestment movement in the United States that barred investments of pension funds in South Africa during the apartheid years was noted earlier. A group called INFACT led many other national organizations in a worldwide boycott of the Nestlé Corporation, whose powdered milk was being widely used in Africa as a substitute for mothers' milk, with numerous infant deaths caused by combining the powdered milk with tainted water. Nestlé eventually acceded to a new marketing code adopted by WHO, which "estimates that the deaths of 1.5 million babies each year could be prevented if women breast-fed their infants."[138] Public awareness of child labor in the production in underdeveloped countries of athletic wear, carpets, and clothing sparked media attention, some positive corporate responses in cooperation with unions and NGOs,[139] and nonprofit organizing in the consumer countries. In the latter category is Rugmark, an international group that puts a tag on carpets to certify that child labor was not used in making them.[140]

Then there are a number of well-established transnational NGOs and civil-society organizations, some activist and confrontational, others nonpolitical in their efforts to promote human rights and related causes. Among the best known are two that have won Nobel Peace Prizes: Amnesty International, based in London, which issues periodic reports on political rights in particular countries and has successfully lobbied for the release of prisoners of conscience; and International Physicians for the Prevention of Nuclear War, founded by Soviet and US doctors. Another prize-winning human-rights group is Survival International, which operates worldwide in support of indigenous peoples. It received the Right Livelihood Award, which has been presented annually since 1980 to individuals and groups that pioneer solutions to global problems.[141] Others are Greenpeace (nuclear-arms reductions and marine ecosystem preservation); International Physicians for Social Responsibility (the hazards of the nuclear arms race); Poètes, Essayistes, Nouvellistes (PEN—a writers' association devoted to freedom of expression); Human Rights Watch; Planned Parenthood (family planning); END (European Nuclear Disarmament, one of many West European groups that galvanized mass protests of Soviet as well as US nuclear-weapons deployments); People-to-People International (international exchange); Fellowship of Reconciliation (Christian peace and human-rights organization); and Médicins sans Frontières (Doctors Without Borders, which has been active throughout Africa during hunger crises and internal conflicts). Finally, we should include civil-society groups of various kinds: the Greens in Europe, whose message of environmental preservation and economic restructuring to reflect human needs has been taken up worldwide;[142] the Templeton Fund (Sir John Templeton) that gives an annual prize in religion; and the Soros Foundation (George Soros) that has established offices in over twenty-five countries, mostly in Eastern Europe, to promote democratization by supporting the independent sector.

Advancing the rights of women has also become a matter of transnational concern, as was dramatized in 1985 at Nairobi, Kenya, and in 1995 at Beijing, when women from all over the world convened to evaluate their progress and the long road yet to be traveled. Several international conventions to end discrimination against women have now been signed or ratified by the overwhelming majority of governments. But many governments have not done either. More to the point, discrimination against women persists, regardless of signatures, paeans of praise, or even elections to national leadership.[143] Clearly, human rights cannot be said to be advancing unless and until women's rights markedly advance.

Central to women's rights is an end to discriminatory laws concerning the acquisition, sale, and inheritance of property, and equality with men in marriage and divorce. Also critical are passage and enforcement of equal educational and economic opportunity laws, provision for child care for working women, and the right of women to vote and compete for any public office. These are among the rights already embodied in international conventions, but they need to be universalized and implemented. International, including corporate, assistance to women's businesses and cooperatives, as noted earlier, should strengthen the case for such laws. So should the appointment of many more women to positions in international organizations, which, by and large, have failed to put their own houses in order with respect to male-female balance.[144] With progress in these areas will come increased (and equal) access to health care and food, acceptance of a woman's right to choose an abortion, and a generalized appreciation of the burdens of womanhood, especially in those parts of the Third World (the Muslim Middle East and parts of South Asia) where women have almost subhuman status. Women's rights are human rights, as the global women's movement is now emphasizing.

The problems women have experienced in securing their rights illustrate an inescapable fact of world politics: the failure of governments to live up to their promises under international agreements, especially where human rights are concerned. It is easier for governments to engage in public posturing about human equality than to yield power, either to persons or to supranational bodies. In fact, there is a resurgence of cynicism, from globalists as well as realists, about the usefulness, and even the desirability, of international governmental organizations as vehicles of humane change.[145] Insofar as critics are concerned that tyrannical power might be vested in a world organization, the cynicism is understandable. But most of their fears stem from the presumed "failures" of the United Nations as a preserver of human rights (for example, in the Israeli-occupied West Bank) and from the use of the General Assembly by Third World representatives as a forum for sometimes abusive criticism of the industrialized countries. Forgotten is the fact that international organizations like the UN can never be more effective than their members wish it to be. As former British prime minister Margaret Thatcher once remarked, the UN is merely a mirror of its members; they would do better to reform themselves than curse the mirror if they don't like what they see. The United Nations' revived peacekeeping role shows that only when states consistently resort to international institutions, use and abide by international law, and give international bodies greater powers and the means of enforcing their charters and the law is it reasonable to expect solutions to the global crisis to come from the supranational level.

The US practice exemplifies the inconsistency and self-interestedness that characterize the way most states treat international law and treaties. In Latin America, for instance, the United States has consistently used force and threats to overthrow legitimate governments or intervene in civil conflicts. Yet the United States is a signatory of the Treaty of the Organization of American States (1948), which specifically prohibits any form of interference in the internal affairs of states in the hemisphere. Its worldwide arms shipments frequently go to governments that systematically violate human rights. US air and naval attacks against Libya in 1986 were justified on the transparent ground of "freedom of the seas" when, in fact, they had no firm basis in international law. Its always qualified support of compulsory jurisdiction by the ICJ (under the Connolly Amendment, which enables a president to withdraw cases he judges to be "essentially within the domestic jurisdiction" of the United States) became a formal rejection in 1985 when the Reagan administration saw no other way to avoid losing a suit brought by Nicaragua over the CIA's mining of its harbors. In the 1980s the United States also withdrew from UNESCO, refused to approve the Law of the Sea Treaty, voted against the World Health Organization's ban on Nestlé infant formula, and agreed to Senate ratification of the 1948 Genocide Convention only with a reservation exempting the United States from being sued in the ICJ for genocide. In the 1990s two US presidents chose to close off access to the United States for Haitian refugees by boarding ships in international waters and forcibly repatriating people fleeing oppression. The Clinton administration also opposed a broad mandate for an international criminal court, a nuclear-weapons convention, and (see below) international treaties to ban landmines and ban or restrict the small-arms trade. And under George W. Bush, the United States showed its near-complete lack of interest in international law, not only by rejecting various international agreements, such as the ICC and the Kyoto Protocol, but also by its illegal prosecution of the Iraq war and its violations of the Geneva Conventions and the Convention Against Torture.[146] Such behavior demonstrates a disregard for international cooperation that is extraordinary for a nation that prides itself on a historical commitment to the rule of law.

In terms of promoting the human interest, realism demands recognition both of the deeply ingrained resistance of state and corporate leaders to supranational authority and of the increasing need for strengthening it. Even when it is not possible to put teeth into global agreements and organiza-tions—such as in the Law of the Sea Treaty, the various human-rights covenants, and the International Criminal Court, none of which can compel adherence by states—the establishment of global standards and of new structures may be worthy accomplishments in their own right. As the expe-rience of the Law of the Sea Treaty shows, sometimes the first step is to gain recognition of the need for global action, then to piece together the means of effective monitoring of the new arrangement, and only later, building on a history of equity and goodwill, to close the loopholes by intro-ducing reliable enforcement mechanisms.

But practice has a way of outrunning theory. As much as states and global corporations will resist encroachments on their authority, break-throughs do occur that create precedents and interesting possibilities for the future of international law and institutions. The Indian government's brief seizure of Union Carbide's top officer after the Bhopal tragedy is one such precedent. (India was unable, however, to sue the company in a US court.) Another was the attempt by a Spanish judge to gain the extradition of the former Chilean dictator, Augusto Pinochet, for trial on genocide and other charges. His effort failed; but it elevated state terrorism to a new level of judicial review.[147] A third precedent was the successful lawsuit against Unocal Corporation for its complicity with the Burmese government in the brutal treatment of villagers so that an oil pipeline could be laid. At this writing, Massachusetts and eleven other US states were seeking a Supreme Court decision to compel US government compliance with tough global warming standards. Many other creative uses of international law on behalf of global betterment are in process, often involving citizens and NGOs in different countries joining together to sue TNCs that pollute the environment or conspire with governments to repress human rights.[148] The operative concept here is not personal injury but *global* injury, an expanded version of the Nuremberg Principle. Until such time as businesses, governments, and NGOs develop an enforceable code of behavior on environmental and labor rights to which TNCs and host countries subscribe, ordinary people will have to rely on new understandings of the rule of international law.[149]

Governments need to be educated to lawfulness and constantly prompted to practice what they preach about justice. Hence the importance, once more, of popular movements and voluntary organizations. But we should also keep in mind that citizen action against oppression has up until now not often been at the global level. Civil wars have been the norm. And whether these have toppled governments or led to the creation of new territories, they have all accepted the state as the appropriate vehicle for their rule.[150] Consequently, we see that among the obstacles to a new globalism is not only the weakness of global consciousness and recourse to law by state leaderships, but also a continuing identification with the state even by those who feel oppressed by it.

### The Prospects for Humanity

Ultimately, the future of the planet rests with individuals—those who, in their daily struggles to survive, create positive examples of courage and self-sacrifice that will empower others; and those who use the fact of not having to struggle as a privileged opportunity to work for human betterment. Both kinds of persons reflect the best of human values and the best hope for humanity.

If it is true, as Richard Falk says, that "the most revealing world order statement each of us makes is with his or her life,"[151] then we are fortunate to have plenty of examples of people who have made the planet a better place—and in the process demonstrated that individuals do make a difference. In an age when personal power exercised on behalf of humanity is infrequently applauded in the global media, we would do well to remind ourselves of those who have fought and are fighting for human rights; of the enormous strides that have been made in a very short time by the women's, environmental, civil rights, and liberation theology movements; of the worldwide support for calls to restore ecological rationality and end the arms race, and the prominent place of religious institutions in catalyzing such support. Just a few concerned citizens were enough to inspire transforming events such as the UN's International Year of Cooperation, the Partial Test Ban, the Bilateral Nuclear Freeze initiative, and the international convention to outlaw landmines.[152] Civil-society organizations are a critical component of the international effort to bring the production and export of small arms under control.[153] In short, world politics is too important to be left to diplomats. As *Star Trek*'s Mr. Spock once observed, "We must acknowledge that the purpose of diplomacy is to prolong a crisis."

Ordinary people acting to make both their communities and the world more secure is one kind of individual empowerment. Another kind has to do with shifts in individual values. In the United States, where this shift has been documented,[154] it seems to be occurring across the political and social spectrum. Its most remarkable feature in world-political terms is that it displays a turn away from many prominent realist and corporate-globalist values (such as competition, materialism, quantity, individualism, and power) and toward many global-humanist values (such as cooperation, spirituality, enoughness, community, and personal growth). Although too much can be made of the political direction and scope of this values shift—there is always backsliding—neither can it be considered spurious or ephemeral. When large numbers of people from all walks of life simplify their lifestyles (their needs) and change their values (their wants), and when they begin to participate in re-creating the substance of their communities and businesses, national and eventually global politics must also change. Growth, expansion, and consumption, which have always characterized state and corporate politics, have to be cast aside as national security is pressured to serve human-security needs more directly.

When and whether such a dramatic transformation—and the prospects for universalizing it—will occur may finally depend on people's beliefs and attitudes at least as much as on their energies. For the global crisis is psychological as well as material, and it starts with us. How much we believe in ourselves, whether or not we question our beliefs as well as those of others, how important we really believe the crisis is, and how seriously we believe in one person's ability to influence it—these, Roger Walsh eloquently tells us, are among the fundamental issues each of us must decide as we confront hunger, the arms race, and pollution.[155]

It takes great inner strength in times of fear and uncertainty to hold to a positive vision of the future. Yet positiveness and hopefulness are essential to creating a humane world. As Patricia Mische perceptively pointed out to an audience of peace workers:

> Many of us are not successful in our efforts for peace because secretly we don't really believe it can happen. Secretly, we don't even know if we want it to happen. And if we do want it to happen, we don't know what a peace system would look like. We know what it is we're working against, but we don't know what it is we want to create. Our images of the future serve like magnets. If we walk around only with images of destruction, we [may] use our energies to bring about the very destruction we fear.[156]

The struggle for dominion that takes place at every level of human activity will surely remain with us for a very long time. But not necessarily forever, in the same forms, or with the same intensities or doomsday potential.

Global humanism contends that it is realistic to be optimistic, fc
stave off worldwide collapse by calling forth the best that is with..
us. Who in 1985 would have believed that the end of Soviet communism
and the Cold War would occur within six years? Who would have believed
that such a strong worldwide consensus could form around the threat of
global warming? Fundamental changes for the better do occur, and suddenly and unpredictably.

The bottom line is that our age is but another phase in the universal
evolutionary process. Like all ages that preceded it and all that will follow,
this one holds out new opportunities for tapping the human potential. It is
demonstrably true that everyone can achieve a fulfilling life, and that the
earth can be kept green and blue—just as true as humanity's ability to
explore distant planets. The real question is whether enough of us will
believe in that prospect and will dedicate our "lives and sacred fortunes" to
realizing it.

The opening pages of this study quoted the warning of then UN
Secretary-General U Thant about an impending planetary crisis brought on
by the arms race and underdevelopment. U Thant's plea was that people
develop a "dual allegiance . . . to the human race as well as to our local
community or nation." "I even believe," he concluded, "that the mark of the
truly educated and imaginative person facing the twenty-first century is that
he feels himself to be a planetary citizen."[157] Perhaps the best argument on
behalf of space travel is that every astronaut and cosmonaut who has gazed
at the planet from the moon and deep space has moved toward that dual
allegiance. The last word belongs to one of them, Edgar Mitchell:

> No man I know of has gone to the moon that has not been affected in some
> way that is similar. It is what I prefer to call instant global consciousness.
> Each man comes back with a feeling that he is no longer only an American
> citizen; he is a planetary citizen. He doesn't like things the way they are,
> and he wants to improve them.

## Notes

1. For instance, Brandt et al. and Commission on Weak States and US
National Security.
2. Richard Rosecrance, *The Rise of the Trading State: Commerce and
Conquest in the Modern World.*
3. "Developing Nations Win by Getting Greener," *Financial Times*, June 28,
2002; Assadourian, "Transforming Corporations," pp. 171–89.
4. Quoted in Marcus G. Raskin, "Progressive Liberalism for the '80s," *The
Nation*, p. 591.
5. On the essentially domestic sources of Soviet and US security, see John W.
Burton, *Global Conflict: The Domestic Sources of International Crisis.*
6. The UNDP's human-development reports consistently show that in the top
twenty industrialized countries and the Asian NICs, government plays a central role
in social welfare, for example, in education and public health. Countries that rank

lowest in human development, such as Pakistan and Peru, spend very little on social well-being.

7. The issue of "peak oil" naturally has its ardent supporters and detractors. For both sides of the issue, see the essays in *World Watch*, vol. 19, no. 1 (January–February 2005).

8. The "conceptual marriage of 'environment' and development . . . aims at new levels of administrative monitoring and control. It treats as a technical problem what amounts to no less than a civilizational impasse, namely that the level of production already achieved in the North—let alone the rest of the globe—is not viable." Wolfgang Sachs, "Ecology vs. Ecocracy," *Amicus Journal*, p. 4.

9. World Bank 1992, p. 9.

10. See the report of the 2050 Project, in which mostly developing-country respondents offer views on sustainable development: Tanvi Nagpal and C. Foltz, eds., *Choosing Our Future: Visions of a Sustainable World*.

11. Denis Goulet, "Authentic Development: Is It Sustainable?" *Hunger TeachNet*. In Goulet's conception, development should have six dimensions: equitable distribution of material goods, social well-being, political freedoms, cultural autonomy, ecological soundness, and meaningful living.

12. See Joseph E. Stiglitz, *Making Globalization Work*, p. 281.

13. Lappé and Collins, pp. 328–39; Cornia et al., chs. 6 and 9; and Smith, *Ending Global Poverty*.

14. As the one-time chief economist of the World Bank and current top US trade official, Lawrence H. Summers, has written, the estimated cost in the Third and Fourth Worlds of educating female children is $2.4 billion, "less than one-quarter of 1 percent of their gross domestic product." Summers, "Best Third World Investment? Girls' Education," *The Oregonian*, May 5, 1993, C9.

15. See William K. Stevens, "Green Revolution Not Enough, Study Finds," *NYT*, September 6, 1994, p. B9; John F. Burns, "Bangladesh Still Poor, Cuts Birth Rate Sharply," *NYT*, September 13, 1994, p. A5; Weiskel, "Vicious Circles."

16. "Credit to the Poor," *The Newsletter from the International Center for Economic Growth*, pp. 3, 7; Paul Ekins, *A New World Order: Grassroots Movements for Social Change*, pp. 122–24; Michael Renner, "Transforming Security," in Brown et al., eds., *State of the World 1997*, p. 129.

17. On microloan experiences, see Paul Lewis, "Small Loans May Be Key to Helping Third World," *NYT*, January 26, 1997, online at www.nytimes.com; Susan E. Reed, "Bangladesh Start-up a Ringing Success," *International Herald Tribune*, May 25–26, 2002; Saritha Rai, "Tiny Loans Have Big Impact on Poor," *NYT*, April 12, 2004, p. C3; Tim Weiner, "With Little Loans, Mexican Women Overcome," *NYT*, March 18, 2003, p. A8; and *NYT*, October 14, 2006, p. 1; Connie Bruck, "Millions for Millions," *The New Yorker*, October 30, 2006, pp. 62–73; and Celia W. Dugger, "Debate Stirs over Tiny Loans for World's Poorest," *NYT*, April 29, 2004, online ed. As Bruck and Dugger report, there is disagreement within the loans-for-the-poor community over issues such as whether to emphasize the poorest of the poor and whether or not to put loans on a commercial, profit-making basis. An organization called Kiva (www.kiva.org) deals with this problem by making small loans directly to African villagers via the Internet. People contribute as little as $25 by credit card to a small business whose owner and project are pictured online.

18. Bruce Stokes, *Helping Ourselves: Local Solutions to Global Problems*, p. 96.

19. Paul Harrison, *The Greening of Africa: Breaking Through in the Battle for Land and Food*, pp. 89–91.

20. Oxfam is headquartered in London; Oxfam America, its US affiliate, is in

Boston. Church World Service, in New York, is part of the National Council of Churches of Christ. Grassroots International is located in Cambridge, Massachusetts. The Plenty Project, which has won international recognition for its self-help teachings in Guatemala (and the South Bronx), is sponsored by The Farm in Tennessee, the largest intentional community in the United States. See Lillie Wilson, "The Plenty Project: Inside the Hippie Peace Corps," *New Age*. An excellent overview of private voluntary organizations (PVOs) is provided by David C. Korten, *Getting to the 21st Century*, ch. 10.

21. John Clark, *Democratizing Development: The Role of Voluntary Organizations*, pp. 39–63, 208–11.

22. See Mary Ann Littrell and Marsha Ann Dickson, eds., *Social Responsibility in the Global Market: Fair Trade of Cultural Products*.

23. See its publication, *The Canopy*, at www.rainforest-alliance.org.

24. See the publication, *Nature Conservancy*, at www.nature.org.

25. Michael Wines, "Hope for Hungry Children, Arriving in a Foil Packet," *NYT*, August 8, 2005, p. A7.

26. The unknowns surrounding biotechnology suggest the need for great caution in relying on such a technical fix to increase food production. A good discussion is in *Amicus Journal*, vol. 15, no. 1 (Spring 1993), pp. 19–30. The Biosafety Protocol (2000) to the 1992 Convention on Biological Diversity, if ratified by fifty governments, would provide one crucial safeguard: the right of a government to decide whether or not to import products containing GMOs.

27. The designer is Nicholas Negroponte at MIT. See John Markoff, "For $150, Third-World Laptop Stirs a Big Debate," *NYT*, November 30, 2006, p. 1.

28. Quoted in Duane Elgin, *Voluntary Simplicity: Toward a Way of Life That Is Outwardly Simple, Inwardly Rich*, p. 190.

29. Professor Paul Wapner of American University, Washington, DC, letter to the *NYT*, December 2, 1994, p. A14.

30. Land conservation programs are outlined in a study by the American Farmland Trust, "Future Policy Directions for American Agriculture," pp. 90–92. Brown et al., *State of the World 1985*, pp. 135–39, notes promising research currently being done on plants and crops to increase food yields, develop new strains, and improve hardiness. The Eugene (Oregon) *Register-Guard* of August 2, 1985, reports on new developments in hydroponics—growing food without soil. Plants thrive by being suspended in fertilizer solutions, and herbicides are not applied.

31. Feeding and grazing cattle require large amounts of grain, land, water, and fossil fuels, all of which contribute to desertification, hunger, and depletion of water tables. So long as meat-for-protein diets are the norm, and grain-fed beef is more profitable than healthy people, livestock will occupy a prominent place in the world political economy. A concise review of findings on this issue is in "The Damage Done by Cattle-Raising," *Washington Spectator*, January 15, 1993, pp. 1–3.

32. The UN claims to have already saved the lives of 1 million children (*Los Angeles Times*, December 12, 1985).

33. Paul Harrison, pp. 261–71.

34. See the Partners in Health program discussed by Howard Hiatt, "Learn from Haiti," *NYT*, December 6, 2001, p. A29.

35. Celia W. Dugger, "A Cure That Really Works: Cambodia Tries the Nonprofit Path to Health Care," *NYT*, January 8, 2006, p. 8.

36. Margaret A. Haapoja, "Tropical Medicine: An Interview with Sadie Brorson," *Hemispheres*.

37. The Andes program is reported in *Los Angeles Times*, February 16, 1985, p. 1. On Brazil, see James Brooke, "Brazilian State Leads Way in Saving Children," *NYT*, May 14, 1993, p. 1.

38. See Stephanie Strom, "Gates Aims Billions to Attack Illnesses of World's Neediest," *NYT*, July 13, 2003, online ed.

39. Bethany McLean, "The Power of Philanthropy," *Fortune*.

40. Amory B. Lovins, *Soft Energy Paths: Toward a Durable Peace*.

41. Good, concise discussions of "soft path" technologies are in Lovins, pp. 38–46; John J. Berger, *Nuclear Power: Unviable Option*, rev. ed., part II; Brown et al., *State of the World 1985*, ch. 8; and Brown, *Building a Sustainable Society*, ch. 9. Emphasis on small-scale energy technologies has been part of US aid programs for about fifteen years.

42. See, for example, Brown, *Building a Sustainable Society*, p. 215; and Paul Harrison, pp. 210–15.

43. Craig Canine, "How to Clean Coal," *OnEarth* (Natural Resources Defense Council), pp. 28–29. BP and Edison International are already planning to build such power plants in California; see *NYT*, February 11, 2006, p. B3.

44. Lester R. Brown et al., "Picturing a Sustainable Society," in Brown, *State of the World 1990*, pp. 177, 179.

45. The economic, health, safety, and energy costs of the nuclear option are briefly discussed in Berger, chs. 3–7; Brown, *Building a Sustainable Society*, pp. 73–81; and Lovins, Lovins, and Ross, pp. 1149–53. Less frequently noted are the potentially astronomical costs (not to mention safety hazards) of decommissioning nuclear plants and disposing of their waste products and equipment. One study by Cynthia Pollock ("Decommissioning: Nuclear Power's Missing Link") observes that over 350 nuclear plants will need to be decommissioned worldwide by 2020; the average lifetime of each is only about thirty-one years. That cost alone could be anywhere from $50 million to $3 billion per plant.

46. See the extensive discussion by Carlos F. Díaz-Alejandro, "Delinking North and South: Unshackled or Unhinged?" in Albert Fishlow et al., *Rich and Poor Nations in the World Economy*, pp. 105–44. On Third World transnational firms, see the study by Sanjaya Lall, *The New Multinationals: The Spread of Third World Enterprises*.

47. These debt-for-nature swaps seem to have lost their popularity. Between 1987 and 1991 there were seventeen such swaps that resulted in the retirement of about $100 million in external debt. But this figure is extremely small in relation to the debt problem. See World Bank 1992, p. 169.

48. Estimate in Brown, *Building a Sustainable Society*, table 10-1, p. 249. On investments in renewables, see Christopher Flavin et al., *American Energy: The Renewable Path to Energy Security*.

49. For an excellent critique, see James Howard Kunstler, *The Long Emergency: Surviving the Converging Catastrophes of the Twenty-first Century*.

50. Finland is among the European countries that is again constructing, or reconsidering, nuclear power plants. See *International Herald Tribune*, December 13, 2005. China, India, and South Korea all have expanded nuclear power production in recent years. See Renner et al., eds., *Vital Signs 2003*, p. 36. On the other hand, in Germany, antinuclear sentiment led to a decision in mid-2001 by the German power industry to close down all nineteen nuclear plants within twenty years. Germany and Austria also urged the Czech Republic to close down its recently upgraded Temelin nuclear plant for safety reasons. In the United States efforts to revive the nuclear industry continue despite the fact that finding a final repository for radioactive waste at Yucca Flats is way over budget and still unsettled.

51. Flavin et al., *American Energy*, pp. 7, 21.

52. Brown et al., eds., *State of the World 1985*, pp. 149–50.

53. *Los Angeles Times*, February 19, 1986.

54. See "A *Practical* Alternative to Mindless Growth?" *New Options,* no. 15 (April 8, 1985), pp. 1–2.

55. Andrew C. Revkin, "British Government Report Calls for Broad Effort on Climate Issues," *NYT,* October 30, 2006, p. A15. The Stern Review on the Economics of Climate Change, the title of the report, is at www.sternreview.org.uk.

56. Christopher Flavin, "The Legacy of Rio," in Brown et al., *State of the World 1997,* table 1-2, p. 11.

57. For brief reviews of the scientific community's overwhelming endorsement of global warming's reality, see Guy Gugliotta, "Warming May Threaten 37% of Species by 2050," *Washington Post,* January 8, 2004; Gregg Easterbrook, "Finally Feeling the Heat," *NYT,* May 24, 2006, p. A27; Michael Janofsky, "6 Ex-Chiefs of E.P.A. Urge Action on Greenhouse Gases," *NYT,* January 19, 2006, p. A17.

58. The former US vice president Al Gore's knockout film, *An Inconvenient Truth,* helped shatter the notion that global warming is at worst a distant threat (see at www.climatecrisis.net). After meeting with Gore, British billionaire Sir Richard Branson (founder of The Virgin Group) pledged $3 billion over ten years to fight global warming—a figure, it might be noted, that is three times the 2006 US budget for research on energy alternatives.

59. For background, see Christopher Flavin and Seth Dunn, "Responding to the Threat of Climate Change," in Brown et al., eds., *State of the World 1998,* pp. 113–30.

60. These and other criticisms by environmental NGOs are contained in a report by Derick Atienza from Kyoto via Kyodo News Service, December 9, 1997, online at http://home.kyodo.co.jp. More upbeat commentary is in Charley Hanley's report for the Associated Press, December 10, 1997, online at www.ap.org.

61. See estimates in Flavin, "The Legacy of Rio," in Brown et al., eds., *State of the World 1997,* p. 13, and Seth Dunn and Christopher Flavin, "Moving the Climate Change Agenda Forward," in Flavin et al., *State of the World 2002,* pp. 30–35.

62. For a more detailed prescription, see Lester R. Brown, *Plan B: Rescuing a Planet Under Stress and a Civilization in Trouble.*

63. Kellogg and Schware, p. 1104; Maranto, p. 49; Seth Zuckerman, "Living According to Nature," *The Nation.*

64. Wolfgang Sachs, "One World," in Sachs, ed., *Development Dictionary: A Guide to Knowledge as Power,* pp. 108–12.

65. Marcus Colchester, "Sustaining the Forests: The Community-Based Approach in South and South-East Asia," *Development and Change.*

66. The 2001 Convention on Persistent Organic Pollutants, which bans nine pesticides and some other dangerous substances, is a good start inasmuch as it establishes a "precautionary principle" as the basis for action and leaves open the possibility of adding other toxins to the list. See Anne Platt McGinn, "Reducing Our Toxic Burden," in Flavin et al., *State of the World 2002,* pp. 75–100.

67. A wide range of NGOs and international organizations have collectively concluded that government energy subsidies primarily benefit the rich, indirectly tax the poor, and cause billions of dollars' worth of environmental destruction. See Barbara Crossette, "Critics Say Industrial Subsidies Hurt Environment," *NYT,* June 23, 1997, online.

68. *Human Development Report 1992,* p. 84.

69. Lester R. Brown and Jennifer Mitchell, "Building a New Economy," in Brown et al., eds., *State of the World 1998,* pp. 181–82.

70. "By 1992, there were more than nine hundred international legal instruments (mostly binding) that either were fully directed to environmental protection or had more than one important provision addressing the issue." Harold K. Jacobson

and Edith Brown Weiss, "Strengthening Compliance with International Environmental Accords," in Paul F. Diehl, ed., *The Politics of Global Governance: International Organizations in an Interdependent World,* p. 305. Some important agreements not mentioned in this chapter are treated by Jacobsen and Weiss, such as the World Heritage Convention of 1972 concerning designation of historic sites, and the 1973 Convention on International Trade in Endangered Species.

71. See Elisabeth Mann Borgese, "The Law of the Sea," *Scientific American,* pp. 42–49.

72. A.W. Harris, "The International Seabed Authority: Enforcement in International Negotiations," paper prepared for the annual convention of the International Studies Association, Acapulco, Mexico, March 23–27, 1993. The convention was ratified by the required sixty states and entered into force in 1994.

73. Seth Dunn and Christopher Flavin, "Moving the Climate Change Agenda Forward," in Flavin et al., *State of the World 2002,* p. 48.

74. Hilary F. French, "Learning from the Ozone Experience," in Brown et al., eds., *State of the World 1997,* pp. 151–52 and table 9-2, p. 166. As French adds, however, record levels of ultraviolet radiation are being reported over populated and agricultural areas of the planet, "a sobering reminder that although action eventually was taken, it came too late to avoid serious consequences for human and ecological health."

75. The Japanese proposal is in Yoichi Kaya et al., "Management of Global Environmental Issues," *World Futures,* pp. 223–31.

76. French, "Learning from the Ozone Experience."

77. For a systematic appraisal of these issues, see P.J. Simmons and Chantal de Jonge Oudraat, eds., *Managing Global Issues: Lessons Learned.*

78. Kirkpatrick Sale, *Dwellers in the Land: The Bioregional Vision.*

79. It had once been widely assumed that only factories and power plants on the US side, mainly in the Ohio River Valley, were responsible. But it is now apparent that the Canadian side is also a source for some pollution. In any case, dealing with the growing problem will require exchanges of information and documentation that so far have not systematically occurred. See Anthony DePalma, "Pollution Flow Between U.S. and Canada Called Mutual," *NYT,* November 11, 1997, p. A9.

80. The antipollution conventions are briefly discussed by Armin Rosencranz, "The Problem of Transboundary Pollution," *Environment,* pp. 16–17.

81. A useful survey of the informal business sector in the Third World is by A. Lawrence Chickering and Mohamed Sahladine, eds., *The Silent Revolution: The Informal Sector in Five Asian and Near Eastern Countries.*

82. See *Utne Reader,* no. 15 (April–May 1986), pp. 24–33.

83. One study concludes that Mexican remittances, which amounted to around $5 billion by 1996, may help reduce future migration to the United States by virtue of the investments they make in local communities back home. "That is, remittance investments—or the indirect effects of their expenditure—provide the basis for humane work conditions and a level of remuneration sufficient to sustain a dignified lifestyle." But the author acknowledges that most households do not use remittances skillfully, thereby perpetuating outward migration. Leigh Binford, "Migrant Remittances and (Under)Development in Mexico," unpublished paper, Instituto de Ciencias Sociales y Humanidades, Puebla, Mexico, n.d., p. 15.

84. Karl W. Deutsch et al., *Political Community and the North Atlantic Area: International Organization in the Light of Historical Experience,* p. 5.

85. See Robert C. Johansen, "Toward an Alternative Security System: Moving Beyond the Balance of Power in the Search for World Security," pp. 33–36.

86. Patricia Mische, "Re-Visioning National Security: Toward a Viable World

Security System," in Carolyn M. Stephenson, ed., *Alternative Methods for International Security,* pp. 82–84.

87. Louis Henkin, *How Nations Behave: Law and Foreign Policy,* p. 113.

88. *NYT,* February 25, 2004, p. A8.

89. The Harvard project's contributions are reflected in the works of Roger Fisher and William L. Ury, starting with *Getting to YES: Negotiating Agreement Without Giving In.* Kelman's, Cohen's, and Saunders's approaches are conveniently available as chapters in Crocker and Hampson, eds., *Managing Global Chaos.*

90. Serge Schmemann, "Negotiators, Arab and Israeli, Built Friendship from Mistrust," *NYT,* September 28, 1995, p. 1. Once Benjamin Netanyahu became prime minister of Israel, a very different domestic political climate and far tougher line on relations with the PLO took over.

91. Text of the accord is in *Tikkun,* vol. 19, no. 1 (January–February 2004), pp. 33–45, and is reported on by Elaine Sciolino, "Self-Appointed Israeli and Palestinian Negotiators Offer a Plan for Middle East Peace," *NYT,* December 2, 2003, p. A8.

92. George F. Kennan, "On Nuclear War," *New York Review of Books,* p. 10. Also see Donald Keys, "The Neglected 'Software' Aspects of Disarmament," in Ervin Laszlo and Donald Keys, eds., *Disarmament: The Human Factor,* p. 19.

93. *NYT,* October 14, 1997, p. A8.

94. R. Jeffrey Smith, "Scientists Fault Charges of Soviet Cheating," *Science.* For a contrary view, see the US State Department's "Soviet Noncompliance with Arms Control Agreements." The list of agreements adhered to by both sides begins with the 1961 Antarctic Treaty and includes the Limited Test Ban (1963), treaties governing outer space (1967) and nuclear proliferation (1968), the Seabed Arms Control Treaty (1971), the "hot line" agreements (1963 and 1971), the ABM Treaty and protocol (1972 and 1974), and the Threshold Test Ban (1974) and Peaceful Nuclear Explosions (1976) treaties limiting the size of underground tests.

95. McGeorge Bundy, George F. Kennan, Robert S. McNamara, and Gerard Smith, "Nuclear Weapons and the Atlantic Alliance," *Foreign Affairs,* pp. 766–77.

96. For further discussion of no-first-use and minimum deterrence, including additional proposals for dealing with nuclear warheads, see Daniel Ellsberg, "Manhattan Project II," and Bundy, Crowe, and Drell. "Reducing Nuclear Danger."

97. See the comments of Robert McNamara and Joseph Rotblat in Schell, "The Gift of Time," pp. 25–28.

98. The overwhelming vote in favor was 115 to 22 (including the United States) with 32 abstentions. It was prompted by a ruling of the International Court of Justice that the threat or use of nuclear weapons is contrary to international law and the rules of conflict except in self-defense, when the survival of a country is at stake. See Schell, "The Gift of Time," pp. 17–18, and the Lawyers' Committee on Nuclear Policy (US), "Model Nuclear Weapons Convention," online at www.LCNP.org. One of the principal objections to eliminating nuclear weapons is the possibility of a "breakout" by a previously non-weapon state, which could then blackmail all other states. But former senior US civilian and military officials discount such a threat, pointing out (for example) that the breakout state would be an international renegade and would invite total destruction by all other states. See, for instance, in Schell, "The Gift of Time," pp. 23, 56, the comments of General Charles Horner and General George Lee Butler.

99. Patterson, p. 197; *The Defense Monitor* 24, no. 8 (September–October 1995), p. 58.

100. For a review of nuclear-free zones, see Zachary S. Davis, "The Spread of Nuclear-Weapon-Free Zones: Building a New Nuclear Bargain," *Arms Control Today.*

101. *NewsHour with Jim Lehrer,* July 18, 2006, at www.pbs.org/newshour/bb/middle_east/july-dec06/mideast_07-18.html.

102. Johansen, "Toward an Alternative Security System," p. 45.

103. Nicole Ball, *Pressing for Peace: Can Aid Induce Reform?* pp. 22, 66–67.

104. *NYT,* November 19, 2003, p. A8.

105. The literature on peacekeeping in all its dimensions is growing rapidly. A good start for understanding the conditions of success and failure is Crocker and Hampson, eds., *Managing Global Chaos;* Jacob Bercovitch, ed., *Resolving International Conflicts: The Theory and Practice of Mediation;* and Chester A. Crocker et al., eds., *Herding Cats: Multiparty Mediation in a Complex World.*

106. Chester A. Crocker, "The Varieties of Intervention: Conditions for Success," in Crocker and Hampson, eds., *Managing Global Chaos,* p. 186.

107. Michael S. Lund, "Early Warning and Preventive Diplomacy," in Crocker and Hampson, eds., *Managing Global Chaos,* ch. 26.

108. Paul F. Diehl ("The Conditions for Success in Peacekeeping Operations," in Diehl, ed., *The Politics of Global Governance,* p. 170) thus observes that we are left "with something of a tautology: peacekeeping is successful only when all parties wish to stop fighting." Crocker agrees with the main point: "It is not an accident that many of the United Nations' successes in peace operations have occurred in cases involving the implementation of a negotiated settlement plan: for example, El Salvador, Cambodia, Mozambique, and Namibia" ("The Varieties of Intervention," p. 195). Large-scale violence against people is not, of course, the only post–Cold War threat to international security. There is also the "willful and serious destruction of the global ecosystem" (as perhaps in Brazil's and Indonesia's rain forests) and "the acquisition by a country, in contravention to treaty obligations, of nuclear weapons or other weapons of mass destruction" (James G. Sutterlin, "United Nations Decisionmaking: Future Initiatives for the Security Council and the Secretary-General," in Thomas G. Weiss, ed., *Collective Security in a Changing World,* p. 122). Dealing with these problems will take approaches at once more delicate than and more forceful than a peacekeeping operation.

109. Among the many recapitulations of the Rwanda debacle, see Milton Leitenberg, "Rwanda and Burundi Genocide: A Case Study of Neglect and Indifference," in Samuel P. Oliner and Phillip T. Gay, eds., *Race, Ethnicity and Gender: A Global Perspective,* ch. 13; Philip Gourevitch, "The Genocide Fax," *The New Yorker*; and testimony of Jeff Drumtra, US Committee for Refugees, "Rwanda: Genocide and the Continuing Cycle of Violence," before the House Committee on International Relations, Subcommittee on International Operations and Human Rights, May 5, 1998, online via www.uscr.org.

110. Ayoob, in Weiss, ed., p. 48.

111. Bruce Russett and James S. Sutterlin, "The U.N. in a New World Order," *Foreign Affairs,* pp. 78–79. In their view each use of a permanent UN force would still require advance approval by the legislatures of participating states and by the Security Council itself.

112. Weiss, pp. 128–29, uses "peace enforcement" to refer (as one example) to armed enforcement of a cease-fire that breaks down. He cites Article 40 of the UN Charter as providing justification.

113. Ibid., p. 130.

114. International Commission on Intervention and State Sovereignty, *The Responsibility to Protect.*

115. David C. Hendrickson, "The Ethics of Collective Security," *Ethics and International Affairs,* pp. 1–16.

116. In April 1998 the Roman Catholic Church in Guatemala, headed by

Bishop Gerardi, issued a report based on human-rights abuses during the long civil war. The report gave estimates of the conflict's casualties—150,000 dead and 50,000 missing—which were mainly (80 percent) attributed to the Guatemalan military. Most of the people killed belonged to Indian tribes. Yet not a single member of the military command was charged with a crime. See *NYT,* May 9, 1998, online. Some observers would no doubt add a fifth case of genocide: the Kurds at the hands of Saddam Hussein.

117. William Shawcross, "Tragedy in Cambodia," *New York Review of Books,* November 14, 1996, at www.nybooks.com/articles/article-preview?article_id=1361.

118. *NYT,* February 14, 1995, pp. 1–2. When the Dayton Accords were signed in November 1995, the indicted Bosnian Serb leaders were merely denied future political power; no one was obliged to turn them over to the international tribunal on war-crimes charges. In fact, the two principal leaders were able to move about quite freely and continue to exercise authority. The progress of the International Criminal Tribunal for the Former Yugoslavia may be followed at www.un.org/icty, and the official tribunal website at http://69.94.11.53/default.htm.

119. *NYT,* May 2, 1998, p. 1.

120. Alessandra Stanley, "U.S. Dissents, but Accord Is Reached on War-Crime Court," *NYT,* July 18, 1998, online.

121. The conversion (or more usually, diversification) of military-industrial plants has a disputed record in the United States. A Pentagon study based mainly on conversion experiences in three communities perhaps predictably found no compelling reasons for establishing a national office to promote or facilitate shifts to nonmilitary production (US Department of Defense, Office of the Assistant Secretary of Defense, Office of Economic Adjustment, and President's Economic Adjustment Committee, *Economic Adjustment/Conversion*). Patricia Mische (in Stephenson, ed., p. 81), on the other hand, cites another Department of Defense study of successful conversions in sixty-one US communities. Both the problems and the opportunities presented by military conversion are clearly outlined in a case study by Joel S. Yudken, "Conversion in the Aerospace Industry: The McDonnell-Douglas Project," in Gordon and McFadden, eds., pp. 130–43; and by Seymour Melman, "Successful Conversion Experiences," in Brunn et al., eds., pp. 338–344.

For Europe, see Renner, "Swords into Plowshares"; Gordon and McFadden, eds.; and Paul Dunne and Sue Willett, "National Case Studies in Conversion: The United Kingdom," in Brunn et al., eds., pp. 209–30.

122. Kirkpatrick Sale, "Conversion to What: A Green View of Economic Planning," *Utne Reader.*

123. Marion Anderson et al., "Converting the American Economy."

124. See Maj. Britt Theorin, "Military Resources to the Environment," in Brunn et al., pp. 247–51. Since military forces are the largest polluters in every society, they might be placed under a special civilian agency with the assignment to dispose of their own as well as civilian toxic wastes and to decontaminate land.

125. Remarks to the State of the World Forum, October 3, 1996. See www.nautilus.org/napsnet (December 9, 1996).

126. Mische, in Stephenson, ed., pp. 75–76; Robert Muller, "A World Core Curriculum," *Education Network News.*

127. The widening interest in peace and global studies is reflected in Barbara J. Wien, ed., *Peace and World Order Studies,* 4th ed.; Robert Woito, *To End War: A New Approach to International Conflict;* and "Teaching for Peace," *Christian Science Monitor* supplement, January 31, 1986.

128. For the many ways "think globally, act locally" can be understood, theoretically and practically, see Elgin; Stokes; Harry C. Boyte, *The Backyard*

*Revolution: Understanding the New Citizen Movement;* Margo Adair, *Working Inside Out: Tools for Change;* Joan Bodner, ed., with the American Friends Service Committee, *Taking Charge of Our Lives: Living Responsibly in a Troubled World;* and Corinne McLaughlin and Gordon Davidson, *Builders of the Dawn: Community Lifestyles in a Changing World.*

129. Hawken, "A Declaration of Sustainability," *Utne Reader,* pp. 54–60.

130. On nonviolent defense, see Gene Sharp, "Making the Abolition of War a Realistic Goal," in Severyn T. Bruyn and Paula M. Rayman, eds., *Nonviolent Action and Social Change.*

131. *Los Angeles Times,* February 16, 1986.

132. From various issues of *Far Eastern Economic Review,* May and June 1992, and C. Douglas Lummis, "People Power in Thailand: Long Parliament in the Streets," *The Nation.*

133. For example, see the reports on successful worker protests against a Mexican firm contracted by Nike and Reebok (Ginger Thompson, "Mexican Labor Protest Gets Results," *NYT,* October 8, 2001, p. A3) and Taco Bell's food suppliers in Florida (Eric Schlosser, "A Side Order of Human Rights," *NYT,* April 6, 2005, p. A29).

134. Two cases may be mentioned here: Niger and Ukraine. Niger has reportedly made significant progress in democratization, but not in dealing with hunger and other human-security issues. (See Lydia Polgreen, "A New Face of Hunger, Without the Old Excuses," *NYT,* July 31, 2005, sec. 4, p. 3.) Ukraine, one of ten countries admitted to the EU in 2004, cannot keep its work force at home—the outflow of workers desperate to earn a living wage is very high—has the lowest birthrate in Europe, and has a higher rate of HIV/AIDS than India or China. Andrew Meier, "Endangered Revolution," *National Geographic.*

135. *Human Development Report 2002,* pp. 56–57.

136. Joseph T. Siegle, Michael M. Weinstein, and Morton H. Halperin, "Why Democracies Excel," *Foreign Affairs.*

137. Global Education Associates of East Orange, New Jersey, is one organization that seeks to forge a transnational network. Patricia Mische, cited above, is its co-founder. Most of the other organizations listed can be found in Woito, pp. 539–604.

138. However, it now appears that the code, signed by nearly two hundred countries, is being widely broken. Twenty-one companies reportedly gave away free milk-substitute samples all around the world, from Poland to Thailand. *NYT,* April 11, 1998, p. A6.

139. The Clinton administration brokered an agreement with some of the leading apparel makers, human-rights NGOs, and unions to create a code of conduct. Among other things, the code is supposed to ensure monitoring of overseas sweatshops and a living wage. Steven Greenhouse, "A New Approach to Eliminating Sweatshops," *NYT,* April 13, 1997, online.

140. Rugmark works with carpet manufacturers in India and Nepal to monitor production and contribute fees raised to schools. There are, however, many difficulties in monitoring carpet production. See the *NYT,* October 16, 1997, p. B1.

141. Paul Ekins, a director of the award, profiles Survival International and most of the other recipients in *A New World Order: Grassroots Movements for Social Change.* The book is an excellent directory of global-change agents.

142. On the Greens, consult Capra and Spretnak.

143. Sivard, *Women: A World Survey,* pp. 29–34; Ellen Dorsey, "The Global Women's Movement: Articulating a New Vision of Global Governance," in Diehl, ed., ch 18. In 2005 women were elected to lead Liberia (a first in Africa), Chile (a first in Latin America), and Germany.

144. The UN's problems and failings as a gender-conscious employer are chronicled in the *NYT*, April 10, 1995, p. 1.

145. Shuman, pp. 29–35.

146. See the scathing criticisms contained in the report of a working group under the UN Economic and Social Council, Commission on Human Rights, "Situation of Detainees at Guantánamo Bay," February 15, 2006, at www.ohchr.org/english/bodies/chr/docs/62chr/E.CN.4.2006.120.pdf.

147. The judge, Baltasar Garzón, did succeed years later in having a former Argentine naval officer extradited from Mexico to face genocide charges in Spain stemming from the "disappearances" that occurred during Argentina's dirty war.

148. Just such a situation occurred in 1998 when a US-based NGO represented an Ecuadoran community in a New York suit against ChevronTexaco's destructive oil spills. (Diana Jean Schemo, "Ecuadoreans Want Texaco to Clear Toxic Residue," *NYT*, February 1, 1998, online.) The New York court decided the case should be heard in Ecuador, but that any penalties against the company would be enforced in the United States. See Juan Forero, "Texaco Goes on Trial in Ecuador Pollution Case," *NYT*, October 23, 2003, p. W1.

149. See Blond, pp. 86–90, for suggestions of a code of TNC conduct.

150. Hedley Bull, "The State's Positive Role in World Affairs," *Daedalus*.

151. Richard A. Falk, introduction to Falk, Kim, and Mendlovitz, p. 14.

152. See, for example, Raymond Bonner, "How a Group of Outsiders Moved Nations to Ban Mines," *NYT*, September 20, 1997, p. 4. The movement to ban land-mines was started by two Americans, who received crucial support from the Canadian government. The United States did not sign the resulting treaty, which was signed in Ottawa in December 1997, mainly because of its stated reliance on land-mines to defend South Korea from invasion. In the wake of the wars in the former Yugoslavia and Cambodia, a worldwide momentum gathered in the mid-1990s to ban landmines, which claim roughly 25,000 lives (mostly civilian) every year. The usual estimate is that there are around 100 million land (antipersonnel) mines world-wide. In Cambodia alone, mines planted by all sides accounted for most of the casu-alties and rendered as much as 5 percent of the land unusable, thus also contributing to problems of resettling refugees. Seth Mydans, "Living with Land Mines: Cambodia's Deadly Toll," *NYT*, May 11, 1996, p. 4.

153. Canada and Norway led the way in convening the first international meet-ing to deal with legal and illegal traffic in small arms in mid-1998. Only twenty countries were represented. As mentioned earlier, international agreement has been difficult; the UN Programme of Action to Prevent, Combat and Eradicate the Illicit Trade in Small Arms and Light Weapons in All Its Aspects is the only one (in July 2001) so far on control of small arms. See Owen Greene et al., *Implementing the Programme of Action 2003: Action by States and Civil Society*.

154. A useful general discussion of a values shift is in Brown, *Building a Sustainable Society*, pp. 349–61. That a shift is taking place in the United States is established in different ways by several writers. See, for instance, Daniel Yankelovich, *New Rules: Searching for Self-Fulfillment in a World Turned Upside Down*, public opinion poll results; Arnold Mitchell, "Changing Values and Lifestyles"; Alvin Toffler, *The Third Wave*; Marilyn Ferguson, *The Aquarian Conspiracy: Personal and Social Transformation in the 1980s*; *The Futurist* vol. 11, no. 3 (May–June 1996), pp. 11–12.

The necessity of a values shift is cogently argued in an expanding number of books, notably Brown, *Building a Sustainable Society*, pp. 345–50; Mark Satin, *New Age Politics: Healing Self and Society*; Theodore Roszak et al., *Person/Planet: The Creative Disintegration of Industrial Society*; and Robert Bellah et al., *Habits of the Heart*. Finally, nothing illuminates better than personal experiences of changed values and attitudes. Norie Huddle's *Surviving: The Best Game on Earth* contains a number of interviews with both well-known and not-so-well-known people (including a few from outside the United States) on the critical question of redefining national security.

155. Roger Walsh, *Staying Alive: The Psychology of Human Survival*, ch. 11.
156. *Los Angeles Times*, September 26, 1984.
157. U Thant, *View from the UN*, p. 454.

or Bane for Asian Security?" *The China and Eurasia Forum Quarterly* 3 (2005): 19–26.

Bercovitch, Jacob, ed. *Resolving International Conflicts: The Theory and Practice of Mediation.* Boulder, Colo.: Lynne Rienner, 1996.

Berger, John J. *Nuclear Power: The Unviable Option.* Rev. ed. Palo Alto, Calif.: Ramparts, 1977.

Bergsten, C. Fred, et al. *China: The Balance Sheet.* New York: Public Affairs, 2006.

Bernstein, Dennis, and Leslie Kean. "People of the Opiate: Burma's Dictatorship of Drugs." *The Nation,* December 16, 1996, 11–18.

Berrigan, Frida, and William D. Hartung. *U.S. Weapons at War 2005: Promoting Freedom or Fueling Conflict?* New York: World Policy Institute, June 2005.

Betts, Richard K. *Nuclear Blackmail and Nuclear Balance.* Washington, D.C.: Brookings Institution, 1987.

Bianco, Lucien. *Origins of the Chinese Revolution, 1915–1949.* Trans. Muriel Bell. Stanford, Calif.: Stanford University Press, 1971.

Bill, James A. *The Eagle and the Lion: The Tragedy of American-Iranian Relations.* New Haven, Conn.: Yale University Press, 1988.

Bilmes, Linda, and Joseph E. Stiglitz. "Encore." *Milken Institute Review* 4 (2006): 76–83.

Binford, Leigh. "Migrant Remittances and (Under)Development in Mexico," unpublished paper, Instituto de Ciencias Sociales y Humanidades, Puebla, Mexico, n.d.

Blake, David H., and Robert S. Walters. *The Politics of Global Economic Relations.* Englewood Cliffs, N.J.: Prentice-Hall, 1976.

Blank, Stephen J. *Why Russian Policy Is Failing in Asia.* Carlisle Barracks, Penn.: US Army War College, 1997.

Block, Fred L. *The Origins of International Economic Disorder: A Study of United States International Monetary Policy from World War II to the Present.* Berkeley: University of California Press, 1977.

Blond, David. "The Future Contribution of Multinational Corporations to World Growth—A Positive Appraisal." *Business Economics* (May 1978): 80–95.

Bodner, Joan, ed., with the American Friends Service Committee. *Taking Charge of Our Lives: Living Responsibly in a Troubled World.* New York: Harper and Row, 1984.

Boff, Leonardo. *Church: Charism and Power; Liberation Theology and the Institutional Church.* Trans. John W. Diercksmeier. New York: Crossroad, 1985.

Bonner, Raymond. *Weakness and Deceit: U.S. Policy and El Salvador.* New York: Times Books, 1984.

Borgese, Elisabeth Mann. "The Law of the Sea." *Scientific American* (March 1983): 42–49.

Boulding, Elise. "The Old and New Transnationalism: An Evolutionary Perspective." *Human Relations* 44, no. 8 (1991): 789–805.

———. "A Post-Military Agenda for the Scientific Community." *International Social Science Journal* 95 (1983): 163–99.

Boyte, Harry C. *The Backyard Revolution: Understanding the New Citizen Movement.* Philadelphia: Temple University Press, 1980.

Brandt, Willy, et al. *North-South, A Program for Survival: Report of the Independent Commission on International Development Issues.* Cambridge, Mass.: MIT Press, 1980.

Brecher, Jeremy, and Tim Costello. *Global Village or Global Pillage: Economic Reconstruction from the Bottom Up.* Boston: South End Press, 1994.

Brooks, Karen M. "Soviet Agriculture Under Perestroika." *Current History* 89 (October 1990): 329–36.

Brown, Cynthia. "The High Cost of Monetarism in Chile." *The Nation,* September 27, 1980, 271–75.

Brown, Lester R. *Building a Sustainable Society.* New York: Norton, 1981.

———. *Plan B: Rescuing a Planet Under Stress and a Civilization in Trouble.* New York: Norton, 2003.

Brown, Lester R., et al., eds. *State of the World 1985: A Worldwatch Institute Report on Progress Toward a Sustainable Society.* New York: Norton, 1985.

———. *State of the World 1992: A Worldwatch Institute Report on Progress Toward a Sustainable Society.* New York: Norton, 1992.

———. *State of the World 1997: A Worldwatch Institute Report on Progress Toward a Sustainable Society.* New York: Norton, 1997.

———. *State of the World 1998: A Worldwatch Institute Report on Progress Toward a Sustainable Society.* New York: Norton, 1998.

———. *State of the World 1990: A Worldwatch Institute Report on Progress Toward a Sustainable Society.* New York: Norton, 1990.

Bruce, James. "Brazil's New Computer Market." *U.S./Latin Trade* 1, no. 3 (March 1993): 48–52.

Bruck, Connie. "Millions for Millions." *The New Yorker,* October 30, 2006, 62–73.

Brundtland, Gro Harlem. *Our Common Future.* New York: Oxford University Press, 1987.

Brunn, A., et al., eds. *Conversion: Opportunities for Development and Environment.* Berlin: Springer-Verlag, 1992.

Bruyn, Severyn T., and Paula M. Rayman, eds. *Nonviolent Action and Social Change.* New York: Irvington, 1979.

Brzezinski, Zbigniew. "How the Cold War Was Played." *Foreign Affairs* 51 (October 1972): 181–209.

Bull, Hedley. "The State's Positive Role in World Affairs." *Daedalus* 108 (Fall 1979): 111–23.

Bundy, McGeorge, George F. Kennan, Robert S. McNamara, and Gerard Smith. "Nuclear Weapons and the Atlantic Alliance." *Foreign Affairs* 60 (Spring 1982): 753–68.

Bundy, McGeorge, William J. Crowe Jr., and Sidney Drell. "Reducing Nuclear Danger," *Foreign Affairs* 72, no. 2 (Spring 1993): 140–55.

Bundy, William P. "Elements of Power." *Foreign Affairs* 56 (October 1977): 1–26.

Bunker, Stephen G. *Extraction, Unequal Exchange, and the Failure of the Modern State.* Urbana: University of Illinois Press, 1985.

Burg, Steven L. "Why Yugoslavia Fell Apart." *Current History* 92, no. 577 (November 1993): 357–63.

Burnett, Alan. *The Western Pacific: Challenge of Sustainable Growth.* Sydney: Allen and Unwin, 1993.

Burrows, William E. "Ballistic Missile Defense: The Illusion of Security." *Foreign Affairs* 62 (Spring 1984): 843–56.

Burton, John W. *Global Conflict: The Domestic Sources of International Crisis.* Brighton, Sussex, England: Wheatsheaf, for the Center for International Development, 1984.

Calabrese, Mike, and Mike Kendall. "The Black Agenda for South Africa." *The Nation,* October 27, 1985, 393, 406–9.

Calder, Nigel. *Nuclear Nightmares: An Investigation into Possible Wars.* Harmondsworth, Middlesex, England: Penguin, 1981.

Calleo, David P. "Inflation and American Power." *Foreign Affairs* 59 (Spring 1981): 781–812.

Camp, Roderic A. "Women and Political Leadership in Mexico: A Comparative Study of Female and Male Political Elites." *Journal of Politics* 41 (May 1979): 417–41.

Canine, Craig. "How to Clean Coal." *OnEarth* 27 (Natural Resources Defense Council) (Fall 2005): 21–29.

Capra, Fritjof, and Charlene Spretnak. *Green Politics.* New York: Dutton, 1984.

Carnegie Commission on Preventing Deadly Conflict. *Preventing Deadly Conflict: Final Report.* New York: Carnegie Corporation, December 1997.

Carothers, Thomas. "The Backlash Against Democracy Promotion." *Foreign Affairs* 85, no. 2 (March–April 2006): 55–68.

Carr, Edward H. *The Twenty-Years' Crisis, 1919–1939: An Introduction to the Study of International Relations.* London: Macmillan, 1939.

Carter, Ashton B., William J. Perry, and John D. Steinbruner, *A New Concept of Cooperative Security.* Washington, D.C.: Brookings Institution, 1992.

Castañeda, Jorge G. "Latin America's Left Turn." *Foreign Affairs* 85 (May–June, 2006): 28–43.

———. "Mexico's Circle of Misery." *Foreign Affairs* 75 (July–August 1996): 92–105.

Cavanagh, John, and Frederick Clairmonte. "The Transnational Economy: Transnational Corporations and Global Markets." Washington, D.C.: Institute for Policy Studies, 1982.

Cecchini, Paolo. *The European Challenge 1992: The Benefits of a Single Market.* Hampshire: Wildwood House, 1988.

"The Challenge of Peace: God's Promise and Our Response." *Origins* 12 (October 28, 1982): 305–28.

Chan, Steve, and Cal Clark, eds. *The Evolving Pacific Basin in the Global Political Economy: Domestic and International Linkages.* Boulder, Colo.: Lynne Rienner, 1992.

Chang, Gordon H. "JFK, China, and the Bomb." *Journal of American History* 74 (March 1988): 1287–1310.

Chang, Ha-Joon. *Kicking Away the Ladder: Development Strategies in Historical Perspective.* London: Anthem, 2002.

Chen, Xiangming, *As Borders Bend: Transnational Spaces on the Pacific Rim.* Lanham, Md.: Rowman & Littlefield, 2005.

Chen Xiaonong. "The Chinese Public Sector: Heading Towards Zero Profit?" *China Focus* 1, no. 2 (March 30, 1993): 1, 4–5.

Chickering, A. Lawrence, and Mohamed Sahladine, eds. *The Silent Revolution: The Informal Sector in Five Asian and Near Eastern Countries.* San Francisco: ICS Press, 1991.

Chivian, Eric, et al., eds. *Last Aid: The Medical Dimensions of Nuclear War.* San Francisco: W. H. Freeman, 1982.

Choi, Jang Jip. *Labor and the Authoritarian State: Labor Unions in South Korean Manufacturing Industries, 1961–1980.* Seoul: Korean University Press, 1989.

Chomsky, Noam. *American Power and the New Mandarins.* New York: Pantheon, 1967.

Clark, John. *Democratizing Development: The Role of Voluntary Organizations.* West Hartford, Conn.: Kumarian Press, 1990.

Clifford, Mark. *Troubled Tiger: Businessmen, Bureaucrats, and Generals in South Korea.* New York: M.E. Sharpe, 1994.

Coates, Gary J., ed. *Resettling America: The Movement Toward Local Self-Reliance.* Andover, Mass.: Brick House, 1982.

Cohen, Roberta, and Francis M. Deng. "Exodus Within Borders." *Foreign Affairs* 77, no. 4 (July–August 1998): Colchester, Marcus. "Sustaining the Forests: The Community-Based Approach in South and South-East Asia." *Development and Change* 25, no. 1 (January 1994): 69–100.

Cohen, Stephen F. *Failed Crusade: America and the Tragedy of Post-Communist Russia.* New York: Norton, 2000.

———. "The New American Cold War." *The Nation*, July 10 2006, 9–17.

———. "The Struggle for Russia." *The Nation*, November 24, 2003, 5–6.

Cole, Paul M., and William J. Taylor Jr., eds. *The Nuclear Freeze Debate: Arms Control Issues for the 1980s.* Boulder, Colo.: Westview, 1983.

Coleman, Kenneth M., and George C. Herring, eds. *The Central American Crisis: Sources of Conflict and the Failure of U.S. Policy.* Wilmington, Del.: Scholarly Resources, 1985.

Coll, Steve. "The Stand-Off." *The New Yorker*, February 13–20, 2006, 126–39.

Collins, Joseph, et al., *What Difference Could a Revolution Make? Food and Family in the New Nicaragua.* San Francisco: Food First/Institute for Food and Development Policy, 1982.

Colton, Timothy J. *The Dilemma of Reform in the Soviet Union.* New York: Council on Foreign Relations, 1984.

Commission on Human Security. *Human Security Now.* New York: Commission on Human Security, 2003.

Committee on International Security and Arms Control, National Academy of Sciences. *The Future of U.S. Nuclear Weapons Policy.* Washington, D.C.: National Academy Press, 1997.

Cook, Blanche Wiesen. *The Declassified Eisenhower: A Divided Legacy of Peace and Political Warfare.* New York: Penguin, 1984.

Cornia, Giovanni Andrea, et al., eds. *Adjustment with a Human Face: Protecting the Vulnerable and Promoting Growth.* Vol. 1. Oxford: Clarendon Press, 1987.

Coronil, Fernando. *The Magical State: Nature, Money, and Modernity in Venezuela.* Chicago: University of Chicago Press, 1997.

Council on Foreign Relations. *Blocking the Spread of Nuclear Weapons: American and European Perspectives.* New York: CFR, 1986.

"Credit to the Poor." *The Newsletter from the International Center for Economic Growth* 3 (April 1990): 3, 7.

Crocker, Chester A., and Fen Osler Hampson, eds. *Managing Global Chaos: Sources of and Responses to International Conflict.* Washington, D.C.: United States Institute of Peace Press, 1996.

Crocker, Chester A., et al., eds. *Herding Cats: Multiparty Mediation in a Complex World.* Washington, D.C.: United States Institute of Peace Press, 1999.

Crozier, Michael J., Samuel P. Huntington, and Joji Watanuki. *The Crisis of Democracy: Report on the Governability of Democracies to the Trilateral Commission.* New York: New York University Press, 1975.

Cusack, Thomas R., and Michael Don Ward. "Military Spending in the United States, the Soviet Union, and the People's Republic of China." *Journal of Conflict Resolution* 25 (September 1981): 429–69.

Daalder, Ivo, and James Goldgeier. "Global NATO," *Foreign Affairs* 85 (September–October 2006): 105–13.

Danaher, Kevin. *In Whose Interest? A Guide to U.S.–South Africa Relations.* Washington, D.C.: Institute for Policy Studies, 1984.

Davis, Zachary S. "The Spread of Nuclear-Weapon-Free Zones: Building a New Nuclear Bargain." *Arms Control Today* 26, no. 1 (February 1996): 15–19.
Dean, Jonathan. *Ending Europe's Wars: The Continuing Search for Peace and Security.* New York: Twentieth Century Fund Press, 1994.
de Castro, Josué. *Death in the Northeast.* New York: Vintage, 1969.
Delamaide, Darrell. *Debt Shock: The Full Story of the World Credit Crisis.* Garden City, N.Y.: Doubleday, 1984.
Deng Xiaoping. *Fundamental Issues in Present-Day China.* Beijing: Foreign Languages Press, 1987.
Dent, Frederick B. "The Multinational Corporation—Toward a World Economy." *Financial Executive,* February 1974, 42–47.
Deutsch, Karl W., et al. *Political Community and the North Atlantic Area: International Organization in the Light of Historical Experience.* Princeton, N.J.: Princeton University Press, 1957.
Deyo, Frederic C., ed. *The Political Economy of the New Asian Industrialism.* Ithaca, N.Y.: Cornell University Press, 1987.
Diehl, Paul F., ed. *The Politics of Global Governance: International Organizations in an Interdependent World.* Boulder, Colo.: Lynne Rienner, 1997.
Dikhanov, Yuri. *Trends in Global Income Distribution, 1970–2000, and Scenarios for 2015.* New York: UN Development Program, 2005
Ding Chen. "The Economic Development of China." *Scientific American* (September 1980): 153–65.
Dittmer, Lowell. *China's Continuous Revolution: The Post-Liberation Epoch, 1949–1981.* Berkeley: University of California Press, 1987.
Donnelly, Jack. "Human Rights and Development: Complementary or Competing Concerns?" *World Politics* 36 (January 1984): 255–83.
Doremus, Paul N., et al. *The Myth of the Global Corporation.* Princeton, N.J.: Princeton University Press, 1998.
Downs, E.S. *China's Quest for Energy Security.* Santa Monica, Calif.: RAND Corporation, 2000.
———. *State of the World 2002: A Worldwatch Report on Progress Toward a Sustainable Society.* New York: Norton, 2002.
Dreifus, Claudia. "Freedom Is the Best Revenge." *The Nation,* August 13–20, 1990, 162–66.
Durning, Alan B. *Apartheid's Environmental Toll.* Worldwatch Paper 95. New York: Worldwatch Institute, 1990.
———. *Poverty and the Environment: Reversing the Downward Spiral.* Worldwatch Paper 92. New York: Worldwatch Institute, 1989.
Ebinger, Charles K., and Ronald A. Morse, eds. *U.S.-Japanese Energy Relations: Cooperation and Competition.* Boulder, Colo.: Westview, 1984.
"Economic Reform, Political Repression: Arrests of Dissidents in China Since Mid–1992." *Asia Watch* 5, no. 4 (March 2, 1993): 1–28.
Ehrlich, Paul R. "North America After the War." *Natural History* 93 (March 1984): 4–8.
Ekins, Paul. *A New World Order: Grassroots Movements for Social Change.* London: Routledge, 1992.
Eklof, Ben. *Soviet Briefing: Gorbachev and the Reform Period.* Boulder, Colo.: Westview, 1989.
Elgin, Duane. *Voluntary Simplicity: Toward a Way of Life That Is Outwardly Simple, Inwardly Rich.* New York: William Morrow, 1981.
El-Khawas, Mohamed A., and Barry Cohen, eds. *The Kissinger Study of Southern Africa: National Security Study Memorandum 39.* Westport, Conn.: Lawrence Hill, 1976.

Ellsberg, Daniel. "Manhattan Project II: The End of the Threat of Nuclear War." *Harvard Journal of World Affairs* (Summer 1992): 1–16.

Emerson, Rupert. "The Fate of Human Rights in the Third World." *World Politics* 27 (January 1975): 201–26.

Engler, Robert. "Technology Out of Control." *The Nation,* April 27, 1985, 488–500.

English, Robert. "Eastern Europe's Doves." *Foreign Policy,* no. 56 (Fall 1984): 44–60.

*Environmental Sustainability Index.* New Haven, Conn.: Yale Center for Environmental Law and Policy and Center for International Earth Science Information Network, Columbia University, 2005.

Esteva, Gustavo. "Regenerating People's Space." *Alternatives* 12 (1987): 125–52.

*Europe Without Frontiers: Completing the Internal Market.* 3rd ed. Luxembourg: Office for Official Publications of the Communities, 1989.

*Facts and Figures of Japan.* Tokyo: Foreign Press Center, 1991.

Falk, Richard A. "In Search of a New World Model." *Current History* 92, no. 573 (April 1993): 145–49.

———. *A Study of Future Worlds.* New York: Free Press, 1975.

———. "World Order Values: Secular Means and Spiritual Ends." New York: Planetary Citizens, n.d.

Falk, Richard A., Samuel S. Kim, and Saul H. Mendlovitz, eds. *Toward a Just World Order.* Vol. 1. Boulder, Colo.: Westview, 1980.

Fall, Bernard B., ed. *Ho Chi Minh on Revolution: Selected Writings, 1920–66.* New York: Praeger, 1967.

Fanon, Frantz. *The Wretched of the Earth.* Trans. Constance Farrington. New York: Grove, 1963.

Farer, Tom. "The United States and the Third World: A Basis for Accommodation." *Foreign Affairs* 54 (October 1975): 79–97.

Feldstein, Martin. "Refocusing the IMF." *Foreign Affairs* 77, no. 2 (March–April 1998): 20–33.

Ferguson, Marilyn. *The Aquarian Conspiracy: Personal and Social Transformation in the 1980s.* Los Angeles: J. P. Tarcher, 1980.

Ferguson, Thomas, and Joel Rogers. "Another Trilateral Election?" *The Nation,* June 28, 1980, 770, 783–87.

Finnegan, William. "The Economics of Empire: Notes on the Washington Consensus." *Harper's,* May 2003, 41–52.

Fischer, Louis, ed. *The Essential Gandhi: His Life, Work, and Ideas.* New York: Vintage, 1962.

Fisher, Roger, and William L. Ury. *Getting to YES: Negotiating Agreement Without Giving In.* New York: Penguin, 1981.

Fishlow, Albert, et al. *Rich and Poor Nations in the World Economy.* New York: McGraw-Hill, for the Council on Foreign Relations, 1978.

Flavin, Christopher, et al. *State of the World 2002: A Worldwatch Institute Report on Progress Toward a Sustainable Society.* New York: Norton, 2002.

———. *American Energy: The Renewable Path to Energy Security.* Washington, D.C.: Worldwatch Institute and Center for American Progress, 2006.

Foer, Franklin. "The Talented Mr. Chávez." *The Atlantic Monthly,* May 2004, 96–105.

Forrest, Richard A. "Japanese Aid and the Environment." *Ecologist* 21, no. 1 (January–February 1991): 24–32.

Forster, E.M. *A Passage to India.* New York: Harcourt, Brace and World, 1952.

Frank, André Gunder. *Crisis: In the World Economy.* New York: Holmes and Meier, 1980.

Frank, Ruediger. "The Political Economy of Sanctions Against North Korea." *Asian Perspective* 30, no. 3 (2006): 5–36.

Frederick, Howard H. *Global Communications and International Relations.* Belmont, Calif.: Wadsworth, 1993.

French, Hilary F. *Costly Tradeoffs: Reconciling Trade and the Environment.* New York: Worldwatch Institute, 1993.

Frieden, Jeff. "Why the Big Banks Love Martial Law." *The Nation,* January 23, 1982, 65, 81–84.

Friedman, Robert I. "India's Shame." *The Nation,* April 8, 1996, 11–20.

Friere, Paolo. *Pedagogy of the Oppressed.* Trans. Myra Bergman Ramos. New York: Herder and Herder, 1972.

Frost, Ellen L. *For Richer, for Poorer: The New U.S.-Japan Relationship.* New York: Council on Foreign Relations, 1987.

Fuentes, Annette, and Barbara Ehrenreich. *Women in the Global Factory.* Boston: South End Press, 1983.

Fukuyama, Francis. "The End of History?" *The National Interest* (Summer 1989), 3–18.

———. "Gorbachev and the Third World." *Foreign Affairs* 64 (Spring 1986): 715–31.

Funabashi, Yoichi. *Asia Pacific Fusion: Japan's Role in APEC.* Washington, D.C.: Institute for International Economics, 1995.

———. "Japan and the New World Order." *Foreign Affairs* 70 (Winter 1991–1992): 58–74.

Gaddis, John Lewis. *Strategies of Containment: A Critical Appraisal of Post-War American National Security Policy.* New York: Oxford University Press, 1982.

Gaddy, Clifford G. *The Price of the Past: Russia's Struggle with the Legacy of a Militarized Economy.* Washington, D.C.: Brookings Institution, 1996.

Galtung, Johan. "The New International Economic Order and the Basic Needs Approach." *Alternatives* 4 (March 1979): 455–76.

———. "A Structural Theory of Imperialism." *Journal of Peace Research,* no. 8 (1971): 81–117.

———. *The True Worlds: A Transnational Perspective.* New York: Free Press, 1980.

Garten, Jeffrey E. "Business and Foreign Policy." *Foreign Policy* 76, no. 3 (May–June 1997): 67–79.

Garvin, Charles, and Greg Rosenbaum. *World Without Plenty: A Basic Overview of World Resources.* Skokie, Ill.: National Textbook, 1975.

Gendzier, Irene L. *Managing Political Change: Social Scientists and the Third World.* Boulder, Colo.: Westview, 1984.

George, Alexander L., ed. *Managing U.S.-Soviet Rivalry: Problems of Crisis Prevention.* Boulder, Colo.: Westview, 1983.

George, Susan. *A Fate Worse Than Debt.* New York: Grove, 1988.

———. *How the Other Half Dies: The Real Reasons for World Hunger.* Montclair, N.J.: Allanheld, Osmun, 1977.

Gereffi, Gary, and Miguel Korzeniewicz, eds., *Commodity Chains and Global Capitalism.* Westport, Conn.: Praeger, 1994.

Gilpin, Robert J. *U.S. Power and the Multinational Corporations.* New York: Basic Books, 1975.

Glennon, John P., et al., eds. *Foreign Relations of the United States 1950.* Vol. 1: *National Security Affairs; Foreign Economic Policy.* Washington, D.C.: U.S. Government Printing Office, 1977.

Goldblat, Jozef, and Peter Lomas. "Disarmament Watch: Nuclear Non-Proliferation; the Problem States." *Transnational Perspectives* 15, no. 1 (1989): 17–21.

Goldman, Marshall I. "Needed: A Russian Economic Revolution." *Current History* 91, no. 567 (October 1992): 314–20.

Goldzimer, Aaron. "Worse Than the World Bank? Export Credit Agencies—The Secret Engine of Globalization." *Food First Backgrounder* (Institute for Food and Development Policy) 9, no. 1 (Winter 2003): 1–7.

Goltz, Thomas. "The Caspian Oil Sweepstakes." *The Nation*, November 17, 1997, 18–21.

Gordon, Suzanne, and Dave McFadden, eds. *Economic Conversion: Revitalizing America's Economy.* Cambridge, Mass.: Ballinger, 1984.

Gould, Jay. "Chernobyl—The Hidden Tragedy." *The Nation,* March 15, 1993, 331–34.

Goulding, Michael. "Flooded Forests of the Amazon." *Scientific American* (March 1993): 114–20.

Goulet, Denis. "Authentic Development: Is It Sustainable?" *Hunger TeachNet* 6, no. 1 (February 1995): 3–8.

Gourevitch, Philip. "The Genocide Fax." *The New Yorker,* May 11, 1998, 42–45.

Grare, Frédéric. "Pakistan: The Myth of an Islamist Peril." *Policy Brief* (Carnegie Endowment for International Peace), no. 45 (February 2006): 1–7.

Greenberg, Stanley B. *Race and State in Capitalist Development: Comparative Perspectives.* New Haven, Conn.: Yale University Press, 1980.

Greene, Owen, et al. *Implementing the Programme of Action 2003: Action by States and Civil Society.* London: International Action Network on Small Arms, 2003.

Greider, William. "Pro Patria, Pro Mundus." *The Nation,* November 12, 2001, 22–25.

Grossman, Karl. *Nicaragua: America's New Vietnam?* Sag Harbor, N.Y.: Permanent Press, 1984.

Guertner, Gary L. "What Is Proof?" *Foreign Policy,* no. 59 (Summer 1985): 73–84.

Guisinger, Stephen, ed. *Private Enterprise and the New Global Economic Challenge.* Indianapolis: Bobbs-Merrill, 1979.

Guo Simian. "'New Political Thinking' and the Soviet Union's Readjustment of Its Asian-Pacific Policy." *Comparative Strategy* 8 (1989): 139–48.

Gurr, Ted Robert. *Minorities at Risk: A Global View of Ethnopolitical Conflicts.* Washington, D.C.: U.S. Institute of Peace, 1993.

Gurtov, Mel. "South Korea's Foreign Policy and Future Security: Implications of the Nuclear Standoff." *Pacific Affairs* 69, no. 1 (Spring 1996): 8–31.

———. *Superpower on Crusade: The Bush Doctrine in U.S. Foreign Policy.* Boulder, Colo.: Lynne Rienner, 2006.

———. "Swords into Market Shares: China's Conversion of Military Industry to Civilian Production." *China Quarterly,* no. 134 (June 1993): 1–29.

———, ed. *The Transformation of Socialism: Perestroika and Reform in the Soviet Union and China.* Boulder, Colo.: Westview, 1990.

Gurtov, Mel, and Byong-Moo Hwang. *China's Security: The New Roles of the Military.* Boulder, Colo.: Lynne Rienner, 1998.

Gurtov, Melvin, and Ray Maghroori, eds. *Roots of Failure: United States Policy in the Third World.* Westport, Conn.: Greenwood, 1984.

Haapoja, Margaret A. "Tropical Medicine: An Interview with Sadie Brorson." *Hemispheres* (March 1997): 19–22.

Haggard, Stephan. *Pathways from the Periphery: The Politics of Growth in the Newly Industrializing Countries.* Ithaca, N.Y.: Cornell University Press, 1990.

Haggard, Stephan and Marcus Noland. *Hunger and Human Rights: The Politics of*

*Famine in North Korea.* Washington, D.C.: US Committee for Human Rights in North Korea, 2005.

Haley, P. Edward, David M. Keithly, and Jack Merritt, eds. *Nuclear Strategy, Arms Control, and the Future.* Boulder, Colo.: Westview, 1985.

Halliday, Fred. *Iran: Dictatorship and Development.* Harmondsworth, Middlesex, England: Penguin, 1979.

Halliday, Jon, and Gavan McCormack. *Japanese Imperialism Today: Co-Prosperity in Greater Asia.* New York: Monthly Review, 1973.

Hallward, Peggy. "The Urgent Need for a Campaign Against Forced Resettlement." *The Ecologist* 22, no. 2 (March–April 1992): 43–44.

Hammond, Allen L., ed. *World Resources 1990–91: A Report by the World Resources Institute.* New York: Oxford University Press, 1990.

Harding, Harry. *China's Second Revolution: Reform After Mao.* Washington, D.C.: Brookings Institution, 1987.

Hardt, John P., and Donna Gold. "Andropov's Economic Future." *Orbis* 27 (Spring 1983): 11–20.

Harris, Albert W. "The International Seabed Authority: Enforcement in International Negotiations." Paper presented at the annual convention of the International Studies Association, Acapulco, Mexico, March 23–27, 1993.

Harris, Richard, and Carlos M. Vilas, eds. *Nicaragua: A Revolution Under Siege.* London: Zed, 1985.

Harrison, Paul. *The Greening of Africa: Breaking Through in the Battle for Land and Food.* Harmondsworth, Middlesex, England: Penguin, 1987.

Harrison, Selig S. *Korean Endgame: A Strategy for Reunification and U.S. Disengagement.* Princeton, N.J., and Oxford: Princeton University Press, 2002.

Hart-Landsberg, Martin. "The Asian Crisis: Causes and Consequences." *Against the Current,* no. 73 (March–April 1998): 26–29.

———. *Rush to Development: Economic Change and Political Struggle in South Korea.* New York: Monthly Review Press, 1993.

Hartmann, Betsy, and James K. Boyce. *Needless Hunger: Voices from a Bangladesh Village.* San Francisco: Institute for Food and Development Policy, 1979.

Hartung, William D. *Welfare for Weapons Dealers: The Hidden Costs of the Arms Trade.* New York: World Policy Institute, 1996.

Hartung, William D., and Rosy Nimroody. "Cutting Up the Star Wars Pie." *The Nation,* September 14, 1985, 200–2.

Hasan, Parvez, and D.C. Rao. *Korea: Policy Issues for Long-Term Development.* Baltimore: Johns Hopkins University Press, for the World Bank, 1979.

Havel, Vàclav. "The Post-Communist Nightmare." *New York Review of Books,* May 27, 1993, 8–10.

Hawk, David. "The Killing of Cambodia." *New Republic,* November 15, 1982, 17–21.

Hawken, Paul. "A Declaration of Sustainability." *Utne Reader,* no. 59 (September–October 1993): 54–60.

Hayter, Teresa. *Aid as Imperialism.* Harmondsworth, Middlesex, England: Penguin, 1971.

Head, Ivan L. "South-North Dangers." *Foreign Affairs* 68 (Summer 1989): 71–86.

Hecht, Susanna, and Alexander Cockburn. "Rhetoric and Reality in Rio." *The Nation,* June 22, 1992, 848–53.

Hedges, Chris. *War Is a Force That Gives Us Meaning.* New York: Public Affairs, 2002.

Held, David, et al. *Global Transformations: Politics, Economics, and Culture.* Cambridge: Polity Press, 1999.

Henderson, Hazel. *The Politics of the Solar Age: Alternatives to Economics.* New York: Doubleday Anchor, 1981.

Hendrickson, David C. "The Ethics of Collective Security." *Ethics & International Affairs* 7 (1993): 1–16.

———. Toward Universal Empire: The Dangerous Quest for Absolute Security." *World Policy Journal* 19 (Fall 2002): 1–10.

Henkin, Louis. *How Nations Behave: Law and Foreign Policy.* New York: Columbia University Press, 1979.

Henry, James S. "Dance of Debt Isn't Over Yet." *U.S. News & World Report,* August 31, 1987, 39–41.

Herken, Gregg. *The Winning Weapon: The Atomic Bomb in the Cold War, 1945–1950.* New York: Vintage, 1982.

Herman, Edward S., and Frank Brodhead. *Demonstration Elections: U.S.-Staged Elections in the Dominican Republic, Vietnam, and El Salvador.* Boston: South End Press, 1984.

Hersh, Seymour. "Last Stand." *The New Yorker,* July 10–17, 2006, 42–49.

———. "The Iran Plans." *The New Yorker,* April 17, 2006, 30–37.

———. "On the Nuclear Edge." *The New Yorker,* March 29, 1993, 56–73.

———. *The Price of Power: Kissinger in the Nixon White House.* New York: Summit, 1983.

———. "The Redirection." *The New Yorker,* March 5, 2007, 55–65.

———. *The Samson Option: Israel's Nuclear Arsenal and American Foreign Policy.* New York: Random House, 1991.

———. "Watching Lebanon." *The New Yorker,* August 21, 2006, 28–33.

Hinchberger, Bill. "Land of No Return? Not Brazil." *The Nation,* March 2, 1998, 20–24.

Hinrichsen, Don. "Russian Roulette." *Amicus Journal* 14, no. 4 (Winter 1993): 35–37.

Hinton, William. *Fanshen: A Documentary of Revolution in a Chinese Village.* New York: Vintage, 1966.

Hodge, Carl Cavanagh. "Botching the Balkans: Germany's Recognition of Slovenia and Croatia." *Ethics & International Affairs* 12 (1988): 1–18.

Hoffmann, Stanley. "France, the United States & Iraq." *The Nation,* February 16 2004, 16–19.

Homer-Dixon, Thomas F. "On the Threshold: Environmental Changes as Causes of Acute Conflict." *International Security* 16, no. 2 (Fall 1991): 76–116.

Howe, Christopher. "China, Japan and Economic Interdependence in the Asia Pacific Region." *China Quarterly,* no. 124 (December 1990): 662–93.

Huddle, Norie. *Surviving: The Best Game on Earth.* New York: Schocken, 1984.

Huey, John. "The World's Best Brand." *Fortune,* May 31, 1993, 44–54.

Hughes, Neil C. "Smashing the Iron Rice Bowl." *Foreign Affairs* 77, no. 4 (July–August 1998): 67–77.

Human Rights Watch/Asia. "Human Rights Crisis in Indonesia: Statement to the Senate Foreign Relations Committee, Subcommittee on East Asia and Pacific Affairs," Washington, D.C., March 24, 1998, 1–10.

Hunter, Robert E. "A Forward-Looking Partnership." *Foreign Affairs* 83, no. 5 (September–October 2004): 14–18.

Hunter, Shireen T. "Nationalist Movements in Soviet Asia." *Current History* 89 (October 1990): 325–28, 337.

Ihonvbere, Julius O. "The State, Governance, and Democratization in Africa: Constraints and Possibilities." *Hunger TeachNet* 6, no. 3 (September 1995): 4–5.

Iklé, Fred Charles. "Nuclear Strategy: Can There Be a Happy Ending?" *Foreign Affairs* 63 (Spring 1985): 810–26.
Iklé, Fred Charles, and Terumasa Nakanishi. "Japan's Grand Strategy." *Foreign Affairs* 69 (Summer 1990): 81–95.
Inoguchi, Takashi. "Four Japanese Scenarios for the Future." *International Affairs* 65 (Winter 1988–1989): 15–28.
Inoguchi, Takashi, and Daniel I. Okimoto, eds. *The Political Economy of Japan: The Changing International Context.* Vol. 2. Stanford, Calif.: Stanford University Press, 1988.
Inoue Nobutaka, ed. *Globalization and Indigenous Culture.* Tokyo: Institute for Japanese Culture and Classics, Kokugakuin University, 1997.
International Business Machines. "IBM Operations in South Africa." Armonk, N.Y.: February 1982. Mimeo.
International Commission on Intervention and State Sovereignty. *The Responsibility to Protect.* Ottowa: International Development Research Centre, 2001.
Isaak, Robert A. *International Political Economy: Managing World Economic Change.* Englewood Cliffs, N.J.: Prentice-Hall, 1991.
Islam, Shafiqul. "Capitalism in Conflict." *Foreign Affairs* 69 (Winter 1989–1990): 172–82.
Jackson, James K. "U.S. Direct Investment Abroad: Trends and Current Issues." Congressional Research Service Report to Congress No. RS21118 (April 29, 2005), p. 2.
Jacobson, Jodi L. *Environmental Refugees: A Yardstick of Habitability.* Washington, D.C.: Worldwatch Institute, 1988.
Jacoby, Henry D., Ronald G. Prinn, and Richard Schmalensee. "Kyoto's Unfinished Business." *Foreign Affairs* 77, no. 4 (July–August 1998): 54–66.
"Japan: The Garbage Superpower—A Round-Table Discussion." *Japan Echo* 21, no. 1 (Spring 1994): 86–92.
*Japan 1988: An International Comparison.* Tokyo: Keizai Koho Center, 1987.
Johansen, Robert C. *The National Interest and the Human Interest: An Analysis of U.S. Foreign Policy.* Princeton, N.J.: Princeton University Press, 1980.
———. "Toward an Alternative Security System: Moving Beyond the Balance of Power in the Search for World Security." New York: World Policy Institute, no. 24, 1983.
Johnson, Chalmers. "Cold War Economics Melt Asia." *The Nation,* February 23, 1998, 16–19.
Johnson, Chalmers, and E.B. Keehn. "The Pentagon's Ossified Strategy." *Foreign Affairs* 74, no. 4 (July–August 1995): 103–14.
Johnson, Ian. *Wild Grass: Three Portraits of Change in Modern China.* New York: Vintage, 2004.
Johnson, Rebecca. "The In-Comprehensive Test Ban." *The Bulletin of the Atomic Scientists* 52, no. 6 (November–December 1996): 30–35.
Jubak, Jim, and Marie D'Amico. "Mighty MITI." *Amicus Journal* 15, no. 2 (Summer 1993): 38–43.
Judt, Tony. "Europe: The Grand Illusion." *New York Review of Books,* July 11, 1996, 6–8.
———. *Postwar: A History of Europe Since 1945.* New York: Penguin, 2005.
Kahl, Colin H. "Population Growth, Environmental Degradation, and State-Sponsored Violence: The Case of Kenya, 1991–1993." Paper prepared for the International Studies Association annual convention, Minneapolis, Minn., March 17–21, 1998.

Kaplan, David E., and Ida Landauer. "Radioactivity for the Oceans." *The Nation,* October 9, 1982, 336–39.

Kapur, Devesh, John P. Lewis, and Richard Webb, eds. *The World Bank: Its First Half Century.* Washington, D.C.: Brookings Institution, 1997.

Karatnycky, Adrian. "Ukraine's Orange Revolution." *Foreign Affairs* 84, no. 2 (March–April 2005): 35–52.

Kaya, Yoichi, et al. "Management of Global Environmental Issues." *World Futures* 19 (1984): 223–31.

Kaysen, Carl, Robert S. McNamara, and George W. Rathjens. "Nuclear Weapons After the Cold War." *Foreign Affairs* 70 (Fall 1991): 95–110.

Keen, David. *Refugees: Rationing the Right to Life.* London: Zed, 1992.

Kegley, Charles W. Jr., and Eugene R. Wittkopf. *World Politics: Trend and Transformation.* 1st, 6th, 8th eds. New York: St. Martin's, 1981, 1997, 2001.

Keller, William W. "The Political Economy of Conventional Arms Proliferation." *Current History* 96, no. 609 (April 1997): 179–83.

Kellogg, William W., and Robert Schware. "Society, Science and Climate Change." *Foreign Affairs* 60 (Summer 1982): 1076–1109.

Kennan, George F. *The Nuclear Delusion: Soviet-American Relations in the Atomic Age.* New York: Pantheon, 1982.

———. "On Nuclear War." *New York Review of Books,* January 21, 1982, 8–12.

———. *Realities of American Foreign Policy.* Princeton, N.J.: Princeton University Press, 1954.

Kennedy, Paul. *The Rise and Fall of the Great Powers: Economic Change and Military Conflict from 1500 to 2000.* New York: Random House, 1987.

Keohane, Robert O. *After Hegemony: Cooperation and Discord in the World Political Economy.* Princeton, N.J.: Princeton University Press, 1984.

Kidder, Rushworth M. "Universal Human Values: Finding an Ethical Common Ground." *The Futurist* (July–August 1994): 8–13.

Kidron, Michael, and Ronald Segal, eds. *The State of the World Atlas.* London: Pan, 1981.

Kim Dae Jung. *Mass-Participatory Economy: A Democratic Alternative for Korea.* Lanham, Md.: University Press of America and Center for International Affairs, Harvard University, 1985.

Kim Eun Mee, ed. *The Four Asian Tigers: Economic Development and the Global Political Economy.* San Diego: Academic Press, 1998.

Kim Hyung Kook, and Guillermo Geisse. "The Political Economy of Outward Liberalization: Chile and South Korea in Comparative Perspective." *Asian Perspective* 12, no. 2 (Fall–Winter 1988): 35–68.

Kim, Samuel S. *The Quest for a Just World Order.* Boulder, Colo.: Westview, 1984.

Kissinger, Henry A. *Nuclear Weapons and Foreign Policy.* Garden City, N.Y.: Doubleday Anchor, 1968.

———. *White House Years.* Boston: Little, Brown, 1979.

Klare, Michael T. "Soviet Arms Transfers to the Third World." *Bulletin of the Atomic Scientists* 40 (May 1984): 26–32.

Klare, Michael T., and Cynthia Arnson. *Supplying Repression: U.S. Support for Authoritarian Regimes Abroad.* Washington, D.C.: Institute for Policy Studies, 1981.

Klarreich, Kathie. "The Fight for Haiti." *The Nation,* March 13, 2006, pp. 19–22.

Kojima, Kiyoshi. *Japan and a New World Economic Order.* London: Croom Helm, 1977.

Kolko, Joyce, and Gabriel Kolko. *The Limits of Power: The World and United States Foreign Policy, 1945–1954.* New York: Harper and Row, 1972.

*Korea Annual 1990.* Seoul: Yonhap News Agency, 1990.

Korten, David C. *Getting to the 21st Century: Voluntary Action and the Global Agenda.* West Hartford, Conn.: Kumarian Press, 1990.

———. *When Corporations Rule the World.* Bloomfield, Conn.: Kumarian Press, 2004.

Kotkin, Joel. *Tribes: How Race, Religion and Identity Determine Success in the New Global Economy.* New York: Random House, 1993.

Kotler, Mindy L., Naotaka Sugawara, and Tetsuya Yamada. "Chinese and Japanese Public Opinion: Searching for Moral Security." *Asian Perspective* 31, no. 1 (2007): 93–125.

Kozol, Jonathan. *Illiterate America.* Garden City, N.Y: Doubleday Anchor, 1985.

Krasner, Stephen D. *Structural Conflict: The Third World Against Global Liberalism.* Berkeley: University of California Press, 1985.

Kunstler, James Howard. *The Long Emergency: Surviving the Converging Catastrophes of the Twenty-First Century.* New York: Atlantic Monthly Press, 2005.

Lagos, Gustavo, and Horacio H. Godoy. *Revolution of Being: A Latin American View of the Future.* New York: Free Press, 1977.

Lairson, Thomas D., and David Skidmore. *International Political Economy: The Struggle for Power and Wealth.* Fort Worth, Tex.: Harcourt Brace Jovanovich, 1993.

Lall, Sanjaya. *The New Multinationals: The Spread of Third World Enterprises.* Chichester, N.Y.: John Wiley, 1983.

Lam Peng Er, ed. *Japan's Relations with China: Facing a Rising Power.* London: Routledge, 2006.

Lambeth, Benjamin. "Russia's Wounded Military." *Foreign Affairs* 74 (March–April 1995): 86–98.

Langewiesche, William. "The Wrath of Khan." *The Atlantic Monthly*, November 2005, 62–85.

Lappé, Frances Moore, and Joseph Collins. *Food First: Beyond the Myth of Scarcity.* Boston: Houghton Mifflin, 1977.

Laszlo, Ervin, and Donald Keys, eds. *Disarmament: The Human Factor.* New York: Pergamon, 1981.

Launis, Michael A. "The State and Industrial Labor in South Korea." *Bulletin of Concerned Asian Scholars* 16 (October–December 1984): 2–10.

Lawyers Committee for Human Rights (LCHR). *Criminal Justice with Chinese Characteristics: China's Criminal Process and Violations of Human Rights.* New York: LCHR, 1993.

———. *"Salvaging" Democracy: Human Rights in the Philippines.* New York: LCHR, 1985.

Lee Sook-Jong. "Democratization and Polarization in Korean Society." *Asian Perspective* 29, no. 3 (2005): 99–125.

Lee, Manwoo. *The Odyssey of Korean Democracy: Korean Politics, 1987–1990.* New York: Praeger, 1990.

Leitenberg, Milton. "Biological Weapons, International Sanctions and Proliferation." *Asian Perspective* 21, no. 3 (Winter 1997): 7–39.

———. "Deaths in Wars and Conflicts in the 20th Century." Cornell University Peace Studies Program, Occasional Papers #29, 3rd. ed., 2006.

———. "The Numbers Game or 'Who's on First?'" *Bulletin of the Atomic Scientists* 38 (June 1982): 27–32.

———. "United States–Soviet Strategic Arms Control: The Decade of Detente, 1970–1980, and a Look Ahead." *Arms Control* 8, no. 3 (December 1987): 213–64.

Lemann, Nicholas. "The Next World Order." *The New Yorker*, April 1, 2002, 42–48.

Lernoux, Penny. *Cry of the People: The Struggle for Human Rights in Latin America—The Catholic Church in Conflict with U.S. Policy.* Harmondsworth, Middlesex, England: Penguin, 1982.

Li Xiaorong. "'Asian Values' and the Universality of Human Rights." *Report from the Institute for Philosophy & Public Policy,* University of Maryland, 1996, 16–23.

Li Yushi. "Prospects for China's Foreign Trade and Investment and Involvement in Regional Economic Cooperation." Paper presented at the conference "New World Order? Issues and Opportunities in Asia and Beyond," Portland State University, Portland, Ore., May 6–7, 1993.

Lieber, Keir A., and Daryl G. Press. "The Rise of U.S. Nuclear Primacy." *Foreign Affairs* 85 (March–April 2006): 42–54.

Lintner, Bertil. "Narcopolitics in Burma." *Current History* 95, no. 605 (December 1996): 432–37.

Lipschutz, Ronnie D., and Ken Conca, eds. *The State and Social Power in Global Environmental Politics.* New York: Columbia University Press, 1993.

Littauer, Raphael, and Norman Uphoff, eds. *The Air War in Indochina.* Rev. ed. Boston: Beacon, 1971.

Littrell, Mary Ann, and Marsha Ann Dickson, eds. *Social Responsibility in the Global Market: Fair Trade of Cultural Products.* New York: Sage, 1999.

Litvak, Lawrence, Robert DeGrasse, and Kathleen McTigue. *South Africa: Foreign Investment and Apartheid.* Washington, D.C.: Institute for Policy Studies, 1978.

Liu Binyan. *A Higher Kind of Loyalty.* Trans. from the Chinese by Zhu Hong. New York: Pantheon, 1990.

Lopez, George A., and Michael Stohl, eds. *Dependence, Development, and State Repression.* Westport, Conn.: Greenwood, 1989.

Lovins, Amory B. *Soft Energy Paths: Toward a Durable Peace.* New York: Harper and Row, 1979.

Lovins, Amory B., L. Hunter Lovins, and Leonard Ross. "Nuclear Power and Nuclear Bombs." *Foreign Affairs* 58 (Summer 1980): 1137–77.

Lummis, C. Douglas. "People Power in Thailand: Long Parliament in the Streets." *The Nation,* June 22, 1992, 858–60.

Ma Jisen. "The Politics of China's Population Growth." *Asian Perspective* 22, no. 1 (Spring 1998): 35–52.

MacFarquhar, Roderick, ed. *The Politics of China: The Eras of Mao and Deng.* 2nd ed. Cambridge: Cambridge University Press, 1997.

MacRae, Phyllis. "Race and Class in Southern Africa." *The African Review* 4 (1974): 237–58.

Macy, Joanna Rogers. "How to Deal with Despair." *New Age,* June 1979, 40–45.

Maghroori, Ray, and Bennett Ramberg, eds. *Globalism Versus Realism: International Relations' Third Debate.* Boulder, Colo.: Westview, 1982.

Maguire, Andrew, and Janet Welsh Brown, eds. *Bordering on Trouble: Resources and Politics in Latin America.* Bethesda, Md.: Adler and Adler, 1986.

Mahbubani, Kishore. "Japan Adrift." *Foreign Policy,* no. 88 (Fall 1992): 126–44.

———. "Understanding China." *Foreign Affairs* 84 (September–October 2005): 49–60.

Malcolm X, with Alex Haley. *The Autobiography of Malcolm X.* New York: Grove, 1969.

Mandelbaum, Michael. "The Post–Cold War Settlement in Europe: A Triumph of Arms Control." *Arms Control Today* 27, no. 1 (March 1997): 3–8.

Mander, Jerry, and Edward Goldsmith, eds. *The Case Against the Global*

*Economy—And for a Turn Toward the Local.* San Francisco: Sierra Club Books, 1996.

Manning, Robert A. "The Philippines in Crisis." *Foreign Affairs* 63 (Winter 1984–1985): 392–410.

Mao Zedong. *Mao Zedong xuan ji* (Selected Works of Mao Zedong). 5 vols. Beijing: People's Publishing House, 1969.

———. *Selected Readings from the Works of Mao Tsetung.* Beijing: Foreign Languages Press, 1971.

Maranto, Gina. "Are We Close to the Road's End?" *Discover* 7 (January 1986): 28–50.

Martin, Hans-Peter, and Harald Schumann. *The Global Trap.* London: Zed, 1996.

Mastny, Lisa, et al. *Vital Signs 2005: The Trends That Are Shaping Our Future.* New York: Norton, 2005.

Mather, Alexander S. *Global Forest Resources.* Portland, Ore.: Timber Press, 1990.

May, Christopher, ed. *Global Corporate Power.* Boulder, Colo.: Lynne Rienner, 2006.

McCormack, Gavan, and Mark Selden, eds. *Korea North and South: The Deepening Crisis.* New York: Monthly Review, 1978.

McKean, Margaret A. *Environmental Protest and Citizen Politics in Japan.* Berkeley: University of California Press, 1981.

McLaughlin, Corinne, and Gordon Davidson. *Builders of the Dawn: Community Lifestyles in a Changing World.* Walpole, N.H.: Stillpoint, 1985.

McLean, Bethany. "The Power of Philanthropy." *Fortune,* September 18, 2006, 40–50.

McLuhan, T.C., ed. *Touch the Earth: A Self-Portrait of Indian Existence.* New York: Simon and Schuster, 1971.

McNamara, Robert S. "The Military Role of Nuclear Weapons: Perceptions and Misperceptions." *Foreign Affairs* 62 (Fall 1983): 59–80.

Medvedev, Roy A., and Zhores A. Medvedev. "Nuclear Samizdat." *The Nation,* January 16, 1982, 38–50.

Meier, Andrew. "Endangered Revolution." *National Geographic* (March 2006), 39–58.

Meier, Gerald M. *The International Environment of Business: Competition and Governance in the Global Economy.* New York: Oxford University Press, 1998.

Meissner, Charles F. "Debt: Reform Without Governments." *Foreign Policy,* no. 56 (Fall 1984): 81–93.

Mendlovitz, Saul H., ed. *On the Creation of a Just World Order.* New York: Free Press, 1975.

Merleau-Ponty, Maurice. *Humanism and Terror: An Essay on the Communist Problem,* trans. from the French by John O'Neill. Boston: Beacon Press, 1969.

Mesler, Bill. "Virtual Nukes—When Is a Test Not a Test?" *The Nation,* June 15–22, 1998, 16–20.

Meyer, William H. *Transnational Media and Third World Development: The Structure and Impact of Imperialism.* Westport, Conn.: Greenwood, 1988.

Michnik, Adam. "The Two Faces of Eastern Europe." *The New Republic,* November 12, 1990, 23–25.

Milewski, Jerzy, et al. "Poland: Four Years After." *Foreign Affairs* 64 (Winter 1985–1986): 337–59.

Millis, Walter, ed. *The Forrestal Diaries.* New York: Viking, 1951.

Mische, Gerald, and Patricia Mische. *Toward a Human World Order: Beyond the National Security Straitjacket.* New York: Paulist Press, 1977.

Mitchell, Arnold. "Changing Values and Lifestyles." Palo Alto, Calif.: Stanford Research Institute, n.d.

Moberg, David. "Decline and Inequality After the Great U-Turn." *In These Times,* May 27–June 9, 1992, 7, 10.

Moravcsik, Andrew. "Taking Preferences Seriously: A Liberal Theory of International Politics." *International Organization* 51, no. 4 (Autumn 1997): 513–53.

Morgenthau, Hans J. *Politics Among Nations: The Struggle for Power and Peace.* 5th rev. ed. New York: Knopf, 1978.

Morse, Ronald A., ed. *The Politics of Japan's Energy Strategy: Resources— Diplomacy—Security.* Berkeley: University of California, Institute of East Asian Studies, 1981.

Mukerjee, Madhusree. "Toxins Abounding." *Scientific American* (July 1995): 22–23.

Muller, Robert. "A World Core Curriculum." *Education Network News* 1 (November 1982): 1–4.

Muñoz, Heraldo, ed. *From Dependency to Development: Strategies to Overcome Underdevelopment and Inequality.* Boulder, Colo.: Westview, 1981.

Murphy, Paul. "The Military Tax Bite 1986." Washington, D.C.: Military Spending Research Services, March 1986.

Myers, Desaix. *Labor Practices of U.S. Corporations in South Africa.* New York: Praeger, 1977.

Myers, Norman. "The Conversion of Tropical Forests." *Environment* 22 (July–August 1980): 6–13.

Myers, Ransom A., and Boris Worm. "Rapid Worldwide Depletion of Predatory Fish Communities." *Nature* (May 15, 2003): 280–83.

Nagpal, T., and C. Foltz, eds. *Choosing Our Future: Visions of a Sustainable World.* Washington, D.C.: World Resources Institute, 1995.

Nair, Kusum. *In Defense of the Irrational Peasant: Indian Agriculture After the Green Revolution.* Chicago: University of Chicago Press, 1979.

Nandy, Ashis. "The Beautiful, Expanding Future of Poverty: Popular Economics as a Psychological Defense." *International Studies Review* 4 (Summer 2002): 107–21.

Nathan, Andrew J. "The Tiananmen Papers." *Foreign Affairs* 80 (January–February 2001): 2–48.

Nathan, James A., and James K. Oliver. *United States Foreign Policy and World Order.* 4th ed. Glenview, Ill.: Scott, Foresman, 1989.

Neame, L.E. *The History of Apartheid: The Story of the Colour War in South Africa.* London: Pall Mall, 1962.

Nehru, Jawaharlal. *Nehru on World History.* Ed. Saul K. Padover. New York: John Day, 1960.

Newfarmer, Richard S. "TNC Takeovers in Brazil: The Uneven Distribution of Benefits in the Market for Firms." *World Development* 7 (January 1979): 25–43.

Nierenberg, Danielle, et al. *State of the World 2006: Special Focus—China and India.* New York: Norton, 2006.

*Nonviolent Sanctions* (Albert Einstein Institution, Cambridge, Mass.). Special Issue (Spring/Summer 1990): 1–24.

Nussbaum, Martha. "Capabilities and Social Justice." *International Studies Review* 4 (Summer 2002): 123–35.

———. *Women and Human Development: The Capabilities Approach.* Cambridge: Cambridge University Press, 2000.

Ohmae Kenichi. "The Rise of the Region State." *Foreign Affairs* 72 (Spring 1993): 78–87.

Olcott, Martha Brill. "The Soviet (Dis)Union." *Foreign Policy,* no. 82 (Spring 1991): 118–36.

Oliner, Samuel P., and Phillip T. Gay, eds. *Race, Ethnicity, and Gender: A Global Perspective.* Dubuque, Iowa: Kendall/Hunt, 1997.

Organization for Economic Cooperation and Development (OECD). *Trends and Recent Developments in Foreign Direct Investment.* OECD: June 2004.

Orr, Robert M. Jr. *The Emergence of Japan's Foreign Aid Power.* New York: Columbia University Press, 1990.

———. "Japan Winks at Peru's Coup." *Nikkei Weekly,* April 25, 1992, 7.

Oxfam America. "Special Report: Women in Development." Winter 1985, 1–8.

Ozaki, Robert S. *The Control of Imports and Foreign Capital in Japan.* New York: Praeger, 1972.

Ozaki, Robert S., and Walter Arnold, eds. *Japan's Foreign Relations: A Global Search for Economic Security.* Boulder, Colo.: Westview, 1985.

Ozawa, Terutomo. *Multinationalism, Japanese Style: The Political Economy of Outward Dependency.* Princeton, N.J.: Princeton University Press, 1979.

Paige, Glenn D. *The Korean Decision: June 24–30, 1950.* New York: Free Press, 1968.

———. "On Values and Science: *The Korean Decision* Reconsidered." *American Political Science Review* 71 (December 1977): 1603–9.

Panofsky, Wolfgang K.H. *Arms Control and Salt II.* Seattle: University of Washington Press, 1979.

Parenti, Christian. "Morales Moves." *The Nation,* June 19, 2006, 20–22.

Paterson, Thomas G., ed. *Kennedy's Quest for Victory: American Foreign Policy, 1961–1963.* New York: Oxford University Press, 1989.

Patterson, Walter C. *The Plutonium Business and the Spread of the Bomb.* San Francisco: Sierra Club, 1984.

Payer, Cheryl. *The Debt Trap: The IMF and the Third World.* New York: Monthly Review, 1974.

———. *The World Bank: A Critical Analysis.* New York: Monthly Review, 1982.

Payne, Keith B., and Colin S. Gray. "Nuclear Policy and the Defensive Transition." *Foreign Affairs* 62 (Spring 1984): 820–42.

Pei, Minxin. "Is China Democratizing?" *Foreign Affairs* 77, no. 1 (January–February 1998): 68–82.

Pei, Minxin, and Michael Swaine. "Simmering Fire in Asia: Averting Sino-Japanese Strategic Conflict." *Policy Brief,* no. 44 (November 2005): 1–7.

Peluso, Nancy Lee. *Rich Forests, Poor People: Resource Control and Resistance in Java.* Berkeley: University of California Press, 1992.

Perkovich, George. *India's Nuclear Bomb: The Impact on Global Proliferation.* Berkeley: University of California Press, 1999.

Petrarolha, Fábio L.S. "Brazil: The Meek Want the Earth Now." *The Bulletin of the Atomic Scientists* 52, no. 6 (November–December 1996): 20–29.

Petras, James. *Critical Perspectives on Imperialism and Social Class in the Third World.* New York: Monthly Review, 1978.

Petras, James, and Morris Morley. *The United States and Chile: Imperialism and the Overthrow of the Allende Government.* New York: Monthly Review, 1975.

Pharr, Susan J. *Political Women in Japan: The Search for a Place in Political Life.* Berkeley: University of California Press, 1981.

Pillar, Paul. "Intelligence, Policy, and the War in Iraq." *Foreign Affairs* 85, no. 2 (March–April 2006): 15–27.

Pitroda, Salil S. "From GATT to WTO: The Institutionalization of World Trade." *Harvard International Review* (Spring 1995): 231–34.

"The Politics of Human Rights." *Trialogue,* no. 19 (Fall 1978): 1–36.

Pollock, Cynthia. "Decommissioning: Nuclear Power's Missing Link." Paper 69. Washington, D.C.: Worldwatch Institute, April 1986.

Porter, Gareth. "The Environmental Hazards of Asia Pacific Development." *Current History* 93, no. 587 (December 1994): 430–34.

Prescott, James W. "Body Pleasure and the Origins of Violence." *The Futurist* (April 1975): 64–74.

Pyle, Kenneth B., ed. *The Trade Crisis: How Will Japan Respond?* Seattle: Society for Japanese Studies, 1987.

Quinlan, Joseph, and Marc Chandler. "The U.S. Trade Deficit: A Dangerous Obsession." *Foreign Affairs* 80, no. 3 (May–June 2001): 87–97.

Raskin, Marcus G. "Progressive Liberalism for the '80s." *The Nation,* May 17, 1980, 577, 587–96.

Raven, Peter. "A Time of Catastrophic Extinction: What We Must Do." *The Futurist* (September–October 1995): 38–41.

Record, Jeffrey. *Bounding the Global War on Terrorism.* Carlisle, Penn.: Strategic Studies Institute, US Army War College, 2003.

Redhead, Brian, ed. *Plato to NATO: Studies in Political Thought.* London: BBC Books, 1990.

Reich, Robert B. "Broken Faith." *The Nation,* February 16, 1998, 11–18.

———. *The Work of Nations: Preparing Ourselves for 21st-Century Capitalism.* New York: Knopf, 1991.

Reinicke, Wolfgang H. "Global Public Policy." *Foreign Affairs* 76, no. 6 (November–December 1997): 127–38.

Renner, Michael. *The Anatomy of Resource Wars.* Paper 162. New York: Worldwatch Institute, October 2002.

———. *Small Arms, Big Impact: The Next Challenge of Disarmament.* Paper 137. New York: Worldwatch Institute, October 1997.

———. *Swords into Plowshares: Converting to a Peace Economy.* Paper 96. Washington, D.C.: Worldwatch Institute, 1990.

Renner, Michael, et al., eds. *Vital Signs 2003: The Trends That Are Shaping Our Future.* New York: Norton 2003.

Rieff, David. "Che's Second Coming?" *New York Times Magazine,* November 20, 2005: 70–77.

Robertson, Benjamin. "China's New Education System." *Far Eastern Economic Review* 169 (July–August 2006): 40–43.

Rogers, Carl R. *On Personal Power.* New York: Delta, 1977.

Romm, Joseph J., and Amory B. Lovins. "Fueling a Competitive Economy." *Foreign Affairs* 71 (Winter 1992–1993): 45–62.

Rosecrance, Richard. *The Rise of the Trading State: Commerce and Conquest in the Modern World.* New York: Basic Books, 1986.

Rosencranz, Armin. "The Problem of Transboundary Pollution." *Environment* 22 (June 1980): 15–20.

Rosset, Peter, and John Vandermeer, eds. *The Nicaragua Reader: Documents of a Revolution Under Fire.* New York: Grove, 1983.

Roszak, Theodore. *Person/Planet: The Creative Disintegration of Industrial Society.* Garden City, N.Y.: Doubleday Anchor, 1978.

Russell, Dick. "In the Shadow of the Bomb." *Amicus Journal* 12, no. 3 (Fall 1990): 18–30.

Russett, Bruce and James S. Sutterlin. "The U.N. in a New World Order." *Foreign Affairs* 70 (Spring 1991): 69–83.

Sachs, Jeffrey D. *The End of Poverty: Economic Possibilities for Our Time.* New York: Penguin Books, 2005.

———. "Making the Brady Plan Work." *Foreign Affairs* 68 (Summer 1989): 87–104.

Sachs, Jeffrey, and David Lipton. "Poland's Economic Reform." *Foreign Affairs* 69 (Summer 1990): 47–66.

Sachs, Wolfgang. "Ecology vs. Ecocracy." *Amicus Journal* 14, no. 2 (Summer 1992): 4.

———, ed. *Development Dictionary: A Guide to Knowledge as Power.* London: Zed, 1992.

Said, Edward W. *Orientalism.* New York: Vintage, 1979.

Sakamato, Yoshikazu. "The Global Crisis and Peace Research." *International Peace Research Newsletter* 21 (1983): 4–7.

SaKong, Il. *Korea in the World Economy.* Washington, D.C.: Institute for International Economics, 1993.

Sale, Kirkpatrick. "Conversion to What: A Green View of Economic Planning." *Utne Reader,* no. 39 (May–June 1990): 46–47.

———. *Dwellers in the Land: The Bioregional Vision.* San Francisco: Sierra Club, 1985.

Satin, Mark. *New Age Politics: Healing Self and Society.* New York: Delta, 1979.

Save the Children. *State of the World's Mothers 2004.* Westport, Conn.: Save the Children, 2004.

Scalapino, Robert A. "The United States and Asia: Future Prospects." *Foreign Affairs* 70, no. 5 (Winter 1991–1992): 19–40.

Scheer, Robert. *With Enough Shovels: Reagan, Bush and Nuclear War.* New York: Vintage, 1983.

Schell, Jonathan. *The Fate of the Earth.* New York: Knopf, 1982.

———. "The Gift of Time: The Case for Abolishing Nuclear Weapons." *The Nation,* February 2–9, 1998, 9–60.

———. "Why War Is Futile." *Harper's,* March 2003, 33–46.

Schiller, Herbert I. "Transnational Media: Creating Consumers Worldwide." *Journal of International Affairs* 47, no. 1 (Summer 1993): 47–58.

———. *Who Knows: Information in the Age of the Fortune 500.* Norwood, N.J.: Ablex, 1981.

Scholte, Jan Aart, et al. *Democratizing the Global Economy: The Role of Civil Society.* Coventry, UK: Centre for the Study of Globalisation and Regionalisation, University of Warwick, 2003.

Schwarz, Adam. "Trade for Trees." *Far Eastern Economic Review,* June 4, 1992, 60–62.

Scott, Antony, and David Gordon. "The Russian Timber Rush." *Amicus Journal* 14, no. 3 (Fall 1992): 15–17.

Seidman, Ann, and Neva Seidman. *South Africa and U.S. Multinational Corporations.* Westport, Conn.: Lawrence Hill, 1977.

Seignious, George M. II, and Jonathan Paul Yates. "Europe's Nuclear Superpowers." *Foreign Policy,* no. 55 (Summer 1984): 40–53.

Selden, Mark. *Reinventing Vietnamese Socialism: Doi Moi in Comparative Perspective.* Boulder, Colo.: Westview, 1993.

Sen, Amartya. *Choice, Welfare, and Measurement.* Cambridge, Mass.: MIT Press, 1982.

———. "Human Rights and Asian Values." *The New Republic,* July 24–31, 1997, 33–40.

Servan-Schreiber, Jean-Jacques. *The World Challenge.* New York: Simon and Schuster, 1980.

Seymour, James D., ed. *The Fifth Modernization: China's Human Rights Movement, 1978–1979.* Stanfordville, N.Y.: Human Rights Publishing Group, 1980.

Shambaugh, David. "China's Military: Real or Paper Tiger?" *The Washington Quarterly* 19, no. 2 (Spring 1996): 19–36.

Sharp, Gene. "Making the Abolition of War a Realistic Goal." New York: Institute for World Order, 1980.

Shibusawa, Masahide, et al. *Pacific Asia in the 1990s.* London: Routledge, for the Royal Institute of International Affairs, 1992.

Shifter, Michael. "In Search of Hugo Chávez." *Foreign Affairs* 85 (May–June 2006): 45–59.

Shiva, Vandana. *The Violence of the Green Revolution: Third World Agriculture, Ecology and Politics.* London: Zed, 1991.

Shoup, Laurence. *The Carter Presidency.* Palo Alto, Calif.: Ramparts, 1980.

Shulman, Seth. "Toxic Travels." *Nuclear Times* 8 (Autumn 1990): 20–31.

Shuman, Michael Harrison. "International Institution Building: The Missing Link for Peace." Center for Innovative Diplomacy, June 1984.

Siegle, Joseph T., Michael M. Weinstein, and Morton H. Halperin. "Why Democracies Excel." *Foreign Affairs* 83 (September–October 2004): 57–71.

Sifry, Micah L., and Christopher Cerf, eds. *The Gulf War Reader: History, Documents, Opinions.* New York: Times Books, 1991.

Silverstein, Ken. "The New China Hands." *The Nation,* February 17, 1997, 11–16.

Silverstein, Ken, and Alexander Cockburn. "The Killers and the Killing." *The Nation,* March 6, 1995, 306–11.

Simmons, P.J., and Chantal de Jonge Oudraat, eds. *Managing Global Issues: Lessons Learned.* Washington, D.C.: Carnegie Endowment for International Peace, 2001.

Singer, Daniel. *The Road to Gdansk: Poland and the USSR.* New York: Monthly Review, 1981.

Singleton, Fred, ed. *Environmental Problems in the Soviet Union and Eastern Europe.* Boulder, Colo.: Lynne Rienner, 1987.

Sivard, Ruth Leger, ed. *Women: A World Survey.* Washington, D.C.: World Priorities, 1985.

———. *World Military and Social Expenditures 1983: An Annual Report on World Priorities.* Washington, D.C.: World Priorities, 1983.

———. *World Military and Social Expenditures 1989.* Washington, D.C.: World Priorities, 1989.

———. *World Military and Social Expenditures 1991.* Washington, D.C.: World Priorities, 1991.

Sivard, Ruth Leger, et al., eds. *World Military and Social Expenditures 1996.* Washington, D.C.: World Priorities, 1996.

Sklar, Holly K., ed. *Trilateralism: The Trilateral Commission and Elite Planning for World Management.* Boston: South End Press, 1980.

Smith, Anthony. *The Geopolitics of Information: How Western Culture Dominates the World.* New York: Oxford University Press, 1980.

Smith, Gerard C., and Helena Cobban. "A Blind Eye to Nuclear Proliferation." *Foreign Affairs* 68 (Summer 1989): 53–70.

Smith, Hazel. *Hungry for Peace: International Security, Humanitarian Assistance, and Social Change in North Korea.* Washington, D.C.: United States Institute of Peace Press, 2005.

Smith, Michael. "A Tale of Death and Destruction." *Geographical* 62 (March 1990): 13.

Smith, Nigel J.H. *Rainforest Corridors: The Transamazon Colonization Scheme.* Berkeley: University of California Press, 1982.

Smith, R. Jeffrey. "Scientists Fault Charges of Soviet Cheating." *Science* 220 (May 13, 1983): 695–97.
———. "Soviets Drop Farther Back in Weapons Technology." *Science* 219 (March 18, 1983): 1300–1.
Smith, Stephen C. *Ending Global Poverty: A Guide to What Works.* New York: Palgrave Macmillan, 2005.
Smith, Tom W., and Lars Jarkko. "National Pride: A Cross-National Analysis." National Opinion Research Center: University of Chicago, 1995.
Snarr, Michael T., and T. Neil Snarr, eds. *Introducing Global Issues.* 3rd. ed. Boulder, Colo.: Lynne Rienner, 2005.
Snow, Edgar. *Red Star over China.* New York: Grove, 1944.
Snyder, Glenn H. *Deterrence and Defense: Toward a Theory of National Security.* Princeton, N.J.: Princeton University Press, 1961.
Solzhenitsyn, Aleksandr I. *The Gulag Archipelago, 1918–1956: An Experiment in Literary Investigation.* Trans. Thomas P. Whitney. New York: Harper and Row, 1973.
Sommer, Mark. "Beating Our Swords into Shields: Forging a Preservative Defense." Miranda, Calif.: Center for a Preservative Defense, 1983.
Spar, Debora L. "The Spotlight and the Bottom Line: How Multinationals Export Human Rights." *Foreign Affairs* 77, no. 2 (March–April 1998): 7–12.
Stein, Jonathan B. *From H-Bomb to Star Wars: The Politics of Strategic Decision Making.* Lexington, Mass.: Lexington, 1984.
Stephenson, Carolyn M., ed. *Alternative Methods for International Security.* Lanham, Md.: University Press of America, 1982.
Stiglitz, Joseph E. *Globalization and Its Discontents.* New York: Norton, 2002.
———. *Making Globalization Work.* New York: Norton, 2006.
Stille, Alexander. "The Ganges' Next Life." *The New Yorker,* January 1998, 58–67.
Stockholm International Peace Research Institute, ed. *SIPRI Yearbook 1992: World Armaments and Disarmament.* Oxford: Oxford University Press, 1992.
———. *SIPRI Yearbook 1993: World Armaments and Disarmament.* Oxford: Oxford University Press, 1993.
Stokes, Bruce. *Helping Ourselves: Local Solutions to Global Problems.* New York: Norton, 1981.
Stopford, John M., ed. *Directory of Multinationals.* Vol. 2. New York: Stockton Press, 1992.
Stopford, John M., and John H. Dunning, eds. *The World Directory of Multinational Enterprises, 1982–83: Company Performance and Global Trends.* 2nd ed. Detroit: Gale Research Company, 1983.
Stover, William James. *Information Technology in the Third World: Can It Lead to Humane National Development?* Boulder, Colo.: Westview, 1984.
Strong, Maurice. "The 'New South.'" *The World Today,* November 1995, 215–19.
Stubbs, Richard. "Asia-Pacific Regionalization and the Global Economy." *Asian Survey* 35, no. 9 (September 1995): 785–97.
Sullivan, Michael J. III. *Measuring Global Values: The Ranking of 162 Countries.* New York: Greenwood Press, 1991.
Suskind, Ron. *The One Percent Doctrine: Deep Inside America's Pursuit of Its Enemies Since 9/11.* New York: Simon & Schuster, 2006.
Sussman, Gerald, and Lawrence Galizio. "The Global Reproduction of American Politics." *Political Communication* 20 (2003): 309–28.
Suu Kyi, Aung San. *Letters from Burma.* London: Penguin, 1997.
Talbot, Stephen. "The H-Bombs Next Door." *The Nation,* February 7, 1981, 129, 143–48.

Tanner, Murray Scot. "China Rethinks Unrest." *The Washington Quarterly* 27, no. 3 (Summer 2004): 137–56.

"Teaching for Peace." *Christian Science Monitor* supplement, January 31, 1986.

Thant, U. "Ten Crucial Years." *United Nations Monthly Chronicle* 6 (July 1969): i–v.

———. *View from the UN.* Garden City, N.Y.: Doubleday, 1978.

Theobald, Robert. *Turning the Century: Personal and Organizational Strategies for Your Changed World.* Indianapolis, Ind.: Knowledge Systems, 1992.

Theroux, Peter. "The Imperiled Nile Delta." *National Geographic* 191, no. 1 (January 1997): 3–35.

Thies, Wallace J. "The Atlantic Alliance, Nuclear Weapons and European Attitudes: Reexamining the Conventional Wisdom." Berkeley: Institute of International Studies, no. 19, University of California, 1983.

Thompson, Clive. "Google's China Problem (and China's Google Problem)." *New York Times Magazine,* April 23, 2006, 65–71, 86, 154–56.

Thompson, E.P., and Dan Smith, eds. *Protest and Survive.* New York: Monthly Review, 1981.

Thorsson, Inga. "Study on Disarmament and Development." *Bulletin of the Atomic Scientists* 38 (June 1982): 41–44.

Thurston, Anne F. *Muddling Toward Democracy: Political Change in Grassroots China.* Washington, D.C.: US Institute of Peace, 1998.

Timerman, Jacobo. *Prisoner Without a Name, Cell Without a Number.* Trans. Toby Talbot. New York: Vintage, 1982.

Todd, Walker F. "Bailing Out the Creditor Class." *The Nation,* February 13, 1995, 193–94.

Toffler, Alvin. *The Third Wave.* New York: William Morrow, 1980.

"Trade, Debt and Plunder in Mexico: An Interview with Cuauhtémoc Cárdenas." *Multinational Monitor,* January–February 1991, 25–27.

Trenin, Dmitri. "Reading Russia Right." *Policy Brief,* no. 42 (October, 2005): 1–7.

———. "Russia Leaves the West." *Foreign Affairs* 85 (July–August 2006): 87–96.

Triska, Jan F., and Robert M. Slusser. *The Theory, Law, and Policy of Soviet Treaties.* Stanford, Calif.: Stanford University Press, 1962.

Tucker, Robert C. "Where Is the Soviet Union Headed?" *World Policy Journal* 4 (Spring 1987): 179–206.

Tunstall, Jeremy. *The Media Are American: Anglo-American Media in the World.* London: Constable, 1977.

ul Haq, Mahbub. "Negotiating the Future." *Foreign Affairs* 59 (Winter 1980–1981): 398–417.

Unger, Danny, and Paul Blackburn, eds. *Japan's Emerging Global Role.* Boulder, Colo.: Lynne Rienner, 1993.

United Nations. *World Social Situation in the 1990s.* New York: UN, 1994.

United Nations Centre for Disarmament. Department of Political and Security Council Affairs. *The United Nations Disarmament Yearbook* 6, 1981.

United Nations Development Program (UNDP). *Human Development Report 1992. 1994. 2000. 2002. 2005.* New York: Oxford University Press, 1992–2005.

United Nations Development Programme, China. *The China Human Development Report.* New York: Oxford University Press, 1999.

United Nations Institute for Disarmament Research, ed. *Proceedings of the Beijing Conference: Conference of Research Institutes in Asia and the Pacific (23–25 March 1992).* New York: United Nations, 1992.

Ury, William L. *Beyond the Hotline: How Crisis Control Can Prevent Nuclear War.* Boston: Houghton Mifflin, 1985.

US Arms Control and Disarmament Agency (ACDA). *Arms Control and Disarmament Agreements: Texts and Histories of Negotiations.* Washington, D.C.: ACDA, 1982.

———. *World Military Expenditures and Arms Transfers, 1985.* Washington, D.C.: ACDA, 1985.

US Bureau of the Census. *Statistical Abstract of the United States: 1992.* Washington, D.C.: US Government Printing Office, 1992.

US Congress, House of Representatives, Committee on International Relations, Subcommittees on International Economic Policy and Trade, Asia and the Pacific, and International Operations and Human Rights. "Hearings: The Future of U.S. Foreign Policy in Asia and the Pacific," 104th Cong., 1st Sess., February 2–June 27, 1995 (Washington, D.C.: US Government Printing Office, 1996).

US Department of Defense. Office of the Assistant Secretary of Defense, Office of Economic Adjustment, and President's Economic Adjustment Committee. *Economic Adjustment/Conversion.* Washington, D.C.: The Pentagon, 1985.

———. *The Military Power of the People's Republic of China.* Washington, DC: Department of Defense, 2005.

US Department of State. *Human Rights.* Selected Documents no. 5. Washington, D.C.: US Government Printing Office, 1977.

———. *Human Rights and Foreign Policy: Commemoration of the Universal Declaration of Human Rights.* Selected Documents no. 22. Washington, D.C.: US Government Printing Office, 1983.

———. *Soviet Noncompliance with Arms Control Agreements.* Special Report no. 122. Washington, D.C.: US Government Printing Office, February 1, 1985.

US Department of State, Bureau of Public Affairs. *Current Policy,* no. 434 (November 17, 1982): p. 2. Washington, D.C.: US Government Printing Office, 1975–1988.

———. *Special Report: Human Rights in the Republic of Korea.* Washington, D.C.: US Government Printing Office, September 1974.

Van Cott, Donna Lee. *Defiant Again: Indigenous Peoples and Latin American Security.* Washington, D.C.: Institute for National Strategic Studies, National Defense University, McNair Paper No. 53, October 1996.

van der Post, Laurens. *The Lost World of the Kalahari.* Harmondsworth, Middlesex, England: Penguin, 1958.

Varshney, Ashutosh. *Democracy, Development, and the Countryside: Urban-Rural Struggles in India.* Cambridge: Cambridge University Press, 1994.

———. *Ethnic Conflict and Civic Life: Hindus and Muslims in India.* New Haven, Conn.: Yale University Press, 2002.

Vasconcellos, John. *A Liberating Vision: Politics for Growing Humans.* San Luis Obispo, Calif.: Impact, 1979.

Viederman, Stephen. "Sustainable Development: What Is It and How Do We Get There?" *Current History* 92, no. 573 (April 1993): 180–85.

Vilas, Carlos M. *The Sandinista Revolution: National Liberation and Social Transformation in Central America.* Trans. Judy Butler. New York: Monthly Review, 1986.

Vogel, Ezra F. "Pax Nipponica?" *Foreign Affairs* 64 (Spring 1986): 752–67.

———, ed. *Living with China: U.S.-China Relations in the Twenty-first Century.* New York: Norton, 1997.

Wade, Robert H. "Questions of Fairness." *Foreign Affairs* 85 (September–October 2006): 136–43.

Wakaizumi, Kei. "Japan's Dilemma: To Act or Not to Act." *Foreign Policy,* no. 16 (Fall 1974): 30–47.

Walker, William, and Mans Lönnroth. "Proliferation and Nuclear Trade: A Look Ahead." *Bulletin of the Atomic Scientists* 40 (April 1984): 29–33.
Walleri, R. Dan. "The Political Economy Literature on North-South Relations: Alternative Approaches and Empirical Evidence." *International Studies Quarterly* 22 (December 1978): 587–623.
Walsh, Roger. *Staying Alive: The Psychology of Human Survival.* Boulder, Colo.: New Science Library, 1984.
Wang Jisi. "China's Search for Stability with America." *Foreign Affairs* 84 (September–October 2005): 39–48.
Wasserman, Harvey. "In the Dead Zone: Aftermath of the Apocalypse." *The Nation,* April 29, 1996, 16–19.
Waters, Tom. "Ecoglasnost." *Discover,* April 1990, 51–53.
Wedel, Janine R. "The Harvard Boys Do Russia." *The Nation,* June 1, 1998, 11–16.
Weidenbaum, Murray. "The Business Response to the Global Marketplace." *The Washington Quarterly* 15, no. 1 (Winter 1992): 173–85.
Weir, David. "The Boomerang Crime." *Mother Jones,* November 1979, 40–49.
Weir, David, and Mark Schapiro. *Circle of Poison: Pesticides and People in a Hungry World.* San Francisco: Institute for Food and Development Policy, 1981.
Weir, Fred. "Whistleblowers Face a Chill Wind in Putin's Russia." *Amnesty Now* (Spring 2002), 6–9.
Weisenborn, Ray E., ed. *Korea's Amazing Century: From Kings to Satellites.* Korea Fulbright Foundation and Korean-American Educational Commission, 1996.
Weiskel, Timothy C. "Vicious Circles: African Demographic History as a Warning." *Harvard International Review* (Fall 1994): 12–16.
Weiss, Thomas G., ed. *Collective Security in a Changing World.* Boulder, Colo.: Lynne Rienner, 1993.
Weschler, Lawrence. "The Other Democratic Revolution of 1989." *Utne Reader,* no. 40 (July–August 1990): 38–44.
Westing, Arthur H., and E.W. Pfeiffer. "The Cratering of Indochina." *Scientific American* (May 1972): 21–29.
White, Richard Alan. *The Morass: The United States' Intervention in Central America.* New York: Harper and Row, 1984.
Wien, Barbara J., ed. *Peace and World Order Studies.* 4th ed. New York: World Policy Institute, 1984.
Wilson, Lillie. "The Plenty Project: Inside the Hippie Peace Corps." *New Age,* July 1981, 18–26.
Wittkopf, Eugene R., and Christopher M. Jones, eds. *The Future of American Foreign Policy.* 3rd ed. New York: St. Martin's/Worth, 1999.
Woito, Robert S. *To End War: A New Approach to International Conflict.* New York: Pilgrim Press, 1982.
Wolfe, Alan. *America's Impasse: The Rise and Fall of the Politics of Growth.* Boston: South End Press, 1981.
Woodall, Pam. "The New Titans." *The Economist,* September 16, 2006, 3–34.
Woodward, Bob. *Plan of Attack.* New York: Simon and Schuster, 2004.
Woodward, Susan L. *Balkan Tragedy: Chaos and Dissolution After the Cold War.* Washington, D.C.: Brookings Institution, 1995.
World Bank. *World Development Report 1984.* New York: Oxford University Press, 1984.
———. *World Development Report 1990.* New York: Oxford University Press, 1990.
———. *World Development Report 1992: Development and the Environment.* New York: Oxford University Press, 1992.

———. *World Development Report 1997: The State in a Changing World.* Washington, D.C.: Oxford University Press, 1997.

*World Scientists' Warning to Humanity.* Pamphlet published by the Union of Concerned Scientists in Cambridge, Massachusetts, 1992.

World Trade Organization. *World Trade Report 2006: Exploring the Links Between Subsidies, Trade and the WTO.* Geneva: WTO, 2006.

Wu Ming. "Disaster in the Making?" *China Rights Forum,* Spring 1998, 4–9.

Wu Xinbo. "The End of the Silver Lining: A Chinese View of the U.S.-Japanese Alliance." *The Washington Quarterly* 29 (Winter 2005–2006): 119–30.

Xie Wenqing. "Post-'9.11' Asia-Pacific Security Situation." *International Strategic Studies,* no. 4 (2002): 41–47.

Yang Sung-chul. "North Korea's Nuclear Blackmail." *Korea Times,* April 11 and 13, 1993, 1.

Yankelovich, Daniel. *New Rules: Searching for Self-Fulfillment in a World Turned Upside Down.* New York: Random House, 1981.

Yavlinsky, Grigory. "Russia's Phony Capitalism." *Foreign Affairs* 77, no. 3 (May–June 1998): 67–79.

Yergin, Daniel. *Shattered Peace: The Origins of the Cold War and the National Security State.* Boston: Houghton Mifflin, 1977.

Yergin, Daniel, and Martin Hillenbrand, eds. *Global Insecurity: A Strategy for Energy and Economic Renewal.* Boston: Houghton Mifflin, 1982.

Zakaria, Fareed. "Culture Is Destiny: A Conversation with Lee Kuan Yew." *Foreign Affairs* 73 (March–April 1994): 109–26.

———. "The Rise of Illiberal Democracy." *Foreign Affairs* 76, no. 6 (November–December 1997): 22–43.

Zuckerman, Seth. "Living According to Nature." *The Nation,* October 17, 1988, 340–42.

Zweig, David. *Democratic Values, Political Structures, and Alternative Politics in Greater China.* Washington, D.C.: US Institute of Peace, 2002.

# Index

Afghanistan: peacekeeping efforts in, 82; possibility of state failure in, 81–82; repression of women in, 154; sanctions on, 168

Africa: child labor in, 155; developed-country subsidies to, 161; failure of democratization in, 20; IMF and World Bank austerity programs in, 50, 166; peacebuilding role training in, 323. *See also* South Africa

African National Congress (ANC): governance of, 177–178; guerrilla war of, 175

Agricultural policy, and population growth, 159. *See also specific country; region*

Ahmadinejad, Mahmoud, 131

Ajami, Fouad, 107

Allende, Salvador, US-backed overthrow of, 37

Al-Qaida, 13, 215; US government portrayals of, 23

Amazonian development, 185–187; competing interests and problems in, 187–188; ecosystem and indigenous communities impacted by, 186; forced labor and violence resulting from, 187; globally responsible options for, 187–188; government export and land-use policies in, 188; sustainable development option in, 187–188; and TNC extraction procedures, 189; tropical deforestation and species extinction in, 184, 187; World Bank subsidies for, 185–186

Annan, Kofi, 6, 13, 18, 25, 147

Anti-Ballistic Missile (ABM) Treaty, 123–124

Aquino, Corazon, 167

Arendt, Hannah, 105

Arms control, 114, 209, 210; of chemical and biological weapons, 220; and Cold War arms race, 128–129; efforts to restrain conventional arms exports, 221; and European security structure, 265–266; and reduction and elimination of nuclear weapons, 219–220; treaties and agreements on, 220–221

Arms race, 113; benefits of reining in, 219–221; clandestine nuclear-materials network and, 217; demand for "smart weapon" components, 221; nonproliferation failures and successes in, 216–218; and nuclear-weapon free zones, 218; social costs of, 226; spending in, 6; and terrorist threats, 212, 215; testing moratoriums in, 210; US domination of, 209–214. *See also* Soviet-US arms race

Arms trade: in Asian states, 16; commercialization of, 213–214; of five permanent Security Council members, 16; post-Cold War factors in, 214; small-arms, 214; Third World clientele in, 221. *See also specific country; region*

Asian Development Bank, 48–49

Asian economy, foreign investment in, 73, 75

Nicaragua, social gains through revolution in, 158
9/11 attacks: Afghanistan and Iraq invasion resulting from, 22; and Bush administration's global crusade, 77; and distortions of terror issue, 22–23; and Islamic fundamentalism, 23
Nixon, Richard, 127; realist politics of, 37; trade deficit and, 42
Nongovernmental organizations (NGOs): civil-society, 13; collective contributions of, 303–304; health-related, 305; and indigenous peoples' rights, 171; and self-reliant development, 303; US-backed, promotion of democracy by, 21, 22
Non-Nuclear Korean Peninsula Peace Initiative, 182
Non-Proliferation Treaty (NPT), 131, 216; 1995 extension of, 210; objections to, 210; weakness of, 122–123
North American Free Trade Agreement (NAFTA), 13; and Chapter 11 foreign investment protections, 72; and Mexico's peso crisis, 69–71; social costs of, 71–72; successes of, 71; and violations of labor standards, 72
North Atlantic Treaty Organization (NATO), 37; Eastern European state's membership in, 266; and European military spending, 267; and reconstruction of Europe, 66; and Russia-US relations, 273–274; and nuclear threat to Europe, 264
North Korea: engagement with South Korea, 182; international aid dependence of, 9; nuclear energy rights of, 130, 131; nuclear program and capacity of, 130–131, 182
North Korea—US nuclear dispute: common-security approach to, 133–134; North Korea's opportunities for reform in, 132–133; perceived threat of US attack/encirclement in, 130–131; US limited options in, 132
Northern Ireland peace process, 315
NSC–68, 77
*National Security Strategy of the United States of America* (NSS), US global strategy redefined in, 77
Nuclear power: and international

inspections of civilian reactors, 217–218; rising global popularity of, 307
Nuclear weapons: accidental launch danger of, 220; active development of, 215; and arms control myth, 115; arsenals, 114, 115*tab*, 117, 118–119, 219; and ballistic missile defense, 124; case for reducing and eliminating, 214, 219–220; and covert acquisition of plutonium, 122–123; and deterrence strategy, 119–121, 220; health and safety dangers of, 117–118; lack of military purpose for, 129–130; official and public debates on, 118; political utility of, 127–129; post-Cold War reductions in, 2, 114, 209; and plutonium commerce, 122–123, 217; space-based, 123–124; species survival as central issue of, 116–117; spending, 1940s to mid–1990s, 126; stockpiling of, 212–213; and strategic nuclear defense, 123–124; target lists and, 118; testing of, 210, 215–216; testing moratorium on, 210; treaties, 210, 212; US policy of first-use of, 127; US presidential threats to use, 127; US resistance to reductions in, 128; US role in proliferation of, 123; and virtual weapons, 210, 212; waste disposal and plutonium recycling dangers from, 117. *See also* Soviet-US arms race; Weapons of mass destruction (WMDs)
Nussbaum, Martha, 101–102

Oil: China's production and import of, 243; economic impact of 1979 shortages in, 258; and Gulf Wars, 78; and Russia-US relations, 275; and state consolidation in Venezuela, 191–192; and Third World debt, 165; US military consumption of, 228; and US-Iran dispute, 132
Oil and petroleum products, alternatives to, 306
Open Skies Treaty, 265
Organization for Economic Cooperation and Development (OECD), 61; countries, transnational investment and loans in, 46

113, 273–275; security in, 273; state takeovers of profitable enterprises in, 275; US arms sales to, 214

Sakamoto, Yoshikazu, 98
Salinas de Gortari, Carlos, 70
Sarney, José, 186
Schell, Jonathan, 108, 116
Second World: and information rights, 54; private sources of aid to, 48–49; sources of insecurity in, 1
Sen, Amartya, 101–102
Services sector, foreign investment in, 41
Shell International, complicity in human rights abuses, 62
Slave labor: charged against transnational corporations, 59, 62; of Third and Fourth World children, 155
Slave trafficking, victims of, 6
Small arms trade, 15
Social and political activism: diverse national groups and entities in, 324–328; globalization and, 10–11; human vision and challenges of, 104–105
Social justice, as primary global-humanist value, 98
Socialist state(s): contradictions between theory and practice in, 103–104; economies, and global capitalist systems, 9; human security contributions of, 103; market systems' similarities with, 103; new political synthesis and new realism proposed for, 103–104
Somalia, as failed state, 12
South Africa: AIDS in, 178; apartheid origins in, 174; apartheid regime in, 172–178; Bantustans (homelands) established in, 172; economic and social inequality in, 173; foreign capital in, 175–177; as international pariah, 172; National Party leadership in, 174; new federal structure in, 177; peaceful transition to democracy in, 176–177; post-apartheid racial inequities in, 178; racial segregation and racial injustice in, 173; rebuilding process in, 178; resistance to black exploitation in, 174–175; tor-ture and assassinations in, 173; transnational corporations in, 175–177; Truth and Reconciliation Commission in, 178; underdevelopment in, 178; and US investments and loans, 176; US sanctions and international oil boycott against, 177; US support for peaceful change in, 176; whites' continuing economic domination in, 178
South Korea: agricultural neglect in, 180; and armed conflict with North Korea, 181; authoritarianism in, 181; chaebol's economic role in, 180–181; corruption in, 181, 183; democratization in, 183; direct presidential elections in, 181, 182; economic success of, 178–184; educational attainment in, 179; engagement with North Korea, 182; export-led industrialization in, 179; human rights abuses in, 181; military spending in, 181; national-security sate in, 181; nuclear policy of, 182; political reforms in, 182–183; relative income equality in, 180; repression of labor in, 180; social equity in, 179; sources of export success in, 179–180; trade ranking of, 44; US economic aid to, 179–180; US tactical nuclear weapons removed from, 182
South Korean financial crisis: and bailout loans, 73–74; causes of, 73; social impacts of, 76; US and IMF interventions in, 74–75, 183
Sovereign statehood: creation and reestablishment of, 14; post-Cold War quest for, 14; and system transformation, 100
Soviet republics: antinuclear platforms of, 265; independence of, 271
Soviet Union, 40; dissolution of, 271; and East-West trade, 270; ecological and environmental disaster in, 269; economy ranking of, 269; military-industrial system, 124–125; perestroika and glasnost impacts in, 268, 270–271; political terror in, 269; price of maintaining empire and military strength in, 268; realist politics in, 36, 38; social gains and living

World aid funding cuts of, 159; Third World's importance to, 144; unilateral stance in, 12; women's status in, 224–225
US economy: and Clinton administration, 222; inequities in, 222; and investments abroad, 40–41; Middle East oil reliance and, 228; military R&D costs in, 259; national debt and, 227; and spending on prisons, 225; traditional social compact of, 222
US Institute of Peace, congressional funding of, 323
US military spending: comparative, 258; hidden costs in, 226; social and economic costs of, 226–229, 259
US military-industrial complex, 211–214; and arms control, 212–213; arms exports and transfers in, 213–214; CTBT support of, 212; incentives for weapons proliferation in, 125, 126; interlocking institutions of, 124; and job creation, 228; and major military contractors, 126; and military doctrine, 212; military economy and spending purposes in, 125–126; and military spending, 211, 212, 213; political influence of, 213; post-Cold War survival of, 211; prime contractors in, 213; research money and talent in, 227–228
US politics and foreign policy: costs of empire in, 226; maintenance of power and privilege in, 226; two-war strategy in, 212. *See also* Soviet-US arms race
US presidents, nuclear threats made by, 127. *See also specific administration*
US trade policy: and dependence on Persian Gulf oil, 116; politicization of, 68; shift from global to short-term objectives in, 67–68. *See also* North American Free Trade Agreement (NAFTA)
US transnational corporations: food aid program and, 60; tobacco exports to Third World, 157

Venezuela: Chávez government policies in, 191–192; economic decline in,

191; human-development indicators in, 192; income inequality in, 191; oil wealth and policy in, 191–192; promise of state recovery in, 190; Washington's view of, 192
Vietnam, loss of forests and arable land in, 164
Vietnam War, 67, 109
Vladivostok Agreement, 128

Waite, Terry, 321
Wal-Mart Stores, 46
War crimes, and strengthening of international tribunals/courts, 321
Wars and armed conflicts: attempts to outlaw, 100; child deaths in, 155; and civil wars since 1990s, 15, 16–17; and common security notion, 102, 108; and costs of militarization, 108–109; destructive and delusional nature of, 108; and expanded access to small arms, 15; and failed peace accords, 15; global-humanist approach to, 108–109; international arms market and, 16; psychological and ecological damages from, 109; realist assumptions about causes of, 115; structural approach to, 100–101; and US nuclear intervention threats, 127. *See also specific war*
Warsaw Pact, 40, 264, 265; collapse of, 114
Warsaw Pact countries, military spending as percent of GNP in, 258
Washington consensus: and American populism, 191; key objectives and unwritten rules of, 49; pressure on governments to implement, 60
Wassenaar Arrangement, 221
Water resources: access and management, 6, 156; privatization of, 155–156
Weapons contractors, Pentagon's dependence on, 213
Weapons of mass destruction (WMDs): contemporary dangers of, 215; international treaties governing, 210, 211*tab*; materials, safeguarding of, 318; and US military requirements, 212
Western Europe: social welfare cutbacks

in, 260; US loss of industrial advantage to, 227; world trade shares of, 44, 258. *See also specific country*
Women: abuse and violence against, 225; as Third World leaders, 154
Women's rights and status: advancement of, 328–329; embodied in international conventions, 328; in political participation and representation, 154; and social and economic benefits of education, 302; as transnational concern, 328. *See also specific country; region*
World Bank: aid program, failure to promote income growth in, 152; Amazonian development subsidized by, 185–186; creation of, 65; functions and loan commitments of, 47–48; and Mexico's peso crisis, 69; politics of, 49; Russia's membership in, 274; shareholder contributors in, 48; structural adjustment loans of, 50; and sustainable development,

301; and Third World indebtedness, 165–168; US role in, 49
World Health Organization (WHO), 163, 164, 235; prevention and social mobilization models of, 305–306
World Order Models Project, 99
World Trade Organization (WTO), 56, 58, 164; binding dispute resolution mechanism of, 42; China's membership in, 234–235; and telecommunication competition, 53; and workers' rights, 42

Yahoo, Chinese market concessions of, 63
Yeltsin, Boris, 125, 209, 220; democratizing reforms of, 272; and formation of Commonwealth of Independent States, 271–272; and NATO enlargement, 274
Yoshida Shigeru, 277; Doctrine of, 282

Zedillo, Ernesto, 68, 70

# About the Book

Traditional studies of world politics emphasize the struggle between states as they search for national security. But increasing interdependence has transformed the world political agenda, creating the need for new tools to explain the changing reality of global politics. *Global Politics in the Human Interest* provides those tools.

This fully revised fifth edition thoroughly covers post–September 11 developments. Addressing such interrelated issues as terrorism, democratic transitions, nationalism, human rights violations, armed conflicts, economic globalization, and sustainable development, Gurtov explores the threats and opportunities posed by the changing world order. The book retains its practical bent, revealing how global politics affects the quality and content of people's lives.

**Mel Gurtov** is professor of political science and international studies at Portland State University. His most recent book is *Superpower on Crusade: The Bush Doctrine in US Foreign Policy.* Professor Gurtov is editor-in-chief of *Asian Perspective,* a quarterly journal in international affairs.